P · O

IT

DICTIONARY

ITALIAN · ENGLISH
ENGLISH · ITALIAN

COVENT
GARDEN
BOOKS

A DORLING KINDERSLEY BOOK

Produced for Dorling Kindersley by
PAGEOne, Cairn House, Elgiva Lane, Chesham,
Buckinghamshire HP5 2JD

PAGEOne team   Chris Clark, Matthew Cook,
Bob Gordon, Helen Parker

DK Managing editor   Jane Yorke

Italian editors   Paola Tite
Loredana Riu
Francesca Logi

Published in Great Britain by
Dorling Kindersley Limited, 9 Henrietta Street,
London WC2E 8PS

2 4 6 8 10 9 7 5 3 1
Copyright © 1998 Dorling Kindersley Limited, London

This edition published in 1999
for Covent Garden Books

A CIP catalogue record for this book is available from
the British Library

ISBN 1-85605-507-8

Printed and bound in Italy by LegoPrint

GUIDE TO THE IMITATED PRONUNCIATION

The imitated pronunciation in the Italian–English section is designed to help English speakers pronounce the Italian words accurately. Read each syllable as though it were an English one, bearing in mind the following conventions.

1 The stressed syllable is printed in **bold** type. This is usually either the last but one syllable, or the third from the end:

    parola, pah-**ro**-lah (word)
    tavolo, **tah**-vo-lo (table)

2 Each Italian vowel is pronounced as a single sound, usually long, but shorter when in the middle of a syllable or in an unstressed syllable.

3 Combinations of vowels in a single syllable are pronounced as separate sounds; this is indicated in the imitated pronunciation by an apostrophe:

    ampio, **ahm**-pe'o (wide)
    annuale, ahn-noo'**ah**-lay (yearly)

4 **r** is printed in bold type after a vowel as a reminder that it should be rolled more than in English. This does not mean that the syllable in which the **r** occurs is stressed:

    berretta, bair-**ret**-tah (cap)

5 The combination l'y represents a sound similar to the lli in million:

    famiglia, fah-**mee**-l'yah (family)

6 The combination n'y sounds like the ni in onion:

    campagna, kahm-**pah**-n'yah (countryside)

7 Doubled consonants in Italian are lingered on, i.e. pronounced more slowly than single consonants. They are represented in the imitated pronunciation either by a double consonant or by two different consonants:

    caffellatte, kahf-fayl-**lat**-tay (white coffee)
    caccia, **kaht**-chah (hunting)
    pacco, **pahk**-ko (parcel)

The sounds represented by pp, tt, kk are produced by a slight pause after the vowel, followed by a forceful pronunciation of the consonant.

ABBREVIATIONS / ABBREVIAZIONI

adj	adjective	aggettivo
adv	adverb	avverbio
art	article	articolo
comm	commerce	commercio
comp	computing	informatica
conj	conjunction	congiunzione
f	feminine	femminile
fam	familiar	familiare
fig	figuratively	figuratamente
gram	grammar	grammatica
interj	interjection	interiezione
law	law	legge, diritto
m	masculine	maschile
mech	mechanics	meccanica
med	medicine	medicina
mil	military	militare
mus	music	musica
n	noun	nome
naut	nautical	nautica
parl	parliament	parlamento
pl	plural	plurale
pref	prefix	prefisso
prep	preposition	preposizione
pron	pronoun	pronome
refl	reflexive	riflessivo
relig	religion	religione
tech	technical	tecnica
v	verb	verbo
vulg	vulgar	volgare

* An asterisk after an Italian adjective shows that the adverb is formed by adding -mente to the feminine singular. A final e following l or r is dropped before the ending: largo = larga + mente; dolce = dolce + mente; facile = facil + mente; particolare = particolare + mente

* L'asterisco appare dopo gli aggettivi inglesi che formano un avverbio in -ly di uso comune.

SPIEGAZIONE DELLA PRONUNCIA IMITATA

La pronuncia imitata della sezione Inglese–Italiano aiuta l'utente italiano a pronunciare le parole inglesi correttamente. Ogni sillaba della pronuncia imitata deve essere letta come se fosse una sillaba italiana, tenendo presente le seguenti convenzioni:

1   La sillaba accentata è indicata dal segno ' alla fine della sillaba stessa.

2   Una vocale in **neretto** deve essere pronunciata più forte di un'altra vocale nella stessa sillaba:

    face, feis (faccia)

    Il gruppo ei si pronuncia come la e chiusa di godere, seguita da una i pronunciata rapidamente.

    Il gruppo ou si pronuncia con una o lunga seguita da una u pronunciata rapidamente.

3   Le vocali lunghe sono indicate da una doppia vocale in **neretto**. Rappresentano un suono unico.

    adore, a-door (adorare)

4   In molte parole inglesi, le vocali delle sillabe non accentate hanno un suono indistinto, simile a quello della e francese in que, me, le. Questo suono è rappresentato nella pronuncia imitata da una vocale in *corsivo: a, e, o* oppure *u* a seconda

dell'ortografia della parola inglese, ma in ogni caso si tratta sempre dello stesso suono:

    acceptance, ak-sept'-ens (accettazione)

5   g o gh rappresenta la g dura di gola:

    ghost, goust (spettro)
    get, ghet (procurare)

    g in corsivo dopo una n indica un suono nasale e non è pronunciato separatamente:

    bring, bring (portare)
    bank, bangk (banca)

6   r in corsivo è muta nell'inglese meridionale, mentre in altre zone è una r pronunciata arrotondola meno che in italiano:

    fair, fer (fiera)
    farm, faarm (fattoria)

7   s rappresenta la s sorda di senso:

    sing, sing (cantare)

s in neretto e corsivo rappresenta la s sonora di chiesa:

vase, va*a*s (vaso)

8 **ch** rappresenta il suono c di cena; **ch** in neretto rappresenta il suono g di già:

change, cheinch (cambiare)

9 **sh** rappresenta il suono sc di scena:

action, ak'-sh*o*n (azione)

sh in neretto rappresenta il suono francese j di jour:

treasure, tresh'-*a* (tesoro)

10 Z e D rappresentano i due suoni del "th" inglese, che non esistono in italiano.

Z si ottiene mettendo la lingua fra i denti e pronunciando una s come in senso:

thing, Zing (cosa)

D si ottiene mettendo la lingua fra i denti e pronunciando una s come in chiesa:

this, Dis (questo)

11 Il simbolo ŏ rappresenta un suono vocalico breve, a metà strada tra la a breve e la o breve:

come, kŏm (venire)

12 h nella pronuncia imitata indica che la h deve essere aspirata distintamente:

hello, hel-ou' (ciao)

ITALIAN · ENGLISH
ITALIANO · INGLESE

a, ah, *prep* to; in, at; by

abate, ah-bah-tay, *m* abbot

abbacchiato, ahb-bahk-ke'**ah**-to, *adj* depressed

abbacinare, ahb-bah-che-**nah**-ray, *v* to dazzle

abbaglianti, ahb-bah-l'**yahn**-te, *mpl* headlights

abbagliare, ahb-bah-l'**yah**-ray, *v* to dazzle; to mislead

abbaglio, ahb-**bah**-l'yo, *m* mistake, blunder

abbaiare, ahb-bah'e-**yah**-ray, *v* to bark; to scream

abbaino, ahb-bah'ee-no, *m* skylight, dormer window

abbandonare, ahb-bahn-do-**nah**-ray, *v* to abandon; to give up

abbandono, ahb-bahn-do-no, *m* abandonment; neglect

abbassamento, ahb-bahss-sah-**men**-to, *m* lowering

abbassare, ahb-bahss-**sah**-ray, *v* to lower

abbassarsi, ahb-bahss-**sar**-se, *v* to stoop down

abbasso...!, ahb-**bahss**-so, *interj* down with...!

abbastanza, ahb-bah-**stahn**-tsah, *adv* enough; quite

abbattere, ahb-**baht**-tay-ray, *v* to knock down; to slaughter; to fell

abbattimento, ahb-bahtte-**men**-to, *m* discouragement

abbattuto, ahb-baht-too-to, *adj* despondent

abbazia, ahb-bah-**tsee**-ah, *f* abbey

abbellire, ahb-bell-**lee**-ray, *v* to embellish; to deck

abbeverare, ahb-bay-vay-**rah**-ray, *v* to water

abbeveratoio, ahb-bay-vay-rah-**to**-e'o, *m* watering place, trough

abbicì, ahb-be-**chee**, *m* alphabet; primer

abbigliamento, ahb-bel-l'yah-**men**-to, *m* dress, clothing

abbigliarsi, ahb-be-l'**yar**-se, *v* to dress oneself

abbiente, ahb-**byen**-tay, *adj* well off

abbinare, ahb-bee-**nah**-ray, *v* to combine; to match

abbindolare, ahb-bin-do-**lah**-ray, *v* to cheat

abboccamento, ahb-bok-kah-**men**-to, *m* interview, talks

abboccare, ahb-bok-**kah**-ray, *v* to bite; to connect

abboccarsi, ahb-bok-**kar**-se, *v* to have a meeting

abbonamento, ahb-bo-nah-**men**-to, *m* subscription; season ticket; radio/television licence

abbonato, ahb-bo-**nah**-to, *m* subscriber

abbonarsi, ahb-bo-**nar**-se, *v* to subscribe

abbondante, ahb-bon-**dahn**-tay, *adj* abundant; loose-fitting

abbondanza, ahb-bon-**dahn**-tsah, *f* abundance; plenty

abbondare, ahb-bon-**dah**-ray, *v* to abound

abbordabile, ahb-bor-**dah**-bee-lay, *adj* approachable

abbordare, ahb-bor-**dah**-ray, *v* to approach; *naut* to draw alongside

abbottonare, ahb-bot-to-**nah**-ray, *v* to button

abbozzare, ahb-bot-**tsah**-ray, *v* to sketch; to rough-hew; to draft

abbozzo, ahb-**bot**-tso, *m* sketch, outline

abbracciare, ahb-braht-**chah**-ray, *v* to embrace

abbraccio, ahb-**braht**-cho, *m* embrace

abbreviare, ahb-bray-ve'**ah**-ray, *v* to abbreviate

abbreviatura, ahb-bray-ve'ah-**too**-rah, *f* abbreviation

abbreviazione, ahb-bray-ve'ah-tse'**o**-nay, *f* abbreviation

abbronzarsi, ahb-bron-**dzar**-se, *v* to get a suntan

abbronzatura, ahb-bron-

dzah-**too**-rah, *f* suntan

abbrustolire, ahb-broos-to-**lee**-ray, *v* to toast, to grill

abbrutire, ahb-broo-**tee**-ray, *v* to degrade; to brutalize

abdicare, ahb-de-**kah**-ray, *v* to abdicate

aberrazione, ah-bair-rah-tse'**o**-nay, *f* aberration

abete, ah-**bay**-tay, *m* fir-tree

abietto*, -a, ahb-be'**ayt**-to, *adj* abject

abile, ah-be-lay, *adj* skilful, able, clever

abilità, ah-be-le-**tah**, *f* cleverness; skill

abilitare, ah-be-le-**tah**-ray, *v* to qualify; to enable

abilitazione, ah-be-le-tah-tse'**o**-nay, *f* qualification

abilmente, ah-bil-**men**-tay, *adv* ably, cleverly

abisso, ah-**biss**-so, *m* abyss

abitante, ah-be-**tahn**-tay, *m* inhabitant

abitare, ah-be-**tah**-ray, *v* to inhabit, to live (in)

abitato, ah-be-**tah**-to, *adj* inhabited; *m* built-up area

abitazione, ah-be-tah-tse'**o**-nay, *f* residence, dwelling

abito, **ah**-be-to, *m* dress; suit; habit

abituale, ah-be-too'**ah**-lay, *adj* usual; regular

abitualmente, ah-be-too'ahl-**men**-tay, *adv* usually

abituare, ah-be-too'**ah**-ray, *v* to accustom

abituarsi, ah-be-too'**ar**-se, *v* to get used to

abitudine, ah-be-**too**-de-nay, *f* habit

abnorme, ahb-**nor**-may, *adj* abnormal

abolire, ah-bo-**lee**-ray, *v* to abolish; to repeal

abominevole, ah-bo-me-**nay**-vo-lay, *adj* abominable

aborigeno, -a ah-boh-**re**-jay-no, *adj* aboriginal; *m/f* aboriginal

aborrire, ah-bor-**ree**-ray, *v* to abhor

abortire, ah-bor-**tee**-ray, *v* to miscarry; to have an abortion

aborto, ah-**bor**-to, *m* miscarriage; abortion

abrasione, ah-brah-ze'**o**-nay, *f* abrasion

abrogare, ah-broh-**gah**-re, *v* to repeal, to abrogate

abside, ahb-se-day, *f* apse

abulico, ah-**boo**-le-ko, *adj* lacking in willpower

abusare, ah-boo-zah-ray, *v* to abuse

abusivo*, -a, ah-boo-zeevo, *adj* illegal, unauthorized

abuso, ah-boo-zo, *m* abuse

accademia, ahk-kah-**day**-me'ah, *f* academy

accadere, ahk-kah-**day**-ray, *v* to happen, to occur

accaduto, ahk-kah-**doo**-to, *m* happening, event

accalappiare, ahk-kah-lahp-pe'**ah**-ray, *v* to ensnare; to dupe

accalcare, ahk-kahl-**kah**-ray, *v* to crowd

accaldato, ahk-kahl-**dah**-to, *adj* hot, sweaty

accalorarsi, ahk-kah-loh-**rar**-se, *v* to get excited

accamparsi, ahk-kahm-**pah**-rse, *v* to camp

accanirsi, ahk-kah-**nee**-rse, *v* to rage; to persist

accanito, ahk-kah-**nee**-to, *adj* fierce; dogged

accanto, ahk-**kahn**-to, *adv* near; **– a,** *prep* next to

accaparrare, ahk-kah-par-**rah**-ray, *v* to buy up; to grab

accappatoio, ahk-kahp-pah-**to**-e'o, *m* bathrobe

accarezzare, ahk-kah-ret-**tsah**-ray, *v* to caress; to stroke

accasarsi, ahk-kah-**zar**-se, *v* to marry

accasciarsi, ahk-kah-

she'**ar**-se, *v* to collapse; to get discouraged

accatastare, ahk-kah-tahss-**tah**-ray, *v* to pile up

accattone, ahk-kaht-to-nay, *m* beggar

accecare, aht-chay-**kah**-ray, *v* to blind; to dazzle

accedere, aht-**chay**-day-ray, *v* to gain access (to)

accelerare, aht-chay-lay-**rah**-ray, *v* to accelerate

accelerato, aht-chay-lay-**rah**-to, *adj* quick; *m* local train

acceleratore, aht-chay-lay-rah-**to**-ray, *m* accelerator

accendere, aht-**chen**-day-ray, *v* to light; to switch on

accendino, aht-chen-**dee**-no, *m* lighter

accennare, aht-chen-**nah**-ray, *v* to point out; to hint

accenno, aht-**chen**-no, *m* nod; hint; sign

accensione, aht-chen-se'o-nay, *f* lighting; switching on

accento, aht-**chen**-to, *m* accent

accentrare, aht-chen-tr'**ah**-ray, *v* to centralize

accentuare, aht-chen-too'**ah**-ray, *v* to

accentuate, to emphasize

accerchiare, aht-chair-ke'**ah**-ray, *v* to encircle

accertamento, aht-chair-tah-**men**-to, *m* ascertainment, check

accertare, aht-chair-**tah**-ray, *v* to verify, to ascertain

accessibile, aht-chess-**see**-be-lay, *adj* accessible; affordable

accesso, aht-**chess**-so, *m* access

accessorio, aht-chess-so-re'o, *adj* secondary; *m* accessory

accetta, aht-**chet**-tah, *f* hatchet

accettabile, aht-chet-**tah**-be-lay, *adj* acceptable

accettare, aht-chet-**tah**-ray, *v* to accept

accettazione, aht-chet-tah-tse'o-nay, *f* acceptance; reception

accezione, aht-chay-tse'o-nay, *f* meaning

acchiappare, ahk-ke'ahp-**pah**-ray, *v* to catch

acciacco, aht-**chahk**-ko, *m* infirmity

acciaio, aht-**chah**-e'o, *m* steel

accidentale, aht-che-den-**tah**-lay, *adj* accidental

accidentato, aht-che-den-

tah-to, *adj* uneven, bumpy

accidente, aht-che-**den**-tay, *m* accident; stroke

accidenti!, aht-che-**den**-te, *interj* damn!; good heavens!

accigliato, aht-che-l'**yah**-to, *adj* sullen, haughty

accingersi, aht-**chen**-jair-se, *v* to set about

acciuga, aht-**choo**-gah, *f* anchovy

acclamare, ahk-klah-**mah**-ray, *v* to acclaim

acclamazione, ahk-klah-mah-tse'o-nay, *f* acclamation

acclimatarsi, ahk-kle-mah-**tar**-se, *v* to acclimatize

accludere, ahk-**kloo**-day-ray, *v* to enclose

accoglienza, ahk-ko-l'**yen**-tsah, *f* reception, welcome

accogliere, ahk-ko-l'**yay**-ray, *v* to receive; to accommodate

accomandante, ahk-ko-mahn-**dahn**-tay, *m* sleeping-partner

accomandatario, ahk-ko-mahn-dah-**tah**-re'o, *m* working-partner

accomandita, ahk-ko-**mahn**-de-tah, *f* limited partnership

accomodare, ahk-ko-mo-**dah**-ray, *v* to repair; to settle

accomodarsi, ahk-ko-mo-**dar**-se, *v* to take a seat

accompagnare, ahk-kom-pah-**n'yah**-ray, *v* to accompany

accompagnatore, ahk-kom-pah-n'yah-**tor**-ay, *m* accompanist; companion

acconciatura, ahk-kon-**chah**-too-rah, *f* hairstyle; headdress

accondiscendere, ahk-kon-de-**shen**-day-ray, *v* to consent, to agree

acconsentire, ahk-kon-sen-**tee**-ray, *v* to consent

accontentare, ahk-kon-ten-**tah**-ray, *v* to satisfy

acconto, ahk-**kon**-to, *m* part payment; instalment

accoppiare, ahk-kop-pe'**ah**-ray, *v* to pair; to match

accorciare, ahk-kor-**chah**-ray, *v* to shorten

accordare, ahk-kor-**dah**-ray, *v* to grant; to tune

accordarsi, ahk-kor-**dah**-rse, *v* to agree

accordo, ahk-**kor**-do, *m* agreement; harmony; chord

accorgersi, ahk-**kor**-jair-se, *v* to perceive; to realize

accorrere, ahk-**kor**-ray-ray, *v* to run up

accorto*, -a, ahk-**kor**-to, *adj* shrewd, cunning, smart

accostare, ahk-koss-**tah**-ray, *v* to approach; to leave ajar

accovacciarsi, ahk-kwoh-vahch-**char**-se, *v* to crouch

accozzaglia, ahk-kot-tsah-l'yah, *f* rabble; heap

accreditare, ahk-kray-de-**tah**-ray, *v* to accredit; to credit

accrescere, ahk-**kray**-shay-ray, *v* to increase

accudire, ahk-koo-dee-ray, *v* to attend to

accumulare, ahk-koo-moo-**lah**-ray, *v* to accumulate

accuratezza, ahk-koo-rah-**tayt**-tsah, *f* accuracy

accurato*, -a, ahk-koo-**rah**-to, *adj* accurate

accusa, ahk-koo-zah, *f* accusation; charge

accusare, ahk-koo-**zah**-ray, *v* to accuse; to charge; to blame

accusatore, ahk-koo-zah-**tor**-ay, *m* accuser; prosecutor

acerbo*, -a, ah-**chair**-bo,

adj unripe, sour

acero, ah-**chay**-ro, *m* maple

aceto, ah-**chay**-to, *m* vinegar

acetone, ah-chay-**to**-nay, *m* acetone; nail varnish remover

acidità, ah-che-dee-**tah**, *f* acidity; heartburn

acido, ah-**che**-do, *m* acid; *adj** acid

acino, ah-**che**-no, *m* grape

acne, ahk-nay, *f* acne

acqua, ahk-kwah, *f* water; – **dolce**, fresh water; – **potabile**, drinking water; – **salata**, salt water

acquaio, ahk-**kwah**-yo, *m* kitchen sink

acquario, ahk-**kwah**-ryo, *m* aquarium; **Acquario**, Aquarius

acquavite, ahk-kwah-**vee**-tay, *f* crude brandy

acquazzone, ahk-kwaht-**tso**-nay, *m* downpour

acquedotto, ahk-kway-**dot**-to, *m* aqueduct

acquerello, ahk-kway-**rell**-lo, *m* water-colour

acquietare, ahk-kwe'ay-**tah**-ray, *v* to appease

acquistare, ahk-kwiss-**tah**-ray, *v* to acquire; to buy

acquisto, ahk-**kwiss**-to, *m* acquisition; shopping; purchase

acquoso, ahk-koo'o-zo, *adj* watery

acre, ah-kray, *adj* acrid; harsh

acrilico, ah-**kre**-le-co, *adj* acrylic

acrobata, ah-**kro**-bah-ta, *m* acrobat

acuire, ah-**kwee**-ray, *v* to sharpen; to embitter

acume, ah-koo-may, *m* acumen; subtleness

acuminato, ah-koo-me-**nah**-to, *adj* pointed, sharp

acutezza, ah-koo-**tayt**-tsah, *f* sharpness

acuto*, -a, ah-koo-to, *adj* sharp, pointed; keen; *m* high note

adagiare, ah-dah-**jah**-ray, *v* to lay down

adagiarsi, ah-dah-**jar**-se, *v* to lie down

adagio, ah-dah-jo, *adv* slowly; *m* adage; adagio

adattamento, ah-daht-tah-**men**-to, *m* adaptation; conversion

adattare, ah-daht-**tah**-ray, *v* to adapt

adatto, ah-**daht**-to, *adj* suitable

addebitare, ahd-day-be-**tah**-ray, *v* to debit

addebito, ahd-**day**-be-to, *m* debit; imputation

addensare, ahd-den-**sah**-ray, *v* to thicken

addentare, ahd-den-**tah**-ray, *v* to seize with the teeth; to bite into

addentrarsi, ahd-den-**trah**-rse, *v* to penetrate

addentro, ahd-**den**-tro, *adv* within; well up on

addestramento, ahd-desss-trah-**men**-to, *m* training

addestrare, ahd-dess-**trah**-ray, *v* to train

addetto, ahd-**det**-to, *adj* in charge, *m* attaché

addietro, ahd-de'ay-tro, *adv* behind; before

addio, ahd-**dee**-o, *interj* goodbye

addirittura, ahd-de-rit-**too**-rah, *adv* absolutely; even, *interj* indeed!

addirsi, ahd-**deer**-se, *v* to be suitable

additare, ahd-de-**tah**-ray, *v* to indicate

additivo, ahd-de-**te**-vo, *m* additive

addizionare, ahd-de-tseo-**na**-ray, *v* to add up

addizione, ahd-de-**tse'o**-nay, *f* addition

addobbare, ahd-dob-**bah**-ray, *v* to decorate

addolcire, ahd-dol-**chee**-ray, *v* to sweeten; *fig* to soothe

addolorare, ahd-do-lo-**rah**-ray, *v* to grieve; to

pain

addome, ahd-**do**-may, *m* abdomen

addomesticare, ahd-do-mess-te-**kah**-ray, *v* to tame; to break in

addormentare, ahd-dor-men-**tah**-ray, *v* to put to sleep

addormentarsi, ahd-dor-men-**tar**-se, *v* to go to sleep

addossare, ahd-doss-**sah**-ray, *v* to lean against; to charge with

addossarsi, ahd-doss-**sar**-se, *v* to take upon oneself

addosso, ahd-**doss**-so, *adv* on, against; – **a,** *prep* on, against

addurre, ahd-**doohr**-ray, *v* to allege; to put forward

adeguare, ah-day-goo'**ah**-ray, *v* to adjust; to bring into line

adeguato*, -a, ah-day-goo'**ah**-to, *adj* adequate

adempiere, ah-dem-pe'**ay**-ray, *v* to fulfil; to perform

adempire, ah- dem-**pee**-ray, *v* to fulfil; to perform

aderente, ah-day-**ren**-tay, *adj* sticking; tight-fitting; *m/f* supporter, follower

aderenza, ah-day-**ren**-tsah, *f* adherence; *fpl* connections

aderire, ah-day-**ree**-ray, *v* to adhere; to join

adescare, ah-dess-**kah**-ray, *v* to bait, to lure; to solicit

adesione, ah-day-ze'o-**nay,** *f* adhesion

adesivo, ah-day-**ze**-vo, *adj* adhesive; *m* adhesive

adesso, ah-**dess**-so, *adv* now; presently

adiacente, ah-de'ah-**chen**-tay, *adj* adjacent

adipe, ah-de-**pay,** *m* fat

adirarsi, ah-de-**rah**-rse, *v* to get angry

adirato, ah-de-**rah**-to, *adj* angry

adire, ah-**dee**-ray, *v* – **le vie legali,** to take legal proceedings

adito, ah-de-to, *m* access; **dare – a,** to give rise to

adocchiare, ah-dock-ke'**ah**-ray, *v* to eye; to observe for a moment

adolescente, ah-do-lay-**shen**-te, *adj* adolescent; *m/f* adolescent

adolescenza, ah-do-lay-**shen**-tsah, *f* adolescence

adoperare, ah-do-pay-**rah**-ray, *v* to use

adorabile, ah-do-**rah**-be-lay, *adj* adorable

adorare, ah-do-**rah**-ray, *v* to adore

adornare, ah-dor-**nah**-ray, *v* to adorn

adottare, ah-dot-**tah**-ray, *v* to adopt

adottivo, ah-dot-**te**-vo, *adj* adopted, adoptive

adozione, ah-do-tse'o-**nay,** *f* adoption

adulare, ah-doo-**lah**-ray, *v* to flatter

adulterare, ah-dool-tay-**rah**-ray, *v* to adulterate

adulterio, ah-dool-**tay**-re'o, *m* adultery

adulto, ah-**dool**-to, *adj* adult; *m* adult, grown-up

adunanza, ah-doo-**nahn**-tsah, *f* meeting

adunare, ah-doo-**nah**-ray, *v* to assemble; to gather

adunco, ah-**doonn**-ko, *adj* hooked

aereo, ah-**ay**-ray-o, *adj* aerial; *m* aeroplane

aerobica, ah-ay-**roh**-be-kah, *f* aerobics

aeronauta, ah-ay-ro-**nah**'oo-tah, *m* aeronaut

aeronave, ah-ay-ro-**nah**-vay, *f* airship

aeroplano, ah-ay-ro-**plah**-no, *m* aeroplane

aeroporto, ah-ay-ro-**por**-to, *m* airport

aerosol, ah-ay-roh-**sol**, *m* aerosol

aerospaziale, ah-ay-ross-pah-tse'a-le, *adj* (of) aerospace

aerostato, ah-ay-ross-tah-to, *m* air-balloon

afa, ah-fah, *f* sultriness

affabile, ahf-fah-be-lay, *adj* affable

affaccendarsi, ahf-faht-chen-**dar**-se, *v* to get busy

affaccendato, ahf-faht-chen-**dah**-to, *adj* busy

affacciarsi, ahf-faht-**char**-se, *v* to look out of the window

affamare, ahf-fah-**mah**-ray, *v* to starve out

affamato, ahf-fah-**mah**-to, *adj* hungry, starved

affannare, ahf-fahn-**nah**-ray, *v* to grieve, to worry

affannarsi, ahf-fahn-**nar**-se, *v* to bustle; to fret

affannato*, ahf-fahn-**nah**-to, *adj* out of breath

affanno, ahf-**fahn**-no, *m* difficulty of breath; anxiety

affare, ahf-**fah**-ray, *m* business; matter; affair; bargain

affarista, ahf-fah-**riss**-tah, *m/f* unscrupulous business man/woman

affascinante, ahf-fah-she-**nahn**-tay, *adj* fascinating

affascinare, ahf-fah-she-**nah**-ray, *v* to fascinate

affaticare, ahf-fah-te-**kah**-ray, *v* to tire, to fatigue

affatto, ahf-**faht**-to, *adv* not at all; entirely

affermare, ahf-fair-**mah**-ray, *v* to affirm

affermazione, ahf-fair-mah-tse'o-nay, *f* statement; achievement

afferrare, ahf-fair-**rah**-ray, *v* to seize

affettare, ahf-fet-**tah**-ray, *v* to pretend; to slice

affettato, ahf-fet-**tah**-to, *adj* affected; *m* sliced cold meat

affetto, ahf-**fet**-to, *m* affection; affected, suffering (from)

affettuoso*, ahf-fet-too'o-zo, *adj* affectionate

affezionato, ahf-fay-tse'o-na-to, *adj* fond (of), attached (to)

affezione, ahf-fay-tse'o-nay, *f* affection; ailment

affiatarsi, ahf-fe'ah-**tah**-rse, *v* to get on well together

affibbiare, ahf-fib-be'**ah**-ray, *v* to buckle; to give (slap, kick)

affidare, ahf-fe-**dah**-ray, *v* to entrust, to rely on

affievolire, ahf-fe'ay-vo-lee-ray, *v* to weaken

affiggere, ahf-**feed**-jay-ray,

v to placard, to stick up

affilare, ahf-fe-**lah**-ray, *v* to sharpen

affilato, ahf-fe-**lah**-to, *adj* sharpened

affinare, ahf-fe-**nah**-ray, *v* to refine

affinché, ahf-fin-**kay**, *conj*, in order that

affine, ahf-**fee**-nay, *adj* akin

affinità, ahf-fee-nee-tah, *f* affinity

affiorare, ahf-fe'o-**rah**-ray, *v* to come to the surface

affittare, ahf-feet-**tah**-ray, *v* to rent; to let; to hire

affitto, ahf-**feet**-to, *m* rent; lease

affliggere, ahf-**fleed**-jay-ray, *v* to afflict; to trouble; to pain

afflitto, ahf-**fleet**-to, *adj* afflicted

afflizione, ahf-flee-tse'o-nay, *f* affliction

afflosciarsi, ahf-flo-shee'a-rse, *v* to go limp, to collapse

affluente, ahf-floo'en-tay, *m* tributary

affluenza, ahf-floo'en-tsah, *f* influx; flow; turn-out

affluire, ahf-floo'ee-ray, *v* to flow (into); to flock (to)

afflusso, ahf-**flooss**-so, *m*

influx, flow

affogare, ahf-fo-**gah**-ray, *v* to drown

affollamento, ahf-fol-lah-**men**-to, *m* gathering

affollare, ahf-fol-**lah**-ray, *v* to crowd

affondare, ahf-fon-**dah**-ray, *v* to sink

affrancare, ahf-frahn-**kah**-ray, *v* to stamp (letters); to prepay; to release; to redeem

affranto, ahf-**frahn**-to, *adj* worn out; overcome

affrettarsi, ahf-fret-**tah**-rse, *v* to hasten

affrontare, ahf-fron-**tah**-ray, *v* to confront; to face

affronto, ahf-**fron**-to, *m* insult, affront

affumicare, ahf-foo-me-**kah**-ray, *v* to fill with smoke, to smoke (food)

afono, ah-fo-no, *adj* voiceless, aphonous

afoso, ah-**fo**-so, *adj* sultry

Africa, ah-free-kah, *f* Africa

africano, -a, ah-free-**kah**-no, *adj* African; *m/f* African

agenda, ah-**jen**-dah, *f* diary

agente, ah-**jen**-tay, *m/f* agent

agenzia, ah-jen-tsee-ah, *f*

agency

agevolare, ah-jay-vo-**lah**-ray, *v* to facilitate

agevole, ah-**jay**-vo-lay, *adj* easy, manageable

agevolazione, ah-jay-vo-lah-tse'o-nay, *f* facility, easy terms (for credit, etc)

agganciare, ahg-gahn-**chah**-ray, *v* to hook, to hang up; to clasp

aggeggio, ahd-**jej**-jo, *m* gadget

aggettivo, ahd-jet-**tee**-vo, *m* adjective

agghiacciante, ahg-ghe'aht-**chan**-tay, *adj* chilling

agghindarsi, ahg-ghin-**dah**-rse, *v* to dress in one's best

aggiornamento, ahd-jor-nah-**men**-to, *m* adjournment, postponement; updating

aggiornare, ahd-jor-**nah**-ray, *v* to postpone; to bring up to date

aggirare, ahd-je-**rah**-ray, *v* to go round; to dupe

aggirarsi, ahd-je-**ras**-se, *v* to wander about

aggiudicare, ahd-joo-de-**kah**-ray, *v* to award

aggiungere, ahd-**joonn**-jay-ray, *v* to add

aggiunta, ahd-**joonn**-tah, *f*

addition

aggiustare, ahd-jooss-**tah**-ray, *v* to adjust; to mend; to settle

agglomerato, ahg-gloh-may-**rah**-to, *m* conglomerate; **– urbano,** built-up area

aggrapparsi, ahg-grahp-**pah**-rse, *v* to cling (to)

aggravare, ahg-grah-**vah**-ray, *v* to aggravate

aggraziato*, ahg-grah-tse'**ah**-to, *adj* graceful

aggredire, ahg-gray-**dee**-ray, *v* to assault

aggregarsi, ahg-gray-**gah**-rse, *v* to join

aggressione, ahg-gress-se'o-nay, *f* aggression; attack

aggressivo, ahg-gress-see-vo, *adj* aggressive

aggressore, ahg-gress-**sor**-ay, *m* aggressor

aggrottare, ahg-grot-**tah**-ray, *v* **– le sopracciglia,** to frown

aggrovigliato, ahg-gro-vee-l'**yah**-to, *adj* entangled

agguantare, ahg-goo'**ahn**-tah-ray, *v* to seize, to catch

agguato, ahg-goo'**ah**-to, *m* ambush

agiatamente, ah-jah-tah-**men**-tay, *adv*

comfortably

agiatezza, ah-jah-**tet**-tsah, *f* comfort

agiato, ah-**jah**-to, *adj* wealthy; comfortable

agile, ah-je-lay, *adj* agile, alert

agio, ah-jo, *m* comfort, ease; convenience

agire, ah-**jee**-ray, *v* to act

agitare, ah-je-**tah**-ray, *v* to shake; to agitate

aglio, ah-**l'yo,** *m* garlic

agnello, ah-n'**yell**-lo, *m* lamb

ago, ah-go, *m* needle

agonia, ah-go-**nee**-ah, *f* agony; death throes

agosto, ah-**goss**-to, *m* August

agrario, ah-**gra**-ree'o, *adj* agrarian, agricultural

agricoltore, ah-gre-kol-**tor**-ay, *m* farmer

agricoltura, ah-gre-kol-**too**-rah, *f* agriculture, farming

agrifoglio, ah-gre-**fo**-l'yo, *m* holly

agrimensore, ah-gre-men-**sor**-ay, *m* land surveyor

agriturismo, ah-gre-too-**res**-mo, *m* farm holidays

agro, ah-gro, *adj* sharp, sour; pungent

agrodolce, ah-gro-**doll**-chay, *adj* bitter-sweet

agronomo, ah-gro-no-mo,

m agronomist

agrume, ah-**groo**-may, *m* citrus fruit

aguzzare, ah-goot-**tsah**-ray, *v* to sharpen

aguzzino, ah-goot-**tsee**-no, *m* tyrant

aguzzo, ah-**goot**-tso, *adj* sharp; pointed

ah!, ah, *interj* oh! ah!

ahi!, ah'e, *interj* ouch!

ahimè, ah'e-**may,** *interj* alas! poor me!

aia, ah'e-ah, *f* threshing-floor

AIDS, ah'eds, *m* AIDS

airone, ah'e-**ro**-nay, *m* heron

aitante, ah'e-**tahn**-tay, *adj* strong, robust

aiuola, ah-yoo-o-lah, *f* flower-bed

aiutante, ah-yoo-**tahn**-tay, *m/f* adjutant; helper

aiutare, ah-yoo-**tah**-ray, *v* to assist, to help

aiuto, ah-**yoo**-to, *m* help; support

aizzare, ah'it-**tsah**-ray, *v* to instigate, to incite

ala, ah-lah, *f* wing

alacre, ah-**lah**-kray, *adj* active, cheerful; brisk

alano, ah-**lah**-no, *m* great Dane

alba, ahl-bah, *f* day-break, dawn

albeggiare, ahl-bayd-**jah**-

ray, *v* to dawn

alberato, ahl-bay-**rah**-to, *adj* lined with trees

alberatura, ahl-bay-rah-**too**-rah, *f* masts

albergatore, ahl-bair-gah-**tor**-ay, *m* hotel owner

albergo, ahl-**bair**-go, *m* hotel

albero, ahl-bay-ro, *m* tree; shaft; mast

albicocca, ahl-be-**kok**-kah, *f* apricot

albicocco, ahl-be-**kok**-ko, *m* apricot-tree

albo, ahl-boh, *m* professional register

album ahl-boom *m* album

albume, ahl-**boo**-may, *m* albumen

alce, ahl-chay, *m* elk, moose

alcolizzato, -a, ahl-ko-led-**zah**-to, *adj* alcoholic; *m/f* alcoholic

alcool, ahl-ko-ol, *m* alcohol

alcova, ahl-ko-vah, *f* alcove

alcuni, ahl-**koo**-ne, *adj &* *pron* a few, some

alcuno, ahl-**koo**-no, *adj* **non –** , not ... any

aldilà, ahl-de-lah, *m* after-life

alfabeto, ahl-fah-**bay**-to, *m* alphabet

alfiere, ahl-fe'**ay**-ray, *m*

ensign; bishop (in chess)

alga, ahl-gah, *f* sea-weed

alibi, ah-lee-be, *m* alibi

alice, ah-lee-chay, *f* anchovy

alienare, ah-le'ay-**nah**-ray, *v* to alienate

alieno, ah-le'**ay**-no, *adj* – **a,** not inclined to, averse to

alimentare, ah-le-men-**tah**-ray, *v* to feed

alimentazione, ah-le-men-tah-tse'o-nay, *f* nutrition, diet

alimento, ah-le-**men**-to, *m* food

aliscafo, ah-le-**skah**-fo, *m* hydrofoil

alitare, ah-le-**tah**-ray, *v* to breeze; to blow gently

alito, ah-le-to, *m* breath

allacciare, ahl-laht-**chah**-ray, *v* to fasten; to lace up; to link

allagare, ahl-lah-**gah**-ray, *v* to flood

allargare, ahl-lar-**gah**-ray, *v* to broaden; to extend; to let out

allarmare, ahl-lar-**mah**-ray, *v* to alarm

allarme, ahl-**lar**-may, *m* alarm

allarmismo, ahl-**lar**-mees-mo, *m* scaremongering

allattare, ahl-laht-**tah**-ray,

v to feed, to nurse

alleanza, ahl-lay-**ahn**-tsah, *f* alliance

alleato, ahl-lay-**ah**-to, *adj* allied, *m* ally

allegare, ahl-lay-**gah**-ray, *v* to allege; to attach

allegato, ahl-lay-**gah**-to, *adj* enclosed; *m* enclosure

alleggerire, ahl-led-jay-**ree**-ray, *v* to lighten

allegria, ahl-lay-**gree**-ah, *f* merriment, joy

allegro, ahl-**lay**-gro, *adj* merry

allenamento, ahl-lay-nah-**men**-to, *m* training

allenare, ahl-lay-**nah**-ray, *v* to exercise, to train

allentare, ahl-len-**tah**-ray, *v* to slacken

allergia, ahl-ler-**je**-ah, *f* allergy

allergico, ahl-**ler**-je-ko, *adj* allergic

allestimento, ahl-less-te-**men**-to, *m* completion; fitting out

allestire, ahl-less-**tee**-ray, *v* to prepare; to stage

allettare, ahl-let-**tah**-ray, *v* to allure

allevamento, ahl-lay-vah-**men**-to, *m* breeding

allevare, ahl-lay-**vah**-ray, *v* to bring up; to breed

alleviare, ahl-lay-ve'**ah**-

ray, *v* to alleviate

allibire, ahl-le-**bee**-ray, *v* to be bewildered

allietare, ahl-le'ay-**tah**-ray, *v* to cheer up

allievo, ahl-le'**ay**-vo, *m* pupil; – **ufficiale,** cadet

allineamento, ahl-le-nay-ah-**men**-to, *m* alignment

allineare, ahl-le-nay-**ah**-ray, *v* to set in line

allocco, ahl-**lok**-ko, *m* owl; *fig* dunce

allodola, ahl-lo-do-lah, *f* lark

alloggiare, ahl-lod-**jah**-ray, *v* to lodge, to dwell

alloggio, ahl-**lod**-jo, *m* lodgings; flat

allontanamento, ahl-lon-tah-nah-**men**-to, *m* removal

allontanare, ahl-lon-tah-**nah**-ray, *v* to send away

allora, ahl-lo-rah, *adv* then; in such a case

allorché, ahl-lor-kay, *conj,* when, as soon as

alloro, ahl-lo-ro, *m* laurel

alluce, ahl-loo-chay, *m* big toe

allucinante, ahl-loo-che-**nahn**-tay, *adj* awful

allucinazione, ahl-loo-che-nah-tse'o-nay, *f* hallucination

alludere, ahl-**loo**-day-ray, *v* to allude

alluminio, ahl-loo-mee-ne'o, *m* aluminium

allungare, ahl-loonn-**gah**-ray, *v* to lengthen; to water down

alluvione, ahl-loo-ve'o-nay, *f* flood

almeno, ahl-**may**-no, *adv* at least

alone, ah-**lo**-nay, *m* halo

Alpi, ahl-pe, *fpl* Alps

alpino, ahl-**pe**-no, *adj* alpine

alquanto, ahl-**kwahn**-to, *adv* somewhat

altalena, ahl-tah-**lay**-nah, *f* see-saw; swing

altare, ahl-**tah**-ray, *m* altar

alterare, ahl-tay-**rah**-ray, *v* to alter; to adulterate

alterco, ahl-**tair**-ko, *m* quarrel

alternare, ahl-tair-**nah**-ray, *v* to alternate

alternativo, ahl-tair-nah-**tee**-vo, *adj* alternative

alterno, ahl-**tair**-no, *adj* alternate

altezza, ahl-**tet**-tsah, *f* height; Highness

altipiano, ahl-te-pe'**ah**-no, *m* plateau

altitudine, ahl-te-too-de-nay, *f* altitude

alto*, ahl-to, *adj* high; tall; loud

altolocato, ahl-to-lo-kah-to, *adj* of high rank

altrettanto, ahl-tret-**tan**-to, *adj & pron* as much, as many; *adv* equally

altri, ahl-tre, *pron* somebody else; others

altrimenti, ahl-tre-**men**-te, *adv* otherwise

altro, ahl-tro, *adj & pron* other

altronde, ahl-**tron**-day, *adv* d'–, besides, on the other hand

altrove, ahl-**tro**-vay, *adv* elsewhere

altrui, ahl-trooe, *adj* somebody else's

altura, ahl-too-rah, *f* hillock

alunno, ah-**loonn**-no, *m* pupil

alveare, ahl-vay-**ah**-ray, *m* beehive

alveo, ahl-vay-o, *m* riverbed

alzare, ahl-tsah-ray, *v* to raise; to hoist

alzarsi, ahl-tsar-se, *v* to get up; to stand up

amaca, ah-mah-kah, *f* hammock

amante, ah-**mahn**-tay, *m/f* lover; *adj* fond (of)

amare, ah-**mah**-ray, *v* to love, to cherish

amareggiare, ah-mah-red-**jah**-ray, *v* to embitter

amarena, ah-mah-**ray**-nah, *f* black cherry

amaretto, ah-mah-**ret**-to, *m* macaroon

amarezza, ah-mah-**ret**-tsah, *f* bitterness; grief

amaro*, ah-**mah**-ro, *adj* bitter

ambasciata, ahm-bah-she'**ah**-tah, *f* embassy

ambasciatore, -trice, ahm-bah-she'ah-**tor**-ay, ahm-bah-she'ah-**tree**-chay, *m/f* ambassador

ambedue, ahm-bay-doo-ay, *adj & pron* both

ambientare, ahm-be'en-**tah**-ray, *v* to acclimatize; to set (novel, film)

ambiente, ahm-be'**en**-tay, *m* environment; room; circle

ambiguo*, ahm-bee-goo'o, *adj* ambiguous

ambire, ahm-bee-ray, *v* to aspire

ambito, ahm-be-to, *m* sphere, area

ambito, ahm-bee-to, *adj* coveted

ambizione, ahm-be-tse'o-nay, *f* ambition

ambizioso*, ahm-be-tse'o-so, *adj* ambitious

ambra, ahm-brah, *f* amber

ambulante, ahm-boo-lahn-tay, *adj* itinerant; *m* pedlar

ambulanza, ahm-boo-lahn-tsah, *f* ambulance

ambulatorio, ahm-boo-lah-**to**-re'oh, *m* surgery

amenità, ah-may-ne-**tah**, *f* amenity

ameno, ah-**may**-no, *adj* pleasant; mild; amusing

America, ah-**may**-re-kah, *f* America

americano, ah-may-re-**kah**-no, *adj* American

ametista, ah-may-**tiss**-tah, *f* amethyst

amianto, ah-me'**ahn**-to, *m* asbestos

amica, ah-**mee**-kah, *f* (lady) friend

amichevole, ah-me-**kay**-vo-lay, *adj* amiable

amicizia, ah-me-**chee**-tse-ah, *f* friendship

amico, ah-**mee**-ko, *m* friend,; *adj* friendly

amido, ah-me-do, *m* starch

ammaccare, ahm-mahk-**kah**-ray, *v* to bruise; to crush

ammaccatura, ahm-mahk-kah-**too**-rah, *f* bruise

ammaestrare, ahm-mah-ess-**trah**-ray, *v* to train

ammainare, ahm-mah'e-**nah**-ray, *v* to take in sails

ammalarsi, ahm-mah-**lah**-rse, *v* to become ill

ammalato, ahm-mah-**lah**-to, *m* sick person; patient; *adj* sick; ailing

ammaliare, ahm-mah-le'**ah**-ray, *v* to bewitch

ammanco, ahm-**mahn**-ko, *m* deficit

ammanettare, ahm-mah-net-**tah**-ray, *v* to handcuff

ammassare, ahm-mahss-**sah**-ray, *v* to amass

ammasso, ahm-**mahss**-so, *m* heap

ammattire, ahm-maht-**tee**-ray, *v* to go mad

ammazzare, ahm-maht-**tsah**-ray, *v* to kill

ammenda, ahm-**men**-dah, *f* fine; amends

ammettere, ahm-**met**-tay-ray, *v* to admit

ammiccare, ahm-mick-**kah**-ray, *v* to wink

amministrare, ahm-me-niss-**trah**-ray, *v* to run, to manage

amministratore, ahm-me-niss-trah-**tor**-ay, *m* managing director; – **fiduciario,** trustee

ammiraglio, ahm-me-**rah**l'yo, *m* admiral

ammirare, ahm-me-**rah**-ray, *v* to admire

ammirevole, ahm-me-**ray**-vo-lay, *adj* admirable

ammissibile, ahm-miss-**see**-be-lay, *adj* admissible

ammobiliare, ahm-mo-be-l'**yah**-ray, *v* to furnish

ammodo, ahm-**mo**-do, *adj* respectable

ammogliarsi, ahm-mo-l'**yar**-se, *v* (man) to marry

ammollo, ahm-**mol**-lo, *m* soaking

ammoniaca, ahm-mo-nee-ah-kah, *f* ammonia

ammonimento, ahm-mo-ne-**men**-to, *m* admonition; warning

ammonire, ahm-mo-**nee**-ray, *v* to admonish

ammontare, ahm-mon-**tah**-ray, *m* sum; *v* to amount

ammonticchiare, ahm-mon-tick-ke'**ah**-ray, *v* to heap together; to hoard

ammorbidire, ahm-mor-be-**dee**-ray, *v* to soften

ammortamento, ahm-mor-tah-**men**-to, *m* settlement of debts by sinking fund

ammortizzare, ahm-mor-tit-**tsah**-ray, *v* to pay off a debt by instalments

ammucchiare, ahm-mook-ke'**ah**-ray, *v* to pile up

ammuffire, ahm-moof-**fee**-ray, *v* to get mouldy

ammutinamento, ahm-moo-te-nah-**men**-to, *m*

mutiny; uprising

ammutinarsi, ahm-moo-te-**nar**-se, *v* to mutiny

ammutolire, ahm-moo-to-**lee**-ray, *v* to be struck dumb

amnistia, ahm-niss-**tee**-ah, *f* amnesty

amnistiare, ahm-niss-te'**ah**-ray, *v* to grant pardon

amo, ah-mo, *m* fishing-hook

amore, ah-**mo**-ray, *m* love

amoreggiare, ah-mo-red-**jah**-ray, *v* to woo

amorevole, ah-mo-**ray**-vo-lay, *adj* loving

amorino, ah-mo-**ree**-no, *m* cupid

amoroso*, ah-mo-**ro**-zo, *adj* amorous

ampio*, ahm-pe'o, *adj* wide, ample, spacious

amplesso, ahm-**pless**-so, *m* embrace

ampliare, ahm-ple'**ah**-ray, *v* to enlarge

ampolla, ahm-**poll**-lah, *f* phial; cruet-bottle

ampolloso*, ahm-poll-**lo**-zo, *adj* bombastic

amputare, ahm-poo-**tah**-ray, *v* to amputate

anagrafe, ah-**nah**-grah-fay, *f* register of births, marriages and deaths

analfabeta, ah-nahl-fah-

bay-tah, *adj* illiterate

analisi, ah-**nah**-le-ze, *f* analysis; **in ultima –**, in short, after all

analizzare, ah-nah-lit-**tsah**-ray, *v* to analyse

analogico, ah-nah-**lo**-je-ko, *adj* analogical; (watch) analog

analogo*, ah-**nah**-lo-go, *adj* analogous

ananas, ah-nah-**nahs**, *m* pineapple

anarchia, ah-nar-**kee**-ah, *f* anarchy

anarchico, ah-**nar**-ke-ko, *m* anarchist

anatomia, ah-nah-to-**mee**-ah, *f* anatomy

anatra, ah-nah-trah, *f* duck

anca, ahn-kah, *f* hip; haunch

anche, ahn-kay, *conj* also, too; even

ancora, ahn-**ko**-rah, *adv* again; more; yet

ancora, ahn-**ko**-rah, *f* anchor

andamento, ahn-dah-**men**-to, *m* trend; progress

andante, ahn-**dahn**-tay, *adj* current; cheap; *m mus* andante

andare, ahn-**dah**-ray, *v* to go

andarsene, ahn-**dar**-say-

nay, *v* to leave, to depart

andata, ahn-**dah**-tah, *f* outward journey

andatura, ahn-dah-**too**-rah, *f* gait, walking

andirivieni, ahn-de-re-ve'**ay**-ne, *m* coming and going

andito, **ahn**-de-to, *m* corridor

androne, ahn-**dro**-nay, *m* entrance; hall

aneddoto, ah-**ned**-do-to, *m* anecdote

anelare, ah-nay-**lah**-ray, *v* to long for

anelito, ah-**nay**-le-to, *m* breath; gasp; craving

anello, ah-**nell**-lo, *m* ring; ringlet; link

anemia, ah-nay-**mee**-ah, *f* anaemia

anestesia, ah-nay-stay-**ze**'ah, *f* anaesthesia

anestetico, ah-nay-**stay**-te-ko, *m* anaesthetic

anfibio, ah-**fee**-be'o, *adj* amphibious; amphibian

angelo, **ahn**-jay-lo, *m* angel

angina, ahn-je-nah, *f* tonsillitis; **– pectoris**, angina

anglicano, -a, ahn-glee-**kah**-no, *adj* Anglican; *m/f* Anglican

angolare, ahn-go-**lah**-ray, *adj* angular

angolo, ahn-go-lo, *m* corner, angle

angoscia, ahn-go-she'ah, *f* anguish

angoscioso*, ahn-go-she'o-zo, *adj* distressing

anguilla, ahn-goo'eel-lah, *f* eel

anguria, ahn-goo-re'ah, *f* watermelon

angustia, ahn-gooss-te'ah, *f* sorrow; misery

angusto*, ahn-gooss-to, *adj* narrow; poor, modest

anice, ah-ne-chay, *m* aniseed

anima, ah-ne-mah, *f* soul

animare, ah-ne-mah-ray, *v* to animate

animarsi, ah-ne-mar-se, *v* to take heart; to come to

animella, ah-ne-mel-lah, *f* sweet-bread

animo, ah-ne-mo, *m* mind, soul; courage; disposition

anitra, ah-ne-trah, *f* duck

annacquare, ahn-nahk-kwah-ray, *v* to dilute

annaffiare, ahn-nahf-fe'ah-ray, *v* to water

annaffiatoio, ahn-nahf-fe'ah-**to**-e'o, *m* watering-can

annali, ahn-nah-le, *mpl* annals

annaspare, ahn-nah-**spah**-ray, *v* to reel; to gasp

annata, ahn-nah-tah, *f* year; year's profits

annebbiare, ahn-neb-be'ah-ray, *v* to cloud

annebbiarsi, ahn-neb-be'ar-se, *v* to become misty

annegare, ahn-nay-gah-ray, *v* to drown

annerire, ahn-nay-ree-ray, *v* to blacken

annessi, ahn-ness-se, *mpl* out-buildings

annessione, ahn-ness-se'o-nay, *f* annexation

annettere, ahn-net-tay-ray, *v* to annex

annichilire, ahn-ne-ke-lee-ray, *v* to annihilate

annientare, ahn-ne'en-tah-ray, *v* to annihilate

anniversario, ahn-ne-vair-**sah**-re'o, *m* anniversary

anno, ahn-no, *m* year

annodare, ahn-no-dah-ray, *v* to tie

annoiare, ahn-no-yah-ray, *v* to bore; to annoy

annotare, ahn-no-tah-ray, *v* to take a note of

annoverare, ahn-no-vay-rah-ray, *v* to number

annuale, ahn-noo'ah-lay, *adj* yearly

annuire, ahn-noo'ee-ray, *v* to assent; to nod

annullare, ahn-nooll-lah-ray, *v* to annul; to cancel; to quash

annunciare, ahn-noon-che'ah-ray, *v* to announce

annuncio, ahn-noon-che'o, *m* advertisement; notice; announcement

annuo, ahn-noo'o, *adj* annual

annusare, ahn-noo-sah-ray, *v* to sniff; to scent

annuvolarsi, ahn-noo-vo-lar-se, *v* to become cloudy

anomalo, ah-no-mah-lo, *adj* anomalous

anonimo, ah-no-ne-mo, *adj* anonymous

anormale, ah-nor-mah-lay, *adj* abnormal

ansa, ahn-sah, *f* loop

ansia, ahn-se'ah, *f* longing; anxiety

ansietà, ahn-se'ay'tah, *f* anxiety; agitation

ansimare, ahn-se-mah-ray, *v* to pant, to be out of breath

antecedente, ahn-tay-chay-**den**-tay, *adj* antecedent

antenato, ahn-tay-nah-to, *m* ancestor

antenna, ahn-ten-nah, *f* antenna; aerial

anteporre, ahn-tay-**por**-

ray, *v* to prefer

anteriore, ahn-tay-re'o-ray, *adj* anterior, prior

antibiotico, ahn-te-be'o-te-ko, *m* antibiotic

anticaglie, ahn-te-**kah**-l'yay, *fpl* antiquities, old curiosities

anticamente, ahn-te-kah-**men**-tay, *adv* in bygone times, formerly

anticamera, ahn-te-**kah**-may-rah, *f* ante-chamber; hall

antichità, ahn-te-ke-**tah**, *f* antiquity

anticipare, ahn-te-che-**pah**-ray, *v* to anticipate; to pay in advance

anticipo, ahn-te-che-po, *m* advance; **in –**, in advance

antico, ahn-**tee**-ko, *adj* antique; ancient

anticoncezionale, ahn-te-con-che-tse'o-**nah**-le, *adj* contraceptive; *m* contraceptive

antifurto, ahn-te-**foor**-to, *m* burglar alarm

antigelo, ahn-te-**jay**-lo, *m* antifreeze

antilope, ahn-**tee**-lo-pay, *f* antelope

antiorario, ahn-te-oh-**rah**-re'o, *adj* anticlockwise

antipasto, ahn-te-**pahss**-to, *m* hors-d'oeuvre

antipatico, ahn-te-**pa**-te-ko, *adj* disagreeable

antipodi, ahn-**tee**-po-de, *mpl* antipodes

antiquato*, ahn-te-**kwah**-to, *adj* obsolete; out-of-date

antistaminico, ahn-te-stah-me-**ne**-ko, *m* antihistamine

antracite, ahn-trah-**chee**-tay, *f* anthracite

antro, **ahn**-tro, *m* cave, den, lair

anulare, ah-noo-**lah**-ray, *m* ring-finger

anzi, **ahn**-tse, *adv* rather; even; just the opposite

anzianità, ahn-tse'ah-ne-**tah**, *f* seniority

anziano, -a, ahn-tse'**ah**-no, *adj* aged, elder, senior; *m/f* old person

anziché, ahn-tse-**kay**, *conj*, rather than

anzitutto, ahn-tse-**toot**-to, *adv* first of all

apatia, ah-pah-**tee**-ah, *f* apathy, insensibility

apatico*, ah-**pa**-te-ko, *adj* apathetic, indifferent

ape, **ah**-pay, *f* bee

aperitivo, ah-pay-re-**tee**-vo, *m* apéritif

aperto*, ah-**pair**-to, *adj* open, candid

apertura, ah-pair-**too**-rah, *f* aperture; opening

apice, **ah**-pe-chay, *m* apex, top; *fig* summit

apoplessia, ah-po-pless-**see**-ah, *f* apoplexy

apostolo, ah-**poss**-to-lo, *m* apostle

appagamento, ahp-pah-gah-**men**-to, *m* satisfaction

appagare, ahp-pah-**gah**-ray, *v* to satisfy, to content

appaltare, ahp-pahl-**tah**-ray, *v* to lease out on contract

appaltatore, ahp-pahl-tah-**tor**-ay, *m* contractor

appalto, ahp-**pahl**-to, *m* contract

appannare, ahp-pahn-**nah**-ray, *v* to mist, to dim

apparato, ahp-pah-**rah**-to, *m* apparatus; *fig* pomp, show

apparecchiare, ahp-pah-reck-ke'**ah**-ray, *v* to prepare; to lay the table

apparecchio, ahp-pah-**reck**-ke'o, *m* apparatus; outfit; aircraft

apparente, ahp-pah-**ren**-tay, *adj* apparent

apparenza, ahp-pah-**ren**-tsah, *f* appearance

apparire, ahp-pah-**ree**-ray, *v* to appear

appartamento, ahp-par-

25

tah-**men**-to, *m* flat

appartarsi, ahp-par-**tar**-se,
v to withdraw oneself

appartenere, ahp-par-tay-
nay-ray, *v* to belong

appassionarsi, ahp-pahss-
se'o-**nar**-se, *v* to become
very interested

appassionato*, ahp-pahss-
se'o-**nah**-to, *adj*
passionate; affectionate

appassire, ahp-pahss-**see**-
ray, *v* to wizen, to fade

appellarsi, ahp-pell-**lah**-
rse, *v law* to appeal

appello, ahp-**pell**-lo, *m*
appeal; roll-call

appena, ahp-**pay**-nah, *adv*
barely, hardly; *conj* as
soon as

appendere, ahp-**pen**-day-
ray, *v* to hang up

appetito, ahp-pay-**tee**-to,
m appetite

appianare, ahp-pe'ah-**nah**-
ray, *v* to smooth; to level

appiattire, ahp-pe'aht-**tee**-
ray, *v* to flatten

appiccicare, ahp-pit-che-
kah-ray, *v* to stick

appiccicaticcio, ahp-pit-
che-kah-**tit**-cho, *adj*
sticky

appieno, ahp-pe'**ay**-no,
adv entirely, completely

appigliarsi, ahp-pe-l'**yar**-
se, *v* to cling

appiglio, ahp-**pee**-l'yo, *m*
pretext; grip

appioppare, ahp-pe'op-
pah-ray, *v fam* to give (a
slap, a punch)

applaudire, ahp-plah'oo-
dee-ray, *v* to applaud

applicare, ahp-ple-**kah**-
ray, *v* to apply

appoggiare, ahp-pod-**jah**-
ray, *v* to lean; to help

appoggiarsi, ahp-pod-**jar**-
se, *v* to lean against; to
rely upon

appoggio, ahp-**pod**-jo, *m*
support, protection

apporre, ahp-**por**-ray, *v* to
affix

apportare, ahp-por-**tah**-
ray, *v* to bring; to carry

apporto, ahp-**por**-to, *m*
contribution

apposito*, ahp-**po**-ze-to,
adj made to order,
appropriate

apposta, ahp-**poss**-tah, *adv*
for the express purpose

appostamento, ahp-poss-
tah-**men**-to, *m* ambush

apprendere, ahp-**pren**-
day-ray, *v* to learn

apprendista, ahp-pren-
diss-tah, *m/f* apprentice;
articled clerk

apprensione, ahp-pren-
se'o-nay, *f* apprehension

appresso, ahp-**press**-so,
adv near, close; after

apprestare, ahp-press-**tah**-
ray, *v* to prepare

apprezzare, ahp-pret-**tsah**-
ray, *v* to appreciate

approccio, ahp-**proch**-
cho, *m* approach

approdare, ahp-pro-
dah-ray, *v* to land; to
arrive at

approdo, ahp-**pro**-do, *m*
landing; landing-place

approfittare, ahp-pro-feet-
tah-ray, *v* to profit

approfondire, ahp-pro-
fon-**dee**-ray, *v* to deepen;
to fathom

approssimarsi, ahp-pross-
se-**mar**-se, *v* to
approach; to
approximate

approvare, ahp-pro-**vah**-
ray, *v* to approve

approvazione, ahp-pro-
vah-tse'o-nay, *f* approval

approvvigionare, ahp-
prov-ve-jo-**nah**-ray, *v* to
supply; to provide

appuntamento, ahp-
poonn-tah-**men**-to, *m*
appointment; meeting

appuntare, ahp-poonn-
tah-ray, *v* to pin

appuntato, ahp-poonn-
tah-to, *m* corporal

appunto, ahp-**poonn**-to, *m*
note; blame; *adv*
precisely, quite so

appurare, ahp-poo-**rah**-
ray, *v* to verify; to

clear up

apribottiglie, ahp-pree-bot-**tee**-l'yay, *m* bottle-opener

aprile, ah-**pree**-lay, *m* April

aprire, ah-**pree**-ray, *v* to open

apriscatole, ahp-pree-skah-**to**-lay, *m* tin opener

aquila, ah-**kwe**-lah, *f* eagle

aquilone, ah-kwe-**lo**-nay, *m* kite

aragosta, ah-rah-**goss**-tah, *f* lobster

araldica, ah-**rahl**-de-kah, *f* heraldry

araldo, ah-**rahl**-do, *m* herald

arancia, ah-**rahn**-chah, *f* orange

aranciata, ah-rahn-**chah**-tah, *f* orangeade

arancio, ah-**rahn**-cho, *m* orange-tree

arancione, ah-rahn-**cho**-nay, *adj & m* orange

arare, ah-**rah**-ray, *v* to plough

aratro, ah-**rah**-tro, *m* plough

arazzo, ah-**raht**-tso, *m* tapestry

arbitrare, ahr-be-**trah**-ray, *v* to arbitrate; to referee

arbitrio, ahr-**bee**-tre'o, *m* arbitrary act; **libero –,**

free will

arbitro, ahr-**be**-tro, *m* arbiter; umpire; referee

arboscello, ahr-bo-**shell**-lo, *m* sapling

arbusto, ahr-**booss**-to, *m* shrub

arca, ahr-kah, *f* ark, chest; tomb

arcata, ahr-**kah**-tah, *f* arcade; arch

archeologia, ahr-ke'o-loh-je-ah, *f* archeology

archeologo, ahr-ke'o-loh-go, *m* archeologist

archetto, ahr-**ket**-to, *m* violin-bow

architetto, ahr-kee-**tet**-to, *m* architect

architettura, ahr-kee-tet-**too**-rah, *f* architecture

archivio, ahr-**kee**-ve'o, *m* archives

arcigno*, ahr-**chee**-n'yo, *adj* surly

arcivescovo, ahr-che-**vess**-ko-vo, *m* archbishop

arco, ahr-ko, *m* arch; bow

arcobaleno, ahr-ko-bah-**lay**-no, *m* rainbow

arcuato, ahr-koo**'ah**-to, *adj* arched, curved

ardente, ahr-**den**-tay, *adj* ardent

ardere, ahr-**day**-ray, *v* to burn

ardesia, ahr-**day**-se'ah, *f*

slate

ardire, ahr-**dee**-ray, *v* to dare

arditezza, ahr-de-**tet**-tsah, *f* boldness, audacity

ardito*, ahr-**dee**-to, *adj* daring

ardore, ahr-**dor**-ay, *m* ardour

arduo*, ahr-**doo**'o, *adj* arduous

arena, ah-**ray**-nah, *f* sand; arena

argano, ahr-**gah**-no, *m* capstan; winch

argenteria, ahr-jen-**tay**-re'ah, *f* silverware

argentiere, ahr-jen-te'**ay**-ray, *m* silversmith

argentino, ahr-jen-**tee**-no, *adj* silvery; harmonious

argento, ahr-**jen**-to, *m* silver

argilla, ahr-**jill**-lah, *f* clay

arginare, ahr-je-nah-ray, *v* to dam

argine, ahr-**je**-nay, *m* embankment, dyke; causeway

argomentare, ahr-go-men-**tah**-ray, *v* to argue

argomento, ahr-go-**men**-to, *m* argument; reason; subject

arguire, ahr-goo'ee-ray, *v* to argue; to infer

arguto*, ahr-**goo**-to, *adj* sharp, witty, acute

aria, ah-re'ah, *f* air; look; aria, tune

arido*, ah-re-do, *adj* dry; barren, sterile

arieggiare, ah-re-aid-**jah**-ray, *v* to ventilate

ariete, ah-re'ay-tay, *m* ram; *naut* ram; **Ariete,** Aries

arietta, ah-re'ayt-tah, *f* light musical aria; breeze

aringa, ah-**reen**-gah, *f* herring

arioso, ah-re'o-zo, *adj* airy, well-aired

aristocrazia, ah-re-sto-krah-**tsee**-ah, *f* aristocracy

aritmetica, ah-rit-**may**-te-kah, *f* arithmetic

arlecchino, ahr-lek-**kee**-no, *m* harlequin

arma, **ahr**-mah, *f* weapon

armadio, ahr-**mah**-de'o, *m* wardrobe

armaiolo, ahr-mah-e'oo-o-lo, *m* gunsmith

armamento, ahr-mah-**men**-to, *m* armament

armare, ahr-**mah**-ray, *v* to arm; *naut* to rig

armata, ahr-**mah**-tah, *f* army

armatore, ahr-mah-**tor**-ay, *m* shipowner

armatura, ahr-mah-**too**-rah, *f* armour; structure

armeria, ahr-may-**ree**-ah, *f* arsenal; armoury

armi, **ahr**-me, *fpl* arms

armistizio, ahr-miss-**tee**-tse'o, *m* armistice

armonia, ahr-mo-**nee**-ah, *f* harmony

armonizzare, ahr-mo-nit-**tsah**-ray, *v* to harmonize

arnese, ahr-**nay**-zay, *m* tool

arnia, **ahr**-nee-ah, *f* bee-hive

arpa, **ahr**-pah, *f* harp

arpione, ahr-pe'o-nay, *m* harpoon; hook

arrabattarsi, ahr-rah-baht-**tar**-se, *v* to take pains, to exert oneself

arrabbiarsi, **ahr**-rahb-be'**ar**-se, *v* to get angry

arrabbiato, ahr-rahb-be'**ah**-to, *v* angry; with rabies

arraffare, ahr-rahf-**fah**-ray, *v* to snatch, to seize

arrampicarsi, ahr-rahm-pe-**kar**-se, *v* to climb up

arrancare, ahr-rahn-**kah**-ray, *v* to limp

arrangiare, ahr-rahn-**jah**-ray, *v* to arrange

arrangiarsi, ahr-rahn-**jahr**-se, *v* to manage

arrecare, ahr-ray-**kah**-ray, *v* to bring about

arredamento, ahr-ray-dah-**men**-to, *m* furnishing; interior design

arredare, ahr-ray-**dah**-ray, *v* to furnish, to fit out

arredo, ahr-**ray**-do, *m* furniture

arrendersi, ahr-**ren**-dair-se, *v* to surrender

arrestare, ahr-ress-**tah**-ray, *v* to arrest, to stop

arretrare, ahr-ray-**tra**-ray, *v* to recede; to draw back

arretrati, ahr-ray-**trah**-te, *mpl* arrears

arricchirsi, ahr-rik-**keer**-se, *v* to grow rich

arricciare, ahr-rit-**chah**-ray, *v* to curl

arringa, ahr-**rin**-gah, *f* harangue; pleading

arringare, ahr-rin-**gah**-ray, *v* to harangue

arrischiare, ahr-riss-ke'**ah**-ray, *v* to risk

arrivare, ahr-re-**vah**-ray, *v* to arrive; to reach

arrivederci, ahr-re-vay-**der**-che, *interj* goodbye

arrivo, ahr-**ree**-vo, *m* arrival; finishing line

arroganza, ahr-ro-**gahn**-tsah, *f* arrogance

arrossire, ahr-ross-**see**-ray, *v* to blush

arrostire, ahr-ross-**tee**-ray, *v* to roast; to toast

arrosto, ahr-**ross**-to, *m* roast

arrotare, ahr-ro-**tah**-ray, *v* to sharpen

arrotolare, ahr-ro-to-**lah**-ray, *v* to roll up

arrotondare, ahr-ro-ton-**dah**-ray, *v* to make round; to round off

arrovellarsi, ahr-ro-vell-**lar**-se, *v* to rack one's brain

arruffare, ahr-roof-**fah**-ray, *v* to ruffle, to dishevel; to entangle

arrugginire, ahr-rood-je-**nee**-ray, *v* to get rusty

arruolare, ahr-roo'o-**lah**-ray, *v* to enlist

arruolarsi, ahr-roo'o-**lar**-se, *v* to enlist; to join up

arsenale, ahr-say-**nah**-lay, *v* arsenal; dockyard

arso, ahr-so, *adj* burnt, scorched

arsura, ahr-**soo**-rah, *f* drought; thirst; stifling heat

arte, ahr-tay, *f* art; skill

artefatto, ahr-tay-**faht**-to, *adj* artificial; adulterated

artefice, ahr-tay-fe-chay, *m/f* creator, maker

arteria, ahr-tay-re'ah, *f* artery

articolare, ahr-te-ko-**lah**-ray, *v* to articulate

articolo, ahr-**tee**-ko-lo, *m* article; clause

artificiale, ahr-te-fe-**chah**-lay, *adj* artificial

artificio, ahr-te-**fee**-cho, *m* artifice, trick

artigiano, ahr-te-**jah**-no, *m* artisan

artigliere, ahr-te-l'**yay**-ray, *m* artilleryman

artiglieria, ahr-te-l'yay-**ree**-ah, *f* artillery

artiglio, ahr-**tee**-l'yo, *m* claw, talon

artista, ahr-**tiss**-tah, *m/f* artist

arto, ahr-to, *m* member, limb

artrite, ahr-**tree**-tay, *f* arthritis

arzigogolare, ahr-dze-go-go-**lah**-re, *v* to muse; to quibble

arzillo, ahr-**dzell**-lo, *adj* vigorous, lively

ascella, ah-**shell**-lah, *f* armpit

ascendente, ah-shen-**den**-tay, *m* ascendant; ascendency

ascendere, ah-**shen**-day-ray, *v* to ascend, to climb

ascensione, ah-shen-se'o-nay, *f* ascent; Ascension

ascensore, ah-shen-**sor**-ay, *m* lift

ascesso, ah-**shess**-so, *m* abscess

asceta, ah-**shay**-tah, *m* ascetic

ascia, ah-she'ah, *f* axe

asciugacapelli, ah-she'oo-gah-cah-**payl**-le, *m* hair dryer

asciugamano, ah-she'oo-gah-**mah**-no, *m* towel

asciugare, ah-she'oo-**gah**-ray, *v* to dry; to wipe

asciutto, ah-she'**oot**-to, *adj* dry; lean

ascoltare, ahss-koll-**tah**-ray, *v* to listen (to)

ascoltatore, -trice, ahss-koll-tah-**tor**-ay, ahss-koll-tah-**tree**-chay, *m/f* listener

ascolto, ahss-**koll**-to, *m* **stare in –,** to be listening; **indice di –,** audience rating

ascrivere, ahss-**kree**-vay-ray, *v* to ascribe

asfalto, ahss-**fahl**-to, *m* asphalt

asfissiare, ahss-fess-se'**ah**-ray, *v* to asphyxiate

Asia, ah-ze'ah, *f* Asia

asiatico, ah-ze-**ah**-te-ko, *adj* Asian

asilo, ah-**zee**-lo, *m* asylum; shelter

asino, ah-ze-no, *m* ass

asma, ass-mah, *f* asthma

asola, ah-zo-lah, *f* buttonhole

asparago, ahss-**pah**-rah-go, *m* asparagus

aspettare, ahss-pet-**tah**-

ray, v to wait (for); to expect

aspettativa, ahss-pet-tah-**tee**-vah, f expectation

aspetto, ahss-**pet**-to, m aspect; appearance

aspirante, ahss-pe-**rahn**-tay, m/f candidate

aspirapolvere, ahss-pe-rah-**poll**-vay-ray, m vacuum cleaner

aspirare, ahss-pe-rah-ray, v to inhale; to aspirate; to aim at

aspirina, ahss-pe-**ree**-nah, f aspirin

asportare, ahss-por-**tah**-ray, v to remove, to extirpate

asprezza, ahss-**pret**-tsah, f harshness; rudeness

aspro*, ahss-pro, adj sour; bitter; rough

assaggiare, ahss-sahd-**jah**-ray, v to taste; to sample

assai, ahss-**sah**'e, adv much, plenty

assalire, ahss-sah-lee-ray, v to assault, to attack

assalto, ahss-**sahl**-to, m attack

assaporare, ahss-sah-po-**rah**-ray, v to taste

assassinare, ahss-sahss-se-**nah**-ray, v to assassinate; to murder

assassinio, ahss-sahss-see-ne'o, m murder

assassino, ahss-sahss-**see**-no, m murderer

asse, ahss-say, f plank; axle; shaft; axis

assecondare, ahss-say-kon-**dah**-ray, v to go along with

assediare, ahss-say-de'**ah**-ray, v to besiege

assedio, ahss-**say**-de'o, m siege; importunity

assegnare, ahss-say-n'**yah**-ray, v to assign; to award

assegno, ahss-**say**-n'yo, m cheque; allowance

assemblea, ahss-sem-**ble**-ah, f assembly

assennato*, ahss-sen-**nah**-to, adj prudent, wise

assentarsi, ahss-sen-**tar**-se, v to absent oneself

assente, ahss-**sen**-tay, adj absent

assentire, ahss-sen-**tee**-ray, v to assent, to agree

assenza, ahss-**sen**-tsah, f absence

asserire, ahss-say-ree-ray, v to assert

asserzione, ahss-sair-tse'o-nay, f assertion

assestare, ahss-sess-**tah**-ray, v to adjust; to put in order

assetato, ahss-say-**tah**-to, adj thirsty

assetto, ahss-**set**-to, m order; arrangement

assicurare, ahss-se-koo-**rah**-ray, v to affirm; to assure, to insure

assicurarsi, ahss-se-koo-**rar**-se, v to make sure; – **contro,** to insure oneself against

assicuratore, -trice, ahss-se-koo-rah-**tor**-ay, ahss-se-koo-rah-**tree**-chay, m/f insurance agent

assicurazione, ahss-se-koo-rah-tse'o-nay, f insurance policy; assurance

assideramento, ahss-se-day-rah-**men**-to, m exposure

assiduità, ahss-se-doo'e-**tah**, f assiduity, diligence

assiduo*, ahss-**see**-doo'o, adj assiduous

assieme, ahss-se'**ay**-may, adv together

assillato, ahss-sill-**lah**-to, adj busy; worried; annoyed

assillo, ahss-**sill**-lo, m worry, anguish

assimilare, ahss-se-me-**lah**-ray, v to assimilate

assioma, ahss-se'o-mah, m axiom

assise, ahss-see-zay, fpl (court of) assizes

assistente, ahss-siss-**ten**-tay, m/f assistant; – **sociale,** social worker; –

di volo, steward, stewardess

assistenza, ahss-siss-**ten**-tsah, *f* assistance

assistere, ahss-**siss**-tay-ray, *v* to assist; to attend

asso, **ahss**-so, *m* ace

associare, ahss-so-**chah**-ray, *v* to associate

associato, ahss-so-**chah**-to, *m* partner, associate

associazione, ahss-so-chah-tse'o-nay, *f* association; company

assodato, ahss-so-**dah**-to, *adj* well-founded

assoggettare, ahss-sod-jet-**tah**-ray, *v* to subdue

assolato, ahss-sol-**lah**-to, *adj* sunny

assoluto*, ahss-so-**loo**-to, *adj* absolute

assoluzione, ahss-so-loo-tse'o-nay, *f* absolution

assolvere, ahss-**soll**-vay-ray, *v* to absolve; *law* to acquit

assomigliare, ahss-so-me-le'**ah**-ray, *v* to resemble

assonnato*, ahss-son-**nah**-to, *adj* sleepy

assopirsi, ahss-so-**peer**-se, *v* to get sleepy, to doze off

assorbente, ahss-sor-**ben**-tay, *adj* absorbing; *m* sanitary towel

assorbimento, ahss-sor-

be-**men**-to, *m* absorption

assorbire, ahss-sor-**bee**-ray, *v* to absorb

assordare, ahss-sor-**dah**-ray, *v* to deafen

assortimento, ahss-sor-te-**men**-to, *m* assortment

assortito, ahss-sor-**tee**-to, *adj* assorted; matched

assorto, ahss-**sor**-to, *adj* absorbed

assottigliare, ahss-sot-te-l'**yah**-ray, *v* to make thin, to reduce

assuefarsi, ahss-soo'ay-**far**-se, *v* to get accustomed

assuefazione, ahss-soo'ay-fah-tse'o-nay, *f* addiction, habit

assumere, ahss-**soo**-may-ray, *v* to assume

assunto, ahss-**soonn**-to, *m* assertion; proposition

assunzione, ahss-soonn-tse'o-nay, *f* employment; Assumption

assurdità, ahss-soohr-de-**tah**, *f* absurdity

assurdo*, ahss-**soohr**-do, *adj* absurd

asta, ahss-tah, *f* staff; pole; auction

astemio, ahss-**tay**-me'o, *m* teetotaller; *adj* abstemious

astenersi, ahss-tay-**nair**-se, *v* to abstain

astensione, ahss-ten-se'o-nay, *f* abstention

astinenza, ahss-te-**nen**-tsah, *f* abstinence

astio, ahss-**te**'o, *m* spite, hatred, resentment

astioso*, ahss-te'o-zo, *adj* malicious

astrarre, ahss-**trar**-ray, *v* to abstract

astratto*, ahss-**traht**-to, *adj* abstract

astrazione, ahss-trah-tse'o-nay, *f* abstraction

astringente, ahss-trin-**jen**-tay, *adj* astringent; *m* astringent

astro, ahss-tro, *m* star

astrologia, ahss-tro-lo-jee-ah, *f* astrology

astronauta, ahss-tro-na'oo-tah, *m/f* astronaut

astronomia, ahss-tro-no-mee-ah, *f* astronomy

astruso*, ahss-**troo**-zo, *adj* abstruse, enigmatic

astuccio, ahss-**toot**-cho, *m* case, box; sheath

astuto*, ahss-**too**-to, *adj* cunning, artful, astute

astuzia, ahss-**too**-tse'ah, *f* astuteness

Atene, ah-**tay**-nay, *f* Athens

ateo, **ah**-tay'o, *m* atheist

atlante, aht-**lahn**-tay, *m* atlas

atleta, aht-**lay**-tah, *m/f*

athlete

atletico, aht-**lay**-tee-ko, *adj* athletic

atmosfera, aht-moss-**fay**-rah, *f* atmosphere

atomo, ah-to-mo, *m* atom

atrio, ah-tre'o, *m* entrance-hall, vestibule

atroce, ah-**tro**-chay, *adj* atrocious

attaccabrighe, aht-tahk-kah-**bree**-gay, *m/f* quarrelsome person

attaccamento, aht-tahk-kah-**men**-to, *m* attachment

attaccare, aht-tahk-**kah**-ray, *v* to attach, to tie; to attack; to begin

attacco, aht-**tahk**-ko, *m* attack; connection

attecchire, aht-teck-**kee**-ray, *v* to take root; to thrive

atteggiamento, aht-ted-jah-**men**-to, *m* attitude; mood

attempato, aht-tem-**pah**-to, *adj* elderly

attendente, aht-ten-**den**-tay, *m* mil orderly

attendere, aht-**ten**-day-ray, *v* to wait for; to attend to

attendibile, aht-tayn-dee-**bee**-lay, *adj* reliable

attenersi, aht-tay-**nair**-se, *v* to abide by

attentare, aht-ten-**tah**-ray, *v* to attack

attentato, aht-ten-**tah**-to, *m* attempt (on life)

attento*, aht-**ten**-to, *adj* attentive

attenuare, aht-tay-noo'**ah**-ray, *v* to attenuate, to lessen

attenzione, aht-ten-tse'o-nay, *f* attention

atterraggio, aht-tair-**rahd**-jo, *m* landing

atterrare, aht-tair-**rah**-ray, *v* (aircraft) to land; to push to the ground

atterrire, aht-tair-**ree**-ray, *v* to terrify

attesa, aht-**tay**-zah, *f* waiting

attestato, aht-tess-**tah**-to, *m* certificate; testimonial

attico, ah-te-ko, *m* attic

attiguo, aht-**tee**-goo'o, *adj* adjoining, contiguous

attillato, aht-till-**lah**-to, *adj* close-fitting

attimo, ah-te-mo, *m* instant

attinente, aht-te-**nen**-tay, *adj* relating to

attingere, aht-**teen**-jay-ray, *v* to draw on, to draw from

attirare, aht-te-**rah**-ray, *v* to attract

attitudine, aht-te-**too**-de-nay, *f* inclination, aptitude

attivare, aht-te-**vah**-ray, *v* to activate, to start

attività, aht-te-ve-**tah**, *f* activity

attivo, aht-**tee**-vo, *adj** active; *m* assets; **in –,** in credit

attizzatoio, aht-tit-tsah-**to**-e'o, *m* poker

atto, aht-to, *m* act; document; **atto** qualified, capable; fit

attonito, aht-**to**-ne-to, *adj* astonished

attorcigliarsi, aht-tor-che-l'**yar**-se, *v* to wind around

attore, aht-**tor**-ay, *m* actor; plaintiff

attorno, aht-**tor**-no, *adv* round, about

attraente, aht-trah-**enn**-tay, *adj* attractive

attrarre, aht-**trar**-ray, *v* to attract

attraversare, aht-trah-vair-**sah**-ray, *v* to cross; to go through

attraverso, aht-trah-**vair**-so, *prep* across; through

attrazione, aht-trat-tse'o-nay, *f* attraction

attrezzare, aht-tret-**tsah**-ray, *v* to fit up; to rig

attrezzo, aht-**tret**-tso, *m* tool, implement; utensil

attribuire, aht-tre-boo'ee-ray, *v* to attribute

attrice, aht-**tree**-chay, *f* actress; plaintiff

attrito, aht-**tree**-to, *m* friction; abrasion

attuabile, aht-too'**ah**-be-lay, *adj* feasible

attuale, aht-too'**ah**-lay, *adj* actual; present

attutire, aht-too-tee-ray, *v* to deaden, to cushion

audace*, ah'oo-**dah**-chay, *adj* audacious, daring

audacia, ah'oo-**dah**-chah, *f* audacity, impudence

auditorio, ah'oo-de-to-ree-o, *m* auditorium

audizione ah'oo-de-tse'o-ne, *f* audition

augurare, ah'oo-goo-**rah**-ray, *v* to wish

augurio, ah'oo-**goo**-re'o, *m* wish; omen

aula, ah'oo-lah, *f* class-room; hall; court

aumentare, ah'oo-men-**tah**-ray, *v* to increase

aumento, ah'oo-**men**-to, *m* increase; rise

aureo, ah'oo-ray'o, *adj* golden

aureola, ah'oo-**ray**-o-lah, *f* halo

aurora, ah'oo-**ro**-rah, *f* dawn

ausiliare, ah'oo-ze-le-'**ah**-ray, *adj* auxiliary; *m* gram auxiliary

ausiliario, -a, ah'oo-ze-le-'**ah**-re'o, *m/f* auxiliary

auspicio, ah'oo-**spe**-cho, *m* omen

austero*, ah'oo-**stay**-ro, *adj* austere, stern

Australia, ah'oo-**strah**-le'ah, *f* Australia

australiano, ah'oo-strah-le-**ah**-no, *adj* Australian

Austria, ah'oo-stre'ah, *f* Austria

austriaco, ah'oo-**stree**-ah-ko, *adj* Austrian

autenticare, ah'oo-ten-te-**kah**-ray, *v* to authenticate; to legalize

autenticità, ah'oo-ten-te-che-**tah**, *f* authenticity

autista, ah'oo-**tiss**-tah, *m/f* driver

autobiografia, ah'oo-to-be'o-grah-**fee**-ah, *f* autobiography

autoblinda, ah'oo-to-**blin**-dah, *f* armoured car

autobus, ah'oo-to-**booss**, *m* bus

autocarro, ah'oo-to-**kar**-ro, *m* lorry

autocrate, ah'oo-to-**krah**-tay, *m* autocrat

autodromo, ah'oo-to-dro-mo, *m* motor-racing track

autografo, ah'oo-to-grah-fo, *m* autograph

autogrill, ah'oo-to-**grill**, *m* motorway café

autolinea, ah'oo-to-lee-nay-ah, *m* bus service

automa, ah'oo-to-mah, *m* automaton

automezzo, ah'oo-to-**med**-dzo, *m* motor vehicle

automobile, ah'oo-to-**moh**-be-lay, *f* car

autonoleggio, ah'oo-to-noh-**lej**-jo, *m* car hire

autonomo, ah'oo-**toh**-noh-mo, *adj* autonomous

autopsia, ah'oo- top-see-ah, *f* post mortem

autore, -trice, ah'oo-**tor**-ay, ah'oo-**tree**-che, *m/f* author

autorevole, ah'oo-to-**ray**-vo-lay, *adj* authoritative

autorimessa, ah'oo-to-re-**mess**-sah, *f* garage

autorizzare, ah'oo-to-rid-**dzah**-ray, *v* to authorize

autostrada, ah'oo-to-**strah**-dah, *f* motorway

autoveicolo, ah'oo-to-vay-ee-ko-lo, *m* motor vehicle

autunnale, ah'oo-toonn-**nah**-lay, *adj* autumnal

autunno, ah'oo-**toonn**-no, *m* autumn

avallo, ah-**vahl**-lo, *m* indorsement; guarantee

avambraccio, ah-vahm-

braht-cho, *m* forearm

avanguardia, ah-vahn-gooar-de'ah, *f* vanguard

avanti, ah-**vahn**-te, *adv* forward

avanzare, ah-vahn-**tsah**-ray, *v* to advance; to be left over

avanzato, ah-vahn-**tsah**-to, *adj* advanced; left over

avanzo, ah-**vahn**-tso, *m* rest, residue; profit

avaria, ah-vah-**ree**-ah, *f* damage

avariare, ah-vah-re'**ah**-ray, *v* to damage

avaro, ah-**vah**-ro, *m* miser; *adj** avaricious

avena, ah-**vay**-nah, *f* oats

avere, ah-**vay**-ray, *m* property; credit, *v* to have, to get, to possess

aviatore, ah-ve'ah-**tor**-ay, *m* aviator

aviazione, ah-ve'ah-tse'o-nay, *f* aviation; air force

avidità, ah-ve-de-**tah**, *f* avidity

avido*, **ah**-ve-do, *adj* greedy; eager

aviolinea, ah-ve'o-**lee**-nay-ah, *f* airline

avo, **ah**-vo, *m* ancestor

avocado, ah-vo-**cah**-do, *m* avocado

avorio, ah-vo-re'o, *m* ivory

avvallamento, ahv-vahl-lah-**men**-to, *m* depression in the ground

avvalorare, ahv-vah-lo-**rah**-ray, *v* to prove, to confirm

avvampare, ahv-vahm-**pah**-ray, *v* to flare up

avvantaggiare, ahv-vahn-tahd-**jah**-ray, *v* to favour

avvantaggiarsi, ahv-vahn-tahd-**jah**-rse, *v* to gain an advantage

avvedersi, ahv-vay-**dair**-se, *v* to perceive; to become aware of

avvedutezza, ahv-vay-doo-**tet**-tsah, *f* foresight

avveduto*, ahv-vay-**doo**-to, *adj* wary; prudent

avvelenare, ahv-vay-lay-**nah**-ray, *v* to poison

avvenente, ahv-vay-**nen**-tay, *adj* attractive, pretty, charming

avvenenza, ahv-vay-**nen**-tsah, *f* charm, prettiness

avvenimento, ahv-vay-ne-**men**-to, *m* event; happening

avvenire, ahv-vay-**nee**-ray, *v* to happen; *m* future

avventarsi, ahv-ven-**tar**-se, *v* to hurl oneself (against)

avventato*, ahv-ven-**tah**-to, *adj* rash; risky

avvento, ahv-**ven**-to, *m* advent

avventura, ahv-ven-**too**-rah, *f* adventure

avventurarsi, ahv-ven-too-**rah**-rse, *v* to venture (into)

avventuroso, ahv-ven-too-**roh**-so, *adj* adventurous

avverarsi, ahv-vay-**rah**-ray, *v* to come true

avverbio, ahv-**vair**-be'o, *m* adverb

avversario, -a, ahv-vair-**sah**-re'o, *adj* unfriendly; *m/f* opponent

avversità, ahv-vair-se-**tah**, *f* adversity

avverso*, ahv-**vair**-so, *adj* adverse, opposed

avvertenza, ahv-vair-**ten**-tsah, *f* warning, attention

avvertimento, ahv-vair-te-**men**-to, *m* warning, notice; admonition

avvertire, ahv-vair-**tee**-ray, *v* to warn, to give notice; to perceive

avvezzo, ahv-**vet**-tso, *adj* **–a,** used to

avviamento, ahv-ve'ah-**men**-to, *m* starting

avviare, ahv-ve'**ah**-ray, *v* to set up in, to start

avvicendarsi, ahv-ve-chen-**dah**-rse, *v* to

alternate

avvicinare, ahv-ve-che-**nah**-ray, *v* to approach

avvilimento, ahv-ve-le-**men**-to, *m* discouragement; degradation; humiliation

avvilire, ahv-ve-lee-ray, *v* to degrade, to lower

avvilirsi, ahv-ve-**leer**-se, *v* to get discouraged

avviluppare, ahv-ve-loop-**pah**-ray, *v* to envelop, to wrap up; to entangle

avvincere, ahv-**veen**-chay-ray, *v* to hug; to tie up; to convince

avvinghiare, ahv-veen-ghe'**ah**-ray, *v* to grip; to clutch

avvisare, ahv-ve-zah-ray, *v* to warn

avviso, ahv-**vee**-zo, *m* notice; warning; advertisement; opinion

avvistare, ahv-ve-**stah**-ray, *v* to see, to sight

avvitare, ahv-ve-**tah**-ray, *v* to screw

avvizzire, ahv-vit-**tsee**-ray, *v* to fade, to wither

avvocato, ahv-vo-**kah**-to, *m* lawyer, barrister

avvolgere, ahv-**voll**-jay-ray, *v* to wrap up

avvoltoio, ahv-voll-**to**-e'o, *m* vulture

azalea, ah-dzah-**lay**-ah, *f* azalea

azienda, ah-dze'**en**-dah, *f* business, firm

azionare, ah-tse'o-**nah**-ray, *v* to start up, to activate

azione, ah-tse'o-nay, *f* action; share

azionista, ah-tse'o-**niss**-tah, *m/f* shareholder

azzannare, ahd-dzahn-**nah**-ray, *v* to snap, to bite

azzardare, ahd-dzar-**dah**-ray, *v* to hazard

azzardo, ahd-**dzar**-do, *m* risk, hazard

azzeccare, ahd-dzeck-**kah**-ray, *v* to guess; to strike

azzuffarsi, ahd-dzoof-**far**-se, *v* to scuffle

azzurro, ahd-**dzoor**-ro, *adj* sky-blue; *m* azure

B

babbeo, bahb-**bay**-o, *m*
fool

babbo, bahb-bo, *m* father,
dad

babbuino, bahb-boo'**ee**-
no, *m* baboon

babordo, bah-**bor**-do, *m*
port side

bacato, bah-**kah**-to, *adj*
worm-eaten; degenerate

bacca, bahk-kah, *f* berry

baccalà, bahk-kah-**lah,** *m*
dried codfish

baccano, bahk-**kah**-no, *m*
row, din

baccello, baht-**chell**-lo, *m*
pod

bacchetta, bahk-**ket**-tah, *f*
rod; wand; baton;
drumstick

bacheca, bahk-**ke**-kah, *f*
notice board; display
case

baciare, bah-**chah**-ray, *v*
to kiss

bacillo, bah-**chill**-lo, *m*
bacillus, germ

bacinella, bah-che-**nell**-
lah, *f* bowl, basin

bacino, bah-**chee**-no, *m*
basin; pelvis; dock; –
petrolifero, oilfield

bacio, bah-cho, *m* kiss

baco, bah-ko, *m* worm; –
da seta, silkworm

bada, bah-dah, *f* tenere a
–, to keep at bay *or* arm's
length

badare, bah-dah-ray, *v* to
mind; to look after

badessa, bah-**dess**-sah, *f*
abbess

badia, bah-**dee**-ah, *f* abbey

badile, bah-dee-lay, *m*
shovel

baffi, bahf-fe, *mpl*
moustache; (animal)
whiskers

bagagli, bah-**gah**-l'y, *mpl*
luggage

bagagliaio, bah-gah-l'**yah**-
e'o, *m* luggage-van

bagaglio, bah-**gah**-l'yo, *m*
luggage

bagattella, bah-gah-**tell**-
lah, *f* trifle

bagliore, bah-l'**yo**-ray, *m*
flash of light; glare; glow

bagnare, bah-n'**yah**-ray, *v*
to wet; to soak

bagnarsi, bah-n'**yah**-rsee,
v to bathe; to wet
oneself; to get soaked

bagno, bah-n'yo, *m* bath;
swim; bathroom

bagnoschiuma, bah-n'yo-
skeoo-ma, *m* bubblebath

baia, bah'e-ah, *f* bay

baio, bah'e-o, *adj* (horse)
chestnut colour, bay

baionetta, bah'e-o-**net**-
tah, *f* bayonet

balaustra, bah-lah'**ooss**-
trah, *f* balustrade

balaustrata, bah-lah'ooss-
trah-tah, *f* balustrade

balbettare, bahl-bet-**tah**-
ray, *v* to stutter

balbuzie, bahl-**boo**-tse'ay, *f*
stutter, stammer

balbuziente, bahl-boo-
tse'**ayn**-tay, *adj*

stammering

balcone, bahl-**ko**-nay, *m* balcony

baldacchino, bahl-dahk-**kee**-no, *m* canopy

baldanza, bahl-**dahn**-tsah, *f* boldness

baldo, bahl-do, *adj* bold, fearless

baldoria, bahl-**do**-re'ah, *f* merrymaking; **fare –,** to have a good time

balena, bah-**lay**-nah, *f* whale

balenare, bah-lay-**nah**-ray, *v* to flash

baleno, bah-**lay**-no, *m* flash of lightning

balia, bah-le'ah, *f* wet-nurse

balia, bah-lee-ah, *f* **in –,** at the mercy

balla, bahl-lah, *f* bale; tall story, lie

ballare, bahl-**lah**-ray, *v* to dance

ballata, bahl-**lah**-tah, *f* ballad

ballerina, bahl-lay-**ree**-nah, *f* dancer; ballerina; pump shoe

balletto, bahl-**let**-to, *m* ballet

ballo, bahl-lo, *m* ball, dance; **essere in –,** to be at stake; to be involved

ballottaggio, bahl-lot-**tahd**-jo, *m* second ballot

ballottare, bahl-lot-tah-ray, *v* to ballot

balneare, bahl-nay-**ah**-ray, *adj* of the seaside

balocco, bah-**lock**-ko, *m* toy

balordo*, bah-**lor**-do, *adj* silly, stupid, foolish

balsamo, bahl-**sa**-mo, *m* balm; hair conditioner

baluardo, bah-loo'**ar**-do, *m* bulwark

balza, bahl-tsah, *f* rock, crag; (dress) frill

balzano, bahl-**tsah**-no, *adj* strange, crazy

balzare, bahl-**tsah**-ray, *v* to leap, to jump

balzo, bahl-tso, *m* bounce; jump

bambagia, bahm-**bah**-jah, *f* cottonwool

bambina, bahm-**bee**-nah, *f* baby girl; little girl

bambinaia, bahm-be-**nah**-yah, *f* nurse

bambinesco, bahm-be-**ness**-ko, *adj* childish

bambino, bahm-**bee**-no, *m* child; baby; little boy

bambola, bahm-bo-lah, *f* doll

bambù, bahm-**booh**, *m* bamboo

banale, bah-**nah**-lay, *adj* commonplace, banal

banana, bah-**nah**-nah, *f* banana

banca, bahn-kah, *f* bank; **– dati,** data bank

bancarella, bahn-kah-**rayl**-lah, *f* market stall

bancario, bahn-**kah**-re'o, *adj* banking

bancarotta, bahn-kah-**rot**-tah, *f* bankruptcy

banchettare, bahn-ket-**tah**-ray, *v* to banquet

banchetto, bahn-**ket**-to, *m* banquet

banchiere, bahn-ke'**ay**-ray, *m* banker

banchina, bahn-**kee**-nah, *f* quay; platform

banco, bahn-ko, *m* pew; bench; counter; school desk; bank; **– degli imputati,** dock; **– di nebbia,** fog patch; **– di prova,** testing ground

banconota, bahn-ko-**no**-tah, *f* banknote

banda, bahn-dah, *f* band; gang; strip; side

banderuola, bahn-day-roo'**o**-lah, *f* weathercock

bandiera, bahn-de'**ay**-rah, *f* flag, banner, colours

bandire, bahn-dee-ray, *v* to proclaim, to announce; to banish, to exile

bandita, bahn-dee-tah, *f* place protected by rights for shooting, fishing, etc.

bandito, bahn-**dee**-to, *m*
bandit; *adj* exiled

banditore, bahn-de-**tor**-ay,
m auctioneer

bando, bahn-do, *m*
proclamation;
banishment, exile

bar, bahr, *m* coffee bar;
bar

bara, bah-rah, *f* coffin

baracca, bah-**rahk**-kah, *f*
wooden shed; piece of
junk; **mandare avanti la
–**, to keep things going

baraonda, bah-rah-**onn**-
dah, *f* chaos, confusion

barare, bah-**rah**-ray, *v* to
cheat (at cards, etc.)

baratro, bah-rah-tro, *m*
abyss

barattare, bah-raht-**tah**-
ray, *v* to barter

baratto, bah-**raht**-to, *m*
barter; exchange; **fare
un –**, to swap

barattolo, bah-**raht**-to-lo,
m jar; tin

barba, bar-bah, *f* beard;
farsi la –, to shave

barbabietola, bar-bah-
be'**ay**-to-lah, *f* beetroot

barbagianni, bar-bah-
jahn-ne, *m* barn owl

barbaro, bar-bah-ro, *adj**
barbarous; *m* barbarian

barbecue, bar-be-keeu, *m*
barbecue

barbiere, bar-be'**ay**-ray, *m*
barber

barbiturico, bar-bee-**too**-
ree-ko, *m* barbiturate

barbone, bar-**bo**-nay, *m*
poodle; *m/f* tramp

barboso, bar-**bo**-so, *adj*
boring

barbottare, bar-bot-**tah**-
ray, *v* to grumble

barbuto, bar-**boo**-to, *adj*
bearded

barca, bar-kah, *f* boat

barcaiolo, bar-kah-e'**o**-lo,
m boatman

barcamenarsi, bar-kah-
may-**nahr**-se, *v* to
manage somehow

barcollare, bar-koll-**lah**-
ray, *v* to stagger; to
totter

barcone, bar-**ko**-nay, *m*
pontoon

bardare, bar-**dah**-ray, *v* to
harness; to dress up

barella, bah-**rell**-lah, *f*
stretcher

baricentro, bah-ree-**chen**-
tro, *m* centre of gravity

barile, bah-**ree**-lay, *m*
cask, barrel

barilotto, bah-ree-**lot**-to,
m small cask, keg

barista, bah-**ree**-stah, *m/f*
barman, barmaid

baritono, bah-**ree**-to-no,
m baritone

barlume, bar-**loo**-may, *m*
gleam, ray

barocco, bah-**rock**-ko, *adj*
baroque; grotesque, odd

barometro, bah-**ro**-may-
tro, *m* barometer

barone, bah-**ro**-nay, *m*
baron

baronessa, bah-ro-**ness**-
sah, *f* baroness

barra, bar-rah, *f* bar;
stroke; *naut* helm

barricare, bar-re-ka-ray, *v*
to barricade

barricata, bar-re-**ka**-tah, *f*
barricade

barriera, bar-re'**ay**-rah, *f*
barrier; gate

barroccio, bahr-**rot**-cho,
m cart

baruffa, bar-**roof**-fah, *f*
squabble

barzelletta, bahr-**dzel**-let-
tah, *f* joke

basamento, bah-zah-**men**-
to, *m* pedestal

basare, bah-**zah**-ray, *v* to
base

base, bah-zay, *f* base,
foundation

basette, bah-**zet**-tay, *fpl*
sideburns, whiskers

basilico, bah-**zee**-lee-ko,
m basil

bassezza, bahss-**set**-tsah, *f*
baseness, meanness

basso, bahss-so, *adj** low,
short; base, vulgar; *m*
bottom, lower part; *mus*
bass

bassofondo, bahss-so-**fon**-do, m shallows

bassotto, bahss-**sot**-to, m dachshund; adj squat

basta! bahss-tah, interj enough!

bastante, bahss-**tahn**-tay, adj sufficient

bastardo, bahss-**tar**-do, m bastard; mongrel

bastare, bahss-**tah**-ray, v to suffice; **basta così**, that's enough

bastimento, bahss-te-**men**-to, m ship

basto, bahss-to, m pack-saddle

bastonare, bahss-to-**nah**-ray, v to thrash

bastonata, bahss-to-**nah**-tah, f thrashing

bastone, bahss-**to**-nay, m stick

batacchio, bah-**tahk**-ke'o, m knocker; clapper

batosta, bah-**toss**-tah, f blow, setback

battaglia, baht-**tah**-l'yah, f battle

battaglio, baht-tah-l'yo, m knocker; clapper

battello, baht-**tell**-lo, m boat

battente, baht-**ten**-tay, m flap, shutter; knocker

battere, **baht**-tay-ray, v to beat; to hit; to knock; to strike

batteria, baht-tay-**ree**-ah, f battery; mus drums

battesimo, baht-**tay**-ze-mo, m christening

battezzare, baht-ted-**dzah**-ray, v to baptize; to christen

battibecco, baht-te-**beck**-ko, m squabble

batticuore, baht-te-koo'o-ray, m palpitation

battimano, baht-te-**mah**-no, m applause

battistero, baht-te-**stay**-ro, m baptistry

battito, **baht**-te-to, m beat, throb; **– cardiaco**, heartbeat

battitore, baht-te-to-ray, m batsman

battuta, baht-**too**-tah, f remark; cue; mus bar

baule, bah'oo-lay, m trunk; (car) boot

bava, bah-vah, f dribble; slobber; slime

bavaglino, bah-vah-**l'y**-no, m bib

bavaglio, bah-**vah**-l'yo, m gag

bavero, bah-vay-ro, m collar

bavoso, bah-vo-zo, adj dribbling

bazar, bah-**dzahr**, m bazaar

bazzecola, bahd-dze-**koh**-lah, f trifle, bagatelle

bazzicare, bahd-dze-**kah**-ray, v to frequent

bearsi, bay-**ar**-se, v to rejoice

beato*, bay-**ah**-to, adj happy; blessed; **beata lei!** how lucky she is!

bebè, bay-**bay**, m baby

beccaccia, beck-**kaht**-chah, f woodcock

beccaccino, beck-kaht-**chee**-no, m snipe

beccare, beck-**kah**-ray, v to peck

beccarsi, beck-**kar**-se, v – **l'influenza**, to catch the flu

beccata, beck-**kah**-tah, f peck

becchino, beck-**kee**-no, m grave-digger

becco, **beck**-ko, m beak; spout; burner; **chiudi il becco!** shut up!

befana, bay-**fah**-nah, f Epiphany; old fairy bringing presents at the Epiphany; old hag

beffa, bef-fah, f practical joke; mockery

beffardo*, bef-**far**-do, adj mocking, scoffing

beffare, bef-**fah**-ray, v to mock, to sneer at

beffeggiare, bef-fed-**jah**-ray, v to mock, to laugh at

bega, bay-gah, f dispute

begonia, bay-**gho**-neah, f

begonia

belare, bay-**lah**-ray, *v* to bleat

belga, bell-gah, *adj* Belgian

Belgio, bell-je'o, *m* Belgium

belletto, bell-**let**-to, *m* rouge

bellezza, bell-**let**-tsah, *f* beauty

bellico, bell-le-ko, *adj* war

bellicoso*, bell-le-**ko**-so, *adj* warlike

bellimbusto, bell-lim-**booss**-to, *m* dandy, beau

bello*, bell-lo, *adj* beautiful; good-looking; handsome

beltà, bell-**tah**, *f* beauty

belva, bell-vah, *f* wild beast

benché, ben-**kay**, *conj*, though, although

benda, ben-dah, *f* bandage; blindfold

bendare, ben-dah-ray, *v* to bandage; to blindfold

bene, bay-nay, *adv* well; properly; *m* good; **per il suo –,** for his/her own good; **beni,** property, goods

benedetto, bay-nay-**det**-to, *adj* blessed, holy

benedire, bay-nay-dee-ray, *v* to bless

beneducato, bay-nay-doo-kah-to, *adj* well-mannered

beneficenza, bay-nay-fee-**chen**-tsah, *f* charity

beneficio, bay-nay-fee-cho, *m* benefit

benefico, bay-**nay**-fe-ko, *adj* beneficial; generous

benemerenza, bay-nay-may-**ren**-tsah, *f* merit

benemerito, bay-nay-**may**-re-to, *adj* meritorious

beneplacito, bay-nay-**plah**-che-to, *m* consent; approval

benessere, bay-**ness**-say-ray, *m* comfort; well-being

benestante, bay-nay-**stahn**-tay, *m/f* well-off person; *adj* well-to-do

benevolo, bay-**nay**-vo-lo, *adj* benevolent

benigno*, bay-**nee**-n'yo, *adj* good, kind; *med* benign

benino, bay-**nee**-no, *adv* pretty well

beninteso, bay-nin-**tay**-zo, *adv* of course

benissimo, bay-**niss**-se-mo, *adv* very well

benone, bay-**bo**-nay, *adv* very well

benservito, ben-sair-vee-to, *m* reference; **dare il –,** to give somebody the sack

bensì, ben-**see**, *adv* on the contrary; but

benzina, ben-**dzee**-nah, *f* petrol; **fare –,** to get petrol; **– senza piombo,** unleaded petrol; **– super,** 4-star petrol

benzinaio, -a, ben-dzee-**nah**-e'o, *m/f* petrol attendant

beone, bay-o-nay, *m* drunkard

bere, bay-ray, *v* to drink

Berlino, bair-lee-no, *f* Berlin

bernoccolo, bair-**nock**-ko-lo, *m* bump; **avere il – di,** to have a flair for

berretta, bair-**ret**-tah, *f* cap

berretto, bair-**ret**-to, *m* cap

bersagliare, bair-sah-l'**yah**-ray, *v* to bombard (with criticism, questions, etc.)

bersaglio, bair-sah-l'yo, *m* target

bestemmia, bess-**tem**-me'ah, *f* blasphemy

bestemmiare, bess-tem-me'**ah**-ray, *v* to swear; to blaspheme

bestia, bess-te'ah, *f* beast; brute; fool

bestiale, bess-te'ah-lay, *adj* brutal; beastly

bestiame, bess-te'**ah**-may,

m cattle; livestock

bettola, bet-to-lah, *f* tavern, pub

betulla, bay-**tooll**-lah, *f* birch-tree

bevanda, bay-**vahn**-dah, *f* beverage

bevibile, bay-vee-be-lay, *adj* drinkable

bevuta, bay-**voo**-tah, *f* drink

biacca, be'**ahk**-kah, *f* white paint

biada, be'**ah**-dah, *f* fodder

biancastro, be'**ahn**-kahsstro, *adj* whitish

biancheria, be'ahn-kayree-ah, *f* linen; lingerie

bianchezza, be'ahn-**ket**-tsah, *f* whiteness

bianco, -a be'**ahn**-ko, *adj* white; *m* white; **assegno in –,** blank cheque; **notte in –,** sleepless night

biancospino, be'ahn-kospee-no, *m* hawthorn

biascicare, be'ah-she-kahray, *v* to mumble

biasimare, be'ah-ze-mahray, *v* to blame

biasimevole, be'ah-zemay-vo-lay, *adj* blameworthy

biasimo, be'**ah**-ze-mo, *m* blame

Bibbia, bib-be'ah, *f* Bible

bibita, bee-be-tah, *f*

beverage, drink

bibliotecario, be-ble'o-taykah-re'o, *m/f* librarian

bicchiere, bik-ke-**ay**-ray, *m* glass; tumbler

bicicletta, be-che-**klet**tah, *f* bicycle

bidè, be-**day**, *m* bidet

bidello, be-**dell**-lo, *m* janitor

bidone, be-**doh**-nay, *m* large can, drum; **fare un –,** to swindle

bieco*, be'**ay**-ko, *adj* sinister

biella, be'**ell**-lah, *f* connecting-rod

biennale, be'**en**-nah-lay, *adj* two-yearly, biennial

bietola, be'**ay**-to-lah, *f* beet

bifolco, be-**fol**-ko, *m* bumpkin

biforcarsi, be-for-**kar**-se, *v* to fork, to branch off

bigamo, bee-gah-mo, *m* bigamist; *adj* bigamous

bighellone, be-ghell-lonay, *m* loafer

bigio, bee-jo, *adj* grey

bigiotteria, bee-jot-tayree-ah, *f* costume jewelllery

biglia, bee-l'yah, *f* billiard ball; marble

bigliardo, be-l'**yar**-do, *m* billiards; billiard table; **sala da –,** poolroom

bigliettaio, be-l'yet-**tah**e'o, *m* booking-office clerk; conductor; ticket inspector

biglietto, be-l'**yet**-to, *m* note; ticket; card; **– di andata e ritorno,** return ticket

bigodino, be-go-**dee**-no, *m* curler, roller

bigotto, f, be-**got**-to, *adj* over-devout, pharisaic; *m/f* bigot

bikini, bee-**kee**-nee, *m* bikini

bilancia, be-**lahn**-chah, *f* scales; weighing machine; **Bilancia,** Libra

bilanciare, be-lahn-**chah**ray, *v* to balance; to weigh up

bilancio, be-**lahn**-cho, *m* budget; balance-sheet

bile, bee-lay, *f* bile; *fig* anger

bilia, bee-le'ah, *f* billiard ball; marble

biliardo, be-l'**yar**-do, *m* billiards; billiard table; **sala da –,** poolroom

bilico, bee-le-ko, *m* **essere in –,** to be balanced; *fig* to be undecided

bilingue, be-**leen**-goo'ay, *adj* bilingual

bilione, be-le'o-nay, *m* thousand million;

billion

bimbo, -a, beem-bo, *m/f* child; baby

bimensile, be-men-**see**-lay, *adj* two-monthly, fortnightly

bimestrale, be-me-**strha**-lay, *adj* two-monthly

binario, be-**nah**-re-o, *m* (railway) track, line; platform

binocolo, be-**no**-ko-lo, *m* binoculars, field glasses; opera glasses

biodegradabile, be'o-de-gra-da-**bee**-lay, *adj* biodegradable

biofisica, be'o-**fee**-se-ka, *f* biophysics

biografia, be'o-gra-**fee**-ah, *f* biography

biografo, -a, be'o-**gra**-fo, *m/f* biographer

biologia, be'o-lo-**jee**-ah, *f* biology

biologico, be'o-lo-**jee**-ko, *adj* biological

biologo, -a, be'o-lo-go, *m/f* biologist

biondo, be'**onn**-do, *adj* fair, blond

birbante, beer-**bahn**-tay, *m* rogue

birichino, -a, be-rick-**kee**-no, *adj* mischievous; *m/f* little rascal

birillo, bee-**reel**-lo, *m* skittle, pin

biro, bee-ro, *f* biro

birra, beer-rah, *f* beer

birraio, beer-**rah**-e'o, *m* brewer

birreria, beer-ray-**ree**-ah, *f* brewery

bis, biss, *interj* encore!

bisavola, be-**zah**-vah, *f* great-grandmother

bisavolo, be-**zah**-vo, *m* great-grandfather

bisbetico, biss-**bay**-te-ko, *adj* crabby, irritable

bisbigliare, biss-be-l'**yah**-ray, *v* to whisper

bisbiglio, biss-**bee**-l'yo, *m* whisper

bisca, biss-kah, *f* gambling den

biscia, bee-she'ah, *f* snake

biscotto, biss-**kot**-to, *m* biscuit

bisestile, be-zess-**tee**-lay, *adj* **anno –,** leap year

bislacco, biss-**lack**-ko, *adj* weird

bislungo, biss-**loonn**-go, *adj* oblong

bisnonna, biss-**non**-nah, *f* great-grandmother

bisnonno, biss-**non**-no, *m* great-grandfather

bisognare, be-zo-n'**yah**-ray, *v* to be necessary; **bisogna che tu venga,** you'll have to come

bisogno, be-zo-n'yo, *m* need, necessity; **avere –**

di, to need; **non c'è – di,** there's no need of/to

bisonte, be-**zon**-tay, *m* bison

bistecca, biss-**teck**-kah, *f* steak

bisticciare, biss-**teet**-cha-ray, *v* to quarrel

bisticcio, biss-**teet**-cho, *m* squabble, dispute; pun

bisturi, biss-**too**-re, *m med* scalpel

bitorzolo, be-**tor**-tso-lo, *m* lump; bump; wart

bivio, bee-ve'o, *m* fork; crossroads

bizza, beed-dzah, *f* tantrum

bizzarro*, beed-**dzar**-ro, *adj* odd, queer

bizzeffe, bit-**tsef**-fay, *adv* **a –,** in abundance

blandire, blahn-**dee**-ray, *v* to soothe; to flatter, to cajole

blando, blahn-do, *adj* soft, mild; bland

blasone, blah-**so**-nay, *m* coat of arms

bloccare, block-**kah**-ray, *v* to block; to stop; to blockade

bloccchetto, block-**ket**-to, *m* notepad

blocco, block-ko, *m* block; *mil* blockade; *med* blockage

blu, bloo, *adj* & *m* dark

blue

boa, boh'a, *m* boa constrictor; *f* buoy

boato, bo'ah-to, *m* roar, loud noise

bobina, bo-bee-nah, *f* reel, spool; coil

bocca, bock-kah, *f* mouth; **– di leone,** snapdragon; **in – al lupo,** good luck!

boccale, bock-kah-lay, *m* jug; mug; tankard

boccetta, bot-**chet-**tah, *f* phial

bocchino, bock-kee-no, *m* mouthpiece; cigarette holder

bocce, bot-chay, *fpl* (game) bowls

bocciare, bot-**cha-**ray, *v* to reject; (at exams) to fail

bocciatura, bot-cha-**too-**rah, *f* (at exams) failure

bocciolo, bot-**cho-**lo, *m* bud

boccone, bock-ko-nay, *m* mouthful

bocconi, bock-ko-ne, *adv* (lying) face downwards

boia, bo-e'ah, *m* executioner

boiata, bo-e'**ah-**ta, *f* rubbish, nonsense

boicottare, bo'ee-kot-**ta-**ray, *v* to boycott

bolla, boll-lah, *f* bubble; blister; **– di consegna,** delivery note

bollare, boll-lah-ray, *v* to stamp; to brand

bollente, boll-len-tay, *adj* boiling; boiling hot

bolletta, boll-let-tah, *f* receipt; bill; **essere in –,** to be broke

bollettino, boll-let-tee-no, *m* bulletin; **– meteorologico,** weather report; **– di spedizione,** consignment note

bollire, boll-lee-ray, *v* to boil

bollito, boll-le-to, *m* boiled meat

bollitore, boll-le-tor-ay, *m* kettle; boiler

bollo, boll-lo, *m* stamp; **– di circolazione,** road tax

bomba, bom-bah, *f* bomb; **– a mano,** hand grenade; **– atomica,** atom bomb

bombardare, bom-bar-**dah-**ray, *v* to bombard; to bomb; to shell

bombetta, bom-**bet-**tah, *f* bowler hat

bombola, bom-bo-lah, *f* (gas) cylinder

bonaccia, bo-**naht-**chah, *f* calm at sea; **in –,** dead calm

bonaccione, bo-naht-**cho-**nay, *adj* good-natured

bonario*, bo-**nah-**re'o, *adj* good-natured; kindly

bonifica, bo-nee-fee-kah, *f* (land) reclamation

bonificare, bo-nee-fee-**kah-**ray, *v* (land) to reclaim; to give a discount

bonifico, bo-**nee-**fee-ko, *m* discount; credit transfer

bontà, bon-**tah,** *f* goodness; good quality

borace, bo-**rah-**chay, *m* borax

borbottare, bor-bot-**tah-**ray, *v* to grumble; to murmur

bordello, bor-**dell-**lo, *m* brothel

bordo, bor-do, *m* edge; hem; brim; margin; **a – di,** on board

borgata, bor-**gah-**tah, *f* suburb; hamlet

borghese, bor-**gay-**zay, *m* bourgeois, middle-class; **in –,** in civilian clothes, plainclothes

borghesia, bor-gay-**zee-**ah, *f* middle classes, bourgeoisie

borgo, bor-go, *m* suburb; hamlet

boria, bo-re'ah, *f* haughtiness

borioso*, bo-re'o-zo, *adj* arrogant

borraccia, bor-**raht-**chah, *f* flask

borsa, bor-sah, *f* bag;

purse; pouch; stock-exchange; **– dell'acqua calda,** hot water bottle; **– di studio,** student's grant

borsaiolo, -a, bor-sah-yo-lo, *m/f* pickpocket

borsellino, bor-sell-lee-no, *m* purse

bosco, boss-ko, *m* wood

bosso, boss-so, *m* box-tree; box-wood

bossolo, boss-so-lo, *m* cartridge case

botanica, bo-**tah**-ne-kah, *f* botany

botola, bo-to-lah, *f* trap-door

botta, bot-tah, *f* blow

botte, bot-tay, *f* cask, barrel

bottega, bot-**tay**-gah, *f* shop; workshop

bottegaio, -a, bot-tay-gah-e'o, *m/f* shopkeeper

botteghino, bot-tay-ghe-no, *m* box office; lottery office

bottiglia, bot-**tee**-l'yah, *f* bottle

bottino, bot-tee-no, *m* booty; loot

botto, bot-to, *m* bang, thud; **di –,** suddenly

bottone, bot-to-nay, *m* button; bud; stud; **attaccare –,** to buttonhole

bove, bo-vay, *m* ox

bovino, bo-vee-no, *adj* bovine

boxe, box, *f* boxing

bozza, bot-tsah, *f* sketch, draft; (in printing) proof

bozzolo, bot-tso-lo, *m* cocoon

braccialetto, braht-chah-**let**-to, *m* bracelet

braccio, braht-cho, *m* arm; **– di mare,** channel

bracciolo, braht-choo'o-lo, *m* arm (of a chair)

bracco, brahk-ko, *m* hound

brace, brah-chay, *f* embers

brache, brah-kay, *fpl* trousers

braciere, brah-**chay**-ray, *m* brazier

braciola, brah-**cho**-lah, *f* chop

brama, brah-mah, *f* longing, yearning

bramare, brah-**mah**-ray, *v* to covet, to long for

bramoso, brah-**mo**-zo, *adj* eager

branca, brahn-kah, *f* branch

branchia, brahn-ke'ah, *f* gill

branco, brahn-ko, *m* flock; pack

brancolare, brahn-ko-**lah**-ray, *v* to grope

branda, brahn-dah, *f* camp bed; hammock

brandello, brahn-**dell**-lo, *m* scrap; rag

brandire, brahn-**dee**-ray, *v* to brandish

brano, brah-no, *m* piece; (book) passage

Brasile, brah-**zee**-lay, *m* Brazil

brasiliano, brah-zee-le'**ah**-no, *adj* Brazilian

bravata, brah-**vah**-tah, *f* act of bravado

bravo, brah-vo, *adj* capable, clever; good, honest; brave; *interj* bravo!

bravura, brah-**voo**-rah, *f* skill, cleverness

breccia, bret-chah, *f* breach

brefotrofio, bray-fo-**tro**-fe'o, *m* orphanage

bretella, bray-**tell**-lah, *f* strap; motorway link; **bretelle,** braces

breve, bray-vay, *adj* brief, short; *f mus* breve

brevettare, bray-vet-**tah**-ray, *v* to patent

brevetto, bray-**vet**-to, *m* patent; (pilot) licence

brezza, bret-tsah, *f* breeze

bricco, brik-ko, *m* jug

briccone, -a, brik-**ko**-nay, *m/f* rascal

briciola, bree-cho-lah, *f* crumb

briciolo, bree-cho-lo, *m* bit, scrap

briga, bree-gah, *f* trouble; **attaccar –,** to start a quarrel; **prendersi la – di,** to take the trouble to

brigante, bre-gan-tay, *m* brigand, bandit; rascal

brigare, bre-gah-ray, *v* to intrigue

brigata, bre-gah-tah, *f* gang; party; *mil* brigade

briglia, bree-l'yah, *f* bridle, rein

brillante, bril-lahn-tay, *m* diamond; *adj* brilliant, sparkling

brillare, bril-lah-ray, *v* to glitter, to shine

brillo, bril-lo, *adj* tipsy

brina, bree-nah, *f* hoar-frost

brindare, brin-dah-ray, *v* to toast, to drink

brindisi, breen-de-ze, *m* toast; **fare un – a,** to drink a toast to

brio, bree-o, *m* liveliness

brioso*, bre'o-zo, *adj* full of life

britannico, bre-than-ne-ko, *adj* British

brivido, bree-ve-do, *m* shiver; thrill

brizzolato, brit-tso-lah-to, *adj* grey-haired

brocca, brock-kah, *f* pitcher, jug

broccolo, brock-ko-lo, *m* broccoli

brodo, bro-do, *m* broth; stock

broglio, bro-l'yo, *m* – **elettorale,** gerrymandering

bromuro, bro-moo-ro, *m* bromide

bronchi, bron-ke, *mpl* bronchial tubes

broncio, bron-cho, *m* sulkiness; **avere il –,** to sulk

brontolare, bron-to-lah-ray, *v* to grumble

brontolio, bron-to-lee-o, *m* muttering; growl; rumbling

brontolone, -a, bron-to-lo-nay, *m/f* grumbler

bronzo, bron-dzo, *m* bronze; **faccia di –,** cheek

bruciare, broo-chah-ray, *v* to burn; to scald

bruciatura, broo-chah-too-rah, *f* burn; scald

bruciore, broo-cho-ray, *m* burning sensation

bruco, broo-ko, *m* caterpillar

brughiera, broo-ghe'ay-rah, *f* moorland; heath

brulicare, broo-le-kah-ray, *v* to swarm

brullo, brooll-lo, *adj* barren

bruma, broo-mah, *f* mist

bruno, broo-no, *adj* brown; dark

brusco, broo-sko, *adj* abrupt; (person) brusque; (taste) sharp

brutale, broo-tah-lay, *adj** brutal

bruto, broo-to, *m* brute; *adj* brute; **forza bruta,** brute force

bruttezza, broot-tet-tsah, *f* ugliness

brutto, broot-to, *adj* ugly; nasty; **– tempo,** bad weather

Bruxelles, broo-sell, *f* Brussels

buca, boo-kah, *f* hole; **– delle lettere,** letterbox

bucare, boo-kah-ray, *v* to pierce, to bore; **– una gomma,** to have a puncture

bucarsi, boo-kahr-se, *v* to prick onself; (drugs) to mainline

bucato, boo-kah-to, *m* washing

buccia, boot-chah, *f* peel; skin; rind

buco, boo-ko, *m* hole

budello, boo-dell-lo, *m* bowel, gut; alley

budino, boo-dee-no, *m* pudding

bue, boo-ay, *m* ox

bufalo, boo-fah-lo, *m*

buffalo

bufera, boo-**fay**-rah, *f* gale, storm

buffo, boof-fo, *adj** funny, comical; comic

buffone, boof-**fo**-nay, *m* clown; jester

buggerare, bood-jay-**rah**-ray, *v fam* to cheat

bugia, boo-**jee**-ah, *f* lie; candleholder

bugiardo, -a, boo-**jar**-do, *adj* lying; *m/f* liar

buio, boo-e'o, *m* darkness; *adj* dark

bulbo, booll-bo, *m* bulb

bulimia, boo-le-**mee**'a, *f* bulimia

bulino, boo-**lee**-no, *m* graver

bulletta, booll-**let**-tah, *f* tack

bullone, booll-**lo**-nay, *m* bolt

buonanotte, boo'o-**nah**-**not**-tay, *interj* good night!

buonasera, boo'o-nah-**se**-rah, *interj* good evening!

buondì, boo'on-**dee**, *interj* hello! good day!

buongiorno, boo'on-**je'or**-no, *interj* good morning!; good afternoon!

buono, boo'o-no, *adj* good, kind; proper; *m* coupon, voucher; **– del Tesoro,** Treasury bond

buontempone, boo'on-tem-**po**-nay, *m* person who enjoys life

burattino, boo-raht-**tee**-no, *m* puppet

burbero*, boor-**bay**-ro, *adj* surly, sullen

burla, boor-lah, *f* jest; trick

burlare, boor-lah-ray, *v* to make a fool of

burlone, boor-**lo**-nay, *m* joker

burrasca, boor-**rahss**-kah, *f* gale, storm

burro, boor-ro, *m* butter

burrone, boor-ro-nay, *m* ravine

buscare, booss-**kah**-ray, *v* to catch, to get

bussare, booss-**sah**-ray, *v* to knock

busse, booss-say, *fpl* thrashing, slapping

bussola, booss-so-lah, *f* compass

busta, booss-tah, *f* envelope; **– paga,** pay packet

busto, booss-to, *m* bust; corset

buttare, boot-**tah**-ray, *v* to throw; to discard

buttarsi, boot-**tar**-say, *v* to jump; to throw oneself

cabala, kah-bah-lah, *f* cabal

cabina, kah-bee-nah, *f* cabin; beach hut; cockpit; **– telefonica**, phone box

cabotaggio, kah-bo-**tahd**-jo, *m naut* coastal navigation

cacao, kah-**kah**-o, *m* cocoa

cacare, kah-**kah**-ray, *v fam* to shit

cacca, kahk-kah, *f fam* shit

caccia, kaht-chah, *f* hunting, shooting; **dare la –**, to give chase

cacciare, kaht-chah-ray, *v* to hunt, to shoot; to send away, to chase away

cacciarsi, kaht-**char**-se, *v* to hide oneself; **– nei guai**, to get into trouble

cacciatore, kaht-chah-tor-ay, *m* hunter

cacciavite, kaht-chah-vee-tay, *m* screwdriver

cacio, kah-cho, *m* cheese

cadavere, kah-**dah**-vay-ray, *m* corpse

cadenza, kah-**dayn**-tsah, *f* cadence, rhythm

cadere, kah-**day**-ray, *v* to fall; **lasciar –**, to drop

cadetto, kah-**det**-to, *m* cadet; *adj* younger

caducità, kah-doo-che-**tah**, *f* transience, short life

caduco, kah-**doo**-ko, *adj* short-lived; deciduous

caduta, kah-**doo**-tah, *f* fall; **la – dei capelli**, hair loss

caffè, kahf-**fay**, *m* coffee; café; **– macchiato**, coffee with a dash of milk; **– ristretto**, strong black coffee; **– solubile**, instant coffee

caffellatte, kahf-fayl-**lat**-tay, *m* white coffee

caffettiera, kahf-fet-te'**ay**-rah, *f* coffee-pot; coffee-maker

cagionare, kah-jo-**nah**-ray, *v* to cause

cagione, kah-jo-nay, *f* cause

cagionevole, kah-jo-**nay**-vo-lay, *adj* delicate

cagliare, kah-**l'ya**-ray, *v* to curdle

caglio, kah-**l'yo**, *m* rennet

cagna, kah-n'yah, *f* bitch

cagnara, kah-n'**yah**-rah, *f* tumult, uproar

cagnolino, kah-n'yo-lee-no, *m* puppy; small dog

caimano, kah'e-**mah**-no, *m* alligator, cayman

cala, kah-lah, *f* cove; *naut* hold

calabrone, kah-lah-**bro**-nay, *m* hornet

calamaio, kah-lah-**mah**-e'o, *m* inkpot

calamaro, kah-lah-**mah**-ro, *m* squid

calamita, kah-lah-meetah, f magnet

calamità, kah-lah-me-**tah**, f calamity; – **naturale**, natural disaster

calamitare, kah-lah-me-**tah**-ray, v to magnetize

calamitato, kah-lah-me-**ta**-to, adj magnetic

calare, kah-**lah**-ray, v to lower; to drop; (sun) to set; (night) to fall

calata, kah-**lah**-tah, f invasion

calca, **kahl**-kah, f crowd, throng

calcagno, kahl-**kah**-n'yo, m heel

calcare, kahl-**kah**-ray, v to press down; to stress; – **la mano**, to exaggerate; m limestone

calce, **kahl**-chay, f lime; **in – a**, at the foot of

calcestruzzo, kahl-chess-**troot**-tso, m concrete

calciare, kahl-**chah**-ray, v to kick

calciatore, kahl-chah-**tor**-ay, m footballer

calcina, kahl-**chee**-nah, f (lime) mortar

calcio, **kahl**-cho, m kick; soccer; butt; calcium; – **d'angolo**, corner; – **di punizione**, free kick; – **di rigore**, penalty kick

calcio-balilla, kahl-cho-bah-**leell**-lah, m table

football

calco, **kahl**-ko, m cast, mould

calcolo, **kahl**-ko-lo, m calculation; med kidney stone

caldaia, kahl-**dah**-e'ah, f boiler

caldeggiare, kahl-dej-**jah**-ray, v to support

calderone, kahl-day-**ro**-nay, m cauldron

caldo, **kahl**-do, m heat, warmth; adj* warm, hot; friendly

calendario, kah-len-**dah**-re'o, m calendar

calibro, **kah**-le-bro, m calibre, bore; callipers

calice, **kah**-le-chay, m stem glass; chalice; calyx

caligine, kah-**lee**-je-nay, f fog; smog

calle, **kahl**-lay, f Venetian street

calligrafia, kahl-lee-grah-**fee**-ah, f handwriting; calligraphy

callista, kahl-**liss**-tah, m/f chiropodist

callo, **kahl**-lo, m corn, hard skin

calma, **kahl**-mah, f calm, peacefulness

calmante, kahl-**mahn**-tay, m painkiller; sedative; adj soothing, calming

calm, **kahl**-mo, m calm,

quiet, peaceful

calo, **kah**-lo, m drop (in prices); loss (in weight)

calore, kah-**lor**-ay, m heat, warmth; fervour

caloria, kah-lo-**ree**'ah, f calorie

calorifero, kah-lo-**ree**-fay-ro, m radiator

caloroso, kah-lo-**ro**-so, adj warm; enthusiastic

calotta, kah-**lot**-tah, f skullcap; – **polare** polar icecap

calpestare, kahl-pay-**stah**-ray, v to trample on

calunnia, kah-**loonn**-ne'ah, f slander

calunniare, kah-loonn-ne'**ah**-ray, v to slander

calunniatore, -trice, kah-loonn-ne'ah-**tor**-ay, kah-loonn-ne'ah-**tree**-chay, m/f slanderer

calvario, kahl-**vah**-ree'o, m calvary; ordeal

calvizie, kahl-**vee**-tse-ay, f baldness

calvo, **kahl**-vo, adj bald

calza, **kahl**-tsah, f stocking; sock

calzare, kahl-**tsah**-ray, v to put on (shoes, gloves)

calzatura, kahl-tsah-**too**-rah, f footwear

calzettone, kahl-tset-**to**-nay, m knee-length sock

calzino, kahl-**tsee**-no, m

short sock

calzolaio, kahl-tso-**lah**-e'o, *m* shoemaker; cobbler

calzoleria, kahl-tso-lay-**ree**-ah, *f* shoe repairs

calzoncini, kahl-tson-**chee**-nee, *mpl* shorts

calzoni, kahl-**tso**-ne, mpl, trousers

camaleonte, kah-mah-lay-**on**-tay, *m* chameleon

cambiale, kahm-be-**ah**-lay, *f* bill of exchange, draft

cambiamento, kahm-be'ah-**men**-to, *m* change

cambiare, kahm-be'ah-ray, *v* to change, to alter

cambiavalute, kahm-be'ah-vah-**loo**-tay, *m* bureau de change

cambio, **kahm**-be'o, *m* change; rate of exchange; gears

camera, **kah**-may-rah, *f* room; bedroom; chamber; – **d'aria**, inner tube; – **dei deputati**, House of Commons; – **matrimoniale**, double room; – **singola**, single room

camerata, kah-may-**rah**-tah, *f* dormitory

cameratismo, kah-may-rah-**tiz**-mo, *m* comradeship

cameriera, kah-may-re'ay-rah, *f* waitress;

chambermaid; maid

cameriere, kah-may-re'ay-ray, *m* waiter; valet

camerino, kah-may-ree-no, *m* dressing room (in theatre)

camice, **kah**-me-chay, *m* (doctor) white coat

camicetta, kah-me-**chet**-tah, *f* blouse

camicia, kah-**mee**-chah, *f* shirt; blouse; – **di forza**, straitjacket; – **da notte**, nightdress

camiciola, kah-me-**cho**-lah, *f* vest

caminetto, kah-me-**net**-to, *m* fireplace

camino, kah-**mee**-no, *m* fireplace; chimney

camion, kah-**mee**'on, *m* lorry; truck

camioncino, kah-me'on-**chee**-no, *m* van

camionetta, kah-me'o-**net**-tah, *f* jeep

camionista, kah-mee'o-**niss**-stah, *m/f* lorry driver

cammello, kahm-**mell**-lo, *m* camel

camminare, kahm-me-**nah**-ray, *v* to walk

camminata, kahm-me-**nah**-tah, *f* walk, stroll

cammino, kahm-**mee**-no, *m* path; way; **un'ora di** –, an hour's walk

camorra, kah-**mor**-rah, *f* camorra; racket

camoscio, kah-mo-she'o, *m* chamois

campagna, kahm-**pah**-n'yah, *f* country, countryside; campaign

campana, kahm-**pah**-nah, *f* bell

campanella, kahm-pah-**nell**-lah, *f* school bell; campanula

campanello, kahm-pah-**nell**-lo, *m* bell

campanile, kahm-pah-**nee**-lay, *m* bell tower

campanula, kahm-pah-**noo**-lah, *f* bellflower

campare, kahm-**pah**-ray, *v* to live; to get by

campeggiare, kahm-ped-**jah**-ray, *v* to camp; to stand out

campeggio, kahm-**ped**-jo, *m* camp site; camping; **fare –, andare in –**, to go camping

campestre, kahm-**pess**-tray, *adj* rural; **corsa –**, cross-country race

campionario, kahm-pe'o-**nah**-re'o, *m* samples

campionato, kahm-pe'o-**nah**-to, *m* championship

campione, kahm-pe'o-nay, *m* sample; champion

campo, **kahm**-po, *m* field; pitch; camp; – **sportivo**, sports ground

camposanto, kahm-po-**sahn**-to, m churchyard, cemetery

camuffare, kah-moof-**fah**-ray, v to disguise

Canada, kah-nah-**dah**, m Canada

canadese, kah-nah-**day**-zay, adj Canadian

canaglia, kah-**nah**-l'yah, f rabble; rogue

canale, kah-**nah**-lay, m channel; canal

canapa, kah-nah-pah, f hemp

canapo, kah-nah-po, m naut hawser

canarino, kah-nah-**ree**-no, m canary

cancellare, kahn-chell-**lah**-ray, v to erase, to rub out; to cancel

cancellatura, kahn-chell-lah-**too**-rah, f erasure

cancellazione, kahn-chell-lah-tse'o-nay, f cancellation

cancelleria, kahn-chell-lay-**ree**-ah, f stationery; chancery

cancelliere, kahn-chell-le'**ay**-ray, m clerk of the court; chancellor

cancello, kahn-**chell**-lo, m gate

cancrena, kahn-**kray**-nah, f gangrene

cancro, kahn-kro, m cancer; **Cancro,** Cancer

candela, kahn-**day**-lah, f candle; spark(ing) plug

candelabro, kahn-day-**lah**-bro, m candelabra

candeliere, kahn-day-le'**ay**-ray, m candlestick

candidato, kahn-de-**dah**-to, m candidate; applicant

candidatura, kahn-de-dah-**too**-rah, f candidature

candido*, kahn-de-do, adj white; fig candid, frank; innocent

candore, kahn-**dor**-ay, m brilliant white; fig candour; innocence

cane, kah-nay, m dog; (gun) cock; **– barbone,** French poodle; **– da guardia,** guard dog; **– lupo,** alsatian

canestro, kah-**ness**-tro, m basket

canfora, kahn-fo-rah, f camphor

cangiante, kahn-**jahn**-tay, adj iridescent

canguro, kahn-**goo**-ro, m kangaroo

canile, kah-**nee**-lay, m kennel, **– municipale,** dog pound

canino, kah-**nee**-no, adj canine; **rosa canina,** dog

rose; **tosse canina,** whooping-cough; m canine

canizie, kah-**nee**-tse'ay, f white hair; fig old age

canna, kahn-nah, f cane; reed; (gun) barrel; **– da pesca,** fishing rod; **– da zucchero,** sugar cane; **– fumaria,** chimney flue

cannella, kahn-**nell**-lah, f cinnamon

cannello, kahn-**nell**-lo, m tube; blowpipe

cannocchiale, kahn-nock-ke'**ah**-lay, m telescope

cannone, kahn-no-nay, m gun; cannon; fig ace

cannuccia, kahn-**noot**-chah, f straw

canone, kah-no-nay, m criterion; relig canon; **– d'abbonamento,** TV/radio licence fee; **– d'affitto,** rent

canonico, kah-no-ne-ko, adj canonical

canoro, kah-no-ro, adj harmonious, singing

canottaggio, kah-not-**tahd**-jo, m rowing

canottiera, kah-not-tee'**ah**-rah, f vest

canotto, kah-not-to, m dinghy; canoe

canovaccio, kah-no-**vaht**-cho, m canvas; dishcloth; (of a play) outline

cantante, kahn-**tahn**-tay, m/f singer

cantare, kahn-**tah**-ray, v to sing; (cockerel) to crow

cantico, kahn-te-ko, m canticle; carol

cantiere, kahn-te'**ay**-ray, m dockyard; building site

cantina, kahn-**tee**-nah, f cellar

canto, kahn-to, m song; lyric poem; canto; **– di Natale,** Christams carol; **d'altro –,** on the other hand

cantonata, kahn-to-**nah**-tah, f corner; **prendere una –,** to blunder

cantone, kahn-**to**-nay, m corner; canton

cantuccio, kahn-**toot**-cho, m nook

canuto, kah-**noo**-to, adj white-haired, white

canzonare, kahn-tso-**nah**-ray, v to make fun of

canzonatura, kahn-tso-nah-**too**-rah, f joke; teasing

canzone, kahn-**tso**-nay, f song; tune; carol

canzoniere, kahn-tso-nee'**ay**-re, m song book; collection of poems

caos, kah-oss, m chaos

capace, kah-**pah**-chay, adj capable, able; capacious

capacità, kah-pah-che-**tah,** f ability; capacity

capacitarsi, kah-pah-che-**tar**-se, v to comprehend

capanna, kah-**pahn**-nah, f hut, shed

capannello, kah-pahn-**nell**-lo, m group (of people)

capannone, kah-pahn-**no**-nay, m hangar; outhouse

caparbietà, kah-par-be'**ay**-tah, f stubborness

caparbio*, kah-**par**-be'o, adj obstinate, stubborn

caparra, kah-**par**-rah, f deposit, down payment

capello, kah-**pell**-lo, m hair

capelluto, kah-pell-**loo**-to, adj **cuoio –,** scalp

capestro, kah-**pess**-tro, m noose; halter

capezzale, kah-pet-**tsah**-lay, m bolster; fig bedside

capezzolo, kah-**pet**-tso-lo, m nipple

capigliatura, kah-pe-l'yah-**too**-rah, f hair

capire, kah-**pee**-ray, v to understand

capitale, kah-pee-**tah**-lay, m capital; f capital city; adj capital; fundamental; **di – importanza,** of capital importanza; **pena**

–, capital punishment

capitalismo, kah-pee-tah-**lees**-mo, m capitalism

capitano, kah-pee-**tah**-no, m captain

capitare, kah-pe-**tah**-ray, v to arrive; to occur, to happen

capitello, kah-pe-**tell**-lo, m (architecture) capital

capitolo, kah-**pee**-to-lo, m chapter

capitombolo, kah-pee-**tom**-bo-lo, m tumble

capo, kah-po, m head; boss; end; cape

Capodanno, kah-po-**dahn**-no, m New Year's Day

capodoglio, kah-po-**do**-l'yo, m sperm whale

capogiro, kah-po-**jee**-ro, m dizziness, giddiness

capolavoro, kah-po-lah-**vo**-ro, m masterpiece

capolinea, kah-po-**lee**-nay-ah, m terminus

caporale, kah-po-**rah**-lay, m corporal

caporeparto, kah-po-re-**pahr**-to, m foreman

caporione, kah-po-re'o-nay, m ringleader

caposala, kah-po-**sah**-lah, m/f head nurse

caposquadra, kah-po-**skwah**-drah, m/f overseer; team captain

capostazione, kah-po-stah-tse'o-nay, *m* station master

capoufficio, kah-po-oof-fee-cho, *m/f* head clerk

capovolgere, kah-po-voll-jay-ray, *v* to turn upside down; to overturn; to capsize

cappa, kahp-pah, *f* cape; (chimney) hood

cappella, kahp-**pell**-lah, *f* chapel

cappellano, kahp-pell-**lah**-no, *m* chaplain

cappellino, kahp-pell-lee-no, *m* (small) hat

cappello, kahp-**pell**-lo, *m* hat; **– a bombetta,** bowler hat; **– a cilindro,** top hat

cappero, kahp-pay-ro, *m* caper; *interj* wonderful! gosh!

cappio, kahp-pe'o, *m* slip-knot; noose

cappone, kahp-po-nay, *m* capon

cappottare, kahp-pot-tah-ray, *v* (car) to overturn

cappotto, kahp-**pot**-to, *m* overcoat

cappuccino, kahp-poot-chee-no, *m* cappuccino, frothy white coffee

cappuccio, kahp-**poot**-cho, *m* hood

capra, kah-prah, *f* she-goat

capretto, kah-**pret**-to, *m* kid

capriccio, kah-**preet**-cho, *m* caprice; tantrum

Capricorno, kah-pree-**kor**-no, *m* Capricorn

caprifoglio, kah-pre-**fo**-l'yo, *m* honeysuckle

capriola, kah-pre'o-lah, *f* somersault

capriolo, kah-pre'o-lo, *m* roe deer

capro, kah-pro, *m* he-goat; **– espiatorio,** scapegoat

capsula, kah-psoo-lah, *f* capsule; (teeth) crown

captare, kahp-**tah**-ray, *v* to pick up (signal); to catch (the eye)

carabina, kah-rah-**bee**-nah, *f* rifle

caraffa, kah-**rahf**-fah, *f* carafe

caramella, kah-rah-**mell**-lah, *f* sweet

caramellato, kah-rah-mell-**lah**-to, *adj* caramelized

carato, kah-**rah**-to, *m* carat

carattere, kah-**raht**-tay-ray, *m* character; trait; (printing) character

caratteristica, kah-raht-tay-**ree**-stee-kah, *f* characteristic, feature

caratterizzare, kah-raht-tay-reed-dzah-ray, *v* to characterize

carboidrato, kar-bo-ee-**drah**-to, *m* carbohydrate

carbonaia, kar-bo-nah-e'ah, *f* coal cellar; charcoal pit

carbonchio, kar-**bon**-ke'o, *m* anthrax

carbone, kar-bo-nay, *m* coal; charcoal

carbonio, kar-bo-ne'o, *m* carbon

carburante, kar-boo-**rahn**-tay, *m* fuel

carburatore, kar-boo-rah-**to**-ray, *m* carburettor

carcassa, kar-**kahs**-sah, *f* carcass; old wreck

carcerato, -a, kar-chay-**rah**-to, *m/f* prisoner

carcere, kar-chay-ray, *m* prison; imprisonment

carceriere, -a, kar-chay-re'ay-ray, *m/f* jailer

carciofo, kar-cho-fo, *m* artichoke

cardellino, kar-dell-lee-no, *m* goldfinch

cardiaco, -a, kar-de'ah-ko, *adj* cardiac

cardinale, kar-dee-nah-lay, *adj* cardinal; *m relig* cardinal

cardine, kar-de-nay, *m* hinge; *fig* cornerstone

cardiologo, -a, kar-de'o-lo-go, *m/f* heart specialist

cardo, kar-do, *m* cardoon; thistle

carena, kah-**ray**-nah, *f* keel

carenza, kah-**rayn**-tsah, *f* lack, shortage

carestia, kah-ress-**tee**-ah, *f* famine; dearth

carezza, kah-**ret**-tsah, *f* caress

carezzare, kah-ret-**tsah**-ray, *v* to caress

carica, kah-re-kah, *f* charge; position, rank

caricare, kah-re-**kah**-ray, *v* to load; (clock) to wind up; (battery) to charge

carico, kah-re-ko, *adj* loaded; (coffee) strong; (clock) wound up; (gun) loaded; (battery) charged; **– di**, loaded with; *m* load, freight; loading; burden, responsibility; **polizza di –**, bill of lading

carie, kah-re-ay, *f* (dental) decay

carino, kah-ree-no, *adj* nice; cosy; charming; dear

carità, kah-re-tah, *f* charity

caritatevole, hah-re-tah-tay-vo-lay, *adj* charitable

carnagione, kar-nah-jo-nay, *f* complexion

carnale, kar-nah-lay, *adj* carnal; **violenza –**, rape

carne, kar-nay, *f* flesh; meat; **– di manzo**, beef; **– di maiale**, pork; **– tritata**, mince; **– di vitello**, veal

carnefice, kar-nay-fe-chay, *m* executioner

carneficina, kar-nay-fe-chee-nah, *f* carnage, massacre

carnevale, kar-nay-vah-lay, *m* carnival

carnivoro, kar-nee-vo-ro, *m* carnivore; *adj* carnivorous

caro*, kah-ro, *adj* dear; expensive

carogna, kah-ro-n'yah, *f* carrion; *fam* swine!

carota, kah-ro-tah, *f* carrot

carovana, kah-ro-vah-nah, *f* convoy; (in desert) caravan

carovita, kah-ro-vee-tah, *m* high cost of living; **indennità di –**, cost of living allowance

carpa, kar-pah, *f* carp

carponi, kar-po-ne, on all fours

carrabile, kar-rah-be-lay, *adj* suitable for vehicles; "**passo –**", "keep clear"

carrello, kar-rell-lo, *m* trolley; undercarriage

carretta, kar-ret-tah, *f* cart

carretto, kar-ret-to, *m* wheel-barrow; hand-cart

carriera, kar-re'ay-rah, *f* career; **di gran –**, at full speed

carro, kar-ro, *m* cart, waggon; **– armato**, tank; **– attrezzi**, breakdown van

carrozza, kar-rot-tsah, *f* carriage; coach; **– letto**, sleeper; **– ristorante**, restaurant car

carrozzeria, kar-rot-tsay-ree-ah, *f* (car) bodywork

carrozzina, kar-rot-tsee-nah, *f* pram

carrucola, kar-roo-ko-lah, *f* pulley

carta, kar-tah, *f* paper; card; map; **– assegni**, cheque card; **– assorbente**, blotting paper; **– di credito**, credit card; **– igienica**, toilet paper; **– straccia**, waste paper

cartapesta, kar-tah-pess-tah, *f* papier-maché

carteggio, kar-ted-jo, *m* correspondence

cartella, kar-tell-lah, *f* folder; satchel; briefcase

cartellino, kar-tell-lee-no, *m* label; card

cartello, kar-tell-lo, *m* notice, sign; poster; (business) cartel

cartellone, kar-tell-lo-nay, *m* poster

cartiera, kar-te'ay-rah, *f* paper mill

cartilagine, kar-te-lah-je-nay, *f* cartilage

cartina, kar-tee-nah, *f* map

cartoccio, kar-tot-cho, *m* paper bag, cornet

cartolaio, -a kar-to-lah-e'o, *m/f* stationer

cartoleria, kar-to-lay-ree-ah, *f* stationer's shop

cartolina, kar-to-lee-nah, *f* postcard; **– di auguri,** greetings card

cartone, kar-to-nay, *m* cardboard; carton; **– animato,** cartoon

cartuccia, kar-toot-chah, *f* cartridge

casa, kah-zah, *f* house; home; firm; **– di cura,** nursing-home; **– editrice,** publishing house; **– popolare,** council house/flat

casacca, kah-zak-kah, *f* jacket, coat

casale, kah-zah-lay, *m* hamlet; farmhouse

casalinga, kah-zah-leen-gah, *f* housewife

casalingo, kah-zah-leen-

go, *adj* home-made; domestic

cascare, kahss-kah-ray, *v* to fall, to tumble

cascata, kahss-kah-tah, *f* waterfall

cascina, kah-shee-nah, *f* farmstead

casco, kahss-ko, *m* helmet; (hairdresser) hairdryer

casella, kah-zell-lah, *f* square; pigeon-hole; **– postale,** PO Box

casellario, kah-zell-lah-re'o, *m* filing cabinet; files

casello, kah-zell-lo, *m* signal box; tollgate

caserma, kah-zair-mah, *f* barracks

casino, kah-zee-no, *m* brothel; mess; racket; **– di caccia,** hunting lodge

caso, kah-zo, *m* case; chance; event; **a –,** at random; **per –,** by chance; **nel – che,** in case

cassa, kahss-sah, *f* case; box; cash desk, checkout; **– da morto,** coffin; **– di risparmio,** savings bank; **– toracica,** chest

cassaforte, kahss-sah-for-tay, *f* safe

cassetta, kahss-set-tah, *f*

box; cassette; box office

cassetto, kahss-set-to, *m* drawer

cassiere, -a, kahss-se'ay-ray, *m/f* cashier

cassone, kahss-so-nay, *m* large case, large chest

casta, kahss-tah, *f* caste

castagna, kahss-tah-n'yah, *f* chestnut

castagno, kahss-tah-n'yo, *m* chestnut-tree

castano, kahss-tah-no, *adj* chestnut brown

castello, kahss-tell-lo, *m* castle; **letti a –,** bunk-beds

castigare, kahss-te-gah-ray, *v* to punish

castigo, kahss-tee-go, *m* punishment

castità, kahss-te-tah, *f* chastity

casto*, kahss-to, *adj* chaste

castoro, kahss-to-ro, *m* beaver

castrare, kahss-trah-ray, *v* to castrate, to doctor

castrato, kahss-trah-to, *m* mutton; eunuch

casuale, kah-zoo'ah-lay, *adj* fortuitous, chance

casupola, kah-zoo-po-lah, *f* hovel

catacomba, kah-tah-kom-bah, *f* catacomb

catalizzatore, kah-tah-

leed-dzah-**to**-ray, *m*
catalytic converter;
catalyst

catalogo, kah-**tah**-lo-go, *m*
catalogue

catapecchia, kah-tah-**peck**-ke'ah, *f* tumble-down house; hovel

cataplasma, kah-tah-**plahss**-mah, *m* poultice

catarro, kah-**tar**-ro, *m* catarrh

catasta, kah-**tahss**-tah, *f* stack; heap

catasto, kah-**tahss**-to, *m* land register

catastrofe, kah-**tahss**-tro-phay, *f* catastrophe

categoria, kah-tay-go-ree-ah, *f* category

catena, kah-tay-nah, *f* chain; – **di montaggio**, assembly line

catenaccio, kah-tay-**naht**-cho, *m* bolt

cateratta, kah-tay-**raht**-tah, *f* cataract

caterva, kah-**tair**-vah, *f* band, troop; **una – di**, heaps of

catinella, kah-te-**nell**-lah, *f* basin

catino, kah-tee-no, *m* basin

catrame, kah-**trah**-may, *m* tar

cattedra, **kaht**-tay-drah, *f* teacher's desk; bishop's

chair; teaching post; professorship

cattedratico, kaht-tay-**drah**-te-ko, *m* professor; *adj* university; pedantic

cattiveria, kah-te-**vay**-re'ah, *f* wickedness

cattività, kaht-te-ve-**tah**, *f* captivity

cattivo, kaht-**tee**-vo, *adj* naughty; wicked; nasty

cattolico, -a, kaht-**to**-lee-ko, *adj* Catholic; *m/f* Catholic

cattura, kaht-**too**-rah, *f* capture; seizure

catturare, kaht-too-**rah**-ray, *v* to capture; to seize

caucciù, kah'oot-**choo**, *m* India rubber

causa, **kah'oo**-zah, *f* cause; case, legal action

causare, kah'oo-**zah**-ray, *v* to cause

cautela, kah'oo-**tay**-lah, *f* caution

cauto*, **kah'**oo-to, *adj* cautious

cauzione, kah'oo-tse'o-nay, *f* bail; security

cava, **kah**-vah, *f* quarry

cavalcare, kah-vahl-**kah**-ray, *v* to ride

cavalcata, kah-vahl-**kah**-tah, *f* ride

cavalcatura, kah-vahl-kah-**too**-rah, *f* mount

cavalcavia, kah-vahl-kah-

vee-ah, *m* flyover

cavalcioni, kah-vahl-**cho**-ne, *adv* **a –**, astride

cavaliere, kah-vah-le'**ay**-ray, *m* rider; knight; cavalryman; partner; gentleman

cavalla, kah-**vahl**-lah, *f* mare

cavalleresco*, kah-vahl-lay-**ress**-ko, *adj* chivalrous

cavalleria, kahl-vahl-lay-ree-ah, *f* cavalry; chivalry

cavalletta, kah-vahl-**let**-tah, *f* grasshopper; locust

cavalletto, kah-vahl-**let**-to, *m* trestle; easel; tripod

cavallino, kah-vahl-**lee**-no, *m* pony

cavallo, kah-**vahl**-lo, *m* horse; (chess) knight; (sport) vaulting horse; – **da corsa**, racehorse

cavallone, kah-vahl-**lo**-nay, *m* (sea) breaker

cavare, kah-**vah**-ray, *v* to take out; to extract; to satisfy; **cavarsela**, to find a way out, to manage

cavatappi, kah-vah-**tap**-pe, *m* corkscrew

caverna, kah-**vair**-nah, *f* cavern, cave

cavezza, kah-**vet**-tsah, *f* halter

cavia, kah-ve'ah, *f* guinea pig

caviale, kah-ve'**ah**-lay, *m* caviar

caviglia, kah-**vee**-l'yah, *f* ankle

cavillare, kah-vil-**lah**-ray, *v* to quibble

cavillo, kah-**vil**-lo, *m* cavil, quibble

cavità, kah-vi-**tah**, *f* hollow; cavity

cavo, kah-vo, *m* cable; *adj* hollow

cavolfiore, kah-vol-fe'o-ray, *m* cauliflower

cavolo, kah-vo-lo, *m* cabbage

cazzotto, kaht-**tsot**-to, *m* blow, punch

cazzuola, kaht-tsoo'o-lah, *f* trowel

ce, chay, *pron & adv* (see **ci**)

cece, chay-chay, *m* chickpea

cecità, chay-che-**tah**, *f* blindness

cedere, chay-day-ray, *v* to give up, to yield; to collapse; to sell

cedibile, chay-**dee**-be-lay, *adj* transferable

cedola, chay-do-lah, *f* coupon; counterfoil

cedro, chay-dro, *m* cedar; (fruit) citron

cefalo, chay-fah-lo, *m* mullet

ceffo, chayf-fo, *m* snout; ugly mug

ceffone, chayf-**fo**-nay, *m* slap

celare, chay-**lah**-ray, *v* to conceal

celebrare, chay-lay-**brah**-ray, *v* to celebrate

celebrazione, chay-lay-brah-tse'o-nay, *f* celebration

celebre, chay-lay-bray, *adj* renowned

celebre, chay-lay-bree-**tah**, *f* fame; celebrity

celere, chay-lay-ray, *adj* rapid; speedy

celeste, chay-**less**-tay, *adj* sky-blue; celestial

celia, chay-le'ah, *f* joke, fun

celiare, chay-le'**ah**-ray, *v* to joke; to make fun

celibato, chay-le-**bah**-to, *m* celibacy

celibe, chay-le-bay, *m* bachelor

cella, chell-lah, *f* cell

celluloide, chell-loo-lo-e-day, *f* celluloid

cemento, chay-**men**-to, *m* cement; **– armato,** reinforced concrete

cena, chay-nah, *f* supper; dinner

cenare, chay-**nah**-ray, *v* to have dinner

cencio, chen-cho, *m* rag, tatter

cencioso, chen-**cho**-zo, *adj* ragged, tattered

cenere, chay-nay-ray, *f* ashes; *adj* ash-colour

Cenerentola, chay-nay-ren-to-lah, *f* Cinderella

cenno, chen-no, *m* nod; signal; hint

censimento, chen-se-men-to, *m* census

censire, chen-**see**-ray, *v* to take a census

censo, chen-so, *m* census

censore, chen-**sor**-ay, *m* censor; critic

censura, chen-**soo**-rah, *f* censorship

censurare, chen-soo-**rah**-ray, *v* to censure

centellinare, chen-tell-le-nah-ray, *v* to sip

centesimo, chen-**tay**-ze-mo, *m* centime, cent; hundredth; *adj* hundredth

centigrado, chen-tee-grah-do, *adj* centigrade

centimetro, chen-tee-may-tro, *m* centimetre

centinaio, chen-te-**nah**-e'o, *m* about a hundred

cento, chen-to, *adj & m* one hundred

centrale, chen-**trah**-lay, *adj* central; *f* head office; **– elettrica,** power station

centralino, chen-trah-**lee**-no, *m* telephone exchange; switchboard

centrare, chen-**trah**-ray, *v* to hit the centre; to centre

centrifuga, chen-**tree**-foo-gah, *f* spin-dryer

centro, chen-tro, *m* centre; **– commerciale,** shopping centre

centuplo, chen-too-plo, *adj* hundredfold; *m* a hundred times

ceppo, chep-po, *m* tree stump; block

cera, chay-rah, *f* wax; look, appearance

ceralacca, chay-rah-**lahk**-kah, *f* sealing wax

cerata, chay-**rah**-tah, *adj* **tela –,** tarpaulin

cerbiatto, chair-**beat**-to, *m* fawn

cerca, chair-kah, *f* **in – di,** in serach of

cercare, chair-**kah**-ray, *v* to seek; to search; to look for

cerchia, chair-**ke**'ah, *f* circle (of friends); **– di mura,** city walls

cerchio, chair-ke'o, *m* circle; ring; hoop

cereale, chay-ray-ah-lay, *m* cereal

cerebrale, chay-ray-**brah**-lay, *adj* cerebral

cerimonia, chay-re-**mo**-ne'ah, *f* ceremony

cerino, chay-**ree**-no, *m* wax match

cerniera, chair-ne'ay-rah, *f* hinge; zip

cero, chay-ro, *m* large wax candle

cerotto, chay-**rot**-to, *m* sticking plaster

certezza, chair-**tet**-tsah, *f* certainty

certificato, chair-te-fe-**kah**-to, *m* certificate

certo, chair-to, *adj* certain, sure; some; *pron* some; *adv* certainly

certuni, chair-**too**-ne, *pron* some

cerume, chay-**roo**-may, *m* ear wax

cerva, chair-vah, *f* doe, female deer

cervella, chair-**vell**-lah, *fpl* brains

cervello, chair-**vell**-lo, *m* brain; intelligence

cervice, chair-vee-chay, *f* cervix

cervo, chair-vo, *m* deer, stag

cesello, chay-**zell**-lo, *m* chisel

cesoie, chay-zo-e'ay, *fpl* shears

cespuglio, chess-poo-l'yo, *m* thicket, bush

cessare, chess-**sah**-ray, *v* to cease, to stop

cessione, chess-se'o-nay, *f* cession; transfer

cesso, chess-so, *m* bog, toilet

cesta, chess-tah, *f* basket, hamper

cestinare, chess-te-**nah**-ray, *v* to throw away; to reject

cestino, chess-**tee**-no, *m* basket

ceto, chay-to, *m* social class

cetra, chay-trah, *f* zither

cetriolino, chay-tre'o-**lee**-no, *m* gherkin

cetriolo, chay-tre'o-lo, *m* cucumber

che, kay, *adj* which, what; *pron* who, whom; which; what; *conj* that; than; *interj* what!

chi, kee, *pron* who, whom; whoever; anyone who; some

chiacchiera, ke'**ahk**-ke'ay-rah, *f* idle talk, gossip

chiacchierare, ke'ahk-ke'ay-**rah**-ray, *v* to chatter, to gossip

chiacchierata, ke'ahk-ke'ay-**rah**-tah, *f* chat

chiacchierone, ke'ahk-ke'ay-ro-nay, *m* chatterbox; gossip

chiamare, ke'ah-**mah**-ray,

v to call

chiamata, ke'ah-**mah**-tah, *f* call

chiappa, ke'**ahp**-pah, *f fam* buttock

chiarezza, ke'ah-**ret**-tsah, *f* clearness, clarity

chiarificare, ke'ah-re-fe-**kah**-ray, *v* to clarify

chiarire, ke'ah-**ree**-ray, *v* to make clear

chiaro, ke'**ah**-ro, *adj** clear; light; bright; *m* daylight; *adv* clearly

chiaroscuro, ke'ah-ro-**skoo**-ro, *m* chiaroscuro

chiaroveggente, ke'ah-ro-ved-**jen**-tay, *m/f* clairvoyant

chiasso, ke'**ahss**-so, *m* noise, uproar

chiatta, ke'**aht**-tah, *f* barge

chiavare, ke'ah-**vah**-ray, *v vulg* to screw

chiave, ke'**ah**-vay, *f* key; – **inglese**, spanner

chiavistello, ke'ah-ve-**stell**-lo, *m* bolt

chiazza, ke'**aht**-tsah, *f* spot, stain

chiazzare, ke'aht-**tsah**-ray, *v* to stain

chicco, **keek**-ko, *m* grain; bean; stone; grape

chiedere, ke'**ay**-day-ray, *v* to ask, to ask for, to demand

chiesa, ke'**ay**-zah, *f* church

chiglia, kee-'l'yah, *f* keel

chilo, **kee**-lo, *m* kilogram

chilogrammo, kee-lo-**gram**-mo, *m* kilogram

chilometro, kee-lo-may-tro, *m* kilometre

chimica, **kee**-me-kah, *f* chemistry

chimico, **kee**-me-ko, *m* chemist; *adj** chemical

china, **kee**-nah, *f* slope, incline

chinarsi, ke-**nar**-se, *v* to bend; to stoop

chincaglieria, keen-kah-l'yay-**ree**-ah, *f* knick-knacks

chinino, ke-**nee**-no, *m* quinine

chioccia, ke'**ot**-chah, *f* broody-hen

chiocciare, ke'ot-**chah**-ray, *v* to cackle

chiocciola, ke'ot-cho-lah, *f* snail; **scala a –**, winding staircase

chiodo, ke'o-do, *m* nail; stud, spike

chioma, ke'o-mah, *f* head of hair

chiosa, ke'o-zah, *f* gloss, note

chiosare, ke'o-zah-ray, *v* to gloss, to annotate

chiostro, ke'**oss**-tro, *m* cloister

chiromante, ke-ro-**mahn**-tay, *m/f* palmist; fortune-teller

chirurgico*, ke-**roohr**-je-ko, *adj* surgical

chirurgo, ke-**roohr**-go, *m* surgeon

chissà, kiss-**sah**, *adv* who knows; perhaps, maybe

chitarra, ke-tar-rah, *f* guitar

chiudere, ke'oo-day-ray, *v* to close, to shut; – **a chiave**, to lock

chiunque, ke'oonn-kway, *pron* whoever; anybody

chiusa, ke'oo-zah, *f* lock; enclosure

chiuso, ke'oo-zo, *adj* shut, closed

chiusura, ke'oo-zoo-rah, *f* lock; closing down; – **lampo**, zip fastener

ci, chee, *pron* us, to us; (refl) ourselves; each other; *adv* there; here

ciabatta, che'ah-**baht**-tah, *f* slipper

ciabattino, che'ah-baht-**tee**-no, *m* cobbler

cialda, che'**ahl**-dah, *f* wafer

cialtrone, che'ahl-**tro**-nay, *m* rogue

ciambella, che'ahm-**bell**-lah, *f* ring-shaped cake

ciambellano, che'ahm-bell-**lah**-no, *m* chamberlain

ciao, chah'o, *interj* hello!,

cheerio!, bye-bye!

ciarlatano, che'ar-lah-**tah**-no, m charlatan; quack

ciarpame, che'ar-**pah**-me, m rubbish

ciascuno, che'ahss-**koo**-no, *pron* each one, every one; *adj* each, every

cibare, che-**bah**-ray, v to feed

cibo, **chee**-bo, m food

cicala, che-**kah**-lah, f cicada

cicatrice, che-kah-**tree**-chay, f scar

cicca, **chick**-kah, f cigarette end, stub

ciclismo, chee-**kles**-mo, m cycling

ciclo, **chee**-klo, m cycle

cicogna, che-**ko**-n'yah, f stork

cicuta, che-**koo**-tah, f hemlock

cieco*, che'**ay**-ko, *adj* blind; **i ciechi**, the blind

cielo, che'**ay**-lo, m sky; *relig* heaven; **santo –!**, good heavens!

cifra, **chee**-frah, f figure; cipher

ciglio, **chee**-l'yo, m eyelash; edge

cigno, **chee**-n'yo, m swan

cigolare, che-go-lah-ray, v to creak

cigolio, che-go-**lee**-o, m creaking

ciliegia, che-le'**ay**-jah, f cherry

ciliegio, che-le'**ay**-jo, m cherry-tree

cilindrata, che-lin-**drah**-tah, f cubic capacity

cilindro, che-**lin**-dro, m cylinder

cima, **chee**-mah, f top; summit

cimelio, che-**may**-l'yo, m relic; old curiosity

cimentare, che-men-**tah**-ray, v to put to the test

cimentarsi, che-men-**tar**-se, v – **in**, to undertake

cimice, **chee**-me-chay, f bug

ciminiera, che-me-ne'**ay**-rah, f funnel; chimney stack

cimitero, che-me-**tay**-ro, m cemetery

cimurro, che-**moohr**-ro, m distemper

cinema, **che**-nay-mah, m cinema

cinepresa, che-nay-**pray**-sah, f cine camera

Cina, **chee**-nah, f China

cinese, chee-**nay**-zay, *adj* Chinese

cingere, **chin**-jay-ray, v to surround; to encircle

cinghia, **chin**-ghe'ah, f strap; belt

cinghiale, chin-ghe'**ah**-lay, m wild boar

cinguettare, chin-goo'et-**tah**-ray, v to chatter; to chirp

cinico, -a, **chee**-ne-ko, *adj** cynical; *m/f* cynic

cinquanta, chin-**kwahn**-tah, *adj & m* fifty

cinquantesimo, chin-kwahn-**tay**-se-mo, *adj & m* one-fiftieth

cinque, **chin**-kway, *adj & m* five

cinquecento, chin-kway-**chen**-to, *adj & m* five hundred; m **il Cinquecento**, the sixteenth century; *f* **la –**, Fiat 500

cintola, **chin**-to-lah, f belt; waist

cintura, chin-**too**-rah, f belt; waist

ciò, cho, *pron* that; it; – **che**, what

ciocca, **chock**-kah, f (hair) lock

cioccolata, chock-ko-**lah**-tah, f (a bar of, a cup of) chocolate

cioccolatino, chock-ko-lah-**tee**-no, m (a small) chocolate

cioccolato, chock-ko-**lah**-to, m (substance) chocolate

cioè, cho-**ay**, *adv* namely, that is to say

ciondolare, chon-do-**lah**-

ray, *v* to dangle; to hang about

ciondolo, chon-do-lo, *m* trinket; pendant

ciononostante, cho-no-no-**stahn**-tay, *adv* nevertheless

ciotola, cho-to-lah, *f* bowl

ciottolo, chot-to-lo, *m* pebble

cipiglio, che-**pee**-l'yo, *m* frown

cipolla, che-**pol**-lah, *f* onion

cipollina, che-pol-lee-nah, *f* spring onion

cipresso, che-**press**-so, *m* cypress

cipria, chee-pre-ah, *f* (face) powder

circa, cheer-kah, *prep* about, regarding; *adv* about

circo, cheer-ko, *m* circus

circolare, cheer-ko-**lah**-ray, *v* to circulate; *f* circular

circolazione, cheer-ko-lah-tse'o-nay, *f* circulation; traffic

circolo, cheer-ko-lo, *m* circle; club

circoncidere, cheer-kon-chee-day-ray, *v* to circumcise

circondare, cheer-kon-dah-ray, *v* to surround

circondario, cheer-kon-dah-re'o, *m* district

circonferenza, cheer-kon-fay-**rayn**-tsah, *f* circumference

circonvallazione, cheer-kon-vahl-lah-tse'o-nay, *f* ring road

circostanza, cheer-ko-**stahn**-tsah, *f* circumstance

circuire, cheer-koo'**ee**-ray, *v* to fool

circuito, cheer-koo'e-to, *m* circuit

cisposo, chiss-**po**-zo, *adj* blear-eyed

cisterna, chees-**tair**-nah, *f* cistern, tank

citare, che-tah-ray, *v* to cite; to summons

citofono, che-to-fo-no, *m* intercom; entry phone

citrullo, -a, che-**trooll**-lo, *adj* stupid; *m/f* blockhead

città, chit-**tah**, *f* city; town

cittadinanza, chit-tah-dee-**nahn**-tsah, *f* citizenship; inhabitants of a town

cittadino, chit-tah-dee-no, *m* citizen; inhabitant

ciuco, choo-ko, *m* donkey

ciuffo, choof-fo, *m* tuft of hair

civetta, che-vet-tah, *f* owl; coquette

civettare, che-vet-tah-ray,

v to flirt

civico, che-vee-ko, *adj* civic, municipal

civile, che-vee-lay, *adj* civil, courteous

civiltà, che-vil-tah, *f* civilization; civility

clacson, klak-son, *m* hooter, horn

clamore, klah-mor-ay, *m* clamour

clamoroso*, klah-mo-ro-zo, *adj* sensational; resounding

clarinetto, klah-ree-**net**-to, *m* clarinet

clarino, klah-ree-no, *m* clarinet

classe, klahss-say, *f* class; classroom

classico, klahss-se-ko, *m* (book) classic; (writer) classical author; *adj* classical

classificare, klahss-se-fe-**kah**-ray, *v* to classify

classificarsi, klahss-se-fe-**kar**-se, *v* to be placed (in a list/league)

clausola, klah'oo-zo-lah, *f* clause

clavicola, klah-**vee**-ko-lah, *f* collar-bone, clavicule

clemenza, klay-men-tsah, *f* clemency; mildness

clericale, klay-re-kah-lay, *adj* clerical

clero, klay-ro, *m* clergy

clessidra, klays-see-drah, *f* hourglass

cliente, kle-en-tay, *m/f* client, customer

clima, klee-mah, *m* climate

clinica, klee-nee-kah, *f* clinic

clistere, kliss-tay-ray, *m* enema

cloaca, klo-ah-kah, *f* sewer, drain

cloro, klo-ro, *m* chlorine

cloruro, klo-roo-ro, *m* chloride

coadiuvare, ko-ah-de'oo-vah-ray, *v* to assist

coagulare, ko-ah-goo-lah-ray, *v* to coagulate; to curdle

coalizione, ko-ah-lee-tse'o-nay, *f* coalition

coatto, ko-aht-to, *adj* compelled

cocaina, ko-kah'i-nah, *f* cocaine

cocca, kock-kah, *f* notch

coccarda, kock-kar-dah, *f* cockade

cocchiere, kock-ke'ay-ray, *m* coachman

cocchio, kock-ke'o, *m* carriage, coach

coccinella, kot-chee-nel-lah, *f* ladybird

coccio, kot-cho, *m* earthenware; fragment of pottery

cocciuto*, kot-choo-to, *adj* stubborn, obstinate

cocco, kock-ko, *m* coconut palm; **noce di –**, coconut

cocco, -a, kock-ko, *m/f* darling

coccodrillo, kock-ko-dreel-lo, *m* crocodile

coccolare, kock-ko-lah-ray, *v* to cuddle

cocente, ko-chen-tay, *adj* burning

cocomero, ko-ko-may-ro, *m* watermelon

cocuzzolo, ko-koot-tso-lo, *m* summit, top

coda, ko-dah, *f* tail; queue; (dress) train

codardia, ko-dar-dee-ah, *f* cowardice

codardo, ko-dar-do, *m* coward

codesto, ko-dess-to, *adj & pron* that, those

codice, ko-de-chay, *m* code; codex; **– a barre**, bar code; **– di avviamento postale**, postcode; **– della strada**, highway code

codino, ko-dee-no, *m* pigtail

coerente, ko-ay-ren-tay, *adj* coherent; consistent

coerenza, ko-ay-ren-tsah, *f* coherence; consistency

coesione, ko-ay-ze'o-nay, *f* cohesion

coetaneo, -a, ko-ay-tah-nay-o, *adj* contemporary; *m/f* contemporary

cofano, ko-fah-no, *m* trunk; (car) bonnet

cogli, ko-l'y, **(con gli)**, with the

cogliere, ko-l'yay-ray, *v* to gather; to catch

coglione, ko-l'yo-nay, *m* *vulg* testicle; *fig* dickhead

cognata, ko-n'yah-tah, *f* sister-in-law

cognato, ko-n'yah-to, *m* brother-in-law

cognizione, ko-n'ye-tse'o-nay, *f* knowledge

cognome, ko-n'yo-may, *m* surname, family name

coi, ko'e, **(con i)**, with the

coincidenza, ko-in-che-den-tsah, *f* coincidence; (train, etc.) connection

coinvolgere, ko-in-vol-jay-ray, *v* involve

coito, ko'e-to, *m* coitus

col, kol, (con il), with the

colapasta, ko-lah-pah-stah, *m* colander

colare, ko-lah-ray, *v* to drip; to run; to strain

colazione, ko-lah-tse'o-nay, *f* breakfast; lunch; **fare –**, to have breakfast; **prima –**, breakfast

colei, ko-**lay**-e, *pron* – **che,** she who

colera, kol-**lay**-rah, *m* cholera

colica, kol-lee-kah, *f* colic

colino, ko-**lee**-no, *m* strainer

colla, koll-lah, *f* glue; paste

colla, koll-lah, **(con la),** with the

collana, koll-**lah**-nah, *f* necklace

collare, koll-**lah**-ray, *m* collar

collasso, koll-**lahss**-so, *m* collapse

collaudare, koll-la'oo-**dah**-ray, *v* to test

colle, koll-lay, *m* hill; pass

collegare, koll-lay-**gah**-ray, *v* to connect, to link

collegio, koll-**lay**-jo, *m* college; community; – **elettorale,** constituency

collera, koll-lay-rah, *f* anger

colletta, koll-**let**-tah, *f* collection

collettivo, koll-let-**tee**-vo, *adj* collective; general

colletto, koll-**let**-to, *m* collar

collezionare, koll-lay-tse'o-**nah**-nay, *v* to collect

collezione, koll-lay-tse'o-nay, *f* collection

collina, koll-**lee**-nah, *f* hill

collirio, koll-**lee**-ree'o, *m* eyedrops

collisione, koll-**lee**-zee'o-nay, *f* collision

collo, koll-lo, *m* neck; parcel; packet

collo, koll-lo, **(con lo),** with the

collocamento, koll-lo-kah-**men**-to, *m* employment; appointment; **ufficio di –,** job centre

collocare, koll-lo-**kah**-ray, *v* to place

colloquio, koll-lo-**kwe**'o, *m* interview; conference; (university) oral exam

colmare, koll-**mah**-ray, *v* to fill up

colmo, koll-mo, *m* top; acme; *adj* full

colomba, ko-**lomm**-bah, *f* dove

colombaia, ko-lomm-bah-e'ah, *f* dovecote; pigeon coop

colombo, ko-**lomm**-bo, *m* pigeon

colonia, ko-lo-ne'ah, *f* colony

coloniale, ko-lo-ne'**ah**-lay, *adj* colonial

colonizzare, ko-lo-need-**dzah**-ray, *v* to colonize

colonna, ko-**lon**-nah, *f* column

colonnello, ko-lon-**nel**-lo, *m* colonel

colono, ko-**lo**-no, *m* colonist, settler; farmer

colorante, ko-lo-**rahn**-tay, *m* (food) colouring

colorare, ko-lo-**rah**-ray, *v* to colour

colore, ko-**lo**-ray, *m* colour

coloro, ko-**lo**-ro, *pron* those; they, them

colpa, koll-pah, *f* fault; guilt; blame

colpevole, koll-**pay**-vo-lay, *adj* guilty; *m/f* culprit

colpire, koll-**pee**-ray, *v* to hit, to strike; to affect

colpo, koll-po, *m* blow; shot; *med* stroke

coltellata, koll-tell-**lah**-tah, *f* stab

coltello, koll-**tell**-lo, *m* knife

colto, koll-to, *adj* educated, cultured

coltre, koll-tray, *f* blanket; coverlet

colui, ko-**loo**-e, *pron* – **che,** he who

comandante, ko-mahn-**dahn**-tay, *m* commander; captain; commanding officer

comandare, ko-mahn-**dah**-ray, *v* to command, to order; to be in charge

comando, ko-**mahn**-do, *m* command, order; (tech) control

combaciare, kom-bah-**chah**-ray, *v* to join, to fit together; to correspond

combattere, kom-**baht**-tay-ray, *v* to fight

combattimento, kom-baht-te-**men**-to, *m* fight, battle

combinare, kom-be-**nah**-ray, *v* to combine; to arrange

combinazione, kom-be-nah-tse'o-nay, *f* coincidence; combination

combriccola, kom-**brick**-ko-lah, *f* gang; clique

combustibile, kom-booss-**tee**-be-lay, *m* fuel

come, ko-may, *adv* so; as; like; while; *conj* how; as; as soon as

cometa, ko-**may**-tah, *f* comet

comico, ko-me-ko, *m* comedian; *adj** comical

comignolo, ko-**mee**-n'yo-lo, *m* chimney top

cominciare, ko-min-**chah**-ray, *v* to begin, to start

comitato, ko-me-**tah**-to, *m* committee, board

comitiva, ko-me-**tee**-vah, *f* party

comizio, ko-**mee**-tse'o,

m rally

commedia, kom-**may**-de'ah, *f* comedy; play

commediante, kom-may-de'**ahn**-tay, *m/f* comedian; actor, actress

commemorare, kom-may-mo-**rah**-ray, *v* to commemorate

commendatore, kom-men-dah-**to**-ray, *m* official title in the Italian republic

commensale, kom-men-**sah**-lay, *m/f* table companion

commentare, kom-men-**tah**-ray, *v* to comment

commento, kom-**men**-to, *m* comment

commerciale, kom-mair-**chah**-lay, *adj* commercial

commercialista, kom-mair-chah-**lee**-stah, *m/f* accountant; business consultant

commerciante, kom-mair-**chahn**-tay, *m/f* trader; shopkeeper

commerciare, kom-mair-**chah**-ray, *v* to trade

commercio, kom-**mair**-cho, *m* commerce, trade

commesso, -a, kom-**mess**-so, *m/f* shop assistant; clerk

commestibile, kom-mess-

tee-be-lay, *adj* edible

commestibili, kom-mess-**tee**-be-lee, *mpl* foodstuffs

commettere, kom-**met**-tay-ray, *v* to commit; to commission

commiato, kom-me'**ah**-to, *m* leave-taking

comminare, kom-me-**nah**-ray, *v law* to threaten, to inflict (sanctions)

commiserare, kom-me-zay-**rah**-ray, *v* to pity

commissariato, kom-miss-sah-re'a-to, *m* police station; commissioner's office

commissario, kom-miss-**sah**-re'o, *m* police superintendent; commissioner

commissionario, kom-miss-se'o-**nah**-re'o, *m* agent, broker

commovente, kom-mo-**ven**-tay, *adj* touching

commuovere, kom-moo'o-vay-ray, *v* to affect

commuoversi, kom-moo'o-vair-se, *v* to be moved

commutare, kom-moo-**tah**-ray, *v law* to commute; to change over

commutatore, kom-moo-tah-**tor**-ay, *m* (electric)

switch

comodino, ko-mo-**dee**-no, *m* bedside table

comodità, ko-mo-de-**tah**, *f* comfort; convenience

comodo*, **ko**-mo-do, *adj* handy; comfortable; convenient

compagnia, kom-pah-n'**yee**-ah, *f* company; society

compagno, -a, kom-**pah**-n'yo, *m/f* companion; partner

comparabile, kom-pah-**rah**-be-lay, *adj* comparable

comparare, kom-pah-**rah**-ray, *v* to compare

compare, kom-pah-ray, *m* godfather; accomplice; *fam* pal

comparire, kom-pah-**ree**-ray, *v* to appear; to come out

comparsa, kom-**par**-sah, *f* appearance; (stage) walk-on, extra

compartecipare, kom-par-tay-che-**pah**-ray, *v* to have a share

compartimento, kom-**par**-te-**men**-to, *m* compartment; district

compassione, kom-pahss-se'o-nay, *f* compassion, pity

compassionevole, kom-

pahss-se'o-**nay**-vo-lay, *adj* compassionate; moving, touching

compasso, kom-**pahss**-so, *m* compasses; callipers

compatimento, kom-pah-te-**men**-to, *m* compassion; indulgence

compatire, kom-pah-**tee**-ray, *v* to pity; to make allowances for

compatto*, kom-**paht**-to, *adj* compact; dense

compendio, kom-**pen**-de'o, *m* compendium; summary

compensare, kom-pen-**sah**-ray, *v* to pay for; to make up for

compenso, kom-**pen**-so, *m* compensation, reward; payment

compera, **kom**-pay-rah, *f* purchase

competente, kom-pay-**ten**-tay, *adj* competent, qualified

competenza, kom-pay-**ten**-tsah, *f* competence; jurisdiction

competere, kom-**pay**-tay-ray, *v* to compete; to be incumbent upon

competizione, kom-pay-tee-**tse'o**-nay, *f* competition

compiacente, kom-pe'ah-**chen**-tay, *adj* obliging

compiacenza, kom-pe'ah-**chen**-tsah, *f* kindness

compiacimento, kom-pe'ah-che-**men**-to, *m* pleasure

compiangere, kom-pe'**ahn**-jay-ray, *v* to feel sorry for

compianto, kom-pe'**ahn**-to, *m* grief

compiere, kom-pe'ay-ray, *v* to complete; to fulfil

compilare, kom-pe-**lah**-ray, *v* to compile

compimento, kom-pe-**men**-to, *m* accomplishment; fulfilment; completion

compire, kom-pee-ray, *v* to complete; to fulfil

compitare, kom-pe-**tah**-ray, *v* to spell

compitezza, kom-pe-**tet**-tsah, *f* politeness

compito, **kom**-pe-to, *m* task; duty; homework

compiuto*, kom-pe'oo-to, *adj* ended, completed

compleanno, kom-play-**ahn**-no, *m* birthday

complementare, kom-play-men-**tah**-ray, *adj* additional; auxiliary

complemento, kom-play-**men**-to, *m* complement

complessità, kom-pless-see-**tah**, *f* complexity

complessivo, kom-pless-

see-vo, *adj*
comprehensive, total

complesso, kom-**pless**-so,
adj complex; whole

completare, kom-**play**-**tah**-ray, *v* to complete

completo*, kom-**play**-to,
adj complete; full up; *m*
suit

complicare, kom-ple-**kah**-ray, *v* to complicate

complice, kom-ple-chay,
m/f accomplice

complimento, kom-ple-**men**-to, *m* compliment;
complimenti,
congratulations; **fare –,**
to stand on ceremony

complotto, kom-**plot**-to,
m conspiracy, plot

componente, kom-po-**nen**-tay, *m* component;
member; *adj* component

componimento, kom-po-ne-**men**-to, *m*
composition

comporre, kom-**por**-ray, *v*
to compose; to arrange;
law to settle

comportamento, kom-por-tah-**men**-to, *m*
behaviour

comportare, kom-por-**tah**-ray, *v* to imply, to
involve

comportarsi, kom-por-**tar**-se, *v* to behave

compositore, -trice, kom-

po-ze-**tor**-ay, kom-po-ze-**tree**-chay, *m/f* composer;
compositor, typesetter

composizione, kom-po-ze-**tse'o**-nay, *f* composition;
typesetting; settlement

composta, kom-**poss**-tah, *f*
stewed fruit

composto, kom-**poss**-to, *m*
mixture, compound; *adj*
compound, composite;
composed, dignified

compra, kom-prah, *f*
purchase

comprare, kom-**prah**-ray,
v to purchase

compratore, -trice, kom-prah-**tor**-ay, kom-prah-**tree**-chay, *m/f* buyer

comprendere, kom-**pren**-day-ray, *v* to understand;
to include

comprensibile, kom-pren-**see**-be-lay, *adj*
comprehensible

comprensione, kom-pren-se'o-nay, *f*
comprehension,
understanding

compressa, kom-**press**-sah, *f* tablet; compress

comprimere, kom-**pree**-may-ray, *v* to compress

compromesso, kom-pro-**mes**-so, *m* compromise

compromettere, kom-pro-**met**-tay-ray, *v* to
compromise

comprovare, kom-pro-**vah**-ray, *v* to prove

compunto*, kom-**poonn**-to, *adj* repentant,
contrite

compunzione, kom-poonn-tse'o-nay, *f*
contrition

computer, kom-pee'**oo**-ter,
m computer

computisteria, kom-poo-tiss-tay-**ree**-ah, *f*
accounting, book-
keeping

computo, kom-poo-to, *m*
calculation

comune, ko-**moo**-nay, *adj*
common, ordinary; *m*
town hall; town council

comunicare, ko-moo-ne-**ka**-ray, *v* to
communicate; *relig* to
administer communion

comunicativo, ko-moo-nee-kah-**tee**-vo, *adj*
communicative

comunicato, ko-moo-nee-**kah**-to, *m* communiqué;
– stampa, press release

comunicazione, ko-moo-nee-kah-tse'o-nay, *f*
communication;
(phone) call;
announcement

comunione, ko-moo-nee'o-nay, *f* communion

comunismo, ko-moo-**niss**-mo, *m* communism

comunità, ko-moo-nee-**tah**, f community; **Comunità Economica Europea**, European Economic Community

comunque, ko-**moon**-kway, adv anyway; nevertheless; conj however

con, kon, prep with; by

conato, ko-**nah**-to, m – **di vomito**, retching

conca, kon-kah, f broad valley

concatenare, kon-kah-tay-**nah**-ray, v to link up

concavo, kon-kah-vo, adj concave

concedere, kon-**chay**-day-ray, v to concede, to allow

concentramento, kon-chen-trah-**men**-to, m concentration

concentrare, kon-chen-**trah**-ray, v to concentrate

concepibile, kon-chay-**pee**-be-lay, adj conceivable

concepire, kon-chay-pee-ray, v to conceive; to imagine

conceria, kon-chay-ree-ah, f tannery

concernere, kon-**chair**-nay-ray, v to concern

concertare, kon-chair-**tah**-ray, v to plan

concerto, kon-**chair**-to, m concert

concessionario, kon-chess-se'o-**nah**-re'o, m concessionary; agent, dealer

concessione, kon-chess-se'o-nay, f concession

concetto, kon-**chet**-to, m concept; opinion

concezione, kon-chay-tse'o-nay, f conception; view

conchiglia, kon-kee-l'yah, f shell

conciare, kon-**chah**-ray, v to tan; to treat badly

conciliare, kon-che-le'**ah**-ray, v to reconcile; to settle

conciliazione, kon-che-le'ah-tse'o-nay, f reconciliation; settlement

concilio, kon-chee-le'o, m council; assembly

concime, kon-**chee**-may, m manure; fertiliser

concisione, kon-che-ze'o-nay, f conciseness

conciso*, kon-**chee**-zo, adj concise

concitato, kon-che-**tah**-to, adj agitated

concittadino, kon-chit-tah-**dee**-no, m fellow citizen

conclave, kon-**klah**-vay, m conclave

concludere, kon-**kloo**-day-ray, v to conclude

conclusione, kon-kloo-see'o-nay, f conclusion; end

conclusivo, kon-kloo-see-vo, adj conclusive

concordare, kon-kor-**dah**-ray, v to agree

concordato, kon-kor-**dah**-to, m settlement; relig concordat

concorde*, kon-**kor**-day, adj unanimous

concordia, kon-**kor**-de'ah, f harmony, concord

concorrente, kon-kor-**ren**-tay, m/f competitor

concorrenza, kon-kor-**ren**-tsah, f competition

concorrere, kon-**kor**-ray-ray, v to compete; – **a**, to contribute to

concorso, kon-**kor**-so, m competition

condanna, kon-**dahn**-nah, f condemnation; law sentence

condannare, kon-dahn-**nah**-ray, v to condemn; law to sentence

condannato, kon-dahn-**nah**-to, m convict

condensare, kon-den-**sah**-ray, v to condense

condensatore, kon-den-sah-**tor**-ay, *m* condenser

condimento, kon-de-**men**-to, *m* seasoning; dressing

condire, kon-**dee**-ray, *v* to season; to dress

condiscendere, kon-de-**shen**-day-ray, *v* to condescend

condividere, kon-de-**vee**-day-ray *v* to share

condizionale, kon-de-tse'o-**nah**-lay, *adj* conditional; *m gram* conditional; *f law* suspended sentence

condizionare, kon-de-tse'o-**nah**-ray, *v* to condition

condizione, kon-de-tse'o-nay, *f* condition; rank; calling

condoglianze, kon-do-l'**yahn**-tsay, *fpl* condolences

condominio, kon-do-mee-ne'o, *m* joint ownership

condonare, kon-do-nah-ray, *v* to pardon

condotta, kon-**dot**-tah, *f* conduct

condottiero, kon-dot-te'**ay**-ro, *m* leader

condotto, kon-**dot**-to, *m* conduit; duct; **medico –**, local authority doctor

conducente, kon-doo-**chen**-tay, *m/f* driver

condurre, kon-**doohr**-ray,

v to lead; to drive; to run, to manage; to conduct

confederazione, kon-fay-day-rah-tse'o-nay, *f* confederation

conferenza, kon-fay-**ren**-tsah, *f* conference; lecture

conferenziere, kon-fay-ren-tse'**ay**-ray, *m* lecturer

conferire, kon-fay-**ree**-ray, *v* to confer, to bestow

conferma, kon-**fair**-mah, *f* confirmation

confermare, kon-fair-**mah**-ray, *v* to confirm; to sanction

confessare, kon-fess-**sah**-ray, *v* to confess

confessione, kon-fess-se'o-nay, *f* confession

confettiera, kon-fet-tee'**ay**-rah, *f* bonbonnière

confetto, kon-**fet**-to, *m* sugared almond

confettura, kon-fet-**too**-rah, *f* preserve; jam

confezionare, kon-fay-tse'o-**nah**-ray, *v* to wrap up; to package; to make (clothes)

confezione, kon-fay-tse'o-nay, *f* packaging; tailoring, dressmaking; – **regalo**, gift pack

conficcare, kon-feeck-**kah**-ray, *v* – **in**, to hammer into; to stick into

confidare, kon-fe-**dah**-ray, *v* to confide; – **in**, to rely upon

confidenza, kon-fe-**den**-tsah, *f* confidence; familiarity

confinare, kon-fe-**nah**-ray, *v* to border upon; to confine

confinato, kon-fe-**nah**-to, *adj* interned

confine, kon-**fee**-nay, *m* border; boundary

confino, kon-**fee**-no, *m* internment

confisca, kon-**fiss**-kah, *f* confiscation

conflitto, kon-**flit**-to, *m* conflict; dispute

confluire, kon-floo'i-ray, *v* (rivers, streets) to meet; to come together

confondere, kon-**fon**-day-ray, *v* to confuse, to mix up; to embarrass

conformare, kon-for-**mah**-ray, *v* to conform

confortare, kon-for-**tah**-ray, *v* to comfort

confortevole, kon-for-**tay**-vo-lay, *adj* comforting

conforto, kon-**for**-to, *m* comfort

confrontare, kon-fron-

tah-ray, v to confront; to compare

confronto, kon-fron-to, m comparison

confusione, kon-foo-zee'o-nay, f confusion; noise; embarrassment

confuso*, kon-foo-zo, adj confused; nuddled; embarrassed

confutare, kon-foo-tah-ray, v to confute

congedare, kon-jay-dah-ray, v to dismiss

congedo, kon-jay-do, m leave; discharge

congegnare, kon-jay-n'yah-ray, v to assemble; to devise

congegno, kon-jay-n'yo, m mechanism; device

congelare, kon-jay-lah-ray, v to freeze

congelatore, kon-jay-lah-to-ray, m freezer

congestione, kon-jay-stee'o-nay, f congestion

congettura, kon-jet-too-rah, f conjecture

congetturare, kon-jet-too-rah-ray, v to surmise

congiungere, kon-joonn-jay-ray, v to join

congiunto, -a, kon-joonn-to, adj* connected; m/f relation

congiuntura, kon-joonn-too-rah, f junction;

occasion; economic situation

congiunzione, kon-joonn-tse'o-nay, f conjunction; connection

congiura, kon-joo-rah, f conspiracy

congiurato, -a, kon-joo-rah-to, m/f conspirator

congratulare, kon-grah-too-lah-ray, v to congratulate

congratulazioni, kon-grah-too-lah-tse'o-nee, fpl congratulations

congregare, kon-gray-gah-ray, v to assemble

congresso, kon-gress-so, m congress; assemble

congruo*, kon-groo'o, adj adequate; consistent

coniare, ko-ne'ah-ray, v to coin; to mint

coniglio, ko-nee-l'yo, m rabbit; fig coward

conio, ko-ne'o, m minting die; coinage

coniugale, ko-ne'oo-gah-lay, adj conjugal

coniugare, ko-ne'oo-gah-ray, v to conjugate

coniugato, ko-ne'oo-gah-to, adj married

coniuge, ko-ne'oo-jay, m/f spouse; **i coniugi,** the husband and wife

connazionale, kon-nah-tse'o-nah-lay, m/f fellow-

countryman/woman

connessione, kon-ness-se'o-nay, f connection

connettere, kon-net-tay-ray, v to connect

connivenza, kon-ne-ven-tsah, f connivance

connotati, kon-no-tah-te, mpl distinguishing marks

cono, ko-no, m cone

conoscente, ko-no-shen-tay, m/f acquaintance

conoscenza, ko-no-shen-tsah, f knowledge; acquaintance

conoscere, ko-no-shay-ray, v to know

conosciuto, ko-no-she'oo-to, adj known, renowned

conquista, kon-kwiss-tah, f conquest

conquistare, kon-kwiss-tah-ray, v to conquer

conquistatore, kon-kwiss-tah-tor-ay, m conqueror

consacrare, kon-sah-krah-ray, v to consecrate

consanguineo, kon-sahn-goo'ee-nay-o, adj related by blood

consapevole, kon-sah-pay-vo-lay, adj conscious, aware

conscio*, kon-she'o, adj conscious

consegna, kon-say-n'yah, f delivery; consignment; mil orders

consegnare, kon-say-n'**yah**-ray, *v* to deliver; *mil* to confine to barracks

conseguente, kon-say-goo'**en**-tay, *adj* consequent, ensuing

conseguire, kon-say-goo'**ee**-ray, *v* to obtain, to achieve; to follow

consenso, kon-**sen**-so, *m* consent

consentire, kon-sen-**tee**-ray, *v* to consent

consenziente, kon-sen-tse'**en**-tay, *adj* consenting

conserva, kon-**sair**-vah, *f* preserve

conservare, kon-sair-**vah**-ray, *v* to keep; to preserve

conservatore, -trice, kon-sair-vah-**tor**-ay, kon-sair-vah-**tree**-chay, *m/f* Conservative

conservazione, kon-sair-vah-tse'**o**-nay, *f* conservation, preservation

considerare, kon-se-day-**rah**-ray, *v* to consider

considerazione, kon-se-day-rah-tse'**o**-nay, *f* consideration; esteem; remark

considerevole, kon-se-day-**ray**-vo-lay, *adj* considerable; important

consigliare, kon-se-l'**yah**-ray, *v* to advise

consigliere, -a, kon-se-l'**yay**-ray, *m/f* adviser; councillor

consiglio, kon-**see**-l'yo, *m* advice; counsel; council; **– di amministrazione,** board of directors

consistente, kon-siss-**ten**-tay, *adj* firm; solid

consistenza, kon-siss-**ten**-tsah, *f* firmness; solidity

consistere, kon-**siss**-tay-ray, *v* to consist

consociata, kon-so-**chah**-tah, *f* associated company

consociato, kon-so-**chah**-to, *adj* associated

consocio, -a, kon-so-cho, *m/f* partner, associate

consolare, kon-so-**lah**-ray, *v* to console; *adj* consular

consolato, kon-so-**lah**-to, *m* consulate

consolazione, kon-so-lah-tse'**o**-nay, *f* consolation

console, kon-so-lay, *m* consul

consolidare, kon-so-le-**dah**-ray, *v* to consolidate

consonante, kon-so-**nahn**-tay, *f* consonant

consono, kon-so-no, *adj* consistent; conforming

consorte, kon-**sor**-tay, *m/f* consort

consorzio, kon-**sor**-tse'o, *m* consortium; cooperative; syndicate

constare, kon-**stah**-ray, *v* to be evident; to consist of; **a quanto mi consta,** as far as I know

constatare, kon-stah-**tah**-ray, *v* to ascertain, to notice

consueto*, kon-soo'**ay**-to, *adj* usual, habitual

consuetudine, kon-soo'ay-**too**-de-nay, *f* custom

consulente, kon-soo-**len**-tay, *adj* consulting; *m/f* consultant

consultare, kon-sooll-**tah**-ray, *v* to consult

consulto, kon-**sooll**-to, *m med* consultation

consumare, kon-soo-**mah**-ray, *v* to consume

consumismo, kon-soo-**mee**-zmo, *m* consumerism

consumo, kon-**soo**-mo, *m* consumption; **società dei consumi,** consumer society

consuntivo, kon-soonn-**tee**-vo, *adj comm* final; *m* final balance

contabile, kon-**tah**-be-lay, *m/f* book-keeper; accountant

contabilità, kon-tah-be-le-tah, f book-keeping

contachilometri, kon-tah-ke-lo-may-tre, m mileometer

contadino, -a, kon-tah-dee-no, m/f farm worker; peasant

contagiare, kon-tah-jah-ray, v to infect

contagio, kon-tah-jo, m infection; contagion; epidemic

contagioso, kon-tah-jo-zo, adj infectious

contaminare, kon-tah-me-nah-ray, v to contaminate

contanti, kon-tahn-te, mpl cash

contare, kon-tah-ray, v to count; – **su,** to rely upon

contatore, kon-tah-tor-ay, m meter

contatto, kon-taht-to, m contact; touch

conte, kon-tay, m count

contea, kon-tay-ah, f county

conteggiare, kon-ted-jah-ray, v to calculate

contegno, kon-tay-n'yo, m behaviour; attitude

contegnoso*, kon-tay-n'yo-zo, adj reserved; haughty

contemplare, kon-tem-plah-ray, v to

contemplate; to gaze at; law to provide for

contemporaneo, -a, kon-tem-po-rah-nay-o, adj* contemporary; m/f contemporary

contendere, kon-ten-day-ray, v to contend; to quarrel

contenere, kon-tay-nay-ray, v to contain; to restrain; to hold back

contenitore, kon-tay-nee-to-ray, m container

contentarsi, kon-ten-tar-se, v to be satisfied

contentezza, kon-ten-tet-tsah, f contentment; pleasure

contento, kon-ten-to, adj happy; satisfied

contenuto, kon-tay-noo-to, m contents

contesa, kon-tay-zah, f dispute; argument

contessa, kon-tess-sah, f countess

contestare, kon-tay-stah-ray, v to contest; to protest against

contestazione, kon-tay-stah-tse'o-nay, f law dispute; anti-establishment activity

contesto, kon-tess-to, m context

contiguo, kon-tee-goo'o, adj adjacent

continente, kon-te-nen-tay, m continent

contingente, kon-tin-jen-tay, m contingent; quantity; share; adj contingent

continuare, kon-te-noo'ah-ray, v to continue

continuazione, kon-te-noo'a-tse'o-nay, f continuation

continuità, kon-te-noo'e-tah, f continuity

continuo*, kon-tee-noo'o, adj continuous

conto, kon-to, m account; bill; calculation; – **corrente,** current account; **tener – di,** to take into consideration

contorcere, kon-tor-chay-ray, v to contort; to twist

contorno, kon-tor-no, m outline, border; vegetables

contorto*, kon-tor-to, adj twisted; crooked; tortuous

contrabbandiere, kon-trahb-bahn-de'ay-ray, m smuggler

contrabbando, kon-trahb-bahn-do, m smuggling; contraband

contrabbasso, kon-trahb-bahss-so, m double bass

contraccambiare, kon-

trahk-kahm-be'**ah**-ray, *v*
to reciprocate

contraccettivo, kon-traht-
chet-**tee**-vo, *m*
contraceptive

contraccolpo, kon-trahk-
koll-po, *m* recoil;
rebound; consequence

contrada, kon-**trah**-dah, *f*
road; country, region

contraddire, kon-trahd-
dee-ray, *v* to contradict

contraddittorio, kon-
trahd-de-**tor**-e'o, *adj*
contradictory;
conflicting; *m* cross-
examination

contraddizione, kon-trah-
de-tse'o-nay, *f*
contradiction

contraente, kon-trah-**en**-
tay, *m/f* contracting
party

contraffare, kon-trahf-
fah-ray, *v* to forge; to
counterfeit; to
adulterate

contraffazione, kon-trahf-
fah-tse'o-nay, *f* forgery;
counterfeiting;
adulteration

contrafforte, kon-trahf-
for-tay, *m* buttress

contralto, kon-**trahl**-to, *m*
contralto

contrappeso, kon-trahp-
pay-zo, *m*
counterweight;

counterbalance

contrapporre, kon-trahp-
por-ray, *v* to oppose, to
counter; to compare

contrapposizione, kon-
trahp-po-zee-tse'o-nay, *f*
contrast; comparison;
juxtaposition

contrariare, kon-trah-
re'**ah**-ray, *v* to oppose; to
annoy

contrarietà, kon-trah-
re'ay-**tah**, *f* adversity;
trouble

contrario, kon-**trah**-re'o,
m contrary; opposite;
adj* opposite; adverse

contrarre, kon-**trar**-ray, *v*
to contract; to tense; to
enter into

contrassegnare, kon-
trahss-say-n'**yah**-ray, *v*
to place a mark upon

contrassegno, kon-trahss-
say-n'yo, *m* mark; proof;
spedire in –, to send
COD

contrastare, kon-trah-
stah-ray, *v* to contrast;
to oppose; to clash

contrasto, kon-**trah**-sto, *m*
contrast; dispute;
disagreement

contrattare, kon-traht-
tah-ray, *v* to negotiate;
to bargain

contrattempo, kon-traht-
tem-po, *m* difficulty,

hitch

contratto, kon-**traht**-to, *m*
contract; *adj* tense;
contracted

contrattuale, kon-traht-
too'**ah**-lay, *adj* in
accordance with
agreement

contravvenire, kon-trahv-
vay-**ne**-ray, *v* to
contravene

contravvenzione, kon-
trahv-ven-tse'o-nay, *f*
fine; contravention

contrazione, kon-trahv-
tse'o-nay, *f* contraction

contribuente, kon-tre-
boo'**en**-tay, *m/f* taxpayer

contribuire, kon-tre-
boo'**ee**-ray, *v* to
contribute, to help

contributo, kon-tre-**boo**-
to, *m* contribution;
**contributi
previdenziali**, national
insurance

contrito*, kon-**tree**-to, *adj*
repentant

contrizione, kon-tre-tse'o-
nay, *f* contrition

contro, **kon**-tro, prep
against; contrary to; *adv*
against; **per –**, on the
other hand

controbattere, kon-tro-
baht-tay-ray, *v* to refute;
to answer back

controcorrente, kon-tro-kor-**ren**-tay, *adv* against the tide; upstream

controfigura, kon-tro-fee-**goo**-rah, *f* stuntman/woman

controindicazione, kon-tro-een-dee-kah-tse'**o**-nay, *f* contraindication

controllare, kon-troll-**lah**-ray, *v* to check, to control

controllo, kon-**troll**-lo, *m* check; control; *med* **visita di –,** checkup

controllore, kon-trol-**lo**-ray, *m* ticket inspector; controller

contrordine, kon-**tror**-dee-nay, *m* counter-order

controspionaggio, kon-tros-speeo-**nad**-jo, *m* counter-espionage

controversia, kon-tro-**vair**-se'ah, *f* controversy; dispute

controverso, kon-tro-**vair**-so, *adj* controversial

controvoglia, kon-tro-vo-**l'**yah, *adv* unwillingly

contumacia, kon-too-**mah**-chah, *f law* default

contundente, kon-toon-**den**-tay, *adj* blunt

conturbante, kon-toohr-**bahn**-tay, *adj* perturbing

contuso, kon-**too**-zo, *adj*

hurt, bruised

conurbazione, kon-noor-bah-tse'**o**-nay, *f* conurbation

convalescente, kon-vah-lay-**shen**-tay, *adj* convalescent

convalescenza, kon-vah-lay-**shen**-tsah, *f* recovery, convalescence

convalidare, kon-vah-le-**dah**-ray, *v* to confirm; to validate

convegno, kon-**vay**-n'yo, *m* meeting; congress

convenevoli, kon-vay-**nay**-vo-le, *mpl* courtesies, compliments

conveniente*, kon-vay-ne'**en**-tay, *adj* convenient, fitting; cheap

convenienza, kon-vay-ne'**ent**-tsah, *f* convenience; advantage; propriety

convenire, kon-vay-**nee**-ray, *v* to agree; to gather

convento, kon-**ven**-to, *m* convent

convenzionale, kon-ven-tse'o-**nah**-lay, *adj* conventional

convenzione, kon-ven-tse'**o**-nay, *f* convention; agreement

convergere, kon-**vair**-jay-ray, *v* to converge

conversare, kon-vair-**sah**-ray, *v* to converse

conversazione, kon-vair-sah-tse'**o**-nay, *f* conversation; chat

convertire, kon-vair-**tee**-ray, *v* to convert

convesso, kon-**vess**-so, *adj* convex

convincente, kon-veen-**chen**-tay, *adj* convincing

convincere, kon-**veen**-chay-ray, *v* to convince, to persuade

convinto, kon-**veen**-to, *adj* convinced, persuaded

convinzione, kon-veen-tse'**o**-nay, *f* conviction

convitato, -a, kon-ve-tah-to, *m/f* guest

convitto, kon-**veet**-to, *m* boarding school

convivenza, kon-vee-**ven**-tsah, *f* cohabitation

convivere, kon-vee-**vay**-ray, *v* to live together, to cohabit

convocare, kon-vo-**kah**-ray, *v* to convene; to call; to summon

convocazione, kon-vo-kah-tse'**o**-nay, *f* meeting; summoning; summons

convogliare, kon-vo-**l'**yah-ray, *v* to channel; to convey

convoglio, kon-vo-**l'**yo, *m*

train; convoy

convulso*, kon-**vooll**-so, *adj* convulsive

cooperare, ko-o-pay-**rah**-ray, *v* to cooperate

coordinare, ko-or-de-**nah**-ray, *v* to coordinate

coperchio, ko-**pair**-ke'o, *m* cover, lid

coperta, ko-**pair**-tah, *f* blanket; cover; upper-deck

copertina, ko-pair-tee-nah, *f* (book) cover; (book) jacket

coperto, ko-**pair**-to, *m* place (at table); *adj* covered; overcast; indoor; **al –**, under cover

copertone, ko-pair-to-nay, *m* tarpaulin; tyre

copertura, ko-pair-too-rah, *f* cover; roofing

copia, ko-**pee**-ah, *f* copy

copiare, ko-pe'ah-ray, *v* to copy

copiativo, ko-pe'ah-tee-vo, *adj* **carta copiativa**, carbon paper

copiatura, ko-pe'ah-too-rah, *f* copying

copione, ko-pe'o-nay, *m* script

copioso, ko-pe'o-zo, *adj* abundant, copious

copisteria, ko-piss-tay-ree-ah, *f* copy bureau

coppa, **kop**-pah, *f* cup; trophy; pork sausage

coppia, **kop**-pe'ah, *f* couple; pair

coprifuoco, ko-pre-foo'o-ko, *m* curfew

copriletto, ko-pre-**let**-to, *m* bedspread

coprire, ko-**pree**-ray, *v* to cover; to hide

copula, **ko**-poo-lah, *f gram* copula; conjunction

coraggio, ko-**rahd**-jo, *m* courage; *fig* cheek

corale, ko-**rah**-lay, *adj* choral; unanimous

corallo, ko-**rahl**-lo, *m* coral

corazza, ko-**raht**-tsah, *f* cuirass, breastplate

corazzata, ko-raht-**tsah**-tah, *f* battleship

corbelleria, kor-bell-lay-ree-ah, *f* tomfoolery; nonsense

corda, **kor**-dah, *f* rope; string; sinew; chord

cordame, kor-**dah**-may, *m* rigging; ropes

cordata, kor-**dah**-tah, *f* roped party

cordiale, kor-de'ah-lay, *adj* cordial, warm

cordialità, kor-de'ah-le-**tah**, *f* cordiality

cordoglio, kor-do-l'yo, *m* grief; mourning

cordone, kor-do-nay, *m* cord; cordon

coreografia, ko-ray'o-grah-**fee**-ah, *f* choreography

coricarsi, ko-re-**kar**-se, *v* to go to bed; to lie down

corista, ko-**riss**-tah, *m/f* chorister

cornacchia, kor-**nahk**-ke'ah, *f* crow

cornamusa, kor-nah-**moo**-zah, *f* bagpipes

cornetta, kor-**net**-tah, *f* (phone) receiver

cornetto, kor-**net**-to, *m* croissant; cone; string bean

cornice, kor-**nee**-chay, *f* cornice; frame

corno, **kor**-no, *m* horn; antler

cornuto, kor-**noo**-to, *adj* horned; *m* cuckold

coro, **ko**-ro, *m* chorus; choir

corona, ko-ro-nah, *f* crown; wreath

coronaria, ko-ro-**nah**-re'ah, *f* coronary artery

corpo, **kor**-po, *m* body; (dead) corpse; (literature) corpus; corps

corporatura, kor-po-rah-too-rah, *f* build, physique

corporazione, kor-po-rah-tse'o-nay, *f* guild

corpulenza, kor-poo-**len**-

tsah, f corpulence

corpuscolo, kor-pooss-ko-lo, m corpuscle

corredare, kor-ray-dah-ray, v to equip

corredo, kor-ray-do, m trousseau; kit

correggere, kor-red-jay-ray, v to correct

correlativo*, kor-ray-lah-tee-vo, adj correlative

corrente, kor-ren-tay, f current; stream; draught; adj running; ordinary; (month) instant; (currency) valid; **essere al –,** to be informed

correntemente, kor-ren-tay-men-tay, adv fluently; commonly

correntista, kor-ren-tiss-tah, m/f current account holder

correre, kor-ray-ray, v to run; to race; **corre voce che,** it is rumoured that

correttezza, kor-ret-tet-tsah, f correctness; fair play

corretto*, kor-ret-to, adj correct; exact

correzione, kor-ret-tse'o-nay, f correction

corridoio, kor-re-do-e'o, m corridor

corridore, kor-re-dor-ay, m runner; (car) racing driver

corriera, kor-re'ay-rah, f coach

corriere, kor-re'ay-ray, m courier; carrier; mail

corrispettivo, kor-riss-pet-tee-vo, m amount due

corrispondente, kor-riss-pon-den-tay, adj corresponding; m/f correspondent

corrispondenza, kor-riss-pon-dent-sah, f correspondence; connection

corrispondere, kor-riss-pon-day-ray, v to correspond; to return

corroborare, kor-ro-bo-rah-ray, v to corroborate

corrodere, kor-ro-day-ray, v to corrode

corrompere, kor-rom-pay-ray, v to corrupt

corrosione, kor-ro-ze'o-nay, f corrosion

corrotto*, kor-rot-to, adj corrupt

corrugare, kor-roo-gah-ray, v to frown

corruttibile, kor-root-tee-be-lay, adj corruptible

corruzione, kor-roo-tse'o-nay, f corruption

corsa, kor-sah, f running; race; racing; trip

corsaro, kor-sah-ro, m corsair

corsia, kor-see-ah, f passage; (motorway) lane; (hospital) ward

corsivo, kor-see-vo, m italics

corso, kor-so, m course; main street; circulation; **in –,** in progress

corte, kor-tay, f court; court-yard

corteccia, kor-tet-chah, f bark; cortex

corteggiare, kor-ted-jah-ray, v to court

corteo, kor-tay-o, m procession

cortese, kor-tay-zay, adj courteous

cortesia, kor-tay-see-ah, f courtesy

cortigiano, kor-te-jah-no, m courtier

cortigiana, kor-te-jah-na, f courtier; courtesan

cortile, kor-tee-lay, m courtyard; forecourt; farmyard

cortina, kor-tee-nah, f curtain; screen

corto, kor-to, adj short

cortometraggio, kor-to-may-trad-jo, m short feature film

corvetta, kor-vet-tah, f corvette

corvo, kor-vo, m raven; rook

cosa, ko-zah, f thing; matter; affair

coscia, ko-she'ah, *f* thigh

cosciente, ko-she'en-tay, *adj* conscious; aware

coscienza, ko-she'en-tsah, *f* conscience; consciousness; awareness

coscienzioso*, ko-she'en-tse'o-zo, *adj* conscientious

coscritto, ko-skrit-to, *m* conscript

così, ko-zee, *adv* so; thus; as; **basta** –! enough!

cosicché, ko-zick-kay, *conj* so that

cosmetico, koz-zmay-tee-ko, *m* cosmetic; *adj* cosmetic

cosmo, koz-zmo, *m* cosmos; outer space

cosmonauta, koz-zmo-nah'oo-tah, *m/f* cosmonaut

cospargere, koss-par-jay-ray, *v* to sprinkle

cospicuo*, koss-pee-koo'o, *adj* considerable

cospiratore, -trice, koss-pe-rah-tor-ay, koss-pe-rah-tree-chay, *m/f* conspirator

cospirazione, koss-pe-rah-tse'o-nay, *f* conspiracy

costa, koss-tah, *f* coast; slope; (ship) rib; (book) spine

costante, koss-tahn-tay, *adj* constant

costanza, koss-tahn-tsah, *f* constancy

costare, koss-tah-ray, *v* to cost

costata, koss-tah-tah, *f* large chop

costato, koss-tah-to, *m* ribs

costeggiare, koss-ted-jah-ray, *v* to skirt, to run alongside

costei, koss-tay-e, *pron* she; this/that woman

costellazione, koss-tell-lah-tse'o-nay, *f* constellation

costernato, koss-tair-nah-to, *adj* dismayed

costiera, koss-te'ay-rah, *f* coast; coast road

costipazione, koss-te-pah-tse'o-nay, *f* cold

costituire, koss-te-too'ee-ray, *v* to constitute; to set up

costituzione, koss-te-too-tse'o-nay, *f* constitution

costo, koss-to, *m* cost

costola, koss-to-lah, *f* rib

costoletta, koss-to-let-tah, *f* cutlet

costoro, koss-to-ro, *pron* they; these/those people

costoso*, koss-to-zo, *adj* costly, expensive

costretto, koss-tret-to, *adj* compelled, forced

costringere, koss-treen-jay-ray, *v* to compel

costruire, koss-troo'ee-ray, *v* to construct, to build

costrutto, koss-troot-to, *gram* construction

costruzione, koss-troot-tse'o-nay, *f* building; construction

costui, koss-too-e, *pron* he; this/that man

costume, koss-too-may, *m* custom; costume; swimsuit; swimming trunks

cotechino, ko-tay-kee-no, *m* pork sausage

cotenna, ko-ten-nah, *f* pigskin

cotogna, ko-to-n'yah, *f* quince

cotogno, ko-to-n'yo, *m* quince-tree

cotoletta, ko-to-let-tah, *f* chop; cutlet

cotone, ko-to-nay, *m* cotton; cotton wool

cotonificio, ko-to-ne-fee-cho, *m* cotton mill

cotta, kot-tah, *f* surplice; chain mail; *fig* blind infatuation

cottimo, kot-te-mo, *m* piecework

cotto, kot-to, *adj* cooked, baked; in love; *m* brickwork

cottura, kot-too-rah, *f*

cooking, baking

covare, ko-**vah**-ray, v to smoulder

covo, ko-vo, m den

covone, ko-vo-nay, m sheaf

cozzare, kot-tsah-ray, v to butt; to collide

cozzo, kot-tso, m butting; collision; clash

crampo, krahm-po, m cramp

cranio, krah-ne'o, m skull

cratere, krah-tay-ray, m crater

cravatta, kra-vat-tah, f tie

cravattino, kra-vat-tee-no, m bow tie

creare, kray-ah-ray, v to create; to set up

creato, kray-ah-to, m universe, Creation

creatore, -trice, kray-ah-tor-ay, kray-ah-tree-chay, m/f creator

creatura, kray-ah-too-rah, f creature; baby

creazione, kray-ah-tse'o-nay, f creation; foundation

credente, kray-den-tay, m/f believer

credenza, kray-den-tsah, f belief; sideboard

credenziali, kray-den-tse'ah-le, fpl credentials

credere, **kray**-day-ray, v to believe, to think

credito, **kray**-de-to, m credit; trust

creditore, -trice, kray-de-tor-ay, kray-de-tree-chay, m/f creditor

credo, **kray**-do, m creed; belief; credo

credulo, **kray**-doo-lo, adj credulous

crema, **kray**-mah, f cream; custard

cremare, kray-**mah**-ray, v to cremate

crematorio, kray-mah-tor-e'o, m crematorium

crepa, **kray**-pah, f crack

crepaccio, kray-**paht**-cho, m crack; crevasse

crepacuore, kray-pah-koo'**or**-ay, m heart-breaking

crepare, kray-**pah**-ray, v to crack; fam to kick the bucket

crepitare, kray-pe-**tah**-ray, v to crackle; to rustle

crepitio, kray-pe-tee-o, m cracking; rustling

crepuscolo, kray-**pooss**-ko-lo, m twilight

crescente, kray-**shen**-tay, adj increasing; growing; (moon) waxing

crescere, **kray**-shay-ray, v to increase; to grow; (moon) to wax

crescione, kray-she'o-nay, m watercress

crescita, **kray**-she-tah, f growth

cresima, **kray**-se-mah, f relig confirmation

cresimare, kray-se-**mah**-ray, v relig to confirm

crespo, **krayss**-po, adj frizzy

cresta, **krayss**-tah, f crest; (bird) comb; ridge

creta, **kray**-tah, f clay

cretino, kray-tee-no, m cretin, idiot

criceto, kri-**che**-to, m hamster

criminale, kree-me-**nah**-lay, adj criminal; m/f criminal

crimine, **kree**-me-nay, m crime

crinale, kree-**nah**-lay, m ridge, crest

crine, **kree**-nay, m horsehair

criniera, kre-ne'**ay**-rah, f mane

crisantemo, kre-zahn-**tay**-mo, m chrysanthemum

crisi, **kree**-ze, f crisis; med fit, attack

cristallo, kriss-**tahl**-lo, m crystal

cristianesimo, kriss-te'ah-**nay**-see-mo, m Christianity

cristiano, -a, kriss-te'**ah**-no, adj Christian; m/f Christian

criterio, kre-**tay**-re'o, *m* criterion

critica, **kree**-te-kah, *f* criticism; review

criticare, kre-te-kah-ray, *v* to criticise

critico, **kree**-te-ko, *adj** critical; *m* critic

croccante, krock-**kahn**-tay, *adj* crunchy, crisp; *m* almond crunch

crocchio, **krock**-ke'o, *m* small gathering, small group

croce, **kro**-chay, *f* cross; *fig* torment

crocevia, kro-chay-**vee**-ah, *f* crossroads

crociata, kro-**chah**-tah, *f* crusade

crocicchio, kro-**cheek**-ke'o, *m* crossroads

crociera, kro-**chay**-rah, *f* cruise

crocifiggere, kro-che-**fid**-jay-ray, *v* to crucify

crocifisso, kro-che-**fiss**-so, *m* crucifix; *adj* crucified

croco, **kro**-ko, *m* crocus

crogiolo, kro-joo'o-lo, *m* crucible; melting pot

crollare, kroll-**lah**-ray, *v* to tumble down; to collapse; to cave in

crollo, **kroll**-lo, *m* collapse; ruin

croma, **kro**-mah, *f* quaver

cromo, **kro**-mo, *m*

chromium, chrome

cromosoma, kro-mo-**so**-mah, *m* chromosome

cronaca, **kro**-nah-kah, *f* chronicle; news

cronico*, **kro**-ne-ko, *adj** chronic

cronista, kro-**nee**-stah, *m/f* columnist; commentator

cronologia, kro-no-lod-**jee**-ah, *f* chronology

crosta, **kross**-tah, *f* crust; scab

crostaceo, kross-**tah**-chay-o, *m* shellfish

crostata, kross-**tah**-tah, *f* tart

crostino, kross-**tee**-no, *m* croûton; canapé

crucciarsi, kroot-**char**-se, *v* to worry oneself

cruccio, **kroot**-cho, *m* worry, torment

cruciale, kroot-**chah**-lay, *adj* crucial

cruciverba, kroot-chee-**ver**-bah, *m* crossword puzzle

crudele, kroo-**day**-lay, *adj* cruel

crudeltà, kroo-dell-**tah**, *f* cruelty

crudo*, **kroo**-do, *adj* raw; *fig* blunt; harsh

cruento, kroo-**en**-to, *adj* bloody

crumiro, -a, kroo-**mee**-ro, *m/f* blackleg

cruna, **kroo**-nah, *f* eye of a needle

crusca, **krooss**-kah, *f* bran

cubo, **koo**-bo, *m* cube; *adj* cubic

cuccagna, kook-**kah**-n'yah, *f* **albero della –,** greasy pole; **paese della –,** land of plenty

cuccetta, koot-**chet**-tah, *f* couchette; berth

cucchiaino, kook-ke-ah-ee-no, *m* coffee spoon; tea spoon

cucchiaio, kook-ke-**ah**-e'o, *m* spoon

cuccia, **koot**-chah, *f* kennel; dog's basket; **a –!,** down!

cucciolata, koot-cho-**lah**-tah, *f* litter

cucciolo, **koot**-cho-lo, *m* puppy; cub

cucina, koo-**chee**-nah, *f* kitchen; cooking; cooker

cucinare, koo-che-**nah**-ray, *v* to cook

cucire, koo-**chee**-ray, *v* to sew; **macchina da –,** sewing machine

cucitrice, koo-che-**tree**-chay, *f* stapler

cucitura, koo-che-**too**-rah, *f* seam

cuculo, **koo**-koo-lo, *m* cuckoo

cuffia, **koof**-fe'ah, *f* cap;

headphone

cugina, koo-**jee**-nah, *f* cousin

cugino, koo-**jee**-no, *m* cousin

cui, koo'e, *pron* whom, which; whose, of which; to whom, to which

culinario, koo-lee-nah-ree'o, *adj* culinary

culla, kooll-lah, *f* cradle

cullare, kooll-**lah**-ray, *v* to rock; to lull

culminare, kooll-me-**nah**-ray, *v* to culminate

culmine, kooll-me-nay, *m* top; summit; peak

culo, koo-lo, *m vulg* arse

culto, kooll-to, *m* worship; cult

cultura, kooll-**too**-rah, *f* culture; learning

culturale, kooll-too-**rah**-lay, *adj* cultural

culturismo, kooll-too-**ree**-zmo, *m* body-building

cumulativo, koo-moo-lah-tee-vo, *adj* cumulative

cumulo, koo-moo-lo, *m* heap, pile, hoard

cuneo, koo-nay-o, *m* wedge

cunetta, koo-**net**-tah, *f* bump (in the road)

cuocere, koo'o-chay-ray, *v* to cook

cuoco, -a, koo'o-ko, *m/f* cook; chef

cuoio, koo'o-e'o, *m* leather, hide

cuore, koo'o-ray, *m* heart

cupidigia, koo-pe-dee-jah, *f* greed

cupido, koo-pe-do, *m* cupid

cupo*, koo-po, *adj* dark; gloomy

cupola, koo-po-lah, *f* dome

cura, koo-rah, *f* care; cure, treament

curare, koo-**rah**-ray, *v* to cure; to treat; to look after; (book) to edit

curato, koo-**rah**-to, *m* vicar; parish priest

curatore, -trice, koo-rah-**tor**-ay, koo-rah-**tree**-chay, *m/f* guardian; trustee; editor

curia, koo-re'ah, *f* diocese

curiosare, koo-re'o-**zah**-ray, *v* to wander round; to browse

curioso*, koo-re'o-zo, *adj* curious; strange

cursore, koohr-**sor**-ay, *m comp* cursor

curva, koohr-vah, *f* curve; bend

curvare, koohr-**vah**-ray, *v* to curve; to bend

curvatura, koohr-vah-**too**-rah, *f* curvature

curvo*, koohr-vo, *adj* curved; warped; bent

cuscinetto, koo-she-**net**-to, *m* pad; **– a sfere**, ball bearing

cuscino, koo-**shee**-no, *m* cushion; pillow

cuspide, kooss-pe-day, *f* spire; cusp

custode, kooss-**to**-day, *m/f* custodian; warden

custodia, kooss-to-de'ah, *f* custody; care

custodire, kooss-to-**dee**-ray, *v* to guard; to keep; to take care of

cutaneo, koo-tah-nay-o, *adj* of the skin

da, dah, *prep* from; by; of; since; on; at; with

dabbene, dahb-**bay**-nay, *adj* good; honest

daccapo, dahk-**kah**-po, *adv* again; once more

dacché, dahk-**kay**, *conj* since; as

dado, dah-do, *m* dice; stock cube; *tech* nut

daino, dah'e-no, *m* deer; **pelle di –**, buckskin

dalia, dah-le'ah, *f* dahlia

d'altronde, dahl-**tron**-day, *adv* besides; moreover; however

dama, dah-mah, *f* lady; (game) draughts

damasco, dah-**mahss**-ko, *m* damask

damigella, dah-me-**jell**-lah, *f* damsel; **– d'onore**, bridesmaid

damigiana, dah-me-**jah**-na, *f* demijohn

danaro, dah-**nah**-ro, *m* money; (cards) diamonds

danaroso, dah-nah-**ro**-zo, *adj* wealthy, well-off

dancing, **dahn**-sing, *m* dance hall

danese, dah-**nay**-zay, *adj* Danish

Danese, dah-**nay**-zay, *m/f* Dane

Danimarca, dah-ne-**mar**-kah, *f* Denmark

dannare, dahn-**nah**-ray, *v* to damn; **far –**, to drive mad

dannazione!, dahn-nah-**tse**'o-nay, *interj* damn!

danneggiare, dahn-ned-jah-ray, *v* to damage, to injure

danno, **dahn**-no, *m* damage; loss

dannoso, dahn-**no**-zo, *adj* detrimental; harmful

Danubio, dah-**noo**-be'o, *m* Danube

danza, **dahn**-tsah, *f* dance; dancing; **– classica**, ballet dancing

danzare, dahn-**tsah**-ray, *v* to dance

dappertutto, dahp-pair-**toot**-to, *adv* everywhere

dappoco, dahp-**po**-ko, *adj* useless, worthless; insignificant

dapprima, dahp-**pree**-mah, *adv* firstly; at first

dardo, dar-do, *m* dart; arrow

dare, dah-ray, *v* to give; to grant; (party) to hold; (film) to show; **– su**, to overlook

darsena, dar-**say**-nah, *f* naut dock

darsi, dar-se, *v* **– a**, to devote oneself to; (drinking, gambling) to take to; **può –**, maybe

data, dah-tah, *f* date; **di fresca –**, of recent date

datare, dah-**tah**-ray, *v* to date; **– da**, to date back to, to date from

dato, dah-to, *m* datum;

fact; *pp* given

datore, -trice, dah-tor-ay, dah-**tree**-chay, *m/f* – **di lavoro,** employer

dattero, daht-tay-ro, *m* date; date palm

dattilografia, daht-te-lo-grah-**fee**-ah, *f* typewriting

dattilografo, -a, daht-te-lo-grah-fo, *m/f* typist

davanti, dah-**vahn**-te, *m* front; *adv* in front; **– a,** *prep* in front of

davanzale, dah-vahn-**tsah**-lay, *m* windowsill

davvero, dahv-**vay**-ro, *adv* indeed; truly

dazio, dah-tse'o, *m* duty, tax; excise

dea, day-ah, *f* goddess

debellare, day-bell-**lah**-ray, *v* to overcome; to suppress

debilitare, day-be-le-**tah**-ray, *v* to debilitate

debito, day-be-to, *m* debt; *adj* due; appropriate

debitore, -trice, day-be-**tor**-ay, day-be-**tree**-chay, *m/f* debtor

debole, day-bo-lay, *adj* weak; dim; faint; *m* weakness; **avere un – per,** to have a weakness for

debolezza, day-bo-**let**-tsah, *f* weakness

debuttare, day-boot-**tah**-ray, *v* to make one's debut

decadenza, day-kah-**den**-tsah, *f* decadence

decadere, day-kah-**day**-ray, *v* to fall into decline

decaduto, day-kah-**doo**-to, *adj* impoverished

decaffeinato, day-kahf-fay'ee-**nah**-to, *adj* decaffeinated

decano, day-**kah**-no, *m* dean

decantare, day-kahn-**tah**-ray, *v* to praise; (liquid) to leave to settle

decapitare, day-kah-pe-**tah**-ray, *v* to behead; to decapitate

deceduto, day-chay-**doo**-to, *adj* deceased

decennio, day-**chen**-ne'o, *m* decade

decente, day-**chen**-tay, *adj* decent

decenza, day-**chen**-tsah, *f* decency, decorum

decesso, day-**chess**-so, *m* death

decidere, day-**chee**-day-ray, *v* to decide

decidersi, day-**chee**-dair-se, *v* to make up one's mind, to come to a decision

decifrare, day-che-**frah**-ray, *v* to decipher, to make out

decilitro, day-che-lee-tro, *m* decilitre

decima, day-che-mah, *f* tenth part; tithe

decimale, day-che-**mah**-lay, *adj* decimal; *m* decimal

decimare, day-che-**mah**-ray, *v* to decimate

decimetro, day-**che**-may-tro, *m* decimetre

decimo, day-che-mo, *adj* & *m* tenth

decina, day-**che**-nah, *f* about ten

decisione, day-che-ze'o-nay, *f* decision

decisivo*, day-che-**zee**-vo, *adj* decisive

deciso*, day-**che**-zo, *adj* determined, resolute; (cut, blow) clean

declamare, day-klah-**mah**-ray, *v* to declaim

declinare, day-kle-**nah**-ray, *v* to decline; to slope

declivio, day-**klee**-ve'o, *m* slope

decodificare, day-ko-dee-fee-**cah**-ray, *v* to decode

decollare, day-koll-**lah**-ray, *v* (aeroplane) to take off

decollo, day-**koll**-lo, *m* take-off

decomporre, day-kom-

por-ray, *v* to decompose

decorare, day-ko-**rah**-ray, *v* to decorate, to award

decorazione, day-ko-rahtse'o-nay, *f* decoration

decoro, day-**ko**-ro, *m* decorum; dignity

decoroso*, day-ko-**ro**-zo, *adj* decorous

decorrenza, day-kor-**ren**-tsah, *f* **con – da,** dating from, as from

decorrere, day-**kor**-ray-ray, *v* to elapse; **– da,** to run from, to have effect from

decotto, day-**kot**-to, *m* decoction

decrepito, day-**kray**-pe-to, *adj* decrepit

decrescere, day-**kray**-shay-ray, *v* to decrease, to diminish

decretare, day-kray-**tah**-ray, *v* to decree

decreto, day-**kray**-to, *m* decree

decuplo, day-**koo**-plo, *adj* tenfold; *m* ten times more

dedalo, day-**dah**-lo, *m* labyrinth, maze

dedica, day-de-kah, *f* dedication

dedicare, day-de-**kah**-ray, *v* to dedicate; to devote

dedito, day-de-to, *adj* **– a,** addicted to; devoted to

dedizione, day-de-tse'o-nay, *f* devotion, dedication

dedurre, day-**doohr**-ray, *v* to deduce; to deduct

deduzione, day-doo-tse'o-nay, *f* deduction

deferente, day-fay-**ren**-tay, *adj* deferent

deferenza, day-fay-**ren**-tsah, *f* deference

deferire, day-fay-**ree**-ray, *v* **– qualcuno a,** to refer somebody to

defezione, day-fay-tse'o-nay, *f* defection; desertion

deficiente, day-fe-**chen**-tay, *adj* half-wit; **– di,** lacking in; *m/f* idiot

deficienza, day-fe-**chen**-tsah, *f* deficiency; shortage; weakness

definire, day-fe-**nee**-ray, *v* to define; to settle

definitivo*, day-fe-ne-**tee**-vo, *adj* definitive

definizione, day-fe-ne-tse'o-nay, *f* definition; settlement

deflazione, day-flah-tse'o-nay, *f* deflation

deflettere, day-**flet**-tay-ray, *v* to deflect

deflusso, day-**floos**-so, *f* flow; (tide) ebb

deformare, day-for-**mah**-ray, *v* to deform; to distort

deforme, day-**for**-may, *adj* deformed, misshapen

deformità, day-for-me-**tah**, *f* deformity

defraudare, day-frah'oo-**dah**-ray, *v* to defraud

defunto, -a, day-**foonn**-to, *adj* late, deceased, dead; *m/f* deceased person

degenerare, day-jay-nay-**rah**-ray, *v* to degenerate

degenere, day-**jay**-nay-ray, *adj* degenerate

degente, day-**jen**-tay, *m/f* in-patient

degenza, day-**jen**-tsah, *f* confinement to bed; **– in ospedale,** period in hospital

deglutire, day-gloo-**tee**-ray, *v* to swallow

degnare, day-n'**yah**-ray, *v* to deign

degno*, day-n'yo, *adj* worthy, deserving; **– di fiducia,** trustworthy

degradare, day-grah-**dah**-ray, *v* to degrade; *mil* to demote

degradazione, day-grah-dah-tse'o-nay, *f* degradation, abasement; *mil* demotion

degrado, day-**grah**-do, *m* decline

degustare, day-gooss-**tah**-ray, *v* to taste

delatore, -trice, day-lah-**tor**-ay, day-lah-**tree**-chay, *m/f* informer, accuser

delazione, day-lah-tse'o-nay, *f* informing

delega, day-lay-gah, *f* delegation; **per –,** by proxy

delegare, day-lay-**gah**-ray, *v* to entrust, to delegate

delegato, day-lay-**gah**-to, *m* delegate; **amministratore –,** managing director

deleterio, day-lay-**tay**-re'o, *adj* deleterious; harmful

delfino, del-**fee**-no, *m* dolphin; dauphin

deliberare, day-le-bay-**rah**-ray, *v* to deliberate

deliberatamente, day-le-bay-rah-tah-**men**-tay, *adv* deliberately

deliberazione, day-le-bay-rah-tse'o-nay, *f* decision; *parl* resolution

delicatezza, day-le-kah-**tet**-tsah, *f* delicacy; softness; fragility; tactfulness

delicato*, day-le-**kah**-to, *adj* delicate; gentle; frail; tactful

delineare, day-le-nay-**ah**-ray, *v* to outline

delinquente, day-lin-**kwen**-tay, *m/f* offender; scoundrel

delinquenza, day-lin-**kwen**-tsah, *f* delinquency; **– minorile,** juvenile delinquency

deliquio, day-**lee**-kwe'o, *m* swoon

delirante, day-le-**rahn**-tay, *adj* delirious

delirare, day-le-**rah**-ray, *v* to be delirious

delitto, day-**lit**-to, *m* crime

delittuoso, day-lit-too-o-zo, *adj* criminal

delizia, day-**lee**-tse'ah, *f* delight

delizioso*, day-le-tse'o-zo, *adj* delicious; delightful

delta, dayl-tah, *m* delta

deltaplano, dayl-tah-**plah**-no, *m* hang-glider

deludere, day-**loo**-day-ray, *v* to disappoint

deluso, day-**loo**-zo, *adj* disappointed

demanio, day-**mah**-ne'o, *m* state property

demagogia, day-mah-go-**jee**-ah, *f* demagogy

demarcazione, day-mar-kah-tse'o-nay, *f* demarcation

demente, day-**men**-tay, *adj* demented; mad; *m/f* lunatic

demenza, day-**men**-tsah, *f* madness; **– senile,** senile dementia

demerito, day-**may**-re-to, *m* demerit

democratico, -a, day-mo-krah-**tee**-ko, *adj* democratic; *m/f* democrat

democrazia, day-mo-krak-**tsee**-ah, *f* democracy

demolire, day-mo-**lee**-ray, *v* to demolish

demolizione, day-mo-le-tse'o-nay, *f* demolition

demone, day-mo-nay, *m* demon

demonio, day-**mo**-ne'o, *m* demon, devil

demoralizzare, day-mo-rah-lid-**dzah**-ray, *v* to demoralize

denaro, day-**nah**-ro, *m* money; **– contante,** cash

denaturato, day-nah-too-**rah**-to, *adj* **alcol –,** methylated spirits

denigrare, day-ne-**grah**-ray, *v* to denigrate; to disparage

denigrazione, day-ne-grah-tse'o-nay, *f* denigration, disparagement

denominare, day-no-me-**nah**-ray, *v* to name

denominazione, day-no-me-nah-tse'o-nay, *f* denomination; name; **– di origine controllata,**

DOC, guarantee of quality and origin of wine

denotare, day-no-**tah**-ray, *v* to denote

densità, den-se-**tah,** *f* density

denso*, **den**-so, *adj* dense; thick

dentale, den-**tah**-lay, *adj* dental

dentatura, den-tah-**too**-rah, *f* set of teeth

dente, **den**-tay, *m* tooth; cog; prong; **– del giudizio,** wisdom tooth; **– da latte,** milk tooth

dentellare, den-tell-**lah**-ray, *v* to indent; to notch

dentice, **den**-tee-chay, *m* sea bream

dentiera, den-te'**ay**-rah, *f* dentures, false teeth

dentifricio, den-te-**free**-cho, *m* toothpaste

dentista, den-**tiss**-tah, *m/f* dentist

dentizione, den-te-tse'o-nay, *f* teething

dentro, **den**-tro, *adv* inside, within; *prep* in, within

denudare, day-noo-**dah**-ray, *v* to bare; to strip

denuncia, day-**noonn**-chah, *f* report (to the police); notification,

declaration; denunciation

denunciare, day-noonn-**chah**-ray, *v* (to the police) to report; (tax) to declare; (accuse) to denounce, to expose

denunzia, day-**noonn**-tse'ah, *f* report (to the police); notification, declaration; denunciation

denutrito, day-noo-**tree**-to, *adj* undernourished

deodorante, day'o-do-**rahn**-tay, *m* deodorant; *adj* deodorant

depauperare, day-pah'oo-pay-**rah**-ray, *v* to impoverish

deperibile, day-pay-**ree**-bee-lay, *adj* perishable

deperire, day-pay-**ree**-ray, *v* to waste away

depilare, day-pe-**lah**-ray, *v* to depilate, to remove hair

depistare, day-pe-**stah**-ray, *v* to set on the wrong track

deplorabile, day-plo-**rah**-be-lay, *adj* deplorable

deplorare, day-plo-**rah**-ray, *v* to deplore

deplorevole, day-plo-**ray**-vo-lay, *adj* deplorable

deporre, day-**por**-ray, *v* (weight) to put down;

(eggs) to lay; (king) to depose; (from office) to remove; *law* to testify

deportare, day-por-**tah**-ray, *v* to deport

deportazione, day-por-tah-tse'o-nay, *f* deportation

depositare, day-po-ze-**tah**-ray, *v* to deposit; to put down

deposito, day-**po**-ze-to, *m* deposit; warehouse; depot; sediment; **– bagagli,** left luggage office

deposizione, day-po-ze-tse'o-nay, *f* deposition; removal

depravato, day-prah-**vah**-to, *adj* depraved

depredare, day-pray-**dah**-ray, *v* to rob, to plunder

depressione, day-press-se'o-nay, *f* depression

depressivo, day-press-**see**-vo, *adj* depressive

depresso, day-**press**-so, *adj* depressed

deprezzamento, day-prett-tsah-**men**-to, *m* depreciation

deprezzare, day-pret-**tsah**-ray, *v* to depreciate

deprimente, day-pree-**men**-tay, *adj* depressing

deprimere, day-**pree**-may-ray, *v* to depress

depurare, day-poo-**rah**-ray, *v* to purify, to cleanse

depurazione, day-poo-rah-tse'o-nay, *f* purification

deputare, day-poo-**tah**-ray, *v* to delegate

deputato, day-poo-**tah**-to, *m* deputy, delegate; member of Parliament, MP

deputazione, day-poo-tah-tse'o-nay, *f* deputation, delegation

deragliamento, day-rah-l'yah-**men**-to, *m* derailment

deragliare, day-rah-l'yah-ray, *v* to derail

derelitto, -a, day-ray-**lit**-to, *adj* abandoned, derelict; *m/f* destitute person

deridere, day-ree-day-ray, *v* to mock, to deride

derisione, day-re-ze'o-nay, *f* derision

deriva, day-ree-vah, *f* drift; **andare alla –,** to drift

derivare, day-re-**vah**-ray, *v* to derive

derivazione, day-re-vah-tse'o-nay, *f* derivation; extension

deroga, **day**-ro-gah, *f* dispensation

derrata, dair-rah-tah, *f* merchandise; **derrate,** foodstuffs

derubare, day-roo-bah-ray, *v* to rob

descrittivo, dess-krit-**tee**-vo, *adj* descriptive

descrivere, dess-**kree**-vay-ray, *v* to describe

descrizione, dess-kre-tse'o-nay, *f* description

deserto, day-**zair**-to, *m* desert; *adj* deserted, bare

desiderabile, day-ze-day-**rah**-be-lay, *adj* desirable

desiderare, day-ze-day-**rah**-ray, *v* to want; to wish; to desire

desiderio, day-ze-**day**-re'o, *m* wish; desire, longing

desideroso, day-ze-day-ro-zo, *adj* eager, longing

designare, day-ze-n'yah-ray, *v* to designate, to appoint

designazione, day-ze-n'yah-tse'o-nay, *f* designation

desinenza, day-ze-**nayn**-tsa, *f gram* ending

desistere, day-ziss-tay-ray, *v* to desist, to leave off

desolato*, day-zo-**lah**-to, *adj* desolate; sorrowful

despota, dess-po-tah, *m* despot, tyrant

dessert, dess-**sert,** *m* dessert

destare, dess-**tah**-ray, *v* to wake up; to arouse, to awaken

destinare, dess-te-**nah**-ray, *v – a,* to destine to, to intend for; to assign to; to set aside for

destinatario, -a, dess-te-nah-**tah**-ree'o, *m/f* addressee

destinazione, dess-te-nah-tse'o-nay, *f* destination

destino, dess-**tee**-no, *m* destiny

destituire, dess-te-too-**ee**-ray, *v* to dismiss

destituzione, dess-te-too-tse'o-nay, *f* dismissal

desto, dess-to, *adj* wide-awake

destra, dess-**trah,** *f* right hand; right-hand side; **tenere la –,** to keep to the right; **di –,** right-wing

destreggiarsi, dess-tred-jar-se, *v* to manoeuvre; to manage

destrezza, dess-**tret**-tsah, *f* dexterity; agility

destro, dess-**tro,** *adj* right; skilful

desumere, day-zoo-may-ray, *v* to deduce, to infer

detenere, day-tay-**nay**-ray, *v* to detain; (record) to hold

detenuto, day-tay-**noo**-to, *m* convict

detenzione, day-ten-tse'o-nay, *f* detention; (record) holding

detergente, day-tayr-jen-tay, *adj* cleansing; *m* cleanser

detergere, day-tayr-jay-ray, *v* to cleanse; to wipe

deteriorare, day-tay-re'o-rah-ray, *v* to cause to deteriorate

deteriorarsi, day-tay-re'o-rahr-se, *v* to deteriorate

determinare, day-tair-me-nah-ray,*v* to determine

determinazione, day-tair-me-nah-tse'o-nay, *f* determination

detersivo, day-tayr-see-vo, detergent; washing powder; **– per i piatti,** washing-up liquid

detestare, day-tess-tah-ray, *v* to detest

detonazione, day-to-nah-tse'o-nay, *f* detonation

detrarre, day-trar-ray, *v* to deduct

detrattore, -trice, day-traht-tor-ay, day-traht-tree-chay, *m/f* slanderer

detrazione, day-trah-tse'o-nay, *f* deduction

detrimento, day-tre-men-to, *m* **a – di,** to the detriment of

detrito, day-tree-to, *m* detritum; silt

dettagliante, det-tah-l'yahn-tay, *m/f* retailer

dettagliare, det-tah-l'yah-ray, *v* to detail

dettaglio, det-tah-l'yo, *m* detail, particular; **vendere al –,** to sell retail

dettare, det-tah-ray, *v* to dictate

dettato, det-tah-to, *m* dictation

dettatura, det-tah-too-rah, *f* dictation; **scrivere sotto –,** to take down from dictation

detto, det-to, *m* saying; *adj* called; named; above-mentioned

deturpare, day-toohr-pah-ray, *v* to disfigure

devastare, day-vahss-tah-ray, *v* to devastate

devastazione, day-vahss-tah-tse'o-nay, *f* devastation, destruction

deviare, day-ve'ah-ray, *v* to divert, deflect; to turn off (from); to go astray

deviazione, day-ve'ah-tse'o-nay, *f* deviation; diversion

devolvere, day-voll-vay-ray, *v* to devolve, to transfer

devoto*, day-vo-to, *adj* devout; devoted; **i**

devoti, the faithful

devozione, day-vo-tse'o-nay, *f* devotion

di, dee, *prep* of; from; by; on; in; with; about; (+ *art*) some; **ci sono dei libri,** there are some books

dì, dee, *m* day

diabetico, de'ah-bay-te-ko, *adj* diabetic

diabolico*, de'ah-bo-le-ko, *adj* diabolical

diacono, de'ah-ko-no, *m* deacon

diadema, de'ah-day-mah, *m* diadem

diaframma, de'ah-frahm-mah, *m* diaphragm

diagnosi, de'ah-n'yo-zee, *f* diagnosis

diagonale, de'ah-go-nah-lay, *adj* diagonal; *f* diagonal

diagramma, de'ah-gram-mah, *m* diagram; **– a torta,** pie chart; **– di flusso,** flow chart

dialetto, de'ah-let-to, *m* dialect

dialogo, de'ah-lo-go, *m* dialogue

diamante, de'ah-mahn-tay, *m* diamond

diametralmente, de'ah-may-trahl-men-tay, *adv* diametrically

diametro, de'ah-may-tro,

m diameter

diamine, de'**ah**-me-nay, *interj fam* good heavens!

diapositiva, de'ah-po-se-**tee**-vah, *f* slide, transparency

diario, de'**ah**-re'o, *m* diary; **– di bordo,** logbook; **– di classe,** class register

diarrea, de'ahr-**ray**-ah, *f* diarrhoea

diavolo, de'**ah**-vo-lo, *m* devil; **che – succede?** what the hell is happening?

dibattere, de-**baht**-tay-ray, *v* to debate, to argue

dibattersi, de-**baht**-tair-se, *v* to struggle

dibattito, de-**baht**-te-to, *m* debate

dicastero, de-kahss-**tay**-ro, *m* government-department, ministry

dicembre, de-**chem**-bray, *m* December

diceria, de-chay-**ree**-ah, *f* rumour

dichiarare, de-ke'ah-**rah**-ray, *v* to declare

dichiarazione, de-ke'ah-rah-tse'**o**-nay, *f* declaration; statement; **– dei redditi,** tax return

diciannove, de-che'ahn-**no**-vay, *adj & m* nineteen

diciannovesimo, de-

che'ahn-no-**vay**-ze-mo, *adj & m* nineteenth

diciassette, de-che'ahss-**set**-tay, *adj & m* seventeen

diciassettesimo, de-che'ahss-set-**tay**-ze-mo, *adj & m* seventeenth

diciottesimo, de-che'ot-**tay**-ze-mo, *adj & m* eighteenth

diciotto, de-che'**ot**-to, *adj & m* eighteen

dicitura, de-che-**too**-rah, *f* text; wording

didascalia, de-dah-skah-**lee**-ah, *f* caption; subtitle

didattica, de-**daht**-tee-kah, *f* didactics, teaching methods

didattico, de-**daht**-tee-ko, *adj* didactic, educational

dieci, de'**ay**-che, *adj & m* ten

dieta, de'**ay**-tah, *f* diet; assembly

dietetica, de'ay-tay-**tee**-kah, *f* dietetics

dietro, de'**ay**-tro, *adv* behind; *prep* behind, after; *m* back, rear

dietro front, de'**ay**-tro front, *m* about-turn

difatti, de-**faht**-tee, *conj* as a matter of fact

difendere, de-fen-**day**-ray, *v* to defend; to protect

difensore, de-fen-**sor**-ay, *m* defender; **avvocato –,** defence counsel

difesa, de-**fay**-zah, *f* defence

difettivo, de-fet-**tee**-vo, *adj gram* defective

difetto, de-**fet**-to, *m* defect, fault, flaw

difettoso*, de-fet-**to**-zo, *adj* defective; faulty

diffamare, dif-fah-**mah**-ray, *v* to defame

diffamatorio, dif-fah-mah-**tor**-e'o, *adj* slanderous

differente, dif-fay-**ren**-tay, *adj* different

differenza, dif-fay-**ren**-tsah, *f* difference

differenziale, dif-fay-rent-tse'a-lay, *adj* differential; *m* differential

differimento, dif-fay-re-**men**-to, *m* postponement

differire, dif-fay-**ree**-ray, *v* to differ; to postpone

difficile*, dif-fee-**che**-lay, *adj* difficult

difficoltà, dif-fee-kol-**tah**, *f* difficulty

diffida, dif-**fee**-dah, *f* warning; notice

diffidare, dif-fee-**dah**-ray, *v* to distrust; to caution

diffidente, dif-fe-den-tay, *adj* diffident

diffidenza, dif-fe-**den**-tsah,

f diffidence

diffondere, dif-**fon**-day-ray, v to diffuse; to broadcast

diffusione, dif-foo-ze'o-nay, f diffusion

diffuso*, dif-**foo**-zo, adj widespread; diffuse

difterite, dif-tay-**ree**-tay, f diphtheria

diga, dee-gah, f dam; dyke; breakwater

digeribile, de-jay-**ree**-be-lay, adj digestible

digerire, de-jay-**ree**-ray, v to digest

digestivo, de-jess-**tee**-vo, adj digestive; m after-dinner liqueur

digitale, de-jee-**tah**-lay, adj digital; **impronta –,** fingerprint; f foxglove

digitare, de-jee-**tah**-ray, v to key in

digiunare, de-joo-**nah**-ray, v to fast

digiuno, de-**joo**-no, m fasting; fast; adj **– di,** ignorant of

dignità, de-n'yee-**tah**, f dignity

dignitoso*, de-n'yee-**to**-so, adj dignified

digradare, de-grah-**dah**-ray, v to slope

digressione, de-grays-see'o-nay, f digression

digrignare, de-gre-n'yah-ray, v **– i denti,** to grind one's teeth; (animal) to bare its teeth

dilagare, de-lah-**gah**-ray, v to overflow, to flood; to spread

dilaniare, de-lah-ne'**ah**-ray, v to tear to pieces

dilapidare, de-lah-pe-**dah**-ray, v to squander

dilatare, de-lah-**tah**-ray, v to dilate

dilazionare, de-lah-tse'o-**nah**-ray, v to delay

dilazione, de-lah-tse'o-nay, f delay, deferment

dileggiare, de-led-**jah**-ray, v to scoff at

dileguarsi, de-led-goo'**ar**-se, v to vanish

dilemma, de-**lem**-mah, m dilemma

dilettante, de-let-**tahn**-tay, adj amateur, dilettante

dilettare, de-let-**tah**-ray, v to delight; to charm

diletto, de-**let**-to, m delight; adj beloved

diligente, de-le-**jen**-tay, adj diligent; accurate

diligenza, de-le-**jen**-tsah, f diligence; care; stagecoach

diluire, de-loo-**ee**-ray, v to dilute

dilungarsi, de-loonn-**gar**-se, v to go into details

diluviare, de-loo-ve'**ah**-ray, v to rain hard, to pour

diluvio, de-loo-ve'o, m deluge, flood

dimagrante, de-mah-**grahn**-tay, adj slimming; **cura –,** slimming diet

dimagrire, de-mah-**gree**-ray, v to grow thin, to lose weight

dimenare, de-may-**nah**-ray, v to shake; (tail) to wag

dimensione, de-men-se'o-nay, f dimension

dimenticanza, de-men-te-**kahn**-tsah, f oversight; oblivion

dimenticare, de-men-te-**kah**-ray, v to forget

dimentico, de-**men**-te-ko, adj forgetful

dimesso*, de-**mess**-so, adj shabby; unassuming

dimestichezza, de-mes-tee-**ket**-sah, f familiarity

dimettere, de-**met**-tay-ray, v to dismiss; to discharge

dimettersi, de-**met**-tair-se, v to resign

dimezzare, de-med-**dzah**-ray, v to halve

diminuire, de-me-noo'**ee**-ray, v to diminish

diminutivo, de-me-noo-**tee**-vo, adj diminutive; m gram diminutive

dimissioni, dee-mes-see'o-nee, *fpl* resignation

dimora, de-mo-rah, *f* abode; sojourn; residence

dimorare, de-mo-**rah**-ray, *v* to dwell, to reside

dimostrare, de-moss-**trah**-ray, *v* to demonstrate

dimostrazione, de-moss-trah-tse'o-nay, *f* demonstration

dinamico*, de-nah-mee-ko, *adj* dynamic

dinamite, de-nah-mee-tay, *f* dynamite

dinamo, dee-nah-mo, *f* dynamo

dinanzi, de-nahn-tse, *prep* – **a**, before; in front of

dinastia, de-nahss-tee-ah, *f* dynasty

diniego, de-ne'**ay**-go, *m* refusal; denial

dinosauro, de-no-sah'oo-ro, *m* dinosaur

dintorni, din-**tor**-nee, *m* neighbourhood, outskirts

dintorno, din-**tor**-no, *adv* around

Dio, dee-o, *m* God

diocesano, de'o-chay-**sah**-no, *adj* diocesan

diocesi, de'**o**-chay-se, *f* diocese

dipanare, de-pah-**nah**-ray, *v* to unravel

dipartimento, de-par-tee-

men-to, *m* department

dipartita, de-par-tee-tah, *f* passing away

dipendente, de-pen-**den**-tay, *adj* dependent; *m/f* employee

dipendere, de-pen-**day**-ray, *v* to depend; – **da**, to depend on

dipingere, de-**pin**-jay-ray, *v* to paint; to describe

dipinto, de-**pin**-to, *m* painting; *adj* painted

diploma, de-plo-mah, *m* diploma, certificate

diplomatico, de-plo-**mah**-tee-ko, *adj** diplomatic; *m* diplomat

diplomazia, de-plo-mah-**tsee**-ah, *f* diplomacy; diplomatic corps

diporto, de-**por**-to, *m* **imbarcazione da –**, pleasure craft

diradare, de-rah-**dah**-ray, *v* to disperse; to clear up; to thin out

diramazione, de-rah-mah-tse'o-nay, *f* branch; (orders) issuing

dire, dee-ray, *v* to say; to tell; to recite; **che ne dici?** what do you think?

diretto*, de-**ret**-to, *adj** direct; straight; *m* through train

direttore, de-re-**tor**-ay, *m* manager; director;

headmaster; – **d'orchestra**, conductor

direttrice, de-re-**tree**-chay, *f* manager; director; headmistress

direzione, de-ray-tse'o-nay, *f* direction; management; editorship; leadership

dirigente, de-ree-**jayn**-tay, *adj* managerial; *m/f* executive

dirigere, de-**ree**-jay-ray, *v* to run; to manage; to direct; to conduct

dirigibile, de-re-**jee**-be-lay, *m* airship

dirimpetto, de-rim-**pet**-to, *adv* facing; opposite; – **a**, *prep* opposite

diritto, de-**rit**-to, *m* right; *adj* straight; upright; *adv* straight; directly

dirittura, de-rit-**too**-rah, *f* rectitude; integrity

diroccato, de-rock-**kah**-to, *adj* in ruins

dirompente, de-rom-**payn**-tay, *adj* explosive

dirottamento, de-rot-tah-**men**-to, *m* hijacking

dirottare, de-rot-**tah**-ray, *v* to hijack; *naut* to change course

dirotto, de-**rot**-to, *adj** (rain) pouring; **pianto –**, floods of tears; **piovere a –**, to pour

dirozzare, de-rod-**dzah**-ray, *v* to rough-hew; to refine

dirupo, de-**roo**-po, *m* precipice

disabitato, de-zah-be-**tah**-to, *adj* uninhabited

disadattato, de-zah-daht-tah-to, *adj* maladjusted

disadatto, de-zah-**daht**-to, *adj* unfit

disadorno, de-zah-**dor**-no, *adj* unadorned; bare

disagevole, de-zah-**jay**-vo-lay, *adj* difficult; uncomfortable

disagiato, de-zah-**jah**-to, *adj* needy

disagio, de-**zah**-jo, *m* discomfort; awkwardness; want; **a –**, uncomfortable

disamina, de-zah-me-nah, *f* careful examination

disapprovare, de-zahp-pro-**vah**-ray, *v* to disapprove; to reproach

disappunto, de-zahp-**poonn**-to, *m* disappointment

disarmare, de-zar-**mah**-ray, *v* to disarm

disarmo, de-**zar**-mo, *m* disarmament

disastro, de-**zahss**-tro, *m* disaster

disattento, de-zaht-**ten**-to, *adj* inattentive, careless

disavanzo, de-zah-**vahn**-tso, *m* deficit

disavventura, de-zahv-ven-**too**-rah, *f* mishap

disboscare, diz-boss-**kah**-ray, *v* (woods) to clear

disbrigo, diz-**bree**-go, *m* handling (of letters, files)

discapito, diss-**kah**-pe-to, *m* detriment, disadvantage

discarica, diss-**kah**-re-kah, *f* rubbish tip

discendente, de-shen-**den**-tay, *m/f* descendant

discendenza, de-shen-**den**-tsah, *f* descent; descendants

discendere, de-**shen**-day-ray, *v* to descend; to derive; to come from

discepolo, de-**shay**-po-lo, *m* disciple; pupil

discernere, de-**shair**-nay-ray, *v* to discern

discesa, de-**shay**-sah, *f* descent; slope

dischetto, de-**sket**-to, *m* floppy disk

dischiudere, diss-ke'**oo**-day-ray, *v* to open; to disclose

discinto, de-**sheen**-to, *adj* scantily dressed

disciogliere, di-she'o-l'**yay**-ray, *v* to dissolve; to melt

disciplina, de-she-**ple**-nah, *f* discipline; subject

disciplinare, de-she-ple-**nah**-ray, *v* to discipline; *adj* disciplinary

disco, **diss**-ko, *m* disc; *comp* disk; *mus* record; (sport) discus

discografico, diss-ko-grah-**fee**-ko, *adj* recording

discolo, **diss**-ko-lo, *adj* undisciplined

discolpare, diss-koll-**pah**-ray, *v* to excuse; to clear of blame

disconoscere, diss-ko-**no**-shay-ray, *v* to ignore

discontinuo, diss-kon-tte-**noo**'o, *adj* discontinuous

discordante, diss-kor-**dahn**-tay, *adj* discordant; conflicting

discordare, diss-kor-**dah**-ray, *v* to disagree; to clash

discorde, diss-**kor**-day, *adj* conflicting

discorrere, diss-**kor**-ray-ray, *v* to chat

discorsivo, diss-kor-rsee-vo, *adj* conversational

discorso, diss-**kor**-so, *m* speech; discourse; **cambiare –**, to change subject

discosto, diss-**koss**-to, *adj* at some distance

discoteca, diss-ko-**tay**-ka, *f*

disco

discretamente, diss-kray-tah-**men**-tay, *adv* discreetly; rather

discretezza, diss-kray-**tet**-tsah, *f* discretion

discreto, diss-**kray**-to, *adj* discreet; fair

discrezione, diss-kray-tse'o-nay, *f* discretion

discriminare, diss-kree-mee-**nah**-ray, *v* to discriminate

discussione, diss-koos-see'o-nay, *f* discussion

discutere, diss-**koo**-tay-ray, *v* to discuss; to dispute

discutibile, diss-koo-tee-**bee**-lay, *adj* questionable

disdegnare, diss-day-n'yah-ray, *v* to disdain

disdetta, diss-**det**-tah, *f* notice to quit; bad luck

disdire, diss-**dee**-ray, *v* to cancel; to give notice

disegnare, de-zay-n'yah-ray, *v* to design, to draw; to describe

disegnatore, -trice, de-zay-n'yah-**to**-ray, de-zay-n'yah-**tree**-chay, *m/f* draughtsman, draughtswoman; designer

disegno, de-**zay**-n'yo, *m* design; drawing; project; **– di legge,** *parl* bill

diserbante, de-zayr-**bahn**-tay, *m* herbicide, weed-killer

diseredare, de-zay-ray-**dah**-ray, *v* to disinherit

disertare, de-zair-tah-ray, *v* to desert

disertore, de-zair-**tor**-ay, *m* deserter

disfare, diss-**fah**-ray, *v* to undo; to untie; to unpack

disfatta, diss-**faht**-tah, *f* defeat, rout

disfunzione, diss-foont-see'o-nay, *f* dysfunction

disgelo, diss-**jay**-lo, *m* thaw

disgiunto, diss-**joonn**-to, *adj* disjointed

disgrazia, diss-**grah**-tse'ah, *f* bad luck; disaster; accident; disgrace

disgraziato*, diss-grah-tse'**ah**-to, *adj* unfortunate

disgregare, diss-gray-**gah**-ray, *v* to break up, to disintegrate

disguido, diss-goo'ee-do, *m* error, hitch

disgustare, diss-gooss-**tah**-ray, *v* to disgust; to vex

disgusto, diss-**gooss**-to, *m* disgust; vexation

disgustoso*, diss-gooss-**to**-zo, *adj* disgusting, unpalatable

disidratato, dee-zee-drah-**tah**-to, *adj* dehydrated

disilludere, de-zill-**loo**-day-ray, *v* to disillusion

disimpegnare, de-zim-pay-n'yah-ray, *v* to free, to release; to redeem

disinfestare, de-zin-fes-**tah**-ray, *v* to disinfest

disinfettante, de-zin-fet-**tahn**-tay, *m* disinfectant; *adj* disinfectant

disinfettare, de-zin-fet-**tah**-ray, *v* to disinfect

disingannare, de-zin-gahn-**nah**-ray, *v* to disillusion

disinnescare, de-zin-nay-**skah**-ray, *v* to defuse

disinvolto*, de-zin-**voll**-to, *adj* free and easy

disinvoltura, de-zin-voll-**too**-rah, *f* ease, nonchalance

dislessico, diss-**les**-see-ko, *adj* dyslexic

dislivello, diss-lee-**vell**-lo *m* gap; difference in height

dislocazione, diss-lo-gah-tse'o-nay, *f* dislocation

dismisura, diss-me-**zoo**-rah, *f* **a –,** excessively

disoccupato, de-zock-koo-**pah**-to, *adj* unemployed

disoccupazione, de-zock-koo-pah-tse'o-nay, *f* unemployment

disonesto*, de-zo-**ness**-to, *adj* dishonest

disonorare, de-zo-no-**rah**-ray, *v* to dishonour

disonore, de-zo-**no**-ray, *m* dishonour; discredit

disonorevole*, de-zo-no-**ray**-vo-lay, *adj* dishonourable; disgraceful

disopra, de-so-prah, *adv* upstairs

disordinato*, de-zor-de-**nah**-to, *adj* disorderly; untidy

disordine, de-**zor**-de-nay, *m* disorder; mess; **disordini**, riots

disorganizzato, de-zor-gah-nit-**tsah**-to, *adj* disorganized

disorientare, de-zor-e'en-**tah**-ray, *v* to disorient

disotto, de-**sot**-to, *adv* downstairs

dispaccio, diss-**paht**-cho, *m* despatch

disparato, diss-pah-**rah**-to, *adj* diverse; disparate

dispari, **diss**-pah-re, *adj* odd; unequal

disparte, diss-**par**-tay, *adv* **in –**, aside, on one side

dispendio, diss-**pen**-de'o, *m* expenditure; waste

dispendioso, diss-pen-de'**o**-zo, *adj* expensive

dispensa, diss-**pen**-sah, *f* (of publication) instalment; exemption; larder

dispensare, diss-pen-**sah**-ray, *v* to dispense; to exempt; to distribute

dispensario, diss-pen-**sah**-re'o, *m* dispensary

disperare, diss-pay-**rah**-ray, *v* to despair

disperato*, diss-pay-**rah**-to, *adj* desperate; in despair

disperazione, diss-pay-rah-tse'**o**-nay, *f* despair

disperdere, diss-**pair**-day-ray, *v* to disperse; to waste

disperso, -a, diss-**pair**-so, *m/f* missing person

dispettoso*, diss-pet-**to**-zo, *adj* spiteful

dispiacere, diss-pe'ah-**chay**-ray, *v* to displease; to upset; *m* pain, sorrow; regret

dispiaciuto, diss-pe'ah-**choo**-to, *adj* sorry

disponibile, diss-po-**nee**-be-lay, *adj* available; (person) helpful

disponibilità, diss-po-nee-be-lee-**tah**, *f* availability; helpfulness

disporre, diss-**por**-ray, *v* to arrange; to order; **– di**, to have at one's disposal

dispositivo, diss-po-zee-**tee**-vo, *m* device

disposizione, diss-po-zee-tse'**o**-nay, *f* arrangement; order, instruction

disposto, diss-**poss**-to, *adj* disposed

dispotico, diss-**po**-te-ko, *adj* despotic

dispotismo, diss-po-**tiss**-mo, *m* despotism

dispregiativo, diss-pred-jah-**tee**-vo, *adj gram* pejorative

disprezzare, diss-pret-**tsah**-ray, *v* to despise

disprezzo, diss-**pret**-tso, *m* contempt, scorn

disputa, **diss**-poo-tah, *f* dispute; discussion

disputare, diss-poo-**tah**-ray, *v* to dispute; to discuss

dissanguato, diss-sahn-goo'a-to, *adj* drained of blood; impoverished

dissapore, diss-sah-**po**-ray, *m* disagreement

disseccare, diss-seck-**kah**-ray, *v* to dry up

disseminare, diss-say-me-**nah**-ray, *v* to spread, to scatter

dissenso, diss-**sen**-so, *m* dissent; disapproval

dissenteria, diss-sen-tay-**ree**-ah, *f* dysentery

dissentire, diss-sen-**tee**-ray, *v* to dissent, to differ

dissertazione, diss-sair-tah-tse'o-nay, *f* dissertation

dissestare, diss-sess-**tah**-ray, *v* to involve in financial difficulties

dissetare, diss-say-**tah**-ray, *v* to quench the thirst

dissidente, diss-see-**den**-tay, *adj* dissident; *m/f* dissident

dissidio, diss-**see**-de'o, *m* dissension, disagreement

dissimile, diss-**see**-me-lay, *adj* unlike, dissimilar

dissimulare, diss-se-moo-**lah**-ray, *v* to hide; to pretend; to camouflage

dissipare, diss-see-**pah**-ray, *v* to squander; to disperse; to dispel

dissipato*, diss-see-**pah**-to, *adj* dissipated, dissolute

dissociare, diss-**sot**-chah-ray, *v* to dissociate

dissodare, diss-so-**dah**-ray, *v* to till

dissoluto*, diss-so-**loo**-to, *adj* dissolute

dissolvere, diss-**soll**-vay-ray, *v* to dissolve; to dipserse

dissonante, diss-so-**nahn**-tay, *adj* discordant, dissonant

dissuadere, diss-soo'ah-**day**-ray, *v* to dissuade

distaccare, diss-tahk-**kah**-ray, *v* to detach, to separate

distacco, diss-**tahk**-ko, *m* detachment, parting

distante, diss-**tahn**-tay, *adj* distant; *adv* far away

distanza, diss-**tahn**-tsah, *f* distance

distanziare, diss-tahn-tse'**ah**-ray, *v* to space out; to outstrip

distare, diss-**tah**-ray, *v* to be a long way; **quanto dista?** how far is it?

distendere, diss-ten-**day**-ray, *v* to stretch; to spread; to unfold

distendersi, diss-ten-**dair**-se, *v* to lie down; to relax

distensione, diss-ten-see'o-nay, *f* relaxation; stretching

distesa, diss-**tay**-zah, *f* expanse; stretch

disteso, diss-**tay**-zo, *adj* wide; extended, spread out; relaxed

distillare, diss-till-**lah**-ray, *v* to distil

distilleria, diss-till-lah-**ree**-ah, *f* distillery

distinguere, diss-**tinn**-goo'ay-ray, *v* to distinguish

distinta, diss-**tinn**-tah, *f* list; invoice; inventory

distintivo, diss-tinn-**tee**-vo, *m* badge, *adj* distinctive

distinto*, diss-**tinn**-to, *adj* distinct; distinguished

distinzione, diss-tinn-tee'o-nay, *f* distinction

distogliere, diss-to-l'**yay**-ray, *v* to dissuade; to distract; **– lo sguardo,** to look away

distorcere, diss-tor-**chay**-ray, *v* to distort

distorsione, diss-tor-see'o-nay, *f* sprain; distortion

distrarre, diss-**trar**-ray, *v* to distract; to amuse

distrarsi, diss-**trar**-se, *v* not to pay attention to; to amuse oneself

distratto*, diss-**traht**-to, *adj* absent-minded

distrazione, diss-traht-tse'o-nay, *f* absent-mindedness; amusement

distretto, diss-**tret**-to, *m* district; territory

distribuire, diss-tree-boo'ee-ray, *v* to distribute; to deliver

distributore, diss-tree-boo-**to**-ray, *m* dispenser; *mech* distributor; petrol pump

distribuzione, diss-tree-boo-tse'o-nay, *f* distribution; delivery

distruggere, diss-**trood**-

jay-ray, v to destroy

distrutto, diss-**troot**-to, adj
destroyed, wasted

disturbare, diss-toohr-**bah**-ray, v to disturb, to
trouble

disturbo, diss-**toohr**-bo, m
disturbance; trouble;
ailment

disubbidiente, de-zoob-be-de**'an**-tay, adj
disobedient

disubbidire, de-zoob-be-dee-ray, v to disobey

disuguale, de-zoo-goo**'ah**-lay, adj uneven; unequal

disumano, de-zoo-**mah**-no, adj inhuman

disunione, de-zoo-ne'o-nay, f disunity

disunire, de-zoo-**nee**-ray, v
to separate

disuso, de-**zoo**-zo, m
disuse

ditale, de-**tah**-lay, m
thimble; finger-stall

dito, dee-to, m finger; toe

ditta, dit-tah, f firm,
business concern; **Spett.
Ditta** (address) Messrs,
(letter) Dear Sirs

dittafono, dit-**tah**-fo-no,
m dictaphone

dittatore, dit-tah-**tor**-ay, m
dictator

dittatura, dit-tah-**too**-rah,
f dictatorship

dittongo, dit-**tonn**-go, m

diphthong

diurno, de-**oohr**-no, adj
daily

diva, dee-vah, f (film) star

divagare, de-vah-**gah**-ray,
v to digress; to wander

divampare, de-vahm-**pah**-ray, v to flare up; to
break out

divano, de-**vah**-no, m
settee, sofa; divan

divario, de-**vah**-re'o, m
variance; difference

divellere, de-**vell**-lay-ray, v
to pluck out, to uproot

divenire, de-vay-**nee**-ray, v
to become, to get

diventare, de-vayn-**tah**-ray, v to become, to get

diverbio, de-**vair**-be'o, m
heated argument

divergenza, de-vair-**gent**-sa, f divergence,
difference

divergere, de-**vair**-jay-ray,
v to diverge

diversità, de-vair-se-**tah**, f
difference; diversity

diversivo, de-vair-**see**-vo,
m diversion, distraction;
adj diversionary

diverso*, de-**vair**-so, adj
diverse; different;
diversi, several

divertente, de-vair-**ten**-tay, adj amusing; funny

divertimento, de-vair-tee-**men**-to, m amusement;

pastime; **buon –!,** enjoy
yourself/yourselves!

divertire, de-vair-**tee**-ray,
v to amuse, to entertain

divertirsi, de-vair-**teer**-se,
v to amuse oneself

divezzare, de-vet-**tsah**-ray,
v to wean

dividendo, de-ve-**den**-do,
m dividend

dividere, de-**vee**-day-ray, v
to divide; to separate; to
cut; to share (out)

divieto, de-ve-**ay**-to, m
prohibition; **– di sosta,**
no waiting

divincolarsi, de-vin-ko-**lah**-ray, v to wriggle
(free)

divinità, de-ve-nee-**tah**, f
divinity

divino*, de-**vee**-no, adj
divine; heavenly

divisa, de-**vee**-zah, f
uniform; foreign
currency

divisione, de-ve-ze'o-nay, f
division; hyphenation

divo, dee-vo, m (film) star

divorare, de-vo-**rah**-ray, v
to devour

divorziare, de-vor-tse'**ah**-ray, v to divorce

divorzio, de-**vor**-tse'o, m
divorce

divulgare, de-vooll-**gah**-ray, v to divulge; to
popularize

dizionario, de-tse'o-nah-re'o, *m* dictionary

dizione, de-tse'o-nay, *f* diction; elocution

do, do, *m mus* C

doccia, dot-chah, *f* shower

docente, do-chen-tay, *m/f* lecturer, professor; *adj* teaching

docile, do-che-lay, *adj* docile, pliable

docilità, do-che-le-tah, *f* docility

documento, do-coo-men-to, *m* document

dodicenne, do-de-chayn-nay, *adj* & *m/f* twelve-year-old

dodicesimo, do-de-chay-ze-mo, *adj* & *m* twelfth

dodici, do-de-che, *adj* & *m* twelve

dogana, do-gah-nah, *f* customs; customs duty

doganiere, do-gah-ne'ay-ray, *m* customs officer

doglie, do-l'yay, *fpl* labour

dogma, dog-mah, *m* dogma

dogmatico, dog-mah-tee-ko, *adj* dogmatic

dolce, doll-chay, *adj* sweet; soft; gentle; *m* sweet, dessert

dolcevita, doll-chay-vee-tah, *f* rollneck sweater

dolcezza, doll-chet-tsah, *f* sweetness; gentleness

dolciumi, doll-choo-me, *mpl* sweets

dolente, do-len-tay, *adj* aching; grieved

dolere, do-lay-ray, *v* to ache

dolersi, do-layr-se, *v* to complain; – **di**, to regret

dollaro, doll-lah-ro, *m* dollar

Dolomiti, do-lo-mee-te, *fpl* Dolomites

dolore, do-lo-ray, *m* pain, sorrow

doloroso*, do-lo-ro-zo, *adj* painful; sore; distressing

doloso, do-lo-zo, *adj* fraudulent; malicious; **incendio** –, arson

domanda, do-mahn-dah, *f* question; request; demand

domandare, do-mahn-dah-ray, *v* to ask; to demand

domandarsi, do-mahn-dar-se, *v* to wonder

domani, do-mah-ne, *adv* tomorrow; **il** –, *m* the future

domare, do-mah-ray, *v* to tame; to master

domatore, -trice, do-mah-tor-ay, do-mah-tree-chay, *m/f* tamer

domattina, do-maht-tee-nah, *adv* tomorrow morning

domenica, do-may-ne-kah, *f* Sunday

domestico, -a, do-mess-te-ko, *m/f* servant; *adj* domestic

domicilio, do-me-chee-le'o, *m* residence; domicile

dominante, do-me-nahn-tay, *adj* dominant, prevailing

dominare, do-me-nah-ray, *v* to dominate; to rule; to master

dominio, do-mee-ne'o, *m* dominion; domain; rule; – **di sé**, self-control

domino, do-mee-no, *m* dominoes

don, don, *m* Father (title for priests); Don (title of respect in Southern Italy)

donare, do-nah-ray, *v* to give; to donate

donatore, -trice, do-nah-to-ray, do-nah-tree-chay, *m/f* giver; donor; – **di sangue**, blood donor

dondolare, don-do-lah-ray, *v* to swing; to dangle; to rock

dondolo, don-do-lo, *m* **a** –, rocking

donna, don-nah, *f* woman; wife; lady; (cards) queen; – **di servizio**, maid

donnaccia, don-**naht**-chah, *f* slut

donnaiolo, don-nah-e'oo-o-lo, *m* womanizer

donnola, don-no-lah, *f* weasel

dono, do-no, *m* gift, present; talent

dopo, do-po, *adv* after, next; *prep* after; past

dopobarba, do-po-**bar**-bah, *m* aftershave

dopoché, do-po-**kay**, *conj* after, when

dopodomani, do-po-do-**mah**-nee, *adv* the day after tomorrow

dopoguerra, do-po-goo'**air**-ra, *m* post-war period

dopopranzo, do-po-**pran**-tso, *m* afternoon

dopotutto, do-po-**toot**-to, *adv* after all

doppiare, dop-pe'**ah**-ray, *v* naut to round; (sport) to lap; (film) to dub

doppietta, dop-pe'**ayt**-tah, *f* double-barrelled gun

doppiezza, dop-pe'**et**-tsah, *f* duplicity

doppio*, dop-pe'o, *adj* double; twofold; *fig* false; *m* twice as much; (tennis) doubles; *adv* double

dorare, do-**rah**-ray, *v* to gild; (in cooking) to

brown

dorato, do-**rah**-to, *adj* gilt; golden

dormicchiare, dor-mick-ke'**ah**-ray, *v* to doze

dormiglione, -a, dor-me-l'yo-nay, *m/f* sleepyhead

dormire, dor-**mee**-ray, *v* to sleep

dormita, dor-**mee**-tah, *f* sleep

dormitorio, dor-mee-**to**-ree'o, *m* dormitory; night shelter

dorso, dor-so, *m* back; (book) spine; (mountain) ridge

dosare, do-**zah**-ray, *v* to dose

dose, do-zay, *f* dose; amount

dosso, doss-so, *m* hillock; bump; **togliersi di –,** to take off

dotare, do-**tah**-ray, *v* **– di,** to equip with; to endow with

dotato, do-**tah**-to, *adj* talented; **– di,** equipped with; endowed with

dotazione, do-tah-tse'o-nay, *f* endowment; equipment; **dare in –,** to issue with

dote, do-tay, *f* dowry; endowment; talent

dotto*, dot-to, *adj* learned

dottore, -essa, dot-tor-ay,

dot-to-**res**-sah, *m/f* doctor; physician; graduate

dottrina, dot-**tree**-nah, *f* doctrine; culture

dove, do-vay, *adv* where; *conj* if

dovere, do-**vay**-ray, *v* to owe; to have to; *m* duty

doveroso*, do-vay-ro-zo, *adj* due; dutiful

dovizia, do-vee-tse'ah, *f* abundance

dovunque, do-**voonn**-kway, *adv* anywhere; wherever; everywhere

dovuto, do-**voonn**-to, *adj* owing; due; *m* due

dozzina, dod-**dzee**-nah, *f* dozen

dozzinale, dod-dze-**nah**-lay, *adj* second-rate; cheap

dragare, drah-**gah**-ray, *v* to dredge

drago, drah-go, *m* dragon

dramma, drahm-mah, *m* drama; tragedy

drammatico, drahm-**mah**-tee-ko, *adj* drama; tragic

drammaturgo, -a, drahm-mah-**toohr**-go, *m/f* playwright

drappeggio, drahp-**ped**-jo, *m* drapery; folds

drappello, drahp-**pell**-lo, *m* squad

drastico, drahs-**stee**-ko,

adj drastic

drenaggio, dray-**nahd**-jo,
m drainage; reclamation

drizzare, drit-**tsah**-ray, *v* to
straighten; to erect

droga, dro-gah, *f* drug

drogato, -a, dro-**gah**-to,
m/f drug addict

drogheria, dro-gay-**ree**-ah,
f grocer's shop

droghiere, dro-ghe'**ay**-ray,
m grocer

dromedario, dro-may-**dah**-
ree'o, *m* dromedary

dubbio, doob-be'o, *m*
doubt; *adj* doubtful;
dubious

dubbioso*, doob-be'o-zo,
adj uncertain

dubitare, doo-be-**tah**-ray,
v to doubt

duca, doo -kah, *m* duke

ducato, doo-**kah**-to, *m*
duchy; (coin) ducat

duce, doo-chay, *m*
commander; (fascism)
Duce

duchessa, doo-**kess**-sah, *f*
duchess

due, doo-ay, *adj* & *m* two

duecento, doo-ay-**chen**-to,
adj & *m* two hundred; **il
Duecento,** the
thirteenth century

duello, doo-**el**-lo, *m* duel

duemila, doo-ay-**mee**-lah,
adj & *m* two thousand; **il
duemila,** the year two

thousand

duetto, doo-**et**-to, *m* duet

duna, doo-nah, *f* sand-
dune

dunque, doonn-kway, *conj*
then, therefore

duomo, doo'o-mo, *m*
cathedral

duplicare, doo-ple-**kah**-
ray, *v* to duplicate

duplice, doo-ple-chay, *adj*
double, twofold

duplicità, doo-ple-che-
tah, *f* duplicity

durante, doo-**rahn**-tay,
prep during

durare, doo-**rah**-ray, *v* to
last

durata, doo-**rah**-tah, *f*
duration

durezza, doo-**ret**-tsah, *f*
hardness; harshness

duro*, doo-ro, *adj* hard;
firm; tough; stale

duttile, doot-te-lay, *adj*
flexible; ductile

E

e, ay, *conj* and

ebano, **ay**-bah-no, *m* ebony; ebony-tree

ebbene, ayb-**bay**-nay, *interj* well then! now then!

ebbrezza, ayb-**bret**-tsah, *f* drunkenness; exhilaration

ebbro, ayb-bro, *adj* drunk

ebete, ay-bay-tay, *adj* slow-witted

ebollizione, ay-boll-lee-**tse'o**-nay, *f* boiling

ebraico, ay-**brah**-ee-ko, *adj* Jewish; Hebraic

ebreo, -a, ay-**bray**-o, *adj* Jewish; *m/f* Jewish man, Jewish woman

ecatombe, ay-kah-**tom**-bay, *f* slaughter

eccedenza, ayt-chay-**den**-tsah, *f* excess

eccedere, ayt-**chay**-day-ray, *v* to exceed

eccellente, ayt-chell-**len**-tay, *adj* excellent

eccellenza, ayt-chell-**len**-tsah, *f* excellence; (title) Excellency

eccellere, ayt-**chell**-lay-ray, *v* to excel

eccelso*, ayt-**chell**-so, *adj* eminent; lofty

eccentrico*, ayt-**chen**-tre-ko, *adj* eccentric

eccepire, ayt-chay-**pee**-ray, *v* to object

eccessivo*, ayt-chayss-**see**-vo, *adj* excessive

eccesso, ayt-**chayss**-so, *m* excess

eccetto, ayt-**chayt**-to, *prep* except; *conj* – **che,** unless

eccettuare, ayt-chayt-too-**ah**-ray, *v* to except

eccezionale*, ayt-chay-tse'o-**nah**-lay, *adj* exceptional

eccezione, ayt-chay-tse'o-nay, *f* exception

eccidio, ayt-**chee**-de'o, *m* slaughter, massacre

eccitabile, ayt-che-**tah**-be-lay, *adj* excitable

eccitante, ayt-che-**tahn**-tay, *adj* exciting; *m* stimulant

eccitare, ayt-che-**tah**-ray, *v* to excite; to incite; (sexually) to arouse

eccitato*, ayt-che-**tah**-to, *adj* excited; (sexually) aroused

ecco, eck-ko, *adv* here is/are, there is/are; **eccomi,** here I am; – **perché,** that's why

echeggiare, ay-ked-**jah**-ray, *v* to echo

eclissi, ay-**kliss**-se, *f* eclipse

eco, ay-ko, *f* echo

ecografia, ay-ko-grah-**fee**-ah, *f* ultrasound, echography

ecologia, ay-ko-lo-**jee**-ah, *f* ecology

ecologico, ay-ko-lo-jee-ko, *adj* ecological; environmentally friendly

economia, ay-ko-no-**mee**-ah, *f* economy; (science) economics

economico*, ay-ko-no-mee-ko, *adj* inexpensive; economical; (science) economic

economizzare, ay-ko-no-mid-**dzah**-ray, *v* to save, to economize

economo, ay-**ko**-no-mo, *m* bursar; *adj* thrifty

ecumenico, ay-koo-**may**-nee-ko, *adj* ecumenical

eczema, ayk-**dzay**-mah, *m* eczema

ed, ayd, *conj* and

edera, ay-day-rah, *f* ivy

edicola, ay-dee-ko-lah, *f* newspaper kiosk

edificare, ay-de-fe-**kah**-ray, *v* to build; to edify

edificio, ay-de-**fee**-cho, *m* building

edilizia, ay-dee-lee-tse'ah, *f* building trade

editore, -trice, ay-de-**tor**-ay, ay-de-**tree**-chay, *m/f* publisher, editor; **casa editrice,** publishing house, publisher

editto, ay-**deet**-to, *m* edict, decree

edizione, ay-de-tse'**o**-nay, *f* edition

educare, ay-doo-**kah**-ray, *v* to educate; to bring up

educato*, ay-doo-**kah**-to,

adj polite; well-behaved

educatore, -trice, ay-doo-kah-**to**-ray, ay-doo-kah-**tree**-chay, *m/f* educationalist

educazione, ay-doo-kah-tse'**o**-nay, *f* good manners; education; upbringing

efelide, ay-**fay**-lee-day, *f* freckle

effeminato*, ef-fay-mee-**nah**-to, *adj* effeminate

efferatezza, ef-fay-rah-**tet**-tsah, *f* cruelty; ferocity

efferato*, ef-fay-**rah**-to, *adj* cruel; brutal

effervescente, ef-fair-vay-**shen**-tay, *adj* effervescent

effettivo, ef-fet-**tee**-vo, *adj** effective; real; (staff) permanent; **ufficiale –,** regular officer

effetto, ef-**fet**-to, *m* effect; impression; bill of exchange; **– serra,** greenhouse effect; **effetti personali,** personal belongings

effettuare, ef-fet-too'**a**-ray, *v* to carry out

efficace*, ef-fe-**kah**-chay, *adj* effective

efficiente*, ef-fee-**chen**-tay, *adj* efficient

efficienza, ef-fee-**chen**-

tsah, *f* efficiency

effigie, ef-**fee**-jay, *f* effigy; portrait

effimero, ef-**fee**-may-ro, *adj* ephemeral

effluvio, ef-**floo**-ve'o, *m* scent

effusione, ef-foo-see'**o**-nay, *f* effusion

Egitto, ey-**jeet**-to, *m* Egypt

egli, ay-l'ye, *pron* he

egocentrico, ay-go-**chen**-tree-ko, *adj* egocentric, self-centred

egoismo, ay-go'**eess**-mo, *m* selfishness, egoism

egoista, ay-go'**eess**-tah, *adj* selfish; *m/f* selfish person

egregio*, ay-**gray**-jo, *adj* egregious; (letters) **Egregio Signore,** Dear Sir

eguaglianza, ay-goo'ah-l'**yahn**-tsah, *f* equality

eguagliare, ay-goo'ah-l'**yah**-ray, *v* to equal

eguale, ay-goo'ah-lay, *adj* the same, equal

eiaculazione, ay-eah-coo-lah-tse'**o**-nay, *f* ejaculation

elaborare, ay-lah-bo-**rah**-ray, *v* to elaborate; *comp* to process

elaboratore, ay-lah-bo-rah-**to**-ray, *m* **– elettronico** computer

elargire, ay-lar-**jee**-ray, *v*

to give generously

elasticità, ay-lahss-te-che-**tah,** f elasticity

elastico, ay-**lahss**-te-ko, adj elastic; springy; lax; m rubber band

elefante, ay-lay-**fahn**-tay, m elephant

elegante, ay-lay-**gahn**-tay, adj elegant, smart

eleganza, ay-lay-**gahn**-tsah, f elegance, smartness

eleggere, ay-**led**-jay-ray, v to elect

elementare, ay-lay-men-**tah**-ray, adj elementary; basic; **scuola –,** primary school

elemento, ay-lay-**men**-to, m element

elemosina, ay-lay-**mo**-ze-nah, f alms

elencare, ay-len-**kah**-ray, v to list

elenco, ay-**len**-ko, m list; – **telefonico,** telephone directory

elettivo, ay-let-**tee**-vo, adj elective

eletto, ay-**let**-to, adj elected; chosen

elettore, -trice, ay-let-**tor**-ay, ay-let-**tree**-chay, m/f elector, voter

elettricista, ay-let-tre-**chiss**-tah, m electrician

elettrico*, ay-let-**tre**-ko,

adj electric; electrical

elettrizzare, ay-let-trid-**dzah**-ray, v to electrify

elettrocardiogramma, ay-let-tro-kar-deo-**gram**-mah, m electrocardiogram

elettrodomestici, ay-let-tro-do-**mes**-stee-chee, mpl electrical appliances

elettronico, ay-let-**tro**-nee-ko, adj electronic

elettrotecnico, ay-let-tro-**tek**-nee-ko, adj electrotechnical; m electrical engineer

elevare, ay-lay-**vah**-ray, v to elevate, to raise

elevato, ay-lay-**vah**-to, adj hign, lofty

elevazione, ay-lay-vah-tse'o-**nay,** f elevation; raising

elezioni, ay-lay-tse'o-ne, fpl election; – **politiche,** general election

elica, ay-le-kah, f propeller, screw

elicottero, ay-le-**kot**-tay-ro, m helicopter

eliminare, ay-le-me-**nah**-ray, v to eliminate

elisione, ay-le-se'o-nay, f gram elision

ella, el-lah, pron she

ellisse, ell-**liss**-say, f ellipse

ellissi, ell-**liss**-se, f gram ellipsis

elmetto, el-**met**-to, m helmet

elmo, el-mo, m helmet

elogiare, ay-lo-**jah**-ray, v to praise, to commend

elogio, ay-**lo**-jo, m praise; eulogy

eloquente, ay-lo-**kwen**-tay, adj eloquent

eloquenza, ay-lo-**kwen**-tsah, f eloquence

elsa, el-sah, f hilt

eludere, ay-loo-day-ray, v to elude; to evade

emaciato, ay-mah-**chah**-to, adj emaciated

emanare, ay-mah-**nah**-ray, v to give off; to radiate; to issue; to emanate

emancipare, ay-mahn-che-**pah**-ray, v to emancipate

emarginare, ay-mahr-jee-**nah**-ray, v to marginalize

ematoma, ay-mah-to-mah, m bruise; haematoma

embargo, em-**bar**-rgo, m embargo

emblema, em-**blay**-mah, m emblem

embolia, em-bo-**lee**-ah, f embolism

embrione, em-bre'o-nay, m embryo

emendare, ay-men-**dah**-ray, v to amend

emergere, ay-**mair**-jay-ray, v to emerge

emerito*, ay-**may**-re-to, *adj* distinguished; emeritus

emettere, ay-**met**-tay-ray, *v* to emit; to issue; to transmit; to output

emicrania, ay-me-**krah**-ne'ah, *f* migraine

emigrante, ay-me-**grahn**-tay, *m/f* emigrant; *adj* emigrant

emigrare, ay-me-**grah**-ray, *v* to emigrate; (animal) to migrate

emigrato, -a, ay-me-**grah**-to, *m/f* emigrant; *adj* emigrant

eminente, ay-me-**nen**-tay, *adj* eminent

emisfero, ay-miss-**fay**-ro, *m* hemisphere

emissione, ay-miss-se'o-nay, *f* emission; issue; output

emittente, ay-mit-**ten**-tay, *adj* transmitting; issuing; *f* broadcasting station

emorragia, ay-mor-rah-jee-ah, *f* haemorrhage

emorroidi, ay-mor-**ro**'e-de, *fpl* haemorrhoids, piles

emotivo, ay-mo-**tee**-vo, *adj* emotional

emozionante, ay-mo-tse'o-**nahn**-tay, *adj* exciting; moving

emozionarsi, ay-mo-tse'o-nar-se, *v* to get excited; to be moved

emozione, ay-mo-tse'o-nay, *f* emotion

empietà, em-pe'ay-**tah**, *f* impiety; cruelty

empio, em-pe'o, *adj* impious; cruel

empirico, em-**pee**-ree-ko, *adj* empirical

emporio, em-po-re'o, *m* emporium

emulare, ay-moo-**lah**-ray, *v* to emulate

enciclopedia, en-chee-klo-**pay**-dee-ah, *f* encyclopaedia

encomio, en-ko-me'o, *m* praise, commendation

endemico, en-**day**-me-ko, *adj* endemic

energia, ay-nair-jee-ah, *f* energy, strength

energico, ay-**nair**-jee-ko, *adj* energetic; forceful

energumeno, ay-nair-goo-**may**-no, *m* brute

enfasi, en-fah-ze, *f* emphasis, stress

enfatico, en-**fah**-tee-ko, *adj* emphatic; pompous

enigma, ay-**neeg**-mah, *m* enigma, riddle, puzzle

enigmatico, ay-neeg-**mah**-tee-ko, *adj* enigmatic

ennesimo, en-**nay**-ze-mo, *adj* nth, umpteenth

enologo, ay-**no**-lo-go, *m* oenologist, wine expert

enorme, ay-**nor**-may, *adj* enormous, huge

enormità, ay-nor-mee-**tah**, *f* hugeness; enormity; blunder, nonsense

ente, en-tay, *m* body, corporation; (philosophy) being

enterite, en-tay-**ree**-tay, *f* enteritis

entrambi, en-**trahm**-be, *pron* both; *adj* both

entrare, en-**trah**-ray, *v* to enter, to go in, to come in

entrata, en-**trah**-tah, *f* entrance; admission; **entrate**, income

entro, en-tro, *prep* within

entroterra, en-tro-**ter**-rah, *m* hinterland

entusiasmare, en-too-ze'ahz-**mah**-ray, *v* to fill with enthusiasm

entusiasmo, en-too-ze'**ahz**-mo, *m* enthusiasm

entusiasta, en-too-ze'**ahss**-tah, *adj* enthusiastic

enumerare, ay-noo-may-**rah**-ray, *v* to enumerate

enunciare, ay-noonn-**chah**-ray, *v* to enunciate

enzima, end-**dzee**-mah, *m* enzyme

epatico, ay-**pah**-te-ko, *adj*

hepatic

epatite, ay-pah-**tee**-tay, *f* hepatitis

epidemia, ay-pe-day-**mee**-ah, *f* epidemic

epidermide, ay-pe-**der**-mee-day, *f* epidermis

Epifania, ay-pe-fah-**nee**-ah, *f* Epiphany

epigrafe, ay-**pee**-grah-fay, *f* epigraph; (on book) dedication

epigramma, ay-pee-**grahm**-mah, *m* epigram

epilessia, ay-pe-less-**see**-ah, *f* epilepsy

epilogo, ay-**pe**-lo-go, *m* epilogue

episodio, ay-pe-zo-de'o, *m* episode, incident

epistola, ay-**piss**-to-lah, *f* epistle

epitaffio, ay-pee-**taf**-fee'o, *m* epitaph

epiteto, ay-pee-**tay**-to, *m* epithet

epoca, **ay**-po-kah, *f* epoch, era; time; **auto d'–**, vintage car

eppure, ayp-**poo**-ray, *conj* and yet

epurare, ay-poo-**rah**-ray, *v* to purge

epurazione, ay-poo-rah-tse'o-nay, *f* purge; **– etnica**, ethnic cleansing

equanime, ay-kwah-nee-may, *adj* impartial

equatore, ay-kwah-**tor**-ay, *m* equator

equazione, ay-kwah-tse'o-nay, *f* equation

equestre, ay-**kwess**-tray, *adj* equestrian

equilibrare, ay-kwe-lee-**brah**-ray, *v* to balance; to counterbalance

equilibrato, ay-kwe-lee-**brah**-to, *adj* balanced; well-balanced

equilibrio, ay-kwe-lee-bree'o, *m* balance, equilibrium

equilibrista, ay-kwe-lee-**bree**-stah, *m/f* tightrope walker

equino, ay-**kwe**-no, *adj* equine, (of) horse

equinozio, ay-kwe-no-tse'o, *m* equinox

equipaggiamento, ay-kwe-pahd-jah-**men**-to, *m* equipment, gear; equipping, fitting out

equipaggiare, ay-kwe-pahd-**jah**-ray, *v* to equip; to kit out

equipaggio, ay-kwe-**pahd**-jo, *m* crew

équipe, ay-**kweep**, *f* team

equità, ay-kwe-**tah**, *f* equity

equivalente, ay-kwee-vah-**len**-tay, *adj* equivalent

equivalenza, ay-kwee-vah-**len**-tsah, *f*

equivalence

equivoco, ay-**kwee**-vo-ko, *adj* equivocal; *m* misunderstanding, mistake

equo*, **ay**-kwo, *adj* equitable, right, fair

era, ay-rah, *f* era; **l'– spaziale**, the space age

erba, **air**-bah, *f* grass, herb

erbaccia, air-**baht**-chah, *f* weed

erbicida, air-bee-**chee**-dah, *m* weedkiller

erborista, air-bo-ree-stah, *m/f* herbalist

erede, ay-**ray**-day, *m/f* heir, heiress

eredità, ay-ray-de-**tah**, *f* inheritance

ereditare, ay-ray-de-**tah**-ray, *v* to inherit

eremita, ay-ray-**mee**-tah, *m* hermit

eresia, ay-ray-**zee**-ah, *f* heresy

eretico, -a, ay-**ray** te-ko, *adj* heretical; *m/f* heretic

erezione, ay-ray-tse'o-nay, *f* erection; building

ergastolo, air-**gass**-to-lo, *m* prison; life imprisonment

ergoterapia, air-go-tay-rah-**pee**-ah, *f* occupational therapy

erica, **ay**-re-kah, *f* heather

erigere, ay-**ree**-jay-ray, *v*

to erect, to build

eritema, ay-re-**tay**-mah, *f med* inflammation (of the skin)

ermellino, air-mell-**lee**-no, *m* ermine, stoat

ermetico, air-**may**-tee-ko, *adj* airtight; impenetrable; hermetic

ernia, air-ne'ah, *f* hernia; – **del disco**, slipped disk

erodere, ay-**ro**-de-ray, *v* to erode

eroe, ay-**ro**-ay, *m* hero

erogare, ay-ro-**gah**-ray, *v* to supply (gas, electricity)

eroina, ay-ro-**ee**-nah, *f* heroine; (drug) heroin

eroismo, ay-ro-**eess**-mo, *m* heroism

erompere, ay-**rom**-pay-ray, *v* to erupt; to burst forth

erotico, air-**ro**-tee-ko, *adj* erotic

erpete, air-**pay**-tay, *m med* herpes

errare, air-**rah**-ray, *v* to make a mistake; to roam

errore, air-**ro**-ray, *m* mistake, error, blunder; – **di stampa**, misprint

erta, air-tah, *f* steep incline; **stare all'–**, to be on the alert

erto, air-to, *adj* steep; rising

erudito, ay-roo-**dee**-to, *m* scholar; *adj* learned

eruttare, ay-root-**tah**-ray, *v* (lava) to spew out

eruzione, ay-roo-tse'**o**-nay, *f* eruption; *med* rash

esagerare, ay-zah-jay-**rah**-ray, *v* to exaggerate

esagerato, ay-zah-jay-**rah**-to, *adj* exaggerated; exorbitant

esagerazione, ay-zah-jay-rah-tse'**o**-nay, *f* exaggeration

esalare, ay-zah-**lah**-ray, *v* to give off; to emanate

esalazione, ay-zah-lah-tse'**o**-nay, *f* exhalation; fumes

esaltare, ay-zahl-**tah**-ray, *v* to exalt, to extol

esame, ay-**zah**-may, *m* examination, exam

esaminare, ay-zah-me-**nah**-ray, *v* to examine

esangue, ay-**zahn**-goo'ay, *adj* bloodless; lifeless

esanime, ay-**zah**-ne-may, *adj* lifeless

esasperare, ay-zahss-pay-**rah**-ray, *v* to exasperate

esattezza, ay-zaht-**tet**-tsah, *f* exactness, precision

esatto*, ay-**zaht**-to, *adj* correct, exact; accurate

esattore, -trice, ay-zaht-**tor**-ay, ay-zaht-**tree**-chay, *m/f* (tax) collector

esaudire, ay-zah'oo-**dee**-ray, *v* to grant, to fulfil

esaurire, ay-zah'oo-**ree**-ray, *v* to exhaust; to deplete

esaurito, ay-zah'oo-**ree**-to, *adj* exhaust; run-down; sold out; out of print

esca, ess-kah, *f* bait

esclamare, ess-klah-**mah**-ray, *v* to exclaim

esclamazione, ess-klah-mah-ze'**o**-nay, *f* exclamation

escludere, ess-**kloo**-day-ray, *v* to exclude; to rule out

esclusione, ess-kloo-ze'**o**-nay, *f* exclusion

esclusivo, ess-kloo-**zee**-vo, *adj* exclusive

escogitare, ess-ko-je-**tah**-ray, *v* to devise

escoriazione, ess-ko-re'ah-tse'**o**-nay, *f* graze

escremento, ess-kray-**men**-to, *m* excrement

escrescenza, ess-kray-**shen**-tsah, *f* excrescence

escursione, ess-koohr-se'**o**-nay, *f* excursion; hike

esecrare, ay-zay-**krah**-ray, *v* to abhor, to loathe

esecutivo*, ay-zay-koo-**tee**-vo, *adj* executive

esecutore, -trice, ay-zay-koo-**tor**-ay, ay-zay-koo-**tree**-chay, *m/f law* executor; *mus* performer

esecuzione, ay-zay-koo-tse'o-nay, f execution; performance; *law* execution

eseguire, ay-zay-goo'ee-ray, v to carry out; to perform, to execute

esempio, ay-**zem**-pe'o, m example

esemplare, ay-zem-**plah**-ray, m specimen; *adj* exemplary

esentare, ay-zen-**tah**-ray, v to exempt

esente, ay-**zen**-tay, *adj* exempt

esenzione, ay-zen-tse'o-nay, f exemption

esercente, ay-zair-**chen**-tay, *m/f* trader; shopkeeper

esercitare, ay-zair-che-**tah**-ray, v to practise; to exercise; to train

esercito, ay-**zair**-che-to, m army

esercizio, ay-zair-**chee**-tse'o, m exercise; practice; management; – **finanziario**, financial year

esibire, ay-ze-**bee**-ray, v to exhibit; (documents) to present

esibizione, ay-ze-be-tse'o-nay, f performance; showing off; presentation

esigente, ay-ze-**jen**-tay, *adj* demanding

esigenza, ay-ze-**jen**-tsah, f requirement, need

esigere, ay-**zee**-jay-ray, v to demand; (debts) to collect

esiguo, ay-**zee**-goo-o, *adj* small, scanty

esile, **ay**-ze-lay, *adj* slender; thin; weak

esiliare, ay-ze-le'**ah**-ray, v to exile

esilio, ay-**zee**-le'o, m exile

esimere, ay-**zee**-may-ray, v to exempt

esistente, ay-ziss-**ten**-tay, *adj* existing, living

esistenza, ay-ziss-**ten**-tsah, f existence

esistere, ay-**ziss**-tay-ray, v to exist

esitante, ay-ze-**tahn**-tay, *adj* hesitating

esitare, ay-ze-**tah**-ray, v to hesitate

esitazione, ay-ze-tah-tse'o-nay, f hesitation

esito, **ay**-ze-to, m result; **buon –**, success

esofago, ay-**zo**-fah-go, m oesophagus

esonerare, ay-zo-nay-**rah**-ray, v to exonerate, to exempt

esorbitante, ay-zor-be-**tahn**-tay, *adj* exorbitant

esordio, ay-**zor**-dee'o, m

first appearance, debut

esordire, ay-zor-**dee**-ray, v to make one's first appearance

esortare, ay-zor-**tah**-ray, v to exhort

esoso, ay-**zo**-zo, *adj* exorbitant; greedy

esotico, ay-**zo**-te-ko, *adj* exotic

espandere, ess-**pahn**-day-ray, v to expand

espansione, ess-pahn-se'o-nay, f expansion

espansivo, ess-pahn-see-vo, *adj* expansive, communicative

espatriare, ess-pah-tre'**ah**-ray, v to expatriate

espediente, ess-pay-de-en-tay, m expedient

espellere, ess-**pell**-lay-ray, v to expel

esperienza, ess-pay-re'en-tsah, f experience

esperimento, ess-pay-re-**men**-to, m experiment

esperto*, **-a**, ess-**pair**-to, *adj* skilled; expert; *m/f* expert

espiare, ess-pe'**ah**-ray, v to expiate, to atone for

espiazione, ess-pe'ah-tse'o-nay, f atonement

espirare, ess-pe-**rah**-ray, v to exhale, to breathe out

esplicare, ess-ple-**kah**-ray, v to carry out

esplicito*, ess-**plee**-che-to, *adj* explicit

esplodere, ess-plo-**day**-ray, *v* to explode; to blow up

esplorare, ess-plo-**rah**-ray, *v* to explore

esploratore, -trice, ess-plo-rah-**tor**-ay, ess-plo-rah-**tree**-chay, *m/f* explorer

esplosione, ess-plo-ze'**o**-nay, *f* explosion; outburst

esplosivo, ess-plo-**zee**-vo, *m* explosive; *adj* explosive

esporre, ess-**por**-ray, *v* to exhibit, to display; to explain; – **a**, to expose to

esportare, ess-por-**tah**-ray, *v* to export

esportazione, ess-por-tah-tse'**o**-nay, *f* export; exportation

esposizione, ess-po-ze-tse'**o**-nay, *f* exhibition; exposition, explanation; – **a**, exposure

espressione, ess-press-se'**o**-nay, *f* expression

espressivo*, ess-press-**see**-vo, *adj* expressive

espresso*, ess-**press**-so, *adj* express; on purpose; *m* espresso (coffee); express letter; express (train)

esprimere, ess-**pree**-may-ray, *v* to express

espropriare, ess-pro-pre'**ah**-ray, *v* to evict, to expropriate

espulsione, ess-pooll-se'**o**-nay, *f* expulsion

essenza, ess-**sen**-tsah, *f* essence

essenziale, ess-sen-tse'**ah**-lay, *adj* essential; *m* most important thing

essere, ess-**say**-ray, *v* to be; *m* being

essi, -e, **ess**-se, **ess**-say, *pron* they; them

esso, -a, **ess**-so, **ess**-sah, *pron* it; he/she; him/her

est, esst, *m* east; *adj* eastern; **in direzione –**, eastwards

estasi, **ess**-tah-ze, *f* ecstasy

estate, ess-**tah**-tay, *f* summer

estendere, ess-**ten**-day-ray, *v* to extend

estensione, ess-ten-see'**o**-nay, *f* extension; extent; expanse

estensivo*, ess-ten-**see**-vo, *adj* extensive

estenuato, ess-tay-noo'**ah**-to, *adj* exhausted, worn out

esteriore, ess-tay-re'**o**-ray, *adj* external

esternare, ess-tair-**nah**-ray, *v* to manifest, to

express

esterno, ess-**tair**-no, *m* outside, exterior; *adj** external

estero, ess-**tay**-ro, *adj* foreign; **all'–**, abroad

esteso, ess-**tay**-zo, *adj* large, vast; **per –**, in full

estetico, ess-te-**tee**-ko, *adj* aesthetic

estetista, ess-te-**tees**-tah, *m/f* beautician

estimo, ess-**te**-mo, *m* valuation

estinguere, ess-**tin**-goo'ay-ray, *v* to extinguish; to put out; (debt) to pay off

estinzione, ess-tin-tse'**o**-nay, *f* extinction

estirpare, ess-**teer**-pah-ray, *v* to uproot; to eradicate

estivo, ess-**tee**-vo, *adj* of summer

estorcere, ess-**tor**-chay-ray, *v* to extort

estorsione, ess-tor-se'**o**-nay, *f* extortion

estradizione, ess-trah-de-tse'**o**-nay, *f* extradition

estraneo, ess-**trah**-nay-o, *m* stranger; *adj* extraneous, foreign

estrarre, ess-**trar**-ray, *v* to extract; – **a sorte**, to draw lots

estratto, ess-**traht**-to, *m*

extract; synopsis

estrazione, ess-trah-tse'o-nay, *f* extraction; draw

estremista, ess-tray-mees-tah, *m/f* extremist

estremità, ess-tray-me-tah, *f* extremity, end

estremo, ess-**tray**-mo, *m* extreme, limit; *adj** extreme; **Estremo Oriente**, Far East

estromettere, ess-tro-**met**-tay-ray, *v* to expel, to exclude

estroverso, ess-tro-**ver**-so, *adj* extrovert

estuario, ess-too'**ah**-re'o, *m* estuary

esuberante, ay-zoo-bay-rahn-tay, *adj* exuberant

esulare, ay-zooll-**lah**-ray, *v* – **da**, to be beyond (one's competence)

esule, ay-zoo-lay, *m* exile

esultare, ay-zooll-**tah**-ray, *v* to rejoice

età, ay-**tah**, *f* age; period

etere, ay-**tay**-ray, *m* ether

eterno*, ay-**tair**-no, *adj* eternal

eterosessuale, ay-tai-ro-ses-soo'**a**-lay, *adj* heterosexual

etica, ay-te-kah, *f* ethics

etichetta, ay-te-ket-tah, *f* label; etiquette

etico*, **ay**-te-ko, *adj* ethical

etilismo, ay-te-lee-smo, *m* alcoholism

etimologia, ay-te-mo-lo-jee-ah, *f* etymology

etnico*, **ay**-tne-ko, *adj* ethnic

ettaro, **ayt**-tah-ro, *m* hectare, 10,000 m²

etto, **ayt**-to, *m* hectogram, 100 grams

eucalipto, ay-oo-kah-lit-to, *m* eucalyptus

eufemismo, ay-oo-fay-mis-mo, *m* euphemism

euforico, ay-oo-fo-ree-ko, *adj* euphoric

Europa, ay'oo-ro-pah, *f* Europe

europeo, ay'oo-ro-**pay**-o, *adj* European

evacuare, ay-vah-koo'ah-ray, *v* to evacuate

evadere, ay-vah-day-ray, *v* to evade; (correspondence) to deal with

evangelico, ay-vahn-**jay**-lee-ko, *adj* evangelical

evaporare, ay-vah-po-**rah**-ray, *v* to evaporate

evasione, ay-vah-zee'o-nay, *f* escape; (tax) evasion

evaso, ay-**vah**-zo, *m* escaped convict

evenienza, ay-vay-ne'en-tsah, *f* eventuality; **nell'– di**, in the event of

evento, ay-**ven**-to, *m* event

eventuale, ay-ven-too'**a**-lay, *adj* possible

eventualità, ay-ven-too'a-lee-**tah**, *f* eventuality, possibility

eventualmente, ay-ven-too-al-**men**-tay, *adv* if need be

evidente, ay-vee-**den**-tay, *adj* obvious, evident

evidenza, ay-vee-**den**-tsah, *f* facts, evidence

evidenziare, ay-vee-den-tse'**ah**-ray, *v* to highlight; to emphasize

evitare, ay-ve-**tah**-ray, *v* to avoid

evo, **ay**-vo, *m* age, period

evocare, ay-vo-kah-ray, *v* to evoke

evoluto, ay-vo-loo-to, *adj* advanced

evoluzione, ay-vo-loo-tse'o-nay, *f* evolution

evviva, ayv-vee-vah, *interj* hurrah!, long live!

extracomunitario, ex-trah-ko-moo-nee-**tah**-re'o, *adj* non-EEC

extraconiugale, ex-tra-ko-ne-oo-**gah**-lay, *adj* extramarital

extraterrestre, ex-tra-ter-res-stray, *adj* extraterrestrial

F

fa, fah, *adv* ago; *m mus* F

fabbisogno, fahb-be-**zo**-n'yo, *m* requirements

fabbrica, **fahb**-bre-kah, *f* factory

fabbricante, fahb-bre-**kahn**-tay, *m/f* manufacturer; maker

fabbricare, fahb-bre-**kah**-ray, *v* to manufacture; to build

fabbro, **fahb**-bro, *m* blacksmith

faccenda, faht-**chen**-dah, *f* business; matter

facchino, fahk-**kee**-no, *m* porter

faccia, **faht**-chah, *f* face; **in/di –**, opposite; **faccia a faccia**, face to face

facciata, faht-**chah**-tah, *f* façade

faceto, fah-**chay**-to, *adj* facetious; witty

facezia, fah-**chay**-tse'ah, *f* witticism

facile, **fah**-che-lay, *adj* easy

facilità, fah-che-le-**tah**, *f* easiness; ease; aptitude

facilitare, fah-che-le-**tah**-ray, *v* to facilitate

facilitazione, fah-che-le-tah-tse'o-nay, *f* facility

facilmente, fah-chill-**men**-tay, *adv* easily

facinoroso, fah-che-no-**ro**-zo, *adj* rebellious, violent; *m* rioter

facoltà, fah-koll-**tah**, *f* faculty

facoltativo, fah-koll-tah-**tee**-vo, *adj* optional

faggio, **fahd**-jo, *m* beech

fagiano, fah-**jah**-no, *m* pheasant

fagiolino, fah-jo-**lee**-no, *m* French bean

fagiolo, fah-**jo**-lo, *m* (kidney) bean

fagotto, fah-**got**-to, *m* bundle; *mus* bassoon

faina, fah-**ee**-nah, *f* stone marten

falce, **fahl**-chay, *f* scythe; sickle

falciare, fahl-**chah**-ray, *v* to mow

falciatrice, fahl-chah-**tree**-chay, *f* mowing machine

falciatura, fahl-chah-**too**-rah, *f* mowing

falco, **fahl**-ko, *m* hawk

falcone, fahl-**ko**-nay, *m* falcon

falda, **fahl**-dah, *f* (hat) brim; (coat) tails; (snow) flake; (mountain) slope; (geology) layer

falegname, fah-lay-n'yah-may, *m* carpenter

falena, fah-**lay**-nah, *f* moth

falla, **fahl**-lah, *f* leak

fallace, fahl-**lah**-chay, *adj* deceptive

fallacia, fahl-**lah**-chah, *f* fallacy

fallimento, fahl-lee-**men**-to, *m* failure; bankruptcy

fallire, fahl-**lee**-ray, *v* to

fail; to go bankrupt; to miss

fallito, -a, fahl-lee-to, *m/f* bankrupt; failure

fallo, fahl-lo, *m* fault, error; **mettere un piede in –,** to slip

falò, fah-lo, *m* bonfire

falsare, fahl-**sah**-ray, *v* to distort

falsariga, fahl-sah-**ree**-gah, *f* ruled paper; **sulla – di,** along the lines of

falsario, fahl-sah-re'o, *m* forger; counterfeiter

falsificare, fahl-se-fe-**kah**-ray, *v* to falsify, to forge, to counterfeit

falsità, fahl-se-tah, *f* falsehood

falso, fahl-so, *adj** false, untrue; forged; *m* forgery; fake

fama, fah-mah, *f* fame, renown

fame, fah-may, *f* hunger **aver –,** to be hungry

famelico, fah-**me**-lee-ko, *adj* ravenous

famigerato, fah-me-jay-**rah**-to, *adj* notorious

famiglia, fah-**mee**-l'yah, *f* family

familiare, fah-me-lee'**ah**-ray, *adj* familiar; *m/f* relative

familiarizzare, fah-mee-lee'ah-rid-**dzah**-ray, *v*

familiarize

famoso, fah-**mo**-zo, *adj* famous

fanale, fah-**nah**-lay, *m* lamp; light

fanatico, -a, fah-**nah**-tee-ko, *adj* fanatical; *m/f* fanatic

fanciullesco, fahn-chool-**less**-ko, *adj* childish

fanciullezza, fahn-chool-**let**-tsah, *f* childhood

fanciullo, -a, fahn-**chool**-lo, fahn-**chool**-lah, *m/f* child

fandonia, fahn-**do**-ne'ah, *f* lie, nonsense

fanello, fah-**nel**-lo, *m* linnet

fanfara, fahn-**fah**-rah, *f* fanfare; brass band

fanfarone, fahn-fah-**ro**-nay, *m* braggart

fango, fahn-go, *m* mud

fangoso, fahn-**go**-zo, *adj* muddy

fannullone, fahn-nool-**lo**-nay, *m* layabout

fantascienza, fahn-taht-**shent**-tsah, *f* science fiction

fantasia, fahn-tah-**zee**-ah, *f* imagination, fancy; pattern

fantasma, fahn-**tahss**-mah, *m* spectre, ghost

fantasticare, fahn-tahss-te-**kah**-ray, *v* to

daydream

fantastico, fahn-**tah**-stee-ko, *adj* fantastic

fante, fahn-tay, *m* infantryman; (cards) jack

fanteria, fahn-tay-**ree**-ah, *f* infantry

fantino, fahn-**tee**-no, *m* jockey

fantoccio, fahn-**tot**-cho, *m* dummy; puppet; doll

farabutto, fah-rah-**boot**-to, *m* blackguard

faraona fah-rah'o-nah, *f* guinea fowl

faraone, fah-rah'o-nay, *m* Pharaoh

farcela, far-chay-lah, *v* to manage

farcire, far-**chee**-ray, *v* to stuff

fardello, far-**dell**-lo, *m* bundle; burden

fare, fah-ray, *v* to do, to make; (profession) to be; *m* manner

farfalla, far-**fahl**-lah, *f* butterfly; bow tie

farina, fah-**ree**-nah, *f* flour

faringe, fah-**reen**-djay, *f* pharynx

farinoso, fah-re-**no**-zo, *adj* floury; powdery

farmacia, far-mah-**chee**-ah, *f* chemist's shop

farmacista, far-mah-**chiss**-tah, *m/f* chemist,

pharmacist

farmaco, far-mah-ko, m
drug; remedy

farneticare, far-nay-te-**kah**-ray, v to be delirious

faro, fah-ro, m lighthouse;
headlight

farsa, far-sah, f farce

fascetta, fah-**shet**-tah, f
corset; small band;
wrapper

fascia, fah-**she'ah**, f
bandage; band; sash

fasciare, fah-**she'ah**-ray, v
to bandage

fasciatura, fah-she'ah-**too**-rah, f bandage;
bandaging

fascicolo, fah-**shee**-ko-lo,
m (magazine) issue;
booklet; dossier

fascina, fah-**shee**-nah, f
faggot

fascino, fah-**she**-no, m
fascination, charm

fascio, fah-**she'o**, m
bundle; sheaf

fascista, fah-**shiss**-tah, m/f
fascist; adj fascist

fase, fah-zay, f phase

fastello, fahss-**tell**-lo, m
faggot; bundle

fastidio, fahss-**tee**-de'o, m
nuisance; trouble; **dare
–**, to annoy

fasto, fahss-to, m pomp

fastoso*, fahss-**to**-zo, adj
ostentatious, sumptuous

fata, fah-tah, f fairy

fatale, fah-**tah**-lay, adj
fatal; inevitable

fatalità, fah-tah-lee-**tah**, f
fate; inevitability

fatica, fah-**tee**-kah, f
fatigue; hard work; **a –**,
with difficulty

faticare, fah-te-**kah**-ray, v
to toil

faticoso*, fah-te-**ko**-zo, adj
tiring; laborious

fato, fah-to, m fate,
destiny

fattaccio, faht-**taht**-cho, m
foul deed

fattibile, faht-**tee**-be-lay,
adj feasible

fatto, faht-to, m fact;
deed; adj made; (drugs)
stoned

fattore, faht-**tor**-ay, m
(element) factor; farmer,
farm manager

fattoria, faht-to-**ree**-ah, f
farm; farmhouse

fattorino, faht-to-**ree**-no,
m errand boy

fattura, faht-**too**-rah, f
invoice

fatturare, faht-too-**rah**-ray, v to invoice

fatturato, faht-too-**rah**-to,
m turnover

fatuo, fah-too'o, adj
conceited

fausto, fahoo-sto, adj
happy, propitious

fautore, -trice, fah'oo-**tor**-ay, fah'oo-**tree**-chay, m/f
supporter, advocate

fava, fah-vah, f broad
bean

favella, fah-**vell**-lah, f
speech; language

favellare, fah-vell-**lah**-ray,
v to talk, to speak

favilla, fah-**vill**-lah, f spark

favo, fah-vo, m
honeycomb

favola, fah-vo-lah, f fairy
tale; fable

favoloso*, fah-vo-**lo**-zo,
adj fabulous

favore, fah-**vo**-ray, m
favour; **per –**, please

favoreggiare, fah-vo-red-**jah**-ray, v to favour; law
to aid and abet

favorevole*, fah-vo-**ray**-vo-lay, adj favourable

favorire, fah-vo-**ree**-ray, v
to favour

fax, fahks, m fax

faxare, fahk-**ksah**-ray, v to
fax

fazione, fah-tse'o-**nay**, f
faction

fazioso*, fah-tse'o-zo, adj
partisan

fazzoletto, faht-tso-**let**-to,
m handkerchief; **– di
carta**, tissue

febbraio, feb-**brah**-e'o, m
February

febbre, feb-bray, f fever; **–**

108

da fieno, hay fever

febbricitante, feb-bre-che-**tahn**-tay, *adj* feverish

febbrile, feb-**bree**-lay, *adj* feverish

feccia, fet-chah, *f* dregs

feci, **fay**-che, *fpl* excrement; faeces

fecola, **fay**-ko-lah, *f* – **di patate**, cornflour

fecondazione, fay-kon-dah-tse'o-nay, *f* fertilization; – **artificiale**, artificial insemination

fecondo, fay-**kon**-do, *adj* fruitful, fertile

fede, **fay**-day, *f* faith; wedding ring; **degno di** –, trustworthy

fedele, fay-**day**-lay, *adj* faithful; *m/f* faithful, believer

fedeltà, fay-dell-**tah**, *f* faithfulness; fidelity

federa, **fay**-day-rah, *f* pillowcase

federazione, fay-day-rah-tse'o-nay, *f* federation

fedina penale, fay-dee-nah pay-**nah**-lay, *f law* record

fegato, **fay**-gah-to, *m* liver; *fam* nerve

felce, **fell**-chay, *f* fern, bracken

felice*, fay-**lee**-chay, *adj* happy

felicitarsi, fay-le-che-**tar**-se, *v* to congratulate

felicitazioni, fay-le-che-tah-tse'o-ne, *fpl* congratulations

felino*, fay-**lee**-no, *adj* feline

felpa, **fell**-pah, *f* sweatshirt

feltro, **fell**-tro, *m* felt

femmina, **fem**-me-nah, *f* female

femminile, fem-me-**nee**-lay, *adj* feminine

femminista, fem-me-**nees**-stah, *adj* feminist; *m/f* feminist

femore, **fay**-mo-ray, *m* thighbone

fendere, **fen**-day-ray, *v* to cut through

fenditura, fen-de-**too**-rah, *f* cleft; crack

fenico, fay-ne-ko, *adj* **acido** –, carbolic acid

fenicottero, fay-ne-**kot**-tay-ro, *m* flamingo

fenomeno, fay-**no**-may-no, *m* phenomenon

feretro, **fay**-ray-tro, *m* coffin

feriale, fay-re'**ah**-lay, *adj* **giorno** –, weekday

ferie, **fay**-re'ay, *fpl* holidays

ferire, fay-**ree**-ray, *v* to wound; to injure; to hurt

ferita, fay-**ree**-tah, *f* wound; injury

ferito, fay-**ree**-to, *m* wounded person; injured person

ferma, **fair**-mah, *f* period of military service; **cane da** –, pointer

fermaglio, fair-**mah**-l'yo, *m* clasp

fermare, fair-**mah**-ray, *v* to stop, to halt; to detain

fermata, fair-**mah**-tah, *f* stop

fermentare, fair-men-**tah**-ray, *v* to ferment

fermento, fair-**men**-to, *m* ferment; yeast

fermezza, fair-**met**-tsah, *f* firmness; steadiness

fermo, **fair**-mo, *adj** still; firm; *interj* stop!; – **posta**, poste restante

feroce, fay-**ro**-chay, *adj* ferocious, fierce

ferragosto, fair-rah-**go**-sto, *m* 15th August, August bank holiday

ferramenta, fair-rah-**men**-tah, *f* ironmongery; hardware shop

ferrare, fair-**rah**-ray, *v* (horse) to shoe

ferrata, fair-**rah**-rah, *adj* **strada** –, railway

ferro, **fair**-ro, *m* iron; – **di cavallo**, horseshoe; – **da stiro**, iron; **carne ai**

ferri, grilled meat

ferrovia, fair-ro-**vee**-ah, *f* railway

ferroviere, fair-ro-ve'**ay**-ray, *m* railwayman

fertile, fair-tee-lay, *adj* fertile

fertilizzante, fair-tee-leed-**zahn**-tay, *adj* fertilizing; *m* fertilizer

fervido, fair-vee-do, *adj* fervent, ardent

fervore, fair-**vor**-ay, *m* fervour

fesso, -a, fess-so, *adj* stupid; cracked; *m/f* idiot

fessura, fess-soo-rah, *f* crack; slot

festa, fess-tah, *f* holiday, feast; party; festival

festeggiare, fess-ted-**jah**-ray, *v* to celebrate

festino, fess-**tee**-no, *m* party

festivo, fess-**tee**-vo, *adj* festive; **giorno –,** holiday

festone, fess-to-nay, *m* festoon

festoso*, fess-to-zo, *adj* merry

fetente, fay-**ten**-tay, *adj* stinky; disgusting

feticcio, fay-**tit**-cho, *m* fetish

feto, fay-to, *m* fetus

fetta, fet-tah, *f* slice

fettuccia, fayt-**toot**-chah, *f* ribbon, tape

fettuccine, fayt-toot-**chee**-nay, *fpl* ribbon-shaped pasta

feudale, fe'oo-**dah**-lay, *adj* feudal

fiaba, fe'**ah**-bah, *f* fairy tale

fiacca, fe'**ahk**-kah, *f* weariness; slackness

fiaccare, fe'**ahk-kah**-ray, *v* to tire out

fiacco*, fe'**ahk**-ko, *adj* weak; tired

fiaccola, fe'**ahk**-ko-lah, *f* torch

fiala, fe'**ah**-lah, *f* phial

fiamma, fe'**ahm**-mah, *f* flame; *naut* pennant

fiammeggiare, fe'ahm-med-**jah**-ray, *v* to blaze; to gleam

fiammifero, fe'ahm-**mee**-fay-ro, *m* match

fiancheggiare, fe'ahn-ked-**jah**-ray, *v* to border; *mil* to flank; to support

fianco, fe'**ahn**-ko, *m* side; hip; flank; slope

fiasco, fe'**ahss**-ko, *m* bottle in a straw holder; *fig* failure, fiasco

fiatare, fe'ah-**tah**-ray, *v* to breathe; to whisper

fiato, fe'**ah**-to, *m* breath; *fig* stamina; **senza –,** breathless

fibbia, feeb-be'ah, *f* buckle

fibra, fee-brah, *f* fibre; strength

fibroso, fe-**bro**-zo, *adj* fibrous

ficcare, feek-**kah**-ray, *v* to drive in; to poke; to thrust

ficcarsi, feek-**kar**-se, *v –* **nei guai,** to get into trouble

fico, fee-ko, *m* fig; figtree

fidanzamento, fe-dahn-tsah-**men**-to, *m* engagement

fidanzarsi, fe-dahn-**tsar**-se, *v* to become engaged

fidanzato, -a, fe-dahn-**tsah**-to, *m/f* fiancé, fiancée

fidarsi, fe-**dar**-se, *v – di,* to rely upon

fidato, fe-**dah**-to, *adj* trustworthy

fiducia, fe-**doo**-chah, *f* trust; **– in se stesso,** self-confidence

fiele, fe'**ay**-lay, *m* gall; bitterness

fieno, fe'**ay**-no, *m* hay

fiera, fe'**ay**-rah, *f* wild beast; fair; **– campionaria,** trade fair

fiero*, fe'**ay**-ro, *adj* proud; bold

fievole, fe'**ay**-vo-lay, *adj* dim, faint

figlia, fee-l'yah, *f* daughter

figliare, fe-l'yah-ray, *v* (animal) to give birth

figliastro, -a, fe-l'yahss-tro, *m/f* stepson, stepdaughter

figlio, fee-l'yo, *m* son; child; **– unico,** only child

figlioccio, -a, fe-l'yot-cho, *m/f* godchild

figura, fe-goo-rah, *f* figure; picture; **fare bella/brutta –,** to make a good/bad impression

figurare, fe-goo-rah-ray, *v* to appear

figurarsi, fe-goo-rar-se, *v* to imagine; **figurati!** not at all!; just imagine!

fila, fee-lah, *f* line, row; **di –,** in succession; **fare la –,** to queue up

filare, fe-lah-ray, *v* to spin; (speech) to be coherent; **– con,** to go steady with; **– via,** to run away

filarmonica, fe-lahr-mo-nee-kah, *f* music society

filastrocca, fe-lah-strok-kah, *f* nursery rhyme

filato, fe-lah-to, *m* yarn; **di –,** without a break; straight off; **zucchero –,** candy floss

filetto, fe-let-to, *m* fillet; thread

filiale, fe-le'ah-lay, *f* branch; subsidiary; *adj* filial

filigrana, fe-le-grah-nah, *f* filigree

film, film, *m* film

filo, fee-lo, *m* thread; string; wire; (knife) edge

filosofia, fe-lo-zo-fee-ah, *f* philosophy

filosofo, -a, fe-lo-zo-fo, *m/f* philosopher

filovia, fe-lo-vee-ah, *f* trolley line; trolley bus

filtrare, feel-trah-ray, *v* to filter

filtro, feel-tro, *m* filter; potion

filza, feel-tsah, *f* string; series

finale, fe-nah-lay, *adj* final; *m* (of book, of film) ending; *f* (sport) final

finalità, fe-nah-lee-tah, *f* aim

finalmente, fe-nahl-men-tay, *adv* finally, at long last

finanza, fe-nahn-tsah, *f* finance; revenue

finanziare, fe-nahn-tse'ah-ray, *v* to finance, to fund

finanziario*, fe-nahn-tse'ah-re'o, *adj* financial

finché, feen-kay, *conj* until; as long as

fine, fee-nay, *m* aim, goal; *f* end, ending; *adj* thin, fine; sharp; refined; **– settimana,** weekend

finestra, fe-ness-trah, *f* window

finezza, fe-net-tsah, *f* fineness; sharpness; refinement

fingere, feen-jay-ray, *v* to feign, to pretend

finimenti, fe-ne-men-tee, *mpl* harness

finimondo, fe-ne-mon-do, *m* pandemonium

finire, fe-nee-ray, *v* to finish, to end; to cease, to stop

fino, fee-no, *prep* **– a,** till; until; as far as; **– da,** from, since; *adj* even; *adj* sharp; (gold) pure

finocchio, fe-nock-ke'o, *m* fennel; *vulg* homosexual, queer

finora, fe-no-rah, *adv* up till now, so far

finta, feen-tah, *f* feint; **far –,** to pretend

finto, feen-to, *adj* false; artificial; feigned

finzione, feen-tse'o-nay, *f* pretence

fiocco, fe'ock-ko, *m* flake; bow

fiocina, fe'o-che-nah, *f* harpoon

fioco*, fe'o-ko, *adj* weak; dim; faint

fionda, fe'**onn**-dah, f sling; catapult

fioraio, -a, fe'o-**rah**-e'o, m/f florist

fiordaliso, fe'or-dah-**lee**-zo, m cornflower

fiore, fe'o-ray, m flower; blossom; bloom

fiorente, fe'o-**ren**-tay, adj blooming; thriving

fioretto, fe'o-**ret**-to, m foil; little flower; small sacrifice

fiori, fe'o-re, mpl (cards) clubs

fiorire, fe'o-**ree**-ray, v to flower, to blossom; to flourish

fioritura, fe'o-re-**too**-rah, f blooming; flourishing

firma, feer-mah, f signature

firmare, feer-**mah**-ray, v to sign

firmatario, -a, feer-mah-**tah**-re'o, m/f signatory

fisarmonica, fe-zar-**mo**-ne-kah, f accordion

fiscale, fiss-**kah**-lay, adj fiscal; **anno –**, tax year

fischiare, fiss-ke'**ah**-ray, v to whistle; to hiss

fischietto, fiss-ke'**et**-to, m (instrument) whistle

fischio, fiss-ke'o, m (act) whistle

fisco, fiss-ko, m Inland Revenue; tax authorities

fisica, fee-ze-kah, f physics

fisico, fee-ze-ko, m (body) physique; (scientist) physicist; adj physical

fisime, fee-ze-may, fpl whims, fixation

fisiologia, fee-zee'o-lo-jee-ah, f physiology

fisionomia, fee-zee'o-no-mee-ah, f physionomy

fisioterapia, fee-zee'o-te-rah-**pee**-ah, f physiotherapy

fissare, fiss-**sah**-ray, v to fix; to book; to stare at

fisso*, **fis**-so, adj fixed; regular; **guardare –**, to stare (at)

fitta, fit-tah, f stitch in the side

fittizio, fit-tee-tse'o, adj fictitious

fitto, fit-to, m rent; adj* thick

fiumana, fe'oo-**mah**-nah, f **una – di**, a stream of

fiume, fe'oo-may, m river; fig stream, flow

fiutare, fe'oo-**tah**-ray, v to sniff

fiuto, fe'oo-to, m sense of smell; fig nose

flagello, flah-**jell**-lo, m scourge

flagrante, flah-**grahn**-tay, adj flagrant; **in –**, in the act

flanella, flah-**nell**-lah, f (fabric) flannel

flauto, flah'oo-to, m mus flute

flebile, flay-be-lay, adj plaintive; feeble

flemma, flem-mah, f coolness, composure

flessibile, fless-**see**-be-lay, adj flexible

flessione, fless-see'o-nay, f bending; press-up; (language) inflection

floppy disk, flop-pee disk, m floppy disk

floricoltura, flo-ree-kol-**too**-rah, f flower-growing

florido, flo-ree-do, adj thriving; healthy

floscio, flo-she'o, adj flabby; floppy

flotta, flot-tah, f fleet

fluido, floo'e-do, m fluid; adj* liquid

fluire, floo'ee-ray, v to flow

fluoro, floo'o-ro, m fluorine

fluoruro, floo'o-**roo**-ro, m fluoride

flusso, flooss-so, m flow; flux; rising tide

flutto, floot-to, m wave, billow

fluttuare, floot-too'**ah**-ray, v to fluctuate

fluttuazione, floot-too'ah-tse'o-nay, f fluctuation

fluviale, floo-vee'**ah**-lay, *adj* (of) river

fobia, fo-**bee**-ah, *f* phobia

foca, fo-kah, *f* seal

focaccia, fo-**kaht**-chah, *f* (sweet) bun; (savoury) kind of pizza

focaia, fo-**kah**-e'ah, *adj* **pietra –**, flint

focalizzare, fo-kah-leed-**dza**-ray, *v* to get into focus

foce, fo-chay, *f* mouth (of river)

focolaio, fo-ko-lah-e'o, *m* centre of infection; breeding ground

focolare, fo-ko-**lah**-ray, *m* hearth, fireplace

focoso*, fo-**ko**-zo, *adj* fiery

fodera, fo-day-rah, *f* lining; (book) dust jacket

foderare, fo-day-**rah**-ray, *v* to line

fodero, fo-day-ro, *m* scabbard; sheath

foga, fo-gah, *f* ardour; **con –**, enthusiastically, excitedly

foggia, fod-jah, *f* shape; fashion

foglia, fo-l'yah, *f* leaf; **mangiar la –**, to catch on

fogliame, fo-l'yah-may, *m* foliage

foglio, fo-l'yo, *m* sheet (of paper, of metal)

fogna, fo-n'yah, *f* sewer; drain

fognatura, fo-n'yah-**too**-rah, *f* sewers, drains

föhn, fon, *m* hairdryer

folata, fo-lah-tah, *f* gust

folclore, fol-**klo**-ray, *m* folklore

folgorare, fol-go-**rah**-ray, *v* to strike down; to electrocute

folgore, fol-**gor**-ay, *f* thunderbolt

folla, fol-lah, *f* crowd; multitude

folle, fol-lay, *adj* mad

folletto, fol-**let**-to, *m* imp, elf

follia, fol-**lee**-ah, *f* madness; folly

folto, fol-to, *adj** thick; **nel – di**, in the thick of

fomentare, fo-men-**tah**-ray, *v* to stir up

fondale, fon-**dah**-lay, *m* (sea) bed; (theatre) backdrop

fondamentale, fon-dah-men-**tah**-lay, *adj* fundamental

fondamento, fon-dah-**men**-to, *m* foundation

fondare, fon-**dah**-ray, *v* to establish, to found

fondatore, -trice, fon-dah-**tor**-ay, fon-dah-**tree**-chay, *m/f* founder

fondere, fon-**day**-ray, *v* to melt; to cast

fonderia, fon-day-**ree**-ah, *f* foundry

fondo, fon-do, *m* bottom; landed property; funds; *adj* deep

fonetica, fo-**nay**-tee-kah, *f* phonetics

fontana, fon-**tah**-nah, *f* fountain

fonte, fon-tay, *f* source; spring; *m* **– battesimale**, font

footing, foo-ting, *m* jogging

foraggio, fo-**rahd**-jo, *m* forage, fodder

forare, fo-**rah**-ray, *v* to pierce; to puncture

forbici, **for**-be-che, *fpl* scissors

forbito, for-**bee**-to, *adj* polished

forca, for-kah, *f* pitchfork; gallows

forchetta, for-**ket**-tah, *f* fork

forcina, for-**chee**-nah, *f* hairpin

forcipe, **for**-chee-pay, *m* forceps

foresta, fo-**ress**-tah, *f* forest

forestiero, -a, fo-**ress**-te'ay-ro, *m/f* foreigner; stranger; visitor; *adj* foreign

forfora, for-fo-rah, f dandruff

forgiare, for-jah-ray, v to mould

forma, for-mah, f form; mould; figure

formaggio, for-mahd-jo, m cheese

formale*, for-mah-lay, adj formal

formalità, for-mah-lee-tah, f formality

formare, for-mah-ray, v to form; to shape

formazione, for-mah-tse'o-nay, f formation; training; education

formica, for-mee-kah, f ant

formicaio, for-me-kah-e'o, m anthill; swarm

formicolio, for-me-ko-lee'o, m (tingling) pins and needles; (multitude) swarming

formidabile, for-me-dah-be-lay, adj formidable

formoso, for-mo-zo, adj shapely

formula, for-moo-lah, f formula

formulare, for-moo-lah-ray, v to formulate

fornace, for-nah-chay, f furnace; kiln

fornaio, for-nah-e'o, m baker

fornello, for-nell-lo, m stove; kitchen-cooker; gas ring

fornire, for-nee-ray, v to supply with

fornitore, for-ne-tor-ay, m supplier

forno, for-no, m oven; furnace; kiln; – a microonde, microwave oven

foro, fo-ro, m hole; law court; forum

forse, for-say, adv perhaps; maybe

forsennato, -a, for-sen-nah-to, adj mad, crazy; m/f lunatic

forte*, for-tay, adj strong; loud; hard; m strong point; mil fort

fortezza, for-tet-tsah, f strength; fortress

fortificare, for-te-fe-kah-ray, v to fortify

fortuito*, for-too-e-to, adj fortuitous, (by) chance

fortuna, for-too-nah, f fortune; luck; wealth; di –, emergency, makeshift

fortunato, -a, for-too-nah-to, adj fortunate, lucky

foruncolo, fo-roonn-ko-lo, m boil

forza, for-tsah, f strength; force; power

forzare, for-tsah-ray, v to force

forzato, for-tsah-to, m convict; adj* forced, artificial

forziere, for-tse'ay-ray, m iron-chest; strongbox

foschia, foss-kee-ah, f mist

fosco*, foss-ko, adj gloomy; dull

fosfato, foss-fah-to, m phosphate

fosforo, foss-fo-ro, m phosphorus

fossa, foss-sah, f pit; trench; grave

fossato, foss-sah-to, m ditch; moat

fossetta, foss-set-tah, f dimple

fossile, foss-se-lay, adj fossil; m fossil

fosso, foss-so, m ditch; moat

foto, fo-to, f photo

fotocopia, fo-to-ko-pe'ah, f photocopy

fotocopiatrice, fo-to-ko-pe'ah-tree-chay, f photocopier

fotografia, fo-to-grah-fee-ah, f photography; photograph

fotografo, -a, fo-to-grah-fo, m/f photographer

fotomodello, -a, fo-to-mo-del-lo, m/f fashion model

fotoreporter, fo-to-ray-por-tayr, m/f newspaper

photographer

fra, frah, *prep* between; amongst; within

fracassare, frah-kahss-**sah**-ray, *v* to smash

fracasso, frah-**kahss**-so, *m* din

fradicio, frah-de-cho, *adj* soaked; **bagnato –,** soaking wet; **ubriaco –,** blind drunk

fragile*, frah-**gee**-lay, *adj* fragile, brittle; delicate

fragola, frah-go-lah, *f* strawberry

fragore, frah-**gor**-ay, *m* rumble, roar

fragoroso, frah-go-**ro**-so, *adj* uproarious

fragranza, frah-**grahn**-tsah, *f* fragrance

fraintendere, frah-in-**ten**-day-ray, *v* to misunderstand

frammentario, frahm-men-**tah**-re'o, *adj* fragmentary

frammento, frahm-**men**-to, *m* fragment

frana, frah-nah, *f* landslide

franare, frah-**nah**-ray, *v* to slide down, to collapse

franchezza, frahn-**ket**-tsah, *f* frankness

francese, frahn-**chay**-zay, *adj* French

Francia, frahn-che'ah, *f* France

franco, frahn-ko, *adj** frank; **– di dazio,** duty free; **– di porto,** carriage free; **farla franca,** to get away with it

francobollo, frahn-ko-**boll**-lo, *m* postage stamp

frangente, frahn-**jayn**-tay, *m* (sea) breaker; *fig* circumstance

frangia, frahn-jah, *f* fringe

frantoio, frahn-to-e'o, *m* olive-press

frantumare, frahn-too-**mah**-ray, *v* to smash

frantumi, frahn-**too**-me, *mpl* **in –,** to smithereens

frapporsi, frahp-**por**-se, *v* to interfere

frasario, frah-**zah**-re'o, *m* jargon; phrase-book

frasca, frahss-kah, *f* leafy bough

frase, frah-zay, *f* sentence; **– fatta,** set phrase

frassino, frahss-se-no, *m* ash-tree

frastagliato, frahss-tah-le'**ah**-to, *adj* indented

frastornato, frahss-tor-**nah**-to, *adj* bewildered

frastuono, frahss-too'**o**-no, *m* uproar, din

frate, frah-tay, *m* friar, monk, brother

fratellanza, frah-tell-**lahn**-tsah, *f* fraternity

fratellastro, frah-tell-**lahss**-tro, *m* stepbrother

fratello, frah-**tell**-lo, *m* brother; **fratelli,** brothers; brother(s) and sister(s); *relig* brethren

fraterno*, frah-**tair**-no, *adj* fraternal, brotherly

frattaglie, fraht-**tah**-l'yay, *fpl* offal

frattanto, fraht-**tahn**-to, *adv* meanwhile

frattempo, fraht-**tem**-po, *adv* **nel –,** in the meanwhile

frattura, fraht-**too**-rah, *f* fracture; split, break

frazione, frah-tse'o-nay, *f* fraction; hamlet

freccia, fret-chah, *f* arrow; (car) indicator

freddare, fred-**dah**-ray, *v* to cool; to shoot dead

freddezza, fred-**det**-tsah, *f* coldness

freddo, fred-do, *m* cold weather, *adj** cold; cool; **avere –,** to be cold

freddoloso, fred-do-**lo**-so, *adj* sensitive to the cold

freddura, fred-**doo**-rah, *f* pun

fregare, fray-**gah**-ray, *v* to rub; to cheat

fregarsene, fray-**gahr**-say-nay, *v* **non –,** not to give a damn

fregata, fray-**gah**-tah, *f*

rub; *naut* frigate

fregatura, fray-gah-**too**-rah, *f* rip-off; let-down

fregio, fray-jo, *m* frieze; decoration

fremere, fray-may-ray, *v* to shake, to tremble

frenare, fray-**nah**-ray, *v* to restrain; to brake; to pull up

frenata, fray-**nah**-tah, *f* braking

frenesia, fray-nay-**zee**-ah, *f* frenzy

freno, fray-no, *m* brake; bit; *fig* control

frequentare, fray-kwen-**tah**-ray, *v* to attend; to frequent

frequente*, fray-**kwen**-tay, *adj* frequent

frequenza, fray-**kwen**-tsah, *f* frequency; attendance

freschezza, frayss-**ket**-tsah, *f* freshness; coolness

fresco, frayss-ko, *m* coolness; *adj* cool, fresh; new

fretta, frayt-tah, *f* haste, hurry

frettoloso*, frayt-to-**lo**-zo, *adj* hasty, in a hurry

friabile, fre-ah-be-lay, *adj* crumbly; (rock) friable

friggere, freed-jay-ray, *v* to fry

friggitoria, freed-je-to-**ree**-ah, *f* fried food shop

frigido*, free-je-do, *adj* frigid

frigo, free-go, *m* fridge

frigobar, free-go-**bahr**, *m* minibar

frigorifero, fre-go-ree-**fay**-ro, *m* refrigerator

fringuello, freen-goo'**ell**-lo, *m* chaffinch

frittata, freet-**tah**-tah, *f* omelette

frittella, freet-**tell**-lah, *f* pancake; fritter

fritto, freet-to, *adj* fried; *m* fried food; **sono –,** I'm done for

frittura, freet-**too**-rah, *f* fried food

frivolo, free-vo-lo, *adj* frivolous

frizione, fre-tse'o-nay, *f* friction; massage; (car) clutch

frizzante, freet-**tsahn**-tay, *adj* fizzy, sparkling

frizzare, freet-**tsah**-ray, *v* to sparkle

frizzo, freet-tso, *m* joke

frodare, fro-**dah**-ray, *v* to defraud

frode, fro-day, *f* fraud

frodo, fro-do, *m* **di –,** illegal; **cacciatore/pescatore di –,** poacher

frollo, frol-lo, *adj* (meat)

tender; **pasta frolla,** shortcrust pastry

fronda, fron-dah, *f* leafy branch; revolt, opposition

frontale*, fron-tah-lay, *adj* frontal; head-on

fronte, fron-tay, *f* forehead; *mil* front; (weather) front

fronteggiare, fron-ted-**jah**-ray, *v* to face

frontiera, fron-te'**ay**-rah, *f* frontier

fronzoli, fron-dzo-le, *mpl* finery, frills

frotte, frot-tay, *fpl* **a –,** in droves

frottola, frot-to-lah, *f* fib, lie

frugare, froo-**gah**-ray, *v* to search; to rummage

fruire, froo'ee-ray, *v* **– di,** to benefit from

frullare, frool-**lah**-ray, *v* to beat (eggs); to liquidize

frullato, frool-**lah**-to, *m* milk shake

frullino, frool-**lee**-no, *m* whisk

frumento, froo-men-to, *m* wheat

frusciare, froos-**shah**-ray, *v* to rustle

frusta, frooss-tah, *f* whip

frustare, frooss-**tah**-ray, *v* to whip

frustrare, frooss-**trah**-ray,

v to frustate

frutta, froot-tah, *f* fruit

fruttare, froot-**tah**-ray, *v* to yield; to give a profit

frutteto, froot-**tay**-to, *m* orchard

fruttivendolo, -a, froot-tee-**ven**-do-lo, *m/f* greengrocer

frutto, froot-to, *m* fruit; profit

fu, foo, *adj* deceased; **il – Aldo Bianchi,** the late Aldo Bianchi

fucilare, foo-che-**lah**-ray, *v* to shoot

fucilata, foo-che-**lah**-tah, *f* gun-shot

fucile, foo-**chee**-lay, *m* gun; rifle

fucina, foo-**chee**-nah, *f* forge

fuga, foo-gah, *f* escape, flight; leak; *mus* fugue

fugace, foo-**gah**-chay, *adj* fleeting, transient

fuggevole, food-**jay**-vo-lay, *adj* fleeting

fuggire, food-**jee**-ray, *v* to flee, to escape; to avoid, to shun

fulgido, fool-jee-do, *adj* shining

fuliggine, foo-**leed**-je-nay, *f* soot

fulminato, fool-me-**nah**-to, struck by lightning; electrocuted; (bulb) blown

fulmine, fool-me-nay, *m* lightning

fulmineo, fool-**mee**-ne'o, *adj* rapid, quick as a flash

fulvo, fool-vo, *adj* tawny

fumaiolo, foo-mah-ee'**o**-lo, *m* funnel; chimney-stack

fumare, foo-**mah**-ray, *v* to smoke; *fig* to fume

fumatore, -trice, foo-mah-**tor**-ay, foo-mah-**tree**-chay, *m/f* smoker

fumetto, foo-**met**-to, *m* comic strip; speech bubble

fumo, foo-mo, *m* smoke; fume

funambolo, -a, foo-**nahm**-bo-lo, *m/f* tightrope walker

fune, foo-nay, *f* rope, cord

funebre, foo-nay-bray, *adj* funereal; **carro –,** hearse

funesto*, foo-**ness**-to, *adj* fatal; distressing

fungere, foonn-**jay**-ray, *v* to act as

fungo, foonn-go, *m* mushroom; fungus

funicolare, foo-nee-ko-**lah**-ray, *f* cable railway

funivia, foo-nee-**vee**-ah, *f* cable car

funzionare, foonn-tse'o-**nah**-ray, *v* to function; to work

funzionario, -a, foonn-tse'o-**nah**-ree'o, *m/f* official; **– statale,** civil servant

funzione, foonn-tse'**o**-nay, *f* function; *relig* service

fuoco, foo'o-ko, *m* fire; focus; **– d'artificio,** fireworks

fuorché, foo'or-**kay**, *conj* except; *prep* except

fuori, foo'o-re, *adv* out; outside; **– di,** *prep* out of, outside

fuoribordo, foo'o-ree-**bor**-do, *m* speedboat

fuorilegge, foo'o-ree-**lej**-jay, *m/f* outlaw

fuoriserie, foo'o-ree-**say**-re'ay, *f* custom-built car

fuoriuscito, foo'o-ree-oo-**shee**-to, *m* exile; outlaw

fuorviare, foo'or-ve'**ah**-ray, *v* to go *or* lead astray

furbizia, foohr-bee-tse'ah, *f* cleverness, cunning

furbo*, foohr-bo, *adj* clever, smart; sly

furente, foo-**ren**-tay, *adj* furious

furetto, foo-**ret**-to, *m* ferret

furfante, foohr-**fahn**-tay, *m* rascal; swindler

furgone, foohr-**go**-nay, *m* lorry; van

furia, foo-re'ah, *f* fury;

hurry

furibondo, foo-ree-**bon**-do, *adj* furious

furioso, foo-ree'**o**-so, *adj* furious; violent

furore, foo-**ro**-ray, *m* fury

furtivo, foor-**tee**-vo, *adj* furtive

furto, foor-to, *m* theft

fusa, foo-zah, *fpl* **fare le –,** to purr

fusibile, foo-**zee**-bee-lay, *m* fuse

fusione, foo-zee'**o**-nay, *f* fusion

fuso, foo-zo, *m* spindle; **– orario,** time zone

fusoliera, foo-zo-le'**ay**-rah, *f* fuselage

fustagno, fooss-**tah**-n'yo, *m* kind of corduroy

fustigare, fooss-tee-**gah**-ray, *v* to flog

fusto, fooss-to, *m* trunk; stem; shaft

futile*, foo-te-lay, *adj* futile, trifling

futuro, foo-**too**-ro, *adj* future; *m* future

gabbare, gahb-**bah**-ray, *v* to deceive

gabbia, gahb-be'ah, *f* cage; crate

gabbiano, gahb-be'**ah**-no, *m* seagull

gabinetto, gah-be-**net**-to, *m* lavatory; (dentist, doctor) surgery; *parl* ministry

gaffe, gahf, *f* blunder

gaggia, gahd-**jee**-ah, *f* acacia

gagliardo*, gah-l'**yar**-do, *adj* sturdy, robust

gaiezza, gah-e-**et**-tsah, *f* gaiety, merriment

gaio*, gah-e'o, *adj* cheerful

gala, gah-lah, *f* bow; **serata di –**, gala evening

galante, gah-**lahn**-tay, *adj* gallant; romantic

galantuomo, gah-lahn-too'**o**-mo, *m* honest man

galassia, gah-lahs-se'ah, *f* galaxy

galateo, gah-lah-**tay**-o, *m* etiquette

galeotto, gah-lay-**ot**-to, *m* convict

galera, gah-**lay**-rah, *f* prison; *naut* galley

galla, gahl-lah, *f* gall; **a –**, afloat

galleggiare, gahl-led-**jah**-ray, *v* to float

galleria, gahl-lay-**ree**-ah, *f* gallery; tunnel; (theatre) circle

Galles, gahl-layss, *m* Wales

gallese, gahl-lay-zay, *adj* Welsh

galletta, gah-**let**-tah, *f* cracker

gallina, gahl-lee-nah, *f* hen

gallo, gahl-lo, *m* cock

gallone, gahl-**lo**-nay, *m* stripe; gallon; braid

galoppare, gah-lop-**pah**-ray, *v* to gallop

galoppo, gah-**lop**-po, *m* gallop; **piccolo –**, canter

gamba, gahm-bah, *f* leg

gamberetto, gahm-bay-**ret**-to, *m* shrimp

gambero, gahm-bay-ro, *m* prawn; crayfish

gambo, gahm-bo, *m* stalk; stem

gamma, gahm-mah, *f mus* scale; range; *adj* **raggi –**, gamma rays

ganascia, gah-**nah**-she'ah, *f* jaw; brake shoes

gancio, gahn-cho, *m* hook

gangheri, gahn-gay-re, *mpl* **uscire dai –**, to lose one's temper

gara, gah-rah, *f* competition

garage, gah-**rahj**, *m* garage

garante, gah-**rahn**-tay, *adj* **farsi – di/per**, to vouch for

garantire, gah-rahn-tee-ray, *v* to guarantee; to assure

garanzia, gah-rahn-**tsee**-ah, *f* guarantee,

warranty
garbato*, gar-**bah**-to, *adj* well-bred; amiable
garbo, gar-bo, *m* good manners; graceful movements
garbuglio, gar-**boo**-l'yo, *m* jumble, tangle
gardenia, gar-**day**-ne'ah, *f* gardenia
gareggiare, gah-red-**jah**-ray, *v* to compete
gargarismo, gar-gah-**reez**-mo, *m* gargle
garofano, gar-**ro**-fah-no, *m* (flower) pink; carnation
garrire, gar-**ree**-ray, *v* to chirp
garza, gar-dsah, *f* gauze
garzone, gar-**tso**-nay, *m* apprentice; boy
gas, gahz, *m* gas; – **lacrimogeno,** tear gas
gasolio, ga-**zo**-le'o, *m* diesel
gassato, gas-**sah**-to, *adj* fizzy
gastronomia, gas-tro-no-**mee**-ah, *f* gastronomy
gatta, gaht-tah, *f* she-cat
gatto, gaht-to, *m* tom-cat, cat
gattopardo, gaht-to-**par**-do, *m* serval
gaudio, gah'oo-de'o, *m* joy, gladness, bliss
gavetta, gah-**vet**-tah, *f*

mess tin
gavitello, gah-ve-**tell**-lo, *m* buoy
gazza, gahd-dzah, *f* magpie
gazzella, gahd-**dzel**-lah, *f* gazelle; police car
gazzetta, gahd-**dzet**-tah, *f* gazette
gazzosa, gahd-**dzo**-za, *f* fizzy drink; lemonade
gelare, jay-**lah**-ray, *v* to freeze
gelata, jay-**lah**-tah, *f* frost
gelatina, jay-lah-**tee**-nah, *f* gelatine; (fruit) jelly
gelato, jay-**lah**-to, *m* ice-cream; *adj* frozen
gelido, jay-lee-do, *adj* freezing, icy; ice-cold
gelo, jay-lo, *m* frost; chill
gelone, jay-**lo**-nay, *m* chilblain
gelosia, jay-lo-**zee**-ah, *f* jealousy; shutter
geloso*, jay-**lo**-zo, *adj* jealous
gelso, jayl-so, *m* mulberry tree
gelsomino, jayl-so-**mee**-no, *m* jasmine
gemelli, jay-**mell**-le, *mpl* cuff-links; twins; **Gemelli,** Gemini
gemere, jay-**may**-ray, *v* to groan, to moan
gemito, jay-me-to, *m* moan
gemma, jaym-mah, *f* gem,

jewel; (plant) bud
generale, jay-nay-**rah**-lay, *adj** general; *m* mil general
generalità, jay-nay-rah-lee-**tah**, *f* generality; majority; **dare le –,** to give one's name and address
generalizzare, jay-nay-rah-lid-**dzah**-ray, *v* to generalize
generare, jay-nay-**rah**-ray, *v* to generate; to produce
generatore, jay-nay-rah-**to**-ray, *m* (electric) generator
generazione, jay-nay-rah-tse'o-nay, *f* generation
genere, jay-nay-ray, *m* kind; gender; (literary) genre; **generi alimentari,** foodstuffs
generico, jay-**nay**-ree-ko, *adj** generic; vague; **medico –,** general practitioner
genero, jay-nay-ro, *m* son-in-law
generosità, jay-nay-ro-ze-**tah**, *f* generosity
generoso*, jay-nay-**ro**-zo, *adj* generous
genetica, jay-**ne**-te-kah, *f* genetics
genetico, jay-**ne**-te-ko, *adj* genetic

gengiva, jen-**jee**-vah, *f* (teeth) gum

geniale, jay-ne'**ah**-lay, *adj* brilliant

genio, **jay**-ne'o, *m* genius; talent

genitali, jay-ne-**tah**-lee, *mpl* genitals

genitori, jay-ne-**to**-re, *mpl* parents

gennaio, jen-**nah**-e'o, *m* January

genocidio, jay-no-**chee**-dee'o, *m* genocide

Genova, **jay**-no-vah, *f* Genoa

gentaglia, jen-**tah**-l'yah, *f* riffraff

gente, jen-tay, *f* people

gentile*, jen-**tse'a**-lay, *adj* kind; polite

gentilezza, jen-te-**let**-tsah, *f* kindness; politeness

gentiluomo, jen-te-loo'**o**-mo, *m* gentleman

genuino, jay-noo'e-no, *adj* genuine; natural

genziana, jen-tse'**a**-nah, *f* gentian

geografia, jay'o-grah-**fee**-ah, *f* geography

geologia, jay'o-lo-**jee**-ah, *f* geology

geometra, jay'o-**may**-trah, *m/f* surveyor

geometria, jay'o-may-**tree**-ah, *f* geometry

geranio, jay-**rah**-ne'o, *m* geranium

gerarchia, jay-rar-**kee**-ah, *f* hierarchy

gerente, jay-**ren**-tay, *m/f* manager, manageress

gerenza, jay-**ren**-tsah, *f* management

gergo, **jayr**-go, *m* slang

geriatria, jay-re'**ah**-**tree**-ah, *f* geriatrics

Germania, jayr-**mah**-ne'ah, *f* Germany

germe, **jayr**-may, *m* germ

germogliare, jayr-mo-**l'yah**-ray, *v* to germinate, to sprout

germoglio, jayr-mo-**l'yo**, *m* shoot; bud

geroglifico, jay-ro-**glee**-fee-ko, *m* hieroglyphic

gesso, **jess**-so, *m* chalk; plaster

gesta, **jess**-tah, *fpl* exploits, deeds

gestante, jess-**tahn**-tay, *f* expectant mother

gesticolare, jess-tee-ko-**lah**-ray, *v* to gesticulate

gestione, jess-te'o-nay, *f* management

gestire, jess-**tee**-ray, *v* to manage, to run

gesto, **jess**-to, *m* gesture, sign

Gesù, Jay-**soo**, *m* Jesus

gesuita, jay-soo'**ee**-tah, *m* Jesuit

gettare, jet-**tah**-ray, *v* to throw; to cast

gettito, jet-**tee**-to, *m* yield, revenue

getto, **jet**-to, *m* jet; throw; shoot

gettone, jet-**to**-nay, *m* token; (games) counter

ghepardo, gay-**pahr**-do, *m* cheetah

ghetto, **gayt**-to, *m* ghetto

ghiacciaia, ghe-aht-**chah**-e'ah, *f* icebox

ghiacciaio, ghe-aht-**chah**-e'o, *m* glacier

ghiacciare, ghe-aht-**chah**-ray, *v* to freeze

ghiaccio, ghe-**aht**-cho, *m* ice

ghiacciolo, ghe-aht-**cho**-lo, *m* ice lolly; icicle

ghiaia, ghe-**ah**-e'ah, *f* gravel; shingle

ghianda, ghe-**ahn**-dah, *f* acorn

ghiandaia, ghe-ahn-**dah**-e'ah, *f* jay

ghiandola, ghe-**ahn**-do-lah, *f* gland

ghigliottina, ghe-l'ye'ot-**tee**-nah, *f* guillotine

ghignare, ghe-n'**yah**-ray, *v* to grin, to sneer

ghigno, ghe-n'yo, *m* sneer; grin; ugly face

ghiotto*, ghe-**ot**-to, *adj* gluttonous

ghiottoneria, ghe-ot-to-nay-**ree**-ah, *f* gluttony;

(food) delicacy

ghiribizzo, ghe-re-**bit**-tso, *m* whim

ghirigoro, ghe-re-**go**-ro, *m* scribble; flourish

ghirlanda, gheer-**lahn**-dah, *f* garland

ghiro, **ghe**-ro, *m* dormouse

ghisa, **ghee**-zah, *f* cast iron

già, je'ah, *adv* already; of course; formerly

giacca, je'**ahk**-ah, *f* jacket

giacché, je'ahk-**kay**, *adv* since; seeing that

giacchetta, je'ahk-**ket**-tah, *f* jacket

giacenza, je'ah-**chen**-tsah, *f* in –, (goods) unclaimed, undelivered; (capital) uninvested

giacere, je'ah-**chay**-ray, *v* to lie

giaciglio, je'ah-**chee**-l'yo, *m* pallet, rough bed

giacimento, je'ah-chee-**men**-to, *m* deposit

giacinto, je'ah-**cheen**-to, *m* hyacinth

giaggiolo, je'ahd-**jo**-lo, *m* iris

giaguaro, je'ah-goo'**ah**-ro, *m* jaguar

giallo, je'**ahl**-lo, *adj & m* yellow; (traffic lights) amber

giammai, je'ahm-**mah**-e, *adv* never

Giappone, je'ahp-po-nay,

m Japan

giapponese, je'ahp-po-**nay**-zay, *adj* Japanese

giara, je'**ah**-rah, *f* jar

giardinaggio, je'ar-de-**nahd**-jo, *m* gardening

giardiniera, je'ar-de-ne'**ay**-rah, *f* mixed pickles

giardiniere, -a, je'ar-de-ne'**ay**-ray, *m/f* gardener

giardino, je'ar-**dee**-no, *m* garden; – **d'infanzia**, nursery school; – **zoologico**, zoo

giarrettiera, je'ar-ret-te'**ay**-rah, *f* garter

giavellotto, je'a-vel-**lot**-to, *m* javelin

Gibilterra, je-beel-**tair**-rah, *f* Gibraltar

gigante, jee-**gahn**-tay, *m* giant

giglio, jee-l'yo, *m* lily

gilè, je-**lay**, *m* waistcoat

gin, jeen, *m* gin

ginecologo, -a, je-nay-ko-lo-go, *m/f* gynaecologist

ginepraio, je-nay-**prah**-e'o, *m fig* muddle

ginepro, je-**nay**-pro, *m* juniper

ginestra, je-**nays**-trah, *f* broom

Ginevra, je-**nay**-vrah, *f* Geneva

gingillarsi, jeen-jeell-**lar**-se, *v* to fool about; –

con, to toy with

gingillo, jeen-**jeell**-lo, *m* plaything; knick-knack

ginnasio, jeen-nah-ze-o, *m* 4th and 5th year of secondary school

ginnastica, jeen-**nahss**-te-kah, *f* gymnastics; gym; physical education

ginnico, jeen-ne-ko, *adj* gymnastic

ginocchio, je-**nock**-ke'o, *m* knee

ginocchioni, je-nock-ke'o-ne, *adv* kneeling

giocare, je'o-**kah**-ray, *v* to play; to gamble; to bet

giocatore, -trice, je'o-kah-**tor**-ay, je'o-kah-**tree**-chay, *m/f* player; gambler

giocattolo, je'o-**kaht**-to-lo, *m* toy, plaything

gioco, je'**o**-ko, *m* game; gambling; – **di parole**, pun; **essere in** –, to be at stake; **fare il doppio** –, to double-cross; **per** –, for fun; **prendersi – di qualcuno**, to pull somebody's leg

giocoliere, je'o-ko-le'**ay**-ray, *m* juggler

giocondo, je'o-**kon**-do, *adj* joyful, cheerful

giogo, je'**o**-go, *m* yoke; ridge; mountain range

gioia, je'o-e'ah, *f* joy

gioielleria, je'o-e-ell-lay-ree-ah, *f* jeweller's; jewels

gioielliere, je'o-e-ell-le'ay-ray, *m* jeweller

gioiello, je'o-e-ell-lo, *m* jewel

gioioso*, je'o-e'o-zo, *adj* joyful, merry

gioire, je'o-ee-ray, *v* to rejoice

giornalaio, -a, je'or-nah-lah-e'o, *m/f* newsagent

giornale, je'or-nah-lay, *m* newspaper; journal; diary; – **radio**, radio news

giornaliero, -a, je'or-nah-le'ay-ro, *adj* daily; *m* day pass; *m/f* day labourer

giornalista, je'or-nah-lees-tah, *m/f* journalist

giornata, je'or-nah-tah, *f* day; day's wages

giorno, je'or-no, *m* day; **al –**, per day; **al – d'oggi**, nowadays; **fra quindici giorni**, in a fortnight

giostra, je'os-strah, *f* merry-go-round; joust

giovamento, je'o-vah-men-to, *m* benefit

giovane, je'o-vah-nay, *adj* young; youthful; *m/f* young man; young woman; youth; **i giovani**, young people

giovanile, je'o-vah-nee-lay, *adj* youthful

giovare, je'o-vah-ray, *v* to be useful

giovedì, je'o-vay-dee, *m* Thursday

gioventù, je'o-ven-too, *f* youth; young people

gioviale, je'o-ve'ah-lay, *adj* jovial

giovinezza, je'o-ve-net-tsah, *f* youth, youthfulness

giradischi, je-rah-dis-kee, *m* record player

giraffa, je-rahf-fah, *f* giraffe

girandola, je-rahn-do-lah, *f* (toy) windmill; Catherine wheel; weathercock

girare, je-rah-ray, *v* to turn; to go round; to endorse; (film) to shoot

girarrosto, je-rar-ross-to, *m* spit

girasole, je-rah-so-lay, *m* sunflower

girata, je-rah-tah, *f* endorsement

giratario, -a, je-rah-tah-re'o, *m/f* endorsee

giravolta, je-rah-voll-tah, *f* turn; about-turn

girevole, je-ray-vo-lay, *adj* revolving

girino, je-ree-no, *m* tadpole

giro, jee-ro, *m* turn,

revolution; tour; stroll; circuit; lap

gironzolare, je-ron-dzo-lah-ray, *v* to wander about

girotondo, je-ron-ton-do, *m* ring-a-ring-o'roses

girovago, je-ro-vah-go, *m* tramp; peddlar

gita, jee-tah, *f* excursion, outing

gitano, -a, je-tah-no, *m/f* gipsy

giù, je'oo, *adv* down; below; downwards; – **di lì**, approximately; **essere –**, to be depressed, to be run down

giubbotto, je'oob-bot-to, *m* bomber jacket

giubileo, je'oo-be-lay-o, *m* jubilee

giubilo, je'oo-be-lo, *m* rejoicing

giudicare, je'oo-de-kah-ray, *v* to judge; to consider

giudice, je'oo-de-chay, *m* judge; umpire

giudiziario, je'oo-dee-tse'a-re'o, *adj* judicial, legal

giudizio, je'oo-dee-tse'o, *m* judgement; opinion; trial; verdict

giugno, je'oo-n'yo, *m* June

giullare, je'ool-lah-ray, *m* jester

giumenta, je'oo-**men**-tah, *f* mare

giunchiglia, je'oonn-**kee**-l'yah, *f* jonquil

giunco, je'**oonn**-ko, *m* rush

giungere, je'**oonn**-jay-ray, *v* to arrive; **– a**, to reach

giungla, je'**oonn**-glah, *f* jungle

giunta, je'**oonn**-tah, *f* council; *mil* junta; addition; **per –**, in addition

giuntare, je'oonn-**tah**-ray, *v* to join

giuntura, je'oonn-**too**-rah, *f* joint

giuramento, je'oo-rah-**men**-to, *m* oath

giurare, je'oo-**rah**-ray, *v* to swear; to take an oath

giurato, -a, je'oo-**rah**-to, *adj* sworn; *m/f* juror

giurì, je'oo-**ree**, *m* jury

giuria, je'oo-**ree**-ah, *f* jury

giuridico*, je'oo-**ree**-de-ko, *adj* legal

giurista, je'oo-**riss**-tah, *m/f* jurist

giustezza, je'ooss-**tet**-tsah, *f* accuracy

giustificare, je'ooss-te-fee-**kah**-ray, *v* to justify

giustificazione, je'ooss-te-fee-kah-tse'o-nay, *f* justification; excuse note

giustizia, je'ooss-**tee**-tse'ah, *f* justice

giustiziare, je'ooss-te-tse'**ah**-ray, *v* to execute

giustiziere, je'ooss-te-tse'**ay**-ray, *m* executioner

giusto*, je'**ooss**-to, *adj* just; right; exact

glabro, **glah**-bro, *adj* hairless

glaciale, glah-**chah**-lay, *adj* glacial, icy; frozen

gli, l'yee, *art* the; *pron* to him; to it; to them

glicerina, gle-chay-**ree**-nah, *f* glycerine

glicine, **glee**-chee-nay, *m* wistaria

glielo, l'**yay**-lo, *pron* it to him/her/them

globale, glo-**ba**-lay, *adj* overall; global

globo, **glo**-bo, *m* globe

globulo, glo-**boo**-lo, *m* globule, corpuscle

gloria, **glo**-re'ah, *f* glory

gloriarsi, glo-re'**ar**-se, *v –* **di**, to glory in

glorioso, glo-re'**o**-so, *adj* glorious

glossario, glo-**ssah**-re'o, *m* glossary

gnocchi, ny-**ok**-kee, *mpl* potato and flour dumplings

gobba, **gob**-bah, *f* hump; bump

gobbo, -a, **gob**-bo, *adj* hunchbacked; curved; *m/f* hunchback

goccia, **got**-chah, *f* drop

gocciolare, got-cho-**lah**-ray, *v* to drip, to trickle

godere, go-**day**-ray, *v* to enjoy; to rejoice; **– di**, to enjoy

godimento, go-de-**men**-to, *m* enjoyment, pleasure

goffaggine, gof-**fahd**-je-nay, *f* clumsiness

goffo*, **gof**-fo, *adj* clumsy

gogna, **go**-n'yah, *f* pillory

gola, **go**-lah, *f* throat; gluttony; gorge; **fare –**, to tempt

goletta, go-**let**-tah, *f* schooner

golf, golf, *m* jumper; cardigan

golfo, **gol**-fo, *m* gulf

goloso*, go-**lo**-zo, *adj* greedy

gomena, go-**may**-nah, *f* cable, hawser

gomitata, go-me-**tah**-tah, *f* nudge (with the elbow)

gomito, **go**-me-to, *m* elbow; **curva a –**, hairpin bend; **tubo a –**, L-shaped tube

gomitolo, go-**mee**-to-lo, *m* ball (of thread, of wool)

gomma, **gom**-mah, *f* gum; rubber; eraser

gommapiuma, gom-mah-pee'**oo**-mah, f foam rubber

gondola, gon-do-lah, f gondola

gonfalone, gon-fah-**lo**-nay, m standard, banner

gonfiare, gon-fe'**ah**-ray, v to inflate, to blow up; to swell

gonfio, gon-fe'o, adj swollen; inflated

gonfiore, gon-fe'o-ray, m swelling

gongolare, gon-go-**lah**-ray, v to look pleased

gonna, gon-nah, f skirt

gonzo, gon-dzo, m simpleton

gorgheggiare, gor-ghed-**jah**-ray, v to warble

gorgo, gor-go, m whirlpool

gorgogliare, gor-go-l'**yah**-ray, v to gurgle

gorgoglìo, gor-go-l'**yo**, m gurgling; bubbling

gorilla, gor-**rel**-lah, m gorilla; bodyguard

gota, go-tah, f cheek

gotta, got-tah, f gout

governante, go-vair-**nahn**-tay, f governess; housekeeper; m ruler

governare, go-vair-**nah**-ray, v to rule; to steer

governo, go-**vair**-no, m government; Cabinet

gozzo, got-tso, m goitre;

crop

gozzovigliare, got-tso-ve-l'**yah**-ray, v to revel, to make merry

gracchiare, grahk-ke'**ah**-ray, v to caw, to croak

gracidare, grah-che-**dah**-ray, v to croak

gracile, grah-che-lay, adj delicate; slim

gracilità, grah-che-le-**tah**, f slenderness; delicateness

gradasso, grah-**dahss**-so, m bully, braggart

gradazione, grah-dah-tse'**o**-nay, f gradation

gradevole*, grah-**day**-vo-lay, adj pleasant

gradimento, grah-de-**men**-to, m pleasure, satisfaction

gradinata, grah-de-**nah**-tah, f flight of steps; terraces; tiers

gradino, grah-**dee**-no, m step; rung

gradire, grah-**dee**-ray, v to appreciate; to accept with pleasure

gradito, grah-**dee**-to, adj pleasing, welcome

grado, grah-do, m degree; rank

graduale*, grah-doo'**ah**-lay, adj gradual

graduare, grah-doo'**ah**-ray, v to graduate

graduato, grah-doo'**ah**-to, m non-commissioned officer; adj graduated, graded

graffetta, grahf-**fet**-tah, f paper clip

graffiare, grahf-fe'**ah**-ray, v to scratch, to claw

graffio, grahf-fe'o, m scratch

grafia, grah-**fee**-ah, f spelling; handwriting

grafico, grah-fee-ko, adj graphic; m graph; graphic designer

gramigna, grah-mee-ny'ah, f couch grass

grammatica, grahm-**mah**-tee-kah, f grammar

grammo, grahm-mo, m gramme

grammofono, grahm-mo-fo-no, m gramophone

grana, grah-na, f (of sandpaper, minerals, etc.) grain; (problem) trouble; (money) cash; type of Parmesan cheese

granaio, grah-nah-e'o, m granary; barn

granata, grah-nah-tah, f grenade

Gran Bretagna, grahn bray-**tah**-n'yah, f Great Britain

grancassa, grahn-**kahss**-sah, f big drum

granchio, grahn-ke'o, m

crab; *fig* blunder

grande, grahn-day, *adj**
big, large; great; high;
m/f grown-up

grandezza, grahn-deht-
sah, *f* size; greatness;
manie di –, delusions of
grandeur

grandinare, grahn-de-
nah-ray, *v* to hail

grandine, grahn-de-nay, *f*
hail

grandioso*, grahn-de'o-zo,
adj imposing; grandiose,
grand

granello, grah-nell-lo, *m*
grain; seed; pip

granita, grah-nee-tah, *f*
iced sherbet drink

granito, grah-nee-to, *m*
granite

grano, grah-no, *m* grain;
wheat; bead

granturco, grahn-toohr-
ko, *m* maize, Indian
corn

grappa, grahp-pah, *f*
grappa, type of strong
brandy

grappolo, grahp-po-lo, *m*
bunch (of grapes)

grassetto, grahss-set-to, *m*
bold (type)

grassezza, grahss-set-tsah,
f fatness

grasso, grahss-so, *m* fat;
grease; *adj* fat, plump;
greasy

grassoccio, grahss-sot-
cho, *adj* plump

grata, grah-tah, *f* grate;
grating

graticola, grah-tee-ko-lah,
f gridiron, grill

gratifica, grah-tee-fe-kah,
f bonus

gratificazione, grah-te-fe-
kah-tse'o-nay, *f*
gratification

gratis, grah-tes, *adv* free,
without paying

gratitudine, grah-te-too-
de-nay, *f* gratitude

grato, grah-to, *adj*
grateful; pleasant

grattacapo, graht-tah-ka-
po, *m* worry, problem

**grattacielo, graht-tah-
chay**-lo, *m* skyscraper

grattare, graht-tah-ray, *v*
to scratch; to scrape; to
grate; *fam* to nick

grattugia, graht-too-jah, *f*
grater

grattugiare, graht-too-jah-
ray, *v* to grate

gratuito, grah-too-ee-to,
adj free; gratuitous

gravare, grah-vah-ray, *v* to
burden

grave*, grah-vay, *adj*
grave, serious; (accent)
grave

gravidanza, grah-ve-dan-
tsah, *f* pregnancy

gravità, grah-ve-tah, *f*
gravity

gravitare, grah-ve-tah-ray,
v to gravitate

gravoso*, grah-vo-zo, *adj*
heavy, onerous

grazia, grah-tse'ah, *f*
grace; favour; mercy;
pardon

graziare, grah-tse'ah-ray, *v*
to pardon

grazie, grah-tse'ay, *interj*
thank you! thanks!; **– a**,
thanks to

grazioso*, grah-tse'o-zo,
adj gracious; pretty,
charming

Grecia, gray-che'ah, *f*
Greece

greco, gray-ko, *adj* Greek

gregario, gray-gah-re'o, *adj*
gregarious

gregge, gred-jay, *m* herd,
flock

greggio, gred-jo, *adj* raw,
unrefined; *m* crude oil

grembiule, grem-be'oo-
lay, *m* apron

grembo, grem-bo, *m* lap;
womb; *fig* bosom

gremire, gray-mee-ray, *v*
to crowd

greppia, grayp-pe'ah, *f*
manger

greto, gray-to, *m* gravel
river-bed

gretto*, gret-to, *adj* mean,
petty

grezzo, gred-zo, *adj* raw,

unrefined; coarse

gridare, gre-dah-ray, v to shout, to yell, to cry (out)

grido, gree-do, m cry; shout; **all'ultimo –**, in the latest style

grigio, gree-jo, adj & m grey

griglia, gree-l'yah, f grill; grate; grid

grilletto, greel-let-to, m trigger

grillo, greel-lo, m cricket; fig whim

grimaldello, gre-mahl-del-lo, m picklock

grinfia, green-fe'ah, f claw; **cadere nelle grinfie di,** to fall into the clutches of

grinta, green-tah, f determination; pluck

grinza, green-tsah, f wrinkle; crease

gronda, gron-dah, f eaves

grondaia, gron-da-e'ah, f gutter

grondare, gron-dah-ray, v to drip; to pour

groppa, grop-pah, f (animal) back; (person) shoulders

grossezza, gross-set-tsah, f size; thickness

grossista, gross-siss-tah, m/f wholesaler

grosso, gross-so, m bulk; adj big; thick; **mare –,** rough sea

grossolano*, gross-so-lah-no, adj coarse

grotta, grot-tah, f grotto; cave

grottesco, grot-tes-ko, adj grotesque

groviera, gro-ve'ay-rah, f gruyère

groviglio, gro-vee-l'yo, m tangle

gru, groo, f crane

gruccia, groot-chah, f crutch; coat hanger

grugnire, groo-n'yee-ray, v to grunt

grugnito, groo-n'yee-to, m grunting, grunt

grugno, groo-n'yo, m snout

grullo, grool-lo, m dolt; idiot

grumo, groo-mo, m clot; lump

gruppo, groop-po, m group

gruzzolo, groot-tso-lo, m hoard

guadagnare, goo-ah-dah-n'yah-ray, v to earn; to gain; to win

guadagno, goo-ah-dah-n'yo, m earnings; gain; profit

guadare, goo-ah-dah-ray, v to ford

guado, goo-ah-do, m ford

guai, goo-ah-e, interj – **a,** woe betide

guaina, goo-ah-ee-nah, f sheath

guaio, goo-ah-e'o, m trouble; disaster

guaire, goo-ah-ee-ray, v to yelp, to whine

guancia, goo-ahn-chah, f cheek

guanciale, goo-ahn-chah-lay, m pillow

guanto, goo-ahn-to, m glove

guardare, goo'ar-dah-ray, v to look at; to watch; to look after

guardaroba, goo'ar-dah-ro-bah, f wardrobe; cloakroom

guardia, goo'ar-de'ah, f guard; sentry; policeman

guardiano, goo'ar-de'ah-no, m warder; caretaker; keeper

guardingo, goo'ah-deen-go, adj cautious

guarigione, goo'ah-re-jo-nay, f recovery

guarire, goo'ah-ree-ray, v to cure; to heal; to recover

guaritore, -trice, goo'ah-ree-to-ray, goo'ah-ree-tree-chay, m/f healer

guarnigione, goo'ar-ne-jo-nay, f garrison

guarnire, goo'ar-nee-ray, v

to trim; to garnish

guarnizione, goo'ar-ne-tse'o-nay, *f* trimming; (of tap) washer; *tech* gasket

guastafeste, goo'ahss-tah-**fess**-tay, *m/f* spoilsport

guastare, goo'ahss-**tah**-ray, *v* to spoil; to break

guasto, goo'**ahss**-to, *adj* broken, out of order; rotten; *m* breakdown; failure

guazzabuglio, goo'aht-tsah-**boo**-l'yo, *m* muddle

guercio, goo'**air**-cho, *adj* squinting, cross-eyed

guerra, goo'**air**-rah, *f* war; warfare

guerriero, goo'air-re-**ay**-ro, *m* warrior; *adj* warlike

guerriglia, goo'air-**ree**-l'yah, *f* guerrilla warfare

guerrigliero, -a, goo'air-ree-**l'yay**-ro, *m/f* guerrilla

gufo, goo-fo, *m* owl

guglia, goo-l'yah, *f* spire

guida, goo'ee-dah, *f* guide; guide-book; driving

guidare, goo'e-**dah**-ray, *v* to guide, to lead; to drive

guidatore, -trice, goo'e-dah-**to**-ray, goo'e-dah-**tree**-chay, *m/f* driver

guinzaglio, goo'een-**tsah**-l'yo, *m* leash

guisa, goo'ee-zah, *f* way; **a – di,** in the manner of

guizzare, goo'eet-**tsah**-ray, *v* to dart; to slip; to flash

guizzo, goo'**eet**-tso, *m* dart; leap; flash

guscio, goo-she'o, *m* shell

gustare, gooss-**tah**-ray, *v* to taste; to savour

gusto, gooss-to, *m* taste, flavour; *fig* pleasure

gustoso*, gooss-**to**-zo, *adj* tasty; pleasing

ha, ah, 3rd pers sing of the present of **avere**

habitat, ah-bee-tat, *m* habitat

hai, ah'ee, 2nd pers sing of the present of **avere**

hall, ohl, *f* (hotel) hall, foyer

hamburger, ahm-**boor**-gher, *m* hamburger

handicappato, -a, ahn-dee-kap-**pah**-to, *adj* handicapped; *m/f* handicapped person, disabled person

hanno, ahn-no, 3rd pers plur of the present of **avere**

hippy, eep-py, *m/f* hippy

ho, oh, 1st pers sing of the present of **avere**

hobby, ohb-bee, *m* hobby

hockey, oh-kee, *m* hockey; **– su ghiacco,** ice hockey

hostess, ohs-stess, *f* air hostess; escort

hotel, oh-**tel,** *m* hotel

i, e, *art* the

iarda, e'**ar**-dah, *f* yard

iato, e'**ah**-to, *m* hiatus

ibrido, **ee**-bre-do, *adj* hybrid; *m* hybrid

iceberg, **ah**'es-berg, *m* iceberg

iconografia, e-ko-no-grah-**fee**-ah, *f* hiconography

Iddio, eed-**dee**-o, *m* God

idea, e-**day**-ah, *f* idea; **cambiare –**, to change one's mind

ideale, e-**day**'ah-lay, *adj* ideal; *m* ideal

ideare, e-day-**ah**-ray, *v* to imagine, to conceive; to plan

identico, e-**den**-te-ko, *adj* identical

identificare, e-den-te-fe-**kah**-ray, *v* to identify

identità, e-den-te-**tah**, *f* identity

idillio, e-**deel**-le'o, *m* idyll

idioma, e-dee'o-mah, *m* language

idiomatico, e-dee'o-**mah**-te-ko, *adj* idiomatic; **frase idiomatica**, idiom

idiota, e-de'o-tah, *adj* stupid; *m/f* idiot

idolatria, e-do-lah-**tree**-ah, *f* idolatry

idolo, **ee**-do-lo, *m* idol

idoneità, e-do-nay-e-**tah**, *f* suitability; fitness

idoneo*, e-do-**nay**-o, *adj* able, fit; suitable

idrante, e-**drahn**-tay, *m* hydrant

idratante, e-drah-**tahn**-tay, *adj* moisturizing

idraulica, e-**drah**'oo-le-kah, *f* hydraulics

idroelettrico, e-dro-ay-**let**-tre-ko, *adj* hydroelectric

idrofobia, e-dro-fo-**bee**-ah, *f* rabies

idrogeno, e-**dro**-jay-no, *m* hydrogen

idropisia, e-dro-pe-**see**-ah, *f* dropsy

idrovolante, e-dro-vo-**lahn**-tay, *m* seaplane

iena, e'**ay**-nah, *f* hyena

ieri, e'**ay**-re, *adv* yesterday

iettatura, e'ayt-tah-**too**-rah, *f* evil eye; spell

igiene, e-je'**ay**-nay, *f* hygiene, health

igienico, e-je'**ay**-ne-ko, *adj* hygienic; **carta igienica**, toilet paper

ignaro, e-n'**yah**-ro, *adj* – **di**, ignorant of, unaware of

ignobile*, e-n'yo-be-lay, *adj* despicable, ignoble

ignorante, e-n'yo-**rahn**-tay, *adj* ignorant

ignoranza, e-n'yo-**rahn**-tsah, *f* ignorance

ignorare, e-n'yo-**rah**-ray, *v* to ignore, to be unaware of

ignoto, e-n'yo-to, *adj* unknown

ignudo, e-n'**yoo**-do, *adj* naked

il, eel, *art* the

ilare, **ee**-lah-ray, *adj*

cheerful, joyous

illanguidire, eel-lahn-goo'e-**dee**-ray, *v* to languish

illazione, ell-lah-tse'**o**-nay, *f* deduction

illecito*, eel-**lay**-che-to, *adj* illicit

illegale*, eel-lay-**gah**-lay, *adj* illegal

illeggibile, eel-layd-**jee**-be-lay, *adj* illegible; unreadable

illegittimo, eel-lay-**jeet**-te-mo, *adj* illegitimate

illeso, eel-**lay**-zo, *adj* unharmed, unhurt

illibato, eel-le-**bah**-to, *adj* pure; virgin

illimitato*, eel-le-me-**tah**-to, *adj* unlimited

illudere, eel-**loo**-day-ray, *v* to deceive

illuminare, eel-loo-me-**nah**-ray, *v* to light

illuminazione, eel-loo-mee-nah-tse'**o**-nay, *f* lighting

illusione, eel-looss-zee'**o**-nay, *f* illusion

illustrare, eel-looss-**trah**-ray, *v* to illustrate

illustrazione, eel-loo-strah-tse'**o**-nay, *f* lighting

illustre, eel-**looss**-tray, *adj* illustrious

imbacuccare, im-bah-

kook-**kah**-ray, *v* to wrap up

imballaggio, im-bahl-**lahd**-jo, *m* packing; wrapper

imballare, im-bahl-**lah**-ray, *v* to pack

imbalsamare, im-bahl-sah-**mah**-ray, *v* to embalm

imbandierare, im-bahn-de'ay-**rah**-ray, *v* to deck with flags

imbandire, im-bahn-**dee**-ray, *v* to set the table (for a lavish feast)

imbarazzare, im-bah-raht-**tsah**-ray, *v* to embarrass; to hinder

imbarazzo, im-bah-**raht**-tso, *m* embarrassment

imbarcadero, im-bar-kah-**day**-ro, *m* landing-stage

imbarcarsi, im-bar-**kahr**-se, *v* to sail; to board; − **in,** to embark on

imbarcazione, im-bar-kah-tse'**o**-nay, *f* boat, craft

imbarco, im-**bar**-ko, *m* embarkation; landing-stage

imbastire, im-bah-**stee**-ray, *v* to tack; *fig* to sketch out

imbattersi, im-**baht**-tair-se, *v* − **in,** to run into; *fig* to come across

imbattuto, im-baht-**too**-to, *adj* unbeaten

imbavagliare, im-bah-vah-l'**yah**-ray, *v* to gag

imbeccata, im-bek-**kah**-tah, *f* prompt

imbecille, im-bay-**cheel**-lay, *m/f* imbecile; *adj* idiotic

imbellettarsi, im-bell-let-**tar**-se, *v* to make oneself up

imbellire, im-bell-**lee**-ray, *v* to adorn; to grow more beautiful

imberbe, im-**bair**-bay, *adj* beardless

imbevere, im-**bay**-vay-ray, *v* to soak

imbiancare, im-be'ahn-**kah**-ray, *v* to whiten; to whitewash

imbianchino, im-be'ahn-**kee**-no, *m* painter and decorator

imbizzarrirsi, im-bid-dzar-**reer**-se, *v* to bolt; to get excited

imboccare, im-bock-**kah**-ray, *v* to enter; to spoon-feed; *fig* to prompt

imbocco, im-**bock**-ko, *m* entrance; mouth

imboscarsi, im-boss-**kar**-se, *v* to hide; to avoid military service

imboscata, im-boss-**kah**-tah, *f* ambush

imboschimento, im-boss-kee-**men**-to, *m* afforestation

imbottigliare, im-bot-te-l'yah-ray, *v* to bottle

imbottire, im-bot-tee-ray, *v* to stuff; to pad

imbottitura, im-bot-te-**too**-rah, *f* stuffing; padding

imbrattare, im-braht-**tah**-ray, *v* to soil, to stain

imbrigliare, im-bre-l'yah-ray, *v* to bridle

imbrogliare, im-bro-l'yah-ray, *v* to mix up; to deceive

imbroglio, im-**bro**-l'yo, *m* muddle, mess; fraud

imbroglione, -a, im-bro-l'yo-nay, *m/f* swindler

imbronciato, im-bron-**cha**-to, *adj* sulky

imbruttire, im-broot-tee-ray, *v* to grow ugly

imbucare, im-boo-**kah**-ray, *v* to post

imburrare, im-boor-**ra**-ray, *v* to butter

imbuto, im-**boo**-to, *m* funnel

imitare, e-me-**tah**-ray, *v* to imitate

immacolato, im-mah-ko-**lah**-to, *adj* immaculate

immagazzinare, im-mah-gahd-dze-**nah**-ray, *v* to store

immaginare, im-mah-je-**nah**-ray, *v* to imagine

immaginazione, im-mah-je-nah-tse'o-nay, *f* imagination

immagine, im-**mah**-je-nay, *f* image; picture

immancabile, im-mahn-**kah**-be-lay, *adj* unfailing

immane, im-**mah**-nay, *adj* huge

immaturo, im-mah-**too**-ro, *adj* immature

immedesimarsi, im-may-day-ze-**mar**-se, *v* to identify with

immediatamente, im-may-de'ah-tah-**men**-tay, *adv* immediately

immemore, in-**may**-mo-ray, *adj* – **di,** forgetful of

immenso, in-**mayn**-so, *adj* immense

immergere, im-**mair**-jay-ray, *v* to submerge; to dip

immersione, im-mair-see'o-nay, *f* immersion; dive

immettere, im-**mait**-tay-ray, *v* to enter (data); to introduce

immigrato, -a, im-me-**grah**-to, *m/f* immigrant

immigrazione, im-me-grah-tse'o-nay, *f* immigration

imminente, im-mee-nen-

tay, *adj* imminent

immischiarsi, im-miss-ke'**ar**-se, *v* to meddle in

immissione, im-miss-se'o-nay, *f* intake; introduction; – **di dati,** data entry

immobile, im-**mo**-bee-lay, *adj* motionless, still

immolare, im-mo-**lah**-ray, *v* to sacrifice

immondizia, im-mon-dee-tse'ah, *f* dirt; rubbish

immondo, im-**mon**-do, *adj* filthy

immorale, im-mo-**rah**-lay, *adj* immoral

immortale, im-mor-**rtah**-lay, *adj* immortal

immune, im-**moo**-nay, *adj* immune; exempt

immutato, im-moo-**tah**-to, *adj* unaltered

impacchettare, im-pahk-ket-**tah**-ray, *v* to wrap up

impacciare, im-paht-**chah**-ray, *v* to embarrass; to get in the way of

impaccio, im-**paht**-cho, *m* embarrassment; obstacle; **essere d'–,** to be in the way

impadronirsi, im-pah-dro-**neer**-se, *v* – **di,** to get hold of

impagabile, im-pah-**gah**-be-lay, *adj* priceless

impagliare, im-pah-l'yah-ray, *v* to stuff (with straw)

impalato, im-pah-**lah**-to, *adj* stiff

impalcatura, im-pahl-kah-**too**-rah, *f* scaffolding

impallidire, im-pahl-le-**dee**-ray, *v* to turn pale

impanare, im-pah-**nah**-ray, *v* to roll in breadcrumbs

impappinato, im-pahp-pe-**nah**-to, *adj* confused; stammering

imparare, im-pah-**rah**-ray, *v* to learn

impareggiabile, im-pah-red-**jah**-be-lay, *adj* incomparable

imparentato, im-pah-ren-**tah**-to, *adj* related

impari, im-**pah**-re, *adj* unequal

impartire, im-par-**tee**-ray, *v* to impart, to give

imparziale, im-par-tse'**ah**-lay, *adj* impartial

impassibile, im-pahss-**see**-be-lay, *adj* impassive

impastare, im-pahss-**tah**-ray, *v* to knead; to mix

impasto, im-**pahss**-to, *m* mixing; kneading; mixture

impatto, im-**paht**-to, *m* impact

impaurire, im-pah'oo-**ree**-ray, *v* to scare

impavido*, im-**pah**-ve-do, *adj* intrepid, fearless

impaziente, im-pah-tse'**en**-tay, *adj* impatient

impazientirsi, im-pah-tse'en-**teer**-se, *v* to lose patience

impazzire, im-paht-**tsee**-ray, *v* to go mad

impedimento, im-pay-de-**men**-to, *m* obstacle; hindrance

impedire, im-pay-**dee**-ray, *v* to prevent; to hinder

impegnare, im-pay-**n'yah**-ray, *v* to pledge

impegnarsi, im-pah-**n'yahr**-se, *v* to undertake

impegnativo, im-pah-n'yah-**te**-vo, *adj* demanding

impegnato, im-pah-**n'yah**-to, *adj* demanding

impegno, im-**pay**-n'yo, *m* pledge; engagement

impellente, im-pel-**len**-tay, *adj* pressing

impenetrabile, im-pay-nay-**trah**-be-lay, *adj* inscrutable, impenetrable

impensabile, im-pen-**sah**-be-lay, *adj* unthinkable

impensato, im-pen-**sah**-to, *adj* unforeseen

impensierito, im-pen-se-ay-**ree**-to, *adj* worried

imperativo, im-pay-rah-**tee**-vo, *adj* imperative; *m* imperative

imperatore, -trice, im-pay-rah-**to**-ray, im-pay-rah-**tree**-chay, *m/f* emperor, empress

imperfetto, im-payr-**fet**-to, *adj* imperfect; *m* imperfect

imperioso, im-pay-re'**o**-so, *adj* urgent, pressing; imperious

imperizia, im-pay-**ree**-tse'ah, *f* lack of experience

impermeabile, im-per-me'**ah**-bee-lay, *m* raincoat; *adj* waterproof

impero, im-**pay**-ro, *m* empire; rule

impersonale, im-pair-so-**nah**-lay, *adj* impersonal

impersonare, im-pair-so-**nah**-ray, *v* to personalify

imperterrito, im-pair-**tair**-re-to, *adj* fearless

impertinente, im-per-tee-**nen**-tay, *adj* impertinent

imperversare, im-pair-vair-**sah**-ray, *v* to rage

impeto, im-**pay**-to, *m* impetus, impulse

impetuoso, im-pay-too'**o**-so, *adj* impetuous; raging

impiantare, im-pe'ahn-**tah**-ray, *v* to install; to found

impianto, im-pe'**ahn**-to, *m* plant, installation

impiastricciare, im-pe'ahss-trit-**chah**-ray, *v* to smear

impiastro, im-pe'**ahss**-tro, *m* poultice; *fam* nuisance

impiccare, im-pick-**kah**-ray, *v* to hang

impicciare, im-pit-**chah**-ray, *v* to embarrass

impiccio, im-**pit**-cho, *m* embarrassment

impiegare, im-pe'ay-**gah**-ray, *v* to employ, to use; to spend (time)

impiegato, -a, im-pe'ay-**gah**-to, *m/f* clerk, employee

impiego, im-pe'**ay**-go, *m* employment; post, job

impietosire, im-pe'ay-to-**zee**-ray, *v* to move to pity

impietrire, im-pe'ay-**tree**-ray, *v* to petrify

impigliare, im-pe-l'**yah**-ray, *v* to entangle

impigrire, im-pe-**gree**-ray, *v* to become indolent

implacabile, im-plah-**kah**-bee-lay, *adj* implacable

implicare, im-ple-**kah**-ray, *v* to implicate

implicito, im-**plee**-che-to, *adj* implicit

impolverare, im-pol-vay-**rah**-ray, *v* to cover with dust

imponente, im-po-**nen**-tay, *adj* imposing

imponibile, im-po-nee-**bee**-lay, *adj* taxable

impopolare, im-po-po-**lah**-ray, *adj* unpopular

imporre, im-**por**-ray, *v* to impose

imporsi, im-**por**-se, *v* to assert oneself; to become necessary

importante, im-por-**tahn**-tay, *adj* important

importanza, im-por-**tahn**-tsah, *f* importance

importare, im-por-**tah**-ray, *v* to import; to matter

importo, im-**por**-to, *m* total amount, sum

importunare, im-por-too-**nah**-ray, *v* to disturb, to bother

impossessarsi, im-pos-says-**sar**-se, *v – di,* to take possession of, to seize

impossibile, im-pos-see-**bee**-lay, *adj* impossible

imposta, im-**poss**-tah, *f* duty, tax; shutter

impostare, im-poss-**tah**-ray, *v* to post; to organize; to set out

impostore, -a, im-poss-**tor**-ay, *m/f* impostor

impotente, im-po-**ten**-tay, *adj* powerless; impotent

impratichirsi, im-prah-te-**keer**-se, *v* to practise

imprecare, im-pray-**kah**-ray, *v* to curse

impregnare, im-pray-n'**yah**-ray, *v* to impregnate

imprendere, im-**pren**-day-ray, *v* to undertake

imprenditore, im-pren-de-**tor**-ay, *m* entrepreneur; contractor

impresa, im-**pray**-zah, *f* undertaking, enterprise; exploit; firm

impresario, -a, im-pray-za-re'o, *m/f* theatre manager

impressionare, im-press-e'o-**nah**-ray, *v* to impress; to upset

impressione, im-press-se'o-nay, *f* impression

imprestare, im-pres-**tah**-ray, *v* to lend

impreveduto, im-pray-vay-**doo**-to, *adj* unforeseen

imprevidente, im-pray-vee-**den**-tay, *adj* improvident

imprevisto, im-pray-**viss**-to, *adj* unexpected

imprigionamento, im-pre-jo-nah-**men**-to, *m* imprisonment

imprigionare, im-pre-jo-nah-ray, v to imprison

imprimere, im-**pree**-may-ray, v to impress

improbabile, im-pro-**bah**-bee-lay, adj improbable

improduttivo, im-pro-doot-**tee**-vo, adj unproductive; unprofitable

impronta, im-**pron**-tah, f impression; footprint; mark

improperio, im-pro-**payr**e'o, m insult, abuse

improprio, im-pro-pre'o, adj improper

improvvisare, im-prov-ve-**zah**-ray, v to improvise

improvvisata, im-prov-ve-**zah**-tah, f agreeable surprise

improvviso*, im-prov-**vee**-zo, adj sudden; unexpected

imprudente, im-proo-**den**-tay, adj careless; unwise

impugnare, im-poo-n'**yah**-ray, v to seize; to contest

impugnatura, im-poo-n'yah-**too**-rah, f hilt; handle

impulsivo*, im-pool-**see**-vo, adj impulsive

impulso, im-**pool**-so, m impulse

impuntarsi, im-poonn-**tar**-se, v to be obstinate

impuro, im-**poo**-ro, adj impure

imputare, im-poo-**tah**-ray, v to attribute; law to charge

imputato, -a, im-poo-**tah**-to, m/f law defendant, accused

in, in, prep in; into; on; upon; at; within

inabile, in-**ah**-be-lay, adj unfit; disable

inabitato, in-ah-be-**tah**-to, adj uninhabited

inaccessibile, in-aht-ches-**see**-be-lay, adj inaccessible

inaccettabile, in-aht-chet-**tah**-be-lay, adj unacceptable

inadeguato*, in-ah-day-goo'**ah**-to, adj inadequate

inalare, in-ah-**lah**-ray, v to inhale

inalberare, in-ahl-bay-**rah**-ray, v naut to hoist

inalterabile, in-ahl-tay-**rah**-be-lay, adj unalterable

inamidare, in-ah-me-**dah**-ray, v to starch

inanimato, in-ah-ne-**mah**-to, adj inanimate; lifeless

inappagato, in-ahp-pah-**gah**-to, adj unfulfilled

inappetenza, in-ahp-pay-**tent**-tsah, f lack of appetite

inappuntabile, in-ahp-poon-**tah**-be-lay, adj irreproachable

inarcare, in-**ar**-kah-ray, v to arch

inaridire, in-ah-re-**dee**-ray, v to dry up

inaspettato*, in-ahss-pet-**tah**-to, adj unexpected

inasprire, in-ahss-**pree**-ray, v to irritate; to make harsher

inatteso, in-aht-**tay**-zo, adj unexpected

inattuabile, in-aht-too'**ah**-be-lay, adj impracticable

inaudito, in-ah'oo-**dee**-to, adj unheard of

inaugurare, in-ah'oo-goo-**rah**-ray, v to inaugurate

incagliare, in-kah-l'**yah**-ray, v naut to run aground

incallito, in-kahl-**lee**-to, adj hardened

incalzare, in-kahl-**tsah**-ray, v to pursue

incamminarsi, in-kahm-me-**nar**-se, v to set out

incandescente, in-kahn-day-**shen**-tay, adj incandescent; white-hot

incantare, in-kahn-**tah**-ray, v to enchant

incantevole, in-kahn-**tay**-vo-lay, adj enchanting

incanto, in-**kahn**-to, m spell; auction

incanutire, in-kah-noo-tee-ray, *v* to go white

incapace, in-kah-**pah**-chay, *adj* incapable, unable

incapacità, in-kah-pah-che-**tah**, *f* incapacity, inability

incarcerare, in-kar-chay-**rah**-ray, *v* to imprison

incarcerazione, in-kar-chay-rah-tse'**o**-nay, *f* imprisonment

incaricare, in-kah-re-**kah**-ray, *v* to entrust

incaricato, in-kah-re-**kah**-to, *adj* responsible, in charge

incarico, in-kah-re-ko, *m* task; charge; post

incarnare, in-kar-**nah**-ray, *v* to embody

incarnarsi, in-kar-**nar**-se, *v* to incarnate

incartamento, in-kar-tah-**men**-to, *m* file

incartare, in-kar-**tah**-ray, *v* to wrap up in paper

incassare, in-kahss-**sah**-ray, *v* to receive; to cash; to pack (in cases); (gem) to set

incasso, in-**kahss**-so, *m* takings

incastrare, in-kahss-**trah**-ray, *v* to fit in; to trap

incastro, in-**kahss**-tro, *m* groove

incatenare, in-kah-tay-**nah**-ray, *v* to chain

incatramare, in-kah-trah-**mah**-ray, *v* to tar

incauto*, in-kah'oo-to, *adj* imprudent

incavare, in-kah-**vah**-ray, *v* to hollow out

incavo, **in**-kah-vo, *m* notch; hollow; groove

incazzato, in-kat-**tsah**-to, *adj vulg* pissed off

incendiare, in-chen-de'**ah**-ray, *v* to set fire to

incendio, in-**chen**-de'o, *m* fire; – **doloso**, arson

incenerire, in-chay-nay-**ree**-ray, *v* to incinerate

incenso, in-**chen**-so, *m* incense

incentivo, in-chen-**tee**-vo, *m* incentive

inceppare, in-chep-**pah**-ray, *v* to hinder; to jam

incerata, in-chay-**rah**-tah, *f* tarpaulin

incertezza, in-**chair**-**tet**-tsah, *f* uncertainty

incerto, in-**chair**-to, *adj* uncertain; unsettled

incessante, in-chess-**sahn**-tay, *adj* incessant

incesto, in-**ches**-to, *m* incest

incetta, in-**chet**-tah, *f* hoarding; **fare – di**, to stockpile, to corner

inchiesta, in-ke'**ess**-tah, *f* inquest; inquiry, investigation

inchinarsi, in-ke-**nar**-se, *v* to bow; to curtsey

inchino, in-**kee**-no, *m* bow, curtsey

inchiodare, in-ke'o-**dah**-ray, *v* to nail

inchiostro, in-ke'**oss**-tro, *m* ink

inciampare, in-chahm-**pah**-ray, *v* to stumble

inciampo, in-**chahm**-po, *m* obstacle

incidente, in-che-**den**-tay, *m* accident; incident; – **aereo**, plane crash

incidenza, in-che-**den**-tsah, *f* effect; **angolo d'–**, angle of incidence

incidere, in-**chee**-day-ray, *v* to cut, to engrave; *mus* to record

incinta, in-**chin**-tah, *adj* pregnant

incipriarsi, in-che-pre'**ar**-se, *v* to powder one's face

incirca, in-**cheer**-kah, *adv* **all'–**, approximately

incisione, in-che-ze'**o**-nay, *f* engraving; incision; *mus* recording

incisore, in-che-**zor**-ay, *m* engraver

incitamento, in-che-tah-**men**-to, *m* incitement

incitare, in-che-**tah**-ray, *v*

to incite

incivile, in-che-**vee**-lay, *adj* impolite; uncivilized

inclinare, in-kle-**nah**-ray, *v* to incline; to tilt, to tip

inclinazione, in-kle-naht-tse'**o**-nay, *f* inclination; slope; gradient

incline, in-**klee**-nay, *adj* – **a,** inclined to, prone to

includere, in-kloo-**day**-ray, *v* to include; to enclose

incluso, in-**kloo**-zo, *adj* included; enclosed

incoerente*, in-ko-ay-**ren**-tay, *adj* incoherent

incognito, in-**ko**-ny-to, *adj* unknown; **mantenere l'–,** to remain incognito

incollare, in-koll-**lah**-ray, *v* to stick; to glue

incolore, in-ko-**lo**-ray, *adj* colourless

incolpare, in-koll-**pah**-ray, *v* to blame; to accuse

incolto, in-**koll**-to, *adj* uncultivated; *fig* rough, uneducated

incolume, in-**ko**-loo-may, *adj* unharmed, safe and sound

incombente, in-kom-**ben**-tay, *adj* impending

incombenza, in-kom-**ben**-tsah, *f* task; errand

incominciare, in-kom-

men-**chah**-ray, *v* to begin, to start

incomodare, in-ko-mo-**dah**-ray, *v* to inconvenience

incomodo, in-**ko**-mo-do, *m* inconvenience; trouble

incomparabile*, in-kom-pa-**rah**-be-lay, *adj* incomparable

incompatibile*, in-kom-pah-**tee**-be-lay, *adj* incompatible

incompetente, in-kom-pay-**ten**-tay, *adj* incompetent

incompiuto, in-kom-pe'**oo**-to, *adj* unfinished

incompleto, in-kom-**play**-to, *adj* incomplete

incomprensibile*, in-kom-pren-**see**-be-lay, *adj* incomprehensible

inconcepibile*, in-kon-chay-**pee**-be-lay, *adj* inconceivable

incondizionato*, in-kon-dee-tse'o-**nah**-to, *adj* unconditional

inconfondibile*, in-kon-fon-**dee**-be-lay, *adj* unmistakable

inconsapevole*, in-kon-sah-**pay**-vo-lay, *adj* unaware

inconscio*, in-**kon**-sho, *adj* unconscious,

unaware

inconsistente, in-kon-siss-**ten**-tay, *adj* inconsistent

inconsolabile*, in-kon-so-**lah**-be-lay, *adj* inconsolable

inconsueto, in-kon-soo'**ay**-to, *adj* unusual

inconsulto, in-kon-**sooll**-to, *adj* hasty, rash

incontentabile*, in-kon-ten-**tah**-be-lay, *adj* insatiable; hard to please

incontrare, in-kon-**trah**-ray, *v* to meet; to come up against

incontro, in-**kon**-tro, *m* meeting; encounter; (sport) match; *prep* – **a,** towards

inconveniente, in-kon-vay-ne'**ayn**-tay, *m* setback; disadvantage

incoraggiamento, in-ko-rahd-jah-**men**-to, *m* encouragement

incoraggiare, in-ko-rah-**jah**-ray, *v* to encourage

incorniciare, in-kor-ne-**chah**-ray, *v* to frame

incoronare, in-ko-ro-**nah**-ray, *v* to crown

incoronazione, in-ko-ro-nah-tse'**o**-nay, *f* coronation

incorporare, in-kor-po-**rah**-ray, *v* to incorporate

incorreggibile*, in-kor-red-**jee**-be-lay, *adj* incorrigible

incorrere, in-**kor**-ray-ray, *v* to incur

incorruttibile*, in-kor-root-**tee**-be-lay, *adj* incorruptible

incosciente*, in-ko-she'**en**-tay, *adj* unconscious

incostante, in-koss-**tahn**-tay, *adj* inconstant; inconsistent

incostanza, in-koss-**tahn**-tsah, *f* fickleness

incredibile*, in-kray-**dee**-be-lay, *adj* incredible

incredulo, in-**kray**-doo-lo, *adj* incredulous

incremento, in-kray-**men**-to, *m* increment, rise

increspare, in-kress-**pah**-ray, *v* to curl; to ripple

incriminare, in-kree-mee-**nah**-ray, *v law* to charge

incrinare, in-kree-**nah**-ray, *v* to crack

incrociare, in-kro-**chah**-ray, *v* to cross; to cruise

incrociatore, in-kro-chah-**tor**-ay, *m* cruiser

incrocio, in-**kro**-cho, *m* crossing; crossroads

incrollabile, in-krol-**lah**-be-lay, *adj* unshakeable

incrostare, in-kross-**tah**-ray, *v* to encrust

incruento, in-kroo'**en**-to, *adj* bloodless

incubatrice, in-koo-bah-**tree**-chay, *f* incubator

incubo, in-**koo**-bo, *m* nightmare

incudine, in-**koo**-de-nay, *f* anvil

inculcare, in-kool-**kah**-ray, *v* to inculcate

incurabile, in-koo-**rah**-be-lay, *adj* incurable

incurante, in-koo-**rahn**-tay, *adj* heedless

incuria, in-koo-re'ah, *f* negligence, carelessness

incuriosito, in-kooh-ree'o-**see**-to, *adj* curious

incursione, in-koohr-se'o-nay, *f* raid

incurvare, in-koohr-**vah**-ray, *v* to bend

incustodito, in-kooss-to-**dee**-to, *adj* unguarded, unattended

incutere, in-**koo**-tay-ray, *v* to induce

indaco, in-**dah**-ko, *m* indigo

indaffarato, in-dahf-fah-**rah**-to, *adj* busy

indagare, in-dah-**gah**-ray, *v* to investigate

indagine, in-**dah**-je-nay, *f* research, enquiry

indebitarsi, in-day-be-**tar**-se, *v* to run into debts

indebito*, in-**day**-be-to,

adj undue; undeserved

indebolire, in-day-bo-lee-ray, *v* to weaken

indecente*, in-day-**chen**-tay, *adj* indecent

indecenza, in-day-**chen**-tsah, *f* indecency

indecisione, in-day-che-ze'o-nay, *f* indecision

indeciso, in-day-**chee**-zo, *adj* undecided; indecisive

indefesso, in-day-**fess**-so, *adj* untiring

indefinito, in-day-fee-**nee**-to, *adj* undefined; indefinite

indegno*, in-**day**-n'yo, *adj* unworthy; shameful

indemoniato, in-day-mo-ne'ah-to, *adj* possessed; *m* one possessed

indenne, in-**den**-nay, *adj* undamaged

indennità, in-den-ne-tah, *f* indemnity; – **di trasferta**, travel allowance

indennizzare, in-den-nid-**dzah**-ray, *v* to indemnify, to compensate

indesiderabile, in-day-ze-day-**rah**-be-lay, *adj* undesirable

indeterminato, in-day-tayr-mee-**nah**-to, *adj* indefinite, unspecified

India, in-de'ah, *f* India

indiano, in-de-**ah**-no, *adj* Indian

indicare, in-de-**kah**-ray, *v* to indicate, to point out

indicatore, in-de-kah-**tor**-ay, *m tech* gauge, indicator

indicazione, in-de-kah-tse'**o**-nay, *f* indication; information; **indicazioni,** directions

indice, in-de-chay, *m* index; forefinger; table of contents; *fig* sign

indicibile*, in-de-**chee**-be-lay, *adj* unutterable, inexpressible

indietreggiare, in-de'ay-tred-**jah**-ray, *v* to draw back; *mil* to retreat

indietro, in-de'**ay**-tro, *adv* backwards

indifeso, in-de-**fay**-zo, *adj* undefended

indifferente*, in-deef-fay-**ren**-tay, *adj* indifferent

indifferenza, in-deef-fay-**ren**-tsah, *f* indifference

indigeno, -a, in-**dee**-jay-no, *adj* native; *m/f* native

indigente, in-de-**jen**-tay, *adj* poor, destitute; *m/f* needy person, pauper

indigenza, in-de-**jen**-tsah, *f* destitution

indigestione, in-de-jay-ste'**o**-nay, *f* indigestion

indigesto, in-de-**jess**-to, *adj* indigestible

indignato, in-de-**n'yah**-to, *adj* indignant

indipendente*, in-de-pen-**den**-tay, *adj* independent

indire, in-**dee**-ray, *v* to announce; (elections) to call

indiretto, in-de-**ret**-to, *adj* indirect

indirizzare, in-de-rit-**tsah**-ray, *v* to direct; to address

indirizzo, in-de-**rit**-tso, *m* address; trend, direction

indisciplinato, in-de-shee-plee-**nah**-to, *adj* undisciplined, unruly

indiscreto, in-diss-**kray**-to, *adj* indiscreet

indiscutibile*, in-diss-koo-**tee**-be-lay, *adj* unquestionable

indispensabile, in-diss-pen-**sah**-be-lay, *adj* indispensable

indisporre, in-diss-**por**-ray, *v* to antagonize

indisposto, in-diss-**poss**-to, *adj* indisposed, unwell

indissolubile*, in-diss-so-**loo**-be-lay, *adj* indissoluble

indistruttibile*, in-diss-troot-**tee**-be-lay, *adj* indestructible

indivia, in-**dee**-ve'ah, *f* endive

individuale, in-de-vee-doo-**ah**-lay, *adj* individual

individuare, in-de-vee-doo-**ah**-ray, *v* to identify, to locate

individuo, in-de-vee-**doo**'o, *m* individual

indivisibile, in-de-ve-zee-be-lay, *adj* indivisible

indiziato, -a, in-dee-tse'**ah**-to, *m/f* suspect

indizio, in-**dee**-tse'o, *m* indication; clue

indole, in-do-lay, *f* nature; bent, disposition

indolente, in-do-**len**-tay, *adj* indolent, lazy

indolenza, in-do-**len**-tsah, *f* indolence

indolenzimento, in-do-len-tse-**men**-to, *m* numbness, stiffness

indolore, in-do-**lo**-ray, *adj* painless

indomani, in-do-**mah**-ne, *m* l'–, the next day

indomito, in-**do**-meeh-to, *adj* indomitable

indorare, in-do-**rah**-ray, *v* – la pillola, to sugar the pill

indossare, in-doss-**sah**-ray, *v* to put on; to wear

indossatore, -trice, in-doss-sah-**to**-ray, in-doss-sah-**tree**-chay, *m/f* model

indovinare, in-do-ve-**nah**-ray, *v* to guess; to predict

indovinello, in-do-ve-**nell**-lo, *m* riddle

indovino, -a, in-do-**vee**-no, *m/f* fortune-teller

indubbio*, in-**doob**-be'o, *adj* undoubted

indugiare, in-doo-**jah**-ray, *v* to delay

indugio, in-**doo**-jo, *m* delay; hesitation

indulgente, in-dool-**jen**-tay, *adj* indulgent

indulgere, in-**dool**-jay-ray, *v* to pardon; to indulge

indumento, in-doo-**men**-to, *m* item of clothing

indurire, in-doo-**ree**-ray, *v* to harden

indurre, in-**doohr**-ray, *v* to induce

industria, in-**dooss**-tre-ah, *f* industry

industriale, in-dooss-tre-**ah**-lay, *m/f* industrialist, *adj* industrial

ineccepibile, in-ayt-chay-**pee**-be-lay, *adj* exemplary

inedia, in-ay-de'ah, *f* starvation

inedito, in-**ay**-de-to, *adj* unpublished

inefficace, in-ef-fe-**kah**-chay, *adj* ineffective

inefficiente, in-ef-fe-chen-tay, *adj* inefficient

ineguaglianza, in-ay-goo'ah-ll'**yan**-tsah, *f* inequality; unevenness

ineguale, in-ay-goo'**ah**-lay, *adj* unequal; uneven

inerente*, in-ay-**ren**-tay, *adj* inherent

inerme, in-**air**-may, *adj* unarmed

inerzia, in-**air**-tse'ah, *f* inertia

inesatto, in-ay-**zaht**-to, *adj* inexact, incorrect

inesauribile*, in-ay-zah'oo-**ree**-be-lay, *adj* inexhaustible

inescusabile, in-ess-koo-**zah**-be-lay, *adj* inexcusable

inesistente, in-ay-ze-**sten**-tay, *adj* non-existent

inesorabile*, in-ay-zo-**rah**-be-lay, *adj* inexorable, relentless

inesperto, in-ess-**pair**-to, *adj* inexpert

inesplicabile*, in-ess-ple-**kah**-be-lay, *adj* inexplicable

inesprimibile, in-ess-pre-**mee**-be-lay, *adj* inexpressible

inespugnabile, in-ess-poo-n'**yah**-be-lay, *adj* impregnable

inetto, in-**et**-to, *adj* inept; incompetent

inevitabile, in-ay-vee-**tah**-be-lay, *adj* inevitable

inezia, in-**ay**-tse'ah, *f* trifle

infallibile, in-fahl-**lee**-be-lay, *adj* infallible

infamante, in-fah-**mahn**-tay, *adj* defamatory

infame, in-**fah**-may, *adj* vile, wicked, infamous

infantile, in-fahn-**tee**-lay, *adj* childlike; infantile; **asilo –,** nursery school

infanzia, in-**fahn**-tse'ah, *f* childhood; infancy

infarcire, in-far-**chee**-ray, *v* to stuff

infarinare, in-fah-re-**nah**-ray, *v* to sprinkle/cover with flour

infarinatura, in-fah-re-nah-**too**-rah, *f* smuttering

infarto, in-**fahr**-to, *m* heart attack

infastidire, in-fahss-te-**dee**-ray, *v* to annoy, to bother

infaticabile, in-fah-te-**kah**-be-lay, *adj* untiring

infatti, in-**faht**-te, *adv* in fact, actually

infatuato, in-fah-too'**ah**-to, *adj* infatuated

infausto, in-**fah'**ooss-to, *adj* unfavourable, unlucky

infecondo, in-fay-**kon**-do, *adj* infertile, barren

infedele, in-fay-**day**-lay, *adj* unfaithful

infelice*, in-fay-**lee**-chay, *adj* miserable, unhappy

inferiore, in-fay-ree'**o**-ray, *adj* inferior

inferire, in-fay-**ree**-ray, *v* to infer

infermeria, in-fair-may-**ree**-ah, *f* infirmary, sick bay

infermiera, in-fair-me'**ay**-rah, *f* nurse

infermiere, in-fair-me'**ay**-ray, *m* male nurse

infermità, in-fair-mee-**tah**, *f* infirmity; illness

infermo, -a, in-**fair**-mo, *adj* sick; *m/f* invalid

infernale, in-fair-**nah**-lay, *adj* infernal

inferno, in-**fair**-no, *m* hell

inferocire, in-fay-ro-**chee**-ray, *v* to infuriate

inferriata, in-fair-re'**ah**-tah, *f* grating

infestare, in-fess-**tah**-ray, *v* to infest

infettare, in-fet-**tah**-ray, *v* to infect

infezione, in-fay-tse'**o**-nay, *f* infection, contagion

infiammabile, in-fee'am-**mah**-be-lay, *adj* inflammable

infiammarsi, in-fee'am-**mar**-se, *v med* to become inflamed

infido, in-fe-do, *adj* unfaithful; unreliable

infierire, in-fe'ay-**ree**-ray, *v* to rage; **– su,** to attack savagely

infiggere, in-**feed**-jay-ray, *v* to drive in

infilare, in-fe-**lah**-ray, *v* (needle) to thread; (key) to insert; (jacket) to put on; (street) to turn into

infilzare, in-feel-**tsah**-ray, *v* to string; to pierce

infimo, in-**fe**-mo, *adj* lowest

infine, in-**fee**-nay, *adv* finally, at last

infinità, in-fe-ne-**tah**, *f* infinity

infinito, in-fe-**nee**-to, *adj** boundless, unlimited; *m* infinite; *gram* infinitive

infinocchiare, in-fe-nock-ke'**ah**-ray, *v* to fool

inflazione, in-flah-tse'**o**-nay, *f* inflation

infliggere, in-**fleed**-jay-ray, *v* to inflict, to impose

influenza, in-floo-**en**-tsah, *f* influence; influenza

influenzare, in-floo-en-**tsah**-ray, *v* to influence

influsso, in-**flooss**-so, *m* influence

infondato, in-fon-**dah**-to, *adj* unfounded

infondere, in-**fon**-day-ray, *v* to infuse

informare, in-for-**mah**-ray, *v* to inform

informatica, in-for-**mah**-tee-kah, *f* computer science

informazione, in-for-mah-tse'**o**-nay, *f* piece of information

informe, in-**for**-may, *adj* shapeless

infornare, in-for-**nah**-ray, *v* to put in the oven

infortunio, in-for-**too**-ne'o, *m* accident

infossato, in-foss-**sah**-to, *adj* sunken, hollow

infradiciarsi, in-frah-de-**char**-se, *v* to get soaked; to rot

infrangere, in-**frahn**-jay-ray, *v* to infringe; to smash

infrazione, in-frah-tse'**o**-nay, *f* infringement

infreddarsi, in-fred-**dar**-se, *v* to catch cold

infreddatura, in-fred-dah-**too**-rah, *f* chill

infrequente, in-fray-**kwen**-tay, *adj* infrequent

infruttuoso*, in-froot-too'**o**-zo, *adj* fruitless

infuocato, in-foo'o-**kah**-to, *adj* red-hot

infuori, in-foo'**o**-ree, *adv* outwards; **all'– di,** apart from

infuriato, in-foo-ree'**ah**-to, *adj* furious

infuso, in-**foo**-so, *m* infusion

ingaggiare, in-gahd-**jah**-ray, *v* to take on, to sign; *mil* to engage

ingannare, in-gahn-**nah**-ray, *v* to deceive; to trick

ingannevole, in-gahn-**nay**-vo-lay, *adj* deceptive, misleading

inganno, in-**gahn**-no, *m* deceit, deception; trick, swindle

ingarbugliare, in-gar-boo-l'**yah**-ray, *v* to tangle; *fig* to muddle

ingegnarsi, in-jay-n'**yar**-se, *v* to try one's best

ingegnere, in-jay-n'**yay**-ray, *m* engineer

ingegno, in-**jay**-n'yo, *m* skill; intelligence; ingenuity

ingegnoso*, in-jay-n'**yo**-so, *adj* ingenious, clever

ingelosire, in-jay-lo-**zee**-ray, *v* to make jealous

ingente, in-**jen**-tay, *adj* huge

ingenuità, in-jay-noo'e-**tah**, *f* ingenuousness

ingenuo*, in-**jay**-noo'o, *adj* ingenuous, naïve, innocent

ingerenza, in-jay-**ren**-tsah,

f interference; charge

ingerirsi, in-jay-**reer**-se, *v* to meddle

ingessare, in-jess-**sah**-ray, *v* to put in plaster

Inghilterra, in-gheel-**tair**-rah, *f* England

inghiottire, in-ghe'ot-**tee**-ray, *v* to swallow, to gulp (down)

ingiallire, in-jahl-**lee**-ray, *v* to turn yellow

inginocchiarsi, in-je-nock-ke'**ar**-se, *v* to kneel (down)

ingiù, in-**joo**, *adv* downwards; down

ingiungere, in-**joonn**-jay-ray, *v* to enjoin

ingiunzione, in-joonn-tse'**o**-nay, *f* injunction

ingiuria, in-**joo**-re'ah, *f* insult, offence

ingiuriare, in-joo-re'**ah**-ray, *v* to insult; to abuse

ingiustizia, in-jooss-**tee**-tse'ah, *f* injustice, wrong

ingiusto*, in-**jooss**-to, *adj* unjust, unfair

inglese, in-**glay**-zay, *adj* English

ingoiare, in-go-**yah**-ray, *v* to swallow, to gulp (down)

ingolfarsi, in-gol-**far**-se, *v* (engine) to flood

ingombrare, in-gom-**brah**-ray, *v* to clutter up

ingombro, in-**gom**-bro, *m* obstacle

ingordigia, in-gor-**dee**-jah, *f* greediness, voracity

ingordo*, in-**gor**-do, *adj* greedy

ingorgarsi, in-gor-**gar**-se, *v* to get blocked

ingorgo, in-**gor**-go, *m* blockage; – **stradale**, traffic jam

ingozzare, in-got-**tsah**-ray, *v* to stuff (with food); to forcefeed

ingranaggio, in-grah-**nahd**-jo, *m* gear; mechanism

ingranare, in-grah-**nah**-ray, *v* to engage (gear)

ingrandimento, in-grahn-dee-**men**-to, *m* enlargement; expansion

ingrandire, in-grahn-**dee**-ray, *v* to enlarge; to expand

ingrassare, in-grahss-**sah**-ray, *v* to fatten; to get fat

ingratitudine, in-grah-te-**too**-de-nay, *f* ingratitude

ingrato, in-**grah**-to, *adj* ungrateful

ingraziarsi, in-grah-tse'**ar**-se, *v* to ingratiate

ingrediente, in-gray-de-en-tay, *m* ingredient

ingresso, in-**gress**-so, *m* entrance, entry; admission; **vietato l'–**, no admittance

ingrossare, in-gross-**sah**-ray, *v* to increase, to swell

ingrosso, in-**gross**-so, *adv* all'–, wholesale

inguaribile, in-goo'ah-**ree**-be-lay, *adj* incurable

inguine, in-goo'e-nay, *m* groin

inibito, in-e-bee-to, *adj* inhibited

inibizione, in-e-bee-tse'o-nay, *f* inhibition

iniettare, in-e-ayt-**tah**-ray, *v* to inject

iniezione, in-e-ay-tse'o-nay, *f* injection

inimicarsi, e-ne-me-**kar**-se, *v* to make an enemy of

ininterrotto*, e-nin-tair-**rot**-to, *adj* uninterrupted

iniquo*, in-ee-koo'o, *adj* iniquitous, wicked

iniziale, in-e-tse'**ah**-lay, *f* initial; *adj** initial

iniziare, in-e-tse'**ah**-ray, *v* to begin; **– a**, to initiate into

iniziativa, in-e-tse'ah-**tee**-vah, *f* initiative

inizio, in-ee-tse'o, *m* beginning

innaffiare, in-nahf-fe'**ah**-ray, *v* to water

innaffiatoio, in-nahf-fe'ah-**to**-e'o, *m* watering-can

innalzare, in-nahl-**tsah**-ray, *v* to raise, to erect

innamorarsi, in-nah-mo-**rar**-se, *v* to fall in love

innamorato, -a, in-nah-mo-**rah**-to, *adj* in love; *m/f* sweetheart

innanzi, in-**nann**-tse, *adv* ahead; before; *prep* in front of; before

innato, in-**nah**-to, *adj* innate

innegabile, in-nay-**gah**-be-lay, *adj* undeniable

innervosirsi, in-nair-vo-**seer**-se, *v* to get irritated; to get worried

innestare, in-ness-**tah**-ray, *v* to graft

innesto, in-**ness**-to, *m* graft

inno, in-no, *m* hymn; anthem

innocente*, in-no-**chen**-tay, *adj* innocent; *law* not guilty

innocenza, in-no-**chen**-tsah, *f* innocence

innocuo*, in-**no**-koo'o, *adj* innocuous, harmless

innovare, in-no-**vah**-ray, *v* to innovate

innumerevole, in-noo-may-**ray**-vo-lay, *adj* innumerable, countless

inoculare, in-o-koo-**lah**-ray, *v* to inoculate

inodoro, in-o-**do**-ro, *adj* inodorous, scentless

inoltrare, in-oll-**trah**-ray, *v* to forward; to pass on

inoltrarsi, in-oll-**trar**-se, *v* to advance further

inoltrato, in-oll-**trah**-to, *adj* late

inoltre, in-**oll**-tray, *adv* besides, moreover

inondare, in-on-**dah**-ray, *v* to flood

inondazione, in-on-dah-tse'o-nay, *f* flood, flooding

inoperoso, in-o-pay-**ro**-zo, *adj* inactive; idle

inopinato*, in-o-pe-**nah**-to, *adj* unexpected

inopportuno*, in-op-por-**too**-no, *adj* ill-timed; inappropriate

inoppugnabile, in-op-poo-n'yah-be-lay, *adj* incontrovertible

inorgoglirsi, in-or-go-l'**yeer**-se, *v* to become proud

inorridire, in-or-re-dee-ray, *v* to horrify; to be horrified

inosservato, in-oss-sair-**vah**-to, *adj* unnoticed

inossidabile, in-oss-se-**dah**-be-lay, *adj* stainless

inquadrare, in-koo'ah-**drah**-ray, *v* to frame

inquieto, in-koo'e-**ay**-to,

adj restless; worried

inquietudine, in-koo'e-ay-**too**-de-nay, *f* worry, uneasiness

inquilino, -a, in-koo'e-**lee**-no, *m/f* lodger; tenant

inquinare, in-koo'e-**nah**-ray, *v* to pollute

inquinamento, in-koo'e-nah-**men**-to, *m* pollution

inquisire, in-koo'e-**see**-ray, *v* to investigate

insaccati, in-sack-**kah**-tee, *mpl* sausages

insalata, in-sah-**lah**-tah, *f* lettuce; salad

insalatiera, in-sah-lah-te'**ay**-rah, *f* salad bowl

insalubre, in-sah-**loo**-bray, *adj* unhealthy

insanabile, in-sah-**nah**-be-lay, *adj* incurable

insanguinato, in-sahn-goo'e-**nah**-to, *adj* blood-stained

insania, in-sah-ne'ah, *f* insanity

insano, in-**sah**-no, *adj* insane; unhealthy

insaponare, in-sah-po-**nah**-ray, *v* to soap

insaputa, in-sah-**poo**-tah, *f* all'– di, without the knowledge of

inscenare, in-shay-**na**-ray, *v* to stage

inscindibile, in-shin-**dee**-be-lay, *adj* inseparable

inscrivere, in-**skree**-vay-ray, *v* to inscribe

insediamento, in-say-de'ah-**men**-to, *m* installation; settlement

insegna, in-**say**-n'yah, *f* sign; ensign, standard

insegnamento, in-say-n'yah-**men**-to, *m* teaching

insegnante, in-say-n'**yahn**-tay, *m/f* teacher

insegnare, in-say-n'**yah**-ray, *v* to teach

inseguimento, in-say-goo'e-**men**-to, *m* pursuit

inseguire, in-say-goo'**ee**-ray, *v* to pursue

insenatura, in-say-nah-**too**-rah, *f* inlet, creek

insensato*, in-sen-**sah**-to, *adj* foolish, senseless

insensibile*, in-sen-**see**-be-lay, *adj* insensitive

inseparabile, in-say-pah-**rah**-be-lay, *adj* inseparable

inserire, in-say-**ree**-ray, *v* to insert

inservibile, in-sair-**vee**-be-lay, *adj* useless

inserzione, in-sair-**tse**'o-nay, *f* advertisement; insertion

insetticida, in-set-te-**chee**-dah, *m* insecticide

insetto, in-**set**-to, *m* insect

insidia, in-**see**-de'ah, *f* snare; danger

insidioso*, in-se-de'**o**-zo, *adj* insidious

insieme, in-se-**ay**-may, *adv* together; at the same time; *prep* –a, together with; l'–, *m* the whole

insigne, in-**see**-n'yay, *adj* renowned

insignificante, in-se-n'yee-fee-**kahn**-tay, *adj* insignificant

insinuare, in-se-noo'**ah**-ray, *v* to insinuate

insipido*, in-see-pe-do, *adj* insipid, tasteless

insistere, in-**siss**-tay-ray, *v* to insist, to persist

insoddisfacente, in-sod-diss-fah-**chen**-tay, *adj* unsatisfactory

insoddisfatto, in-sod-diss-**faht**-to, *adj* dissatisfied

insofferente, in-soff-fay-**ren**-tay, *adj* impatient; intolerant

insolazione, in-so-lah-**tse**'o-nay, *f* sunstroke

insolente, in-so-**len**-tay, *adj* insolent

insolito*, in-**so**-le-to, *adj* unusual; rare

insolubile, in-so-**loo**-be-lay, *adj* insoluble

insolvenza, in-soll-**ven**-tsah, *f law* insolvency

insolvibile, in-soll-**vee**-be-lay, *adj law* insolvent

insomma, in-**som**-mah, *adv* in short; *interj* for heaven's sake

insonne, in-**son**-nay, *adj* sleepless

insonnia, in-**son**-ne'ah, *f* insomnia

insopportabile*, in-sop-por-**tah**-be-lay, *adj* unbearable

insorgere, in-**sor**-jay-ray, *v* to rebel

insospettirsi, in-soss-pet-**teer**-se, *v* to become suspicious

insostenibile, in-soss-tay-**nee**-be-lay, *adj* intolerable; untenable

insostituibile, in-soss-tee-too'e-be-lay, *adj* irreplaceable

insperabile, in-spay-**rah**-be-lay, *adj* hopeless

insperato, in-spay-**rah**-to, *adj* unhoped-for

inspiegabile, in-spe-ay-**gah**-be-lay, *adj* inexplicable

inspirare, in-spe-**rah**-ray, *v* to inhale

instabile, in-**stah**-be-lay, *adj* unstable; changeable

installare, in-stahl-**lah**-ray, *v* to install

installazione, in-stahl-lah-tse'o-nay, *f* installation

instancabile, in-stahn-**kah**-be-lay, *adj* tireless

instaurare, in-stah-oo-**rah**-ray, *v* to institute

instillare, in-stel-**lah**-ray, *v* to instil

insù, in-**soo**, *adv* upwards

insuccesso, in-soot-**chess**-so, *m* failure

insufficiente*, in-soof-fe-**chen**-tay, *adj* insufficient

insulina, in-soo-**lee**-na, *f* insulin

insulso*, in-**sool**-so, *adj* dull, silly

insultare, in-sool-**tah**-ray, *v* to insult

insulto, in-**sool**-to, *m* insult

insurrezione, in-soor-ray-tse'o-nay, *f* insurrection

intaccare, in-tahk-**kah**-ray, *v* to corrode; to damage

intagliare, in-tah-l'**yah**-ray, *v* to carve, to engrave

intanto, in-**tahn**-to, *adv* in the meantime

intarsio, in-**tar**-se'o, *m* marquetry; inlay

intasare, in-tah-**zah**-ray, *v* to block

intascare, in-tahss-**kah**-ray, *v* to pocket

intatto, in-**taht**-to, *adj* intact

intavolare, in-tah-vo-**lah**-ray, *v* to start, to enter into

integrale, in-tay-**grah**-lay, *adj* integral, essential; (bread; flour) wholemeal

integrare, in-tay-**grah**-ray, *v* to supplement; to integrate

integratori, in-tay-grah-**to**-ree, *mpl* nutritional supplements

integrità, in-tay-gre-**tah**, *f* integrity

integro*, in-tay-gro, *adj* upright; whole

intelaiatura, in-tay-lah-e'ah-**too**-rah, *f* framework

intelletto, in-tell-**let**-to, *m* intellect

intellettuale*, in-tell-let-too'**ah**-lay, *adj* intellectual

intelligente*, in-tell-le-**jen**-tay, *adj* intelligent

intelligenza, in-tell-le-**jen**-tsah, *f* intelligence

intelligibile, in-tell-le-**jee**-be-lay, *adj* intelligible

intemperanza, in-tem-pay-**rahn**-tsah, *f* intemperance

intemperie, in-tem-**pay**-re-ay, *fpl* bad weather

intendere, in-**ten**-day-ray, *v* to understand; to intend

intendersi, in-ten-**dair**-se, v to be in agreement with; to understand one another; **– di,** to be a connoisseur of

intensità, in-ten-se-**tah**, f intensity; violence

intenso*, in-**ten**-so, adj intense; strong

intento, in-**ten**-to, m aim, intent; adj intent

intenzionale*, in-ten-tse'o-**nah**-lay, adj intentional

interagire, in-tair-ah-jee-ray, v to interact

intercedere, in-tair-**chay**-day-ray, v to intervene

intercessione, in-tair-chess-se'o-nay, f intercession

intercettare, in-tair-chet-**tah**-ray, v to intercept

intercorrere, in-tair-**kor**-ray-ray, v to elapse

interdetto, in-tair-**det**-to, adj prohibited; dumbfounded; m relig interdict

interdire, in-tair-**dee**-ray, v to forbid; relig to interdict

interdizione, in-tair-de-tse'o-nay, f prohibition; relig interdict

interessante, in-tay-ress-**sahn**-tay, adj interesting

interessare, in-tay-ress-**sah**-ray, v to interest; to concern

interessato*, in-tay-ress-**sah**-to, adj interested, involved; self-interested

interesse, in-tay-**ress**-say, m interest; advantage

interfaccia, in-tair-**fach**-chah, f interface

interferire, in-tair-fay-**ree**-ray, v to interfere

interiore, in-tay-re'or-ay, adj inner; internal

interlocutore, **-trice**, in-tair-lo-koo-**to**-ray, in-tair-lo-koo-**tree**-chay, m/f speaker

interludio, in-tair-**loo**-de'o, m interlude

intermedio, in-tair-**may**-de'o, adj intermediate

intermezzo, in-tair-**med**-dzo, m interval; interlude

intermittente, in-tair-mit-**ten**-tay, adj intermittent

internazionale, in-tair-nah-tse'o-**nah**-lay, adj international

interno*, in-tair-no, adj internal; interior; m inside; **Ministero degli Interni,** Home Office

intero*, in-**tay**-ro, adj entire, whole; **per –,** in full

interpellare, in-tair-pel-**lah**-ray, v to consult; parl

to question

interporre, in-tair-**porr**-ray, v to interpose

interpretare, in-tair-pray-**tah**-ray, v to interpret

interpretazione, in-tair-pray-tah-tse'o-nay, f interpretation

interprete, in-tair-pray-tay, m/f interpreter

interrato, in-tair-**rah**-to, m **piano –,** basement

interrogare, in-tair-ro-**gah**-ray, v to question; to examine

interrogatorio, in-tair-ro-gah-tor-e'o, m questioning

interrogazione, in-tair-ro-gah-tse'o-nay, f (school) oral examination; parl question

interrompere, in-tair-**rom**-pay-ray, v to interrupt; to cut off

interruttore, in-tair-**root**-to-ray, m switch

interruzione, in-tair-roo-tse'o-nay, f interruption; **senza –,** without a break

interurbana, in-tair-oor-**bah**-na, f long-distance call

intervallo, in-tair-**vahl**-lo, m interval

intervenire, in-tair-vay-**nee**-ray, v to intervene; med to operate

intervento, in-tair-**vayn**-to, *m* intervention; speech; *med* operation

intervista, in-tair-**viss**-tah, *f* interview

intervistare, in-tair-viss-**tah**-ray, *v* to interview

intesa, in-**tay**-zah, *f* understanding; agreement

intestare, in-tess-**tah**-ray, *v* – **a**, to address to; to register in the name of

intestino, in-tess-**tee**-no, *m* intestine; *adj* internal

intimare, in-te-**mah**-ray, *v* to order; – **lo sfratto**, to serve an eviction order

intimidatorio, in-te-me-dah-**to**-re'o, *adj* threatening

intimidire, in-te-me-**dee**-ray, *v* to intimidate

intimità, in-te-me-**tah**, *f* intimacy

intimo, in-te-mo, *adj* intimate; **biancheria intima**, underwear

intimorire, in-te-mo-**ree**-ray, *v* to frighten

intirizzito, in-te-rit-**tsee**-to, *adj* numb with cold

intitolare, in-te-to-**lah**-ray, *v* to entitle; to dedicate; to give a title to

intollerabile, in-toll-lay-**rah**-be-lay, *adj*

intolerable

intollerante, in-toll-lay-**rahn**-tay, *adj* intolerant

intolleranza, in-toll-lay-**rahn**-tsah, *f* intolerance

intonacare, in-to-nah-**kah**-ray, *v* to plaster

intonare, in-to-**nah**-ray, *v* to match (colours); to sing the opening bars of

intonazione, in-to-nah-**tse'o**-nay, *f* intonation; pitch

intontito, in-ton-**tee**-to, *adj* dazed; dizzy

intoppo, in-**top**-po, *m* hindrance, obstruction

intorbidire, in-tor-be-**dee**-ray, *v* to make turbid/cloudy/muddy

intorno, in-**tor**-no, *adv* about, around; *prep* – **a**, around, about

intossicazione, in-tos-see-kah-**tse'o**-nay, *f* poisoning; – **alimentare**, food poisoning

intralciare, in-trahl-**chah**-ray, *v* to hamper

intrallazzare, in-trahl-lat-**tsah**-ray, *v* to intrigue, to scheme

intransigente*, in-trahn-ze-**jen**-tay, *adj* intransigent

intrappolare, in-trahp-po-**lah**-ray, *v* to trap

intraprendere, in-trah-**pren**-day-ray, *v* to undertake

intrattenere, in-traht-tay-**nay**-ray, *v* to entertain

intravedere, in-trah-vay-**day**-ray, *v* to catch a glimpse of

intrecciare, in-tret-**chah**-ray, *v* to interweave; to plait

intreccio, in-**tret**-cho, *m* plot; weave

intrepido*, in-**tray**-pe-do, *adj* fearless, dauntless

intricato, in-tre-**kah**-to, *adj* tangled; complicated

intrigare, in-tre-**gah**-ray, *v* to intrigue; to plot

intrigo, in-**tree**-go, *m* intrigue

intrinseco*, in-**trin**-say-ko, *adj* intrinsic

introdurre, in-tro-**doohr**-ray, *v* to introduce

introduzione, in-tro-doo-**tse'o**-nay, *f* introduction

introito, in-**tro**-ee-to, *m* revenue

intromettersi, in-tro-**met**-tair-se, *v* to meddle, to interfere

introverso, in-tro-**ver**-so, *adj* introvert

intrusione, in-troo-**ze'o**-nay, *f* intrusion

intruso, -a, in-**troo**-zo, *m/f* intruder

intuire, in-too'**ee**-ray, *v* to

realize; to know intuitively

intuitivo*, in-too'e-tee-vo, *adj* intuitive

intuizione, in-too'e-tse'o-nay, *f* intuition

inumano*, in-oo-mah-no, *adj* inhuman; pitiless

inumare, in-oo-mah-ray, *v* to inter

inumidire, in-oo-me-dee-ray, *v* to moisten

inusitato, in-oo-ze-tah-to, *adj* unusual

inutile, in-oo-te-lay, *adj* useless; needless

inutilmente, in-oo-til-men-tay, *adv* uselessly; unnecessarily

invadere, in-vah-day-ray, *v* to invade

invalidità, in-vah-le-de-tah, *f* disability; *law* invalidity

invalido, -a, in-vah-le-do, *adj** invalid, disabled; *m/f* disabled person; invalid

invano, in-vah-no, *adv* in vain, vainly

invariabile, in-vah-re-ah-be-lay, *adj* invariable

invasione, in-vah-ze'o-nay, *f* invasion

invasore, in-vah-zor-ay, *m* invader

invecchiare, in-vek-ke'ah-ray, *v* to grow old, to age

invece, in-vay-chay, *adv* instead

inveire, in-vay-ee-ray, *v* to inveigh

invendibile, in-ven-dee-be-lay, *adj* unsaleable

inventare, in-ven-tah-ray, *v* to invent, to devise

inventario, in-ven-tah-re'o, *m* inventory, list

inventore, -trice, in-ven-tor-ay, in-ven-tree-chay, *m/f* inventor

invenzione, in-ven-tse'o-nay, *f* invention

invernale, in-vair-nah-lay, *adj* wintry

inverno, in-vair-no, *m* winter; winter season

inverosimile, in-vay-ro-see-me-lay, *adj* unlikely, improbable

inversione, in-vair-se'o-nay, *f* inversion, U-turn

invertire, in-vair-tee-ray, *v* to invert

invertito, -a, in-vair-tee-to, *m/f* homosexual

investigare, in-vess-te-gah-ray, *v* to investigate

investigatore, -trice, in-vess-te-gah-to-ray, in-vess-te-gah-tree-chay, *m/f* detective

investimento, in-vess-te-men-to, *m* investment; knocking down

investire, in-vess-tee-ray,

v to invest; (pedestrian) to run over

inviare, in-ve'ah-ray, *v* to send, to dispatch

inviato, -a, in-ve'ah-to, *m/f* envoy; (newspaper) correspondent

invidia, in-vee-de'ah, *f* envy

invidiabile, in-ve-de'ah-be-lay, *adj* enviable

invidiare, in-ve-de'ah-ray, *v* to envy

invidioso*, in-ve-de'o-zo, *adj* envious, invidious

invincibile, in-vin-chee-be-lay, *adj* invincible

invio, in-vee-o, *m* sending; consignment

inviolabile, in-ve'o-lah-be-lay, *adj* inviolable

invisibile, in-ve-zee-be-lay, *adj* invisible

invitare, in-ve-tah-ray, *v* to invite

invitato, -a, in-ve-tah-to, *m/f* guest

invito, in-vee-to, *m* invitation

invocare, in-vo-kah-ray, *v* to invoke, to call upon

invogliare, in-vo-lyah-ray, *v* to tempt, to induce

involontariamente, in-vo-lon-tah-re'ah-men-tay, *adv* unintentionally

involto, in-voll-to, *m* parcel, bundle

involucro, in-vo-loo-kro, *m* wrapping; outer cover

invulnerabile, in-vooll-nay-**rah**-be-lay, *adj* invulnerable

inzaccherare, in-dzahk-kay-**rah**-ray, *v* to splash with mud

inzuppare, in-dzoop-**pah**-ray, *v* to soak; to dip

io, ee-o, *pron* I; **sono –**, it is me; **– stesso**, I myself; **m l' –**, the ego, the self

iodio, e'o-de-o, *m* iodine

ionizzazione, e'o-need-dza-tse'**o**-nay, *f* ionization

ipermercato, e-per-mer-**kah**-to, *m* hypermarket

ipertensione, e-per-ten-se'**o**-nay, *f* high blood pressure

ipnotismo, ip-no-**teess**-mo, *m* hypnotism

ipocrisia, e-po-kre-**see**-ah, *f* hypocrisy

ipocrita, e-po-kre-tah, *m/f* hypocrite; *adj** hypocritical

ipoteca, e-po-**tay**-kah, *f* mortgage

ipotecare, e-po-tay-**kah**-ray, *v* to mortgage

ipotesi, e-po-**tay**-ze, *f* hypothesis

ippopotamo, ip-po-**po**-tah-mo, *m* hippopotamus

ira, ee-rah, *f* anger

irascibile, e-rah-**shee**-be-lay, *adj* irascible, bad-tempered

iride, ee-re-day, *f* iris; rainbow

Irlanda, eer-**lahn**-dah, *f* Ireland

irlandese, eer-lahn-**day**-zay, *adj* Irish

ironia, e-ro-**nee**-ah, *f* irony

irradiare, eer-rah-de'**ah**-ray, *v* to radiate

irragionevole*, eer-rah-jo-**nay**-vo-lay, *adj* unreasonable

irrazionale*, eer-rah-tse'o-**nah**-lay, *adj* irrational

irregolare*, eer-ray-go-**lah**-ray, *adj* irregular

irregolarità, eer-ray-go-lah-re-**tah**, *f* irregularity

irremovibile, eer-ray-mo-**vee**-be-lay, *adj* unyielding; adamant

irreparabile*, eer-ray-pah-**rah**-be-lay, *adj* irreparable

irreprensibile*, eer-ray-pren-**see**-be-lay, *adj* blameless

irrequieto, eer-ray-kwee'**ay**-to, *adj* restless

irresistibile*, eer-ray-ziss-**tee**-be-lay, *adj* irresistible

irresoluto, eer-ray-zo-**loo**-to, *adj* wavering, irresolute

irrespirabile, eer-ray-spee-**rah**-be-lay, *adj* unbreathable; stifling

irrestringibile, eer-ray-strin-**jee**-be-lay, *adj* unshrinkable

irrevocabile*, eer-ray-vo-**kah**-be-lay, *adj* irrevocable

irrigare, eer-re-**gah**-ray, *v* to irrigate

irrigazione, eer-re-gah-tse'**o**-nay, *f* irrigation

irrigidirsi, eer-re-jee-**deer**-se, *v* to stiffen

irrilevante, eer-re-lay-**vahn**-tay, *adj* irrelevant

irrimediabile, eer-re-may-de'**ah**-be-lay, *adj* irremediable

irrispettoso, eer-re-spet-**to**-so, *adj* disrespectful

irritabile, eer-re-tah-be-lay, *adj* irritable

irritare, eer-re-**tah**-ray, *v* to irritate

irriverente, eer-re-vay-**ren**-tay, *adj* irreverent

irrompere, eer-**rom**-pay-ray, *v* **– in**, to burst into

irrorare, eer-ro-**rah**-ray, *v* to bathe; (fields) to spray

irruente, eer-roo-**en**-tay, *adj* impetuous

irruzione, eer-roo-tse'**o**-nay, *f* **fare –**, to burst into

irsuto, eer-soo-to, *adj* hairy, bristly

irto, eer-to, *adj* – **di**, bristling with

iscrivere, iss-kre-ve-ray, *v* to enroll, to register

iscrizione, iss-kre-tse'o-nay, *f* inscription; enrolment, registration

islamico, ee-zlah-me-ko, *adj* Islamic

isola, ee-zo-lah, *f* island; – **pedonale**, pedestrian precinct

isolamento, e-zo-lah-**men**-to, *m* isolation; insulation

isolare, e-zo-lah-ray, *v* to isolate; to insulate

isolato, e-zo-**lah**-to, *m* block (of houses)

isolatore, e-zo-lah-**tor**-ay, *m* insulator

ispettore, -**trice**, iss-pet-**tor**-ay, iss-pet-**tree**-chay, *m/f* inspector

ispezionare, iss-pay-tse'o-**nah**-ray, *v* to inspect

ispezione, iss-pay-tse'o-nay, *f* inspection

ispirare, iss-pe-**rah**-ray, *v* to inspire

ispirazione, iss-pe-rah-tse'o-nay, *f* inspiration

istantaneo*, iss-tahn-**tah**-nay-o, *adj* instantaneous

istante, iss-**tahn**-tay, *m* instant; moment; **all'–**, **sull'–**, instantly

istanza, iss-**tahn**-tsah, *f* petition; *law* instance

isterico*, iss-**tay**-re-ko, *adj* hysterical

istigare, iss-te-**gah** ray, *v* to instigate

istigazione, iss-te-gah-tse'o-nay, *f* instigation

istintivo*, iss-tin-**tee**-vo, *adj* instinctive

istinto, iss-**tin**-to, *m* instinct

istituire, iss-te-too'ee-ray, *v* to institute; to establish

istituto, iss-te-too-to, *m* institute; college; institution

istitutore, -**trice**, iss-te-too-**tor**-ay, iss-te-too-**tree**-chay, *m/f* tutor, governess; founder

istituzione, iss-te-too-tse'o-nay, *f* institution

istmo, eest-mo, *m* isthmus

istrice, eess-tree-chay, *m* porcupine

istruire, iss-troo-ee-ray, *v* to instruct; to educate; – **un processo**, to prepare a case

istruito, iss-troo'ee-to, *adj* learned, informed, educated

istruttivo*, iss-troot-**tee**-vo, *adj* instructive

istruttore, -**trice**, iss-troot-**to**-ray, iss-troot-**tree**-chay, *m/f* instructor; **giudice –**, examining magistrate

istruttoria, iss-troot-to-re'ah, *f law* preliminary investigation and hearing

istruzione, iss-troo-tse'o-nay, *f* instruction; **Ministero della pubblica –**, Ministry of Education

istupidire, iss-too-pe-**dee**-ray, *v* to daze; to stupefy

Italia, e-**tah**-le'ah, *f* Italy

italiano, e-tah-le'**ah**-no, *adj* Italian

itinerante, e-te-nay-**rahn**-tay, *adj* itinerant; travelling

itinerario, e-te-nay-**rah**-re'o, *m* itinerary; route

itterizia, it-tay-**ree**-tse'ah, *f* jaundice

iuta, e'oo-tah, *f* jute

IVA, ee-vah, *f* VAT

jazz, jaz, *m* jazz
jeans, jeenz, *mpl* jeans
jeep, jeep, *f* jeep
jolly, jol-lee, *m* (cards)
   joker
judo, joo-do, *m* judo
jukebox, jook-box, *m*
   jukebox
junior, e'oo-ne'or, junior
juta, e'oo-tah, *f* jute

K

kaki, kah-kee, *adj* khaki

kamikaze, kah-mee-**kahd**-dzay, *m* kamikaze

kaputt, kah-**poott**, *adj* kaput

karakiri, kah-rah-**kee**-ree, *m* hara-kiri

karatè, kah-rah-**tay**, *m* karate

kg, kee-lo-**gram**-mo, kg

kibbutz, keeb-**boots**, *m* kibbutz

killer, keel-ler, *m* killer

km, kee-lo-may-tro, km

know-how, nou-ahoo, *m* know-how

koala, ko-**ah**-lah, *m* koala

krapfen, kraf-fen, *m* doughnut

la, lah, *art* the; *pron* her; it; you (courtesy form); *m mus* A

là, lah, *adv* there; **qua e –,** here and there

labbro, lahb-bro, *m* lip

labile, lah-be-lay, *adj* ephemeral

labirinto, lah-be-**ren**-to, *m* labyrinth; maze

laboratorio, lah-bo-rah-**to**-re'o, *m* laboratory

laborioso, lah-bo-re'o-so, *adj* hard-working; laborious

laburista, lah-boo-**riss**-tah, *m/f* Labour party member; Labour supporter

lacca, lahk-kah, *f* lacquer, varnish; hairspray

laccio, laht-cho, *m* lace, string; **lacci delle scarpe,** shoelaces

lacerare, lah-chay-**rah**-ray, *v* to lacerate; to tear

lacrima, lah-kre-mah, *f* tear

lacrimare, lah-kre-**mah**-ray, *v* (eyes) to water; to cry

lacrimogeno, lah-kre-moh-**jay**-no, *adj* **gas –,** tear gas

lacuna, lah-**koo**-nah, *f* gap; blank

ladro, lah-dro, *m* thief

ladrocinio, lah-dro-**chee**-ne'o, *m* robbery

laggiù, lahd-**joo**, *adv* down there

lagnanza, lah-n'**yahn**-tsah, *f* complaint

lagnarsi, lah-n'**yar**-se, *v* to complain; to moan

lago, lah-go, *m* lake

lagrima, lah-gre-mah, *f* tear

laguna, lah-**goo**-nah, *f* lagoon

laico, -a, lah-e-ko, *adj* lay; *m/f* layman, laywoman

laido*, lah-e-do, *adj* filthy; obscene

L'Aja, lah-yah, *f* The Hague

lama, lah-mah, *f* blade; *m* (animal) llama; *relig* lama

lambiccarsi, lahm-beek-**kar**-se, *v* **– il cervello,** to rack one's brains

lambire, lahm-**bee**-ray, *v* (flames) to lick; (water) to lap

lamentare, lah-men-**tah**-ray, *v* to lament

lamentarsi, lah-men-**tar**-se, *v* complain

lamento, lah-**men**-to, *m* moan; lament

lamentoso, lah-men-**to**-so, *adj* plaintive, sad

lametta, lah-**met**-tah, *f* razor blade

lamiera, lah-me'**ay**-rah, *f* sheet (metal)

lamina, lah-me-nah, *f* thin sheet of metal

lampada, lahm-pah-dah, *f* lamp

lampadario, lahm-pah-

dah-re'o, *m* chandelier

lampadina, lahm-pah-**dee**-nah, *f* light bulb; –
tascabile, torch

lampante, lahm-**pahn**-tay, *adj* obvious, crystal clear

lampeggiare, lahm-pej-**jah**-ray, *v* to flash;
lampeggia, there's lightning

lampione, lahm-pe'o-nay, street lamp; lamppost

lampo, lahm-po, *m* lightning; flash;
cerniera –, zip

lampone, lahm-**po**-nay, *f* raspberry

lana, lah-nah, *f* wool;
pura – vergine, pure new wool

lancetta, lahn-**chet**-tah, *f* pointer; (clock, watch) hand

lancia, lahn-chah, *f* lance; launch

lanciare, lahn-**chah**-ray, *v* to hurl; to launch

lancinante, lahn-chee-**nahn**-tay, *adj* throbbing, piercing

lancio, lahn-cho, *m* throwing, flinging; launching; throw; – **del disco,** throwing the discus; – **del peso,** putting the shot

landa, lahn-dah, *f* heath, moor

languido*, lahn-goo'e-do, *adj* languid

languire, lahn-goo'**ee**-ray, *v* to languish; to flag

languore, lahn-goo'**o**-ray, *m* languor; faintness

lanificio, lah-nee-**fee**-cho, *m* wool mill

lanoso, lah-**no**-zo, *adj* woolly

lanterna, lahn-**tair**-nah, *f* lantern

lanugine, lah-**noo**-je-nay, *f* down; soft hair

lapidare, lah-pe-**dah**-ray, *v* to stone (to death)

lapide, lah-pe-day, *f* tombstone; plaque

lapilli, lah-**peel**-le, *mpl* ashes from volcano

lapis, lah-pis, *m* pencil

laptop, lahp-top, *m* laptop

lardo, lar-do, *m* lard

larghezza, lar-**ghet**-tsah, *f* width, breadth; generosity

largire, lar-**jee**-ray, *v* to give liberally

largo*, lar-go, *adj* wide, broad; *m naut* largo; open sea; **al – di,** off the coast of

larice, lah-ree-chay, *m* larch

laringe, lah-**reen**-jay, *f* larynx, windpipe

larva, lar-vah, *f* larva; zombie

lasagne, lah-**zah**-ny'ay, *fpl* lasagna

lasciare, lah-she'**ah**-ray, *v* to leave; to let

lasciarsi, lah-she'**ar**-se, *v* to part; to split up

lascito, lah-she-to, *m* legacy

lascivo, lah-**shee**-vo, *adj* wanton

laser, lah-ser, *adj* **raggio –,** laser beam

lassativo, lahss-sah-**tee**-vo, *adj* laxative; *m* laxative

lasso, lahss-so, *m* – **di tempo,** lapse of time

lassù, lahss-**soo,** *adv* up there

lastra, lahss-trah, *f* slab; sheet; plate; paving stone

lastrico, lahss-tre-ko, *m* paving; **essere sul –,** to be penniless

laterale, lah-te-**rah**-lay, *adj* lateral, side

latitante, lah-te-**tahn**-tay, *adj* absconding; *m/f* fugitive

latitudine, lah-te-**too**-de-nay, *f* latitude

lato, lah-to, *m* side; point of view; *adj* broad, wide; **in senso –,** broadly speaking

latore, -trice, lah-**tor**-ay, lah-**tree**-chay, *m/f* bearer

latrare, lah-**trah**-ray, *v* to bark

latrina, lah-**tree**-nah, *f* public lavatory

latta, laht-tah, *f* tin plate; can

lattaio, -a, laht-**tah**-e'o, *m/f* milkman, milkwoman

latte, laht-tay, *m* milk; – **detergente**, cleansing lotion; – **intero**, full-cream milk; – **magro/scremato**, skimmed milk

latteo, laht-tay-o, *adj* milky

latteria, laht-tay-**ree**-ah, *f* dairy

latticini, laht-te-**chee**-ne, *mpl* dairy products

lattina, laht-**tee**-nah, *f* can

lattuga, laht-**too**-gah, *f* lettuce

laurea, lah'oo-ray'ah, *f* degree

laurearsi, lah'oo-ray-**ar**-se, *v* to graduate

laureato, -a, lah'oo-ray-**ah**-to, *m/f* graduate

lauro, lah'oo-ro, *m* laurel

lauto*, lah'oo-to, *adj* lavish; sumptuous

lava, lah-vah, *f* lava

lavabile, lah-vah-be-lay, *adj* washable

lavabo, lah-vah-bo, *m* washbasin

lavaggio, lah-**vahj**-jo, *m* washing; – **auto**, car wash; – **del cervello**, brainwashing

lavagna, lah-vah-n'yah, *f* blackboard; slate

lavanda, lah-**vahn**-dah, *f* lavender; *med* wash; – **gastrica**, stomach pump

lavanderia, lah-vahn-day-**ree**-ah, *f* laundry, launderette; dry-cleaner's

lavandino, lah-vahn-**dee**-no, *m* sink

lavapiatti, lah-vah-pe'**at**-tee, *f* dishwasher

lavare, lah-**vah**-ray, *v* to wash; *fig* to cleanse, to purify

lavasecco, lah-vah-**sayk**-ko, *f* dry-cleaner's

lavastoviglie, lah-vah-sto-vee-ly'ay, *f* dishwasher

lavatrice, lah-vah-**tree**-chay, *f* washing machine

lavorante, lah-vo-**rahn**-tay, *m/f* worker; labourer

lavorare, lah-vo-**rah**-ray, *v* to work; to toil; – **a maglia**, to knit; – **in proprio**, to be self-employed

lavoro, lah-**vo**-ro, *m* work; job; task; labour; – **nero**, moonlighting; – **straordinario**, overtime

le, lay, *art* the; *pron* them;

to her; to you (courtesy form)

leale, lay-**ah**-lay, *adj* loyal, faithful; fair

lealmente, lay-ahl-**men**-tay, *adv* loyally, faithfully

lealtà, lay-ahl-tah, *f* loyalty; fairness

lebbra, leb-brah, *f* leprosy

lebbroso, -a, leb-**bro**-zo, *adj* leprous; *m/f* leper

lecca lecca, leck-kah **leck**-kah, *m* lollipop

leccare, leck-kah-ray, *v* to lick; *fig* to flatter

leccata, leck-kah-tah, *f* lick

leccio, let-cho, *m* ilex

leccornia, leck-kor-ne'ah, *f* titbit, delicacy

lecito*, lay-che-to, *adj* permissible; legal

ledere, lay-day-ray, *v* to injure, to damage

lega, lay-gah, *f* league; alloy

legaccio, lay-**gaht**-cho, *m* lace, string

legale, lay-gah-lay, *adj* legal; *m/f* lawyer

legalizzare, lay-gah-lit-tsah-ray, *v* to legalize

legame, lay-**gah**-may, *m* bond; link

legare, lay-**gah**-ray, *v* to bind; to tie

legatario, -a, lay-gah-**tah**-re'o, *m/f* legatee

legato, lay-**gah**-to, *m law* legacy, bequest

legatura, lay-gah-**too**-rah, *f* (book) binding; *mus* ligature

legazione, lay-gah-tse'o-nay, *f* legation, embassy

legge, led-jay, *f* law

leggenda, led-**jen**-dah, *f* legend; (map, graph, etc.) key

leggere, led-jay-ray, *v* to read

leggero*, led-**jay**-ro, *adj* (weight) light; (pain) slight; (physique) nimble; (tea, coffee) weak

leggiadro, led-**jah**-dro, *adj* graceful, pretty

leggio, led-**jee**-o, *m* music stand; lectern; bookrest

legione, lay-je'o-nay, *f* legion

legislazione, lay-je-slah-tse'o-nay, *f* legislation

legittimo, lay-**jit**-te-mo, *adj* legitimate; justified; *law* **legittima difesa**, self-defence

legna, lay-n'yah, *f* firewood

legname, lay-n'yah-may, *m* timber

legno, lay-n'yo, *m* wood; piece of wood

legnoso, lay-n'yo-zo, *adj* woody; wooden

legumi, lay-**goo**-mee, *mpl* pulses

lei, lay-e, *pron* she; her; you (courtesy form)

lembo, **lem**-bo, *m* edge, strip; hem

lena, lay-nah, *f* stamina, energy

lenire, lay-**nee**-ray, *v* to soothe; to calm

lente, **len**-tay, *f* lens; **lenti a contatto**, contact lenses

lentezza, len-**ted**-dzah, *f* slowness, slackness

lenticchia, len-**tick**-ke'ah, *f* lentil

lentiggine, len-**tej**-jee-nay, *f* freckle

lento*, **len**-to, *adj* slow; loose; slack

lenza, **len**-tsah, *f* fishing line

lenzuolo, len-tsoo'o-lo, *m* bed-sheet

leone, lay-o-nay, *m* lion; **Leone**, Leo

leonessa, lay-o-**ness**-sah, *f* lioness

leopardo, lay-o-**par**-do, *m* leopard

lepre, lay-pray, *f* hare

lercio, **lair**-cho, *adj* filthy

lesbica, layz-zbee-kah, *f* lesbian

lesinare, lay-ze-**nah**-ray, *v* to be stingy with

lesione, lay-ze'o-nay, *f med* lesion; *law* injury

lessare, less-**sah**-ray, *v* to boil

lessico, **less**-e-ko, *m* lexis, vocabulary

lesso, **less**-so, *m* boiled meat; *adj* boiled

lesto*, **less**-to, *adj* quick, nimble, agile

letale, lay-**tah**-lay, *adj* lethal, deadly

letame, lay-**tah**-may, *m* dung, manure

letargo, lay-**tar**-go, *m* hibernation; lethargy

letizia, lay-**tee**-tse'ah, *f* joy

lettera, let-tay-rah, *f* letter; – **maiuscola**, capital letter; – **minuscola**, small letter; – **raccomandata**, recorded delivery

letterale*, let-tay-**rah**-lay, *adj* literal

letterario, let-tay-**rah**-re'o, *adj* literary

letterato, -a, let-tay-**rah**-to, *adj* learned; *m/f* scholar

letteratura, let-tay-rah-**too**-rah, *f* literature

lettiga, let-**tee**-gah, *f* stretcher; litter

letto, let-to, *m* bed

lettore, -trice, let-**tor**-ay, let-**tree**-chay, *m/f* reader

lettura, let-**too**-rah, *f* reading

leucemia, leoo-chay-**mee**-ah, *f* leukaemia

leva, lay-vah, *f* lever; conscription

levante, lay-**vahn**-tay, *m* east; east wind

levare, lay-**vah**-ray, *v* to take off; to raise, to lift

levarsi, lay-**var**-se, *v* to rise

levata, lay-**vah**-tah, *f* (mail) collection; *mil* reveille

levatoio, lay-vah-**to**-ee'o, *adj* **ponte –,** drawbridge

levatrice, lay-vah-**tree**-chay, *f* midwife

levigare, lay-ve-**gah**-ray, *v* to smooth; to sand; to polish

levriere, lay-vre-**ay**-ray, *m* greyhound

lezione, lay-tse'**o**-nay, *f* lesson

li, le, *pron* them

lì, le, *adv* there

libbra, lib-brah, *f* (weight) pound

libeccio, le-**bet**-cho, *m* south-west wind

libello, le-**bell**-lo, *m* libel

libellula, le-**bell**-loo-lah, *f* dragonfly

liberale, le-bay-**rah**-lay, *adj* liberal; *m/f* Liberal

liberare, le-bay-**rah**-ray, *v* to free; to release; to clear

libero*, lee-**bay**-ro, *adj* free; clear; vacant; – **professionista,** self employed person; freelancer

libertà, le-bair-**tah**, *f* freedom; liberty; **in – provvisoria,** released on bail; **in – vigilata,** on probation

libidine, le-**bee**-de-nay, *f* lust

libraio, -a, le-**brah**-e'o, *m/f* bookseller

libreria, le-bray-**ree**-ah, *f* bookshop; bookcase

libretto, le-**bret**-to, *m* booklet; *mus* libretto; – **degli assegni,** chequebook; – **di circolazione,** logbook; – **di risparmio,** bankbook

libro, lee-bro, *m* book; register

licenza, le-**chen**-tsah, *f* permission; (authorization) licence, permit; *mil* leave; school-leaving certificate; licentiousness

licenziamento, le-chen-tse'ah-**men**-to, *m* dismissal; redundancy

licenziare, le-chen-tse'**ah**-ray, *v* to dismiss; to make redundant

licenziarsi, le-chen-tse'**ar**-se, *v* to resign

liceo, le-**chay**-o, *m* secondary school

lichene, le-**kay**-nay, *m* lichen

lido, lee-do, *m* shore, beach

lieto*, le'**ay**-to, *adj* glad, merry

lieve*, le'**ay**-vay, *adj* light, soft; trifling

lievitare, le'ay-ve-**tah**-ray, *v* to rise; to leaven

lievito, le'**ay**-ve-to, *m* yeast; – **di birra,** brewer's yeast; – **in polvere,** baking powder

lignaggio, le-n'**yad**-jo, *m* lineage

lilla, lil-lah, *adj* (colour) lilac

lillà, lil-**lah**, *m* (plant) lilac

lima, lee-mah, *f* file

limaccioso, le-maht-**cho**-so, *adj* muddy; miry

limare, le-**mah**-ray, *v* to file; *fig* to polish

limitare, le-me-**tah**-ray, *v* to limit; to bound

limite, lee-me-tay, *m* limit; boundary

limonata, le-mo-**nah**-tah, *f* lemonade

limone, le-mo-nay, *m* lemon; lemon tree

limpido*, lim-pe-do, *adj* limpid, clear

lince, lin-chay, *f* lynx

linciare, lin-**chah**-ray, *v* to lynch

lindo, lin-do, *adj* clean, trim, tidy

linea, lee-nay-ah, *f* line; figure; **– aerea,** airline; **volo di –,** scheduled flight

lineamenti, le-nay-ah-**men**-te, *mpl* features

lineare, le-nay-**ah**-ray, *adj* linear; coherent

lineetta, le-nay-**ayt**-tah, *f* dash; hyphen

lingua, lin-goo'ah, *f* tongue; language; **– madre,** mother tongue

linguaggio, lin-goo'**ahd**-jo, *m* language

linguistica, lin-goo'ee-ste-ka, *f* linguistics

lino, lee-no, *m* (plant) flax; (fabric) linen

liquefare, le-kway-**fah**-ray, *v* to liquify; to melt

liquidare, le-kwe-**dah**-ray, *v* to liquidate; (goods) to sell off; (matter) to settle

liquido, lee-kwe-do, *m* liquid; *adj* liquid, fluid; **denaro –,** ready cash

liquirizia, le-kwe-**rit**-tse'ah, *f* liquorice

liquore, le-**kwo**-ray, *m* liqueur; **liquori,** spirits

lira, lee-rah, *f* (coin) lira;

mus lyre; **– sterlina,** pound sterling

lirico, lee-re-ko, *adj* lyric, lyrical

Lisbona, le-**zbo**-nah, *f* Lisbon

lisca, liss-kah, *f* fishbone

lisciare, le-she'**ah**-ray, *v* to smooth; *fig* to flatter

liscio, lee-she-o, *adj* smooth, sleek; (hair) stright; (liqueur) neat

liso, lee-zo, *adj* threadbare

lista, liss-tah, *f* list; **– elettorale,** electoral roll

listino, liss-**tee**-no, *m* list; **– di borsa,** Stock Exchange listing; **– dei prezzi,** price list

lite, lee-tay, *f* quarrel; *law* lawsuit

litigare, le-te-**gah**-ray, *v* to quarrel; *law* to litigate

litigio, le-**tee**-jo, *m* dispute; quarrel

litorale, le-to-**rah**-lay, *m* coastline

litro, lee-tro, *m* litre

liuto, lee'oo-to, *m* lute

livellare, le-vell-**lah**-ray, *v* to level

livello, le-**vell**-lo, *m* level; standard

livido, lee-ve-do, *m* bruise; *adj* livid; bruised; (sky) leaden

livore, le-vo-ray, *m* grudge

livrea, le-**vray**-ah, *f* livery

lo, lo, *art* the; *pron* him; it

locale, lo-kah-lay, *adj* local; *m* room; premises; stopping train

località, lo-kah-le-**tah**, *f* locality; resort

localizzare, lo-kah-lid-**dzah**-ray, *v* to locate

locanda, lo-**kahn**-dah, *f* inn

locatario, -a, lo-kah-**tah**-re'o, *m/f* tenant

locazione, lo-kah-tse'o-nay, *f* renting; renting out; **contratto di –,** lease

locomotiva, lo-ko-mo-**tee**-vah, *f* locomotive, engine

locusta, lo-**kooss**-tah, *f* locust

locuzione, lo-koo-tse'o-nay, *f* phrase

lodare, lo-**dah**-ray, *v* to praise

lode, lo-day, *f* praise

lodevole*, lo-**de**-vo-lay, *adj* praiseworthy

logaritmo, lo-gah-**rit**-mo, *m* logarithm

loggia, **lod**-jah, *f* lodge

loggione, lod-jo-nay, *m* (theatre) the gods

logorare, lo-go-**rah**-ray, *v* to wear out

logoro, lo-go-ro, *adj* worn out; wasted

lombaggine, lom-**bahd**-je-nay, *f* lumbago

lombata, lom-**bah**-tah, *f* loin (of meat)

lombo, **lom**-bo, *m* loin

lombrico, lom-**bree**-ko, *m* earthworm

Londra, **lon**-drah, *f* London

longanime, lon-**gah**-ne-may, *adj* patient

longevo, lon-**jay**-vo, *adj* long-lived

longitudine, lon-je-**too**-de-nay, *f* longitude

lontananza, lon-tah-**nahn**-tsah, *f* distance; absence

lontano, lon-**tah**-no, *adj* far-away; distant; remote; *adv* far, a long way off; **più –,** farther

lontra, **lon**-trah, *f* otter

loquace, lo-**kwah**-chay, *adj* loquacious

lordo, **lor**-do, *adj* dirty; foul; gross; **peso –,** gross weight

loro, **lo**-ro, *pron* they; them; to them; theirs; *adj* their

lotta, **lot**-tah, *f* struggle; (sport) wrestling

lottare, lot-**tah**-ray, *v* to strive; to wrestle

lottatore, -trice, lot-tah-**tor**-ay, lot-tah-**tree**-chay, *m/f* wrestler

lotteria, lot-te-**ree**-ah, *f* lottery

lotto, **lot**-to, *m* lot; (piece of land) plot; state lottery

lozione, lo-tse'o-nay, *f* lotion

lubrificante, loo-bre-fe-**kahn**-tay, *m* lubricant; *adj* lubricating

lubrificare, loo-bre-fe-**kah**-ray, *v* to lubricate

lucchetto, look-**ket**-to, *m* padlock

luccicare, loot-che-**kah**-ray, *v* to glitter, to shine, to sparkle

luccio, **loot**-cho, *m* pike

lucciola, **loot**-cho-lah, *f* firefly; glowworm

luce, **loo**-chay, *f* light; daylight; **luci della ribalta,** footlights; **luci di posizione,** sidelights

lucente, loo-**chen**-tay, *adj* shining, luminous

lucerna, loo-**chair**-nah, *f* oil lamp

lucertola, loo-**chair**-to-lah, *f* lizard

lucidare, loo-che-**dah**-ray, *v* to polish

lucidatrice, loo-che-dah-**tree**-chay, *f* floor polisher

lucido, **loo**-che-do, *adj** bright; lucid; *m* shoe polish

lucignolo, loo-**che**-n'yo-lo, *m* wick

lucrativo, loo-krah-**tee**-vo, *adj* lucrative

lucro, **loo**-kro, *m* profit

ludibrio, loo-**dee**-bre-o, *m* mockery, derision

luglio, **loo** l'yo, *m* July

lugubre, **loo**-goo-bray, *adj* lugubrious, mournful

lui, **loo**-e, *pron* he; him

lumaca, loo-**mah**-kah, *f* snail; *fig* slowcoach

lume, **loo**-may, *m* light; lamp; **a – di naso,** by rule of thumb

luminoso*, loo-me-**no**-zo, *adj* luminous; radiant

luna, **loo**-nah, *f* moon; **– di miele,** honeymoon

lunedì, loo-nay-**dee**, *m* Monday

lunghezza, loonn-**get**-tsah, *f* length, duration

lungi, **loonn**-je, *prep* **– da,** far from

lungo, **loonn**-go, *adj* long; (person) slow; (coffee) weak; *prep* along; **alla lunga,** in the long run; **di gran lunga,** far and away, by far

lungofiume, loon-go-fee'**oo**-may, *m* embankment

lungomare, loon-go-**mah**-ray, *m* promenade

luogo, loo'**o**-go, *m* place; site; **aver –,** to take place; **dar – a,** to give rise to

luogotenente, loo'o-go-tay-**nen**-tay, *m* lieutenant

lupa, loo-pah, *f* she-wolf

lupo, loo-po, *m* wolf; **cane –,** alsatian; **in bocca al –!,** good luck!

luppolo, loop-po-lo, *m* hop

lurido, loo-re-do, *adj* foul

lusinga, loo-**sin**-gah, *f* flattery

lusingare, loo-sin-**gah**-ray, *v* to flatter

lussazione, looss-sa-tse'o-nay, *f* dislocation

lusso, looss-so, *m* luxury

lussuoso, looss-soo'o-so, *adj* luxurious

lussuria, looss-**soo**-re'ah, *f* lust

lustrare, looss-**trah**-ray, *v* to polish

lustrascarpe, loos-tras-**kahr**-pay, *m/f* shoeshine

lustrino, loos-**tree**-no, *m* sequin

lustro, looss-tro, *m* shine; gloss; prestige; five-year period

lutto, loot-to, *m* mourning; bereavement

ma, mah, *conj*, but

macabro, mah-**kah**-bro, *adj* macabre, gruesome

macché, mahk-**kay**, *interj* certainly not

maccheroni, mahk-kay-ro-ne, *mpl* macaroni

macchia, mahk-ke'ah, *f* stain, spot; (wood) scrub

macchiare, mahk-ke'ah-ray, *v* to stain, to mark

macchina, mahk-ke-nah, *f* car; machine; engine; – **da cucire,** sewing machine; – **fotografica,** camera; – **da presa,** cine camera; – **da scrivere,** typewriter

macchinare, mahk-ke-nah-ray, *v* to plot

macchinario, mahk-ke-nah-re'o, *m* machinery

macchinista, mahk-ke-niss-tah, *m* engine-driver; *naut* engineer; (theatre) stagehand

macedonia, mah-chay-do-ne'ah, *f* fruit salad

macellaio, mah-chayl-lah-e'o, *m* butcher

macellare, mah-chayl-lah-ray, *v* to slaughter

macello, mah-chell-lo, *m* slaughter-house; *fig* massacre

macerare, mah-chay-rah-ray, *v* to macerate; to marinate

macerie, mah-chay-re'ay, *fpl* rubble

macigno, mah-chee-n'yo, *m* boulder

macilento, mah-che-len-to, *adj* emaciated

macina, mah-che-nah, *f* millstone

macinapepe, mah-che-nah-**pay**-pay, *m* pepper mill

macinare, mah-che-**nah**-ray, *v* to grind, to mill

macinino, mah-che-nee-no, *m* coffee grinder; pepper mill; (car) old banger

maculato, mah-koo-lah-to, spotted

madido, mah-de-do, *adj* moist

madonna, mah-don-nah, *f* (art) madonna; **Madonna,** Our Lady

madornale, mah-dor-nah-lay, *adj* enormous, huge

madre, mah-dray, *f* mother; counterfoil

madrelingua, mah-dray-lin-goo'ah, *f* native language, mother tongue

madreperla, mah-dray-pair-lah, *f* mother of pearl

madrina, mah-dree-nah, *f* godmother

maestà, mah-ess-tah, *f* majesty; dignity

maestoso*, mah-ess-to-zo *adj* majestic

maestrale, mah-ess-trah-lay, *m* north-west wind

maestranze, mah-ess-

trahn-dzay, *fpl* workforce

maestria, mah-ess-**tree**-ah, *f* mastery, skill

maestro, -a, mah-**ess**-tro, *m/f* primary school teacher; expert; instructor; *m mus* maestro; (crafts) master; *adj* masterly

mafioso, -a, mah-fe'o-so, *m/f* member of the Mafia

maga, mah-gah, *f* sorceress

magagna, mah-gah-n'yah, *f* defect; blemish; problem

magari, mah-**gah**-re, *interj* if only!, you bet!; *adv* perhaps

magazzino, mah-gahd-dze-no, *m* warehouse; **grande –,** department store

maggio, mahd-jo, *m* May

maggiorana, mahd-jo-**rah**-nah, *f* marjoram

maggioranza, mahd-jo-**rahn**-dzah, *f* majority

maggiore*, mahd-**jor**-ay, *m* major; *adj* bigger; greater; elder; biggest; greatest; eldest

maggiorenne, mahd-jo-**ren**-nay, *adj* of age

magia, mah-**jee**-ah, *f* magic

magico, mah-je-ko, *adj* magic; magical; enchanting

magistero, mah-jiss-**tay**-ro, *m* teachers' training college

magistrale, mah-jiss-**trah**-lay, *adj* masterly; **istituto –,** type of secondary school

magistrato, mah-jiss-**trah**-to, *m* magistrate

maglia, mah-l'yah, *f* sweater; vest; mesh; stitch; knitting

maglieria, mah-l'yay-**ree**-ah, *f* knitwear

maglietta, mah-l'**yet**-tah, *f* t-shirt; vest

maglio, mah-l'yo, *m* mallet

magnanimo*, mah-n'**yah**-ne-mo, *adj* magnanimous

magnate, mah-n'**yah**-tay, *m* tycoon

magnesia, mah-n'**yah**-se'ah, *f* magnesia

magnesio, mah-n'**yah**-se'o, *m* magnesium

magnete, mah-n'**yay**-tay, *m* magnet

magnetico*, mah-n'**yay**-te-ko, *adj* magnetic

magnetizzare, mah-n'yay-tid-**dzah**-ray, *v* to magnetize; to mesmerize

magnificenza, mah-n'ye-fe-**chen**-tsah, *f* magnificence

magnifico*, mah-n'**yee**-fe-ko, *adj* magnificent

magnolia, mah-n'**yee**-o-le'ah, *f* magnolia

mago, mah-go, *m* magician

magrezza, mah-**gret**-tsah, *f* thinness; scarcity

magro, mah-gro, *adj* thin, slim; poor, meager; (meat) lean; (milk) skimmed

mai, mah-e, *adv* never; ever

maiale, mah-e'**ah**-lay, *m* pig; (meat) pork

maionese, mah-ee'o-**nay**-say, *f* mayonnaise

mais, mah-iss, *m* maize

maiuscola, mah-e'**ooss**-ko-lah, *f* capital letter

malaccorto, mah-lahk-**kor**-to, *adj* rash, inconsiderate

malafede, mah-lah-**fay**-day, *f* bad faith

malandato, mah-lahn-**dah**-to, *adj* in poor health; badly off; shabby

malandrino, mah-lahn-**dree**-no, *m* ruffian

malanno, mah-**lahn**-no, *m* ailment; misfortune

malapena, mah-lah-**pay**-nah, **a –,** *adv* hardly, scarcely

malaria, mah-lah-re'ah, *f* malaria

malaticcio, mah-lah-**tit**-cho, *adj* sickly

malato, -a, mah-**lah**-to, *adj* unwell, ill; *m/f* sick person; patient

malattia, mah-laht-**tee**-ah, *f* illness; disease

malavita, mah-lah-**vee**-tah, *f* underworld

malavoglia, mah-lah-**vo**-ly'ah, **di –,** *avv* unwillingly

maldicenza, mahl-de-**chen**-tsah, *f* slander, malicious gossip

male, **mah**-lay, *m* harm; evil; *adv* badly; **far –,** to hurt, **far – a,** to harm; **sentirsi –,** to feel ill

maledetto, mah-lay-**det**-to, *adj* cursed, confounded

maledire, mah-lay-**dee**-ray, *v* to curse

maledizione, mah-lay-deet-**se'o**-nay, *f* curse; *interj* damn it!

maleducato, mah-lay-doo-**kah**-to, *adj* ill-mannered

malessere, mah-**lays**-say-ray, *m* slight illness; uneasiness

malevolo, mah-**lay**-vo-lo, *adj* malevolent

malfatto, mahl-**faht**-to, *adj* badly done; misshapen

malfermo, mahl-**fair**-mo, *adj* unsteady; shaky

malformazione, mahl-for-mah-te'o-nay, *f* malformation

malgrado, mahl-**grah**-do, *prep* in spite of; *conj* although

maligno*, mah-**lee**-n'yo, *adj* malicious; *med* malignant

malinconia, mah-lin-ko-nee-ah, *f* melancholy

malinconico*, mah-lin-**ko**-ne-ko, *adj* melancholic

malincuore, mah-lin-koo'o-ray, *adv* **a –,** reluctantly

malinteso, mah-lin-**tay**-zo, *m* misunderstanding; *adj* misunderstood; misguided

malizia, mah-lee-**tse'ah**, *f* malice; craftiness

malizioso*, mah-le-**tse'o**-zo, *adj* malicious; mischievous

malmenare, mahl-may-**nah**-ray, *v* to ill-treat; to beat up

malmesso, mahl-**mays**-so, *adj* shabby

malnutrito, mahl-noo-**tree**-to, *adj* undernourished

malocchio, mah-**lock**-ke'o, *m* evil eye

malora, mah-lo-rah, *f* ruin; **andare in –,** to go

to the dogs

malore, mah-**lo**-ray, *m* sudden illness

malsano, mahl-**sah**-no, *adj* unhealthy

malsicuro, mahl-se-**koo**-ro, *adj* unsafe

maltrattare, mahl-traht-**tah**-ray, *v* to ill-treat

malumore, mah-loo-**mo**-ray, *m* bad mood

malva, mahl-vah, *f* mallow; *adj* mauve

malvagio, mahl-**vah**-jo, *adj* wicked

malversazione, mahl-vair-sah-tse'**o**-nay, *f* embezzlement

malvolentieri, mahl-vo-len-te'**ay**-re, *adv* unwillingly

mamma, mahm-mah, *f* mum, mummy

mammella, mahm-**mel**-lah, *f* breast; udder

mammifero, mahm-mee-**fay**-ro, *m* mammal

mammola, mahm-mo-lah, *f* violet

manager, mah-nah-jair, *m/f* manager

manata, mah-**nah**-tah, *f* slap; (quantity) handful

mancanza, mahn-**kahn**-tsah, *f* lack, want; shortage; fault, error

mancare, mahn-kah-ray, *v* to be lacking; to be

missing; to fail; to die; –
a, to fail to keep

mancato, mahn-**kah**-to *adj*
unsuccessful; missed;
wasted

mancia, mahn-chah, *f* tip

manciata, mahn-**chah**-
tah, *f* handful

mancino, mahn-**che**-no,
adj left-handed; **tiro –,**
dirty trick

mandare, mahn-**dah**-ray, *v*
to send; **– a chiamare,**
to send for

mandato, mahn-**dah**-to, *m*
mandate; *law* warrant

mandibola, mahn-**dee**-bo-
lah, *f* jawbone

mandorla, mahn-dor-lah,
f almond

mandria, mahn-**dre**'ah, *f*
herd

mandriano, mahn-dre-**ah**-
no, *m* herdsman

maneggevole, mah-ned-
jay-vo-lay, *adj* easy to
handle

maneggiare, mah-ned-**jah**-
ray, *v* to handle; to use

maneggio, mah-**ned**-jo, *m*
riding-school; handling;
scheme

manesco, mah-**ness**-ko,
adj ready with one's fists

manette, mah-**net**-tay, *fpl*
handcuffs

manganello, mahn-gah-
nayl-lo, *m* cudgel;

truncheon

manganese, mahn-gah-
nay-say, *m* manganese

mangiabile, mahn-jah-be-
lay, *adj* eatable, edible

mangiadischi, mahn-jah-
dee-skee, *m* portable
record-player

mangiare, mahn-**jah**-ray, *v*
to eat; *fig* to squander; *m*
food

mangime, mahn-**jee**-may,
m fodder

mania, mah-**nee**-ah, *f*
mania

manica, mah-ne-kah, *f*
sleeve; **la Manica,** the
Channel; **il tunnel sotto
la Manica,** the Channel
Tunnel

manico, mah-ne-ko, *m*
handle

manicomio, mah-ne-ko-
me'o, *m* lunatic asylum

manicotto, mah-ne-**kot**-
to, *m* muff

manicure, mah-ne-**koo**-
ray, *f* manicure

maniera, mah-ne'**ay**-rah, *f*
manner, way; **alla – di,**
in the style of; **in – che,**
so that

manierato, mah-ne'ay-
rah-to, *adj* affected

manifattura, mah-ne-
faht-**too**-rah, *f*
manufacture, make;
factory

manifestare, mah-ne-fess-
tah-ray, *v* to show, to
reveal; to demonstrate

manifesto, mah-ne-**fess**-
to, *adj** evident, clear; *m*
poster; manifesto

maniglia, mah-**nee**-l'yah, *f*
handle; strap; *naut*
shackle

manipolare, mah-nee-po-
lah-ray, *v* to handle; to
manipulate; to fiddle

maniscalco, mah-niss-
kahl-ko, *m* blacksmith

mano, mah-no, *f* hand; (of
paint) coat; (at cards)
hand; **a portata di –,** ay
hand; **di seconda mano,**
second-hand; **man –,**
little by little; **man –
che,** as

manodopera, mah-no-**do**-
pay-rah, *f* labour,
manpower

manomettere, mah-no-
met-tay-ray, *v* to tamper
with; to force, to break
open

manopola, mah-**no**-po-
lah, *f* knob, hand-grip

manoscirtto, mah-no-
skrit-to, *m* manuscript

manovale, mah-no-**vah**-
lay, *m* labourer

manovella, mah-no-**vell**-
lah, *f mech* crank;
handle

manovra, mah-no-vrah, *f*

manoeuvre; drill; shunting

manovrare, mah-no-**vra**-ray, *v* to manoeuvre; to operate

mansarda, mahn-**sahr**-dah, *f* attic

mansione, mahn-see'o-nay, *f* duty, task

mansueto, mahn-soo-**ay**-to, *adj* (animal) tame; (person) meek, docile

mantello, mahn-**tell**-lo, *m* cloak; (animal) coat; (snow) blanket, mantle

mantenere, mahn-tay-**nay**-ray, *v* to maintain, to keep, to uphold; (family) to support

mantenimento, mahn-tay-ne-**men**-to, *m* maintenance

manuale, mah-noo'**ah**-lay, *adj* manual; *m* handbook, manual

manubrio, mah-**noo**-bre-o, *m* handlebars; handle

manutenzione, mahn-noo-ten-tse'o-nay, *f* maintenance, upkeep

manzo, mahn-dzo, *m* beef; **arrosto di –,** roastbeef

mappa, mahp-pah, *f* map

mappamondo, mahp-pah-**mon**-do, *m* globe; map of the world

maratona, mah-rah-to-nah, *f* marathon

marca, mar-kah, *f* brand; make; trademark; stamp; **– da bollo,** official stamp

marcare, mar-kah-ray, *v* to mark

marchesa, mar-kay-zah, *f* marchioness

marchese, mar-kay-zay, *m* marquis

marchio, mar-ke'o, *m* mark; brand; **– di fabbrica,** trademark

marcia, mar-chah, *f* march; (car) gear; **fare – indietro,** to reverse; *fig* to backtrack; **mettere in –,** to start up

marciapiede, mar-chah-pe'**ay**-day, *m* pavement; platform

marciare, mar-chah-ray, *v* to march; (vehicle) to travel

marcio, mar-cho, *adj* rotten; *med* festering; (morally) corrupt

marcire, mar-chee-ray, *v* to rot; *med* to fester

marco, mar-ko, *m* (currency) mark

mare, mah-ray, *m* sea; seaside

marea, mah-**ray**-ah, *f* tide; ebb and flow

maresciallo, mah-ray-**shall**-lo, *m* marshal

margarina, mar-ghah-ree-nah, *f* margarine

margherita, mar-ghay-**ree**-tah, *f* daisy

margine, mar-je-nay, *m* margin; edge

marijuana, mahr-e'oo-**ah**-nah, *f* marijuana

marina, mah-**ree**-nah, *f* coast; seascape; navy

marinaio, mah-re-**nah**-e'o, *m* sailor; mariner

marinare, mah-re-**nah**-ray, *v* to marinate; to pickle; **– la scuola,** to play truant

marino, mah-**ree**-no, *adj* marine; **cavalluccio –,** sea horse; **fondo –,** sea bed

marionetta, mah-re'o-**net**-tah, *f* puppet; marionette

maritare, mah-re-tah-ray, *v* to give in marriage

maritarsi, mah-re-**tar**-se, *v* to get married

marito, mah-**ree**-to, *m* husband

marittimo, mah-**rit**-te-mo, *adj* maritime

marmellata, mar-mell-**lah**-tah, *f* jam; (citrus fruit) marmalade

marmitta, mar-**mit**-tah, *f* cauldron; pothole; (car) silencer; **– catalitica,** catalytic converter

marmo, mar-mo, *m*

marble

marmocchio, mar-**mock**-ke'o, *m* little kid; brat

marmotta, mar-**mot**-tah, *f* marmot

maroso, mah-**ro**-so, *m* billow, breaker

marrone, mar-**ro**-nay, *adj* & *m* brown, chestnut

Marsiglia, mar-**see**-l'yah, *f* Marseilles

marsina, mar-**see**-nah, *f* tail coat

martedì, mar-tay-**dee**, *m* Tuesday

martellare, mar-tell-**lah**-ray, *v* to hammer

martello, mar-**tell**-lo, *m* hammer; knocker

martinetto, mar-te-**net**-to, *m* (tool) jack

martire, mar-te-ray, *m/f* martyr

martirio, mar-**tee**-re'o, *m* martyrdom

martora, mar-to-rah, *f* marten

martoriare, mar-to-re'**ah**-ray, *v* to torture

marxista, mar-**ksee**-stah, *m/f* Marxist; *adj* Marxist

marzapane, mar-tsah-**pah**-nay, *m* marzipan

marziale, mar-tse'**ah**-lay, *adj* martial

marziano, mar-tse'**ah**-no, *adj* Martian; creature from outer space

marzo, mar-tso, *m* March

mascalzone, mahss-kahl-**tso**-nay, *m* rogue, scoundrel

mascella, mah-**shel**-lah, *f* jaw

maschera, **mahss**-kay-rah, *f* mask; fancy dress; (traditional comedy) stock character; (in cinema) usher, usherette

mascherare, mahss-kay-**rah**-ray, *v* to mask; to conceal; *mil* to camouflage

mascherata, mahss-kay-**rah**-tah, *f* masquerade

maschile, mahss-**kee**-lay, *adj* masculine; male

maschio, **mahss**-ke'o, *m* male; *adj* masculine; manly

massa, **mahss**-sah, *f* mass; pile, heaps; (electricity) earth

massacro, mahss-**sah**-kro, *m* slaughter, massacre

massaggio, mahss-**sahd**-jo, *m* massage

massaia, mahss-sah-e'ah, *f* housewife

masseria, mahss-say-**ree**-ah, *f* farm

masserizie, mahss-say-**ree**-tse'ay, *fpl* household furnishings

massiccio, mahss-**sit**-cho, *adj* massive; solid

massima, mahss-se-mah, *f* maxim; maximum temperature

massimo, mahss-se-mo, *m* maximum; *adj* highest, greatest

masso, **mahss**-so, *m* rock

massone, mahss-**so**-nay, *m* freemason

masticare, mahss-te-**kah**-ray, *v* to masticate, to chew

mastice, mahss-te-chay, *m* mastic; putty

mastino, mahss-**tee**-no, *m* mastiff

mastro, mahss-tro, *m* : **libro –**, ledger

masturbazione, mahss-toor-bah-tse'**o**-nay, *f* masturbation

matassa, mah-**tahss**-sah, *f* skein

matematica, mah-tay-**mah**-te-kah, *f* mathematics

matematico, -a, mah-tay-**mah**-te-ko, *adj* mathematical; *m/f* mathematician

materasso, mah-tay-**rahss**-so, *m* mattress

materia, mah-**tay**-re'ah, *f* matter; (school) subject; (substance) material; **materie plastiche**, plastics; **materie prime**, raw materials

materiale, mah-tay-re'**ah**-lay, *adj* material; *m* material, equipment

maternità, mah-tair-nee-**tah,** *f* motherhood; maternity hospital

materno, mah-**tair**-no, *adj* maternal; motherly; **lingua materna,** mother tongue; **scuola materna,** nursery school

matita, mah-**tee**-tah, *f* pencil

matrice, mah-**tree**-chay, *f* matrix; stub; origin

matricola, mah-**tree**-ko-lah, *f* register; registration number; (university) freshman

matrigna, mah-**tree**-n'yah, *f* stepmother

matrimonio, mah-tre-mo-ne'o, *m* marriage; (ceremony) wedding; matrimony

matrona, mah-**tro**-nah, *f* matron

mattina, maht-**tee**-nah, *f* morning

mattinata, maht-te-**nah**-tah, *f* morning; (performance) matinée

mattiniero, maht-te-ne'**ay**-ro, *adj* essere –, to be an early riser

mattino, maht-**tee**-no, *m* morning

matto, maht-to, *adj* mad;

crazy; insane; *m* lunatic

mattone, maht-to-nay, *m* brick

mattonella, maht-to-**nel**-lah, *f* tile

maturare, mah-too-**rah**-ray, *v* to ripen; to mature

maturità, mah-too-ree-**tah,** *f* maturity; school-leaving examination

maturo, mah-**too**-ro, *adj* ripe, mature

mazza, maht-tsah, *f* club; mace; bat

mazzo, maht-tso, *m* bundle; pack

me, may, *pron* me, to me

meandro, may-**ahn**-dro, *m* meander

meccanica, meck-**kah**-ne-kah, *f* mechanics

meccanico, meck-**kah**-ne-ko, *adj* mechanical; *m* mechanic

medaglia, may-**dah**-l'yah, *f* medal

medaglione, may-dah-l'**yo**-nay, *m* medallion

medesimo, may-**day**-se-mo, *adj* same; *pron* (the) same one; **io –,** I myself

media, may-de'ah, *f* average; mean

mediante, may-de'**ahn**-tay, *prep* by means of

mediare, may-de'ah-ray, *v* to mediate

mediazione, may-de'ah-

tse'o-nay, *f* mediation; brokerage

medicare, may-de-**kah**-ray, *v* to treat (patient); to dress (wound)

medicazione, may-de'kah-tse'**o**-nay, *f* medication, treatment; dressing

medicina, may-de-**chee**-nah, *f* medicine

medicinale, may-de-**chee**-**nah**-lay, *adj* medicinal; *m* drug, medicine

medico, may-de-ko, *m* doctor; – **generico,** general practitioner; *adj* medical; **visita medica,** medical examination

medievale, may-de'ay-**vah**-lay, *adj* medieval

medio, may-de'o, *adj* average; middle; medium; **dito –,** middle finger; **scuola media,** secondary school for 11- to 14-year-olds

mediocre, may-de'o-kray, *adj* mediocre, middling

medioevale, may-de'o-ay-**vah**-lay, *adj* medieval

meditare, may-de-**tah**-ray, *v* to meditate

mediterraneo, may-de-tair-**rah**-nay-o, *adj* Mediterranean; **il Mediterraneo–,** *m* the Mediterranean

medusa, may-**doo**-zah, *f*

jellyfish; Medusa

megafono, may-**ghah**-fo-no, *m* megaphone

megera, may-**jay**-rah, *f* shrew

meglio, may-l'yo, *adv* better, best; *adj* better, best; *m* best; *f* avere la – su, to get the better of

mela, may-lah, *f* apple

melanzana, may-lahnd-dzah-nah, *f* aubergine

melassa, may-**lahss**-sah, *f* treacle; molasses

melma, mell-mah, *f* mud

melo, may-lo, *m* apple tree

melodia, may-lo-**dee**-ah, *f* melody

melodioso*, may-lo-de'o-zo, *adj* melodious

melone, may-**lo**-nay, *m* melon

membrana, mem-**brah**-nah, *f* membrane

membro, mem-bro, *m* limb; member

memorabile, may-mo-**rah**-be-lay, *adj* memorable

memore, may-mo-ray, *adj* mindful

memoria, may-mo-re'ah, *f* memory; recollection; a –, by heart

menare, may-**nah**-ray, *v* to lead; to hit

mendicante, men-de-**kahn**-tay, *m/f* beggar

mendicare, men-de-kah-ray, *v* to beg

menestrello, may-ness-**trel**-lo, *m* minstrel

meningite, may-nin-jee-tay, *f* meningitis

meno, may-no, *adv* less; *adj* less, fewer; *m* least; (in sums) minus; a – che/di, unless; per lo –, at least

menomare, may-no-**mah**-ray, *v* to maim, to disable

menopausa, may-no-pa'oo-zah, *f* menopause

mensa, men-sah, *f* canteen; refectory; *mil* mess

mensile, men-**see**-lay, *adj* monthly; *m* monthly magazine; monthly salary

mensola, men-so-lah, *f* shlef; bracket

menta, men-tah, *f* mint

mente, men-tay, *f* mind; imparare a –, to learn by heart

mentire, men-**tee**-ray, *v* to lie

mento, men-to, *m* chin

mentre, men-tray, *conj* while; whereas

menzionare, men-tse'o-**nah**-ray, *v* to mention

menzione, men-tse'o-nay, *f* mention; far – di, to

mention

menzogna, men-**tso**-n'yah, *f* untruth, lie

meraviglia, may-rah-vee-l'yah, *f* amazement; marvel

meravigliarsi, may-rah-ve-l'**yar**-se, *v* – di, to be amazed at

meraviglioso*, may-rah-ve-l'yo-zo, *adj* marvellous, wonderful

mercante, mair-**kahn**-tay, *m* merchant; dealer, trader

mercantile, mair-kahn-**tee**-lay, *adj* mercantile; merchant; *m* (ship) merchantman

mercanzia, mair-kahn-**tsee**-ah, *f* goods, merchandise

mercato, mair-**kah**-to, *m* market; a buon –, cheap; il Mercato Comune (Europeo), the (European) Common Market

merce, mair-chay, *f* merchandise; goods; wares

mercenario, mair-chay-**nah**-re'o, *m* mercenary; *adj* mercenary

merceria, mair-chay-**ree**-ah, *f* haberdashery

merciaio, -a, mair-**chah**-e'o, *m/f* haberdasher

mercoledì, mair-ko-lay-**dee**, m Wednesday

mercurio, mair-koo-re'o, m mercury

merenda, may-**ren**-dah, f light afternoon meal

meridiana, may-re-de'**ah**-nah, f sundial

meridiano, may-re-de'**ah**-no, adj midday; m meridian

meridionale, may-re-de'o-**nah**-lay, adj southern; m/f southerner

meridione, may-re-de'o-nay, m south; Southern Italy

meringa, may-**rin**-gah, f meringue

meritare, may-re-**tah**-ray, v to merit, to deserve

meritevole, may-re-**tay**-vo-lay, adj worthy

merito, **may**-re-to, m merit; worth; **in – a**, as regards

merletto, mair-**let**-to, m lace

merlo, mair-lo, m blackbird; battlement

merluzzo, mair-**loot**-tso, m cod-fish

mero*, **may**-ro, adj mere

meschino*, mess-**kee**-no, adj mean; petty; meagre

mescolanza, mess-ko-**lahn**-tsah, f mixture

mescolare, mess-ko-**lah**-ray, v to mix; to blend; to shuffle

mese, may-zay, m month

messa, **mess**-say, f mass; **– a fuoco**, focusing; **– in piega**, set; **– in scena**, production

messaggero, mess-sahd-jay-ro, m messenger

messaggio, mess-**sahd**-jo, m message

messe, mess-say, f crop, harvest

messia, mess-**see**-ah, m messiah

Messico, **mess**-se-ko, m Mexico

mestiere, mess-te'**ay**-ray, m job; trade; craft

mesto*, **mess**-to, adj sad, melancholic

mestolo, **mess**-to-lo, m ladle

mestruazione, may-stroo'ah-tse'**o**-nay, f menstruation, period

meta, **may**-tah, f destination; aim

metà, may-**tah**, f half; middle; **a – settimana**, mid-week; **a – strada**, halfway; **fare a –**, to go halves

metafora, may-**tah**-fo-rah, f metaphor

metallo, may-**tahl**-lo, m metal

metano, may-**tah**-no, m methane

meteora, may-**tay**-o-rah, f meteor

meteorologico, may-tay'o-ro-lo-gee-ko, adj meteorological; **bollettino –**, weather report

meticcio, -a, may-**tit**-cho, m/f half-cast

meticoloso, may-tee-ko-**lo**-zo, adj meticulous

metodo, **may**-to-do, f method

metraggio, may-**trahd**-jo, m **a –**, by the metre

metrico, **may**-tre-ko, adj metric; (in poetry) metrical

metro, **may**-tro, m metre; tape measure; metre rule

metrò, may-**tro**, m underground

metropolitana, may-tro-po-lee-**tah**-nah, f underground

mettere, **met**-tay-ray, v to put; to place; (clothes) to put on

mezzaluna, med-dzah-**loo**-nah, f crescent, half-moon; chopping knife

mezzanotte, med-dzah-**not**-tay, f midnight

mezzo, med-dzo, adj half; m middle; half; means, way; **mezzi di trasporto**, means of transport

mezzogiorno, med-dzo-**jor**-no, *m* midday, noon; south

mi, mee, *pron* me; to me; *refl* myself; *m mus* E

miagolare, me'ah-go-**lah**-ray, *v* to mew, to miaow

mica, mee-kah, *adv* not at all, not a bit

miccia, mit-chah, *f* fuse

microfono, me-**kro**-fo-no, *m* microphone

microonda, me-kro-**on**-dah, *f* microwave

microscopio, me-kro-**sko**-pe'o, *m* microscope

microspia, me-kro-**spee**-ah, *f* hidden microphone, bug

midollo, me-**doll**-lo, *m* marrow; **– spinale,** spinal cord

miele, me'ay-lay, *m* honey; **luna di –,** honeymoon

mietere, me'ay-tay-ray, *v* to reap, to harvest; **– vittime,** to claim victims

mietitrebbiatrice, me'ay-te-treb-be'ah-**tree**-chay, *f mech* combine harvester

mietitrice, me'ay-te-**tree**-chay, *f mech* harvester

migliaio, me-l'**yah**-e'o, *m* thousand

miglio, mee-l'yo, *m* mile; millet

miglioramento, me-l'yo-rah-**men**-to, *m* improvement

migliorare, me-l'yo-**rah**-ray, *v* to improve

migliore, me-l'**yor**-ay, *adj* better, best; *m/f* **il/la –,** the best (person)

mignolo, mee-n'yo-lo, *m* little finger; little toe

migrare, me-**grah**-ray, *v* to migrate

Milano, me-**lah**-no, *f* Milan

miliardo, me-le'**ar**-do, *m* thousand million, billion

milione, me-le'o-nay, *m* million

militare, me-le-**tah**-ray, *adj* military; *m* serviceman; *v* to serve in

milite, mee-le-tay, *m* soldier

militesente, me-le-tay-**sen**-tay, *m* exempt from National Service

mille, mil-lay, *adj* & *m* one thousand, a thousand; **duemila,** two thousand

millepiedi, mil-lay-pe'**ay**-de, *m* millipede

millesimo, mil-**lay**-ze-mo, *adj* & *m* thousandth

milligrammo, mil-lee-**grahm**-mo, *m* milligram, milligramme

millimetro, mil-lee-may-tro, *m* millimetre

milza, mil-tsah, *f* spleen

mimetizzarsi, mee-me-tid-**dzar**-se, *v* to camouflage oneself

mimica, mee-me-kah, *f* mime; gestures

mimo, mee-mo, *m* mime

mina, mee-nah, *f* mine

minaccia, me-**naht**-chah, *f* threat

minacciare, me-naht-**chah**-ray, *v* to threaten

minaccioso*, me-naht-**cho**-zo, *adj* threatening

minare, me-**nah**-ray, *v* to mine; to undermine

minatore, me-nah-**tor**-ay, *m* miner

minerale, me-nay-**rah**-lay, *adj* mineral; *m* mineral; *f* mineral water

minestra, me-**ness**-trah, *f* soup

miniatura, me-ne'ah-**too**-rah, *f* miniature

miniera, me-ne'**ay**-rah, *f* mine

minigonna, me-ne-**ghon**-nah, *f* miniskirt

minimo, mee-ne-mo, *adj* minimum, least, minimal; *m* minimum

ministero, me-niss-**tay**-ro, *m* ministry; *law* **pubblico –,** State prosecutor

ministro, me-**niss**-tro, *m* minister

minoranza, me-no-**rahn**-

tsah, *f* minority

minorato, me-no-**rah**-to, *adj* handicapped; **–a,** *m/f* handicapped person

minore, me-**nor**-ay, *adj* less, smaller; lower, inferior; younger; *m/f* under age; **opere minori,** minor works; **do –,** C minor

minorenne, me-no-**ren**-nay, *adj* under age

minuscolo, me-**nooss**-ko-lo, *adj* minute; tiny; small; **in –,** in small letters

minuta, me-**noo**-tah, *f* rough copy, draft

minuto, me-**noo**-to, *adj** tiny; minute; detailed; *m* minute; **al –,** retail

mio, **mee**-o, *adj* my; *pron* mine

miope, **mee**-o-pay, *adj* short-sighted

mira, **mee**-rah, *f* aim; **prendere la –,** to take aim

mirabile, me-**rah**-be-lay, *adj* wonderful

miracolo, me-**rah**-ko-lo, *m* miracle; prodigy

miracoloso*, me-rah-ko-lo-zo, *adj* miraculous

miraggio, me-**rahd**-jo, *m* mirage, illusion

mirare, me-**rah**-ray, *v* to aim at

mirino, me-**ree**-no, *m* (gun) sight; (photo) viewer

mirra, **meer**-rah, *f* myrrh

mirtillo, meer-**til**-lo, *m* bilberry, blueberry

miscela, me-**shay**-lah, *f* mixture; blend

miscellaneo, me-shell-**lah**-nay-o, *adj* miscellaneous

mischia, **miss**-ke'ah, *f* scuffle; (rugby) scrum

mischiare, miss-ke'**ah**-ray, *v* to mix; to blend; (cards) to shuffle

miscredente, miss-**kray**-den-tay, *m/f* unbeliever

miscuglio, miss-**koo**-l'yo, *m* mixture; jumble

miserabile, me-zay-**rah**-be-lay,*adj* miserable; wretched; needy; *m/f* wretch

miseria, me-**zay**-re'ah, *f* poverty; **essere pagato una –,** to be paid a pittance

misericordia, me-zay-re-**kor**-de'ah, *f* mercy; compassion

misericordioso*, me-zay-re-kor-de'o-zo, *adj* merciful

misero, **mee**-zay-ro, *adj* miserable, wretched; poor

misfatto, miss-**faht**-to, *m* crime; wicked action

missile, **miss**-see-lay, *m* missile

missione, miss-se'o-nay, *f* mission

misterioso*, miss-tay-re'o-zo, *adj* mysterious

mistero, miss-**tay**-ro, *m* mystery

misto, **miss**-to, *adj* mixed

mistura, miss-**too**-rah, *f* mixture

misura, me-**zoo**-rah, *f* measure; measurement, size; **in che –,** to what extent

misurare, me-zoo-**rah**-ray, *v* to measure; (land) to survey; (clothes) to try on; (words) to weigh up

misurino, me-zoo-**ree**-no, *m* measuring cup

mite, **mee**-tay, *adj* mild; gentle

mitezza, me-**tet**-tsah, *f* mildness

mitigare, me-te-**gah**-ray, *v* to mitigate; to alleviate

mito, **mee**-to, *m* myth

mitologia, me-to-lo-jee-ah, *f* mythology

mitra, **mee**-trah, *m* submachine gun; *f relig* mitre

mitragliare, me-trah-l'yah-ray, *v* to machin-gun

mitragliatrice, me-trah-l'yah-**tree**-chay, *f*

machine gun

mittente, met-**ten**-tay, *m/f*
sender

mobile, mo-be-lay, *adj*
mobile; movable; *m*
piece of furniture; *f*
flying squad

mobilia, mo-**bee**-le'ah, *f*
furniture

mobilitare, mo-be-le-**tah**-
ray, *v* to mobilize

moccio, **mot**-cho, *m fam*
snot

moda, mo-dah, *f* fashion;
essere di –, to be
fashionable

modalità, mo-dah-lee-**tah,**
f formality

modella, mo-**dell**-lah, *f*
model

modellare, mo-dell-**lah**-
ray, *v* to model, to
mould

modello, mo-**dell**-lo, *m*
model; type; pattern

moderare, mo-day-**rah**-
ray, *v* to moderate

moderato*, mo-day-**rah**-
to, *adj* moderate

moderno*, mo-**dair**-no,
adj modern

modestia, mo-**dess**-te'ah, *f*
modesty

modesto*, mo-**dess**-to, *adj*
modest

modico*, **mo**-de-ko, *adj*
moderate

modifica, mo-de-fe-kah, *f*

modification; alteration;
adjustment

modificare, mo-de-fe-**kah**-
ray, *v* to modify; to alter

modista, mo-**diss**-tah, *f*
milliner

modo, **mo**-do, *m* manner,
way; means; *gram* mood

modulo, **mo**-**doo**-lo, *m*
form; module; **– di**
domanda, application
form

mogano, mo-**gah**-no, *m*
mahogany

moglie, mo-l'yay, *f* wife

mole, **mo**-lay, *f* mass;
massive shape; huge
building

molestare, mo-less-**tah**-
ray, *v* to annoy, to
bother; (sexually) to
molest; to harass

molesto, mo-**less**-to, *adj*
annoying

molla, **moll**-lah, *f* spring;
a –, clockwork; **molle,**
tongs

mollare, moll-**lah**-ray, *v* to
let go; to give in; (slap,
punch) to give

molle, **moll**-lay, *adj* soft;
flabby

molletta, moll-**let**-tah, *f*
hairgrip; clothes peg

mollica, moll-**le**-kah, *f* soft
part of bread

mollusco, moll-**loos**-ko, *m*
mollusc

molo, **mo**-lo, *m* pier, jetty,
mole

molteplice, moll-**tay**-ple-
chay, *adj* manifold,
complex; **molteplici,**
numerous

moltiplicare, moll-te-ple-
kah-ray, *v* to multiply

moltitudine, moll-te-**too**-
de-nay, *f* multitude

molto, **moll**-to, *adj* much,
many, a lot of; *adv* a lot;
very much; very; *pron*
much, many, a lot; **per –**
tempo, for a long time

momentaneo*, mo-men-
tah-nay-o, *adj*
momentary

momento, mo-**men**-to, *m*
moment; **dal – che,**
since; **per il –,** for the
time being

monaca, mo-**nah**-kah, *f*
nun

monaco, mo-**nah**-ko, *m*
monk

monarca, mo-**nar**-kah, *m*
monarch

monarchia, mo-nar-**kee**-
ah, *f* monarchy

monastero, mo-nahss-**tay**-
ro, *m* monastery

moncherino, mon-kay-
ree-no, *m* stump

monco, **mon**-ko, *adj*
maimed, mutilated

mondano, mon-**dah**-no,
adj worldly; fashionable

mondare, mon-**dah**-ray, *v*
to peel; to clean

mondiale, mon-de'**ah**-lay,
adj world-wide; **la
seconda guerra –,** the
Second World War; **i
mondiali di calcio,**
World Football
Championship

mondo, mon-do, *m* world;
adj cleaned

monellerie, mo-nell-lay-
ree-ay, *fpl* pranks

monello, mo-**nell**-lo, *m*
urchin

moneta, mo-**nay**-tah, *f*
money; currency; small
change

monetario, mo-nay-**tah**-
re'o, monetary

mongoloide, mon-go-lo-
ee-day, *adj* mongol

monile, mo-**nee**-lay, *m*
jewel; necklace

monito, mo-ne-to, *m*
warning

monografia, mo-no-grah-
fee-ah, *f* monograph

monologo, mo-**no**-lo-go,
m monologue

monopolio, mo-no-**po**-
le'o, *m* monopoly

monosillabo, mo-no-**sil**-
lah-bo, *m* monosyllable;
adj monosyllabic

monotono, mo-**no**-to-no,
adj monotonous, dull

monsignore, mons-see-

n'yo-ray, *m* monsignor;
Your Grace

monsone, mon-so-nay, *m*
monsoon

montacarichi, mon-tah-
kah-re-ke, *m* goods lift

montaggio, mon-**tahd**-jo,
m assembly; **catena di –,**
assembly line; (film)
editing

montagna, mon-**tah**-
n'yah, *f* mountain; **in –,**
in the mountains

montagnoso, mon-tah-
n'**yo**-zo, *adj*
mountainous

montanaro, -a, mon-tah-
nah-ro, *m/f* mountain
dweller

montare, mon-**tah**-ray, *v*
to go up; to climb; to
ride; to assemble; to
mount

monte, mon-tay, *m*
mountain; **– Bianco,**
Mont Blanc; **– Everest,**
Mount Everest; **– di
pietà,** pawnshop

montatura, mon-tah-**too**-
rah, *f* (glasses) frames;
(jewel) mounting;
assembling

montone, mon-**to**-nay, *m*
ram; (meat) mutton

montuoso, mon-too'o-zo,
adj mountainous

monumento, mo-noo-
men-to, *m* monument

mora, mo-rah, *f*
blackberry; mulberry;
law delay

morale, mo-**rah**-lay, *adj*
moral; *f* morals,
morality; *m* morale

moralità, mo-rah-lee-**tah**,
f morality, morals

morbido, **mor**-be-do, *adj*
soft; smooth; tender

morbillo, mor-**beel**-lo, *m*
measles

morbo, mor-bo, *m* disease

morboso*, mor-**bo**-zo, *adj*
morbid

mordace, mor-**dah**-chay,
adj biting, cutting

mordere, mor-day-ray, *v*
to bite

morfina, mor-**fee**-nah, *f*
morphia, morphine

moribondo, mo-re-**bonn**-
do, *adj* moribund, dying

morire, mo-**ree**-ray, *v* to
die; (light) to fade;
(fire) to die out

mormorare, mor-mo-**rah**-
ray, *v* to murmur, to
whisper; to grumble

mormorio, mor-mo-**ree**-o,
m murmur; muttering

moro, mo-ro, *adj* dark-
haired; dark-skinned;
i Mori, the Moors

morsa, mor-sah, *f tech*
vice; grip

morso, mor-so, *m* bite;
mouthful; (insect) sting;

(bridle) bit

mortaio, mor-**tah**-e'o, *m*
mortar

mortale, mor-**tah**-lay, *adj*
mortal; deadly; fatal; *m/f*
mortal

mortalità, mor-tah-le-**tah**,
f mortality; death rate

morte, mor-tay, *f* death

mortificare, mor-te-fe-
kah-ray, *v* to mortify

morto, mor-to, *adj* dead;
-a, *m/f* dead man, dead
woman; **il giorno dei
morti,** All Souls' Day

mosaico, mo-**zah**'e-ko, *m*
mosaic

mosca, moss-kah, *f* fly; **–
cieca,** (game)
blindman's buff

moscato, moss-**skah**-to, *m*
muscatel; muscat grape

moscerino, mos-shay-**ree**-
no, *m* midge, gnat

moschea, moss-**kay**-ah, *f*
mosque

moscone, moss-**ko**-nay, *m*
bluebottle; (boat)
pedalo

mossa, moss-sah, *f*
movement; (at chess)
move

mostarda, moss-**tar**-dah, *f*
mustard

mostra, moss-trah, *f*
exhibition, show; **in –,**
on display

mostrare, moss-**trah**-ray, *v*

to show, to display

mostrarsi, moss-**trar**-se, *v*
to appear

mostro, moss-tro, *m*
monster

mostruoso*, moss-troo'o-
zo, *adj* monstrous

motivare, mo-te-**vah**-ray,
v to give a reason for; to
motivate

motivo, mo-**tee**-vo, *m*
motive; reason; motif,
theme, pattern

moto, mo-to, *m* motion,
movement; tumult; *f*
motorbike

motocicletta, mo-to-che-
klet-tah, *f* motorcycle

motociclismo, mo-to-che-
kliss-mo, *m*
motorcycling

motociclista, mo-to-che-
kliss-tah, *m/f*
motorcyclist

motore, mo-**tor**-ay, *m*
engine, motor

motorizzato, mo-to-rid-
dzah-to, *adj* motorized;
having transport

motoscafo, mo-to-**skah**-
fo, *m* motorboat

motteggio, mot-**ted**-jo, *m*
jest; banter

motto, mot-to, *m* motto;
witty remark

movente, mo-**ven**-tay, *m*
law motive

movimento, mo-ve-**men**-

to, *m* movement;
exercise

mozione, mo-tse'o-nay, *f*
motion

mozzare, mot-**tsah**-ray, *v*
to cut off

mozzicone, mot-tse-**ko**-
nay, *m* stub, end

mozzo, mot-tso, *m* cabin-
boy; **– di stalla,** stable-
boy

mucca, mook-kah, *f* cow

mucchio, mook-ke'o, *m*
heap, pile

muco, moo-ko, *m* mucus

muffa, moof-fah, *f* mould;
mildew

muggire, mood-**jee**-ray, *v*
to moo, to low; to
bellow; to roar

mughetto, moo-**get**-to, *m*
lily of the valley

mugnaio, -a, moo-n'yah-
e'o, *m/f* miller

mugolare, moo-go-**lah**-ray,
v to whimper, to whine

mulinare, moo-lee-**nah**-
ray, *v* to whirl

mulino, moo-**lee**-no, *m*
mill; **– a vento,**
windmill

mulo, moo-lo, *m* mule

multa, mool-tah, *f* fine

multare, mool-**tah**-ray, *v*
to fine

multimediale, mool-te-
may-de'**ah**-lay, *adj*
multimedia

multiplo, mool-te-plo, *adj*
multiple; *m* multiple

multiuso, mool-te-**oo**-so,
adj multipurpose

mummia, moom-me'ah, *f*
mummy

mungere, moonn-jay-ray,
v to milk

municipio, moo-ne-**chee**-
pe'o, *m* town-hall; town
council

munificenza, moo-ne-fe-
chen-tsah, *f*
munificence

munifico, moo-**nee**-fe-ko,
adj munificent, generous

munire, moo-**nee**-ray, *v* –
di, to provide with

munizioni, moo-ne-tse'o-
ne, *fpl* ammunition

muovere, moo'o-**vay**-ray, *v*
to move

muraglia, moo-rah-l'yah, *f*
wall

murale, moo-**rah**-lay, *adj*
mural; *m* mural

murare, moo-**rah**-ray, *v* to
wall up

muratore, moo-rah-**tor**-ay,
m bricklayer; mason

muro, moo-ro, *m* wall;
armadio a –, built-in
cupboard; **– del suono,**
sound barrier

muschio, mooss-ke'o, *m*
musk; moss

muscolare, mooss-ko-**lah**-
ray, *adj* muscular

muscolo, mooss-ko-lo, *m*
muscle

museo, moo-**zay**-o, *m*
museum

museruola, moo-zay-
roo'o-lah, *f* muzzle

musica, moo-ze-kah, *f*
music

musicale, moo-ze-kah-lay,
adj musical

musicista, moo-ze-**chee**-
stah, *m/f* musician

muso, moo-zo, *m* (animal)
muzzle; (vehicle) front,
nose; **fare il –,** to pull a
long face; **tenere il –,** to
sulk

mussola, mooss-so-lah, *f*
muslin

mussulmano, -a, mooss-
sool-**mah**-no, *adj*
Muslim; *m/f* Muslim

muta, moo-tah, *f*
moulting; shedding of
skin; (for diving) wet
suit; (of dogs) pack

mutamento, moo-tah-
men-to, *m* change

mutande, moo-tahn-day,
fpl pants

mutandine, moo-tahn-
dee-nay, *fpl* pants;
knickers

mutandoni, moo-tahn-**do**-
nee, *mpl* long johns

mutare, moo-**tah**-ray, *v* to
change

mutilare, moo-te-**lah**-ray,

v to mutilate, to maim

mutilato, -a, moo-te-**lah**-
to, *adj* disabled;
mutilated; *m/f* disabled
person

muto, -a, moo-to, *adj*
dumb; *gram* mute, silent;
il cinema –, silent
cinema; *m/f* mute, dumb
person

mutua, moo-too-ah, *f*
National Health Service

mutuo, moo-too-o, *adj*
mutual; *m* loan; –
ipotecario, mortgage

nacchere, nahk-kay-ray, *fpl* castanets

nafta, nahf-tah, *f* naptha; diesel oil

naftalina, nahf-tah-lee-nah, *f* mothballs; naphthalene

nailon, na'ee-lon, *m* nylon

nanna, nahn-nah, *f fam* bye-byes

nano, -a, nah-no, *m/f* dwarf

Napoli, nah-po-le, *f* Naples

nappa, nahp-pah, *f* tassel; soft leather

narciso, nar-chee-so, *m* narcissus

narcosi, nar-ko-se, *f* narcosis, general anaesthesia

narcotico, nar-ko-te-ko, *m* narcotic; *adj* narcotic

narcotraffico, nar-ko-trahf-fee-ko, *m* drug trade

narice, nah-ree-chay, *f* nostril

narrare, nar-rah-ray, *v* to relate, to recite, to tell, to report

narrativa, nar-rah-tee-vah, *f* fiction

narratore, -trice, nar-rah-tor-ay, nar-rah-tree-chay, *m/f* narrator

narrazione, nar-rah-tse'o-nay, *f* account; story

nasale, nah-sah-lay, *adj* nasal; *f* nasal consonant

nascere, nah-shay-ray, *v* to be born; to rise

nascita, nah-she-tah, *f* birth

nascondere, nah-skon-day-ray, *v* to conceal

nascondersi, nah-skon-dair-se, *v* to hide oneself

nascondiglio, nah-skon-dee-l'yo, *m* hiding place

nascosto*, nah-skoss-to, *adj* hidden; **di –,** secretly

nasello, nah-zell-lo, *m* whiting; hake

naso, nah-zo, *m* nose

nastro, nah-stro, *m* ribbon

natale, nah-tah-lay, *adj* native; *m* **Natale,** Christmas; **di umili natali,** of humble birth

natalità, nah-tah-le-tah, *f* birth rate

natica, nah-te-kah, *f* buttock

nativo, -a, nah-tee-vo, *adj* native; *m/f* native

natura, nah-too-rah, *f* nature; kind; temper; **– morta,** still life

naturale, nah-too-rah-lay, *adj* natural

naturalizzare, nah-too-rah-lit-tsah-ray, *v* to naturalize

naturalmente, nah-too-rahl-men-tay, *adv* naturally, of course

naufragare, nah'oo-frah-gah-ray, *v* to be shipwrecked

naufragio, nah'oo-frah-jo, *m* shipwreck

naufrago, -a, nah'oo-**frah**-go, *m/f* shipwrecked person

nausea, nah'oo-zay-ah, *f* nausea; **avere la –,** to feel sick

nauseabondo, nah'oo-zay-ah-**bon**-do, *adj* nauseous; nauseating

nautica, nah'oo-te-kah, *f* nautical science

navale, nah-**vah**-lay, *adj* naval; **cantiere –,** shipyard

navata, nah-**vah**-tah, *f* nave; aisle

nave, nah-vay, *f* ship

navetta, nah-**vayt**-tah, *f* shuttle; shuttle service

navigabile, nah-ve-**gah**-be-lay, *adj* navigable

navigare, nah-ve-**gah**-ray, *v* to sail

navigatore, -trice, nah-ve-gah-**tor**-ay, nah-ve-gah-**tree**-chay, *m/f* navigator

navigazione, nah-ve-gah-tse'o-nay, *f* navigation

naviglio, nah-**vee**-l'yo, *m* navigable canal; ship; fleet

nazionale, nah-tse'o-**nah**-lay, *adj* national; *f* national team

nazionalità, nah-tse'o-nah-le-**tah**, *f* nationality

nazione, nah-tse'o-nay, *f* nation

nazista, nah-**dzee**-stah, *m/f* Nazi; *adj* Nazi

ne, nay, *pron* of it, of them; from it, from them; some of it, some of them; of him, of her, of them; from there, from here

né… né…, nay nay, *conj* neither … nor …

neanche, nay-**ahn**-kay, *adv* not even; *conj* not even

nebbia, nayb-be'ah, *f* fog

nebbioso, nayb-be'o-zo, *adj* foggy; misty

nebulizzatore, nay-boo-leed-dzah-**to**-ray, *m* atomizer

nebuloso, nay-boo-**lo**-zo, *adj* hazy

necessario*, nay-chess-**sah**-re'o, *adj* necessary

necessità, nay-chess-se-**tah**, *f* necessity; need

necessitare, nay-chess-se-**tah**-ray, *v* to be needed; **– di,** to need

necrologio, nay-kro-**lo**-jo, *m* obituary notice

nefando, nay-**fahn**-do, *adj* vile

nefasto, nay-**fahss**-to, *adj* inauspicious; fateful

nefrite, nay-**free**-tay, *f* nephritis

negare, nay-**gah**-ray, *v* to deny, to refuse

negativa, nay-gah-tee-vah, *f* negative

negato, nay-**gah**-to, *adj* **– per/in,** hopeless at

negletto, nay-**glet**-to, *adj* neglected

negligente, nay-glee-**jayn**-tay, *adj* negligent, careless

negligenza, nay-glee-**jaynt**-tsah, *f* negligence, carelessness

negoziante, nay-go-tse'**ahn**-tay, *m/f* shopkeeper

negoziare, nay-go-tse'**ah**-ray, *v* to negotiate

negozio, nay-**go**-tse'o, *m* shop

negro, nay-gro, *adj* black

nembo, nem-bo, *m* nimbus

nemico, -a, nay-**mee**-ko, *adj* hostile, adverse; *m/f* enemy

nemmeno, nem-**may**-no, *adv* not even; *conj* not even

nenia, nay-ne'ah, *f* monotonous song; dirge

neo, nay-o, *m* mole; spot; slight flaw

neoclassico, nay-o-**klas**-se-ko, *adj* neoclassical

neolaureato, nay-o-lah'oo-ray'**ah**-to, *adj* recently graduated

neon, nay-on, *m* neon

neonato, -a, nay-o-nah-to,

m/f new-born baby

neppure, nayp-**poo**-ray, *adv* not even; *conj* not even

nero, -a, nay-ro, *adj* black; dark; (race) black; **Mar Nero,** *m* Black Sea; *m/f* black man, black woman

nervo, nair-vo, *m* nerve

nervosismo, nair-vo-**zee**-zmo, *m* nervousness; irritability

nervoso*, nair-**vo**-zo, *adj* nervous; irritable; sinewy

nespolo, nay-spo-lo, *m* medlar-tree

nesso, ness-so, *m* connection, link

nessuno, ness-**soo**-no, *adj* no, not any; *pron* nobody, no one, (not) anyone

nettare, nayt-tah-ray, *m* nectar

nettare, nayt-**tah**-ray, *v* to clean, to cleanse

nettezza, nayt-**tet**-tsah, *f* cleanliness

netto*, nayt-to, *adj* clean; clear; (weight) net

netturbino, nayt-toor-**bee**-no, *m* dustman

neurologia, nay'oo-ro-lo-**jee**-ah, *f* neurology

neutrale, nay'oo-**trah**-lay, *adj* neutral

neutro, nay'**oo**-tro, *adj* neuter

neve, nay-vay, *f* snow

nevicare, nay-ve-**kah**-ray, *v* to snow

nevicata, nay-ve-**kah**-tah, *f* snowfall

nevischio, nay-**vee**-ske'o, *m* sleet

nevoso, nay-**vo**-zo, *adj* snowy

nevralgia, nay-vrahl-**jee**-ah, *f* neuralgia

nevrosi, nay-**vro**-se, *f* neurosis

nevrotico, nay-**vro**-te-ko, *adj* neurotic

nibbio, neeb-be'o, *m* kite (bird)

nicchia, neek-ke'ah, *f* niche; hollow

nicchiare, neek-ke'**ah**-ray, *v* to hesitate

nichel, nee-kayl, *m* nickel

nicotina, ne-ko-**tee**-nah, *f* nicotine

nidiata, ne-de'**ah**-tah, *f* brood

nidificare, ne-de-fe-**kah**-ray, *v* to make a nest

nido, nee-do, *m* nest; **asilo –,** crèche

niente, ne-**en**-tay, *pron* nothing, anything

nientemeno, ne-en-tay-**may**-no, *adv* actually, no less; *interj* really!

Nilo, nee-lo, *m* Nile

ninfa, neen-fah, *f* nymph

ninfea, neen-**fay**-ah, *f* water-lily

ninnananna, neen-nah-**nahn**-nah, *f* lullaby

ninnolo, neen-no-lo, *m* knick-knack

nipote, ne-**po**-tay, *m/f* nephew; niece; grandson, granddaughter, grandchild

nitidezza, ne-te-**det**-tsah, *f* clearness; sharpness

nitido*, nee-te-do, *adj* clear; sharp

nitrato, ne-**trah**-to, *m* nitrate

nitrire, ne-**tree**-ray, *v* to neigh

nitrito, ne-**tree**-to, *m* (horse) neighing; (chemistry) nitrite

nitroglicerina, nee-tro-gle-chay-ree-nah, *f* nitroglycerine

no, no, *adv & m* no; *adv* not; **o –,** or not; **perché –?,** why not?

nobile, no-be-lay, *adj* noble; *m/f* nobleman, noblewoman

nobilitare, no-be-le-**tah**-ray, *v* to ennoble

nobiltà, no-beel-**tah**, *f* nobility; nobleness

nocca, nock-kah, *f* knuckle

nocciola, not-**cho**-lah, f hazelnut; adj light brown

nocciolo, not-**cho**-lo, m kernel, stone

nocciolo, not-**cho**-lo, m (tree) hazel

noce, no-chay, f walnut; m walnut-tree; **– moscata,** nutmeg

nocepesca, no-chay-**pess**-kah, f nectarine

nocivo*, no-**chee**-vo, adj noxious; harmful

nodo, no-do, m knot; tie; node; **– scorsoio,** slip-knot

nodoso, no-**do**-zo, adj gnarled

noi, no-e, pron we; us; **– stessi,** ourselves

noia, no-e'ah, f boredom; nuisance

noioso, no-e'o-zo, adj boring; annoying

noleggiare, no-led-**jah**-ray, v to hire, to rent; to hire out, to rent out; (ship, plane) to charter

noleggio, no-**led**-jo, m hire, rental; charter; freight

nolo, no-lo, m hire; freight charge

nomade, no-**mah**-day, adj nomadic; m/f nomad

nome, no-may, m name; gram noun

nomignolo, no-mee-n'yo-lo, m nickname

nomina, no-me-nah, f appointment; nomination

nominale*, no-me-**nah**-lay, adj nominal

nominare, no-me-**nah**-ray, v to mention; to name; to appoint

non, non, adv not

noncurante, non-koo-**rahn**-tay, adj **– di,** careless of

nondimeno, non-de-**may**-no, conj nevertheless; however

nonna, non-nah, f grandmother

nonni, non-ne, mpl grandparents

nonno, non-no, m grandfather

nono, no-no, adj & m ninth

nonostante, no-no-**stahn**-tay, prep notwithstanding; conj even though

nord, nord, m north; adj northern; **in direzione –,** northwards; **Mare del Nord,** m North Sea

nord-est, nord-**esst,** m north-east

nordico, nor-de-ko, adj northern

nord-ovest, nord-o-vest,

m north-west

norma, nor-mah, f norm, rule; custom; **a – di legge,** according to the law

normale*, nor-**mah**-lay, adj normal

norvegese, nor-vay-**jay**-zay, adj Norwegian

Norvegia, nor-vay-je'ah, f Norway

nostalgia, no-stahl-jee-ah, f nostalgia, homesickness

nostrano, no-**strah**-no, adj local; home-grown

nostro, noss-tro, adj our; pron ours

nota, no-tah, f note; list

notaio, no-tah-e'o, m notary

notare, no-**tah**-ray, v to note, to notice

notarile, no-tah-**ree**-lay, adj **atto –,** legal document; **studio –,** notary's office

notevole*, no-**tay**-vo-lay, adj remarkable; considerable

notificare, no-te-fe-**kah**-ray, v to notify

notificazione, no-te-fe-kah-tse'o-nay, f notification

notizia, no-tee-tse'ah, f news; piece of information

noto, no-to, *adj* noted; evident

notorietà, no-to-re'ay-tah, *f* fame; notoriety

notorio*, no-**to**-re'o, *adj* notorious

nottambulo, -a, not-tahm-boo-lo, *m/f* night owl *fig*

notte, **not**-tay, *f* night; darkness

nottola, **not**-to-lah, *f* noctule

notturno, not-**toohr**-no, *adj* nocturnal; *m mus* nocturne

novanta, no-**vahn**-tah, *adj* & *m* ninety

novantesimo, no-vahn-**tay**-ze-mo, *adj* & *m* ninetieth

nove, **no**-vay, *adj* & *m* nine

novecento, no-vay-**chayn**-to, *adj* & *m* nine hundred; *m* **il Novecento**, the twentieth century

novella, no-**vell**-lah, *f* short story

novello, no-**vell**-lo, *adj* new, fresh

novembre, no-**vem**-bray, *m* November

novero, no-vay-ro, *m* group; **essere nel – di**, to be counted among

novità, no-ve-**tah**, *f* novelty; news

novizio, no-vee-**tse**'o, *m* novice; apprentice

nozione, no-tse'o-nay, *f* notion

nozze, **not**-tsay, *fpl* wedding; **– d'argento**, silver wedding; **– d'oro**, golden wedding

nube, **noo**-bay, *f* cloud

nubile, **noo**-be-lay, *adj* unmarried, single (woman)

nuca, **noo**-kah, *f* nape of the neck

nucleare, noo-klay'**ah**-ray, *adj* nuclear

nucleo, **noo**-klay-o, *m* nucleus; core; group; **– familiare**, family unit

nudità, noo-de-**tah**, *f* nudity, nakedness

nudo, **noo**-do, *adj* naked; bare; *m* nude

nulla, **nooll**-lah, *pron* nothing; *m* nothingness; **non fa –**, it does not matter

nullità, nooll-le-**tah**, *f* nullity; insignificance

nullo*, **nooll**-lo, *adj* worthless; *law* null

numerale, noo-may-**rah**-lay, *m* numeral; *adj* numeral

numerare, noo-may-**rah**-ray, *v* to number

numerico*, noo-**may**-re-ko, *adj* numerical

numero, **noo**-may-ro, *m* number; numeral; (magazine) issue

numeroso, noo-may-**ro**-zo, *adj* numerous

nunzio, **noonn**-tse'o, *m* nuncio, papal ambassador

nuocere, noo'o-chay-ray, *v* **– a**, to harm, to damage

nuora, noo'o-rah, *f* daughter-in-law

nuotare, noo'o-**tah**-ray, *v* to swim

nuotata, noo'o-**tah**-tah, *f* swim

nuotatore, -trice, noo'o-tah-**tor**-ay, noo'o-tah-**tree**-chay, *m/f* swimmer

Nuova York, noo'o-vah york, *f* New York

Nuova Zelanda, noo'o-vah zay-**lahn**-dah, *f* New Zealand

nuovo*, noo'o-vo, *adj* new; **di –**, again

nutrice, noo-**tree**-chay, *f* wet-nurse

nutrimento, noo-tre-**men**-to, *m* nourishment

nutrire, noo-**tree**-ray, *v* to nourish, to feed; (feelings) to feel

nutritivo, noo-tre-**tee**-vo, *adj* nourishing

nutrizione, noo-tre-tse'o-nay, *f* nutrition

nuvola, **noo**-vo-lah, *f*

cloud; **cadere dalle
nuvole,** to be taken
aback

nuvoloso, noo-vo-**lo**-zo,
adj cloudy

nuziale, noo-tse'**ah**-lay, *adj*
nuptial

nylon, na'ee-lon, *m* nylon

o, o, *conj* or; **o... o...**, either... or...

oasi, o-ah-ze, *f* oasis

obbediente, ob-bay-de'en-tay, *adj* obedient

obbedienza, ob-bay-de'en-tsah, *f* obedience

obbedire, ob-bay-dee-ray, *v* to obey

obbligare, ob-ble-gah-ray, *v* to compel, to oblige, to force

obbligatorio, ob-ble-gah-to-re'o, *adj* compulsory

obbligazione, ob-ble-gah-tse'o-nay, *f* obligation; bond, debenture

obbligo, ob-ble-go, *m* obligation, duty

obeso, o-bay-so, *adj* obese

obiettare, o-be'et-tah-ray, *v* to object

obiettivo, o-be'et-tee-vo, *adj* objective; *m* lens; objective

obiettore, o-be'et-to-ray, *m* objector; **– di coscienza**, conscientious objector

obiezione, o-be'ay-tse'o-nay, *f* objection

obitorio, o-be-to-re'o, *m* mortuary, morgue

oblio, o-blee-o, *m* oblivion

obliquo*, o-blee-kwo, *adj* oblique; indirect

oblò, o-blo, *m naut* porthole

oboe, o-bo-ay, *m* oboe

oboista, o-bo-ees-tah, *m/f* oboist

oca, o-kah, *f* goose

occasionale, ok-kah-ze'o-nah-lay, *adj* casual, occasional, chance

occasionare, ok-kah-ze'o-nah-ray, *v* to cause

occasione, ok-kah-ze'o-nay, *f* opportunity, chance; occasion

occhiaia, ok-ke'ah-e'ah, *f* (eye) socket; **avere le occhiaie**, to have bags under one's eyes

occhiali, ok-ke'ah-le, *mpl* spectacles, glasses; goggles

occhiata, ok-ke'ah-tah, *f* glance, look

occhiello, ok-ke'el-lo, *m* button-hole; eyelet

occhio, ok-ke'o, *m* eye

occhiolino, ok-ke'o-lee-no, *m* **fare l'– a**, to wink at

occidentale, ot-che-den-tah-lay, *adj* western; westerly

occidente, ot-che-den-tay, *m* west; **l'Occidente**, the West

occorrente, ok-kor-ren-tay, *adj* necessary; *m* equipment, materials

occorrenza, ok-kor-ren-tsah, *f* necessity; **all'–**, if need be

occorrere, ok-kor-ray-ray, *v* to be required; **occorre**, it is necessary

occultare, ok-kool-tah-ray, *v* to hide, to conceal

occulto*, ok-**kool**-to, *adj* occult; secret

occupare, ok-koo-**pah**-ray, *v* to occupy; to employ

occuparsi, ok-koo-**pahr**-se, *v* to take an interest in; to look after

occupazione, ok-koo-pah-tse'**o**-nay, *f* occupation; employment

oceano, o-**chay**-ah-no, *m* ocean

ocra, o-krah, *f* ochre

oculatezza, o-koo-lah-**tet**-tsah, *f* caution

oculista, o-koo-lee-stah, *m* eye specialist, oculist

odiare, o-de'**ah**-ray, *v* to hate, to detest

odio, o-de'o, *m* hatred, strong dislike

odioso*, o-de'o-so, *adj* hateful; obnoxious

odontoiatria, o-don-to-e'ah-**tree**-ah, *f* dentistry

odorare, o-do-**rah**-ray, *v* to smell

odorato, o-do-**rah**-to, *m* sense of smell

odore, o-**do**-ray, *m* scent, smell

offendere, of-fen-**day**-ray, *v* to offend; to insult; to infringe

offensiva, of-fen-see-vah, *f* offensive

offensivo*, of-fen-see-vo, *adj* offensive, insulting

offerente, of-fen-**ren**-tay, *m/f* (auction) bidder

offerta, of-**fair**-tah, *f* offer, bid; **offerte d'impiego**, situations vacant

offesa, of-**fay**-zah, *f* offence, insult, affront

officina, of-fe-**chee**-nah, *f* workshop

offrire, of-**free**-ray, *v* to offer, to present

offuscare, of-fooss-**kah**-ray, *v* to darken

oftalmia, of-tahl-**mee**-ah, *f* ophthalmia

oggettivo, od-jet-**tee**-vo, *adj* objective

oggetto, od-**jet**-to, *m* object; **oggetti smarriti**, lost property

oggi, od-je, *adv* today, nowadays

oggigiorno, od-je-**jor**-no, *adv* nowadays

ogni, o-n'ye, *adj* each, every; **– tanto**, every now and then

Ognissanti, o-n'yeess-**sahn**-te, *m* All Saints' Day

ognuno, o-n'yoo-no, *pron* everyone, each one

ohi, o'ee, *interj* hey!; ow!

ohimè, o'ee-may, *interj* oh dear!

okay, o-kay'ee, *interj* okay

Olanda, o-lahn-dah, *f* Holland

olandese, o-lahn-**day**-zay, *adj* Dutch

oleandro, o-lay'**ahn**-dro, *m* oleander

oleodotto, o-lay'o-**dot**-to, *m* oil pipeline

olfatto, ol-**faht**-to, *m* sense of smell

oliare, o-le'**ah**-ray, *v* to lubricate; to grease

oliera, o-le'**ay**-rah, *f* cruet-stand

Olimpiadi, o-lim-pee-ah-de, *fpl* Olymic games

olio, o-l'yo, *m* oil

oliva, o-lee-vah, *f* olive

olivastro, o-le-**vah**-stro, *adj* olive-coloured

oliveto, o-le-**vay**-to, *m* olive grove

olivo, o-lee-vo, *m* olive-tree

olmo, ol-mo, *m* elm

olocausto, o-lo-kah'oo-sto, *m* holocaust; sacrifice

oltraggiare, ol-trahd-**jah**-ray, *v* to offend, to insult

oltraggio, ol-**trahd**-jo, *m* insult, offence

oltre, ol-tray, *adv* farther; further; *prep* beyond; over; **– a**, besides

oltremare, ol-tray-**mah**-ray, *adv* overseas

oltremodo, ol-tray-**mo**-do, *adv* greatly

oltrepassare, ol-traypahss-**sah**-ray, *v* to go beyond; to exceed

omaggio, o-**mahd**-jo, *m* homage; gift; **omaggi**, regards; **in –**, free, complimentary

ombelico, om-bay-**lee**-ko, *m* navel

ombra, om-brah, *f* (area) shade; (silhouette) shadow; ghost; **governo –**, shadow cabinet

ombrellino, om-brell-**lee**-no, *m* parasole

ombrello, om-**brell**-lo, *m* umbrella

ombrellone, om-brell-**lo**-nay, *m* beach umbrella, sunshade

ombretto, om-**bret**-to, *m* eyeshadow

ombroso, om-**bro**-zo, *adj* shady; touchy

omelette, o-mel-**let**, *f* omelette

omeopatia, o-may-o-pah-**tee**-ah, *f* homoeopathy

omertà, o-mer-**tah**, *f* conspiracy of silence

omettere, o-**met**-tay-ray, *v* to omit, to leave out

omicida, o-me-**chee**-dah, *m/f* murderer, murderess

omicidio, o-me-**chee**-de'o, *m* murder; **– colposo,** man-slaughter

omissione, o-mis-se'o-nay, *f* omission

omogeneizzato, o-mo-jay-nay-eed-**dzah**-to, *adj* homogenized; *m* baby food

omogeneo, o-mo-**jay**-nay'o, *adj* homogeneous

omonimo, o-**mo**-ne-no, *adj* with the same name; *m gram* homonym

omosessuale, o-mo-ses-soo'**a**-lay, *adj* homosexual; *m/f* homosexual

oncia, on-chah, *f* ounce; *fig* small quantity

onda, on-dah, *f* wave, billow; **mandare in –**, to broadcast

ondeggiare, on-ded-**jah**-ray, *v* to flutter; to sway; to hesitate

ondulare, on-doo-**lah**-ray, *v* to wave

ondulato*, on-doo-**lah**-to, *adj* undulating; wavy; **lamiera di ferro ondulata,** corrugated iron

onere, o-nay-ray, *m* burden

oneroso, o-nay-**ro**-zo, *adj* onerous, heavy

onestà, o-nay-**stah**, *f* honesty; fairness; virtue

onesto*, o-**nay**-sto, *adj* honest; fair; virtuous

onice, o-ne-chay, *f* onyx

onnipotente, on-nee-po-

ten-tay, *adj* omnipotent; *m* l'**Onnipotente,** the Almighty

onomastico, o-no-**mahs**-te-ko, *m* name day

onorare, o-no-**rah**-ray, *v* to honour

onorario, o-no-**rah**-re'o, *m* fee; *adj* honorary

onore, o-**no**-ray, *m* honour; **farsi –**, to distinguish oneself

onorevole, o-no-**ray**-vo-lay, *adj* honourable; *m/f* Member of Parliament

onorificenza, o-no-re-fe-**chent**-tsah, *f* honour, decoration

onta, on-tah, *f* shame; affront

ontano, on-**tah**-no, *m* alder

opacità, o-pah-che-**tah**, *f* opacity

opaco, o-**pah**-ko, *adj* opaque

opale, o-**pah**-lay, *m & f* opal

opera, o-pay-rah, *f* work, deed; opera; **– d'arte,** work of art; **– pia,** religious charity

operaio, -a, o-pay-**rah**-e'o, *m/f* worker; *adj* worker; **classe operaia,** working class

operare, o-pay-**rah**-ray, *v* to carry out; to act; *med* to operate (on)

operatore, -trice, o-pay-rah-**tor**-ay, o-pay-rah-**tree**-chay, m/f operator; agent; dealer; cameraman; camerawoman

operazione, o-pay-rah-tse'o-nay, f operation; business transaction

operetta, o-pay-**ret**-tah, f operetta

operoso*, o-pay-**ro**-zo, adj industrious; hard-working

opificio, o-pe-**fee**-cho, m mill; factory

opinabile, o-pe-**nah**-be-lay, adj debatable, questionable

opinione, o-pe-ne'o-nay, f opinion

oppio, **op**-pe'o, m opium

opporre, op-**por**-ray, v to oppose

opportunità, op-por-too-ne-**tah**, f timeliness; opportunity

opportuno*, op-por-**too**-no, adj timely; appropriate

oppositore, -trice, op-po-se-**to**-ray, op-po-se-**tree**-chay, m/f opponent

opposizione, op-po-ze-tse'o-nay, f opposition; law objection

opposto, op-**poss**-to, adj

opposite; conflicting; m opposite

oppressione, op-press-se'o-nay, f oppression

oppressivo*, op-press-**see**-vo, adj oppressive

opprimere, op-**pree**-may-ray, v to oppress

oppure, op-**poo**-ray, conj or, or else

opuscolo, o-**poo**-sko-lo, m pamphlet, leaflet

opzionale, op-tse'o-**nah**-lay, adj optional

ora, o-rah, f hour; time; adv now

oracolo, o-**rah**-ko-lo, m oracle

orafo, o-**rah**-fo, m goldsmith

orale, o-**rah**-lay, adj oral

oramai, o-rah-**mah**-e, adv by now; by then

orario, o-**rah**-re'o, m time-table; adj hourly; **in senso –**, clockwise

orata, o-**rah**-tah, f sea bream

oratore, -trice, o-rah-**tor**-ay, o-rah-**tree**-chay m/f orator, public speaker

orazione, o-rah-tse'o-nay, f prayer; oration

orbita, or-**be**-tah, f eye-socket; orbit; sphere of influence

orca, or-kah, f killer whale

orchestra, or-kes-trah, f orchestra; band; orchestra pit

orchidea, or-kee-**day**'ah, f orchid

orco, or-ko, m ogre

orda, or-dah, f horde

ordigno, or-dee-n'yo, m device

ordinale, or-de-nah-lay, adj ordinal; m ordinal number

ordinamento, or-de-nah-**men**-to, m arrangement; rules

ordinanza, or-de-**nahn**-tsah, decree; law, mil order

ordinare, or-de-nah-ray, v to arrange, to put in order; to order; to prescribe; relig to ordain

ordinario*, or-de-**nah**-re'o, adj ordinary; poor-quality; common

ordinazione, or-de-nah-tse'o.nay, f order; relig ordination

ordine, or-de-nay, m order

ordire, or-de-ray, v to plot

orecchino, o-reck-**kee**-no, m ear-ring

orecchio, o-**reck**-ke'o, m ear; hearing

orecchioni, o-reck-kee'o-nee, mpl mumps

orefice, o-**ray**-fe-chay, m goldsmith; jeweller

orfano, -a, or-fah-no, *m/f* orphan

orfanotrofio, or-fah-no-tro-fe'o, *m* orphanage

organetto, or-gah-net-to, *m* street-organ

organico, or-gah-nee-ko, *adj* organic; *m* personnel; *mil* cadre

organismo, or-gah-nee-smo, *m* organism; body

organizzare, or-gah-need-dzah-ray, *v* to organize

organizzazione, or-gah-need-dzah-tse'o-nay, *f* organization

organo, or-gah-no, *m* organ

orgasmo, or-gahz-mo, *m* orgasm; anxiety

orgia, or-jah, *f* orgy

orgoglio, or-go-l'yo, *m* pride

orgoglioso*, or-go-l'yo-zo, *adj* proud

orientale, o-re-en-tah-lay, *adj* oriental; eastern

orientamento, o-re-en-tah-men-to, *m* orientation; positioning; directing

orientare, o-re-en-tah-ray, *v* to orientate; to position; to direct

orientativo, o-re-en-tah-tee-vo, *adj* approximate, indicative

oriente, o-re-en-tay, *m*

east; **l'Oriente,** the East; **l'Estremo Oriente,** the Far East; **il Medio Oriente,** the Middle East

origano, o-ree-gah-no, *m* oregano

originale, o-re-je-nah-lay, *adj* original; eccentric; *m* original

originario, o-re-je-nah-re'o, *adj* native

origine, o-ree-je-nay, *f* origin; source; cause

orina, o-ree-nah, *f* urine

orinale, o-re-nah-lay, *m* chamber-pot

orizzontale, o-rit-tson-tah-lay, *adj* horizontal

orizzonte, o-rit-tson-tay, *m* horizon

orlare, or-lah-ray, *v* to hem; to edge

orlo, or-lo, *m* edge; brim; hem

orma, or-mah, *f* footprint; trace, mark

ormai, or-mah-e, *adv* by now; by then

ormeggio, or-mej-jo, *m* mooring; moorings

ormone, or-mo-nay, *m* hormone

ornamentale, or-nah-men-tah-lay, *adj* decorative, ornamental

ornamento, or-nah-men-to, *m* decoration,

ornament

ornare, or-nah-ray, *v* to adorn, to decorate; to embellish

ornitologia, or.ne-to-lo-jee-ah, *f* ornithology

oro, o-ro, *m* gold

orologiaio, o-ro-lo-jah-e'o, *m* watchmaker

orologio, o-ro-lo-je'o, *m* watch; clock; **– da polso,** wrist-watch; **– digitale,** digital watch

oroscopo, o-ro-sko-po, *m* horoscope

orrendo*, or-ren-do, *adj* horrible; dreadful

orribile*, or-ree-be-lay, *adj* horrible; horrid

orrore, or-ro-ray, *m* horror; disgust

orsa, or-sah, *f* she-bear; **Orsa Maggiore/Minore,** Great/Little Bear

orsacchiotto, or-sahk-ke'ot-to, *m* bear cub; teddy bear

orso, or-so, *m* bear

ortaggio, or-tahj-jo, *m* vegetable

ortica, or-tee-kah, *f* nettle

orticaria, or-te-kah-re'ah, *f* nettle rash

orticultore, -trice, or-te-kool-tor-ay, or-te-kool-tree-chay, *m/f* horticulturalist

orto, or-to, *m* kitchen-garden; vegetable-garden

ortodosso, or-to-**doss**-so, *adj* orthodox

ortografia, or-to-grah-**fee**-ah, *f* spelling, orthography

ortolano, **-a**, or-to-**lah**-no, *m/f* kitchen-gardener

ortopedico, **-a**, or-to-**pay**-de-ko, *adj* orthopaedic; *m/f* orthopaedic specialist

orzaiolo, or-dzah-e'o-lo, *m* (eye-lid) sty

orzata, or-dzah-tah, *f* barley water

orzo, or-dzo, *m* barley

osare, o-zah-ray, *v* to dare

oscenità, o-shay-ne-tah, *f* obscenity

osceno*, o-**shay**-no, *adj* obscene

oscillare, o-sheel-**lah**-ray, *v* to oscillate; to fluctuate

oscillazione, o-sheel-laht-se'o-nay, *f* oscillation; fluctuation

oscurare, oss-koo-**rah**-ray, *v* to darken; to obscure

oscurità, oss-koo-re-**tah**, *f* darkness; obscurity

oscuro*, oss-**koo**-ro, *adj* dark; obscure

ospedale, oss-pay-**dah**-lay, *m* hospital

ospitale, oss-pe-tah-lay, *adj* hospitable

ospitare, oss-pe-**tah**-ray, *v* to accommodate; to put up

ospite, oss-pe-tay, *m/f* host, hostess; visitor, guest

ospizio, oss-**pee**-tse'o, *m* old people's home; hospice

ossatura, oss-sah-**too**-rah, *f* bone structure; framework

ossequio, oss-**say**-kwe-o, *m* respect, deference

ossequioso*, oss-say-kwe'o-zo, *adj* respectful; obsequious

osservanza, oss-sair-**vahn**-tsah, *f* observance

osservare, oss-sair-**vah**-ray, *v* to observe

osservatorio, oss-sair-vah-**to**-re'o, *m* observatory

osservazione, oss-sair-vah-tse'o-nay, *f* observation; comment, remark

ossessione, oss-ses-se'o-nay, *f* obsession

ossessivo, oss-ses-see-vo, *adj* obsessive

ossia, osss-ee-ah, *conj* or rather; that is

ossidare, oss-se-dah-ray, *v* to oxidize

ossido, oss-se-do, *m* oxide; **– di carbonio**, carbon monoxide

ossigeno, oss-**see**-jay-no, *m* oxygen

osso, oss-so, *m* bone; (fruit) stone

ossuto, oss-**soo**-to, *adj* bony

ostacolare, oss-tah-ko-**lah**-ray, *v* to hinder

ostacolo, oss-**tah**-ko-lo, *m* obstacle; (sport) hurdle; fence

ostaggio, oss-**tahd**-jo, *m* hostage

oste, **-essa**, oss-tay, oss-**tes**-sah, *m/f* inn-keeper

ostello, oss-**tel**-lo, *m* hostel; **– della gioventù**, youth hostel

ostentare, oss-ten-**tah**-ray, *v* to show off; to feign

ostentazione, oss-ten-tah-tse'o-nay, *f* ostentation

osteria, oss-tay-**ree**-ah, *f* pub, inn

ostetrico, **-a**, oss-**tay**-tree-ko, *adj* obstetric; *m/f* obstetrician; *f* midwife

ostia, oss-te-ah, *f relig* host; wafer

ostile*, oss-**tee**-lay, *adj* hostile

ostilità, oss-te-le-**tah**, *f* hostility

ostinarsi, oss-te-nar-se, *v* to persist obstinately

ostinato*, oss-te-**nah**-to, *adj* obstinate, stubborn

ostinazione, oss-te-nah-tse'o-nay, *f* obstinacy, stubborness

ostrica, oss-tre-kah, *f* oyster

ostruire, oss-troo-ee-ray, *v* to obstruct, to block

ostruzione, oss-troo-tse'o-nay, *f* obstruction, blockage

otite, o-tee-tay, *f* ear infection

otre, o-tray, *m* goatskin (container)

ottagono, ot-tah-go-no, *m* octagon

ottano, ot-tah-no, *m* octane

ottanta, ot-tahn-tah, *adj* & *m* eighty

ottantesimo, ot-tahn-tay-ze-mo, *adj* & *m* eightieth

ottava, ot-tah-vah, *f mus* octave

ottavo, ot-tah-vo, *adj* & *m* eighth

ottemperare, ot-tem-pay-rah-ray, *v* to comply

ottenere, ot-tay-nay-ray, *v* to obtain

ottico, ot-te-ko, *m* optician; *adj* optical, optic

ottimismo, ot-te-miss-mo, *m* optimism

ottimo*, ot-te-mo, *adj* excellent; perfect

otto, ot-to, *adj* & *m* eight

ottobre, ot-to-bray, *m* October

ottocento, ot-to-chen-to, *adj* & *m* eight hundred; **l'Ottocento,** the nineteenth century

ottone, ot-to-nay, *m* brass; **gli ottoni** *mus* the brass

otturare, ot-too-rah-ray, *v* to block up; (teeth) to fill

ottuso*, ot-too-zo, *adj* stupid; obtuse

ovaia, o-vah-e'ah, *f* ovary

ovale, o-vah-lay, *adj* oval

ovatta, o-vaht-tah, *f* wadding; cotton-wool

ovattare, o-vaht-tah-ray, *v* to pad

ovazione, o-vaht-tse'o-nay, *f* ovation

ovest, o-vest, *m* west; *adj* western; **in direzione –,** westwards

ovile, o-vee-lay, *m* sheepfold, pen

ovunque, o-voonn-kway, *adv* everywhere

ovvero, ov-vay-ro, *conj*, or rather; or else

ovviare, ov-ve'ah-ray, *v* to obviate; to remedy

ovvio*, ov-ve'o, *adj* obvious

oziare, o-tse'ah-ray, *v* to idle

ozio, o-tse'o, *m* idleness; free time

ozioso*, o-tse'o-zo, *adj* idle, lazy, indolent

ozono, o-dzo-no, *m* ozone; **lo strato d'–,** the ozone layer

pacato, pah-**kah**-to, *adj* quiet

pacca, pahk-kah, *f* slap; pat on the shoulder

pacchetto, pahk-**ket**-to, *m* packet; parcel

pacchiano, pahk-ke'**ah**-no, *adj* garish

pacco, pahk-ko, *m* parcel

pace, pah-chay, *f* peace

pacifico, pah-**chee**-fe-ko, *adj* pacific

padella, pah-**dell**-lah, *f* frying pan

padiglione, pah-de-l'yo-nay, *m* pavilion; tent

padre, pah-dray, *m* father

padrino, pah-**dree**-no, *m* godfather

padrona, pah-**dro**-nah, *f* owner; **– di casa** landlady

padrone, pah-**dro**-nay, *m* owner; **– di casa** landlord

paesaggio, pah-ay-**sahd**-jo, *m* landscape

paesano, pah-ay-**zah**-no, *adj* country

paese, pah-**ay**-zay, *m* country; village; **Paesi Bassi,** *mpl* Netherlands

paffuto, pahf-**foo**-to, *adj* plump

paga, pah-gah, *f* salary

pagaia, pah-**gah**-e'ah, *f* paddle

pagamento, pah-gah-**men**-to, *m* payment

pagare, pah-**gah**-ray, *v* to pay

pagella, pah-**jel**-lah, *f* school report

paggio, pahd-jo, *m* page(boy)

pagherò, pah-gay-**ro**, *m* promissory note

pagina, pah-je-nah, *f* page

paglia, pah-l'yah, *f* straw

pagliaccio, pah-**l'yaht**-cho, *m* clown

pagnotta, pah-n'yot-tah, *f* loaf

paio, pah-e'o, *m* pair; **un – di,** a pair of

pala, pah-lah, *f* shovel; blade

palato, pah-**lah**-to, *m* palate

palazzina, pah-laht-**tsee**-nah, *f* villa

palazzo, pah-**laht**-tso, *m* palace; building

palco, pahl-ko, *m* platform; (theatre) box

palcoscenico, pahl-ko-**shay**-ne-ko, *m* stage

palesare, pah-lay-**zah**-ray, *v* to reveal

palese, pah-**lay**-zay, *adj* clear

palestra, pah **less**-trah, *f* gymnasium; gym

paletta, pah-**let**-tah, *f* spade; signalling disc; dustpan

paletto, pah-**let**-to, *m* stake; bolt; pole

palio, pah-l'yo, *m* **in –,** as a prize

palizzata, pah-**lit**-tsah-tah, *f* fence

palla, pahl-lah, *f* ball

pallacanestro, pahl-lah-kah-**ness**-tro, *f* basketball

pallanuoto, pahl-lah-noo'o-to, *f* water polo

pallavolo, pahl-lah-vo-lo, *f* volleyball

pallido, pahl-le-do, *adj* pale

pallino, pahl-**lee**-no, *m* dot

palloncino, pahl-lon-**chee**-no, *m* balloon

pallone, pahl-**lo**-nay, *m* ball; football; balloon

pallore, pahl-**lor**-ay, *m* pallor

pallottola, pahl-**lot**-to-lah, *f* bullet; pellet

palma, pahl-mah, *f* palm, palm-tree

palmo, pahl-mo, *m* palm

palo, pah-lo, *m* post; pole

palombaro, pah-lom-**bah**-ro, *m* diver

palpare, pahl-**pah**-ray, *v* to touch, to feel

palpebra, pahl-**pay**-brah, *f* eye-lid

palpitare, pal-pe-**tah**-ray, *v* to palpitate

palude, pah-**loo**-day, *f* marsh, swamp

paludoso, pah-loo-**do**-zo, *adj* marshy, swampy

panca, pahn-kah, *f* bench

pancarrè, pahn-kahr-**ray**, *m* sliced bread

pancetta, pahn-**chet**-tah, *f* bacon

pancia, pahn-chah, *f* belly

panciotto, pahn-**chot**-to, *m* waistcoat

pane, pah-nay, *m* bread; loaf of bread; **– a cassetta,** sliced bread

panetteria, pah-net-tay-**ree**-ah, *f* bakery

panettiere, -a, pah-net-te'**ay**-ray, *m/f* baker

panico, pah-ne-ko, *m* panic

paniere, pah-ne'**ay**-ray, *m* basket

panino, pah-**nee**-no, *m* roll; **– imbottito** sandwich

panna, pahn-nah, *f* cream

panno, pahn-no, *m* cloth

pannocchia, pahn-**nok**-ke'ah, *f* cob

pannolino, pahn-no-lee-no, *m* nappy

panorama, pah-no-**rah**-mah, *m* panorama

pantaloni, pahn-tah-**lo**-ne, *mpl* trousers

pantera, pahn-**tay**-rah, *f* panther

pantofola, pahn-to-fo-lah, *f* slipper

Papa, pah-pah, *m* Pope

papà, pah-**pah**, *m* dad

papale, pah-**pah**-lay, *adj* papal

papavero, pah-**pah**-vay-ro, *m* poppy

papero, pah-pe-ro, *m* gosling

papillon, pah-pee-yon, *m* bow tie

pappagallo, pahp-pah-**gahl**-lo, *m* parrot

paracadute, pah-rah-kah-**doo**-tay, *m* parachute

para, pah-rah, *f* crepe rubber

parabrezza, pah-rah-**bret**-tsah, *m* windscreen

paradiso, pah-rah-**dee**-zo, *m* paradise, heaven

paradosso, pah-rah-**doss**-so, *m* paradox

parafango, pah-rah-**fahn**-go, *m* mud-guard

parafulmine, pah-rah-**fool**-me-nay, *m* lightning conductor

paragonare, pah-rah-go-**nah**-ray, *v* to compare

paragone, pah-rah-go-nay, *m* comparison

paragrafo, pah-**rah**-grah-fo, *m* paragraph

paralisi, pah-**rah**-le-ze, *f* paralysis

parallelo, pah-rahl-**lay**-lo, *adj* parallel; *m* parallel

paralume, pah-rah-**loo**-may, *m* lamp-shade

parapetto, pah-rah-**pet**-to, *m* parapet

parapiglia, pah-rah-peel'yah, f turmoil

parare, pah-**rah**-ray, v to parry; to save; to shield

parassita, pah-rahs-**see**-tah, m parasite

parata, pah-**rah**-tah, f parade; save

paraurti, pah-rah-**oor**-te, m bumper

paravento, pah-rah-**ven**-to, m screen

parcella, pahr-**chel**-lah, f fee

parcheggiare, pahr-kej-**jah**-ray, v to park

parcheggio, pahr-**kej**-jo, m car park; parking

parchimetro, pahr-kee-me-tro, m parking meter

parco, par-ko, m park; adj moderate

parecchi, pah-**reck**-ke, adj & pron several

parecchio, pah-**reck**-ke'o, adj quite a lot of; pron quite a lot; adv quite; quite a lot

pareggiare, pah-red-**jah**-ray, v to equalize; to make equal

parente, pah-**ren**-tay, m/f relative

parentesi, pah-**ren**-tay-ze, f bracket

parere, pah-**ray**-ray, m opinion; v to seem; to look

parete, pah-**ray**-tay, f wall

pari, **pah**-re, adj equal; level; even; m/f peer

Parigi, pah-**ree**-dje, f Paris

parità, pah-re-**tah**, f equality

parlamentare, par-lah-men-**tah**-ray, adj parliamentary; m/f MP

parlare, par-**lah**-ray, v to speak, to talk

parmigiano, pahr-mee-**jah**-no, m Parmesan cheese

parola, pah-**ro**-lah, f word

parolaccia, pah-ro-**laht**-chah, f swearword

parrocchia, par-**rock**-ke'ah, f parish; parish church

parrocchiano, par-rock-ke'ah-no, m parishioner

parroco, par-ro-ko, m parish priest

parrucca, par-**rock**-kah, f wig

parrucchiere, -a, par-rook-ke'**ay**-ray, m/f hairdresser

parsimonia, par-se-mo-n'yah, f parsimony

parte, par-tay, f part; side; way; **da –**, aside; **in –**, partly

partecipare, par-tay-che-**pah**-ray, v to take part, participate; to share

partenza, par-ten-tsah, f departure; start

particella, par-te-**chell**-lah, f particle

participio, par-te-**chee**-pe'o, m participle

particolare, par-te-ko-**lah**-ray, adj particular

partigiano, par-te-**jah**-no, m partisan

partire, par-tee-ray, v to leave; to depart

partita, par-tee-tah, f game, match; consignment

partito, par-tee-to, m party

partitura, par-te-too-rah, f mus score

parto, par-to, m birth

partorire, par-to-ree-ray, v to give birth to

parziale, par-tse'ah-lay, adj partial; biased

pascolo, pahss-ko-lo, m pasture

Pasqua, pahss-kwah, f Easter

passabile, pahss-sah-be-lay, adj passable

passaggio, pahss-**sahd**-jo, m passage; change; lift

passante, pahss-**sahn**-tay, m/f passer-by

passare, pahss-sah-ray, v to pass; to go by; to go through; to call in; to spend; to go beyond

passatempo, pahss-sah-**tem**-po, m pastime

passato, pahss-**sah**-to, *adj*
past; last; *m* past

passeggero, -a, pahss-sed-**jay**-ro, *m/f* passenger

passeggiare, pahss-sed-**jah**-ray, *v* to walk

passeggiata, pahss-sed-**jah**-tah, *f* walk, stroll

passeggio, pahss-**sed**-jo, *m*
andare a –, to go for a walk

passeggino, pahss-sed-**jee**-no, *m* pushchair

passero, pahss-say-ro, *m*
sparrow

passione, pahss-se'o-nay, *f*
passion

passivo, pahss-**see**-vo, *adj**
passive; *m gram* passive;
liabilities

passo, pahss-so, *m* step;
footstep; pace

pasta, pahss-tah, *f* paste;
pastry; dough; – **sfoglia,**
puff pastry; – **frolla,**
shortcrust pastry

pastasciutta, pahss-tah-**shoot**-tah, *f* pasta

pastello, pahss-**tell**-lo, *m*
crayon

pasticca, pahss-**tick**-kah, *f*
pastille

pasticceria, pahss-tit-chay-**ree**-ah, *f* cake shop

pasticciere, -a, pahss-tit-**chay**-ray, *m/f* pastry-cook

pasticcino, pahss-tit-**chee**-no, *m* cake

pasticcio, pahss-**tit**-cho, *m*
pie; *fig* mix up

pasticcione, pahss-tit-**cho**-nay, *m* bungler

pastiglia, pahss-**tee**-l'yah, *f*
pastille

pastinaca, pahss-te-**nah**-kah, *f* parsnip

pasto, pahss-to, *m* meal

pastore, pahss-**tor**-ay, *m*
shepherd; minister

pastorizzato, pahss-to-reed-**dzah**-to, *adj*
pasteurized

pastura, pahss-**too**-rah, *f*
pasture

patata, pah-**tah**-tah, *f*
potato

patatine, pah-tah-**tee**-nay,
fpl crisps; chips

patente, pah-**ten**-tay, *f*
driving licence

paternità, pah-tair-nee-**tah**, *f* paternity

paterno, pah-**tair**-no, *adj*
fatherly

patetico*, pah-**tay**-te-ko,
adj pathetic

patibolo, pah-**tee**-bo-lo, *m*
gallows

patire, pah-**tee**-ray, *v* to
suffer

patria, pah-tre'ah, *f*
homeland

patrigno, pah-**tree**-n'yo, *m*
stepfather

patrimonio, pah-tree-**mo**-ne'o, *m* property; *fig*
heritage

patrocinare, pah-tro-che-**nah**-ray, *v* to sponsor

patrocinio, pah-tro-**chee**-ne'o *m* patronage

patrono, pah-**tro**-no, *m*
patron

pattinaggio, paht-te-**nahd**-jo, *m* skating

pattinare, paht-te-**nah**-ray, *v* to skate

pattini, paht-te-ne, *mpl*
skates

patto, paht-to, *m*
agreement; condition

pattuglia, paht-**too**-l'yah, *f*
patrol

pattugliare, paht-too-**l'yah**-ray, *v* to patrol

pattuire, paht-too-**ee**-ray,
v to agree

pattumiera, paht-too-me-**ay**-rah, *f* dustbin

paura, pah'oo-rah, *f* fear

pauroso, pah'oo-**ro**-zo, *adj*
fearful; frightening

pausa, pah'oo-zah, *f* break;
pause

pavimentare, pah-ve-men-**tah**-ray, *v* to pave

pavimento, pah-ve-**men**-to, *m* floor

pavone, pah-**vo**-nay, *m*
peacock

paziente, pah-tse'en-tay,
adj patient; *m/f* patient

pazienza, pah-tse'en-tsah,

f patience

pazzia, paht-tsee-ah, *f* madness; crazy thing

pazzesco, paht-tses-ko, *adj* crazy

pazzo, **paht**-tso, *adj* mad, crazy

pecca, peck-kah, *f* fault, flaw, defect

peccaminoso, peck-kah-me-**no**-zo, *adj* sinful

peccare, peck-kah-ray, *v* to sin

peccato, peck-kah-to, *m* sin

peccatore, -trice, peck-kah-**tor**-ay, peck-kah-**tree**-chay, *m/f* sinner

pece, pay-chay, *f* pitch

pecora, **pay**-ko-rah, *f* sheep

pecoraio, pay-ko-**rah**-e'o, *m* shepherd

pedaggio, pay-**dahd**-jo, *m* toll

pedalare, pay-dah-lah-ray, *v* to pedal

pedale, pay-**dah**-lay, *m* pedal

pedana, pay-**dah**-nah, *f* footboard

pedante, pay-**dahn**-tay, *adj* pedantic

pedata, pay-**dah**-tah, *f* kick; foot-print

pediatra, pay-de'**ah**-trah, *m/f* pediatrician

pedina, pay-**dee**-nah, *f* (draughts) piece

pedinare, pay-de-**nah**-ray, *v* to shadow, to follow closely

pedonale, pay-do-**nah**-lay, *adj* pedestrian

pedone, pay-**do**-nay, *m/f* pedestrian

peggio, **ped**-jo, *adv* worse, worst; *adj* worse, worst; *m* worst; *f* **avere la –**, to come off worse

peggioramento, ped-jo-rah-**men**-to, *m* worsening

peggiorare, ped-jo-**rah**-ray, *v* to worsen

peggiore, ped-**jo**-ray, *adj* worse, worst; *m/f* **il/la –**, the worst (person)

pegno, **pay**-n'yo, *m* pledge; forfeit

pelare, pay-**lah**-ray, *v* to peel; to pluck

pelato, pay-**lah**-to, *adj* bald

pelle, **pell**-lay, *f* skin; leather

pellegrinaggio, pell-lay-gre-**nahd**-jo, *m* pilgrimage

pellegrino, pell-lay-**gree**-no, *m* pilgrim

pelliccia, pell-**lit**-chah, *f* fur (coat)

pellicciaio, pell-lit-**chah**-e'o, *m* furrier

pellicola, pell-**lee**-ko-lah, *f* film

pelo, **pay**-lo, *m* hair; coat; **– dell'acqua**, surface of the water

peloso, pay-**lo**-zo, *adj* hairy

peltro, **pell**-tro, *m* pewter

pena, **pay**-nah, *f law* sentence; sorrow

penalità, pay-nah-le-**tah**, *f* penalty

penalizzare, pay-nah-lid-**dzah**-ray, *v* (games) to penalize

pendente, pen-**den**-tay, *adj* hanging; leaning; *m* pendant

pendenza, pen-**den**-tsah, *f* slope; *comm* outstanding account

pendere, pen-**day**-ray, *v* to hang; to lean

pendio, pen-**dee**-o, *m* slope

pendola, **pen**-do-lah, *f* clock

pendolare, pen-doh-**lah**-ray, *m/f* commuter

pendolo, **pen**-do-lo, *m* pendulum

pene, **pay**-nay, *m* penis

penetrare, pay-nay-**trah**-ray, *v* to penetrate

penetrazione, pay-nay-trah-tse'o-nay, *f* penetration

penicillina, pay-ne-cheell-**le**-na, *f* penicillin

penisola, pay-**nee**-zo-lah, *f* peninsula

penitenza, pay-ne-ten-tsah, *f* penitence; (games) forfeit

penitenziario, pay-ne-ten-tse'ah-re'o, *m* prison

penna, pen-nah, *f* pen; feather; – **stilografica**, fountain-pen

pennarello, pen-nah-rell-lo, *m* felt-tip pen

pennello, pen-nell-lo, *m* paint-brush

pennino, pen-nee-no, *m* nib

pennone, pen-no-nay, *m* *naut* yard; banner

penombra, pay-nom-brah, *f* half-light

penoso, pay-no-zo, *adj* painful

pensare, pen-sah-ray, *v* to think

pensiero, pen-se'ay-ro, *m* thought

pensieroso*, pen-se'ay-ro-zo, *adj* thoughtful

pensilina, pen-se-lee-nah, *f* bus shelter; platform roof

pensionato, -a, pen-se'o-nah-to, *m/f* pensioner

pensione, pen-se'o-nay, *f* pension; boarding house; board and lodging; **andare in –**, to retire

Pentecoste, pen-tay-koss-tay, *f* Whit Sunday

pentimento, pen-te-men-to, *m* repentance

pentirsi, pen-teer-se, *v* to repent; to regret

pentola, pen-to-lah, *f* pot

penultimo, pay-nool-te-mo, *adj* penultimate

penzolare, pen-tso-lah-ray, *v* to dangle, to hang

pepe, pay-pay, *m* pepper

peperone, pay-pay-ro-nay, *m* pepper, capsicum

pepita, pay-pee-tah, *f* nugget

per, pair, *prep* for; by; through

pera, pay-rah, *f* pear

percento, pair-chen-to, *m* per cent

percentuale, pair-chen-too'ah-lay, *f* percentage

percepire, pair-chay-pee-ray, *v* to perceive

percezione, pair-chay-tse'o-nay, *f* perception

perché, pair-kay, *adv* why; *conj* because; so that; *m* **il –**, the reason why

perciò, pair-cho, *conj* therefore

percorrere, pair-kor-ray-ray, *v* to travel; to cover

percorso, pair-kor-so, *m* journey

percossa, pair-kos-sah, *f* blow

percuotere, pair-koo'o-tay-ray, *v* to strike

perdere, pair-day-ray, *v* to lose; to miss; to waste

perdigiorno, pair-de-jor-no, *m* idler

perdita, pair-de-tah, *f* loss; waste; leak

perdonare, pair-do-nah-ray, *v* to forgive; to excuse

perdono, pair-do-no, *m* pardon; forgiveness

perdurare, pair-doo-rah-ray, *v* to last

peregrinare, pay-ray-gre-nah-ray, *v* to wander

perentorio*, pay-ren-to-re'o, *adj* peremptory

perfetto*, pair-fet-to, *adj* perfect

perfezionare, pair-fay-tse'o-nah-ray, *v* to improve

perfezione, pair-fay-tse'o-nay, *f* perfection

perfidia, pair-fee-de'ah, *f* perfidy

perfido*, pair-fe-do, *adj* perfidious

perfino, pair-fee-no, *adv* even

perforare, pair-fo-rah-ray, *v* to pierce

pergamena, pair-gah-may-nah, *f* parchment

pericolo, pay-ree-ko-lo, *m* danger

pericoloso*, pay-re-ko-lo-zo, *adj* dangerous

periodico, pay-re'o-de-ko, *adj* periodical; *m* periodical

periodo, pay-**ree**-o-do, *m* period

perire, pay-**ree**-ray, *v* to perish

perito, pay-**ree**-to, *m* expert

perizia, pay-**ree**-tse'ah, *f* survey

perla, pair-lah, *f* pearl

perlustrare, pair-loo-**strah**-ray, *v* to explore

permaloso, pair-mah-lo-so, *adj* touchy

permanente, pair-mah-**nen**-tay, *adj* permanent

permeare, pair-may-**ah**-ray, *v* to permeate

permesso, pair-**mess**-so, *m* permission, permit

permettere, pair-**met**-tay-ray, *v* to allow, to permit

permuta, pair-moo-tah, *f* exchange

permutare, pair-moo-**tah**-ray, *v* to exchange

pernice, pair-**nee**-chay, *f* partridge

pernicioso, pair-ne-cho-zo, *adj* pernicious

perno, pair-no, *m* pivot

pernottare, pair-not-**tah**-ray, *v* to spend the night

pero, pay-ro, *m* pear-tree

però, pay-ro, *conj* but; however

perorare, pay-ro-**rah**-ray, *v* to plead

perpendicolare, pair-pen-de-ko-**lah**-ray, *adj* perpendicular

perpetuare, pair-pay-too-**ah**-ray, *v* to perpetuate

perpetuo, pair-**pay**-too-o, *adj* perpetual

perplesso, pair-**pless**-so, *adj* perplexed

perquisire, pair-kwe-**see**-ray, *v* to search

persecutore, pair-say-koo-**tor**-ay, *m* persecutor

persecuzione, pair-say-koo-tse'o-nay, *f* persecution

perseguire, pair-say-goo'ee-ray, *v* to pursue

perseguitare, pair-say-goo'e-**tah**-ray, *v* to persecute

perseveranza, pair-say-vay-**rahn**-tsah, *f* perseverance

perseverare, pair-say-vay-**rah**-ray, *v* to persevere

persiana, pair-se'ah-nah, *f* shutter; Venetian blind

persino, pair-**see**-no, *adv* even

persistenza, pair-siss-**ten**-tsah, *f* persistence

persistere, pair-siss-**tay**-ray, *v* to persist, to continue

persona, pair-**so**-nah, *f* person, individual

personaggio, pair-so-**nahd**-jo, *m* personality; character

personale, pair-so-**nah**-lay, *adj* personal; *m* personnel

personalità, pair-so-nah-le-**tah**, *f* personality

perspicace, pair-spe-**kah**-chay, *adj* shrewd

persuadere, pair-soo'ah-**day**-ray, *v* to persuade; to convince

persuasione, pair-soo'ah-ze'o-nay, *f* persuasion

pertanto, pair-**tahn**-to, *conj* therefore

pertica, pair-te-kah, *f* pole

pertinenza, pair-te-**nen**-tsah, *f* pertinence, relevance

pertugio, pair-**too**-jo, *m* opening, hole

perturbare, pair-toohr-**bah**-ray, *v* to upset

perversità, pair-vair-se-**tah**, *f* perversity

perverso*, pair-**vair**-so, *adj* perverted

pervinca, pair-**vin**-kah, *f* (flower) periwinkle

pesante, pay-**zahn**-tay, *adj* heavy; dull

pesantezza, pay-zahn-**tet**-tsah, *f* weight

pesare, pay-**zah**-ray, *v* to

weigh

pesca, pess-kah, *f* peach; fishing

pescare, pess-kah-ray, *v* to fish

pescatore, pess-kah-tor-ay, *m* fisherman, angler

pesce, pay-shay, *m* fish; **Pesci,** Pisces

pescecane, pay-shay-kah-nay, *m* shark

pescheria, pess-kay-ree-ah, *f* fishmonger's

pescivendolo, -a, pay-she-**ven**-do-lo, *m/f* fishmonger

pesco, pess-ko, *m* peach-tree

peso, pay-zo, *m* weight; load

pessimismo, pess-se-mees-mo, *m* pessimism

pessimista, pess-se-mees-tah, *m/f* pessimist

pessimo*, pess-se-mo, *adj* very bad, awful

pestare, pess-tah-ray, *v* to tread on; to crush; to beat

peste, pess-tay, *f* plague; pest

pesto, pess-to, *m* pesto

petalo, pay-tah-lo, *m* petal

petardo, pay-tahr-do, *m* banger

petizione, pay-te-tse'o-nay, *f* petition

petroliera, pay-tro-le'ay-rah, *f* oil tanker

petrolio, pay-tro-le'o, *m* oil, petroleum

pettegolezzo, pet-tay-go-let-tso, *m* gossip

pettegolo, -a, pet-tay-go-lo, *m/f* gossip

pettinare, pet-te-nah-ray, *v* to comb

pettine, pet-te-nay, *m* comb; scallop

pettirosso, pet-te-ross-so, *m* robin

petto, pet-to, *m* breast, chest

petulante, pay-too-lahn-tay, *adj* insolent

pezzo, pet-tso, *m* piece; part

piacere, pe'ah-chay-ray, *m* pleasure; favour; *v* to please; to like

piacevole, pe'ah-chay-vo-lay, *adj* pleasant

piaga, pe'ah-gah, *f* sore; wound

pialla, pe'ahl-lah, *f* carpenter's plane

piallare, pe'ahl-lah-ray, *v* to plane

pianerottolo, pe'ah-nay-rot-to-lo, *m* landing

pianeta, pe'ah-nay-tah, *m* planet; *f relig* chasuble

piangere, pe'ahn-jay-ray, *v* to cry, to weep

piano, pe'ah-no, *m* floor; plain; plane; *adj* flat,

level; smooth; *adv* softly

pianoforte, pe'ah-no-for-tay, *m* piano

pianta, pe'ahn-tah, *f* plant; plan; (foot) sole; – **grassa,** succulent

piantagione, pe'ahn-tah-jo-nay, *f* plantation

piantare, pe'ahn-tah-ray, *v* to plant

pianterreno, pe'ahn-tair-ray-no, *m* ground-floor

pianto, pe'ahn-to, *m* tears, weeping

pianura, pe'ah-noo-rah, *f* plain

piastrella, pe'as-strel-lah, *f* tile

piattaforma, pe'aht-tah-for-mah, *f* platform

piattino, pe'aht-tee-no, *m* saucer

piatto, pe'aht-to, *m* plate; dish; course; *adj* flat

piazza, pe'aht-tsah, *f* square

piazzale, pe'aht-tsah-lay, *m* square

picca, pick-kah, *f* pike; **picche** (cards) spades

piccante, pick-kahn-tay, *adj* spicy

picchetto, pick-ket-to, *m* peg; picket

picchiare, pick-ke'ah-ray, *v* to knock; to beat

picchio, pick-ke'o, *m* woodpecker

piccino, pit-**chee**-no, *adj* small, little

piccionaia, pit-cho-**nah**-e'ah, *f* pigeon-house; *fig* gallery

piccione, pit-**cho**-nay, *m* pigeon

picco, **pick**-ko, *m* peak

piccolo, **pick**-ko-lo, *adj* small; little

piccone, pick-**ko**-nay, *m* pick-axe

pidocchio, pe-**dock**-ke'o, *m* louse

piede, pe'**ay**-day, *m* foot

piedi, pe'**ay**-de, **in –**, standing

piedistallo, pe'ay-de-**stahl**-lo, *m* pedestal

piega, pe'**ay**-gah, *f* fold; crease

piegare, pe'ay-**gah**-ray, *v* to fold; to bend

pieghevole, pe'ay-**gay**-vo-lay, *adj* pliable; folding

piena, pe'**ay**-nah, *f* flood

pieno*, pe'**ay**-no, *adj* full

pietà, pe'ay-**tah**, *f* pity; piety

pietanza, pe'ay-**tahn**-tsah, *f* dish, course

pietoso, pe'ay-**to**-zo, *adj* compassionate; pitiful

pietra, pe'**ay**-trah, *f* stone; **– di paragone**, touchstone

pietrificare, pe'ay-tre-fe-**kah**-ray, *v* to petrify

piffero, pif-**fay**-ro, *m* fife

pigiama, pe-**jah**-mah, *m* pyjamas

pigiare, pe-**jah**-ray, *v* to press; to crush

pigione, pe-**jo**-nay, *f* rent

pigliare, pe-l'**yah**-ray, *v* to take; to catch

pigmeo, pig-**may**-o, *m* pigmy

pigna, **pee**-n'yah, *f* fir-cone

pignolo, pe-n'**yo**-lo, *adj* fussy

pignorare, pe-n'yo-**rah**-ray, *v* to distrain

pigolare, pe-go-**lah**-ray, *v* to chirp

pigrizia, pe-**gree**-tse'ah, *f* laziness

pigro*, **pee**-gro, *adj* lazy

pila, **pee**-lah, *f* pile; battery

pilastro, pe-**lahss**-tro, *m* pillar

pillola, **pil**-lo-lah, *f* pill

pilone, pe-**lo**-nay, *m* pylon; pier

pilota, pe-**lo**-tah, *m* pilot; driver

pilotare, pe-lo-**tah**-ray, *v* to pilot

pinacoteca, pe-nah-ko-**tay**-kah, *f* art gallery

pineta, pe-**nay**-tah, *f* pinewood

ping-pong, ping-**pong**, *m* table tennis

pingue, pin-**goo'ay**, *adj* fat

pinguino, pin-goo'**ee**-no, *m* penguin

pinna, **pin**-nah, *f* fin; flipper

pino, **pee**-no, *m* pine-tree

pinolo, pe-**no**-lo, *m* pine kernel

pinze, **pin**-tsay, *fpl* pliers

pinzette, pin-**tset**-tay, *fpl* tweezers

pio, **pee**-o, *adj* pious; charitable

pioggia, pe'**od**-jah, *f* rain

piolo, pe'**o**-lo, *m* rung

piombare, pe'om-**bah**-ray, *v* to swoop down; to seal with lead; **– addosso**, to assail

piombino, pe'om-**bee**-no, *m* sinker; lead seal

piombo, pe'**om**-bo, *m* lead

pioniere, pe'o-ne'**ay**-ray, *m* pioneer

pioppo, pe'**op**-po, *m* poplar

piovere, pe'o-**vay**-ray, *v* to rain

piovigginare, pe'o-vid-je-**nah**-ray, *v* to drizzle

piovoso, pe'o-**vo**-zo, *adj* rainy

pipa, **pee**-pah, *f* pipe

pipì, pe-**pee**, *f* wee, pee

pipistrello, pe-pe-**strell**-lo, *m* bat

pirata, pe-**rah**-tah, *m* pirate

Pirenei, pe-ray-**nay**-e, *mpl*
Pyrenees

piroscafo, pe-ro-**skah**-fo,
m steamer

piscina, pe-**shee**-nah, *f*
swimming pool;
swimming baths

piselli, pe-**zell**-le, *mpl* peas

pista, pees-tah, *f* trail;
track; run; runway; – **da
ballo**, dance floor

pistacchio, piss-**tak**-ke'o,
m pistachio

pistola, piss-**to**-lah, *f*
pistol, gun

pistone, piss-**to**-nay, *m*
piston

pittore, -**trice**, pit-**tor**-ay,
pit-**tree**-chay, *m/f*
painter

pittoresco, pit-to-**ress**-ko,
adj picturesque

pittura, pit-**too**-rah, *f*
painting

pitturare, pit-too-**rah**-ray,
v to paint

più, pe'oo, *adv* more;
most; plus; *adj* more; the
most; several; *m* plus;
the most; **i –**, the
majority; **per lo –**, in
most cases

piuma, pe'**oo**-mah, *f*
feather

piumaggio, pe'oo-**mahd**-
jo, *m* plumage

piumino, pe'oo-**mee**-no, *m*
duvet; quilted jacket

piuttosto, pe'oot-**toss**-to,
adv rather

pizza, pit-tsa, *f* pizza

piviere, pe-ve'**ay**-ray, *m*
plover

pizzicagnolo, pit-tse-**kah**-
n'yo-lo, *m* delicatessen
owner

pizzicare, pit-tse-**kah**-ray,
v to pinch; to sting; to
itch; (food) to be spicy

pizzico, pit-**tse**-ko, *m*
pinch

placare, plah-**kah**-ray, *v* to
pacify; to satisfy

placca, **plahk**-kah, *f* plate;
plaque

placcare, plahk-**kah**-ray, *v*
to plate

placido, **plah**-che-do, *adj*
placid

plagio, **plah**-jo, *m*
plagiarism

planare, plah-**nah**-ray, *v* to
glide

plancia, **plahn**-cha, *f*
bridge

plastica, **plahs**-te-kah, *f*
plastic

platano, **plah**-tah-no, *m*
plane-tree

platea, plah-**tay**-ah, *f*
(theatre) stalls;
audience

platino, **plah**-te-no, *m*
platinum

plauso, **plah**-oo-zo, *m*
approval

plebe, **play**-bay, *f* common
people

plebeo, -**a**, play-**bay**-o, *adj*
plebeian; coarse; *m/f*
plebeian

plico, **plee**-ko, *m* parcel

plurale, ploo-**rah**-lay, *adj*
plural; *m* plural

pneumatico, pnay'oo-
mah-te-ko, *adj*
pneumatic; inflatable; *m*
tyre

po´, po, *adj* & *adv* (see
poco)

pochino, po-**kee**-no, *m*
very very little; wee bit

poco, po-ko, *adj* & *pron*
little; few; *adv* little; not
very; *m* little; **durare –**,
not to last long; **un po´**,
a little

poema, po-**ay**-mah, *m*
poem

poesia, po'ay-**zee**-ah, *f*
poem; poetry

poeta, -**essa**, po'**ay**-tah,
po'ay-**tays**-sah, *m/f* poet

poetico*, po'**ay**-te-ko, *adj*
poetic

poggiarsi, pod-**jar**-se, *v* to
rest

poggiatesta, pod-jah-**tays**-
sta, *m* headrest

poggio, **pod**-jo, *m* hillock

poi, po'e, *adv* then; later

poiché, po'e-**kay**, *conj*
since, as

polare, po-**lah**-ray, *adj*

polar

polemica, po-**lay**-me-ka, *f* controversy

poliestere, po-lee-**ays**-te-ray, *m* polyester

polipo, po-le-po, *m* polyp

polistirolo, po-le-ste-**ro**-lo, *m* polystyrene

politica, po-lee-te-kah, *f* politics; policy

politico, po-lee-te-ko, *adj** political; *m* politician

polizia, po-le-**tsee**-ah, *f* police

polizza, po-lit-tsah, *f* policy; bill; **– di assicurazione**, insurance policy; **– di carico**, bill of lading

pollaio, poll-**lah**-e'o, *m* hen house

pollame, poll-**lah**-may, *m* poultry

pollastra, poll-**lahss**-trah, *f* pullet

pollastro, poll-**lahss**-tro, *m* cockerel

pollice, poll-le-chay, *m* thumb; inch

polline, poll-le-nay, *m* pollen

pollo, poll-lo, *m* chicken

polmone, poll-**mo**-nay, *m* lung

polmonite, poll-mo-**nee**-tay, *f* pneumonia

polo, po-lo, *m* pole; *f* polo shirt

polpa, poll-pah, *f* pulp; flesh

polpaccio, poll-**paht**-cho, *m* (leg) calf

polpastrello, poll-pah-**strell**-lo, *m* fingertip

polpetta, poll-**pet**-tah, *f* meatball

polpo, poll-po, *m* octopus

polsino, poll-**see**-no, *m* cuff

polso, poll-so, *m* pulse; wrist; *fig* vigour

poltiglia, poll-**tee**-l'yah, *f* paste; pulp; slush

poltrona, poll-**tro**-nah, *f* armchair

poltrone, poll-**tro**-nay, *m* idler

polvere, poll-**vay**-ray, *f* dust; powder

polveriera, poll-vay-re'**ay**-rah, *f* powder magazine

polverizzare, poll-vay-rid-**dzah**-ray, *v* to pulverize

polveroso, poll-vay-**ro**-zo, *adj* dusty

pomata, po-**mah**-tah, *f* ointment

pomeriggio, po-may-**rid**-djo, *m* afternoon

pomice, po-me-chay, *f* pumice

pomo, po-mo, *m* apple; knob; pommel

pomodoro, po-mo-**do**-ro, *m* tomato

pompa, pom-pah, *f* pump;

pomp; **pompe funebri**, undertakers

pompare, pom-**pah**-ray, *v* to pump

pompelmo, pom-**pell**-mo, *m* grapefruit

pompiere, pom-pe'**ay**-ray, *m* fireman

pomposo*, pom-**po**-zo, *adj* pompous

ponderare, pon-day-**rah**-ray, *v* to ponder

ponente, po-**nen**-tay, *m* west

ponte, pon-tay, *m* bridge; deck; scaffold

pontefice, pon-**tay**-fe-chay, *m* pontiff

ponticello, pon-te-**chell**-lo, *m* small bridge

popolare, po-po-**lah**-ray, *adj* popular; working-class; *v* to populate

popolazione, po-po-lah-tse'o-nay, *f* population

popolo, po-po-lo, *m* people

poppa, pop-pah, *f naut* stern; breast

poppare, pop-**pah**-ray, *v* to suck

porcellana, por-chell-**lah**-nah, *f* china, porcelain

porcellino, por-chell-**lee**-no, *m* piglet; **– d'India**, guinea-pig

porcheria, por-chay-**ree**-ah, *f* filth; obscenity

porcile, por-**chee**-lay, *m*
pig-sty

porcino, por-**chee**-no, *m*
cep

porco, por-ko, *m* pig; pork

porcospino, por-ko-spee-no, *m* porcupine; hedgehog

porgere, por-jay-ray, *v* to
hold out; to hand

pornografia, por-no-grah-fee-ah, *f* pornography

poro, po-ro, *m* pore

poroso, po-ro-zo, *adj*
porous

porpora, por-po-rah, *f*
crimson

porre, por-ray, *v* to place,
to put; to suppose

porro, por-ro, *m* leek; *med*
wart

porta, por-tah, *f* door; –
girevole, revolving door

portabagagli, por-tah-bah-gah-ly'e, *m* boot; roof
rack

portacenere, por-tah-chay-nay-ray, *m* ashtray

portachiavi, por-tah-ke'ah-ve, *m* key ring

portaerei, por-tah'ay-ray'e, *f* aircraft carrier

portafoglio, por-tah-fo-l'yo, *m* wallet

portafortuna, por-tah-for-too-nah, *m* lucky charm

portalettere, por-tah-let-tay-ray, *m* postman

portamento, por-tah-men-to, *m* bearing

portamonete, por-tah-mo-nay-tay, *m* purse

portapenne, por-tah-pen-nay, *m* pen-holder

portare, por-tah-ray, *v* to
carry; to bring; to take;
to wear

portasigari, por-tah-see-gah-re, *m* cigar-case

portaspilli, por-tah-spil-le, *m* pin-cushion

portata, por-tah-tah, *f*
range; course; flow;
capacity

portatile, por-tah-te-lay,
adj portable

portatore, por-tah-tor-ay,
m bearer; carrier

portento, por-ten-to, *m*
marvel

portiere, por-te'ay-ray, *m*
caretaker; porter; goalkeeper

porto, por-to, *m* port;
comm carriage; – **d'armi,**
gun licence

Portogallo, por-to-gahl-lo, *m* Portugal

portoghese, por-to-gay-zay, *adj* Portuguese

portone, por-to-nay, *m*
main door

porzione, por-tse'o-nay, *f*
portion

posa, po-zah, *f* pose;
exposure

posamine, po-zah-mee-nay, *m* mine-layer

posare, po-zah-ray, *v* to
put (down); to rest; to
pose

posata, po-zah-tah, *f* piece
of cutlery

posato, po-zah-to, *adj*
steady

poscritto, po-skrit-to, *m*
postscript

positivo*, po-ze-tee-vo,
adj positive

posizione, po-ze-tse'o-nay,
f position

posologia, po-zo-lo-jee-ah,
f dosage

posporre, poss-por-ray, *v*
to postpone

possedere, poss-say-day-ray, *v* to possess

possesso, poss-sess-so, *m*
possession

possessore, poss-sess-sor-ay, *m* owner

possibile, poss-see-be-lay,
adj possible

possibilità, poss-se-be-le-tah, *f* possibility; chance

posta, poss-tah, *f* post,
mail; post-office

postale, poss-tah-lay, *adj*
postal; **vaglia –,** *m*
money-order

posteggiare, poss-ted-jah-ray, *v* to park

posteggio, poss-ted-jo, *m*
car-park; parking

posteri, poss-tay-re, *mpl*
descendants

posteriore, poss-tay-re'or-ay, *adj* back; later

posterità, poss-tay-re-tah, *f* posterity

postino, -a, poss-tee-no, *m/f* postman, postwoman

posto, poss-to, *m* place; (job) position; room, space

potabile, po-tah-be-lay, *adj* drinkable; **acqua –**, drinking water

potare, po-tah-ray, *v* to prune

potente, po-ten-tay, *adj* powerful, strong

potenza, po-ten-tsah, *f* power, strength

potere, po-tay-ray, *m* power; *v* can, to be able

povero, -a, po-vair-ro, *adj** poor; *m/f* poor man, poor woman; **i poveri,** the poor

povertà, po-vair-tah, *f* poverty

pozione, po-tse'o-nay, *f* potion

pozza, pot-tsah, *f* pool

pozzanghera, pot-tsahn-ghay-rah, *f* puddle

pozzo, pot-tso, *m* well; pit

pranzare, prahn-dzah-ray, *v* to have lunch

pranzo, prahn-dzo, *m* lunch

prateria, prah-tay-ree-ah, *f* prairie

pratica, prah-te-kah, *f* practice; experience

praticabile, prah-te-kah-be-lay, *adj* practicable; passable

praticare, prah-te-kah-ray, *v* to practise; to play

pratico*, prah-te-ko, *adj* practical; experienced

prato, prah-to, *m* meadow; lawn

preavviso, pray-ahv-ve-so, *m* notice

precario*, pray-kah-re'o, *adj* precarious

precauzione, pray-kah'oo-tse'o-nay, *f* precaution

precedente, pray-chay-den-tay, *adj** previous; *m* precedent

precedenza, pray-chay-den-tsah, *f* precedence, priority; right of way

precedere, pray-chay-day-ray, *v* to precede

precetto, pray-chet-to, *m* precept

precettore, pray-chet-tor-ay, *m* tutor

precipitare, pray-che-pe-tah-ray, *v* to fall; to come to a head; to rush

precipitoso*, pray-che-pe-to-zo, *adj* headlong; rash; rushed

precipizio, pray-che-pee-tse'o, *m* precipice

precipuo, pray-chee-poo-o, *adj* principal, main

precisione, pray-che-ze'o-nay, *f* precision; accuracy

preciso*, pray-chee-zo, *adj* precise; accurate

precoce, pray-ko-chay, *adj* precocious, premature

preda, pray-dah, *f* prey

predica, pray-de-kah, *f* sermon; *fig* lecture

predicare, pray-de-kah-ray, *v* to preach

predicatore, pray-de-kah-tor-ay, *m* preacher

prediletto, pray-de-let-to, *adj* favourite

predire, pray-dee-ray, *v* to predict, to foretell

predisporre, pray-diss-por-ray, *v* to prepare; to predispose

predominare, pray-do-me-nah-ray, *v* to predominate

predone, pray-do-nay, *m* plunderer

prefabbricato, pray-fahb-bre-kah-to, *adj* prefabricated

prefazione, pray-fah-tse'o-nay, *f* preface

preferenza, pray-fay-ren-tsah, *f* preference

preferire, pray-fay-ree-ray,

v to prefer; to like better

prefetto, pray-**fet**-to, *m* prefect

prefiggersi, pray-**feed**-jayrse, *v* – **uno scopo**, to set oneself a goal

prefisso, pray-**fees**-so, *m* dialling code; *gram* prefix

pregare, pray-**gah**-ray, *v* to pray (to); to beg

pregevole, pray-**jay**-vo-lay, *adj* valuable

preghiera, pray-ghe'**ay**-rah, *f* prayer

pregio, pray-jo, *m* value; merit; esteem

pregiudizio, pray-joo-dee-tse'o, *m* prejudice

prego, pray-go, *interj* you're welcome

preistoria, pray-ees-to-re'ah, *f* prehistory

prelavaggio, pray-lah-**vahj**-jo, *m* prewash

prelevare, pray-lay-**vah**-ray, *v* to withdraw; to take

preliminare, pray-le-me-**nah**-ray, *adj* preliminary

premere, pray-**may**-ray, *v* to press; – **a qualcuno**, to matter to sb

premettere, pray-**met**-tay-ray, *v* to start by saying

premiare, pray-me'**ah**-ray, *v* to award a prize to; to reward

premiato, -a, pray-me'**ah**-to, *adj* prizewinning; *m/f* prizewinner

premio, pray-me'o, *m* prize; reward; premium

premunirsi, pray-moo-**neer**-se, *v* – **contro**, to protect oneself against

premura, pray-**moo**-rah, *f* haste; care

prendere, pren-day-ray, *v* to take; to get

prenotare, pray-no-**tah**-ray, *v* to book

prenotazione, pray-no-tah-tse'o-nay, *f* booking

preoccupare, pray-ock-koo-**pah**-ray, *v* to worry

preoccupato, pray-ock-koo-**pah**-to, *adj* worried

preparare, pray-pah-**rah**-ray, *v* to prepare; to get ready

preparazione, pray-pah-rah-tse'o-nay, *f* preparation

preposizione, pray-po-se-tse'o-nay, *f* preposition

presa, pray-zah, *f* taking; grip; pinch; socket

presagio, pray-**zah**-jo, *m* omen

presagire, pray-zah-jee-ray, *v* to foresee

presbite, press-be-tay, *adj* long-sighted

presbiterio, press-be-**tay**-re'o, *m* presbytery

prescrivere, pray-**skree**-vay-ray, *v* to prescribe

prescrizione, pray-skre-tse'o-nay, *f* prescription

presentare, pray-zen-**tah**-ray, *v* to present; to submit; to introduce

presentazione, pray-zen-tah-tse'o-nay, *f* presentation

presente, pray-**zen**-tay, *m* present; *adj* present

presentimento, pray-zen-te-**men**-to, *m* premonition

presenza, pray-**zen**-tsah, *f* presence

presenziare, pray-zen-tse'**ah**-ray, *v* to be present

presepio, pray-**zay**-e'o, *m* crib

preservare, pray-zair-**vah**-ray, *v* to protect

preservativo, pray-zair-vah-**tee**-vo, *m* condom

preside, pray-se-day, *m/f* headteacher

presidente, pray-se-**den**-tay, *m* president

presidenza, pray-se-**den**-tsah, *f* presidency

presidio, pray-**see**-de'o, *m* garrison

presiedere, pray-se'**ay**-day-ray, *v* to preside over

pressa, press-sah, *f* press

pressante, press-**sahn**-tay,

adj pressing

pressare, press-**sah**-ray, *v* to press

pressione, press-se'o-nay, *f* pressure

presso, **press**-so, *prep* near; for; care of

pressoché, press-so-**kay**, *adv* almost

prestabilire, press-tah-be-lee-ray, *v* to arrange beforehand

prestante, press-**tahn**-tay, *adj* good-looking

prestare, press-**tah**-ray, *v* to lend

prestigiatore, press-tee-jah-**to**-ray, *m* conjurer

prestigio, press-**tee**-jo, *m* prestige; **gioco di –**, conjuring trick

prestito, **press**-te-to, *m* loan

presto, **press**-to, *adv* soon; early; quickly

presumere, pray-**zoo**-may-ray, *v* to presume

presuntuoso, pray-zoonn-too'o-zo, *adj* presumptuous, conceited

presunzione, pray-zoonn-tse'o-nay, *f* presumptuousness

prete, pray-tay, *m* priest

pretendere, pray-**ten**-day-ray, *v* to demand; to expect; to claim

pretesa, pray-**tay**-zah, *f* claim; pretension

pretesto, pray-**tess**-to, *m* pretext

pretura, pray-**too**-rah, *f* magistrate's court

prevalere, pray-vah-**lay**-ray, *v* to prevail

prevaricare, pray-vah-re-**kah**-ray, *v* to abuse one's power

prevaricazione, pray-vah-re-kah-tse'o-nay, *f* abuse of power

prevedere, pray-vay-**day**-ray, *v* to foresee; to forecast; to make provision for; to expect

prevenire, pray-vay-**nee**-ray, *v* to prevent; to forestall

preventivo, pray-ven-**tee**-vo, *adj** preventive; *m* estimate

prevenuto, pray-vay-**noo**-to, *adj* prejudiced

prevenzione, pray-ven-tse'o-nay, *f* prevention

previdenza, pray-ve-**den**-tsah, *f* foresight; **– sociale**, social security

previo, pray-ve'o, *adj comm* upon

previsione, pray-ve-ze'o-nay, *f* prediction; expectation; **previsioni del tempo**, weather forecast

previsto, pray-**viss**-sto, *adj* expected; *m* **più del –**, more than expected

prezioso, pray-tse'o-zo, *adj* precious, valuable

prezzemolo, pret-tsay-mo-lo, *m* parsley

prezzo, **pret**-tso, *m* price

prigione, pre-jo-nay, *f* prison

prigionia, pre-jo-nee-ah, *f* imprisonment

prigioniero, -a, pre-jo-ne'ay-ro, *m/f* prisoner

prima, pree-mah, *adv* before; earlier; first; once; *f* (theatre) first night; (car) first gear

primario, pre-**mah**-re'o, *adj* primary; *m* chief physician

primato, pre-**mah**-to, *m* (sport) record

primavera, pre-mah-**vay**-rah, *f* spring

primitivo, pre-me-**tee**-vo, *adj* primitive

primizie, pre-**mee**-tse'ay, *fpl* early produce

primo, pree-mo, *adj & m* first; early; *m* first course

primogenito, -a, pre-mo-**jay**-ne-to, *m/f* first child

primula, pree-mo-lah, *f* primrose

principale, prin-che-**pah**-lay, *adj* principal, main; *m/f* boss

principe, prin-che-pay, *m* prince

principessa, prin-che-pess-sah, *f* princess

principiante, prin-che-pe'ahn-tay, *m/f* beginner

principio, prin-chee-pe'o, *m* beginning; principle

priorità, pre-o-re-tah, *f* priority

privare, pre-vah-ray, *v* to deprive

privativa, pre-vah-tee-vah, *f* monopoly

privato, -a, pre-vah-to, *adj** private; *m/f* private citizen; **in –,** in private

privazione, pre-vah-tse'o-nay, *f* privation; loss

privilegiare, pre-ve-lay-jah-ray, *v* to favour

privilegio, pre-ve-lay-jo, *m* privilege

privo, pree-vo, *adj* – **di,** without; lacking in

pro, pro, *prep* in favour of; *m* advantage; good; **i – e i contro,** pros and cons

probabile, pro-bah-be-lay, *adj* probable, likely

probabilità, pro-bah-be-le-tah, *f* probability

problema, pro-blay-mah, *m* problem

proboscide, pro-bo-she-day, *f* trunk

procacciare, pro-kaht-chah-ray, *v* to get

procace, pro-kah-chay, *adj* provocative

procedere, pro-chay-day-ray, *v* to proceed

procedimento, pro-chay-de-men-to, *m* procedure; *law* proceedings

procedura, pro-chay-doo-rah, *f* procedure

processare, pro-chess-sah-ray, *v law* to try

processione, pro-chess-se'o-nay, *f* procession

processo, pro-chess-so, *m* trial; process

proclama, pro-klah-mah, *m* proclamation

proclamare, pro-klah-mah-ray, *v* to proclaim

proclamazione, pro-klah-mah-tse'o-nay, *f* proclamation

procura, pro-koo-rah, *f* power of attorney; proxy

procurare, pro-koo-rah-ray, *v* to get

procuratore, pro-koo-rah-tor-ay, *m* solicitor; holder of power of attorney

prode, pro-day, *adj* brave

prodigare, pro-de-gah-ray, *v* to be lavish with

prodigarsi, pro-de-gar-se, *v* – **per,** to do all one can for

prodigio, pro-dee-jo, *m* prodigy; marvel

prodigioso, pro-de-jo-zo, *adj* extraordinary, astonishing

prodigo, pro-de-go, *adj* lavish

prodotto, pro-dot-to, *m* product

produrre, pro-doohr-ray, *v* to produce

produttore, pro-doot-tor-ay, *m* producer

produzione, pro-doo-tse'o-nay, *f* production

proemio, pro'ay-me'o, *m* introduction

profanare, pro-fah-nah-ray, *v* to profane

profano, -a, pro-fah-no, *adj* profane; *m/f* lay person

proferire, pro-fay-ree-ray, *v* to utter; to express

professare, pro-fess-sah-ray, *v* to profess

professionale, pro-fess-se'o-nah-lay, *adj* professional

professione, pro-fess-se'o-nay, *f* profession

professore, -essa, pro-fess-so-ray, pro-fess-so-ress-sah, *m/f* teacher; professor

profeta, pro-fay-tah, *m* prophet

profetico, pro-fay-te-ko, *adj* prophetic

profetizzare, pro-fay-tiddzah-ray, v to prophesy

profezia, pro-fay-tsee-ah, f prophecy

profilo, pro-fee-lo, m profile

profittare, pro-fit-tah-ray, v to profit; to take advantage

profitto, pro-fit-to, m profit; advantage

profondere, pro-fon-day-ray, v to lavish

profondità, pro-fon-de-tah, f depth

profondo*, pro-fon-do, adj profound; deep

profugo, -a, pro-foo-go, m/f refugee

profumare, pro-foo-mah-ray, v to perfume; to smell good

profumeria, pro-foo-may-ree-ah, f perfumery

profumo, pro-foo-mo, m perfume; fragrance

profusione, pro-foo-ze'o-nay, f profusion

progettare, pro-jet-tah-ray, v to plan

progetto, pro-jet-to, m plan, project

programma, pro-grahm-mah, m programme; program

progredire, pro-gray-dee-ray, v to progress

progressivo*, pro-gress-see-vo, adj progressive

progresso, pro-gress-so, m progress

proibire, pro-e-bee-ray, v to prohibit

proibizione, pro-e-be-tse'o-nay, f prohibition

proiettare, pro-e'et-tah-ray, v to project

proiettile, pro-e'et-te-lay, m projectile

proiettore, pro-e'et-tor-ay, m projector; search-light; head-lamp

proiezione, pro-e'ay-tse'o-nay, f projection; showing

prole, pro-lay, f children, offspring

prolifico*, pro-lee-fe-ko, adj prolific

prolisso, pro-liss-so, adj verbose

prologo, pro-lo-go, m prologue, introduction

prolunga, pro-loonn-gah, f extension

prolungare, pro-loonn-gah-ray, v to prolong; to extend

promessa, pro-mess-sah, f promise

promettere, pro-met-tay-ray, v to promise; to be promising

promozione, pro-mo-tse'o-nay, f promotion

promulgare, pro-mool-gah-ray, v to promulgate

promuovere, pro-moo'o-vay-ray, v to promote

pronome, pro-no-may, m pronoun

pronostico, pro-noss-te-ko, m forecast

prontezza, pron-tet-tsah, f readiness; promptness; quickness

pronto, pron-to, adj * prompt; ready; quick; interj hello

prontuario, pron-too'ah-re'o, m manual, hand-book

pronuncia, pro-noonn-chah, f pronunciation

pronunciare, pro-noonn-chah-ray, v to pronounce; to utter

propagare, pro-pah-gah-ray, v to propagate; to spread

propensione, pro-pen-se'o-nay, f propensity

propizio, pro-pee-tse'o, adj favourable; suitable

proporre, pro-por-ray, v to suggest; propose

proporzionale, pro-por-tse'o-nah-lay, adj proportional

proporzionato*, pro-por-tse'o-nah-to, adj proportionate

propozione, pro-por-tse'o-nay, f proportion; ratio

proposito, pro-po-ze-to, m

intention; purpose; **a –**, by the way

proposta, pro-**poss**-tah, *f* proposal

proprietà, pro-pre-ay-**tah**, *f* property

proprietario, -a, pro-pre-ay-**tah**-re'o, *m/f* owner

proprio, pro-**pre**'o, *adj* own; exact; characteristic; *adv* really; exactly

propulsore, pro-pooll-**sor**-ay, *m* propeller

prora, pro-**rah**, *f* prow, bow

proroga, pro-**ro**-gah, *f* extension; postponement

prorogare, pro-ro-**gah**-ray, *v* to extend; to postpone

prorompere, pro-**rom**-pay-ray, *v* to burst out

prosa, pro-**zah**, *f* prose

prosciugare, pro-she'oo-**gah**-ray, *v* to drain; to reclaim; to dry up

prosciutto, pro-she'**oot**-to, *m* ham

proscritto, pro-**skrit**-to, *m* outlaw

proseguire, pro-say-goo'ee-ray, *v* to carry on

prosperare, pross-pay-**rah**-ray, *v* to thrive

prosperità, pross-pay-re-**tah**, *f* prosperity

prospero, pross-**pay**-ro,

adj flourishing

prospettiva, pross-pet-**tee**-vah, *f* perspective; prospect

prospetto, pross-**pet**-to, *m* elevation; table; summary

prossimità, pross-se-me-**tah**, *f* proximity

prossimo*, pross-**se**-mo, *adj* next; *m* neighbour

prostituta, pross-te-**too**-tah, *f* prostitute

prostrazione, pross-trah-tse'o-**nay**, *f* prostration

protagonista, pro-tah-go-**niss**-stah, *m/f* protagonist

proteggere, pro-**ted**-jay-ray, *v* to protect

protendere, pro-**ten**-day-ray, *v* to stretch out

protervo, pro-**tair**-vo, *adj* arrogant

protesi, pro-**tay**-ze, *f* prosthesis

protesta, pro-**tess**-tah, *f* protest

protestante, pro-tess-**tahn**-tay, *adj* Protestant; *m/f* Protestant

protestare, pro-tess-**tah**-ray, *v* to protest

protesto, pro-**tess**-to, *m* protest

protettore, -trice, pro-tet-**tor**-ay, pro-tet-**tree**-chay, *m/f* protector

protezione, pro-tay-tse'o-nay, *f* protection

prototipo, pro-**to**-te-po, *m* prototype

protrarre, pro-**trar**-ray, *v* to prolong

prova, pro-**vah**, *f* trial, test; proof, evidence; experiment; rehearsal; exam

provare, pro-**vah**-ray, *v* to try; to try on; to prove; to feel

provenienza, pro-vay-ne'en-tsah, *f* source, origin

provenire, pro-vay-**nee**-ray, *v – da*, to come from

proventi, pro-**ven**-te, *mpl* proceeds

proverbio, pro-**vair**-be'o, *m* proverb

provetta, pro-**vet**-tah, *f* test tube

provincia, pro-**vin**-chah *f* province

provinciale, pro-vin-**chah**-lay, *adj* provincial

provino, pro-**vee**-no, *m* audition

provocante, pro-vo-**kahn**-tay, *adj* provocative

provocare, pro-vo-**kah**-ray, *v* to provoke

provocazione, pro-vo-kah-tse'o-nay, *f* provocation

provvedere, prov-vay-

day-ray, *v* to take measures; to provide for

provvedimento, prov-vay-de-**men**-to, *m* measure

provveditore, prov-vay-de-**tor**-ay, *m* – agli studi, director of education

provvidenza, prov-ve-**den**-tsah, *f* providence

provvigione, prov-ve-jo-nay, *f* commission

provvisorio*, prov-ve-**zo**-re'o, *adj* temporary

provvista, prov-**viss**-tah, *f* supply; provision

prua, proo-ah, *f* prow

prudente, proo-**den**-tay, *adj* prudent, cautious; sensible

prudenza, proo-**den**-tsah, *f* prudence, caution

prudere, proo-day-ray, *v* to itch

prugna, proo-n'yah, *f* plum; – secca, prune

pruriginoso, proo-re-je-no-zo, *adj* itchy

prurito, proo-**ree**-to, *m* itch

pseudonimo, psay'oo-do-ne-mo, *m* pseudonym

psicanalisi, pse-kah-**nah**-le-ze, *f* psychoanalysis

psicanalista, pse-kah-nah-**liss**-stah, *m/f* psychoanalyst

psiche, psee-kay, *f* psyche

psichiatria, pse-ke'ah-tree-ah, *f* psychiatry

psichico, psee-ke-ko, *adj* psychic

psicologia, pse-ko-lo-jee-ah, *f* psychology

psicologico, pse-ko-lo-je-ko, *adj* psychological

psicologo, -a, pse-ko-lo-gho, *m/f* psychologist

psicopatico, -a, pse-ko-**pah**-te-ko, *m/f* psychopath

psoriasi, pso-re'**ah**-ze, *f* psoriasis

pubblicare, poob-ble-**kah**-ray, *v* to publish

pubblicazione, poob-ble-kah-tse'**o**-nay, *f* publication; **pubblicazioni matrimoniali,** marriage banns

pubblicità, poob-ble-che-**tah**, *f* publicity; advertising; advertisement

pubblico, poob-ble-ko, *m* public; *adj** public

pube, poo-bay, *m* pubis

pudico, poo-**dee**-ko, *adj* modest

pudore, poo-**dor**-ay, *m* modesty

puerile, poo'ay-**ree**-lay, *adj* childish, puerile

pugilato, poo-ge-**lah**-to, *m* boxing

pugile, poo-ge-lay, *m* boxer

pugnalare, poo-n'yah-**lah**-ray, *v* to stab

pugnale, poo-n'**yah**-lay, *m* dagger

pugno, poo-n'yo, *m* fist; punch; fistful

pulce, pooll-chay, *f* flea

Pulcinella, pooll-che-**nell**-lah, *m* Punch

pulcino, pooll-**chee**-no, *m* chick

puledra, poo-lay-drah, *f* filly

puledro, poo-lay-dro, *m* colt

puleggia, poo-**led**-jah, *f* pulley

pulire, poo-lee-ray, *v* to clean; to polish

pulito, poo-lee-to, *adj* clean; polished

pulizia, poo-le-tsee-ah, *f* cleanliness; cleaning

pullman, pooll-mahn, *m* coach

pullover, pooll-lo-vair, *m* pullover, sweater

pullulare, pooll-loo-**lah**-ray, *v* to swarm, to teem

pulmino, pooll-**mee**-no, *m* minibus

pulpito, pooll-pe-to, *m* pulpit

pulsante, pooll-**sahn**-tay, *m* button

pulsare, pooll-**sah**-ray, *v* to pulsate, to beat

pulsazione, pooll-sah-tse'o-nay, *f* beat

pungere, poonn-jay-ray, *v* to prick; to sting

pungiglione, poonn-je-l'yo-nay, *m* sting

pungolo, poonn-go-lo, *m* goad

punire, poo-nee-ray, *v* to punish

punizione, poo-ne-tse'o-nay, *f* punishment

punta, poonn-tah, *f* point; end, tip

puntare, poonn-**tah**-ray, *v* to point; to bet; to plant; – **a,** to aim at

puntata, poonn-**tah**-tah, *f* episode; bet

punteggiatura, poonn-ted-jah-**too**-rah, *f* punctuation

punteggio, poonn-**ted**-jo, *m* score

puntellare, poonn-tell-**lah**-ray, *v* to shore; to prop up

punteruolo, poonn-tay-roo'o-lo, *m* punch; bodkin

punto, poonn-to, *m* dot; point; full stop; spot; stitch; – **esclamativo,** exclamation mark; – **interrogativo,** question mark

puntuale, poonn-too'ah-lay, *adj* punctual

puntualità, poonn-too'ah-le-**tah**, *f* punctuality

puntura, poonn-**too**-rah, *f* sting; prick; injection

pupazzo, poo-**pat**-tso, *m* puppet

pupilla, poo-**pill**-lah, *f* (eye) pupil

purché, poohr-**kay**, *conj* provided that

pure, poo-ray, *conj* yet; even if; *adv* also, too

purezza, poo-**ret**-tsah, *f* purity

purgare, poohr-gah-ray, *v* to purge

purgatorio, poohr-gah-tor-e'o, *m* purgatory

purificare, poo-re-fe-**kah**-ray, *v* to purify

puro, poo-ro, *adj* pure

purosangue, poo-ro-**sahn**-goo'ay, *adj* thoroughbred

purpureo, poohr-**poo**-ray-o, *m* purple

purtroppo, poohr-**trop**-po, *adv* unfortunately

pus, pooss, *m* pus

pustola, pooss-to-lah, *f* pustule; pimple

putrefare, poo-tray-**fah**-ray, *v* to putrify; to decompose

putrido, poo-tre-do, *adj* putrid; decomposed

puttana, poot-**tah**-nah, *f* prostitute

puzza, poot-tsah, *f* stink, stench

puzzare, poot-**tsah**-ray, *v* to stink

puzzo, poot-tso, *m* stink, stench

puzzola, poot-**tso**-lah, *f* polecat

puzzolente, poot-tso-**len**-tay, *adj* stinking

qua, kwah, *adv* here; **– e là,** here and there

quacchero, -a, kwahk-kay-ro, *m/f* Quaker

quaderno, kwah-**dair**-no, *m* exercise book

quadrante, kwah-**drahn**-tay, *m* quadrant; face

quadrare, kwah-**drah**-ray, *v* to square; to balance

quadrato, kwah-**drah**-to, *adj* square; *m* square

quadretto, kwah-**dret**-to, *m* **a quadretti,** squared; checked

quadrifoglio, kwah-dree-**fo**-l'yo, *m* four-leaf clover

quadrimestre, kwah-dree-**mes**-tray, *m* term; four-months period

quadro, kwah-dro, *m* square; picture; (cards) diamonds; *adj* square

quadruplo, kwah-**droo**-plo, *m* quadruple

quaggiù, kwahd-**joo,** *adv* here below

quaglia, kwah-l'yah, *f* quail

qualche, kwahl-kay, *adj* some; any; **– volta,** sometimes

qualcosa, kwahl-ko-zah, *pron* something; anything; **qualcos'altro,** something else

qualcuno, kwahl-**koo**-no, *pron,* someone; anyone; **– di noi,** some of us

quale, kwah-lay, *adj & pron* which; who; what

qualifica, kwah-le-fe-kah, *f* qualification

qualificarsi, kwah-le-fe-**kahr**-se, *v* to qualify

qualità, kwah-le-tah, *f* quality; kind

qualitativo*, kwah-le-tah-**tee**-vo, *adj* qualitative

qualora, kwah-**lor**-ah, *conj* if

qualsiasi, kwahl-**see**-ah-se, *adj* any; whatever

qualunque, kwah-**loonn**-kway, *adj* any; whatever

quando, kwahn-do, *adv & conj* when

quantificabile, kwahn-te-fe-**kah**-be-lay, *adj* quantifiable

quantificare, kwahn-te-fe-**kah**-ray, *v* to quantify

quantità, kwahn-te-**tah,** *f* quantity

quantitativo, kwahn-te-tah-**tee**-vo *adj** quantitative; *m* amount, quantity

quanto, kwahn-to, *adj & pron* how much, how many; *adv* how much, how long; how far; **– a,** with regard to; as for;

per –, however, although

quantunque, kwahn-**toonn**-kway, *conj* although

quaranta, kwah-**rahn**-tah, *adj & m* forty

quarantena, kwah-rahn-**tay**-nah, *f* quarantine

quarantesimo, kwah-rahn-**tay**-ze-mo, *adj & m* fortieth

quaresima, kwah-**ray**-ze-mah, *f* Lent

quartiere, kwahr-te'**ay**-ray, *m* district, neighbourhood

quarta, kwahr-tah, *f* fourth gear

quarto, kwahr-to, *adj & m* fourth; *m* quarter

quarzo, kwahr-tso, *m* quartz

quasi, kwah-ze, *adv* almost

quassù, kwahss-**soo**, *adv* up here

quatto, kwaht-to, *adj* **andarsene quatto quatto**, to slip away

quattordicesimo, kwaht-tor-de-**chay**-se-mo, *adj & m* fourteenth

quattordici, kwaht-**tor**-de-che, *adj & m* fourteen

quattrini, kwaht-**tree**-ne, *m* money

quattro, kwaht-tro, *adj &*

m four

quattrocento, kwaht-tro-**chen**-to, *adj & m* four hundred; **il Quattrocento**, the fifteenth century

quegli, kway-l'ye, *adj* those

quei, kway-e, *adj* those

quello, kwayl-lo, *adj & pron* that, those

quercia, kwayr-chah, *f* oak

querela, kway-**ray**-lah, *f* legal action

querelante, kway-ray-**lahn**-tay, *m/f* plaintiff

querelare, kway-ray-**lah**-ray, *v* to bring a legal action against

querelato, kway-ray-**lah**-to, *m* defendant

quesito, kway-**zee**-to, *m* question

questionario, kwess-te'o-**nah**-re'o, *m* questionnaire

questione, kwess-te'o-nay, *f* matter, question

questo, kwess-to, *adj & pron* this, these

questore, kwess-**tor**-ay, *m* chief constable

questura, kwess-**too**-rah, *f* police headquarters

qui, kwee, *adv* here; **di – a pochi giorni**, in a few days

quiete, kwe'**ay**-tay, *f* quiet, peace

quieto, kwe'**ay**-to, *adj* quiet

quindi, kwin-de, *conj* therefore; *adv* then

quindicesimo, kwin-de-**chay**-se-mo, *adj & m* fifteenth

quindici, kwin-de-che, *adj & m* fifteen

quindicina, kwin-de-**chee**-nah, *f* about fifteen

quindicinale, kwin-de-che-**nah**-lay, *adj* fortnightly; *m* fortnightly magazine

quinta, kwin-tah, *f* fifth gear; **quinte**, (theatre) wings

quintale, kwin-**tah**-lay, *m* one hundred kilograms

quinto, kwin-to, *adj & m* fifth

quiz, kwidz, *m* quiz game

quota, kwo-tah, *f* altitude; share; fee

quotare, kwo-**tah**-ray, *v* to quote; to value

quotazione, kwo-tah-tse'o-nay, *f* quotation

quotidiano, kwo-te-de'**ah**-no, *adj** daily; *m* daily paper

quoziente, kwod-dze'**ayn**-tay, *m* quotient; – **d'intelligenza**, IQ

R

rabarbaro, rah-**bar**-bah-ro, *m* rhubarb

rabbia, rabb-be'ah, *f* anger, rage; fury; *med* rabies

rabbino, rahb-**bee**-no, *m* rabbi

rabbioso*, rahb-be'o-so, *adj* angry; furious; rabid

rabbonire, rahb-bo-**nee**-ray, *v* to calm down

rabbrividire, rahb-bre-ve-**dee**-ray, *v* to shudder, to shiver

rabbuiare, rahb-boo-e'ah-ray, *v* to darken

raccapezzarsi, rahk-kah-pet-**tsahr**-se, *v* to make it out

raccapricciante, rahk-kah-prit-**chahn**-tay, *adj* horrifying

raccattapalle, rahk-kaht-tah-**pahl**-lay, *m/f* ball-boy, ball-girl

raccattare, rahk-kaht-**tah**-ray, *v* to pick up

racchetta, rahk-**ket**-tah, *f* racket; bat; (ski) stick

raccogliere, rahk-ko-l'ye'ay-ray, *v* to pick up; to pick; to gather

raccoglitore, rahk-ko-l'ye-**tor**-ay, *m* folder

raccolta, rahk-**koll**-tah, *f* collection; harvest

raccomandare, rahk-ko-mahn-**dah**-ray, *v* to recommend; to entrust; **mi raccomando!**, don't forget!

raccomandata, rahk-ko-mahn-**dah**-tah, *f* registered letter

raccomandazione, rahk-ko-mahn-dah-tse'**o**-nay, *f* recommendation

raccontare, rahk-kon-**tah**-ray, *v* to tell

racconto, rahk-**kon**-to, *m* story; account

raccordare, rahk-kor-**dah**-ray, *v* to connect

raccordo, rahk-**kor**-do, *m* connection; slip road

rachitico, rah-**kee**-te-ko, *adj* suffering from rickets

rachitismo, rah-kee-**teez**-mo, *m* rickets

rada, rah-dah, *f* harbour

radar, rah-**dahr**, *m* radar

raddolcire, rahd-doll-**chee**-ray, *v* to soften

raddoppiare, rahd-dop-pe'**ah**-ray, *v* to double

raddrizzare, rahd-drit-**tsah**-ray, *v* to straighten

radere, rah-day ray, *v* to shave

radiante, rah-de'**ahn**-tay, *adj* radiant

radiare, rah-de'**ah**-ray, *v* to strike off

radiatore, rah-de'ah-**tor**-ay, *m* radiator

radiazione, rah-de'ah-tse'o-nay, *f* radiation

radica, rah-**de**-kah, *f* briar

radicale, rah-de-**kah**-lay, *adj* radical

radicare, rah-de-**kah**-ray, *v* to take root

radicchio, rah-**dik**-ke'o, *m* chicory

radice, rah-**dee**-chay, *f* root

radio, **rah**-de'o, *f* radio; *m* radium

radioascoltatore, **-trice**, rah-de'o-ahs-kol-tah-**to**-ray, rah-de'o-ahs-kol-tah-**tree**-chay, *m/f* listener

radioattivo, rah-de'o-aht-**tee**-vo, *adj* radioactive

radiocomandato, rah-de'o-ko-mahn-**dah**-to, *adj* remote-controlled

radiografia, rah-de'o-grah-**fee**-ah, *f* X-ray

radiotaxi, rah-de'o-**tahk**-se, *m* minicab

radiotelegrafia, rah-de'o-tay-lay-grah-**fee**-ah, *f* radiotelegraphy

rado, **rah**-do, *adj* sparse, thin; **di –**, rarely

radunare, rah-doo-**nah**-ray, *v* to assemble, to gather

raduno, rah-**doo**-no, *m* gathering, meeting

radura, rah-**doo**-rah, *f* clearing

rafano, **rah**-fah-no, *m* horseradish

raffazzonare, rahf-faht-tso-**nah**-ray, *v* to patch up

raffermo, rahf-**fair**-mo, *adj* stale

raffica, **rahf**-fe-kah, *f* gust; burst

raffigurare, rahf-fe-goo-**rah**-ray, *v* to represent, to portray

raffinare, rahf-fe-**nah**-ray, *v* to refine

raffinato, rahf-fe-**nah**-to, *adj* refined; sophisticated

raffineria, rahf-fe-nay-**ree**-ah, *f* refinery

rafforzare, rahf-for-**tsah**-ray, *v* to reinforce

raffreddare, rahf-fraid-**dah**-ray, *v* to cool; *fig* to dampen

raffreddore, rahf-fraid-**dor**-ay, *m* cold

raffronto, rahf-**fron**-to, *m* comparison

ragazza, rah-**gaht**-tsah, *f* girl; girlfriend

ragazzo, rah-**gaht**-tso, *m* boy; lad; boyfriend

raggiante, rahd-**jahn**-tay, *adj* beaming

raggio, **rahd**-jo, *m* ray; radius; spoke

raggirare, rahd-jee-**rah**-ray, *v* to cheat, to trick

raggiro, rahd-**jee**-ro, *m* trick

raggiungere, rahd-**djoonn**-jay-ray, *v* to reach; to catch up; to hit; to achieve

raggomitolarsi, rahg-go-

me-to-**lar**-se, *v* to curl up

raggranellare, rahg-grah-nell-**lah**-ray, *v* to scrape together

raggruppare, rahg-groop-**pah**-ray, *v* to assemble; to group together

ragguagliare, rahg-goo'ah-l'yah-ray, *v* to to inform

ragguardevole, rahg-goo'ar-**day**-vo-lay, *adj* considerable; remarkable

ragionamento, rah-jo-nah-**men**-to, *m* reasoning

ragionare, rah-jo-**nah**-ray, *v* to reason

ragione, rah-**jo**-nay, *f* reason; right

ragioneria, rah-jo-nay-**ree**-ah, *f* accountancy; accounts

ragionevole, rah-jo-**nay**-vo-lay, *adj* reasonable

ragioniere, **-a**, rah-jo-ne'**ay**-ray, *m/f* accountant

ragliare, rah-l'**yah**-ray, *v* to bray

ragnatela, rah-n'yah-**tay**-lah, *f* cobweb, spider's web

ragno, **rah**-n'yo, *m* spider

rallegramenti, rahl-lay-grah-**men**-te, *mpl* congratulations

rallegrare, rahl-lay-**grah**-ray, *v* to rejoice; to cheer up

rallentare, rahl-len-**tah**-ray, *v* to slow down

ramaiolo, rah-mah-e'o-lo, *m* ladle

ramanzina, rah-mahn-dzee-nah, *f* telling-off

rame, rah-may, *m* copper

ramificare, rah-me-fe-**kah**-ray, *v* to ramify

ramino, rah-mee-no, *m* rummy

rammarico, rahm-**mah**-re-ko, *m* regret

rammendare, rahm-men-**dah**-ray, *v* to mend; to darn

rammentare, rahm-men-**tah**-ray, *v* to remind; to remember

rammollire, rahm-moll-**lee**-ray, *v* to soften; to go soft

ramo, rah-mo, *m* branch

ramoscello, rah-mo-**shell**-lo, *m* twig

rampa, rahm-pah, *f* flight (of stairs); slope; **– di lancio**, launching pad

rampicante, rahm-pe-**kahn**-tay, *adj* climbing

rampino, rahm-pee-no, *m* hook

rampone, rahm-po-nay, *m* harpoon

rana, rah-nah, *f* frog

rancido, **rahn**-che-do, *adj* rancid

rancore, rahn-**kor**-ay, *m* rancour; grudge

randagio, rahn-**dah**-jo, *adj* stray

randello, rahn-**dell**-lo, *m* cudgel

rango, **rahn**-go, *m* rank

rannicchiarsi, rahn-nick-ke'**ar**-se, *v* to crouch

rannuvolare, rahn-noo-vo-**lah**-ray, *v* to cloud

ranocchio, rah-**nock**-ke'o, *m* small frog

rantolo, **rahn**-to-lo, *m* (death) rattle

rapa, rah-pah, *f* turnip

rapace, rah-**pah**-chay, *adj* predatory; *fig* rapacious

rapare, rah-**pah**-ray, *v* to crop

rapide, rah-pe-day, *fpl* rapids

rapidità, rah-pe-de-**tah**, *f* rapidity

rapido*, **rah**-pe-do, *adj* fast, rapid, swift

rapimento, rah-pe-**men**-to, *m* kidnapping; *fig* rapture

rapina, rah-pee-nah, *f* robbery

rapinare, rah-pee-**nah**-ray, *v* to rob

rapinatore, **-trice**, rah-pee-nah-**to**-ray, rah-pee-nah-**tree**-chay, *m/f*

robber

rapire, rah-**pee**-ray, *v* to kidnap

rapitore, **-trice**, rah-pee-**to**-ray, rah-pee-**tree**-chay, *m/f* kidnapper

rapportare, rahp-por-**tah**-ray, *v* to compare; to reproduce

rapporto, rahp-**por**-to, *m* report; relationship; ratio; **rapporti sessuali**, sexual intercourse

rapprendersi, rahp-**pren**-der-se, *v* to curdle

rappresaglia, rahp-pray-zah-l'yah, *f* reprisal

rappresentante, rahp-pray-sen-**tahn**-tay, *m/f* representative

rappresentare, rahp-pray-sen-**tah**-ray, *v* to represent; to depict; to perform

rappresentazione, rahp-pray-sen-tah-tse'o-**nay**, *f* performance; representation

rarità, rah-re-**tah**, *f* rarity

raro*, **rah**-ro, *adj* rare

raschiare, rahss-ke'**ah**-ray, *v* to scrape

raschiatura, rahss-ke'ah-**too**-rah, *f* scraping

rasentare, rah-zen-**tah**-ray, *v* to graze; to keep close to; to border on

rasente, rah-**zen**-tay, *prep*

close to

raso, rah-zo, *m* satin; *adj* level

rasoio, rah-zo-e'o, *m* razor

raspa, rahss-pah, *f* rasp

raspare, rahss-pah-ray, *v* to rasp; to scratch

rassegna, rahss-say-n'yah, *f* review; exhibition; season

rassegnare, rahss-say-n'yah-ray, *v* to resign; to give up; – **le dimissioni**, to resign

rassegnazione, rahss-say-n'yah-tse'o-nay, *f* resignation

rasserenare, rahss-say-ray-nah-ray, *v* to clear up

rassettare, rahss-set-tah-ray, *v* to tidy

rassicurare, rahss-se-koo-rah-ray, *v* to reassure

rassodare, rahss-so-dah-ray, *v* to harden

rassomiglianza, rahss-so-me-l'yahn-tsah, *f* resemblance

rassomigliare, rahss-so-me-l'yah-ray, *v* to resemble

rastrellare, rahss-trell-lah-ray, *v* to rake; *fig* to comb

rastrelliera, rahss-trell-le'ay-rah, *f* rack

rastrello, rahss-trell-lo, *m* rake

rata, rah-tah, *f* instalment

ratificare, rah-te-fe-kah-ray, *v* to ratify

ratto, raht-to, *m* rat

rattoppare, raht-top-pah-ray, *v* to patch

rattrappirsi, raht-trahp-peer-se, *v* to become numb

rattristare, raht-triss-tah-ray, *v* to sadden

raucedine, rah'oo-chay-de-nay, *f* hoarseness

rauco, rah'oo-ko, *adj* hoarse

ravanello, rah-vah-nell-lo, *m* radish

ravvedersi, rahv-vay-dair-se, *v* to mend one's ways

ravviare, rahv-ve'ah-ray, *v* (hair) to tidy

ravvicinare, rahv-ve-che-nah-ray, *v* to bring near again; (friends, etc.) to reconcile

ravvivare, rahv-ve-vah-ray, *v* to revive; to brighten up

ravvolgere, rahv-vohl-jay-ray, *v* to wrap up

raziocinio, rah-tse'o-che-ne'o, *m* reasoning; common sense

razionale, rah-tse'o-nah-lay, *adj* rational

razionare, rah-tse'o-nah-ray, *v* to ration

razza, raht-tsah, *f* race;

kind; (fish) skate

razzia, raht-tsee-ah, *f* raid

razziale, raht-tse'ah-lay, *adj* racial

razzismo, raht-tsee-zmo, *m* racism

razzista, raht-tsee-stah, *adj* racist; *m/f* racist

razzo, raht-tso, *m* rocket

razzolare, raht-tso-lah-ray, *v* to scratch about

re, ray, *m* king; *mus* D

reagire, ray-ah-jee-ray, *v* to react

reale, ray-ah-lay, *adj* royal; real

realista, ray-ah-leess-tah, *adj* realistic; *m/f* realist; royalist

realizzare, ray-ah-lid-dzah-ray, *v* to realize; to achieve; to score

realizzazione, ray-ah-lid-dzah-tse'o-nay, *f* realization; achievement

realtà, ray-ahl-tah, *f* reality

reato, ray-ah-to, *m* crime; offence

reattore, ray-aht-to-ray, *m* reactor; jet; jet engine

reazionario, ray-ah-tse'o-nah-re'o, *adj* reactionary; **–a**, *m/f* reactionary

reazione, ray-ah-tse'o-nay, *f* reaction

recapitare, ray-kah-pe-

tah-ray, *v* to deliver

recapito, ray-kah-**pe**-to, *m* address; delivery

recare, ray-kah-ray, *v* to bring; to cause

recarsi, ray-**kar**-se, *v* to go

recedere, ray-**chay**-day-ray, *v* to withdraw

recensione, ray-chen-se'o-nay, *f* review

recensire, ray-chen-**see**-ray, *v* to review

recente,* ray-**chen**-tay, *adj* recent, new

recessione, ray-chess-se'o-nay, *f* recession

recesso, ray-**chess**-so, *m* recess

recidere, ray-**chee**-day-ray, *v* to cut off

recidiva, ray-che-**dee**-vah, *f* relapse

recidivo, -a, ray-che-**dee**-vo, *m/f* recidivist

recinto, ray-**chin**-to, *m* enclosure; fence

recipiente, ray-che-pe'**en**-tay, *m* container

reciproco*, ray-**chee**-pro-ko, *adj* mutual

recita, ray-**che**-tah, *f* performance

recitare, ray-che-**tah**-ray, *v* to recite; to perform; to play

recitazione, ray-che-tah-**tse'o**-nay, *f* acting; recitation

reclamare, ray-klah-**mah**-ray, *v* to complain

reclamo, ray-**klah**-mo, *m* complaint

réclame, ray-**klahm**, *f* advertisement

reclinare, ray-kle-**nah**-ray, *v* to tilt; (head) to bow

reclusione, ray-kloo-**ze'o**-nay, *f* imprisonment

recluso, -a, ray-**kloo**-zo, *m/f* prisoner; *fig* recluse

recluta, ray-**kloo**-tah, *f* recruit

reclutare, ray-kloo-**tah**-ray, *v* to recruit

recondito, ray-**kon**-de-to, *adj* hidden, secret

recriminare, ray-kre-me-**nah**-ray, *v* to recriminate

redattore, -trice, ray-daht-**tor**-ay, ray-daht-**tree**-chay, *m/f* editor

redazione, ray-dah-**tse'o**-nay, *f* editorial department; editorial staff; writing, editing

redditizio, ryad-de-**tee**-tse'o, *adj* profitable

reddito, rayd-**de**-to, *m* income; revenue

redenzione, ray-den-**tse'o**-nay, *f* redemption

redigere, ray-**dee**-jay-ray, *v* to write; to draw up

redimere, ray-**dee**-may-ray, *v* to redeem

redine, ray-**de**-nay, *f* rein

reduce, ray-**doo**-chay, *adj* returning; *m* veteran

refe, ray-**fay**, *m* thread

referendum, ray-fay-**ren**-doom, *m* referendum

referenza, ray-fay-**rent**-tsah, *f* reference

referto, ray-**fair**-to, *m* medical report

refrattario, ray-fraht-**tah**-re'o, *adj* refractory

refrigerio, ray-fre-**jay**-re'o, *m* coolness; relief

regalare, ray-gah-**lah**-ray, *v* to give (as present)

regale, ray-gah-**lay**, *adj* regal

regalo, ray-gah-lo, *m* present, gift

regata, ray-gah-tah, *f* regatta

reggenza, red-**jen**-tsah, *f* regency

reggere, red-jay-ray, *v* to hold; to support, to bear; to hold; to take; to last; to withstand

reggia, red-jah, *f* royal palace

reggicalze, red-je-**kahl**-tsay, *m* suspender belt

reggimento, red-je-**men**-to, *m* regiment

reggiseno, red-je-**say**-no, *m* bra

regia, ray-jee-ah, *f* direction

regime, ray-jee-may, *m*

regime; system; diet

regina, ray-jee-nah, *f* queen

regionale, ray-jo-**nah**-lay, *adj* regional

regione, ray-jo-nay, *f* region; country

regista, ray-jiss-tah, *m/f* director

registrare, ray-jiss-**trah**-ray, *v* to record; to register; to enter

registratore, ray-jiss-trah-**tor**-ay, *m* tape recorder; recorder

registrazione, ray-jiss-trah-tse'o-nay, *f* recording; registration; check-in; *comm* entry

registro, ray-**jiss**-tro, *m* register; registry

regnare, ray-n'yah-ray, *v* to reign

regno, ray-n'yo, *m* kingdom; realm

regola, ray-go-lah, *f* rule

regolamento, ray-go-lah-**men**-to, *m* regulations; settlement

regolare, ray-go-**lah**-ray, *adj** regular; *v* to regulate; to govern; to determine

reintegrare, ray-een-tay-**grah**-ray, *v* to reinstate

reiterare, ray-e-tay-**rah**-ray, *v* to reiterate

relativo*, ray-lah-tee-vo,

adj relative

relatore, -trice, ray-lah-**tor**-ay, ray-lah-**tree**-chay, *m/f* (university) supervisor

relax, ray-laks, *m* relaxation

relazione, ray-lah-tse'o-nay, *f* relation; relationship; report

relegare, ray-lay-**gah**-ray, *v* to banish; to relegate

religione, ray-le-jo-nay, *f* religion

religioso, ray-le-jo-zo, *adj* religious, pious; *m* monk; **-a,** *f* nun

reliquia, ray-**lee**-kwe-ah, *f* relic

reliquiario, ray-le-kwe-**ah**-re'o, *m* reliquary

relitto, ray-**leet**-to, *m* wreck, piece of wreckage

remare, ray-**mah**-ray, *v* to row

rematore, -trice, ray-mah-**tor**-ay, ray-mah-**tree**-chay, *m/f* oarsman, oarswoman

reminiscenza, ray-me-ne-**shen**-tsah, *f* reminiscence

remissione, ray-miss-se'o-nay, *f* remission

remo, ray-mo, *m* oar

rendere, ren-day-ray, *v* to give back, to return; to

make; to yield; to do well

rendimento, ren-de-**men**-to, *m* efficiency; performance

rendita, ren-de-tah, *f* unearned income

rene, ray-nay, *m* kidney

renitente, ray-ne-**ten**-tay, *adj* reluctant

renna, ren-nah, *f* reindeer

reo, ray-o, *adj* guilty

reparto, ray-**par**-to, *m* department; ward; unit

repellere, ray-**pell**-lay-ray, *v* to repel

repentaglio, ray-pen-**tah**-l'yo, *m* : **a –,** at risk

repentino*, ray-pen-tee-no, *adj* sudden

reperibile, ray-pay-ree-be-lay, *adj* available; on call

repertorio, ray-pair-tor-e'o, *m* repertory; index

replica, ray-ple-kah, *f* reply; repeat, repeat performance

replicare, ray-ple-**kah**-ray, *v* to reply; to repeat

repressione, ray-pres-se'o-nay, *f* repression

reprimere, ray-**pree**-may-ray, *v* to repress, to suppress

repubblica, ray-**poob**-ble-kah, *f* republic

repubblicano, -a, ray-poob-ble-**kah**-no, *adj*

republican; *m/f*
republican

reputare, ray-poo-**tah**-ray,
v to consider

reputazione, ray-poo-tah-
tse'o-nay, *f* reputation;
good name

requie, ray-kwe-ay, *f* :
senza –, unceasingly

requisire, ray-kwe-**zee**-ray,
v to requisition

requisito, ray-kwe-**zee**-to,
m requisite

requisizione, ray-kwe-zee-
tse'o-nay, *f* requisition

resa, ray-zah, *f* surrender

rescindere, ray-**sheen**-day-
ray, *v* to rescind

rescissione, ray-shiss-se'o-
nay, *f* rescission

residente, ray-ze-**den**-tay,
m/f resident

residenza, ray-ze-**den**-tsah,
f residence

residenziale, ray-ze-den-
tse'**ah**-lay, *adj* residential

residuo, ray-**zee**-doo-o, *m*
remainder; residue; *adj*
left over

resina, ray-ze-nah, *f* resin

resistente, ray-ziss-**ten**-tay,
adj resistant; strong;
durable

resistenza, ray-ziss-**ten**-
tsah, *f* resistance;
endurance

resistere, ray-**ziss**-tay-ray,
v to resist; to withstand;

to hold out

resoconto, ray-zo-**kon**-to,
m account

respingere, ress-**peen**-jay-
ray, *v* to reject; to repel;
to fail

respirare, ress-pe-**rah**-ray,
v to breathe

respiratore, ress-pe-rah-
to-ray, *m* respirator

respirazione, ress-pe-rah-
tse'o-nay, *f* breathing

respiro, ress-**pee**-ro, *m*
breath; breathing

responsabile, ress-pon-
sah-be-lay, *adj*
responsible; *m/f* person
in charge; culprit

responso, ress-**pon**-so, *m*
answer

ressa, ress-sah, *f* crowd

restare, ress-**tah**-ray, *v* to
remain

restaurare, ress-tah'oo-
rah-ray, *v* to restore

restauro, ress-**tah'oo**-ro, *m*
restoration

restituire, ress-te-too'**ee**-
ray, *v* to give back

restituzione, ress-te-too-
tse'o-nay, *f* return;
repayment

resto, ress-to, *m* rest,
remainder; (small
money) change; **resti,**
ruins; left-overs; remains

restringere, ress-**trin**-jay-
ray, *v* to reduce; to

shrink; to restrict; to
narrow

restrittivo, ress-treet-**tee**-
vo, *adj* restrictive

restrizione, ress-tre-tse'o-
nay, *f* restriction

retaggio, ray-**tahd**-jo, *m*
heritage

retata, ray-**tah**-tah, *f* raid

rete, ray-tay, *f* net;
network; bedsprings;
wire fence; goal

reticente, ray-te-**chen**-tay,
adj reticent

reticolato, ray-te-ko-**lah**-
to, *m* wire netting,
fencing

retina, ray-tee-nah, *f*
retina

retorica, ray-**to**-re-kah, *f*
rhetoric

retorico, ray-**to**-re-ko, *adj*
rhetorical

retribuire, ray-tre-boo'**e**-
ray, *v* to pay, to
remunerate

retribuzione, ray-tre-boo-
tse'o-nay, *f* pay,
remuneration

retro, ray-tro, *m* back

retrocedere, ray-tro-**chay**-
day-ray, *v* to recede; to
be relegated

retrogrado, ray-**tro**-grah-
do, *adj* retrograde

retroguardia, ray-tro-
goo'**ar**-de'ah, *f* rear-
guard

retromarcia, ray-tro-**mahr**-chah, *f* reverse

retta, ret-tah, *f* straight line; fee

rettangolare, ret-tahn-go-**lah**-ray, *adj* rectangular

rettangolo, ret-**tahn**-go-lo, *m* rectangle

rettifica, ret-**tee**-fe-kah, *f* rectification

rettile, ret-te-lay, *m* reptile

retto, ret-to, *m* rectum; *adj* straight; upright

rettore, ret-**tor**-ay, *m* rector; (university) chancellor

reumatismo, ray'oo-mah-**teez**-mo, *m* rheumatism

revisione, ray-ve-ze'o-nay, *f* revision; review; servicing; auditing

revisore, ray-ve-**zor**-ay, *m* **– di conti,** auditor

revoca, ray-vo-kah, *f* revocation

revocare, ray-vo-**kah**-ray, *v* to revoke

riabilitazione, re'ah-be-le-tah-tse'o-nay, *f* rehabilitation

rialzare, re'ahl-**tsah**-ray, *v* to raise; to lift; to rise, to increase

rialzista, re'ahl-**tsiss**-tah, *m* (stock-exchange) bull

rialzo, re'ahl-tso, *m* rise, increase

rianimazione, re'an-ee-mah-tse'**o**-nay, *f* intensive care

riapparire, re'ahp-pah-**ree**-ray, *v* to reappear

riassumere, re'ahss-**soo**-may-ray, *v* to resume; to sum up; to re-employ

riassunto, re'ahss-**soon**-to, *m* summary

riaversi, re'ah-**vair**-se, *v* to come round

ribadire, re-bah-**dee**-ray, *v* to confirm

ribalta, re-**bahl**-tah, *f* front of the stage; foot-light; bureau

ribassista, re-bahss-**siss**-tah, *m* (stock-exchange) bear

ribasso, re-**bahss**-so, *m* fall; reduction

ribattere, re-**baht**-tay-ray, *v* to return; to answer back

ribellarsi, re-bell-**lar**-se, *v* to rebel

ribelle, re-**bell**-lay, *adj* rebellious; *m/f* rebel

ribellione, re-bell-le'o-nay, *f* revolt

ribes, ree-bess, *m* currant

ribollire, re-boll-**lee**-ray, *v* to boil

ribrezzo, re-**bret**-tso, *m* disgust

ributtante, re-boot-**tahn**-tay, *adj* disgusting

ricacciare, re-kaht-**chah**-ray, *v* to drive back

ricaduta, re-kah-**doo**-tah, *f* relapse

ricalcitrare, re-kahl-che-**trah**-ray, *v* to kick; to be recalcitrant

ricamare, re-kah-**mah**-ray, *v* to embroider

ricambiare, re-kahm-be'**ah**-ray, *v* to return; to reciprocate

ricambio, re-**kahm**-be'o, *m* **pezzi di –,** spare parts

ricamo, re-kah-mo, *m* embroidery

ricapitolare, re-kah-pe-to-**lah**-ray, *v* to summarize

ricaricare, re-kah-re-**kah**-ray, *v* to reload; to recharge; to rewind

ricattare, re-kaht-**tah**-ray, *v* to blackmail

ricattatore, -trice, re-kaht-tah-**to**-ray, re-kaht-tah-**tree**-ray, *m/f* blackmailer

ricatto, re-**kaht**-to, *m* blackmail

ricavare, re-kah-**vah**-ray, *v* to extract; to obtain

ricchezza, reek-**ket**-tsah, *f* wealth; richness; abundance; **ricchezze,** riches

riccio, reet-cho, *adj* curly; *m* curl; hedgehog; sea urchin

ricco, reek-ko, *adj* rich; fertile

ricerca, re-**chair**-kah, *f* research; search

ricercare, re-chair-**kah**-ray, *v* to search for

ricercato, -a, re-chair-**kah**-to, *adj* refined; in demand; *m/f* wanted man, wanted woman

ricetta, re-**chet**-tah, *f* prescription; recipe

ricettatore, re-chet-tah-**tor**-ay, *m* (of stolen goods) receiver

ricettazione, re-chet-tah-tse'o-nay, *f* receiving (stolen goods)

ricevere, re-**chay**-vay-ray, *v* to receive

ricevimento, re-chay-ve-**men**-to, *m* reception

ricevitore, re-chay-ve-**tor**-ay, *m* receiver

ricevuta, re-chay-**voo**-tah, *f* receipt

ricezione, re-chay-tse'o-nay, *f* reception

richiamare, re-ke'ah-**mah**-ray, *v* to call back; to attract; to recall

richiamo, re-ke'**ah**-mo, *m* call; *med* booster **uccello da –**, decoy-bird

richiedere, re-ke'**ay**-day-ray, *v* to require; to ask again; to ask back

richiesta, re-ke'**ess**-tah, *f* request; demand

ricino, **ree**-che-no, *m* castor-oil

ricompensa, re-kom-**pen**-sah, *f* reward

ricompensare, re-kom-pen-**sah**-ray, *v* to reward

ricomprare, re-kom-**prah**-ray, *v* to buy back

riconciliare, re-kon-che-le'ah-ray, *v* to reconcile

riconoscente, re-ko-no-**shen**-tay, *adj* grateful

riconoscenza, re-ko-no-**shen**-tsah, *f* gratitude

riconoscere, re-ko-no-shay-ray, *v* to recognize

ricoprire, re-ko-pree-ray, *v* to cover; to hold

ricordare, re-kor-**dah**-ray, *v* to remember; to remind of

ricordo, re-**kor**-do, *m* memory; keepsake

ricorrente, re-kor-**ren**-tay, *adj* recurring

ricorrenza, re-kor-**ren**-tsah, *f* anniversary

ricorrere, re-kor-ray-ray, *v* to recur; to resort

ricorso, re-**kor**-so, *m* appeal

ricostituire, re-koss-te-too'ee-ray, *v* to buil up again; to re-form

ricostruire, re-koss-troo'ee-ray, *v* to reconstruct

ricoverare, re-ko-vay-**rah**-ray, *v* – **in ospedale,** to admit into hospital

ricreare, re-kray-**ah**-ray, *v* to recreate

ricreazione, re-kray-ah-tse'o-nay, *f* recreation; break

ricredersi, re-**krav**-dair-se, *v* to change one's mind

ricucire, re-koo-**chee**-ray, *v* to stich; to mend

ricuperare, re-koo-pay-**rah**-ray, *v* to recover; to make up; to salvage

ricupero, re-**koo**-pay-ro, *m* recovery; salvage; rehabilitation

ricurvo, re-**koohr**-vo, *adj* bent, curved

ricusare, re-koo-zah-ray, *v* to refuse, to reject

ridare, re-**dah**-ray, *v* to give again; to give back

ridere, re-**dee**-ray, *v* to laugh

ridestare, re-day-**stah**-ray, *v* to reawaken

ridicolo, re-**dee**-ko-lo, *adj* ridiculous

ridimensionare, re-de-men-se'o-**nah**-ray, *v* to get into perspective

ridire, re-**dee**-ray, *v* to repeat; to object to

ridotto, re-**dot**-to, *adj* reduced; smaller

ridurre, re-**doohr**-ray, *v* to

reduce

riduzione, re-doo-tse'o-nay, *f* reduction

riempire, re'em-pee-ray, *v* to fill; to fill in

riepilogare, re'ay-pe-lo-gah-ray, *v* to summarize

rifare, re-fah-ray, *v* to do again; to rebuild; to make

rifarsi, re-far-se, *v – di*, to recover from

riferimento, re-fay-re-men-to, *m* reference

riferire, re-fay-ree-ray, *v* to refer; to report

rifinire, re-fe-nee-ray, *v* to finish off

rifiutare, re-fe'oo-tah-ray, *v* to refuse; to turn down

rifiuto, re-fe'oo-to, *m* refusal; **rifiuti**, rubbish

riflessione, re-fless-se'o-nay, *f* reflection

riflessivo, re-fless-see-vo, *adj* thoughtful; *gram* reflexive

riflesso, re-fless-so *m* reflection; reflex

riflettere, re-flet-tay-ray, *v* to reflect

riflettore, re-flet-tor-ay, *m* reflector; floodlight; spotlight

riflusso, re-flooss-so, *m* flow; ebb

rifocillarsi, re-fo-chill-lah-se, *v* to take

refreshments

riforma, re-for-mah, *f* reform

riformare, re-for-mah-ray, *v* to reform; to declare unfit

rifornimento, re-for-ne-men-to, *m* : **fare – di**, to stock up with; **rifornimenti**, supplies

rifuggire, re-food-jee-ray, *v* to shun

rifugio, re-foo-jo, *m* refuge, shelter

rifulgere, re-fooll-jay-ray, *v* to shine

riga, ree-gah, *f* line; ruler; parting

rigagnolo, re-gah-n'yo-lo, *m* rivulet

rigare, re-gah-ray, *v* to rule; to score

rigattiere, re-gaht-te'ay-ray, *m* second-hand dealer

rigettare, re-jet-tah-ray, *v* to reject; to vomit

rigetto, re-jet-to, *m* rejection

rigidezza, re-je-det-tsah, *f* rigidity; strictness

rigido*, ree-je-do, *adj* rigid; harsh; strict

rigirare, re-je-rah-ray, *v* turn over, to turn round

rigoglioso*, re-go-l'yo-zo, *adj* flourishing

rigore, re-go-ray, *m* rigour;

penalty

riguardare, re-goo'ar-dah-ray, *v* to look at again; to check; to concern

riguardo, re-goo'ar-do, *m* regard; care; respect

riguardoso, re-goo'ar-do-zo, *adj* respectful; considerate

rigurgitare, re-goohr-je-tah-ray, *v* to bring up

rilasciare, re-lah-she'ah-ray, *v* to release; to issue; to relax

rilascio, re-lah-she'o, *m* release; issue

rilassamento, re-lahss-sah-men-to, *m* relaxation

rilassare, re-lahss-sah-ray, *v* to relax

rilegare, re-lay-gah-ray, *v* to bind

rilegatore, re-lay-gah-tor-ay, *m* bookbinder

rilento, re-len-to, **a –** *adv* slowly

rilevare, re-lay-vah-ray, *v* to notice, to point out; to collect; to take over

rilievo, re-le'ay-vo, *m* importance; relief; survey

rilucere, re-loo-chay-ray, *v* to shine, to glitter

riluttante, re-loot-tahn-tay, *adj* reluctant

rima, ree-mah, *f* rhyme

rimandare, re-mahn-**dah**-ray, *v* to send back; to postpone

rimando, re-**mahn**-do, *m* cross-reference

rimanente, re-mah-**nen**-tay, *m* remainder

rimanere, re-mah-**nay**-ray, *v* to remain; to be left

rimarchevole, re-mar-**kay**-vo-lay, *adj* remarkable

rimare, re-**mah**-ray, *v* to rhyme

rimarginare, re-mar-jee-**nah**-ray, *v* to heal

rimbalzare, reem-bahl-**tsah**-ray, *v* to rebound; to ricochet

rimbambito, reem-bahm-**bee**-to, *adj* daft

rimbeccare, reem-beck-**kah**-ray, *v* to reply abruptly

rimboccare, reem-bock-**kah**-ray, *v* to tuck in; to turn up

rimbombare, reem-bom-**bah**-ray, *v* to roar; to rumble

rimborsare, reem-bor-**sah**-ray, *v* to reimburse, to refund

rimborso, reem-**bor**-so, *m* reimbursement, refund

rimediare, re-may-de'**ah**-ray, *v* to remedy; to scrape up

rimedio, re-**may**-de'o, *m* remedy

rimescolare, re-mess-ko-**lah**-ray, *v* to mix well; to shuffle

rimessa, re-**mess**-sah, *f* garage; hangar; consignment; remittance; (tennis) return; (football) throw-in

rimettere, re-**met**-tay-ray, *v* to put back; to put back on; to replace; to remit; to pardon; to vomit; to lose

rimettersi, re-met-**tair**-se, *v* to get well again; (weather) to get fine again

rimonta, re-**mon**-tah, *f* recovery

rimorchiare, re-mor-ke'**ah**-ray, *v* to tow

rimorchiatore, re-mor-ke'ah-**tor**-ay, *m* tug

rimorchio, re-**mor**-ke'o, *m* tow; trailer

rimorso, re-**mor**-so, *m* remorse

rimozione, re-mo-tse'**o**-nay, *f* removal; dismissal; repression

rimostranza, re-moss-**trahn**-tsah, *f* complaint

rimpatriare, reem-pah-tre'**ah**-ray, *v* to repatriate

rimpiangere, reem-

pe'**ahn**-jay-ray, *v* to regret; to look back on with regret; to miss

rimpianto, reem-pe'**ahn**-to, *m* regret

rimpiattino, reem-pe'aht-**tee**-no, *m* hide-and-seek

rimpiazzare, reem-pe'aht-**tsah**-ray, *v* to replace

rimpicciolire, reem-peech-cho-**lee**-ray, *v* to make smaller; to become smaller

rimproverare, reem-pro-vay-**rah**-ray, *v* to reprimand; to tell off

rimprovero, reem-**pro**-vay-ro, *m* reproach, reprimand

rimunerare, re-moo-nay-**rah**-ray, *v* to remunerate

rimuovere, re-moo'o-**vay**-ray, *v* to remove

Rinascimento, re-nah-shee-**men**-to, *m* Renaissance

rinascita, re-**nah**-shee-ta, *f* rebirth; revival

rincalzare, reen-kahl-**tsah**-ray, *v* to tuck in; to prop up

rincarare, reen-kah-**rah**-ray, *v* to go up (in price)

rinchiudere, reen-ke'oo-day-ray, *v* to lock up

rincontrare, reen-kon-**trah**-ray, *v* to meet again

rincorrere, reen-**kor**-ray-

ray, v to run after

rincrescere, reen-**kray**-she'ay-ray, v to be sorry

rinculare, reen-koo-**lah**-ray, v to recoil

rinfacciare, reen-faht-**chah**-ray, v to reproach

rinforzare, reen-for-**tsah**-ray, v to reinforce, to strengthen

rinfrancare, reen-frahn-**kah**-ray, v to reassure

rinfrescare, reen-fress-**kah**-ray, v to cool; to freshen up; to grow cooler

rinfresco, reen-**fress**-ko, m reception; party

rinfusa, reen-**foo**-zah, f : **alla –**, higgledy-piggledy

ringhiare, reen-ghe'ah-ray, v to snarl, to growl

ringhiera, reen-ghe'ay-rah, f banisters; railing

ringiovanire, reen-jo-vah-**nee**-ray, v to rejuvenate

ringraziare, reen-grah-tse'ah-ray, v to thank

rinoceronte, re-no-chair-**on**-tay, m rhinoceros

rinnegare, reen-nay-**gah**-ray, v to renounce; to disown

rinnegato, -a, reen-nay-**gah**-to, m/f renegade

rinnovabile, reen-no-**vah**-be-lay, adj renewable

rinnovamento, reen-no-vah-**men**-to, m renewal

rinnovare, reen-no-**vah**-ray, v to renovate

rinomato, re-no-**mah**-to, adj renowned

rinsaldare, reen-sahl-**dah**-ray, v to strengthen

rinserrare, reen-sair-**rah**-ray, v to lock up

rintocco, reen-**tock**-ko, m toll

rintracciare, reen-traht-**chah**-ray, v to track down; to trace

rintronare, reen-tro-**nah**-ray, v to deafen; to stun

rintuzzare, reen-toot-**tsah**-ray, v to refute

rinuncia, re-**noonn**-che'ah, f renunciation

rinunciare, re-noonn-**chah**-ray, v to renounce

rinvenimento, reen-vay-ne-**men**-to, m discovery; recovery

rinvenire, reen-vay-**nee**-ray, v to find (out); to come round

rinviare, reen-ve'ah-ray, v to send back; to return; to postpone

rinvio, reen-**vee**-o, m return; postponement; cross-reference

rinvolgere, reen-**voll**-jay-ray, v to wrap up

rione, re'o-nay, m district

riorganizzare, re-or-gah-

ned-**dzah**-ray, v to reorganize

ripagare, re-pah-**gah**-ray, v to pay again; to repay

riparare, re-pah-**rah**-ray, v to repair; to protect

riparazione, re-pah-rah-tse'o-nay, f repair, repairing

riparo, re-**pah**-ro, m shelter

ripartire, re-par-**tee**-ray, v to leave again; to divide up, to share out

ripassare, re-pahss-**sah**-ray, v to go back, to come back; to go over (again)

ripensare, re-pen-**sah**-ray, v to think over; to change one's mind

ripercuotersi, re-pair-**kwo**-tair-se, v to have repercussions

ripetere, re-**pay**-tay-ray, v to repeat

ripetitore, re-pay-te-**tor**-ay, m relay

ripiano, re-pe'ah-no, m shelf; terrace

ripido*, ree-pe-do, adj steep

ripiegare, re-pe'ay-**gah**-ray, v to fold; to retreat

ripiegarsi, re-peay-**gar**-se, v to bend

ripiego, re-pe'ay-go, m expedient

ripieno, re-pe'ay-no, *adj* full, stuffed, filled; *m* stuffing, filling

ripigliare, re-pe-l'yah-ray, *v* to take again; to take back

riporre, re-por-ray, *v* to replace; to put away

riportare, re-por-tah-ray, *v* to take back, to bring back; to tell, to repor; to obtain

riporto, re-por-to, *m* amount brought forward

riposare, re-po-zah-ray, *v* to rest

riposo, re-po-zo, *m* rest

ripostiglio, re-poss-tee-l'yo, *m* store room

riprendere, re-pren-day-ray, *v* to take again; to take back; to reproach; to resume; to film

riprendersi, re-pren-dair-se *v* to recover

ripresa, re-pray-zah, *f* resumption; recovery; acceleration; shot; (sport) round

ripristinare, re-prees-te-nah-ray, *v* to restore

riprodurre, re-pro-doohr-ray, *v* to reproduce

riprova, re-pro-vah, *f* confirmation

riprovare, re-pro-vah-ray, *v* to try again

ripugnare, re-poo-n'yah-

ray, *v* to repel

riquadro, re-kwah-dro, *m* square; box

risa, ree-zah, *fpl* laughing

risacca, re-zahck-kah, *f* backwash

risaia, re-zah-e'ah, *f* rice-field

risalire, re-zah-lee-ray, *v* to go back up; – **a**, to go back to

risaltare, re-zahl-tah-ray, *v* to stand out

risalto, re-zahl-to, *m* prominence

risanamento, re-sah-nah-men-to, *m* (economy) improvement

risanare, re-sah-nah-ray, *v* to cure; (land) to reclaim; to improve; to reorganize

risaputo, re-sah-poo-to, *adj* : **è – che**, it's common knowledge that

risarcimento, re-zar-che-men-to, *m* compensation

risarcire, re-zar-chee-ray, *v* to compensate, to pay compensation for

risata, re-zah-tah, *f* laugh

riscaldamento, reess-kahl-dah-men-to, *m* heating

riscaldare, reess-kahl-dah-ray, *v* to warm; to heat; to heat up

riscattare, reess-kaht-tah-ray, *v* to redeem; to pay ransom for

riscatto, reess-kaht-to, *m* ransom; redemption

rischiarare, reess-ke'ah-rah-ray, *v* to clear up; to light up

rischiare, reess-ke'ah-ray, *v* to risk

rischio, reess-ke'o, *m* risk, danger

rischioso*, reess-ke'o-zo, *adj* dangerous; risky

risciacquare, re-she'ahk-kwah-ray, *v* to rinse

riscontrare, reess-kon-trah-ray, *v* to compare; to find

riscontro, reess-kon-tro, *m* confirmation; comparison, check; *comm* reply

riscossa, reess-koss-sah, *f* recovery

riscossione, reess-koss-se'o-nay, *f* collection

riscuotere, reess-koo'o-tay-ray, *v* to draw; to collect; to win

risentimento, re-sen-te-men-to, *m* resentment

risentire, re-sen-tee-ray, *v* to hear again; to feel; to resent

riserbo, re-sair-bo, *m* reserve, discretion

riserva, re-sair-vah, *f*

reserve; preserve; reservation

riservare, re-sair-**vah**-ray, *v* to reserve, to book; to save

risiedere, re-se'**ay**-day-ray, *v* to reside

risma, reez-mah, *f* ream; kind

riso, ree-zo, *m* rice; laughter

risolare, re-so-**lah**-ray, *v* to resole

risoluto*, re-so-**loo**-to, *adj* resolute

risolvere, re-**soll**-vay-ray, *v* to resolve; to solve

risonanza, re-so-**nahn**-tsah, *f* resonance

risorsa, re-**sor**-sah, *f* resort; **risorse,** resources

risparmiare, reess-par-me'**ah**-ray, *v* to spare; to save

risparmio, reess-**par**-me'o, *m* saving; savings

rispecchiare, reess-peck-ke'**ah**-ray, *v* to reflect

rispettabile, reess-pet-**tah**-be-lay, *adj* respectable

rispettare, reess-pet-**tah**-ray, *v* to respect

rispettoso*, reess-pet-to-zo, *adj* respectful

rispondere, reess-**pon**-day-ray, *v* to answer

risposta, reess-**poss**-tah, *f* answer; reply

rissa, reess-sah, *f* brawl

rissoso, reess-so-zo, *adj* quarrelsome

ristabilire, reess-tah-be-lee-ray, *v* to re-establish; to restore; to recover

ristagno, reess-**tah**-n'yo, *m* stagnation

ristampa, reess-**tahm**-pah, *f* reprint

ristoro, reess-**to**-ro, *m* refreshment

ristrettezza, reess-tret-**tet**-tsah, *f* shortage; **ristrettezze,** poverty

ristretto, reess-**tret**-to, *adj* restricted; (coffee) extra-strong

risultare, re-sooll-**tah**-ray, *v* to turn out to be; result

risultato, re-sooll-**tah**-to, *m* result

risuonare, re-soo'o-**nah**-ray, *v* to resound

risvegliare, reess-vay-l'**yah**-ray, *v* to awaken; to wake up

risveglio, reess-vay-l'yo, *m* awakening; waking-up

ritagli, re-**tah**-l'ye, *mpl* scraps; cuttings

ritardare, re-tar-**dah**-ray, *v* to be late; to delay; to slow down

ritardatario, -a, re-tar-dah-**tah**-re'o, *m/f* latecomer

ritardo, re-**tar**-do, *m* delay

ritegno, re-**tay**-n'yo, *m* restraint

ritemprare, re-tem-**prah**-ray, *v* to strengthen

ritenere, re-tay-**nay**-ray, *v* to retain; to believe; to deduct

ritentare, re-ten-**tah**-ray, *v* to try again

ritenuta, re-tay-**noo**-tah, *f* deduction

ritirare, re-te-**rah**-ray, *v* to withdraw

ritirata, re-te-**rah**-tah, *f* retreat

ritiro, re-**tee**-ro, *m* retirement; collection; confiscation; retreat

ritmo, reet-mo, *m* rhythm

rito, ree-to, *m* rite

ritoccare, re-tock-**kah**-ray, *v* to touch up; to alter

ritorcere, re-tor-chay-ray, *v* to twist; to throw back

ritornare, re-tor-**nah**-ray, *v* to return; to go back, to come back; to become again

ritornello, re-tor-**nell**-lo, *m* refrain

ritorno, re-**tor**-no, *m* return

ritrarre, re-**trar**-ray, *v* to portray, to depict; to withdraw

ritrattare, re-traht-**tah**-ray, *v* to retract

ritratto, re-**traht**-to, *m* portrait

ritrosia, re-tro-**zee**-ah, *f* reluctance; shyness

ritroso, re-**tro**-zo, *adj* shy; reluctant

ritrovare, re-tro-**vah**-ray, *v* to find again, to recover; to meet again

riunire, re-oo-**nee**-ray, *v* to reunite; to join

riunirsi, re-oo-**neer**-se, *v* to meet; to be reunited

riuscire, re-oo-**shee**-ray, *v* to succeed; to go out again

riuscita, re-oo-**shee**-tah, *f* success

riva, **ree**-vah, *f* bank; shore

rivaleggiare, re-vah-led-**jah**-ray, *v* to compete

rivangare, re-vahn-**gah**-ray, *v* to dig up

rivedere, re-vay-**day**-ray, *v* to see again; to revise; to review

rivelare, re-vay-**lah**-ray, *v* to reveal

rivelazione, re-vay-lah-tse'o-**nay**, *f* revelation

rivendere, re-ven-**day**-ray, *v* to sell again

rivendicare, re-ven-de-**kah**-ray, *v* to claim; to claim responsibility for

rivendita, re-**ven**-de-tah, *f* (shop) dealer

riverberare, re-vair-bay-**rah**-ray, *v* (heat, etc.) to reflect

riverenza, re-vay-**ren**-tsah, *f* reverence

riverire, re-vay-**ree**-ray, *v* to revere

riversare, re-vair-**sah**-ray, *v* to pour; to lavish; to heap

riversarsi, re-vair-**sahr**-se, *v* to pour

rivestimento, re-vess-te-**men**-to, *m* covering; coating

rivestire, re-vess-**tee**-ray, *v* to cover; to hold; to dress again

riviera, re-ve'**ay**-rah, *f* coast

rivincita, re-**vin**-che-tah, *f* return match; revenge

rivista, re-**viss**-tah, *f* magazine

rivivere, re-**vee**-vay-ray, *v* to live through again

rivolgere, re-**voll**-jay-ray, *v* to turn; to address

rivolgersi, re-**voll**-jair-se, *v* to turn round; – **a**, to go and speak to

rivolta, re-**voll**-tah, *f* revolt

rivoltare, re-voll-**tah**-ray, *v* to turn over

rivoltella, re-voll-**tell**-lah, *f* revolver

rivoltoso, re-voll-**to**-zo, *adj* rebel

rivoluzione, re-vo-loo-tse'o-**nay**, *f* revolution

rizzare, rit-**tsah**-ray, *v* to raise

rizzarsi, rit-**tsar**-se, *v* to stand up

roba, **ro**-bah, *f* things; stuff

robaccia, ro-**baht**-chah, *f* rubbish

robusto, ro-**boos**-to, *adj* robust, sturdy; strong

rocca, **rock**-kah, *f* fortress

rocchetto, rock-**ket**-to, *m* spool

roccia, **rot**-chah, *f* rock

roccioso, rot-**cho**-zo, *adj* rocky

roco, **ro**-ko, *adj* hoarse

rodaggio, ra-**daj**-jo, *m* running in

rodere, **ro**-day-ray, *v* to gnaw at

roditore, ro-de-**to**-ray, *m* rodent

rogito, **ro**-je-to, *m law* deed

rogna, **ro**-n'yah, *f* scabies; mange; *fig* trouble

rognone, ro-n'yo-nay, *m* kidney

rognoso, ro-n'yo-zo, *adj* scabby; mangy

rogo, **ro**-go, *m* pyre; stake

Roma, **ro**-mah, *f* Rome

romanico, ro-**mah**-nee-ko, *adj* Romanesque

romano, ro-**mah**-no, *adj* Roman

romanticismo, ro-mahn-te-**cheez**-mo *m* romanticism

romantico, ro-**mahn**-te-ko, *adj* romantic

romanza, ro-**mahn**-tsah, *f* romance

romanzo, ro-**mahn**-tso, *m* novel; *adj* Romance

rombare, rom-**bah**-ray, *v* to rumble

rombo, **rom**-bo, *m* rumble, roar; rhombus; turbot

rompere, rom-**pay**-ray, *v* to break; to crush

rompicapo, rom-pe-**kah**-po, *m* puzzle

rompiscatole, rom-piss-**kah**-to-lay, *m* pain in the neck

ronda, **ron**-dah, *f* patrol; rounds, beat

rondella, ron-**del**-lah, *f* washer

rondine, **ron**-de-nay, *f* swallow

rondone, ron-**do**-nay, *m* swift

ronfare, ron-**fah**-ray, *v* to snore

ronzare, ron-**dzah**-ray, *v* to buzz, to hum

ronzino, ron-**dzee**-no, *m* nag

ronzio, ron-**dzee**-o, *m* buzzing, droning

rosa, **ro**-zah, *f* rose; *adj* pink

rosario, ro-**zah**-re'o, *m* rosary

roseto, ro-**zay**-to, *m* rose-garden

rosicchiare, ro-zick-ke'**ah**-ray, *v* to nibble

rosmarino, ross-mah-**ree**-no, *m* rosemary

rosolare, ro-zo-**lah**-ray, *v* to brown

rosolia, ro-zo-**lee**-ah, *f* measles

rosone, ro-zo-**nay**, *m* rosette; rose window

rospo, **ross**-po, *m* toad

rossastro, ross-**sahss**-tro, *adj* reddish

rossetto, ross-**set**-to, *m* lipstick

rosso, **ross**-so, *adj & m* red; **– d'uovo**, egg yolk

rossore, ross-**sor**-ay, *m* blush; redness

rosticceria, ross-tit-chay-**ree**-ah, *f* shop selling cooked food such as roast meat, lasagne, etc.

rostro, **ross**-tro, *m* beak; rostrum

rotaia, ro-**tah**-e'ah, *f* rail, railway-track

rotare, ro-**tah**-ray, *v* to rotate

rotazione, ro-tah-tse'**o**-nay, *f* rotation

roteare, ro-te'**ah**-ray, *v* to

whirl; to roll

rotella, ro-**tell**-lah, *f* little wheel; cog

rotolare, ro-to-**lah**-ray, *v* to roll

rotolo, **ro**-to-lo, *m* roll

rotonda, ro-**ton**-dah, *f* circular terrace; round about

rotondo, ro-**ton**-do, *adj* round

rotta, **rot**-tah, *f* rout; route; via; **in – per**, bound for

rottami, rot-**tah**-me, *mpl* fragments; wreckage

rotto, **rot**-to, *adj* broken

rottura, rot-**too**-rah, *f* breaking; break; fracture

rotula, **ro**-too-lah, *f* knee-cap

roulotte, roo-**lot**, *f* caravan

rovente, ro-**ven**-tay, *adj* red-hot

rovere, ro-**vay**-ray, *m* oak

rovesciamento, ro-vay-she'ah-**men**-to, *m* overturning; capsizing; reversal

rovesciare, ro-vay-she'**ah**-ray, *v* to spill; to overturn; to capsize; to reverse

rovescio, ro-**vay**-she'o, *m* wrong side; reverse; setback; downpour; backhand

rovina, ro-vee-nah, *f* ruin

rovinare, ro-ve-nah-ray, *v* to ruin, to spoil; to fall

rovinoso, ro-ve-no-zo, *adj* ruinous

rovistare, ro-viss-tah-ray, *v* to rummage

rovo, ro-vo, *m* bramble

rozzo, rod-dzo, *adj* rough; uncouth

ruba, roo-bah, *f* : **andare a –,** to sell like hot cakes

rubacuori, roo-bah-koo'o-re, *m/f* heart-breaker

rubare, roo-bah-ray, *v* to steal

rubicondo, roo-be-kon-do, *adj* ruddy

rubinetto, roo-be-net-to, *m* tap

rubino, roo-bee-no, *m* ruby

rubrica, roo-bree-ka, *f* address book; column

rude, roo-day, *adj* rude

ruderi, roo-day-re, *mpl* ruins

rudimentale, roo-de-men-tah-lay, *adj* rudimentary, basic

rudimenti, roo-de-men-te, *mpl* rudiments; principles

ruffiano, roo-fe'ah-no, *m* pimp; bootlicker

ruga, roo-gah, *f* wrinkle

ruggine, rood-je-nay, *f* rust

rugginoso, rood-je-no-zo, *adj* rusty

ruggire, rood-jee-ray, *v* to roar

ruggito, rood-jee-to, *m* roar, roaring

rugiada, roo-jah-dah, *f* dew

rugoso, roo-go-zo, *adj* wrinkled

rullare, rooll-lah-ray, *v* to roll

rullio, rooll-lee-o, *m* rolling

rullo, rooll-lo, *m* roller; roll

rum, room, *m* rum

ruminare, roo-me-nah-ray, *v* to ruminate

rumore, roo-mor-ay, *m* noise; sound

rumoreggiare, roo-mo-red-jah-ray, *v* to rumble; to clamour

rumoroso*, roo-mor-o-zo, *adj* noisy

ruolo, roo'o-lo, *m* role; list

ruota, roo'o-tah, *f* wheel

rupe, roo-pay, *f* rock; cliff

rurale, roo-rah-lay, *adj* rural

ruscello, roo-shell-lo, *m* stream

ruspa, rooss-pha, *f* excavator

russare, rooss-sah-ray, *v* to snore

Russia, rooss-se'ah, *f* Russia

russo, rooss-so, *adj* Russian

rustico, rooss-te-ko, *adj* rustic

rutilante, roo-te-lahn-tay, *adj* beaming, gleaming

ruttare, root-tah-ray, *v* to belch

ruvido*, roo-ve-do, *adj* rough

ruzzolare, root-tso-lah-ray, *v* to tumble down; to roll over

ruzzoloni, root-tso-lo-ne, *adv* rolling down (*or* over)

sabato, sah-**bah**-to, *m* Saturday

sabbia, sahb-be'ah, *f* sand

sabbioso, sahb-be'**o**-zo, *adj* sandy

sabotaggio, sah-bo-**tahj**-jo, *m* sabotage

sabotare, sah-bo-**tah**-ray, *v* to sabotage

sacca, sahk-kah, *f* bag

saccarina, sahk-ka-**ree**-na, *f* saccharin

saccente, saht-**chen**-tay, *adj* conceited; *m/f* know-all

saccheggiare, sahk-ked-**jah**-ray, *v* to plunder

saccheggio, sahk-**ked**-jo, *m* plundering

sacchetto, sahk-**ket**-to, *m* bag

sacco, sahk-ko, *m* sack; bag; **un – di,** heaps of; – **a pelo,** sleeping bag

sacerdote, sah-chair-do-tay, *m* priest

sacerdozio, sah-chair-**dot**-tse'o, *m* priesthood

sacramento, sah-krah-**men**-to, *m* sacrament

sacrificare, sah-kre-fe-**kah**-ray, *v* to sacrifice

sacrificio, sah-kre-**fee**-cho, *m* sacrifice

sacrilegio, sah-kre-**lay**-jo, *m* sacrilege

sacro, sah-kro, *adj* sacred

sadico, sah-de-ko, *adj* sadistic

saetta, sah-et-tah, *f* arrow; flash of lightning

safari, sah-fah-re, *m* safari

sagace, sah-**gah**-chay, *adj* shrewd

saggezza, sahd-**jet**-tsah, *f* wisdom

saggiare, sahd-**jah**-ray, *v* to assay; to test

saggio, sahd-jo, *m* essay; sample; wise man; *adj** wise

Sagittario, sah-jit-**tah**-re'o, *m* Sagittarius

sagoma, sah-go-mah, *f* outline; shape; template; target

sagra, sah-grah, *f* festival

sagrestano, sah-gress-**tah**-no, *m* sacristan; sexton

sagrestia, sah-gress-**tee**-ah, *f* sacristy

saio, sah-e'o, *m* habit

sala, sah-lah, *f* hall; living room

salame, sah-**lah**-may, *m* salami

salamoia, sah-lah-**mo**-e'ah, *f* brine

salare, sah-**lah**-ray, *v* to salt

salariato, sah-lah-re'**ah**-to, *adj* wage-earning

salario, sah-lah-re'o, *m* wage, pay

salassare, sah-lahss-**sah**-ray, *v* to bleed

salato, sah-lah-to, *adj* salted; salty; salt; dear

saldare, sahl-dah-ray, *v* to solder; to settle

saldatura, sahl-dah-**toohr**-ah, *f* soldering; soldered joint

saldezza, sahl-**det**-tsah, f firmness

saldo, sahl-do, adj* sound; steady; m balance; settlement; **saldi,** sales

sale, sah-lay, m salt

salice, sah-le-chay, m willow

saliera, sah-le'**ay**-rah, f salt-cellar

salina, sah-lee-nah, f salt-works

salire, sah-lee-ray, v to go up, to come up; to get on; to rise; to climb

saliscendi, sah-le-**shen**-de, m latch

salita, sah-lee-tah, f ascent; slope

saliva, sah-lee-vah, f saliva

salma, sahl-mah, f body (of dead person)

salmastro, sahl-**mahss**-tro, adj salty; salt

salmo, sahl-mo, m psalm

salmone, sahl-**mo**-nay, m salmon

salnitro, sahl-nee-tro, m saltpetre

salone, sah-lo-nay, m lounge; show

salotto, sahl-**lot**-to, m sitting-room

salpare, sahl-**pah**-ray, v to weigh anchor

salsa, sahl-sah, f sauce

salsiccia, sahl-**sit**-chah, f sausage

salsiera, sahl-se'**ay**-rah, f sauceboat

saltare, sahl-**tah**-ray, v to jump; to skip

saltellare, sahl-tell-**lah**-ray, v to hop

salto, sahl-to, m jump; – **mortale,** somersault

saltuario *, sahl-too'**ah**-re'o, adj occasional

salumi, sah-**loo**-me, mpl cured pork meats

salumiere, sah-loo-me'**ay**-ray, m delicatessen owner

salutare, sah-loo-**tah**-ray, v to greet; to say goodbye; adj healthy

salute, sah-loo-tay, f health; interj bless you!

saluto, sah-**loo**-to, m salute; greeting; wave

salva, sahl-vah, f salvo

salvacondotto, sahl-vah-kon-**dot**-to, m safe-conduct

salvadanaio, sahl-vah-dah-**nah**-e'o, m money-box

salvagente, sahl-vah-**jen**-tay, m life-belt, life-jacket; traffic island

salvaguardare, sahl-vah-goo'ar-**dah**-ray, v to safeguard

salvare, sahl-**vah**-ray, v to

rescue; to save

salvataggio, sahl-vah-**taj**-jo, m rescue

salve, sahl-vay, interj hello!

salvezza, sahl-**vet**-tsah, f salvation; safety

salvia, sahl-ve'ah, f sage

salvietta, sahl-ve'**et**-tah, f towel; wet wipe

salvo, sahl-vo, adj safe; prep except for

sambuco, sahm-**boo**-ko, m elder-tree

san (see **santo**)

sanabile, sah-**nah**-be-lay, adj curable

sanare, sah-**nah**-ray, v to heal; to cure

sancire, sahn-**chee**-ray, v to sanction

sangue, sahn-goo'ay, m blood

sanguinaccio, sahn-goo'e-**naht**-cho, m black-pudding

sanguinare, sahn-goo'e-**nah**-ray, v to bleed

sanguinoso, sahn-goo'e-**no**-so, adj bloody

sanguisuga, sahn-goo'e-**soo**-gah, f leech

sanità, sah-ne-**tah**, f health

sanitario, sah-ne-**tah**-re'o, adj health; sanitary; **sanitari,** bathroom fittings

sano, sah-no, *adj* healthy

santificare, sahn-te-fe-**kah**-ray, *v* to sanctify; to observe

santità, sahn-te-**tah**, *f* sanctity; holiness

santo, -a, **sahn**-to *adj* holy; saint; *m/f* saint

santuario, sahn-too'a-re'o, *m* sanctuary

sanzionare, sahn-tse'o-**nah**-ray, *v* to sanction

sanzione, sahn-tse'o-nay, *f* sanction

sapere, sah-**pay**-ray, *m* knowledge; *v* to know; to smell; to be able to

sapiente, sah-pe-**en**-tay, *adj* learned; *m* sage

sapienza, sah-pe-**en**-tsah, *f* wisdom

sapone, sah-**po**-nay, *m* soap

saponetta, sah-po-**net**-tah, *f* bar of soap

sapore, sah-**por**-ay, *m* taste, flavour

saporito, sah-po-**ree**-to, *adj* tasty

saracinesca, sah-rah-chee-**ness**-kah, *f* rolling shutter

sardina, sar-**dee**-na, *f* sardine

sarta, sar-tah, *f* dressmaker

sartiame, sar-te'**ah**-may, *m* stays

sarto, sar-to, *m* tailor

sartoria, sar-to-**ree**-ah, *f* tailor's shop

sasso, **sahss**-so, *m* pebble; rock

sassofono, sahss-**so**-fo-no, *m* saxophone

sassoso, sahss-**so**-zo, *adj* stony

satellite, sah-**tell**-le-tay, *m* satellite; *adj* satellite

satira, **sah**-te-rah, *f* satire

satirico, sah-**tee**-re-ko, *adj* satirical

satollo, sah-**toll**-lo, *adj* full

saturo, **sah**-too-ro, *adj* saturated; *fig* full

sauna, **sah**'oo-nah, *f* sauna

sauro, **sah**'oo-ro, *adj* sorrel; *m* sorrel

savio, **sah**-ve'o, *adj* wise

saziare, sah-tse'**ah**-ray, *v* to satiate

sazio, **sah**-tse'o, *adj* sated; full

sbadato*, zbah-**dah**-to, *adj* careless

sbadigliare, zbah-de-l'**yah**-ray, *v* to yawn

sbadiglio, zbah-**de**-l'yo, *m* yawn

sbagliare, zbah-l'**yah**-ray, *v* to get wrong; to make a mistake; to be wrong

sballare, zbahl-**lah**-ray, *v* to unpack; to overestimate

sballottare, zbahl-lot-**tah**-ray, *v* to toss about

sbalordire, zbah-lor-**dee**-ray, *v* to astonish, to amaze

sbalzare, zbahl-**tsah**-ray, *v* to throw; to emboss

sbalzo, zbahl-tso, *m* sudden change

sbancare, zbahn-**kah**-ray, *v* to break the bank

sbandare, zbahn-**dah**-ray, *v* to skid

sbaragliare, zbah-rah-l'**yah**-ray, *v* to rout; to beat

sbarazzare, zbah-raht-**tsah**-ray, *v* to clear

sbarazzarsi, zbah-raht-**tsar**-se, *v* – **di**, to get rid of

sbarbarsi, zbar-**bar**-se, *v* to shave

sbarcare, zbar-**kah**-ray, *v* to disembark; to unload

sbarco, **zbar**-ko, *m* landing; unloading

sbarra, **zbar**-rah, *f* bar; barrier

sbarrare, zbar-**rah**-ray, *v* to bar; to block

sbatacchiare, zbah-tahk-ke'**ah**-ray, *v* to bang

sbattere, **zbaht**-tay-ray, *v* to beat; to bang; to whisk

sbavare, zbah-**vah**-ray, *v* to dribble

sbevazzare, zbay-vaht-

tsah-ray, *v* to booze

sbiadire, zbe'ah-dee-ray, *v* to fade

sbiancare, zbe'ahn-kah-ray, *v* to grow pale; to whiten; to bleach

sbieco, zbe'ay-ko, *adj* squint, askew; **di** –, at an angle

sbigottire, zbe-got-tee-ray, *v* to dismay

sbilanciare, zbe-lahn-chah-ray, *v* to throw off balance

sbilanciarsi, zbe-lahn-char-se, *v* to lose one's balance

sbilancio, zbe-lahn-cho, *m* deficit

sbilenco, zbe-len-ko, *adj* crooked; rickety

sbirciare, zbeer-chah-ray, *v* to peep at; to eye

sbirro, zbeer-ro, *m* (pejorative) cop

sbizzarrirsi, zbeed-dzar-reer-se, *v* to indulge one's whims

sbloccare, zblock-kah-ray, *v* to unblock; to release

sboccare, zbock-kah-ray, *v* to flow into; to lead into; to end up in

sboccato*, zbock-kah-to, *adj* foul-mouthed

sbocciare, zbot-chah-ray, *v* to open, to blossom

sbocco, zbock-ko, *m*

outlet; (of river) mouth; end

sbocconcellare, zbock-kon-chell-lah-ray, *v* to nibble

sbollire, zboll-lee-ray, *v* to cool down

sbornia, zbor-ne'ah, *f* : **prendersi una** –, to get plastered

sborsare, zbor-sah-ray, *v* to pay out

sbottonare, zbot-to-nah-ray, *v* to unbutton

sbozzare, zbot-tsah-ray, *v* to sketch out; to outline

sbracciato, zbraht-chah-to, *adj* sleeveless; bare-armed

sbraitare, zbrah'e-tah-ray, *v* to shout

sbranare, zbrah-nah-ray, *v* to tear to pieces

sbriciolare, zbre-cho-lah-ray, *v* to crumble

sbrigare, zbre-gah-ray, *v* to deal with

sbrigarsi, zbre-gar-se, *v* to hurry

sbrigativo*, zbre-gah-tee-vo, *adj* expeditious; hasty

sbrogliare, zbro-l'yah-ray, *v* to disentangle

sbronzo, zbron-dzo, *adj* plastered

sbucare, zboo-kah-ray, *v* to come out; to spring

out

sbucciare, zboot-chah-ray, *v* to peel; to skin

sbudellare, zboo-del-lah-ray, *v* to disembowel

sbuffare, zboof-fah-ray, *v* to puff; to snort

scabro, skah-bro, *adj* rough

scabroso, skah-bro-zo, *adj* difficult; *fig* indecent

scacchiera, skahk-ke'ay-rah, *f* chess-board

scacciare, skaht-chah-ray, *v* to drive out

scacco, skahk-ko, *m* check; chessman; **scacchi**, chess; **a scacchi**, checked

scadente, skah-den-tay, *adj* of poor quality

scadenza, skah-den-tsah, *f* deadline; expiry date; sell-by date, use-by date

scadere, skah-day-ray, *v* to expire; to fall due; to decline

scafandro, skah-fahn-dro, *m* diving-suit; space-suit

scaffale, skahf-fah-lay, *m* shelf

scafo, skah-fo, *m* hull

scagionare, skah-jo-nah-ray, *v* to exonerate, to free from blame

scaglia, skah-l'yah, *f* chip; (fish) scale

scagliare, skah-l'yah-ray, *v*

to hurl

scagliarsi, skah-l'**yar**-se, *v* – **su**, to attack

scaglione, skah-l'**yo**-nay, *m* echelon

scala, **skah**-lah, *f* stairs; ladder

scalare, skah-**lah**-ray, *v* to climb; to knock off; to layer

scalatore, **-trice**, skah-lah-**to**-ray, skah-lah-**tree**-chay, *m/f* climber

scaldabagno, skahl-dah-**bah**-n'yo, *m* water heater

scaldare, skahl-**dah**-ray, *v* to heat

scaldarsi, skahl-**dar**-se, *v* to warm oneself; to get excited

scalfire, skahl-**fee**-ray, *v* to scratch

scalinata, skah-lee-**nah**-tah, *f* staircase

scalino, skah-**lee**-no, *m* step

scalo, **skah**-lo, *m* stop; port of call; stopover

scaloppina, skah-lop-**pee**-nah, *f* escalope

scalpello, skahl-**pell**-lo, *m* chisel

scalpitare, skahl-pe-**tah**-ray, *v* to paw the ground

scalpore, skahl-**por**-ay, *m* stir

scaltro*, **skahl**-tro, *adj*

shrewd; cunning

scalzare, skahl-**tsar**-ay, *v* to bare the roots of; to undermine

scalzo, **skahl**-tso, *adj* barefoot

scambiare, skahm-be'**ah**-ray, *v* to exchange; to mistake

scambio, **skahm**-be'o, *m* exchange; mistake; trade; points

scampagnata, skahm-pah-n'**yah**-tah, *f* trip to the country

scampanare, skahm-pah-**nah**-ray, *v* to peal

scampanato, skahm-pah-**nah**-to, *adj* flared

scampanio, skahm-pah-**nee**-o, *m* (bells) peal

scampare, skahm-**pah**-ray, *v* to escape

scampo, **skahm**-po, *m* escape; safety; prawn

scampolo, **skahm**-po-lo, *m* remnant

scanalatura, skah-nah-lah-**too**-rah, *f* groove

scandagliare, skahn-dah-l'**yah**-ray, *v* to sound

scandalizzare, skahn-dah-lid-**dzah**-ray, *v* to scandalize; to shock

scandalo, **skahn**-dah-lo, *m* scandal

scandire, skahn-**dee**-ray, *v* to articulate;

mus to beat

scannare, skahn-**nah**-ray, *v* to butcher; to slit the throat of

scanno, **skahn**-no, *m* pew; bench

scansare, skahn-**sah**-ray, *v* to move, to shift; to dodge; to shun

scanso, **skahn**-so, *m* a – **di**, in order to avoid

scantinato, skahn-te-**nah**-to, *m* basement

scapestrato, **-a**, skah-pess-**trah**-to, skah-pess-**trah**-tah, *m/f* dissolute person

scapito, **skah**-pe-to, *m* a – **di**, to the detriment of

scapola, **skah**-po-lah, *f* shoulder-blade

scapolo, **skah**-po-lo, *m* bachelor

scappamento, skahp-pah-**men**-to, *m* exhaust; **tubo di –**, exhaust pipe

scappare, skahp-**pah**-ray, *v* to escape; to run away; to rush

scappata, skahp-**pah**-tah, *f* **fare una – a**, to pop over to

scappatella, skahp-pah-**tell**-lah, *f* escapade

scappatoia, skahp-pah-**to**-e'ah, *f* way out; loophole

scappellarsi, skahp-pell-**lar**-se, *v* to raise hat

scappellotto, skahp-pell-**lot**-to, *m* smack on head

scarabeo, skah-rah-**bay**'o, *m* beetle

scarabocchiare, skah-rah-bock-ke'**ah**-ray, *v* to scrawl; to scribble

scarafaggio, skah-rah-**fahd**-jo, *m* cockroach

scaramuccia, skah-rah-**moot**-chah, *f* skirmish

scaraventare, skah-rah-ven-**tah**-ray, *v* to hurl

scarcerare, skar-chay-**rah**-ray, *v* to release (from prison)

scarica, **skah**-re-kah, *f* shot; *fig* shower; *fig* flood; discharge

scaricare, skah-re-**kah**-ray, *v* to unload; to set down; to discharge

scaricarsi, skah-re-**kahr**-se, *v* to run down; to go flat

scaricatore, skah-re-kah-**to**-ray, *m* loader; docker

scarico, **skah**-re-ko, *adj* unloaded; run down; flat; *m* unloading; dumping; dump; exhaust

scarno, **skar**-no, *adj* thin, bony

scarpa, **skar**-pah, *f* shoe

scarpata, skar-**pah**-tah, *f* escarpment

scarpiera, skar-pe'**ay**-rah, *f* shoe rack

scarpinata, skar-pe-**nah**-tah, *f* trek

scarseggiare, skar-sej-**jah**-ray, *v* to be scarce; **– di**, to be short of

scarso*, **skar**-so, *adj* scarce; **– di**, short of, lacking in

scartare, skar-**tah**-ray, *v* to reject; to discard; to unwrap

scarto, **skar**-to, *m* reject; discarding; gap

scassinare, skahss-se-**nah**-ray, *v* to break open

scatenare, skah-tay-**nah**-ray, *v* to provoke

scatenarsi, skah-tay-**nar**-se, *v* to break; to go wild

scatola, **skah**-to-lah, *f* box; tin, can

scattare, skaht-**tah**-ray, *v* (picture) to take; to be released; to spring up; to go off

scatto, **skaht**-to, *m* release; click; shot; jump

scaturire, skah-too-**ree**-ray, *v* **– da**, to gush from; to come from

scavalcare, skah-vahl-**kah**-ray, *v* to climb over; to overtake

scavare, skah-**vah**-ray, *v* to dig; to hollow out; to excavate

scavatrice, skah-vah-**tree**-chay, *f* excavator

scavo, **skah**-vo, *m* excavation

scegliere, shay-l'**yay**-ray, *v* to choose

scellerato, shell-lay-**rah**-to, *adj* wicked, evil

scelta, **shell**-tah, *f* choice; option

scelto, **shell**-to, *adj* select; choice; *mil* highly skilled

scemare, shav-**mah**-ray, *v* to diminish

scemo, **shay**-mo, *adj* silly, stupid

scempio, shem-pe'o, *m* massacre; destruction

scena, shay-nah, *f* scene; stage

scenario, shay-**nah**-re'o, *m* scenery; backdrop

scenata, shay-**nah**-tah, *f* scene

scendere, shen-day-ray, *v* to go down, to come down; to get off; to descend; to alight

scendiletto, shen-de-**let**-to, *m* bed-side rug

scettico, **shet**-te-ko, *adj** sceptical; *m* sceptic

scettro, **shet**-tro, *m* sceptre

scevro, shay-vro, *adj* **– di**, free from

scheda, skay-dah, *f* card; form; ballot paper

schedario, skay-dah-re'o,

m file; filing cabinet

scheggia, sked-jah, *f* splinter; chip

scheggiare, sked-**jah**-ray, *v* to chip; to splinter

scheletro, skay-lay-tro, *m* skeleton

schema, skay-mah, *m* outline; diagram

scherma, skair-mah, *f* fencing

schermaglia, skair-**mah**-l'yah, *f* skirmish

schermirsi, skair-**meer**-se, *v* to defend oneself

schermo, skair-mo, *m* screen

schernire, skair-**nee**-ray, *v* to sneer at

scherno, skair-no, *m* scorn

scherzare, skair-**tsah**-ray, *v* to joke

scherzo, skair-tso, *m* joke; fun

scherzoso,* skair-**tso**-zo, *adj* playful; facetious

schiaccianoci, ske'aht-chah-**no**-che, *m* nut-cracker

schiacciare, ske'aht-**chah**-ray, *v* to crush; to crack; to mash; to press

schiaffeggiare, ske'ahf-fed-**jah**-ray, *v* to slap, to smack

schiaffo, ske'**ahf**-fo, *m* slap (in the face)

schiamazzare, ske'ah-maht-**tsah**-ray, *v* to squawk; to make a racket

schiamazzo, ske'ah-**maht**-tso, *m* racket

schiantare, ske'ahn-**tah**-ray, *v* to break

schiantarsi, ske'ahn-**tar**-se, *v* to break up; to crash

schianto, ske'**ahn**-to, *m* crash

schiarire, ske'ah-**ree**-ray, *v* to clear up

schiattare, ske'aht-**tah**-ray, *v* to burst

schiavitù, ske'ah-ve-**too**, *f* slavery

schiavo, -a, ske'**ah**-vo, *adj* enslaved; *m/f* slave

schiena, ske'**ay**-nah, *f* (body) back

schienale, ske'**ay**-**nah**-lay, *m* (chair) back

schiera, ske'**ay**-rah, *f* rank; group

schierare, ske'ay-**rah**-ray, *v* to line up

schierarsi, ske'ay-**rar**-se, *v* – con/contro, to side with/to oppose

schietto, ske'**et**-to, *adj* frank, sincere; pure

schifezza, ske-**fet**-tsah, *f* : **essere una –,** to be disgusting, to be awful

schifiltoso,* ske-fill-**to**-zo,

adj difficult

schifo, skee-fo, *m* disgust

schifoso,* ske-**fo**-zo, *adj* disgusting, awful

schioccare, ske'ock-**kah**-ray, *v* to snap; to click

schiudere, ske'**oo**-day-ray, *v* to open

schiuma, ske'**oo**-mah, *f* foam; froth; lather

schiumare, ske'oo-**mah**-ray, *v* to foam; to skim

schivare, ske-**vah**-ray, *v* to dodge; to avoid

schivo, skee-vo, *adj* reserved

schizzare, skit-**tsah**-ray, *v* to splash; to sketch; to spurt; to dart away

schizzettare, skit-tset-**tah**-ray, *v* to drizzle

schizzo, skit-tso, *m* splash; sketch

sci, shee, *m* ski; skiing

scia, she'ah, *f* (ship's) wake; trail

sciabola, she'**ah**-bo-lah, *f* sabre

sciacallo, she'ah-**kahl**-lo, *m* jackal

sciacquare, she'ahk-**kwah**-ray, *v* to rinse; to wash

sciagura, she'ah-**goo**-rah, *f* misfortune, calamity

scialacquare, she'ah-lahk-**kwah**-ray, *v* to squander

scialacquatore, -trice,

she'ah-lahk-kwah-**tor**-ay, she'ah-lahk-kwah-**tree**-chay, *m/f* spendthrift

scialbo*, she'**ahl**-bo, *adj* dull

scialle, she'**ahl**-lay, *m* shawl

scialuppa, she'ah-**loop**-pah, *f* boat, launch

sciamare, she'ah-**mah**-ray, *v* to swarm

sciame, she'**ah**-may, *m* swarm; *fig* crowd

sciare, she'**ah**-ray, *v* to ski

sciarpa, she'**ar**-pah, *f* scarf

sciatica, she'**ah**-te-kah, *f* sciatica

sciatore, -**trice**, she'ah-**to**-ray, she'ah-**tree**-chay, *m/f* skier

scibile, shee-be-lay, *m* knowledge

scientifico, she'en-**tee**-fe-ko, *adj* scientific

scienza, she'**en**-tsah, *f* science; knowledge

scienziato, -**a**, she'en-tse'**ah**-to, *m/f* scientist

scimmia, shim-me'ah, *f* monkey

scimmiottare, shim-me'ot-**tah**-ray, *v* to ape

scimunito, -**a**, she-moo-**nee**-to, *m/f* idiot

scindere, sheen-**day**-ray, *v* to separate

scintilla, sheen-till-lah, *f* spark

scintillare, sheen-till-**lah**-ray, *v* to spark; to sparkle

sciocchezza, she'ock-**ket**-tsah, *f* stupidity; silly thing

sciocco, -**a**, she'**ock**-ko, *adj** stupid; *m/f* fool

sciogliere, she'o-l'yay-ray, *v* to untie; to loosen; to let loose; to melt; to dissolve

sciogliersi, she'o-l'yair-se, *v* to come untied; to melt

scioglimento, she'o-l'ye-**men**-to, *m* dissolution

sciolto, she'**ol**-to, *adj* loose; nimble; melted

scioperante, she'o-pay-**rahn**-tay, *m/f* striker

scioperare, she'o-pay-**rah**-ray, *v* to strike

sciopero, she'**o**-pay-ro, *m* strike

scipito, shee-pe-to, *adj* insipid

sciroppo, she-**rop**-po, *m* syrup

sciupare, she'oo-**pah**-ray, *v* to waste; to spoil; to ruin

sciuparsi, she'oo-**pahr**-se, *v* to get spoilt; to get ruined

scivolare, she-vo-**lah**-ray, *v* to slip; to slide

scoccare, skock-**kah**-ray, *v* to shoot; to strike

scocciare, skock-**chah**-ray, *v* to bother, to annoy

scocciarsi, skock-**char**-se, *v* to get fed up; to get annoyed

scodella, sko-**dell**-lah, *f* bowl

scodinzolare, sko-din-tso-**lah**-ray, *v* to wag its tail

scogliera, sko-**l'yay**-rah *f* reef, cliff

scoglio, sko-l'yo, *m* rock

scoiattolo, sko'e-**aht**-to-lo, *m* squirrel

scolapiatti, sko-lah-pe'**aht**-te, *m* draining board; plate rack

scolare, sko-**lah**-ray, *adj* (age) school; *v* to drain; to drip

scolaro, -**a**, sko-**lah**-ro, *m/f* pupil

scolastico, sko-**lahs**-ste-ko, *adj* school, scholastic

scoliosi, sko-le'o-se, *f* scoliosis

scollarsi, skoll-**lar**-se, *v* to come unstuck, to come off

scollatura, skoll-lah-**too**-rah, *f* neckline

scolo, sko-lo, *m* drainage

scolorire, sko-lo-ree-ray, *v* to fade

scolpire, skoll-**pee**-ray, *v* to carve; to sculp

scombussolare, skom-

booss-so-**lah**-ray,
v to upset

scommessa, skom-**mess**-sah, *f* bet

scommettere, skom-**met**-tay-ray, *v* to bet

scomodare, sko-mo-**dah**-ray, *v* to upset

scomodo, **sko**-mo-do, *adj* uncomfortable; inconvenient

scomparire, skom-pah-**ree**-ray, *v* to disappear, to vanish

scomparsa, skom-**par**-sah, *f* disappearance

scompartimento, skom-par-te-**men**-to, *m* compartment

scompigliare, skom-pe-l'**yah**-ray, *v* to upset; to muddle

scompiglio, skom-**pee**-l'yo, *m* confusion

scomporre, skom-**por**-ray, *v* to break up; to decompose

scomporsi, skom-**por**-se, *v* *fig* to lose one's composure

scomposto, skom-**poss**-to, *adj* broken up; unseemly

scomunicare, sko-moo-ne-**kah**-ray, *v* excommunicate

sconcertare, skon-chair-**tah**-ray, *v* to disconcert

sconcio, **skon**-cho, *adj* indecent

sconfessare, skon-fess-**sah**-ray, *v* to retract

sconfiggere, skon-**fid**-jay-ray, *v* to defeat

sconfinare, skon-fe-**nah**-ray, *v* to cross the border; to trespass; – **da**, *fig* to stray from

sconfinato, skon-fe-**nah**-to, *adj* without limits; *fig* unlimited

sconfitta, skon-**fit**-tah, *f* defeat

sconfortante, skon-for-**tahn**-tay, *adj* disheartening

sconforto, skon-**for**-to, *m* dejection

scongiurare, skon-joo-**rah**-ray, *v* to beseech; to avert

sconnesso, skon-**ness**-so, *adj* incoherent

sconosciuto, -a, sko-no-**shoo**-to, *adj* unknown; *m/f* stranger

sconquassare, skon-kwahss-**sah**-ray, *v* to shatter

sconsigliare, skon-se-l'**yah**-ray, *v* to advise against

sconsolato*, skon-so-**lah**-to, *adj* disconsolate

scontare, skon-**tah**-ray, *v* to deduct; to serve;

to pay for

scontentare, skon-ten-**tah**-ray, *v* to displease

scontentezza, skon-ten-**tet**-tsah, *f* dissatisfaction

sconto, **skon**-to, *m* discount

scontrino, skon-**tree**-no, *m* till receipt; ticket

scontro, **skon**-tro, *m* clash; collision

scontroso, skon-**tro**-so, *adj* surly

sconveniente, skon-vay-ne'**ayn**-tay, *adj* unseemly; improper

sconvolgere, skon-**voll**-jay-ray, *v* to shake; to upset

scopa, **sko**-pah, *f* broom

scopare, sko-**pah**-ray, *v* to sweep

scoperta, sko-**pair**-tah, *f* discovery

scoperto, sko-**pair**-to, *adj* uncovered; bare; open; *m* – **di conto**, bank overdraft

scopo, **sko**-po, *m* aim, purpose

scoppiare, skop-pe'**ah**-ray, *v* to burst; to explode

scoppiettare, skop-pe'et-**tah**-ray, *v* to crackle; to chug

scoppio, **skop**-pe'o, *m* explosion; burst; bang; outbreak

scoprire, sko-**pree**-ray, v to discover, to find out; to uncover; to unveil; to reveal

scoraggiamento, sko-rahd-jah-**men**-to, m discouragement

scoraggiare, sko-rahd-**jah**-ray, v to discourage

scoraggiarsi, sko-rahd-**jar**-se, v to lose heart

scorbuto, skor-**boo**-to, m scurvy

scorciare, skor-**chah**-ray, v to shorten

scorciatoia, skor-chah-**to**-e'ah, f short-cut

scorgere, skor-**jay**-ray, v to catch sight of

scoria, sko-**re**'ah, f slag; scoria; **scorie radioattive**, radioactive waste

scorpacciata, skor-paht-**chah**-tah, f **fare una –**, to stuff oneself

scorpione, skor-pe'**o**-nay, m scorpion; **Scorpione**, Scorpio

scorrazzare, skor-raht-**tsah**-ray, v to run about

scorrere, skor-ray-ray, v to flow; to run; to pass (by); to glance through

scorreria, skor-ray-ree-ah, f raid; incursion

scorretto*, skor-**ret**-to, adj incorrect; unfair

scorrevole, skor-**ray**-vo-lay, adj sliding; fluent

scorribanda, skor-re-**bahn**-dah, f incursion

scorsa, skor-sah, f glance

scorso, skor-so, adj last

scorsoio, skor-so-e'o, adj : **nodo –**, slipknot, noose

scortare, skor-**tah**-ray, v to escort

scortecciare, skor-tet-**chah**-ray, v (strip) to bark

scortese, skor-**tay**-zay, adj impolite

scortesia, skor-tay-**zee**-ah, f impoliteness

scorticare, shor-te-**kah**-ray, v to skin

scorza, skor-tsah, f bark; rind

scosceso, sko-**shay**-zo, adj steep

scossa, skoss-sah, f jerk, shake; shock; tremor

scostare, skoss-**tah**-ray, v to push aside

scostarsi, skoss-**tar**-se, v to move aside

scostumatezza, skoss-too-mah-**tet**-tsah, f dissoluteness

scotennare, sko-ten-**nah**-ray, v to skin; to scalp

scottare, skot-**tah**-ray, v to scald, to burn; to be very hot

scotto, skot-to, m : **pagare**

lo –, to pay the consequences

scovare, sko-**vah**-ray, v to drive out; to discover

Scozia, sko-tse'ah, f Scotland

scozzese, skot-**tsay**-zay, adj Scottish

screanzato*, skray-ahn-**tsah**-to, adj ill-mannered

screditare, skray-de-**tah**-ray, v to discredit

screpolare, skray-po-**lah**-ray, v to crack; to chap

screpolatura, skray-po-lah-**too**-rah, f chap; crack

screziato, skray-tse'**ah**-to, adj variegated

scribacchiare, skre-bahk-ke'**ah**-ray, v to scribble

scricchiolare, skrik-ke'o-**lah**-ray, v to creak

scricciolo, skrit-cho-lo, m wren

scrigno, skree-n'yo, m casket

scriminatura, skre-me-nah-**too**-rah, f parting

scritto, skrit-to, adj written; m work

scrittoio, skrit-**to**-e'o, m writing-desk

scrittore, -trice, skrit-**tor**-ay, skrit-**tree**-chay, m/f writer

scrittura, skrit-**too**-rah, f handwriting; entry;

contract; **la Sacra Scrittura,** the Scriptures

scrivania, skre-vah-**nee**-ah, *f* desk

scrivere, skree-**vay**-ray, *v* to write

scroccare, skrock-**kah**-ray, *v* to scrounge

scroccone, -a, skrock-ko-nay, *m/f* scrounger

scrofa, skro-fah, *f* sow

scrollare, skroll-**lah**-ray, *v* to shake (off); to shrug

scrosciare, skro-she'**ah**-ray, *v* to pelt down; to thunder

scroscio, skro-she'o, *m* pelting; thunder

scrostare, skro-**stah**-ray, *v* to scrape off

scrupolo, skroo-po-lo, *m* scruple; care

scrutare, skroo-**tah**-ray, *v* to scrutinize

scucire, skoo-**chee**-ray, *v* to unstitch; to fork out

scuderia, skoo day-**ree**-ah, *f* stable

scudo, skoo-do, *m* shield

sculacciare, skoo-laht-**chah**-ray, *v* to spank

scultore, -trice, skooll-tor-ay, skooll-**tree**-chay, *m/f* sculptor

scuola, skoo'o lah, *f* school

scuotere, skoo'o-tay-ray, *v* to shake

scure, skoo-ray, *f* axe

scuro, skoo-ro, *adj* dark, grim; *m* dark colour

scusa, skoo-zah, *f* excuse

scusare, skoo-**zah**-ray, *v* to excuse; **scusi,** I'm sorry; excuse me

scusarsi, skoo-**zar**-se, *v –* **(di),** to apologize (for)

sdebitarsi, zday-be-**tar**-se, *v* to repay

sdegnare, zday-n'**yah**-ray, *v* to despise

sdegnato*, zday-n'**yah**-to, *adj* indignant

sdegno, zday-n'yo, *m* indignation; contempt

sdoganare, zdo-gah-**nah**-ray, *v* to clear through customs

sdraiarsi, zdrah-e'**ar**-se, *v* to lie down, to stretch out

sdrucciolare, zdrooht-cho-**lah**-ray, *v* to slip

sdrucciolevole, zdrooht-cho-**lay**-vo-lay, *adj* slippery

se, say, *conj* if, whether

sé, say, *pron* oneself; himself; herself; itself; themselves

sebbene, seb-**bay**-nay, *conj* although, though

secca, seck-kah, *f* shallows

seccare, seck-**kah**-ray, *v* to dry; to dry up; to bother,

to annoy

seccarsi, seck-**kar**-se, *v* to get annoyed

seccatore, -trice, seck-kah-tor-ay, seck-kah-tree-chay, *m/f* bother; nuisance

seccatura, seck-kah-too-rah, *f* bother; nuisance

secchio, seck-ke'o, *m* bucket

secco*, seck-ko, *adj* dry; dried; withered; skinny; abrupt; sharp

secolare, say-ko-**lah**-ray, *adj* secular; centuries-old

secolo, say-ko-lo, *m* century; age

seconda, say-kon-dah, *f* second gear

secondo, say-**kon**-do, *adj & m* second; *m* (time) second; main course; *prep* according to; **secondo!** it depends!

secrezione, say-kray-tse'o-nay, *f* secretion

sedano, say-dah-no, *m* celery

sede, say-day, *f* seat; headquarters; head office; branch; [Holy] See

sedere, say-**day**-ray, *v* to sit; *m* bottom

sedersi, say-**dair**-se, *v* to sit down

sedia, say-de'ah, *f* chair

sedicesimo, say-de-chay-ze-mo, *adj & m* sixteenth

sedici, say-de-che, *adj & m* sixteen

sedile, say-dee-lay, *m* seat

seducente, say-doo-chen-tay, *adj* seductive

sedurre, say-doohr-ray, *v* to seduce

seduta, say-doo-tah, *f* sitting, session; meeting

sega, say-gah, *f* saw

segale, say-gah-lay, *f* rye

segare, say-gah-ray, *v* to saw; to saw off

seggio, sed-jo, *m* seat

seggiolone, sed-jo-lo-nay, *m* highchair

seggiovia, sed-jo-ve'ah, *f* chair lift

segheria, say-gay-ree-ah, *f* saw-mill

segnalare, say-n'yah-lah-ray, *v* to signal, to indicate; to notify; to point out

segnale, say-n'yah-lay, *m* signal; sign

segnalibro, say-n'yah-lee-bro, *m* book-mark

segnare, say-n'yah-ray, *v* to mark; to score; to note

segno, say-n'yo, *m* sign; mark

segregare, say-gray-gah-ray, *v* to segregate

segretario, -a, say-gray-tah-re'o, *m/f* secretary

segreteria, say-gray-tay-re'ah, *f* secretary's office; position of Secretary; – **telefonica,** answering machine

segretezza, say-gray-tet-tsah, *f* secrecy

seguace, say-goo'ah-chay, *m/f* follower

segugio, say-goo-jo, *m* hound

seguire, say-goo'ee-ray, *v* to follow; to attend; to continue

seguitare, say-goo'e-tah-ray, *v* to continue

seguito, say-goo'e-to, *m* continuation; sequel; rest; retinue; followers

sei, say-e, *adj & m* six

seicento, say'ee-chen-to; *adj & m* six hundred; **il Seicento,** the seventeenth century

selciato, sell-chah-to, *m* cobbled surface

selezionare, say-lay-tse'o-nah-ray, *v* to select

selezione, say-lay-tse'o-nay, *f* selection

sella, sell-lah, *f* saddle

sellare, sell-lah-ray, *v* to saddle

selvaggina, sell-vahd-jee-nah, *f* (animals) game

selvaggio, -a, sell-vahd-jo, *adj** savage; wild; *m/f* savage

selvatico, sell-vah-te-ko, *adj* wild

semaforo, say-mah-fo-ro, *m* traffic lights

sembrare, sem-brah-ray, *v* to seem; to look like

seme, say-may, *m* seed; *med* semen; (cards) suit

semestre, say-mess-tray, *m* half-year

semifinale, say-me-fe-nah-lay, *f* semifinal

seminare, say-me-nah-ray, *v* to sow

seminario, say-me-nah-re'o, *m relig* seminary; seminar

semola, say-mo-lah, *f* bran

semolino, say-mo-lee-nah, *m* semolina

semplice, sem-ple-chay, *adj* simple; single; easy

semplicità, sem-ple-che-tah, *f* simplicity

sempre, sem-pray, *adv* always; still; **per –,** forever

senape, say-nah-pay, *f* mustard

senato, say-nah-to, *m* senate

seno, say-no, *m* breast; (mat) sine

sensato*, sen-sah-to, *adj* sensible

sensazione, sen-sah-tse'o-nay, *f* sensation, feeling

sensibile, sen-see-be-lay, *adj* sensitive; noticeable

sensibilità, sen-see-be-le-**tah**, *f* sensitivity

senso, sen-so, *m* sense; feeling; meaning, sense; direction; – **unico,** one way street

sensuale, sen-soo'a-lay, *adj* sensual; sensuous

sentenza, sen-ten-tsah, *f law* sentence; maxim

sentiero, sen-te'ay-ro, *m* path

sentimentale, sen-te-men-**tah**-lay, *adj* sentimental

sentimento, sen-te-**men**-to, *m* feeling

sentinella, sen-te-nell-lah, *f* sentry

sentire, sen-tee-ray, *v* to hear; to feel; to smell; to taste

sentirsi, sen-teer-se, *v* to feel; – **di fare qualcosa,** to feel like doing something

senza, sen-tsah, *prep* & *conj* without; **senz' altro,** certainly; – **dubbio,** undoubtedly

separare, say-pah-**rah**-ray, *v* to separate; to divide; to distinguish

separarsi, say-pah-**rar**-se,

v to separate, to part

separato, say-pah-**rah**-to, *adj* separate; separated

sepolcro, say-**poll**-kro, *m* sepulchre

sepoltura, say poll-**too**-rah, *f* burial

seppellire, sep-pell-**lee**-ray, *v* to bury

seppia, sep-pe'ah, *f* cuttle-fish; sepia

sequela, say-**kway**-lah, *f* series; string

sequestrare, say-kwess-**trah**-ray, *v* to confiscate; to sequestrate; to kidnap

sera, say-rah, *f* evening; night

serata, say-**rah**-tah, *f* evening; party

serbare, sair-**bah**-ray, *v* to keep; to put aside

serbatoio, sair-bah-**to**-e'o, *m* tank; cistern

sereno, say-**ray**-no, *adj* clear; serene; *m* fine weather

serie, say-re-ay, *f* series; set; division, league

serietà, say-re-ay-**tah**, *f* seriousness; reliability

serio, say-re'o, *adj* serious; reliable

serpeggiare, sair-ped-jah-ray, *v* to wind; to spread

serpente, sair-**pen**-tay, *m* snake

serra, sair-rah, *f* green-house

serrata, sair-**rah**-tah, *f* lock-out

serratura, sair-rah-**too**-rah, *f* lock

serva, sair-vah, *f* maidservant

servire, sair-vee-ray, *v* to serve; to wait on; (cards) to deal; to be of use

servirsi, sair-**veer**-se, *v* to help oneself; – **di,** to use

servitù, sair-ve-**too**, *f* domestic staff

servizio, sair-vee-**tse'o**, *m* service; set; report

servo, sair vo, *m* servant

sessanta, sess-**sahn**-tah, *adj* & *m* sixty

sessantesimo, sess-sahn-**tay**-ze-mo, *adj* & *m* sixtieth

sesso, sess-so, *m* sex

sessuale, sess-soo'a-lay, *adj* sexual

sestante, sess-**tahn**-tay, *m* sextant

sesto, sess-to, *adj* & *m* sixth

seta, say-tah, *f* silk

sete, say-tay, *f* thirst; *fig* longing

setola, say-to-lah, *f* bristle

setta, set-tah, *f* sect

settanta, set-tahn-tah, *adj* & *m* seventy

settantesimo, set-tahn-

tay-ze-mo, *adj & m* seventieth

sette, set-tay, *adj & m* seven

settecento, set-tay-**chen**-to; *adj & m* seven hundred; **il Settecento,** the eighteenth century

settembre, set-**tem**-bray, *m* September

settentrionale, set-ten-tre'o-**nah**-lay, *adj* northern

settimana, set-te-**mah**-nah, *f* week

settimanale, set-te-**mah**-nah-lay, *adj* weekly; *m* weekly publication

settimo, **set**-te-mo, *adj & m* seventh

settore, set-**tor**-ay, *m* sector

severo,* say-**vay**-ro, *adj* strict

sevizie, say-vee-tse'ah, *fpl* tortures

sezione, say-tse'o-nay, *f* section; portion

sfaccendato, sfaht-chah-**dah**-to, *adj* idle

sfacciato*, sfaht-**chah**-to, *adj* cheeky

sfamare, sfah-**mah**-ray, *v* to feed

sfamarsi, sfah-**mar**-se, *v* to satisfy one's hunger

sfarzo, sfar-tso, *m* pomp, magnificence

sfatare, sfah-**tah**-ray, *v* to explode, to discredit

sfavorevole, sfah-vo-**ray**-vo-lay, *adj* unfavourable

sfegatato, sfay-gah-**tah**-to, *adj* fanatical

sfera, sfay-rah, *f* sphere

sferrare, sfair-**rah**-ray, *v* to launch; **– un colpo a,** to lash out at

sferzare, sfair-tsah-ray, *v* to whip

sferzata, sfair-tsah-tah, *f* whipping; *fig* lashing

sfida, sfee-dah, *f* challenge

sfidare, sfe-**dah**-ray, *v* to challenge; to defy

sfiducia, sfe-doo-chah, *f* mistrust

sfiduciato*, sfe-doo-**chah**-to, *adj* disheartened

sfigurare, sfe-goo-**rah**-ray, *v* to disfigure

sfilata, sfe-lah-tah, *f mil* parade; **– di moda,** fashion show

sfinge, sfin-jay, *f* sphinx

sfinire, sfe-**nee**-ray, *v* to exhaust

sfinito, sfe-**nee**-to, *adj* exhausted

sfiorare, sfe'o-**rah**-ray, *v* to skim

sfiorire, sfe'o-**ree**-ray, *v* to wither

sfoderare, sfo-day-**rah**-ray, *v* to unsheathe, to draw

sfogare, sfo-**gah**-ray, *v* to give vent to

sfoggiare, sfod-**jah**-ray, *v* to show off

sfoggio, sfod-jo, *m* pomp; show

sfogliare, sfo-l'yah-ray, *v* to leaf through

sfogo, sfo-go, *m* rash; outburst; outlet

sfollare, sfoll-**lah**-ray, *v* to empty

sfondare, sfon-**dah**-ray, *v* to break down; to break the bottom of

sfondarsi, sfon-**dar**-se, *v* to burst at the bottom

sfondo, sfon-do, *m* background

sfortuna, sfor-**too**-nah, *f* misfortune

sfortunato*, sfor-too-**nah**-to, *adj* unfortunate, unlucky

sforzare, sfor-tsah-ray, *v* to force; to strain

sforzarsi, sfor-**tsar**-se, *v* to make an effort

sforzo, sfor-zo, *m* effort

sfracellare, sfrah-**chell**-lah-ray, *v* to shatter

sfrattare, sfraht-**tah**-ray, *v* to evict

sfregiare, sfray-**jah**-ray, *v* to disfigure; to slash

sfregio, sfray-jo, *m* scar; gash; scratch

sfrenato*, sfray-**nah**-to,

adj unrestrained; uncontrolled

sfrondare, sfron-**dah**-ray, *v* to prune

sfrontatezza, sfron-tah-**tet**-tsah, *f* impudence

sfrontato*, sfron-**tah**-to, *adj* cheeky

sfruttare, sfroot-**tah**-ray, *v* to exploit; to take advantage of

sfuggire, sfood-**jee**-ray, *v* to escape; to shun

sfumare, sfoo-**mah**-ray, *v* to shade off ; to vanish

sfumatura, sfoo-mah-**too**-rah, *f* shade; hint

sfuriata, sfoo-re-**ah**-tah, *f* outburst of anger

sgabello, zgah-**bell**-lo, *m* stool

sganciare, zgahn-**chah**-ray, *v* to unfasten; to uncouple; to drop; to fork out

sgangherato, zgahn-gay-**rah**-to, *adj* ramshackle; off its hinges

sgarbato*, zgar-**bah**-to, *adj* impolite

sghembo, zghem-bo, *adj* crooked; aslant

sghignazzare, zghe-n'yaht-**tsah**-ray, *v* to laugh loudly

sgocciolare, zgot-cho-**lah**-ray, *v* to drip; to drain

sgolarsi, zgo-**lar**-se, *v* to

become hoarse

sgomberare, zgom-bay-**rah**-ray, *v* to clear; to vacate; to evacuate

sgombro, zgom-bro, *m* mackerel; clearing

sgomentarsi, zgo-men-**tahr**-se, *v* to be dismayed

sgomento, zgo-**men**-to, *m* dismay

sgonfiare, zgon-fe'**ah**-ray, *v* to deflate

sgorgare, zgor-**gah**-ray, *v* to stream out

sgozzare, zgot-**tsah**-ray, *v* to slit the throat of

sgradevole, zgrah-**day**-vo-lay, *adj* unpleasant

sgranare, zgrah-**nah**-ray, *v* (peas, etc.) to shell

sgranchire, zgrahn-kee-ray, *v* to stretch

sgravio, zgrah-ve'o, *m* – **fiscale**, tax relief

sgraziato*, zgrah-tse'**ah**-to, *adj* awkward, clumsy

sgretolare, zgray-to-lah-ray, *v* to cause to crumble

sgridare, zgre-**dah**-ray, *v* to scold; to tell off

sgridata, zgre-**dah**-tah, *f* scolding

sguainare, zgoo'ah-e-**nah**-ray, *v* to unsheathe

sgualcire, zgoo'ahl-**chee**-ray, *v* to crumple, to

crease

sguardo, zgoo'**ar**-do, *m* look, glance

sguazzare, zgoo'aht-**tsah**-ray, *v* to splash about

sgusciare, zgoo-she'**ah**-ray, *v* to shell; to slip

shampoo, shahm-po, *m* shampoo

si, se, *pron* oneself; himself; herself; itself; themselves; each other; one; you; **lavarsi le mani**, to wash one's hands; *m mus* B

sì, se, *adv & m* yes

sia, see-ah, *conj* **sia ... che/sia**, both ... and; **sia che ... sia che ...,** whether ... or ...

sibilare, se-be-lah-ray, *v* to hiss; to whistle

sibilo, see-bi-lo, *m* hiss, hissing; whistling

sicario, se-kah-re'o, *m* hired assasin, killer

sicché, sick-**kay**, *conj* and so

siccità, sit-che-**tah**, *f* drought

siccome, sick-ko-may, *conj* since; as

sicurezza, se-koo-**ret**-tsah, *f* security, safety; certainty

sicuro*, se-koo-ro, *adj* safe; secure; confident; sure, certain; reliable;

adv sure, certainly

siderurgia, se-day-roohr-jee-ah, *f* iron and steel industry

sidro, see-dro, *m* cider

siepe, se'ay-pay, *f* hedge

siero, se'ay-ro, *m* serum

sieropositivo, se'ay-ro-po-se-tee-vo, *adj* HIV-positive

sigaretta, se-gah-ret-tah, *f* cigarette

sigaro, see-gah-ro, *m* cigar

sigillare, se-jil-lah-ray, *v* to seal

sigillo, se-jil-lo, *m* seal

sigla, see-glah, *f* acronym

significare, se-n'yee-fe-kah-ray, *v* to mean

significato, se-n'yee-fe-kah-to, *m* meaning

signora, se-n'yor-ah, *f* lady; madam; Mrs.

signore, se-n'yor-ay, *m* gentleman; sir; Mr.

signorina, se-n'yor-ee-nah, *f* Miss; young lady

silenzio, see-len-tse'o, *m* silence

sillaba, seel-lah-bah, *f* syllable

siluro, se-loo-ro, *m* torpedo

simbolo, seem-bo-lo, *m* symbol

simile, see-me-lav, *adj* similar

simpatico*, seem-pah-te-ko, *adj* nice

simulare, se-moo-lah-ray, *v* to sham; to simulate

sinagoga, se-nah-go-gah, *f* synagogue

sincerarsi, seen-chay-rar-se, *v* to assure oneself

sincero*, seen-chay-ro, *adj* sincere

sindacato, seen-dah-kah-to, *m* trade union; syndicate

sindaco, seen-dah-ko, *m* mayor

sinfonia, seen-fo-nee-ah, *f* symphony

singhiozzare, seen-ghe'ot-tsah-ray, *v* to sob

singhiozzo, seen-ghe'ot-tso, *m* sob; hiccup

singolare, seen-go-lah-ray, *adj* singular

singolo, seen-go-lo, *adj* single; each

sinistra, se-niss-trah, *f* left; left-hand side

sinistro, se-niss-tro, *adj* left; sinister; *m* accident

sintassi, seen-tahss-se, *f* syntax

sintetico, seen-tay-te-ko, *adj* synthetic

sintomo, seen-to-mo, *m* symptom; sign

sinuoso*, se-noo'o-zo, *adj* sinuous; winding

sipario, se-pah-re'o, *m* curtain

sirena, se-rav-nah, *f* mermaid; siren

siringa, se-reen-gah, *f* syringe

sistema, siss-tay-mah, *m* system; method

sito, see-to, *m* site

slacciare, zlaht-chah-ray, *v* to undo, to unfasten

slanciarsi, zlahn-char-se, *v* to throw oneself

slancio, zlahn-cho, *m* dash, leap; surge

sleale, zlay'ah-lay, *adj* disloyal; unfair

slegare, zlay-gah-ray, *v* to untie

slitta, zlit-tah, *f* sledge; sleigh

slittare, zlit-tah-ray, *v* to slide; to skid

slittamento, zlit-tah-men-to, *m* sliding; skidding

slogare, zlo-gah-ray, *v* to sprain; to dislocate

slogatura, zlo-gah-too-rah, *f* dislocation, sprain

sloggiare, zlod-jah-ray, *v* to move out

smacchiare, zmahk-ke'ah-ray, *v* to remove stains from

smagliante, zmah-l'yahn-tay, *adj* brilliant, dazzling

smagliare, zmah-l'yah-ray, *v* to break; to ladder

smagliatura, zmah-l'yah-too-rah, *f* ladder; stretch

mark

smaltare, zmahl-**tah**-ray, *v* to enamel

smaltire, zmahl-**tee**-ray, *v* to digest; to sell off; to discharge; **– la sbornia**, to get over one's hangover

smalto, **zmahl**-to, *m* enamel; nail varnish

smania, **zmah**-ne'ah, *f* restlessness; craving

smanioso*, zmah-ne'**o**-zo, *adj* eager; furious

smantellare, zmahn-tell-**lah**-ray, *v* to dismantle; to demolish

smarrire, zmar-**ree**-ray, *v* to lose, to mislay

smarrirsi, zmar-**reer**-se, *v* to get lost

smarrito, zmar-**ree**-to, *adj* lost; bewildered

smascherare, zmahss-kay-**rah**-ray, *v* to unmask

smemorato, zmay-mo-**rah**-to, *adj* forgetful, absent-minded

smentire, zmen-**tee**-ray, *v* to deny; to refute

smentita, zmen-**tee**-tah, *f* denial

smeraldo, zmay-**rahl**-do, *m* emerald

smerciare, zmair-**chah**-ray, *v* to sell; to sell off

smercio, **zmair**-cho, *m* sale

smeriglio, zmay-**ree**-l'yo, *m* emery

smettere, **zmet**-tay-ray, *v* to stop; to stop wearing

smilzo, **zmeel**-tso, *adj* lean, thin

sminuire, zme-noo'**ee**-ray, *v* to diminish

sminuzzare, zme-noot-**tsah**-ray, *v* to crumble

smistare, zme-**stah**-ray, *v* to sort out; to shunt

smisurato*, zme-zoo-**rah**-to, *adj* huge

smoderato*, zmo-day-**rah**-to, *adj* immoderate

smoking, **zmo**-king, *m* dinner jacket

smontare, zmon-**tah**-ray, *v* to take to pieces; to dismount; to finish work

smorfia, **zmor**-fe'ah, *f* grimace

smorfioso, zmor-fe'**o**-zo, *adj* simpering

smorto, **zmor**-to, *adj* pale; dull

smottamento, zmot-tah-**men**-to, *m* landslide

smuovere, zmoo'o-**vay**-ray, *v* to move, to shift; to deter

snaturato, znah-too-**rah**-to, *adj* cruel

snello, **znell**-lo, *adj* slender, slim

snervare, znair-**vah**-ray, *v* to wear out

snidare, zne-**dah**-ray, *v* to drive out

snobbare, znob-**bah**-ray, *v* to snub

snodare, zno-**dah**-ray, *v* to loosen

sobbalzare, sob-bahl-**tsah**-ray, *v* to jolt; to jump

sobborgo, sob-**bor**-go, *m* suburb

sobillare, so-bill-**lah**-ray, *v* to instigate

socchiudere, sock-ke'**oo**-day-ray, *v* to half close; to leave ajar

soccorrere, sock-**kor**-ray-ray, *v* to help

soccorso, sock-**kor**-so, *m* help; aid

società, so-chay-**tah**, *f* society; company; club

socievole, so-chay-vo-lay, *adj* sociable

socio, -a, so-cho, so-chah, *m/f* partner; member

soddisfacente, sod-diss-fah-**chen**-tay, *adj* satisfactory

soddisfare, sod-diss-**fah**-ray, *v* to satisfy; to fulfil; to meet

soddisfatto, sod-diss-**faht**-to, *adj* satisfied

sodo, **so**-do, *adj* firm, hard; *adv* hard

sofà, so-**fah**, *f* sofa

sofferente, sof-fay-**ren**-tay, *adj* suffering

sofferenza, sof-fay-ren-tsah, *f* suffering

soffiare, sof-fe'ah-ray, *v* to blow

soffice, sof-fe-chay, *adj* soft

soffio, sof-fe'o, *m* breath

soffitta, sof-fit-tah, *f* attic

soffitto, sof-fit-to, *m* ceiling

soffocare, sof-fo-kah-ray, *v* to suffocate

soffriggere, sof-freed-jay-ray, *v* to fry slowly

soffrire, sof-free-ray, *v* to suffer

soggetto, sod-jet-to, *adj* liable; *m* subject

soggezione, sod-jay-tse'o-nay, *f* subjection; awe

sogghignare, sog-ghe-n'yah-ray, *v* to grin

sogghigno, sog-ghe-n'yo, *m* grin

soggiogare, sod-jo-gah-ray, *v* to subjugate

soggiornare, sod-jor-nah-ray, *v* to stay

soglia, so-l'yah, *f* threshold; doorstep

sogliola, so-l'yo-lah, *f* (fish) sole

sognare, so-n'yah-ray, *v* to dream

sogno, so-n'yo, *m* dream

soia, so-e'ah, *f* soya

sol, sol, *m mus* G

solco, soll-ko, *m* furrow; track; groove; wrinkle

soldato, soll-dah-to, *m* soldier

soldo, soll-do, *m* : **non avere un –,** to be pennyless; **soldi,** money

sole, so-lay, *m* sun; sunshine

solenne*, so-len-nay, *adj* solemn

solere, so-lay-ray, *v* to be used to

solerte, so-lair-tay, *adj* industrious

soletta, so-let-tah, *f* insole

solido, so-le-do, *adj* solid; *m* (matter) solid

solito*, so-le-to, *adj* usual

solitudine, so-le-too-de-nay, *f* solitude

sollecito*, soll-lay-che-to, *adj* prompt, quick

solletico, soll-lay-te-ko, *m* tickling; **fare il – a,** to tickle

sollevare, soll-lay-vah-ray, *v* to raise, to lift; to comfort

sollevarsi, soll-lay-var-se, *v* to get up; to rise up

sollievo, soll-le'ay-vo, *m* relief

solo*, so-lo, *adj* alone; lonely; only; *adv* only

soltanto, sol-tahn-to, *adv* only

solubile, so-loo-be-lay, *adj* soluble; instant

soluzione, so-loo-tse'o-nay, *f* solution; answer

somaro, so-mah-ro, *m* donkey

somiglianza, so-me-l'yahn-tsah, *f* resemblance

somigliare, so-me-l'yah-ray, *v* – a, to be like; to look like

somma, som-mah, *f* sum; amount

sommare, som-mah-ray, *v* to add up; to add

sommario, som-mah-re'o, *m* summary

sommergere, som-mair-jay-ray, *v* to submerge

sommergibile, som-mair-jee-be-lay, *m* submarine

sommesso*, som-mess-so, *adj* subdued

somministrare, som-me-niss-trah-ray, *v* to administer

sommità, som-me-tah, *f* summit; top

sommo, som-mo, *adj* highest

sommossa, som-moss-sah, *f* riot

sonaglio, so-nah-l'yo, *m* bell; rattle

sonda, son-dah, *f* probe; drill

sondaggio, son-dahj-jo, *m* survey

sonnecchiare, son-neckke'**ah**-ray, *v* to doze

sonnellino, son-nell-**lee**-no, *m* nap

sonnifero, son-**nee**-fay-ro, *m* sleeping drug, sleeping pill

sonno, son-no, *m* sleep; avere –, to be sleepy

sonoro*, so-**no**-ro, *adj* sonorous; sound

sontuoso*, son-too'o-zo, *adj* sumptuous

sopore, so-**po**-ray, *m* torpor

soppiantare, sop-pe'ahn-**tah**-ray, *v* to supplant

soppiatto, sop-pe'**aht**-to, *adv* di –, secretly

sopportare, sop-por-**tah**-ray, *v* to support, to bear; to stand

sopprimere, sop-**pree**-may-ray, *v* to suppress

sopra, so-prah, *prep* on; above; over; *adv* above; di –, upstairs

soprabito, so-**prah**-be-to, *m* overcoat

sopracciglio, so-praht-**chee**-l'yo, *m* eyebrow

sopraffare, so-prahf-**fah**-ray, *v* to overcome

sopraggiungere, so-prahd-**joonn**-jay-ray, *v* to arrive unexpectedly; to occur unexpectedly

sopralluogo, so-prah-loo'o-go, *m* inspection; on-the-spot investigation

soprannaturale, so-prahn-nah-too-**rah**-lay, *adj* supernatural

soprannome, so-prahn-**no**-may, *m* nickname

soprassedere, so-prahss-say-**day**-ray, *v* – a, to put off

soprattutto, so-praht-**toot**-to, *adv* above all, especially

sopravvento, so-prahv-**ven**-to, *m* avere il – su, to have the upper hand over

sopravvivere, so-prahv-**vee**-vay-ray, *v* to survive

soprintendere, so-prin-**ten**-day-ray, *v* to supervise

sorbetto, sor-**bet**-to, *m* sorbet

sorbire, sor-**bee**-ray, *v* to sip; *fig* to put up with

sordità, sor-de-**tah**, *f* deafness

sordo, sor-do, *adj* deaf; muffled

sorella, so-**rell**-lah, *f* sister

sorellastra, so-rell-**lahss**-trah, *f* step-sister

sorgente, sor-**jen**-tay, *f* spring; source

sorgere, sor-**jay**-ray, *v* to rise; to arise

sormontare, sor-mon-**tah**-ray, *v* to surmount

sorpassare, sor-pahss-**sah**-ray, *v* to overtake; to surpass; to go past

sorprendente, sor-pren-**den**-tay, *adj* surprising

sorprendere, sor-**pren**-day-ray, *v* to surprise

sorpresa, sor-**pray**-zah, *f* surprise

sorreggere, sor-**red**-jay-ray, *v* to support

sorridere, sor-**ree**-day-ray, *v* to smile

sorriso, sor-**ree**-zo, *m* smile

sorseggiare, sor-sed-**jah**-ray, *v* to sip

sorso, sor-so, *m* sip; gulp

sorta, sor-tah, *f* sort

sorte, sor-tay, *f* destiny; chance

sorteggiare, sor-ted-**jah**-ray, *v* to draw for

sorvegliare, sor-vay-l'**yah**-ray, *v* to watch; to oversee

sorvolare, sor-vo-**lah**-ray, *v* to fly over

sosia, so-ze'ah, *m* (person) double

sospendere, soss-**pen**-day-ray, *v* to suspend, to interrupt; to hang

sospettare, soss-pet-**tah**-ray, *v* to suspect

sospetto, -a, soss-**pet**-to, *adj* suspicious; *m*

suspicion; *m/f* suspect

sospingere, soss-**pin**-jay-ray, *v* to push

sospirare, soss-pe-**rah**-ray, *v* to sigh

sospiro, soss-**pee**-ro, *m* sigh

sosta, **soss**-tah, *f* stop; pause, break

sostantivo, soss-tahn-**tee**-vo, *m* noun

sostanza, soss-**tahn**-tsah, *f* substance

sostare, soss-**tah**-ray, *v* to stop

sostegno, soss-**tay**-n'yo, *m* support

sostenere, soss-tay-**nay**-ray, *v* to support; to maintain

sostituire, soss-te-too'ee-ray, *v* to substitute; to replace; to take over from

sottana, sot-**tah**-nah, *f* skirt

sotterraneo, sot-tair-**rah**-nay-o, *adj* underground; *m* cellar

sotterrare, sot-tair-**rah**-ray, *v* to bury

sottigliezza, sot-te-l'**yay**-tsah, *f* subtlety

sottile, sot-**tee**-lay, *adj* thin; subtle

sottintendere, sot-tin-**ten**-day-ray, *v* to imply

sotto, **sot**-to, *prep* under;

below; *adv* underneath; below; **di –**, downstairs

sottolineare, sot-to-le-nay-**ah**-ray, *v* to underline

sottomano, sot-to-**mah**-no, *adv* at hand

sottomarino, sot-to-mah-**ree**-no, *m* submarine

sottomettere, sot-to-**met**-tay-ray, *v* to subdue

sottomettersi, sot-to-**met**-tair-se, *v* to submit

sottopassaggio, sot-to-pahs-**sahj**-jo, *m* subway; underpass

sottoporre, sot-to-**por**-ray, *v* to subject; to submit

sottoporsi, sot-to-**por**-se, *v* **– a**, to undergo

sottosopra, sot-to-**so**-prah, *adv* topsy-turvy

sottostare, sot-to-**stah**-ray, *v* **– a**, to submit to; to give in to; to undergo

sottosuolo, sot-to-soo'**o**-lo, *m* subsoil

sottrarre, sot-**trar**-ray, *v* to subtract; to deduce; to take away ; to steal

sottrarsi, sot-**trar**-se, *v* **– a**, to escape; to avoid

sovente, so-**ven**-tay, *adv* frequently

sovrano, **-a**, so-**vrah**-no, *m/f* sovereign

sovrapporre, so-vrahp-**por**-ray, *v* to place on

top of; to superimpose

sovrumano, so-vroo-**mah**-no, *adj* superhuman

sovvenzione, sov-ven-tse'**o**-nay, *f* subsidy

sovvertire, sov-vair-**tee**-ray, *v* to subvert

spaccare, spahk-**kah**-ray, *v* to break, to split; to chop

spaccatura, spahk-kah-**too**-rah, *f* split

spacciare, spaht-**chah**-ray, *v* to push

spacciarsi, spaht-**chah**-rse, *v* **– per**, to pass oneself off as

spacciatore, -trice, spaht-chah-**to**-ray, spaht-chah-**tree**-chay, *m/f* pusher; dealer

spaccio, **spaht**-cho, *m* trafficking; shop

spacco, **spahk**-ko, *m* slit

spaccone, -a, spahk-**ko**-nay, *m/f* braggart

spada, **spah**-dah, *f* sword; **spade** (cards) spades

Spagna, **spah**-ny'ah, *f* Spain

spagnolo, spah-n'yo-lo, *adj* Spanish

spago, **spah**-go, *m* twine, string

spalancare, spah-lahn-**kah**-ray, *v* to open wide

spalla, **spahl**-lah, *f* shoulder; back

spalliera, spahl-l'**yay**-rah, *f* (bed) head; wall bars

spallina, spahl-**lee**-nah, *f* strap; shoulder pad; *mil* epaulet

spalmare, spahl-**mah**-ray, *v* to spread

spandere, spahn-day-ray, *v* to spread; to pour; to scatter

sparare, spah-**rah**-ray, *v* to fire; to shoot

sparecchiare, spah-reck-ke'**ah**-ray, *v* to clear (the table)

spargere, spahr-jay-ray, *v* to spread; to scatter

sparire, spah-**ree**-ray, *v* to disappear

sparlare, spahr-lah-ray, *v* : **– di,** to run down

sparpagliare, spahr-pah-l'**yah**-ray, *v* to scatter

sparso, spahr-so, *adj* scattered

spartire, spahr-tee-ray, *v* to share out

sparuto, spah-**roo**-to, *adj* haggard; small; thin

sparviero, spahr-ve'**ay**-ro, *m* sparrowhawk

spasimare, spah-ze-**mah**-ray, *v* to be in agony; **– per,** to be madly in love with

spasmo, spah-zmo, *m* spasm

spassarsela, spahss-**sar**-say-lah, *v* to have fun

spassionato*, spahss-se'o-nah-to, *adj* dispassionate, unbiassed

spasso, spahss-so, *m* amusement; **andare a –,** to go for a walk

spauracchio, spah'oo-**rahk**-ke'o, *m* scare-crow

spaurire, spah'oo-**ree**-ray, *v* to scare

spavaldo, spah-**vahl**-do, *adj* bold

spaventare, spah-ven-**tah**-ray, *v* to frighten

spavento, spah-**ven**-to, *m* fear; fright

spaventoso, spah-ven-**to**-so, *adj* frightening; terrible

spazio, spah-tse'o, *m* space; room

spazioso, spah-tse'**o**-zo, *adj* spacious

spazzacamino, spaht-tsah-kah-**mee**-no, *m* chimney-sweep

spazzaneve, spaht-tsah-**nay**-vay, *m* snowplough

spazzare, spaht-**tsah**-ray, *v* to sweep

spazzatura, spaht-tsah-**too**-rah, *f* rubbish

spazzino, spaht-**tsee**-no, *m* sweeper; dustman

spazzola, spaht-tso-lah, *f* brush

spazzolare, spaht-tso-**lah**-ray, *v* to brush

spazzolino, spaht-tso-**lee**-no, *m* toothbrush

specchiarsi, spayk-ke'**ahr**-se, *v* to look at oneself in the mirror

specchio, spayk-ke'o, *m* mirror

specialità, spay-chah-le-**tah,** *f* speciality

specie, spay-chay, *f* species; kind

specificare, spay-che-fe-**kah**-ray, *v* to specify

spedire, spay-**dee**-ray, *v* to send

spedizione, spay-de-tse'o-nay, *f* sending; expedition

spedizioniere, spay-de-tse'o-ne'**ay**-ray, *m* forwarding agent, shipping agent

spegnere, spay-n'yay-ray, *v* to turn off; to put out; to extinguish

spegnersi, spay-n'yair-se, *v* to go out; to go off

spendere, spen-day-ray, *v* to spend

spennare, spen-**nah**-ray, *v* to pluck; to fleece

spensierato*, spen-se'ay-rah-to, *adj* carefree

spento, spen-to, *adj* out; dull; lifeless

speranza, spay-**rahn**-tsah, *f* hope

sperare, spay-**rah**-ray, *v* to hope

spergiuro, spair-joo-ro, *m* perjury; perjurer

sperimentare, spay-re-men-**tah**-ray, *v* to experiment with; to test out

sperone, spay-**ro**-nay, *m* spur

sperperare, spair-pay-**rah**-ray, *v* to squander

sperpero, spair-pay-ro, *m* squandering, waste

spesa, spay-zah, *f* expense; shopping; purchase; cost; **fare la –**, to do the shopping

spesso, spess-so, *adj* thick; *adv* often

spessore, spess-**sor**-ay, *m* thickness

spettacolo, spet-**tah**-ko-lo, *m* show, performance

spettare, spet-**tah**-ray, *v* : **– a**, to be up to; to be due to

spettatore, -trice, spet-tah-**tor**-ay, spet-tah-**tree**-chay, *m/f* member of the audience; viewer; spectator; onlooker

spettinato, spet-tee-**nah**-to, *adj* dishevelled

spettrale, spet-**trah**-lay, *adj* spectral

spettro, spet-tro, *m* ghost

spezie, spay-tse-ay, *fpl* spices

spezzare, spet-**tsah**-ray, *v* to break (up)

spia, spee-ah, *f* spy; informer; warning light; sign; **fare la –**, to give sb away; to be a telltale

spiacente, spe'ah-**chen**-tay, *adj* sorry

spiacevole, spe'ah-**chay**-vo-lay, *adj* unpleasant

spiaggia, spe'**ahd**-jah, *f* beach

spianare, spe'ah-**nah**-ray, *v* to level

spiare, spe'ah-ray, *v* to spy on, to watch

spiccare, speek-**kah**-ray, *v* to stand out; **– un balzo**, to jump

spicchio, speek ke'o, *m* (of fruit) slice; segment; **– d'aglio**, clove of garlic

spicciarsi, speet-**char**-se, *v* to hurry up

spiccioli, speet-cho-le, *mpl* small change

spiegare, spe'ay-**gah**-ray, *v* to explain; to unfold; to unfurl

spiegarsi, spe'ay-**gar**-se, *v* to make oneself clear; to become clear

spiegazione, spe'ay-gah-**tse**'o-nay, *f* explanation

spiegazzare, spe'ay-gaht-**tsah**-ray, *v* to crumple, to crease

spietato*, spe'ay-**tah**-to, *adj* cruel; pitiless; fierce

spiga, spee-gah, *f* (corn) ear

spillare, spil-**lah**-ray, *v* (cask) to tap; to clip together

spillo, spil-lo, *m* pin; brooch

spilorcio, spe-**lor**-cho, *adj* stingy; *m* miser

spina, spee-nah, *f* thorn; (fish) bone; spine; prickle; **– dorsale**, backbone; **alla –**, draught

spinaci, spe-**nah**-che, *mpl* spinach

spinello, spe-**nel**-lo, *m* joint

spingere, speen-jay-ray, *v* to push; to drive; to press, to urge

spinoso, spe-**no**-so, *m* thorny

spinta, speen-tah, *f* push; thrust; *fig* incentive

spione, spe-o-nay, *m* sneak, telltale

spira, spee-rah, *f* coil; curl

spiraglio, spe-**rah**-l'yo, *m* chink; glimmer

spirale, spe-**rah**-lay, *f* spiral; coil

spirare, spe-**rah**-ray, *v* (to die) to expire

spirito, spee-re-to, *m* spirit; mind; wit

spiritoso*, spe-re-**to**-zo, *adj* witty, funny

splendere, splen-**day**-ray, *v* to shine

spoglia, spo-**l'yah**, *f* slough; **spoglie**, remains

spogliare, spo-**l'yah**-ray, *v* to undress; to strip; to count; to deprive

spogliatoio, spo-**l'yah**-to-e'o, *m* changing room

spola, spo-**lah**, *f* spool; **fare la –**, to go to and fro

spoletta, spo-**let**-tah, *f* fuse; spool

spolpare, spoll-**pah**-ray, *v* to strip the flesh off bone

spolverare, spoll-vay-**rah**-ray, *v* to dust

spolverizzare, spoll-vay-rid-**dzah**-ray, *v* to sprinkle

sponda, spon-**dah**, *f* shore, bank; edge

spontaneo, spon-**tah**-nay-o, *adj* spontaneous, natural

spopolare, spo-po-**lah**-ray, *v* to depopulate

sporcaccione, spor-kaht-**cho**-nay, *m* dirty old man

sporcare, spor-**kah**-ray, *v* dirty, to make dirty; to stain; to soil

sporcizia, spor-**chee**-tse'ah, *f* filth, dirt

sporco, spor-**ko**, *adj* dirty, filthy

sporgere, spor-**jay**-ray, *v* to put out; to stick out; to jut out

sporgersi, spor-**jair**-se, *v* : **– da**, to lean out of

sport, sport, *m* sport

sportello, spor-**tell**-lo, *m* (car, train) door; window, counter; **automatico**, cash dispenser

sposa, spo-**zah**, *f* bride; wife

sposalizio, spo-zah-lee-**tse'o**, *m* wedding

sposare, spo-**zah**-ray, *v* to marry

sposarsi, spo-**zar**-se, *v* to get married, to marry

sposo, spo-**zo**, *m* husband; bridegroom

spossatezza, sposs-sah-**tet**-tsah, *f* weariness

spostare, sposs-**tah**-ray, *v* to move, to shift; to change

spranga, spranh-**gah**, *f* (rod) bar

sprazzo, spraht-**tso**, *m* flash; burst

sprecare, spray-**kah**-ray, *v* to waste

spreco, spray-**ko**, *m* waste

sprecone, -a, spray-**ko**-nay, *m/f* waster

spregio, spray-**jo**, *m* scorn, disdain

spremere, spray-**may**-ray, *v* to squeeze

spremuta, spray-**moo**-tah, *f* fresh fruit juice

sprezzante, spret-**tsahn**-tay, *adj* contemptuous

sprigionare, spre-jo-**nah**-ray, *v* to give off; to unleash

sprigionarsi, spre-jo-**nar**-se, *v* to emanate

sprizzare, spreet-**tsah**-ray, *v* to spurt

sprofondare, spro-fon-**dah**-ray, *v* to sink; to collapse; to subside

spronare, spro-**nah**-ray, *v* to spur

sprone, spro-**nay**, *m* spur

sproporzionato*, spro-por-tse'o-**nah**-to, *adj* out of all proportion

sproposito, spro-po-ze-to, *m* blunder

sprovvisto, sprov-**viss**-to, *adj* **– di**, without, lacking in

spruzzare, sproot-**tsah**-ray, *v* to spray, to sprinkle

spruzzo, sproot-**tso**, *m* spray; splash

spudoratezza, spoo-do-rah-**tet**-tsah, *f* impudence

spugna, spoo-**n'yah**, *f* sponge

spuma, spuma, spoo-mah, *f* foam, froth; fizzy drink; mousse

spumante, spoo-**mahn**-tay, *m* sparkling wine

spuntare, spoonn-**tah**-ray, *v* break the point of; to trim; to dawn; to begin to grow; to sprout; to appear suddenly; **spuntarla,** to make it

spuntato, spoonn-**tah**-to, *adj* blunt

spuntino, spoonn-**tee**-no, *m* snack

spurgare, spoohr-**gah**-ray, *v* to clean; to bleed

sputare, spoo-**tah**-ray, *v* to spit; to spit out

sputo, spoo-to, *m* spittle, spit

squadra, skwah-drah, *f* team; squad; square

squadrare, skwah-**drah**-ray, *v* to square; to look at closely

squagliarsi, skwah-l'**yar**-se, *v* to melt; to sneak off

squalificare, skwah-le-fe-**kah**-ray, *v* to disqualify

squalo, skwah-lo, *m* shark

squama, skwah-mah, *f* scale

squarcio, skwar-cho, *m* rip; hole; gash

squartare, skwar-**tah**-ray, *v* to quarter; to dismember

squilibrato, skwe-le-**brah**-to, *m* deranged person

squilibrio, skwe-lee-bre-o, *m* imbalance; derangement

squillare, skweel-**lah**-ray, *v* to ring; to blare

squillo, skweel-lo, *m* ring, ringing; blare

squisito*, skwe-zee-to, *adj* exquisite; delicious

sradicare, zrah-de-**kah**-ray, *v* to eradicate; to uproot

sregolato*, zray-go-**lah**-to, *adj* disorderly; immoderate; dissolute

stabile, stah-be-lay, *adj* stable, steady; settled; *m* building

stabilimento, stah-be-le-**men**-to, *m* factory, plant

stabilire, stah-be-lee-ray, *v* to establish; to fix; to decide

stabilirsi, stah-be-leer-se, *v* to settle

staccare, stahk-**kah**-ray, *v* to detach; to separate; to tear off; to leave behind

stadio, stah-de'o, *m* stadium; stage, phase

staffa, stahf-fah, *f* stirrup

staffetta, stahf-**fet**-tah, *f* relay race

stagionare, stah-jo-**nah**-ray, *v* to season; to mature

stagione, stah-**jo**-nay, *f* season

stagnare, stah-n'**yah**-ray, *v* to stagnate; to tin-plate; to stop

stagno, stah-n'yo, *m* pond; tin

stagnola, stah-**n'yo**-lah, *f* tinfoil

stalla, stahl-lah, *f* stable; cowshed

stallo, stahl-lo, *m* stall; stalemate

stamani, stah-**mah**-ne, *adv* this morning

stamattina, stah-maht-**tee**-nah, *adv* this morning

stampa, stahm-pah, *f* print; press; printed matter

stampante, stahm-**pahn**-tay, *f* printer

stampare, stahm-**pah**-ray, *v* to print; to publish; to strike

stampatello, stahm-pah-**tel**-lo, *m* block capitals

stampella, stahm-**pell**-lah, *f* crutch

stampo, stahm-po, *m* mould

stancare, stahn-**kah**-ray, *v* to tire; to bore; to annoy

stancarsi, stahn-**kar**-se, *v* to get tired; **– di,** to grow tired of

stanchezza, stahn-**ket**-tsah, *f* tiredness, fatigue

stanco, stahn-ko, *adj* tired

stanga, stahn-gah, *f* bar; shaft

stanghetta, stahn-**ghet**-tah, *f* (glasses) leg

stanotte, stah-**not**-tay, *adv* tonight

stante, stahn-tay, *adj* : **a sé –,** independent, separate; **seduta –,** on the spot

stantio, stahn-**tee**-o, *adj* stale; rancid

stantuffo, stahn-**toof**-fo, *m* piston

stanza, stahn-tsah, *f* room

stanziare, stahn-tse'**ah**-ray, *v* to allocate

stappare, stahp-**pah**-ray, *v* to uncork; to uncap

stare, stah-ray, *v* to be; to stand; to stay, to live; to suit; to fit

starnutire, star-noo-**tee**-ray, *v* to sneeze

starnuto, star-**noo**-to, *m* sneeze

stasera, stah-**say**-rah, *adv* this evening, tonight

statista, stah-**tiss**-tah, *m* statesman

statistica, stah-**tiss**-te-kah, *f* statistics; statistic

stato, stah-to, *m* state; condition; status; **gli Stati Uniti,** *mpl* the United States

statua, stah-too'ah, *f* statue

statura, stah-**too**-rah, *f* height; stature

statuto, stah-**too**-to, *m* statute

stazionario, stah-tse'o-**nah**-re'o, *adj* stable, unchanged

stazione, stah-tse'o-**nay,** *f* station; resort

stazza, staht-tsah, *f* tonnage

stecca, stek-kah, *f* stick; rib; carton; splint; cue; **fare una –,** to sing the wrong note

stecchino, stek-**kee**-no, *m* tooth-pick

steccato, stek-**kah**-to, *m* fence

stella, stell-lah, *f* star; **– alpina,** edelweiss; **– di mare,** starfish

stelo, stay-lo, *m* stem

stemma, stem-mah, *m* coat of arms

stendere, sten-**day**-ray, *v* to stretch; to spread; to hang out; to lay down; to draw up

stenodattilografo, -a, stay-no-daht-te-lo-grah-fo, *m/f* shorthand-typist

stenografia, stay-no-grah-fe'ah, *f* shorthand

stentare, sten-**tah**-ray, *v* : **– a,** to find it hard to

stento, sten-to, *m* **a –,** with difficulty; **stenti,** hardship

sterco, stair-ko, *m* dung

stereo, stay-ray'o, *m* stereo

stereotipo, stay-ray'o-te-po, *m* stereotype

sterile, stay-ree-lay, sterile; barren; futile

sterilizzare, stay-re-lid-dzah-ray, *v* to sterilize

sterlina, stair-**lee**-nah, *f* pound (sterling)

sterminare, stair-me-**nah**-ray, *v* to exterminate

sterminio, stair-**mee**-ne'o, *m* extermination

sterno, stair-no, *m* breastbone

sterzo, stair-tso, *m* steering wheel

stesso, stess-so, *adj & pron* same; **lei stessa,** she herself; **fa lo –,** it doesn't matter

stesura, stay-**soo**-rah, *f* drafting; draft

stile, stee-lay, *m* style

stilista, stee-**leess**-stah, *m/f* designer

stilla, still-lah, *f* drop

stillare, still-**lah**-ray, *v* to drip; to ooze

stima, stee-mah, *f* esteem; estimate, assessment,

valuation

stimare, ste-**mah**-ray, *v* to respect; to value

stimolo, stee-mo-lo, *m* stimulus

stinco, stin-ko, *m* shin

stingere, stin-jay-ray, *v* to fade

stipare, ste-**pah**-ray, *v* to cram

stipendio, ste-**pen**-de'o, *m* salary

stipulare, ste-poo-**lah**-ray, *v* to draw up

stirare, ste-**rah**-ray, *v* to iron; to stretch

stirpe, steer-pay, *f* descent; descendants

stitichezza, ste-te-**ket**-tsah, *f* constipation

stiva, stee-vah, *f* (ship) hold

stivale, ste-**vah**-lay, *m* boot

stivaletti, ste-vah-**let**-te, *mpl* ankle boots

stivare, ste-**vah**-ray, *v* to stow

stizza, steet-tsah, *f* anger

stizzirsi, steet-**tsir**-se, *v* to become vexed

stoccata, stock-**kah**-tah, *f* stab; thrust; shot

stoffa, **stoff**-fah, *f* cloth, material

stomachevole, sto-mah-**kay**-vo-lay, *adj* disgusting

stomaco, sto-**mah**-ko, *m* stomach

stonare, sto-**nah**-ray, *v* to be out of tune

stonatura, sto-nah-**too**-rah, *f* false note

stop, stop, *m* brake-light; stop sign; stop

stoppa, stop-pah, *f* tow

stoppia, stop-pe'ah, *f* stubble

stoppino, stop-**pee**-no, *m* wick

storcere, stor-chay-ray, *v* to twist

stordire, stor-**dee**-ray, *v* to stun

storia, sto-re'ah, *f* history; tale; story; business

storione, sto-re'o-nay, *m* sturgeon

stormire, stor-**mee**-ray, *v* to rustle

stormo, stor-mo, *m* flock

stornare, stor-**nah**-ray, *v* to transfer

storpiare, stor-pe'**ah**-ray, *v* to cripple; to mangle

storpio, stor-pe'o, *m* cripple

storta, stor-tah, *f* sprain, twist

storto, stor-to, *adj* bent; twisted; crooked

stoviglie, sto-vee-l'yay, *fpl* dishes, crockery

strabico, **strah**-be-ko, *adj* squint; **essere –**, to have

a squint

strabiliante, strah-be-l'**yahn**-tay, *adj* amazing

strabismo, strah-**biss** mo, *m* squinting

stracciare, straht-**chah**-ray, *v* to tear; to beat

straccio, **straht**-cho, *m* rag; cloth; *adj* : **carta straccia**, wastepaper

straccione, **-a**, straht-cho-nay; *m/f* ragamuffin

stracotto, strah-**kot**-to, *adj* overcooked

strada, **strah**-dah, *f* road, street; way

strage, strah-jay, *f* massacre

stralunato, strah-loo-**nah**-to, *adj* staring; dazed

stramazzare, strah-**maht**-tsah-ray, *v* to fall heavily

stramberia, strahm-bay-**ree**-ah, *f* eccentricity

stranezza, strah-**net**-tsah, *f* strangeness; odd thing

strangolare, strahn-go-**lah**-ray, *v* to strangle

straniero, **-a**, strah-ne'**ay**-ro, *adj* foreign; *m/f* foreigner

strano*, **strah**-no, *adj* strange, odd

straordinario, strah-or-de-**nah**-re'o, *adj* extraordinary; special; *m* overtime

strapazzare, strah-**paht**-

tsah-ray, *v* to ill-treat; to tire out

strapazzo, strah-**paht**-tso, *m* fatigue, strain; **da –**, third rate

strappare, strahp-**pah**-ray, *v* to tear, to rip; to tear off; to pull up; to snatch

strappo, **strahp**-po, *m* tear; **– muscolare**, torn muscle

straripare, strah-re-**pah**-ray, *v* to overflow

strascicare, strah-she-**kah**-ray, *v* to drag; to drawl

strascico, strah-**she**-ko, *m* (gown) train; *fig* after-effects

strato, **strah**-to, *m* stratum; layer; coat, coating

stratosfera, strah-tos-**sfay**-rah, *f* stratosphere

stravagante, strah-vah-**gahn**-tay, *adj* eccentric

stravolgere, strah-**voll**-jay-ray, *v* to upset; to contort; to shake; to distort

straziare, strah-tse'**ah**-ray, *v* to torture, to torment

strazio, **strah**-tse'o, *m* torture; disaster

strega, **stray**-gah, *f* witch

stregare, stray-**gah**-ray, *v* to bewitch

stregone, stray-**go**-nay, *m* wizard; witch doctor

stremare, stray-**mah**-ray, *v* to exhaust

stremo, **stray**-mo, *m* very end, limit

strenna, **stren**-nah, *f* Christmas present

strepitare, stray-pe-**tah**-ray, *v* to yell and shout

strepito, **stray**-pe-to, *m* din

stress, stress, *m* stress

stressante, stress-**sahn**-tay, *adj* stressful

stressato, stress-**sah**-to, *adj* under stress

stretta, **stret**-tah, *f* grip; squeeze; **una – di mano**, a handshake

strettezza, stret-**tet**-tsah, *f* narrowness

stretto, **stret**-to, *adj** narrow; tight; close; exact; *m* strait

strettoia, stret-to-e'**ah**, *f* bottleneck

stria, **stree**-ah, *f* streak

stridere, **stree**-day-ray, *v* to shriek; to clash

stridore, **stree**-do-ray, *m* shrieking

strigare, stre-**gah**-ray, *v* to unravel

strigliare, stre-l'**yah**-ray, *v* to curry

strillare, streel-**lah**-ray, *v* to scream

strillo, **streel**-lo, *m* cry, scream

strimpellare, streem-pell-**lah**-ray, *v* to strum away on; to plonk away on

stringa, **streen**-gah, *f* (shoes, etc.) lace

stringere, **streen**-jay-ray, *v* to tighten; to squeeze; to clench; to grip; to conclude; to be tight

stringersi, **streen**-jair-se, *v* to squeeze up

striscia, **stree**-she'ah, *f* strip; stripe; **strisce pedonali**, zebra crossing

strisciare, stre-she'**ah**-ray, *v* to creep, to crawl; to drag

stritolare, stre-to **lah**-ray, *v* to crush, to grind

strizzare, street-**tsah**-ray, *v* to wring; **– l'occhio**, to wink

strofa, **stro**-fah, *f* strophe

strofinaccio, stro-fe-**naht**-cho, *m* duster, cloth

strofinare, stro-fe-**nah**-ray, *v* to rub

stropicciare, stro-pit-**chah**-ray, *v* to rub; to crease

strozzare, strot-**tsah**-ray, *v* to choke; to strangle

strozzino, strot-**tsee**-no, *m* shark, moneylender

struggere, strood-**jay**-ray, *v* to melt

struggersi, strood-**jair**-se, *v* to melt; to be

consumed

strumento, stroo-**men**-to, *m* instrument; tool

strutto, stroot-to, *m* lard

struttura, stroot-**too**-rah, *f* structure

struzzo, stroot-tso, *m* ostrich

studente, -essa, stoo-den-tay, stoo-den-**tess**-sah, *m/f* student

studiare, stoo-de-**'ah**-ray, *v* to study

studio, stoo-de'o, *m* studying; study; office; studio

stufa, stoo-fah, *f* stove; – **elettrica,** electric heater

stufare, stoo-**fah**-ray, *v* to stew; to bore

stufato, stoo-**fah**-to, *m* stew

stufo, stoo-fo, *adj* fed up

stuoia, stoo'o-e'ah, *f* mat

stuolo, stoo'o-lo, *m* crowd

stupefacente, stoo-pay-fah-**chen**-tay, *adj* amazing; *m* drug, narcotic

stupido, -a, stoo-pe-do, *adj* stupid; *m/f* fool

stupire, stoo-pee-ray, *v* to amaze

stuprare, stoo prah-ray, *v* to rape

sturare, stoo-**rah**-ray, *v* to uncork; to unblock

stuzzicadenti, stoot-tse-

kah-**den**-te, *m* toothpick

stuzzicare, stoot-tse-**kah**-ray, *v* to poke (at); to whet; to tease

su, soo, *prep* on; about; around; by; *adv* up; upstairs; *interj* come on!

subacqueo, soob-**ack**-kway'o, *adj* underwater; *m* skindiver

subbuglio, soob-**boo**-l'yo, *m* turmoil

subconscio, soob-**kon**-sho, *m* subconscious

subdolo*, soob-do-lo, *adj* underhand

subire, soo-bee-ray, *v* to suffer; to undergo

subitaneo*, soo-be-**tah**-nay-o, *adj* sudden

subito, soo-be-to, *adv* straight away, immediately, at once

succedere, soot-**chay**-day-ray, *v* to happen; – **a,** to succeed; to follow

successivo, soot-ches-**see**-vo, *adj* following

successo, soot-**chays**-so, *m* success

successore, soot-ches-**so**-ray, *m* successor

succhiare, sook-ke'**ah**-ray, *v* to suck

succhiotto, sook-ke'ot-to, *m* dummy; lovebite

succo, sook-ko, *m* juice;

fig gist

succursale, sook-koor-sah-lay, *f* (office) branch

sud, sood, *m* south; *adj* southern; **in direzione** –, southwards

sudare, soo-dah-ray, *v* to sweat; *fig* to work hard

sudario, soo-dah-re'o, *m* shroud

suddetto, sood-det-to, *adj* above-mentioned

suddito, sood-de-to, *m* subject

suddividere, sood-de-vee-day-ray, *v* to subdivide

sud-est, sood-esst, *m* south-east

sudicio, soo-de-cho, *adj* dirty, filthy; *m* dirt, filth

sudore, soo-**dor**-ay, *m* sweat

sud-ovest, sood-o-vest, *m* south-west

sufficiente, soof-fe-**chen**-tay, *adj* sufficient, enough

suffisso, soof-fiss-so, *m* suffix

suffragio, soof-**frah**-jo, *m* vote, suffrage

suggellare, sood-jell-lah-ray, *v* to seal

suggerimento, sood-jay-re-**men**-to, *m* suggestion; piece of advice

suggerire, sood-jay-ree-ray, *v* to suggest; to advise; to tell; to prompt

suggeritore, sood-jay-re-**tor**-ay, *m* prompter

suggestionare, sood-jay-ste'o-**nah**-ray, *v* to influence

sughero, soo-**gay**-ro, *m* cork

sugo, soo-go, *m* sauce; gravy; juice

sugoso, soo-**go**-zo, *adj* succulent, juicy

suicida, soo'e-**chee**-dah, *adj* suicidal; *m/f* (person) suicide

suicidarsi, soo'e-che-**dar**-se, *v* to commit suicide

suicidio, soo'e-**chee**-de-o, *m* suicide

suino, soo'e-no, *adj* pork; *m* pig; **i suini,** swine

sulfureo, sool-**foo**-ray-o, *adj* sulphureous

sunto, soonn-to, *m* synopsis

suo, soo-o, *adj* his; her; its; your; *pron* his; hers; its; yours

suocera, soo-o-**chay**-rah, *f* mother-in-law

suocero, soo-o-**chay**-ro, *m* father-in-law

suola, soo-o-lah, *f* (foot, shoe, etc.) sole

suolo, soo-o-lo, *m* soil; ground

suonare, soo-o-**nah**-ray, *v* to ring; to play; to sound; to strike

suono, soo-o-no, *m* sound

suora, soo-o-rah, *f* nun

superare, soo-pay-**rah**-ray, *v* to overcome; to surpass; to cross; to pass; to be over

superbia, soo-**pair**-be'ah, *f* pride

superbo, soo-**pair**-bo, *adj* proud; superb

superficiale, soo-pair-fe-**chah**-lay, *adj* superficial; light

superficie, soo-pair-**fee**-chay, *f* surface

superiore, soo-pair-re'o-ray, *adj* upper; higher; superior; *m* superior; **le superiori** secondary school

superlativo, soo-pair-lah-**tee**-vo, *adj* superlative; *m* superlative

supermercato, soo-pair-mayr-**kah**-to, *m* supermarket

superstite, soo-**pair**-ste-tay, *adj* surviving; *m/f* survivor

superstizione, soo-pair-stee-tse'o-nay, *f* superstition

suppellettile, soop-pell-**let**-te-lay, *m* utensil

suppergiù, soop-pair-joo,

adv more or less

supplente, soop-**plen**-tay, *m/f* supply teacher

supplica, soop-**ple**-kah, *f* request; plea

supplicare, soop-ple-**kah**-ray, *v* to implore

supplire, soop-**plee**-ray, *v* to stand in for

supplizio, soop-**plee**-tse'o, *m* torture; torment

supporre, soop-**por**-ray, *v* to suppose

supposta, soop-**poss**-stah, *f* suppository

suppurare, soop-poo-**rah**-ray, *v* to suppurate

supremo*, soo-**pray**-mo, *adj* supreme

surgelare, soor-jay-**lah**-ray, *v* to (deep-)freeze

surgelato, soor-jay-**lah**-to, *adj* (deep-)frozen; *m* **surgelati,** frozen food

surriscaldare, soor-riss-kahl-**dah**-ray, *v* to overheat

suscettibile, soo-shet-**tee**-be-lay, *adj* touchy; **– a,** subject to

suscitare, soo-she-**tah**-ray, *v* to raise; to cause

susina, soo-**zee**-nah, *f* plum

susino, soo-**zee**-no, *m* plum-tree

susseguente, sooss-say-

goo'**en**-tay, *adj*
subsequent, consecutive

sussidio, sooss-**see**-de'o, *m*
subsidy, benefit; aid

sussistere, sooss-**siss**-tay-ray, *v* to exist; to be valid

sussultare, soooss-sool-**tah**-ray, *v* to start

sussulto, sooss-**sool**-to, *m* start

sussurrare, soooss-soohr-**rah**-ray, *v* to whisper

sussurro, soooss-**soohr**-ro, *m* murmur; whisper

svagare, zvah-**gah**-ray, *v* to amuse

svago, zvah-go, *m* pastime; relaxation

svaligiare, zvah-le-**jah**-ray, *v* to rob, to burgle

svalutare, zvah-loo-**tah**-ray, *v* to devalue; to belittle

svalutazione, zvah-loo-tah-tse'**o**-nay, *f* devaluation

svanire, zvah-**nee**-ray, *v* to vanish

svantaggio, zvahn-**tahd**-jo, *m* disadvantage

svaporare, zvah-po-**rah**-ray, *v* to evaporate

svariato, zvah-re'**ah**-to, *adj* varied; various

svarione, zvah-re'o-nay, *m* blunder; misprint

svedese, zvay-**day**-zay, *adj* Swedish

sveglia, zvay-l'yah, *f* alarm-clock; reveille

svegliare, zvay-l'yah-ray, *v* to wake up; to awaken, to arouse

svegliarsi, zvay-l'**yar**-se, *v* to wake up

sveglio, zvay-l'yo, *adj* awake; smart

svelare, zvay-**lah**-ray, *v* to reveal

svelto, zvell-to, *adj* quick; brisk

svendere, zven-day-ray, *v* to sell off

svendita, zven-de-tah, *f* clearance sale

svenimento, zvay-ne-**men**-to, *m* fainting fit

svenire, zvay-**nee**-ray, *v* to faint

sventare, zven-**tah**-ray, *v* to foil

sventato*, zven-**tah**-to, *adj* scatterbrained; thoughtless, rash

sventolare, zven-to-**lah**-ray, *v* to wave; to flutter

sventrare, zven-**trah**-ray, *v* to disembowel; to rip open

sventura, zven-**too**-rah, *f* misfortune

sventurato*, zven-too-**rah**-to, *adj* unfortunate; unhappy

svenuto, zvay-**noo**-to, *adj* fainted

svergognare, zvair-go-n'**yah**-ray, *v* to shame

svergognato*, zvair-go-n'**yah**-to, *adj* shameless; impudent

svernare, zvair-**nah**-ray, *v* to winter

svestire, zvess-**tee**-ray, *v* to undress

Svezia, zvay-**tse**'ah, *f* Sweden

svezzare, zvet-**tsah**-ray, *v* to wean

sviare, zve'**ah**-ray, *v* to divert; to lead astray

svignarsela, zve-n'**yar**-say-lah, *v* to sneak off

sviluppare, zve-loop-**pah**-ray, *v* to develop

sviluppo, zve-**loop**-po, *m* development

svincolare, zvin-ko-**lah**-ray, *v* to free; to clear

svista, zviss-tah, *f* oversight, slip

svitare, zve-**tah**-ray, *v* to unscrew

Svizzera, zveet-tsay-rah, *f* Switzerland

svizzero, zveet-tsay-ro, *adj* Swiss

svogliato*, zvo-l'**yah**-to, *adj* lazy; listless

svolazzare, zvo-laht-**tsah**-ray, *v* to flutter

svolgere, zvoll-jay-ray,

v to unwind; to unroll;
to carry out; to
write

svolgersi, zvoll-jair-se, *v*
to unwind; to unroll; to
take place

svolta, zvoll-tah, *f* turn;
turning point

svoltare, zvoll-**tah**-ray, *v*
to turn

svuotare, zvoo'o-**tah**-ray, *v*
to empty

tabaccaio, -a, tah-bahk-**kah**-e'o, *m/f* tobacconist

tabaccheria, tah-bahk-kay-**ree**-ah, *f* tobacconist's

tabacco, tah-**bahk**-ko, *m* tobacco

tabella, tah-**bell**-lah, *f* table; list

tabulato, tah-boo-**lah**-to, *m* printout

tacca, **tahk**-kah, *f* notch, nick

taccagno, tahk-**kah**-n'yo, *adj* mean, stingy

tacchino, tahk-**kee**-no, *m* turkey

tacciare, taht-**chah**-ray, *v* to accuse

tacco, **tahk**-ko, *m* heel

taccuino, tahk-koo'**e**-no, *m* notebook

tacere, tah-**chay**-ray, *v* to keep silent (about)

tachimetro, tah-**kee**-may-tro, *m* speedometer

tacito*, **tah**-che-to, *adj* silent; tacit

tafano, tah-**fah**-no, *m* horse-fly

tafferuglio, tahf-fay-**roo**-l'yo, *m* scuffle

taglia, **tah**-l'yah, *f* size; reward

tagliacarte, tah-l'yah-**kar**-tay, *m* paper-knife

taglialegna, tah-l'yah-**lay**-n'yah, *m* wood-cutter

tagliando, tah-l'**yahn**-do, *m* coupon

tagliare, tah-l'**yah**-ray, *v* to cut; to slice; to chop; to cut off; (tree) to fell

tagliente, tah-l'**yen**-tay, *adj* sharp

taglio, **tah**-l'yo, *m* cut; cutting; edge; (meat) joint; length

tagliuzzare, tah-l'yoot-**tsah**-ray, *v* to cut into small pieces; to shred

talco, **tahl**-ko, *m* talcum powder

tale, **tah**-lay, *adj* such; **tale ... tale ...,** like ... like ...; *pron* **un –,** someone

talento, tah-**len**-to, *m* talent

talloncino, tahl-lon-**chee**-no, *m* counterfoil; coupon

tallone, tahl-**lo**-nay, *m* heel

talmente, tahl-**men**-tay, *adv* so; so much

talora, tah-**lor**-ah, *adv* sometimes

talpa, **tahl**-pah, *f* mole

talvolta, tahl-**vol**-tah, *adv* sometimes

tamburellare, tahm-boo-rel-**lah**-ray, *v* to drum

tamburo, tahm-**boo**-ro, *m* drum; drummer; cylinder

Tamigi, tah-**mee**-je, *m* Thames

tamponamento, tahm-po-nah-**men**-to, *m* collision

tamponare, tahm-po-**nah**-ray, *v* to bump into; to plug

tampone, tahm-**po**-nay, *m med* wad, pad; buffer; tampon

tana, tah-nah, *f* den; lair

tanfo, tahn-fo, *m* stench

tangente, tahn-**jen**-tay, *f* tangent; share; kickback

tantino, tahn-**tee**-no, *adv* : **un –,** a bit, a little

tanto, tahn-to, *adj* a lot of, much, many; so much, so many; *pron* a lot, much, many; *adv* so much; very; so; – ... **quanto,** as much ... as; as ... as

tappa, tahp-pah, *f* stop; stage; lap

tappare, tahp-**pah**-ray, *v* to cork; to plug

tappeto, tahp-**pay**-to, *m* carpet; rug

tappezzeria, tahp-pet-tsay-**ree**-ah, *f* soft furnishings; upholstery; wallpaper

tappezziere, tahp-pet-tse'**ay**-ray, *m* upholsterer

tappo, tahp-po, *m* top, stopper; cork; lid

tara, tah-rah, *f* tare; hereditary defect

tarchiato, tar-ke'**ah**-to, *adj* sturdy

tardare, tar-**dah**-ray, *v* to be late; to delay

tardi, tar-de, *adv* late; **più –,** later

tardo, tar-do, *adj* late; slow

targa, tar-gah, *f* number plate; name plate

tarlo, tar-lo, *m* wood-worm

tarma, tar-mah, *f* moth

tartagliare, tar-tah-l'**yah**-ray, *v* to stammer

tartaruga, tar-tah-**roo**-gah, *f* tortoise; turtle; tortoiseshell

tartina, tar-**tee**-nah, *f* canapé

tartufo, tar-**too**-fo, *m* truffle

tasca, tahss-kah, *f* pocket

tassa, tahss-sah, *f* tax; duty; fee

tassametro, tahss-**sah**-may-tro, *m* taximeter

tassare, tahss-**sah**-ray, *v* to tax

tassativo*, tahss-sah-**tee**-vo, *adj* peremptory

tassista, tahss-**see**-stah, *m/f* taxi driver

tasso, tahss-so, *m* rate; percentage; badger; yew-tree

tastare, tahss-**tah**-ray, *v* to feel

tastiera, tahss-te'**ay**-rah, *f* key-board

tasto, tahss-to, *m* key, button; touch

tatuaggio, tah-too'**ahd**-jo, *m* tattoo

tatto, taht-to, *m* tact; touch

tavola, tah-**vo**-lah, *f* table; index; plank; plate; tablet; panel painting

tavolato, tah-vo-**lah**-to, *m* boarding; wooden floor

tavoletta, tah-vo-**let**-tah, *f* tablet; bar

tavolo, tah-vo-lo, *m* table

tavolozza, tah-vo-**lot**-tsah, *f* palette

taxi, tahk-se, *m* taxi

tazza, taht-tsah, *f* cup, mug

te, tay, *pron* you, to you

tè, tay, *m* tea

teatro, tay-**ah**-tro, *m* theatre

tecnico, -a, tek-ne-ko, *adj* technical; *m/f* technician; expert

tecnologia, tek-no-lo-jee-ah, *f* technology

tediare, tay-de'**ah**-ray, *v* to bore

tegame, tay-**gah**-may, *m* pan

tegola, tay-go-lah, *f* tile

teiera, tay-yay-rah, *f* tea-pot

tela, tay-lah, *f* cloth; canvas; – **cerata,** oilskin; tarpaulin

telaio, tay-lah-e'o, *m* loom; frame

telecamera, tay-lay-**kah**-may-rah, *f* television

camera

telecomando, tay-lay-ko-**mahn**-do, *m* remote control

telefonare, tay-lay-fo-**nah**-ray, *v* to (tele)phone, to ring

telefonata, tay-lay-fo-**nah**-tah, *f* telephone-call; – **interurbana,** long-distance call

telefono, tay-**lay**-fo-no, *m* telephone, phone

telegiornale, tay-lay-jor-**nah**-lay, *m* (television) news

televisione, tay-lay-ve-ze'o-nay, *f* television

televisore, tay-lay-ve-**zo**-ray, *m* television set

tema, **tay**-mah, *m* theme; essay

temerario, tay-may-**rah**-re'o, *adj* reckless

temere, tay-**may**-ray, *v* to fear, to be afraid (of)

tempaccio, tem-**paht**-cho, *m* very bad weather

tempera, **tem**-pay-rah, *f* tempera

temperino, tem-pay-**ree**-no, *m* penknife

temperatura, tem-pay-rah-**too**-rah, *f* temperature

tempestivo*, tem-pess-**tee**-vo, *adj* timely

tempia, **tem**-pe'ah, *f*

(forehead) temple

tempio, **tem**-pe'o, *m* *relig* temple

tempo, **tem**-po, *m* time; weather

temporale, tem-po-**rah**-lay, *adj* temporal; *m* storm

temporaneo*, tem-po-**rah**-nay-o, *adj* temporary

temporeggiare, tem-po-red-**jah**-ray, *v* to temporize

tenace, tay-**nah**-chay, *adj* tenacious

tenaglie, tay-**nah**-l'yay, *fpl* pincers

tenda, **ten**-dah, *f* tent; awning; curtain

tendere, **ten**-day-ray, *v* to stretch; to hold out; – **a,** to tend towards

tendina, ten-**dee**-nah, *f* curtain; blind

tendine, **ten**-de-nay, *m* tendon, sinew

tenebre, **tay**-nay-bray, *fpl* darkness

tenebroso, tay-nay-**bro**-zo, *adj* dark, gloomy

tenente, tay-**nen**-tay, *m* lieutenant

tenere, tay-**nay**-ray, *v* to hold; to keep; – **a,** to care about

tenerezza, tay-nay-**ret**-tsah, *f* tenderness

tenero*, **tay**-nay-ro, *adj*

tender, delicate

tenia, tay-**ne**'ah, *m* tapeworm

tennis, **tenn**-neess, *m* tennis

tennista, tenn-**neess**-tah, *m/f* tennis player

tenore, tay-**nor**-ay, *m* tenor; standard

tentare, ten-**tah**-ray, *v* to tempt; to try

tentoni, ten-**to**-ne, *adv* : **andare a –,** to grope one's way

tenue, **tay**-noo'ay, *adj* thin; slender

tenuta, tay-**noo**-tah, *f* capacity; outfit; estate

teoria, tay-o-**ree**-ah, *f* theory

teppista, tayp-**piss**-tah, *m/f* hooligan

tergicristallo, tair-je-kriss-**stahll**-lo, *m* windscreen wiper

tergiversare, tair-je-vair-**sah**-ray, *v* to shilly-shally

tergo, **tair**-go, *m* : **vedi a –,** please turn over

terme, **tair**-may, *fpl* spa; baths

terminal, tair-me-**nahl**, *m* (air) terminal

terminale, tair-me-**nah**-lay, *adj* final; *m* terminal

terminare, tair-me-**nah**-ray, *v* to end, to finish

termine, **tair**-me-nay, *m*

term; limit; end; word

termometro, tair-mo-may-tro, *m* thermometer

termosifone, tair-mo-se-fo-nay, *m* radiator

termostato, tair-mo-stah-to, *m* thermostat

terra, tair-rah, *f* earth; country; land; **per –**, on the floor, on the ground

terrazza, tair-raht-tsah, *f* balcony; terrace

terremoto, tair-ray-mo-to, *m* earthquake

terreno, tair-ray-no, *adj* worldly, earthly; *m* land; ground

terrestre, tair-ress-tray, *adj* of the earth, earth's; land; earthly, worldly

terribile, tair-ree-be-lay, *adj* dreadful, terrible

terriccio, tair-rit-cho, *m* soil

territorio, tair-re-to-re'o, *m* territory

terrore, tair-ro-ray, *m* terror

terrorismo, tair-ro-riz-mo, *m* terrorism

terrorista, tair-ro-riss-tah, *m/f* terrorist

terza, tair-tsah, *f* third gear

terzo, tair-tso, *adj & m* third; **terzi**, others

teschio, tess-ke'o, *m* skull

tesi, tay-ze, *f* thesis; theory

teso, tay-zo, *adj* taut; tense; strained

tesoreria, tay-zo-ray-ree-ah, *f* treasury

tesoro, tay-zo-ro, *m* treasure; *fig* riches

tessera, tess-say-rah, *f* season-ticket; member's card

tessere, tess-say-ray, *v* to weave

tessile, tess-se-lay, *adj* textile

tessitore, -**trice**, tess-se-tor-ay, tess-se-tree-chay, *m/f* weaver

tessitura, tess-se-too-rah, *f* weaving

tessuto, tess-soo-to, *m* material, cloth

testa, tess-tah, *f* head

testamento, tess-tah-men-to, *m* will

testardo, tess-tar-do, *adj* stubborn, pig-headed

testare, tess-tah-ray, *v* to test

teste, tess-tay, *m & f* witness

testicolo, tess-tee-ko-lo, *m* testicle

testimone, tess-te-mo-nay, *m/f* witness

testimonianza, tess-te-mo-ne'ahn-tsah, *f* deposition; evidence; proof

testimoniare, tess-te-mo-ne'ah-ray, *v* to testify

testo, tess-to, *m* text

testuggine, tess-tood-je-nay, *f* tortoise; turtle

tetano, tay-tah-no, *m* tetanus

tetro, tay-tro, *adj* gloomy

tetta, tet-tah, *f fam* tit

tetto, tet-to, *m* roof

tettoia, tet-to-e'ah, *f* canopy; roof

Tevere, tay-vay-ray, *m* Tiber

thermos, tair-mos, *m* Thermos (flask) TM

ti, tee, *pron* you; to you; *refl* yourself

tibia, tee-be'ah, *f* shin-bone

ticchettio, tik-ket-te'o, *m* ticking; clatter; patter

tiepido, te'ay-pe-do, *adj* lukewarm, tepid

tifo, tee-fo, *m* typhus; **fare il – per**, to be a fan of

tifone, te-fo-nay, *m* typhoon

tifoso, te-fo-zo, *m* (enthusiast) fan

tiglio, tee-l'yo, *m* lime-tree

tiglioso, te-l'yo-zo, *adj* tough

tigna, tee-n'yah, *f* ringworm

tigre, tee-gray, *f* tiger, tigress

timbrare, teem-brah-ray, *v* to stamp

timbro, teem-bro, *m* stamp

timido*, tee-me-do, *adj* shy

timo, tee-mo, *m* thyme

timone, te-**mo-**nay, *m* rudder

timoniere, te-mo-ne'**ay-**ray, *m* helmsman

timore, te-**mo-**ray, *m* fear

tingere, tin-jay-ray, *v* to dye

tino, tee-no, *m* vat

tinozza, tin-**not-**tsah, *f* tub

tinta, tin-tah, *f* dye; paint; colour, shade

tintinnio, tin-tin-**nee-**o, *m* tinkling

tintoria, tin-to-**ree-**ah, *f* dyeworks; dry cleaners

tipo, tee-po, *m* type

tipografo, te-**po-**grah-fo, *m* typographer

tir, teer, *m* heavy goods vehicle

tiraggio, te-**rahd-**jo, *m* draught

tiranneggiare, te-rahn-ned-**jah-**ray, *v* to tyrannize

tiranno, te-**rahn-**no, *m* tyrant

tirare, te-**rah-**ray, *v* to pull; to throw; to draw; to fire; to be tight; – **calci,** to kick

tirata, te-**rah-**tah, *f* pull; tedious speech

tirato, te-**rah-**to, *adj* drawn; taut; mean

tiratura, te-**rah-**too-rah, *f* circulation; printing

tirchio, teer-ke'o, *adj* stingy

tiro, tee-ro, *m* shooting; shot; throwing; throw; draught; trick

tirocinio, te-ro-**chee-**ne'o, *m* apprenticeship; training

tisana, te-**zah-**nah, *f* herbal tea

tisi, tee-ze, *f* consumption

tisico, tee-ze-ko, *adj* consumptive

titolare, te-to-**lah-**ray, *m* holder, incumbent; owner

titolo, tee-to-lo, *m* title; headline; qualifications; security; share, stock

titubare, te-too-**bah-**ray, *v* to hesitate

tizio, teet-tse'o, *m* fellow

tizzone, tit-**tso-**nay, *m* brand; live coal

toccare, tock-**kah-**ray, *v* to touch; to feel; to concern; to mention; – **a,** to happen to; to be up to

tocco, tock-ko, *m* touch; stroke

togliere, to-l'yay-ray, *v* to take away; to take off

tolda, toll-dah, *f* deck

tolleranza, toll-lay-**rahn-**tsah, *f* tolerance

tollerare, toll-lay-**rah-**ray, *v* to tolerate

tomaia, to-mah-e'ah, *f* (shoe) upper

tomba, tom-bah, *f* tomb

tombino, tom-**bee-**no, *m* manhole

tombola, tom-bo-lah, *f* bingo

tomo, to-mo, *m* volume

tondo, ton-do, *adj* round

tonfo, ton-fo, *m* thud

tonnellaggio, ton-nell-**lahd-**jo, *m* tonnage

tonnellata, ton-nell-**lah-**tah, *f* ton

tonno, ton-no, *m* tuna (fish)

tono, to-no, *m* tone; key; shade

tonsille, ton-**sill-**lay, *fpl* tonsils

topo, to-po, *m* mouse

toppa, top-pah, *f* keyhole; patch

torace, to-**rah-**chay, *m* chest

torba, tor-bah, *f* peat

torbido, tor-be-do, *adj* cloudy; *fig* dark

torcere, tor-chay-ray, *v* to twist

torchio, tor-ke'o, *m* press

torcia, tor-chah, *f* torch

torcicollo, tor-che-**kol-**lo, *m* stiff-neck

tordo, tor-do, *m* thrush

tormentare, tor-men-tah-ray, *v* to torment; to pester

tormentarsi, tor-men-tar-se, *v* to fret

tornaconto, tor-nah-kon-to, *m* advantage, benefit; interest

tornare, tor-nah-ray, *v* to come back, to go back, to return; to become again; to work out

torneo, tor-nay-o, *m* tournament

tornio, tor-ne'o, *m* lathe

toro, to-ro, *m* bull; **Toro,** Taurus

torpedine, tor-pay-de-nay, *f* torpedo

torpediniera, tor-pay-de-ne'ay-rah, *f* torpedo-boat

torpido, tor-pe-do, *adj* torpid

torre, tor-ray, *f* tower

torrefare, tor-ray-fah-ray, *v* to roast

torreggiare, tor-red-jah-ray, *v* to tower

torrente, tor-ren-tay, *m* torrent

torretta, tor-ret-tah, *f* turret

torrido, tor-re-do, *adj* torrid

torrone, tor-ro-nay, *m* nougat

torso, tor-so, *m* trunk, torso

torsolo, tor-so-lo, *m* core; stump

torta, tor-tah, *f* cake; pie

torto, tor-to, *adj* twisted; crooked; *m* wrong; fault; **aver –,** to be wrong

tortora, tor-to-rah, *f* turtle-dove

torturare, tor-too-rah-ray, *v* to torture

tortura, tor-too-rah, *f* torture

torvo, tor-vo, *adj* surly

tosare, to-zah-ray, *v* to shear, to clip

tosse, toss-say, *f* cough

tossico, toss-se-ko, *adj* toxic

tossicodipendente, toss-se-ko-de-pen-den-tay, *m/f* drug addict

tossire, toss-see-ray, *v* to cough

tostapane, toss-tah-pah-nay, *m* toaster

tostare, toss-tah-ray, *v* to toast; to roast

tosto, toss-to, *adj* : **faccia tosta,** cheek

tovaglia, to-vah-l'yah, *f* table-cloth

totale,* to-tah-lay, *adj* total; *m* total

tovagliolo, to-vah-l'yo-lo, *m* napkin

tozzo, tot-tso, *adj* stocky;

m – **di pane,** crust of bread

tra, trah, *prep* among; between; within, in

traballare, trah-bahl-lah-ray, *v* to stagger; to be shaky

traboccare, trah-bock-kah-ray, *v* to overflow

trabocchetto, trah-bock-ket-to, *m* trap

tracannare, trah-kahn-nah-ray, *v* to gulp down

traccia, traht-chah, *f* trace; mark; footprint; trail, track

tracciare, traht-chah-ray, *v* to trace; to draw

trachea, trah-kay-ah, *f* windpipe

tracolla, trah-kohl-lah, *f* shoulder strap; **portare a –,** to carry over one's shoulder

tracollo, trah-kol-lo, *m* ruin, collapse

tracotanza, trah-ko-tahn-tsah, *f* arrogance

tradimento, trah-de-men-to, *m* betrayal; treason

tradire, trah-dee-ray, *v* to betray; to be unfaithful to; to reveal

traditore, -trice, trah-de-tor-ay, trah-de-tree-chay, *m/f* traitor

traducibile, trah-doo-chee-be-lay, *adj*

translatable

tradurre, trah-**doohr**-ray, *v* to translate

traduttore, **-trice**, trah-doot-**tor**-ay, trah-doot-**tree**-chay, *m/f* translator

traduzione, trah-doo-tse'o-nay, *f* translation

traente, trah-**en**-tay, *m/f* (cheque) drawer

trafelato*, trah-fay-**lah**-to, *adj* out of breath

trafficare, trahf-fe-**kah**-ray, *v* to trade; to deal in

traffico, **trahf**-fe-ko, *m* traffic; trade

trafiggere, trah-**fid**-jay-ray, *v* to run through, to stab; to pierce

trafiletto, trah-fe-**let**-to, *m* short article

traforare, trah-fo-**rah**-ray, *v* to pierce; to drill; to tunnel trough

traforo, trah-**fo**-ro, *m* tunnel

trafugare, trah-foo-**gah**-ray, *v* to purloin

tragedia, trah-**jay**-de'ah, *f* tragedy

traghettare, trah-ghet-**tah**-ray, *v* to ferry

traghetto, trah-**ghet**-to, *m* ferry

tragittare, trah-jit-**tah**-ray, *v* to cross

tragitto, trah-**jit**-to, *m* crossing, passage;

journey

traguardo, trah-goo'**ar**-do, *m* finishing line; goal

trainare, trah-e-**nah**-ray, *v* to haul; to tow

traino, trah-e-no, *m* pulling; towing

tralasciare, trah-lah-she'**ah**-ray, *v* to omit

traliccio, trah-**lit**-cho, *m* pylon

trama, trah-mah, *f* weft; plot

tramandare, trah-mahn-**dah**-ray, *v* to pass on

tramare, trah-**mah**-ray, *v* to plot; to weave

trambusto, trahm-**booss**-to, *m* hubbub

tramezzino, trah-med-**dzee**-no, *m* sandwich

tramite, trah-me-tay, *prep* through

tramontana, trah-mon-**tah**-nah, *f* north wind

tramontare, trah-mon-**tah**-ray, *v* to set

tramonto, trah-**mon**-to, *m* setting; sunset

tramortire, trah-mor-**tee**-ray, *v* to stun

trampoli, **trahm**-po-le, *mpl* stilts

trampolino, trahm-po-lee-no, *m* springboard, diving board; ski jump

tramutare, trah-moo-**tah**-ray, *v* – **in**, to change

into

tranello, trah-**nell**-lo, *m* trap

trangugiare, trahn-goo-jah-ray, *v* to gulp

tranne, trahn-nay, *prep* except (for)

tranquillante, trahn-kwil-**lahn**-tay, *m* tranquillizer

tranquillità, trahn-kwil-le-tah, *f* calm; peacefulness; peace of mind

tranquillo*, trahn-**kwill**-lo, *adj* quiet; calm

transazione, trahn-zah-tse'o-nay, *f* transaction

transenna, trahn-**senn**-nah, *f* barrier

transitabile, trahn-ze-tah-be-lay, *adj* passable

trapanare, trah-pah-**nah**-ray, *v* to drill

trapassare, trah-pahss-**sah**-ray, *v* to pierce

trapelare, trah-pay-**lah**-ray, *v* to filter through; to leak out

trapezio, trah-**pay**-tse'o, *m* trapezium; trapeze

trapiantare, trah-pe'ahn-**tah**-ray, *v* to transplant

trapianto, trah-pe'**ahn**-to, *m* transplant; transplanting

trappola, **trahp**-po-lah, *f* trap

trapunta, trah-**poonn**-tah,

f quilt

trarre, trahr-ray, *v* to draw, to pull; to obtain, to get

trasalire, trah-sah-lee-ray, *v* to jump

trasandato, trah-sahn-**dah**-to, *adj* shabby

trasbordare, trahss-bor-**dah**-ray, *v* to transfer; to tranship

trascendere, trah-**shen**-day-ray, *v* to transcend; to go beyond

trascinare, trah-she-**nah**-ray, *v* to drag; to haul

trascorrere, trahss-**kor**-ray-ray, *v* to pass; (time) to spend

trascrivere, trahss-**kree**-vay-ray, *v* to write down; to transliterate; to transcribe

trascurare, trahss-koo-**rah**-ray, *v* to neglect; to overlook

trasferire, trahss-fay-**ree**-ray, *v* to transfer

trasferirsi, trahss-fay-**reer**-se, *v* to move

trasformare, trahss-for-**mah**-ray, *v* to transform

trasfusione, trahss-foo-ze'o-nay, *f* transfusion

trasgredire, trahss-gray-**dee**-ray, *v* to trespass; to infringe

traslocare, trahss-lo-**kah**-

ray, *v* to move

trasloco, trahss-**lo**-ko, *m* removal; move

trasmettere, trahss-**met**-tay-ray, *v* to pass on (to); to send; to transmit; to broadcast

trasmissione, trahss-miss-se'o-nay, *f* transmission; broadcast; programme

trasognato, trah-so-n'yah-to, *adj* dreamy

trasparente, trahss-pah-**ren**-tay, *adj* transparent; see-through

traspirare, trahss-pe-**rah**-ray, *v* to perspire

traspirazione, trahss-pe-rah-tse'o-nay, *f* perspiration

trasporre, trahss-**por**-ray, *v* to transpose

trasportare, trahss-por-**tah**-ray, *v* to carry; to transport

trasporto, trahss-**por**-to, *m* transport

trastullarsi, trahss-tooll-**lar**-se, *v* to play

trastullo, trahss-**tooll**-lo, *m* game

trasvolare, trahss-vo-**lah**-ray, *v* to fly across, to fly over

tratta, traht-tah, *f* draft; (slave) trade

trattamento, traht-tah-**men**-to, *m* treatment;

service

trattare, traht-**tah**-ray, *v* to treat; to handle; to discuss; to deal in; to negotiate; – **di**, to deal with; **si tratta di …,** it's about …

trattativa, traht-tah-**tee**-vah, *f* negotiation

trattato, traht-**tah**-to, *m* treatise; treaty

trattenere, traht-tay-**nay**-ray, *v* to detain; to hold back; to deduct

trattenersi, traht-tay-**nair**-se, *v* to stay; to stop oneself

tratto, traht-to, *m* stroke; stretch; period (of time); expanse; **ad un –,** *adv* suddenly

trattore, traht-**tor**-ay, *m* tractor

trattoria, traht-to-**ree**-ah, *f* restaurant

trauma, trah-oo-mah, *m* trauma

travasare, trah-vah-**zah**-ray, *v* to decant

trave, trah-vay, *f* beam

traversa, trah-**vair**-sah, *f* side-street; sleeper; crossbar

traversare, trah-vair-**sah**-ray, *v* to cross

traverso, trah-**vair**-so, *adj* oblique; **di –,** *adv* crosswise

travestimento, trah-vess-te-**men**-to, *m* disguise

travestire, trah-vess-**tee**-ray, *v* to disguise

traviare, trah-ve'**ah**-ray, *v* to lead astray

travisare, trah-ve-**zah**-ray, *v* to distort

travolgere, trah-**vol**-jay-ray, *v* to sweep away; to overwhelm

trazione, trah-tse'o-nay, *f* traction; drive

tre, tray, *adj & m* three

trebbiare, treb-be'**ah**-ray, *v* to thresh

treccia, **tret**-chah, *f* plait

trecento, tray-**chen**-to, *adj & m* three hundred; **il Trecento**, the fourteenth century

tredicesimo, tray-de-chay-ze-mo, *adj & m* thirteenth

tredici, **tray**-de-che, *adj & m* thirteen

tregua, **tray**-goo'ah, *f* truce; respite

tremare, tray-**mah**-ray, *v* to shiver; to shake

tremarella, tray-mah-**rell**-lah, *f* shivers

trementina, tray-men-**tee**-nah, *f* turpentine

tremito, **tray**-me-to, *m* shiver; tremor

tremolio, tray-mo-**lee**-o, *m* shaking

treno, **tray**-no, *m* train

trenta, **tren**-tah, *adj & m* thirty

trentesimo, tren-**tay**-ze-mo, *adj & m* thirtieth

trepidare, tray-pe-**dah**-ray, *v* to be anxious

tresca, **tress**-kah, *f* intrigue; affair

triangolo, tre-**ahn**-go-lo, *m* triangle

tribordo, tre-**bor**-do, *m* starboard

tribù, tre-**boo**, *f* tribe

tribuna, tre-**boo**-nah, *f* platform; stand; gallery

tribunale, tre-boo-**nah**-lay, *m* court

tricheco, tre-**kay**-ko, *m* walrus

triciclo, tre-**chee**-klo, *m* tricycle

trifoglio, tre-**fo**-l'yo, *m* clover

triglia, **tree**-l'yah, *f* red mullet

trillo, **trill**-lo, *m* trill; ring

trimestre, tre-**mess**-tray, *m* quarter, period of three months

trina, **tree**-nah, *f* point-lace

trincea, trin-**chay**-ah, *f* trench

trincerare, trin-chay-**rah**-ray, *v* to entrench

trinchetto, trin-**ket**-to, *m* foresail

trinciare, trin-**chah**-ray, *v* to cut up

trionfare, tre-on-**fah**-ray, *v* to triumph

triplice, **tree**-ple-chay, *adj* triple

triplo, **tree**-plo, *adj* triple; treble; **m il –**, three times as much

trippa, **trip**-pah, *f* tripe

tripudio, tre-**poo**-de'o, *m* jubilation; (colours) galaxy

triste, **triss**-tay, *adj* sad

tritare, tre-**tah**-ray, *v* to mince

trivella, tre-**vell**-lah, *f* auger; drill

trivellare, tre-vell-**lah**-ray, *v* to drill

trofeo, tro-**fay**-o, *m* trophy

tromba, **trom**-bah, *f* trumpet

troncare, tron-**kah**-ray, *v* to cut off; to break off

tronco, **tron**-ko, *m* trunk; section

tronfio, **tron**-fe'o, *adj* conceited

trono, **tro**-no, *m* throne

tropico, **tro**-pe-ko, *m* tropic

troppo, **trop**-po, *adj & pron* too much, too many; *adv* too; too much; too long

trota, **tro**-tah, *f* trout

trottare, trot-**tah**-ray, *v* to

trot

trotto, trot-to, *m* trot

trottola, trot-to-lah, *f* spinning top

trovare, tro-**vah**-ray, *v* to find; to come across; to meet; to call on

trovarsi, tro-**var**-se, *v* to be; to meet

trovatello, tro-vah-**tell**-lo, *m* foundling

truccare, trook-**kah**-ray, *v* to make up; to soup up; to fix

truccarsi, trook-**kar**-se, *v* to make oneself up

trucco, trook-ko, *m* trick; make-up

truce, troo-chay, *adj* fierce

trucidare, troo-che-**dah**-ray, *v* to slaughter

trucioli, troo-cho-le, *mpl* shavings

truffa, troof-fah, *f* fraud; swindle

truffare, troof-**fah**-ray, *v* to cheat; to swindle

truppa, troop-pah, *f* troop

tu, too, *pron* you; – **stesso,** yourself; *m* **darsi del –,** to be on first-name terms

tubetto, too-**bet**-to, *m* tube

tubo, too-bo, *m* tube, pipe; hose

tuffare, toof-**fah**-ray, *v* to dip

tuffarsi, toof-**far**-se, *v* to dive

tuffo, toof-fo, *m* dive, dip

tugurio, too-goo-re'o, *m* hovel

tulipano, too-le-**pah**-no, *m* tulip

tumore, too-**mo**-ray, *m* tumour

tumulare, too-moo-**lah**-ray, *v* to inter

tumulo, too-moo-lo, *m* tumulus

tuo, too-o, *adj* your; *pron* yours

tuonare, too'o-**nah**-ray, *v* to thunder

tuono, too'o-no, *m* thunder

tuorlo, too'or-lo, *m* yolk

turacciolo, too-**raht**-cho-lo, *m* cork

turare, too-**rah**-ray, *v* to cork; to plug

turba, toohr-bah, *f* multitude, mob; disorder

turbamento, toohr-bah-**men**-to, *m* confusion

turbare, toohr-**bah**-ray, *v* to trouble

turbinare, toohr-be-**nah**-ray, *v* to whirl

turbine, toohr-be-nay, *m* whirlwind

turchese, toohr-**kay**-say, *adj & m* turquoise; *f* turquoise

Turchia, toohr-kee-ah, *f* Turkey

turchino, toohr-kee-no, *adj* deep blue

turco, toohr-ko, *adj* Turkish

turismo, too-**riz**-mo, *m* tourism

turista, too-**riss**-tah, *m/f* tourist

turistico, too-**riss**-te-ko, *adj* tourist

turno, toohr-no, *m* turn; shift

turpe, toohr-pay, *adj* vile

turpiloquio, toohr-pe-lo-kwe-o, *m* foul language

tuta, too-tah, *f* overalls; tracksuit

tutela, too-**tay**-lah, *f* guardianship; protection; defence

tutore -trice, too-**tor**-ay, too-**tree**-chay, *m/f*, guardian

tuttavia, toot-tah-**vee**-ah, *adv* yet; nevertheless

tutto, toot-to, *adj* all (of); every; *pron* all; everyone; *adv* completely; *m* **il –,** the lot

tuttora, toot-**tor**-ah, *adv* still

ubbidiente, oobb-be-de'**ayn**-tay, *adj* obedient

ubbidire, oobb-be-**dee**-ray, *v* to obey

ubriacarsi, oo-bre-ah-**kar**-se, *v* to get drunk

ubriachezza, oo-bre-ah-**ket**-tsah, *f* drunkenness

ubriaco, oo-bre-**ah**-ko, *adj* drunk; **–a,** *m/f* drunkard

uccello, oot-**chell**-lo, *m* bird

uccidere, oot-**chee**-day-ray, *v* to kill; to murder

uccisione, oot-che-ze'o-nay, *f* killing; murder

udienza, oo-de-en-tsah, *f* audience; *law* hearing

udire, oo-**dee**-ray, *v* to hear

udito, oo-**dee**-to, *m* hearing

uditorio, oo-de-**tor**-e'o, *m* audience

ufficiale, oof-fe-**chah**-lay, *adj* official; *m* officer

ufficio, oof-**fee**-cho, *m* office

Ufo, oo-fo, *m* UFO

uggioso, ood-**jo**-zo, *adj* dull

uguaglianza, oo-goo'ah-l'**yahn**-tsah, *f* equality

uguagliare, oo-goo'ah-l'**yah**-ray, *v* to equal

uguale, oo-goo'ah-lay, *adj* the same; equal

ulcera, **ool**-chay-rah, *f* ulcer

ulivo, oo-**lee**-vo, *m* olive-tree

ulteriore, ool-tay-re'o-ray, *adj* further

ultimare, ool-te-**mah**-ray, *v* to finish

ultimo, **ool**-te-mo, *adj* last; latest

ululare, oo-loo-**lah**-ray, *v* to howl

umanità, oo-mah-ne-**tah**, *f* mankind

umano, oo-**mah**-no, *adj* human

umidità, oo-me-de-**tah**, *f* dampness; humidity

umido, oo-me-do, *adj* damp; humid

umile, oo-me-lay, *adj* humble

umiliare, oo-me-l'**yah**-ray, *v* to humiliate

umore, oo-**mor**-ay, *m* mood, temper

umorismo, oo-mo-**riz**-mo, *m* humour

un, oon, *art* a, an

una, oo-nah, *art* a, an

unanime, oo-**nah**-ne-may, *adj* unanimous

uncinetto, oonn-chee-**net**-to, *m* crochet hook

uncino, oonn-**chee**-no, *m*, hook

undicesimo, oonn-de-**chay**-ze-mo *adj & m* eleventh

undici, oonn-de-che, *adj & m* eleven

ungere, oonn-**jay**-ray, *v* to oil

unghia, oonn-**ghe**'ah, *f* nail

unguento, oonn-goo'**en**-to, *m* ointment

unico*, oo-ne-ko, *adj* only; unique; sole

unificare, oo-ne-fe-**kah**-ray, *v* to unify

uniformare, oo-ne-for-**mah**-ray, *v* to conform

uniforme, oo-ne-**for**-may, *f* uniform; *adj* uniform

unione, oo-ne'**o**-nay, *f* union

unire, oo-**nee**-ray, *v* to unite; to connect

unità, oo-nee-**tah**, *f* unit

unito, oo-**nee**-to, *adj* united; close

università, oo-nee-vair-se-**tah**, *f* university

universo, oo-nee-**vair**-so, *m* universe

uno, oo-no, *adj & m* one; *art* a, an; *pron* one; somebody

unto, oonn-to, *adj* greasy; *m* grease

untuoso, oonn-too-o-zo, *adj* greasy; oily

uomo, oo'**o**-mo, *m* man

uovo, oo'**o**-vo, *m* egg; – **sodo,** hard-boiled egg

uragano, oo-rah-**gah**-no, *m* hurricane

urbano, oohr-**bah**-no, *adj* urban

urgente, oohr-**jen**-tay, *adj* urgent

urina, oo-**ree**-nah, *f* urine

urlare, oohr-**lah**-ray, *v* to shout

urlo, oohr-lo, *m* yell

urna, oohr-nah, *f* urn; ballot-box

urtare, oohr-**tah**-ray, *v* to bump against

urto, oohr-to, *m* crash

usanza, oo-**zahn**-tsah, *f* custom

usare, oo-**zah**-ray, *v* to use

usato, oo-**zah**-to, *adj* used, second-hand

usciere, oo-she'**ay**-ray, *m* usher

uscire, oo-**shee**-ray, *v* to go out

uscita, oo-**shee**-tah, *f* exit

usignolo, oo-ze-n'**yo**-lo, *m* nightingale

uso, oo-zo, *m* use; custom

usura, oo-**zoo**-rah, *f* usury

usurpare, oo-zoohr-**pah**-ray, *v* to usurp

utensile, oo-**ten**-se-lay, *m* utensil

utero, oo-**tay**-ro, *m* womb

utile, oo-te-lay, *adj* useful

utilitaria, oo-te-le-**tah**-re'ah, *f* economy car

utilizzare, oo-te-lid-**dzah**-ray, *v* to use

uva, oo-vah, *f* grapes; – **passa,** raisins; – **spina,** gooseberry

vacanza, vah-**kahn**-tsah, *f*
holiday

vacca, **vahk**-kah, *f* cow

vaccinare, vaht-che-**nah**-ray, *v* to vaccinate

vaccinazione, vaht-che-nah-tse'**o**-nay, *f*
vaccination

vaccino, vaht-**chee**-no, *m*
vaccine

vacillare, vah-chill-**lah**-ray, *v* to sway

vacuo, vah-**koo**'o, *adj*
vacuous, empty

vagabondare, vah-gah-bon-**dah**-ray, *v* to
wander

vagabondo, -a, vah-gah-**bon**-do, *adj* idle; *m/f*
tramp

vagamente, vah-gah-**men**-tay, *adv* vaguely

vagare, vah-**gah**-ray, *v* to
wander about; to roam

vagina, vah-**jee**-nah, *f*
vagina

vagire, vah-**jee**-ray, *v*
(baby) to wail

vaglia, vah-**l'yah**, *m*
money-order

vagliare, vah-**l'yah**-ray, *v*
to sift; to weigh up

vaglio, vah-**l'yo**, *m* sieve;
passare al –, to examine

vago, **vah**-go, *adj* vague

vagone, vah-**go**-nay, *m*
coach; waggon, truck

vaiolo, vah-e'**o**-lo, *m*
small-pox

valanga, vah-**lahn**-gah, *f*
avalanche

valere, vah-**lay**-ray, *v* to be
valid; to apply; to be
worth; to be equal to

valevole, vah-**lay**-vo-lay,
adj valid

valicare, vah-le-**kah**-ray, *v*
to cross

valico, vah-**le**-ko, *m* pass

valido*, vah-**le**-do, *adj*
valid; effective;
worthwhile

valigia, vah-**lee**-jah, *f* suitcase; **fare le valigie**, to
pack

vallata, vahll-**lah**-tah, *f*
valley

valle, **vahll**-lay, *f* valley

valletta, vahll-**let**-ta, *f*
(TV) assistant

valore, vah-**lor**-ay, *m*
value; merit; bravery;
security; **valori**,
valuables

valorizzare, vah-lo-rid-**dzah**-ray, *v* to make the
most of; to enhance

valuta, vah-**loo**-tah, *f*
currency

valutare, vah-loo-**tah**-ray,
v to value; to estimate

valvola, vahll-**vo**-lah, *f*
valve

valzer, vahll-**zair**, *m* waltz

vampata, vahm-**pah**-tah, *f*
blaze; blast; flush

vampiro, vahm-**pee**-ro, *m*
vampire

vandalismo, vahn-dah-**liz**-zmo, *m* vandalism

vaneggiare, vah-ned-**jah**-ray, *v* to rave

vanga, vahn-gah, *f* spade

vangare, vahn-**gah**-ray, *v* to dig

vangelo, vahn-**jay**-lo, *m* Gospel

vaniglia, vah-**nee**-l'yah, *f* vanilla

vanità, vah-nee-**tah,** *f* vanity; futility

vano, vah-no, *adj** vain; *m* room

vantaggio, vahn-**tahd**-jo, *m* advantage

vantare, vahn-**tah**-ray, *v* to praise

vantarsi, vahn-**tar**-se, *v* to boast

vanto, vahn-to, *m* boasting; merit

vapore, vah-**por**-ay, *m* vapour, steam

vaporetto, vah-po-**ret**-to, *m* steamer

vaporizzatore, vah-po-rid-dzah-**to**-ray, *m* spray

varare, vah-**rah**-ray, *v* to launch; *law* to pass

varcare, vahr-**kah**-ray, *v* to cross

variare, vah-ree-**ah**-ray, *v* to vary; to range

variato, vah-re'**ah**-to, *adj* varied

varice, vah-**ree**-chay, *f* varicose vein

varicella, vah-ree-**chell**-lah, *f* chickenpox

vario*, vah-re'o, *adj* varied; various

variopinto, vah-re'o-**pin**-to, *adj* multicoloured

varo, vah-ro, *m* launching; *law* passing

Varsavia, var-sah-ve'ah, *f* Warsaw

vasaio, vah-**zah**-e'o, *m* potter

vasca, vahss-kah, *f* basin; bath; tank; length

vascello, vah-**shell**-lo, *m* ship; vessel

vasellame, vah-zell-**lah**-may, *m* crockery

vaso, vah-zo, *m* pot; vase

vassoio, vahss-**so**-e'o, *m* tray

vasto*, vahss-to, *adj* vast; ample

ve, vay, *pron & adv* (see **vi**)

vecchiaia, vek-ke'**ah**-e'ah, *f* old age

vecchio, -a, vek-**ke**'o, *adj* old, antique; second-hand; *m/f* old man, old woman

vedere, vay-**day**-ray, *v* to see

vedetta, vay-**det**-tah, *f* look-out

vedova, vay-do-vah, *f* widow

vedovo, vay-do-vo, *m* widower

veduta, vay-**doo**-tah, *f* view

veemente, vay-ay-**men**-tay, *adj* vehement

vegetale, vay-jay-**tah**-lay, *adj* vegetable; *m* plant

vegetariano, vay-jay-tah-re'**ah**-no, *adj* vegetarian

veggente, ved-**jen**-tay, *m/f* clairvoyant

vegliare, vay-l'**yah**-ray, *v* to watch over

veglione, vay-l'**yo**-nay, *m* ball, dance

veicolo, vay-**ee**-ko-lo, *m* vehicle

vela, vay-lah, *f* sail; sailing

velare, vay-**lah**-ray, *v* to veil, to cover

veleggiare, vay-led-**jah**-ray, *v* to sail

veleno, vay-**lay**-no *m* poison

velenoso, vay-lay-**no**-zo, *adj* poisonous

veletta, vay-**let**-tah, *f* veil

veliero, vay-l'**yay**-ray, *m* sailing-ship

velivolo, vay-**lee**-vo-lo, *m* aircraft

velleità, vel-lay-e-**tah,** *f* vain ambition

vello, vell-lo, *m* fleece

velluto, vell-**loo**-to, *m* velvet; **– a coste,** corduroy

velo, vay-lo, *m* veil; voile

veloce, vay-lo-chay, *adj* fast, swift, quick; *adv* fast, quickly

velocità, vay-lo-chee-**tah,** *f* speed

vena, vay-nah, *f* vein; **non essere in – di,** not to be in the mood for

vendemmia, ven-demme'ah, *f* grape harvest

vendere, ven-day-ray, *v* to sell

vendetta, ven-det-tah, *f* revenge

vendicare, ven-de-kahray, *v* to avenge

vendicarsi, ven-de-kar-se, *v* to avenge oneself; – **di,** to take one's revenge for

vendita, ven-de-tah, *f* sale

venditore, -trice, ven-detor-ay, ven-de-tree-chay, *m/f* seller, vendor, salesman, saleswoman

venerare, vay-nay-rah-ray, *v* to venerate

venerdì, vay-nair-dee, *m* Friday

Venezia, vay-nay-tse'ah, *f* Venice

venire, vay-nee-ray, *v* to come; to turn out

ventaglio, ven-tah-l'yo, *m* fan

ventata, ven-tah-tah, *f* (wind) gust

ventesimo, ven-tay-ze-mo, *adj & m* twentieth

venti, ven-te, *adj & m* twenty

ventilare, ven-te-lah-ray, *v* to ventilate

vento, ven-to, *m* wind

ventola, ven-to-lah, *f* fan

ventre, ven-tray, *m* stomach

venturo, ven-too-ro, *adj* next, coming

venuta, vay-noo-tah, *f* arrival

verace, vay-rah-chay, *adj* real

veramente, vay-rah-mentay, *adv* really

verbo, vair-bo, *m* verb

verde, vair-day, *adj & m* green; **essere al –,** to be broke

verderame, vair-day-rahmay, *m* verdigris

verdetto, vair-det-to, *m* verdict

verdura, vair-doo-rah, *f* vegetables

vergine, vair-je-nay, *adj* virgin; blank; *f* virgin; **Vergine,** Virgo

vergogna, vair-go-n'yah, *f* shame

vergognarsi, vair-gon'yahr-se, *v* to be ashamed; to be shy

veridicità, vay-re-de-chetah, *f* truthfulness

veritiero, vay-re-te'ay-ro, *adj* truthful; true

verme, vair-may, *m* worm

vermicelli, vair-me-chell-le, *mpl* vermicelli

vermiglio, vair-mee-l'yo, *m* vermilion

vernice, vair-nee-chay, *f* varnish; paint; patent leather

verniciare, vair-ne-chahray, *v* to varnish; to paint

vero, vay-ro, *adj* true; real

verosimile, vay-ro-seeme-lay, *adj* likely

verruca, vair-roo-kah, *f* wart

versamento, vair-sah-men-to, *m* payment; deposit; *med* effusion

versante, vair-sahn-tay, *m* side; slopes

versare, vair-sah-ray, *v* to pour; to spill; to pay; to deposit

verso, vair-so, *m* verse, line; cry; direction; way; *prep* towards; near; around, about

vertere, vair-tay-ray, *v* – **su,** to be about

verticale, vair-te-kah-lay, *adj* vertical; *f* vertical

vertice, vair-te-chay, *m* vertex; peak; summit

vertigine, vair-tee-je-nay, *f* dizziness; **soffrire di vertigini,** to be afraid of heights

vescica, vay-shee-kah, *f* bladder; blister

vescovado, vess-ko-**vah**-do, *m* bishopric

vescovile, vess-ko-vee-lay, *adj* episcopal

vescovo, vess-ko-vo, *m* bishop

vespa, vess-pah, *f* wasp

vespaio, vess-**pah**-e'o, *m* wasps' nest

vespasiano, vess-pah-ze'**ah**-no, *m* urinal

vespri, vess-pre, *mpl* vespers

vessillo, vess-**sill**-lo, *m* flag, banner, standard

vestaglia, vess-**tah**-l'yah, *f* dressing gown

veste, vess-tay, *f* garment; dress; **in – di,** as

vestiario, vess-te-**ah**-re'o, *m* clothes; **capo di –,** garment

vestire, vess-**tee**-ray, *v* to dress

vestirsi, vess-**teer**-se, *v* to get dressed

vestito, vess-**tee**-to, *m* dress; suit

veterinario, -a, vay-tay-re-**nah**-re'o, *m/f* vet, veterinary surgeon

vetraio, vay-**trah**-e'o, *m* glazier

vetreria, vay-tray-**ree**-ah, *m* glass-ware; glassworks

vetrina, vay-**tree**-nah, *f* shop-window

vetro, vay-tro, *m* glass;

piece of glass; windowpane; window

vetta, vet-tah, *f* peak, top

vettovaglie, vet-to-**vah**-l'yay, *fpl* supplies

vettura, vet-**too**-rah, *f* car; carriage

vezzeggiativo, vet-tsed-jah-**tee**-vo, *m* term of endearment

vi, vee, *pron* you; to you; *refl* yourselves; each other; *adv* there

via, vee-ah, *f* street; road; way; *adv* away; *prep* via; *interj* go away!; go!; come on!; *m* starting signal; *fig* green light

viabilità, ve'ah-be-le-**tah**, *f* road conditions

viadotto, ve'ah-**dot**-to, *m* viaduct

viaggiare, ve'ahd-**jah**-ray, *v* to travel

viaggiatore, -trice, ve'ahd-jah-**tor**-ay, ve'ahd-jah-**tree**-chay, *m/f* traveller

viaggio, ve'**ahd**-jo, *m* travel; journey; trip; flight; voyage

viale, ve'**ah**-lay, *m* avenue; drive

viavai, ve'ah-**vah**-e, *m* bustle

vibrare, ve-**brah**-ray, *v* to vibrate

vicario, ve-**kah**-re'o, *m* vicar

vicenda, ve-**chen**-dah, *f* event

vicepresidente, ve-chay-pray-se-**den**-tay, *m* vicepresident

vicinanza, ve-che-**nahn**-tsah, *f* proximity; **vicinanze,** vicinity

vicinato, ve-che-**nah**-to, *m* neighbourhood; neighbours

vicino, -a, ve-**chee**-no, *adj* near, nearby; close; *adv* nearby; *m/f* neighbour

vicolo, vee-ko-lo, *m* alley

video, vee-de'o, *m* screen; video-clip

videocamera, vee-de'o-**kah**-may-rah, *f* camcorder

videocassetta, vee-de'o-**kahss-set**-tah, *f* video(cassette)

videogioco, vee-de'o-**jo**-ko, *m* videogame

videoregistratore, vee-de'o-ray-jiss-strah-**to**-ray, *m* video(recorder)

videoterminale, vee-de'o-**tair**-me-**nah**-lay, *m* visual display unit

vidimare, ve-de-**mah**-ray, *v* to authenticate

vietare, ve'ay-**tah**-ray, *v* to forbid; to prohibit

vigente, ve-**jen**-tay, *adj* existing; in force

vigere, vee-**jay**-ray, *v* to be

in force

vigilare, ve-je-lah-ray, *v* to watch over

vigile, ve-je-lay, *adj* vigilant; *m* (traffic) policeman, policewoman; **vigili del fuoco**, fire brigade

vigilia, ve-jee-le'ah, *f* eve

vigliacco, -a, ve-l'yahk-ko, *adj** cowardly; *m/f* coward

vigna, vee-n'yah, *f* vineyard

vignetta, ve-n'yet-tah, *f* cartoon

vigore, ve-gor-ay, *m* vigour

vile, vee-lay, *adj* vile, contemptible; cowardly

vilipendere, ve-le-pen-day-ray, *v* to scorn

villa, **vill**-lah, *m* rural or suburban residence

villaggio, vill-lahd-jo, *m* village

villania, vill-lah-nee-ah, *f* lack of manners

villano, vill-lah-no, *adj** ill-mannered, rude

villeggiante, vill-led-jahn-tay, *m/f* holiday-maker

villetta, vill-let-tah, *f* detached house; cottage

viltà, vill-tah, *f* cowardice

vimine, vee-me-nay, *m* wicker

vinaio, ve-nah-e'o, *m*

wine-merchant

vincente, vin-chen-tay, *adj* winning

vincere, vin-chay-ray, *v* to win; to defeat; to overcome

vincita, vin-che-tah, *f* winnings; win

vincitore, -trice, vin-che-tor-ay, vin-che-tree-chay, *m/f* winner

vincolare, vin-ko-lah-ray, *v* to bind; to tie up

vincolo, vin-ko-lo, *m* bond

vino, vee-no, *m* wine

viola, ve'o-lah, *f* violet; *m* purple

violacciocca, ve'o-lahch-chock-kah, *f* stock

violare, ve'o-lah-ray, *v* to violate

violentare, ve'o-len-tah-ray, *v* to rape

violento, ve'o-len-to, *adj* violent

violino, ve'o-lee-no, *m* violin

viottolo, ve'ot-to-lo, *m* path

vipera, vee-pay-rah, *f* viper, adder

viraggio, ve-rahd-jo, *m* turn; toning

virare, ve-rah-ray, *v* to haul (in); to turn; to tone

virgola, veer go-lah, *f*

comma

virgolette, veer-go-let-tay, *fpl* quotation marks

virile, ve-ree-lay, *adj* virile

virtù, veer-too, *f* virtue

virtuale, veer-too'ah-lay, *adj* virtual

virtuoso, veer-too'o-zo, *adj* virtuous

virus, vee-roos, *m* virus

viscere, vee-shay-ray, *fpl* entrails; *fig* bowels

vischio, viss-ke'o, *m* mistletoe; bird-lime

visconte, viss-kon-tay, *m* viscount

visibile, ve-zee-be-lay, *adj* visible

visione, ve-ze'o-nay, *f* vision

visitare, ve-ze-tah-ray, *v* to visit; to examine

visitatore, -trice, ve-ze-tah-tor-ay, ve-ze-tah-tree-chay, *m/f* visitor

viso, vee-zo, *m* face

vispo, viss-po, *adj* lively

vista, viss-tah, *f* view; eyesight

visto, viss-to, *m* visa

vistoso*, viss-to-zo, *adj* gaudy

vita, vee-tah, *f* life; waist; existence

vitalizio, ve-tah-lee-tse'o, *m* life-annuity

vite, vee-tay, *f* vine; screw

vitello, ve-tell-lo, *m* calf;

veal; calfskin

viticoltore, ve-te-koll-**tor**-ay, *m* vine grower

vittima, vit-te-mah, *f* victim

vitto, vit-to, *m* food

vittoria, vit-**tor**-e'ah, *f* victory

vittorioso, vit-to-re'**o**-zo, *adj* victorious, triumphant

viuzza, ve'**oot**-tsah, *f* alley

viva, vee-vah, *interj* hurrah!; long live!

vivacchiare, ve-vahk-ke'ah-ray, *v* to scrape a living

vivace, ve-vah-chay, *adj* lively; bright

vivacità, ve-vah-che-tah, *f* vivacity; liveliness; brightness

vivamente, ve-vah-**men**-tay, *adv* deeply; sincerely

vivanda, ve-**vahn**-dah, *f* food; dish

vivente, ve-ven-tay, *adj* living

vivere, vee-**vay**-ray, *v* to live; to live through; *m* existence

viveri, vee-vay-re, *mpl* supplies

vivo, vee-vo, *adj* alive, living; live; lively; bright

viziare, ve-tse'**ah**-ray, *v* to spoil

vizio, vee-tse'o, *m* vice; bad habit; defect

vizioso, ve-tse'o-zo, *adj* depraved

vizzo, vit-tso, *adj* withered

vocabolario, vo-kah-bo-**lah**-re'o, *m* vocabulary; dictionary

vocabolo, vo-**kah**-bo-lo, *m* word

vocale, vo-kah-lay, *adj* vocal; *f* vowel

vocazione, vo-kah-tse'o-nay, *f* vocation; natural bent

voce, vo-chay, *f* voice

voga, vo-gah, *f* vogue; rowing

vogare, vo-gah-ray, *v* to row

voglia, vo-l'yah, *f* wish, fancy; craving; birthmark; **aver – di (fare) qualcosa**, to feel like (doing) something

voi, vo-e, *pron* you; – **stessi**, yourselves

volante, vo-lahn-tay, *adj* flying; loose, *m* steering wheel

volantino, vo-lahn-tee-no, *m* flier

volare, vo-lah-ray, *v* to fly

volatile, vo-lah-te-lay, *adj* volatile; *m* bird

volatilizzare, vo-lah-te-lid-dzah-ray, *v* to volatilize

volatilizzarsi, vo-lah-te-lid-dzar-se, *v* to volatilize; to vanish

volentieri, vo-len-te'ay-re, *adv* willingly

volere, vo-lay-ray, *v* to want; to need; *m* will, wish; **voler bene a qn**, to love sb; **voler dire**, to mean

volgare, voll-gah-ray, *adj* vulgar

volgarità, voll-gah-re-tah, *f* vulgarity

volgere, voll-jay-ray, *v* to turn

volo, vo-lo, *m* flight

volontà, vo-lon-tah-*f* will

volontario, -a, vo-lon-tah-re'o, *adj** voluntary; *m/f* volunteer

volpe, voll-pay, *f* fox

volta, voll-tah, *f* time; vault; **una –**, once; **due volte**, twice

voltaggio, voll-tahj-jo, *m* voltage

voltare, voll-tah-ray, *v* to turn; to turn over; to turn round

voltarsi, voll-tar-se, *v* to turn; to turn over; to turn round

volteggiare, voll-ted-jah-ray, *v* to vault; to circle

volto, voll-to, *m* face

volubile, vo-loo-be-lay, *adj* fickle

volume, vo-**loo**-may, *m*
volume

voluminoso, vo-loo-me-**no**-zo, *adj* voluminous,
bulky

voluttà, vo-loot-**tah**, *f*
sensual delight

vomere, **vo**-may-ray, *m*
ploughshare

vomitare, vo-me-**tah**-ray,
v to vomit, to throw up

vorace, vo-**rah**-chay, *adj*
voracious

voracità, vo-rah-che-**tah**, *f*
greediness

voragine, vo-**rah**-je-nay, *f*
abyss

vortice, **vor**-te-chay, *m*
vortex; whirl

vostro, **voss**-tro, *adj* your;
pron yours

votante, vo-**tahn**-tay, *m/f*
voter

votare, vo-**tah**-ray, *v* to
vote

votarsi, vo-**tar**-se, *v* to
devote oneself

voto, **vo**-to, *m* vote; mark;
vow

vulcano, vooll-**kah**-no, *m*
volcano

vulcanico, vooll-**kah**-ne-ko, *adj* volcanic

vulnerabile, vooll-nay-**rah**-be-lay, *adj*
vulnerable

vuotare, voo'o-**tah**-ray, *v*
to empty

vuoto, voo'**o**-to, *adj*
empty; *m* empty space;
vacuum

Walkman, oo'ok-mahn, *m*
Walkman TM, personal
stereo

water, vah-tair, *m* toilet
(bowl)

watt, oo'ot, *m* watt

weekend, oo'eek-**end**, *m*
weekend

whisky, oo'iss-ke, *m*
whisky

windsurf, oo'**ind-**serf, *m*
windsurfing; windsurf
board

würstel, vyr-stel, *m*
frankfurter

xenofobia, ksay-no-fo-
bee-ah, *f* xenophobia
xilofono, ksee-**lo**-fo-no, *m*
xylophone

yacht, ee-ot, *m* yacht
yoga, ee'o-gah, *m* yoga
yogurt, ee'o-goort, *m*
 yoghurt

zabaglione, dzah-bah-**ly'o**-nay, m zabaglione

zafferano, dzahf-fay-**rah**-no, m saffron

zaffiro, dzahf-**fee**-ro, m sapphire

zaino, dzah-e-no, m rucksack

zampa, tsahm-pah, f paw

zampillare, tsahm-pill-**lah**-ray, v (fluid) to jet

zampillo, tsahm-**pill**-lo, m jet

zampirone, dzam-pe-ro-nay, m mosquito repellent

zampogna, tsahm-**po**-n'yah, f bag-pipe

zangola, tsahn-go-lah, f churn

zanna, tsahn-nah, f tusk; fang

zanzara, dzahn-dzah-rah, f mosquito

zanzariera, dzahn-dzah-re'**ay**-rah, f mosquito-net

zappa, tsahp-pah, f hoe

zappare, tsahp-**pah**-ray, v to hoe

zar, tsahr, m tsar

zarina, tsah-**ree**-nah, f tsarina

zattera, tsaht-tay-rah, f raft

zavorra, dzah-vor-rah, f ballast

zebra, dzay-brah, f zebra

zecca, tsek-kah, f (parasite) tick; (money) mint

zelante, dzay-**lahn**-tay, adj zealous

zelo, dzay-lo, m zeal

zenzero, dzen-**dzay**-ro, m ginger

zeppa, tsep-pah, f wedge; (shoe) platform

zeppo, tsep-po, adj crammed

zerbino, dzer-**bee**-no, m doormat

zero, dzay-ro m zero, nought; (sport) nil

zeta, dzay-tah, f zed

zia, tsee-ah, f aunt

zibellino, dze-bell-**lee**-no, m sable

zigomo, dzee-go-mo, m cheekbone

zimbello, tsim-bell-lo, m laughing stock

zinco, tsin-ko, m zinc

zingaro, -a, tsin-gah-ro, m/f gipsy

zio, tsee-o, m uncle

zitella, tse-**tell**-lah, f spinster

zittire, tsit-**tee**-ray, v to hush

zitto, tsit-to, adj silent; interj shut up!

zizzania, dzit-dzah-ne'ah, f discord

zoccolo, tsock-ko-lo, m clog; hoof

zodiaco, dzo-**dee**'ah-ko, m zodiac

zolfanello, tsoll-fah-**nell**-lo, m sulphur-match

zolfo, tsoll-fo, m sulphur

zolla, dzoll-lah, f clod

zolletta, dzoll-**let**-tah, *f* lump

zona, dzo-nah, *f* zone; – **pedonale,** pedestrian precinct

zoo, dzo'o, *m* zoo

zoologico, dzo-o-**lo**-je-ko, *adj* zoological

zoppicare, tsop-pe-**kah**-ray, *v* to limp

zoppo, tsop-po, *adj* lame

zotico, dzo-te-ko, *m* boor

zucca, tsook-kah, *f* pumpkin

zuccherare, tsook-kay-**rah**-ray, *v* to sweeten

zuccheriera, tsook-kay-ree'**ay**-rah, *f* sugar bowl

zucchero, tsook-kay-ro, *m* sugar; – **filato,** candy floss; – **a velo,** icing sugar

zuccheroso, tsook-kay-ro-so, *adj* sugary

zucchetto, tsook-**ket**-to, *m* skull-cap

zucchino, tsook-**kee**-no, *m* courgette

zuccone, -a, tsook-**ko**-nay, *m/f* blockhead

zuffa, tsoof-fah, *f* scuffle

zufolare, tsoo-fo-**lah**-ray, *v* to whistle

zuppa, tsoop-pah, *f* soup

zuppiera, tsoop-pe'**ay**-rah, *f* tureen

zuppo, tsoop-po, *adj* soaked

ENGLISH • ITALIAN
INGLESE • ITALIANO

a, ei, *art* un, uno, una

abandon, *a*-ban´-don, *v* abbandonare

abandoned, *a*-ban´-dond, *adj* abbandonato

abashed, *a*-basht´, *adj* sconcertato, imbarazzato

abate, *a*-beit´, *v* (weather) calmarsi; (noise) diminuire

abattoir, ab´-*a*-tuaar, *n* mattatoio *m*, macello *m*

abbot, ab´-ot, *n* abate *m*

abbreviate, *a*-brii´-vi-eit, *v* abbreviare

abbreviation, *a*-bri-vi-ei´-shon, *n* abbreviazione *f*

abdicate, ab´-di-keit, *v* abdicare

abdomen, ab´-do-men, *n* addome *m*

abduction, ab-dŏk´-shon,

n rapimento *m*

aberration, ab-e-rei´-shon, *n* aberrazione *f*

abhor, ab-hoor´, *v* aborrire

abhorrent, ab-ho´-rent, *adj* ripugnante

abide, *a*-baid´, *v* dimorare; **to – by,** attenersi a

ability, *a*-bil´-i-ti, *n* abilità *f*

abject, ab´-chekt, *adj* abietto

ablaze, *a*-bleis´, *adv* in fiamme

able, ei´-bl, *adj* capace, abile; **to be –,** potere

ably, ei´-bli, *adv* abilmente

abnormal*, ab-noor´-mal, *adj* anormale

aboard, *a*-boord´, *adv* a bordo

abode, *a*-boud´, *n* dimora

f, abitazione *f*

abolish, *a*-bol´-ish, *v* abolire

abominable, *a*-bom´-in-*a*-bl, *adj* abominevole, orribile

aboriginal, ab-o-rich´-in-al, *adj* aborigeno

abortion, *a*-boor´-shon, *n* aborto *m*; **to have an –,** abortire

abound, *a*-baund´, *v* abbondare

about, *a*-baut´, *adv* circa; intorno; quasi; *prep* intorno a; riguardo a; **to be – to,** essere sul punto di

above, *a*-bŏv´, *adv* al di sopra; *prep* sopra

abrasion, *a*-brei´-shon, *n* abrasione *f*, escoriazione *f*

abreast, *a*-brest´, *adv* fianco a fianco

abridge, *a*-brich´, *v* riassumere; ridurre

abroad, *a*-brood´, *adv* all'estero

abrupt*, *a*-brŏpt´, *adj* brusco; (steep) scosceso, ripido

abscess, ab´-ses, *n* ascesso *m*

abscond, ab-skond´, *v* fuggire; rendersi latitante

abseil, ab´-seil, *v* scendere

a corda doppia

absence, ab´-sens, *n*
assenza *f*

absent, ab´-sent, *adj*
assente

absent-minded, ab-sent-
main´-did, *adj* distratto

absent oneself, ab-sent'
uŏn-self´, *v* assentarsi;
non presentarsi

absentee, ab-sen-tii´,
n assente *m/f*

absolute*, ab´-so-lut, *adj*
assoluto

absolve, ab-solv´, *v*
assolvere; **– from,**
assolvere da

absorb, ab-soorb´, *v*
assorbire

absorbed, ab-soorbd´, *adj*
assorto

abstain, ab-stein´, *v*
astenersi

abstainer, ab-stein´-a, *n*
astemio *m*

abstemious*, ab-stii´-mi-
os, *adj* sobrio, moderato

abstinence, ab´-sti-nens,
n astinenza *f*

abstract, ab-strakt´, *v*
astrarre; riassumere;
estrarre

abstract, ab´-strakt, *n*
estratto *m*, compendio
m; *adj* astratto

absurd*, ab-serd´, *adj*
assurdo

abundance, a-bŏn´-dans,

n abbondanza *f*

abundant, a-bŏn´-dant,
adj abbondante

abuse, a-biuus´, *v* abusare
di; maltrattare; (affront)
insultare

abuse, a-biuus´, *n* abuso
m; maltrattamento *m*;
(affront) insulto *m*

abusive*, a-biuus´-iv, *adj*
offensivo

abyss, a-bis´, *n* abisso *m*

acacia, a-kei´-sha, *n*
acacia *f*

academy, a-kad´-e-mi, *n*
accademia *f*

accede, ak-siid´, *v*
accedere

accelerate, ak-sel´-e-reit,
v accelerare

accent, ak´-sent, *n*
accento *m*

accent, ak-sent´, *v*
accentare; evidenziare

accentuate, ak-sent´-iu-
eit, *v* accentuare

accept, ak-sept´, *v*
accettare

acceptance, ak-sept´-ens,
n accettazione *f*

acceptable, ak-sept´-a-bl,
adj accettabile, gradito

access, ak´-ses, *n* accesso
m; entrata *f*

accessible, ak-ses´-si-bl,
adj accessibile

accession, ak-se´-shon, *n*
accessione *f*; ascesa al

trono *f*

accessory, ak-ses´-o-ri, *n*
accessorio *m*; (person)
complice *m/f*

accident, ak´-si-dent, *n*
incidente *m*

accidental*, ak-si-den´-tl,
adj accidentale, fortuito

acclaim, a-kleim´, *v*
acclamare, applaudire

accommodate, a-kom´-o-
deit, *v* (lodge)
alloggiare; (have space
for) accogliere

accommodation, a-kom-o-
dei´-shon, *n* (lodging)
alloggio *m*; (room)
posto *m*

accompaniment, a-kŏm´-
pa-ni-ment, *n*
accompagnamento *m*

accompanist, a-kŏm´-pa-
nist, *n* accompagnatore
m, accompagnatrice *f*

accompany, a-kŏm-pa-ni,
v accompagnare

accomplice, a-kŏm´-plis,
n complice *m/f*

accomplish, a-kŏm´-plish,
v compiere; (purpose)
realizzare

accomplishment, a-kŏm´-
plish-ment, *n*
compimento *m*;
risultato *m*

accord, a-koord´, *n*
accordo *m*; **of one's own
–,** di propria volontà; *v*

accordare

accordance, a-koord´-ans, n **in – with,** in conformità a

according to, a-koord´-ing tu, *prep* secondo; a seconda di

accordingly, a-koord´-ing-li, *adv* in conseguenza; conformemente

accordion, a-koor´-di-on, n fisarmonica f

accost, a-kost´, v accostare, avvicinare

account, a-kaunt´, n (bill) conto m; (report) resoconto, rapporto m; **on – of,** a causa di; **on no –,** in nessun modo; – **for,** v rendere conto di, spiegare

accountable for, a-kaun´-ta-bl foor, *adj* responsabile di

accountant, a-kaun´-tant, n ragioniere m, ragioniera f; commercialista m/f

accrue, a-kruu´, v maturare

accumulate, a-kiuu´-miu-leit, v accumulare

accuracy, ak´-iu-ra-si, n accuratezza f

accurate*, ak´-iu-rat, *adj* accurato, esatto

accursed, a-kerst´, *adj* maledetto

accuse, a-kiuus´, v accusare

accustom, a-kŏs´-tom, v abituare

accustomed, a-kŏs´-tomd, *adj* abituale; **– to,** abituato a

ace, eis, n asso m

ache, eik, n dolore m; v far male, dolere

achieve, a-chiiv´, v (success) conseguire; (aim) raggiungere

achievement, a-chiiv´-ment, n (attainment) realizzazione f; (result) risultato m, successo m

acid, as´-id, n acido m; *adj* acido

acid rain, as´-id rein, n pioggia acida f

acidity, a-sid´-i-ti, n acidità f

acknowledge, ak-nol´-ich, v riconoscere; (receipt) accusare

acknowledgment, ak-nol´-ich-ment, n riconoscimento m; (receipt) conferma f

acne, ak´-ni, n acne f

acorn, ei´-koorn, n ghianda f

acoustics, a-kus´-tiks, n acustica f

acquaint, a-kueint´, v informare; far conoscere

acquaintance, a-kueint´-ans, n conoscenza f; (person) conoscente m/f

acquiesce, ak-ui-es´, v accondiscendere

acquiescence, ak-ui-es´-ans, n consenso m

acquire, a-kuair´, v acquistare; apprendere

acquisition, a-kui-si´-shon, n acquisto m

acquit, a-kuit´, v *law* prosciogliere

acquittal, a-kuit´-l, n *law* assoluzione f

acre, ei´-ke, n acro m

acrid, ak´-rid, *adj* acre, pungente

acrobat, ak´-ro-bat, n acrobata m/f

across, a-kros´, *prep* attraverso; dall'altra parte; *adv* dall'altra parte; di traverso; in larghezza

acrylic, a-kri´-lik, *adj* acrilico; n acrilico m

act, akt, n azione f; (of a play) atto m; *law* legge f; v agire, comportarsi; (in a theatre) recitare

action, ak´-shon, n azione f; *law* processo m; (war) combattimento m

active*, ak´-tiv, *adj* attivo

activity, ak-tiv´-i-ti, n attività f

actor, ak´-ta, n attore m

actress, ak´-tris, n attrice f

actual, ak´-chu-al, *adj*

reale, effettivo

actually, ak´-chu-a-li, *adv*
veramente, davvero

actuate, ak´-tiu-eit, *v*
incitare; mettere in
azione; attivare

acumen, ak´-iu-men, *n*
acume *m*

acute, a-kiuut´, *adj* acuto;
fine; perspicace

acuteness, a-kiuut´-nis, *n*
acutezza *f*

adamant, ad´-a-mant, *adj*
inflessibile

adapt, a-dapt´, *v* adattare,
modificare

adaptation, ad-ap-tei´-
shon, *n* adattamento *m*

adaptor, a-dap´-ta, *n* presa
multipla *f*; riduttore *m*,
adattatore *m*

add, ad, *v* aggiungere;
(sum) addizionare

adder, ad´-a, *n* vipera *f*

addict, ad´-ikt, *n* drogato
m, drogata *f*,
tossicomane *m/f*

addicted to, a-dik´-tid tu,
adj dedito a; dipendente
da

addiction, a-dik´-shon, *n*
assuefazione *f*;
tossicodipendenza *f*

addition, a-di´-shon, *n*
addizione *f*; aggiunta *f*

additional, a-di´-shon-al,
adj aggiunto,
supplementare

additive, ad-i-tiv, *n*
additivo *m*

address, a-dres´, *v*
indirizzare; (orally) fare
un discorso a, rivolgersi
a; *n* indirizzo *m*;
discorso *m*

adduce, a-diuus´, *v*
addurre

adequacy, ad´-i-kua-si,
n adeguatezza *f*

adequate, ad´-i-kuat, *adj*
adeguato; adatto;
all'altezza di

adhere, ad-hier´, *v* aderire;
rimanere fedele a

adherence, ad-hie-rens,
n (loyalty) adesione *f*

adherent, ad-hie-rent, *n* &
adj aderente

adhesion, ad-hii´-shon, *n*
(grip) aderenza *f*

adhesive, ad-hii´-siv, *adj*
adesivo; *n* adesivo *m*

adjacent, ad-chei´-sent,
adj adiacente

adjective, ad´-chek-tiv, *n*
aggettivo *m*

adjoin, ad-choin´, *v* essere
attiguo

adjoining, ad-choin´-ing,
adj vicino a, attiguo a

adjourn, ad-chern´, *v*
rinviare, aggiornare;
sospendere

adjournment, ad-chern´-
ment, *n* rinvio *m*

adjust, ad-chŏst´, *v*

adattare, aggiustare;
mech regolare

adjustment, ad-chŏst´-
ment, *n* modifica *f*,
adattamento *m*;
regolazione *f*

administer, ad-min´-is-ta,
v gestire, amministrare;
(medicine)
somministrare

admirable, ad´-mi-ra-bl,
adj ammirevole

admiral, ad´-mi-ral, *n*
ammiraglio *m*

admire, ad-mair´, *v*
ammirare

admission, ad-mi´-shon, *n*
ammissione *f*; entrata *f*

admit, ad-mit´, *v*
ammettere; fare entrare

admittance, ad-mit´-ans, *n*
entrata *f*, ingresso *m*

admonish, ad-mon´-ish, *v*
ammonire

admonition, ad-mo-ni´-
shon, *n* ammonizione *f*

ado, a-duu´, *n* scalpore *m*;
(noise) agitazione *f*

adolescence, ad-a-le´-sens,
n adolescenza *f*

adolescent, ad-a-le´-sent,
n adolescente *m/f*

adopt, a-dopt´, *v* adottare

adore, a-door´, *v* adorare

adorn, a-doorn´, *v*
adornare

adornment, a-doorn´-
ment, *n* ornamento *m*

adrift, a-drift´, adv alla deriva

adulation, ad-iu-lei´-shon, n adulazione f

adult, ad´-ŏlt, n adulto m; adj adulto

adulterate, a-dŏl´-te-reit, v adulterare; falsificare

adultery, a-dŏl´-te-ri, n adulterio m

advance, ad-vaans´, v avanzare; (science) progredire; (lend) anticipare; n (progress) progresso m; (money) anticipo m; mil avanzata f; **in –,** anticipatamente

advancement, ad-vaans´-ment, n promozione f; progresso m

advantage, ad-vaan´-tich, n vantaggio m; **to take – of,** approfittare di

advantageous*, ad-vaan-tei´-chos, adj vantaggioso

advent, ad´-vent, n avvento m

adventure, ad-ven´-cha, n avventura f

adventurer, ad-ven´-cha-ra, n avventuriero m

adventurous, ad-ven´-cha-ros, adj avventuroso

adverb, ad´-verb, n avverbio m

adversary, ad´-ve-sa-ri, n avversario m

adverse*, ad´-vers, adj avverso; contrario

advert, ad´-vert, n annuncio m, inserzione f, pubblicità f

advertise, ad´-ve-tais, v fare pubblicità (a), mettere un annuncio (per)

advertisement, ad-ver´-tis-ment, n annuncio m, inserzione f, pubblicità f

advertiser, ad´-ve-tais-a, n inserzionista m/f

advertising, ad´-ve-tais-ing, n pubblicità f

advice, ad-vais´, n consiglio m, consigli mpl

advisable, ad-vais´-a-bl, adj consigliabile, opportuno

advise, ad-vais´, v consigliare; avvisare

advised, ad-vaisd´, adj **to be ill –,** far male a; **to be well –,** far bene a

adviser, ad-vais´-a, n consulente m/f

advocate, ad´-vo-kat, n avvocato m

advocate, ad´-vo-keit, v difendere, propugnare

aerial, er´-ri-al, n (radio, TV) antenna f; adj aereo

aerobics, er-rou´-biks, n aerobica f

aerodrome, er´-ro-droum, n aerodromo m

aeroplane, er´-ro-plein, n aereo m, aeroplano m

aerosol, er´-ro-sol, n aerosol m

afar, a-faar´, adv lontano; **from –,** da lontano

affable, af-a-bl, adj affabile, cortese

affably, af-a-bli, adv affabilmente

affair, a-fer´, n affare m; faccenda f; relazione amorosa f

affect, a-fekt´, v toccare; (influence) influire su; (move) commuovere; (pretend) fingere

affected, a-fek´-tid, adj affettato; (moved) commosso

affection, a-fek´-shon, n affetto m

affectionate*, a-fek´-shon-at, adj affezionato

affidavit, af-i-dei´-vit, n law affidavit m

affiliate, a-fil´-i-eit, v affiliare, associare

affinity, a-fin´-i-ti, n affinità f

affirm, a-ferm´, v affermare

affirmation, af-e-mei´-shon, n affermazione f

affirmative*, a-ferm´-a-tiv, adj affermativo

affix, a-fiks´, v apporre; attaccare

afflict, a-flikt´, v affliggere

affliction, a-flik´-shon, n afflizione f; infermità f

affluence, af´-lu-ens, n opulenza f; ricchezza f

affluent, af´-lu-ent, adj abbondante; ricco

afford, a-foord´, v (means) permettersi; (opportunity) offrire

affray, a-frei´, n rissa f

affront, a-frönt´, n affronto m; v insultare, oltraggiare

aflame, a-fleim´, adj in fiamme

afloat, a-flout´, adj & adv a galla

aforesaid, a-foor´-sed, adj suddetto

afraid, a-freid´, adj spaventato, impaurito; **to be – of,** aver paura di

afresh, a-fresh´, adv di nuovo

Africa, af´-ri-ca, n Africa f

African, af´-ri-can, adj africano

aft, aaft, adv a poppa

after, aaft´-a, prep dopo; adv dopo, seguente; conj dopo che

aftermath, aaft´-e-maaZ, n conseguenze fpl; **in the –,** nel periodo seguente

afternoon, aaft´-e-nuun, n pomeriggio m

afterthought, aaft´-e-

Zoot, n ripensamento m

afterwards, aaft´-e-ueds, adv in seguito

again, a-ghein´, adv nuovamente; ripetutamente; **not –,** non più

against, a-gheinst´, prep contro

age, eich, n età f; (period) epoca f; **to be of –,** essere maggiorenne

aged, eich´-id, adj vecchio; **a child – five,** un bambino di cinque anni

agency, ei´-chen-si, n agenzia f

agenda, a-chen´-da, n ordine del giorno m, agenda f

agent, ei´-chent, n agente m/f, rappresentante m/f

aggravate, ag´-ra-veit, v aggravare; irritare

aggregate, ag´-ri-gheit, v aggregare; adj aggregato, complessivo; n aggregato m; insieme m

aggression, a-gre´-shon, n aggressione f

aggressive, a-gres´-iv, adj aggressivo

aggrieved, a-griivd´, adj afflitto, addolorato

aghast, a-gaast´, adj sbigottito

agile, a´-chail, adj agile

agitate, a´-chi-teit, v (shake) agitare; (mental) turbare; (stir up) eccitare

agitation, a-chi-tei´-shon, n agitazione f; turbamento m; (strife) turbolenza f

ago, a-gou´, adv fa; **long –,** molto tempo fa

agonize, ag´-o-nais, v angosciarsi

agonizing, ag´-o-nais-ing, adj angoscioso

agony, ag´-o-ni, n agonia f, tormento m

agree, a-grii´, v convenire, essere d'accordo

agreable, a-grii´-e-bl, adj gradevole, piacevole

agreement, a-grii´-ment, n accordo m; (contract) contratto m

agricultural, ag-ri-köl´-cha-ral, adj agricolo

agriculture, ag´-ri-köl-cha, n agricoltura f

aground, a-graund´, adj incagliato, arenato

ahead, a-hed´, adv avanti; in testa; in anticipo

aid, eid´, n aiuto m; v aiutare

AIDS, eids, n AIDS m

ailing, ei´-ling, adj sofferente

ailment, eil´-ment, n male m, malanno m

aim, eim, n (arms) mira f; (object) scopo m; v mirare

aimless, eim´-les, adj senza scopo

air, er, n aria f; (mien) aria f; by –, per via aerea; in aereo; **on the –,** (radio, tv) in onda; v arieggiare, far prendere aria; (ideas) esprimere

air-conditioning, er-kondi´-shon-ing, n aria condizionata f

airgun, er´-gŏn, n fucile ad aria compressa m

airing, er´-ring, n ventilazione f

airlift, er´-lift, n ponte aereo m

airport, er´-poort, n aeroporto m

airship, er´-ship, n dirigibile m

airtight, er´-tait, adj a chiusura ermetica

airy, er-ri, adj arioso, arieggiato

aisle, ail, n navata f

ajar, a-chaar´, adj socchiuso

akimbo, a-kim´-bou, adv (appoggiato) sui fianchi

akin to, a-kin´ tu, adj simile a

alabaster, al´-a-baas-ta, n alabastro m

alacrity, a-lak´-ri-ti, n

alacrità f

alarm, a-laarm´, v allarmare; n allarme m

alarm-clock, a-laarm´-klok, n sveglia f

alarming, a-laarm´-ing, adj allarmante

album, al´-bum, n album m

alcohol, al´-ko-hol, n alcol m

alcoholic, al-ko-hol´-ik, adj alcolizzato; n alcolizzato m

ale, eil, n birra f

alert, a-lert´, adj vigile, all'erta

alertess, a-lert´-nis, n vigilanza f; prontezza f

alias, ei´-li-as, adv altrimenti detto; n falso nome m

alibi, al´-i-bai, n alibi m

alien, ei´-li-en, n straniero m; extraterrestre m; adj straniero; **– to,** estraneo a

alienate, ei´-li-en-eit, v alienare

alight, a-lait´, adj acceso; in fiamme; v scendere (da un veicolo)

align, a-lain´, v allineare

alike, a-laik´, adj simile; adv allo stesso modo

alive, a-laiv´, adj vivo, vivente

all, ool, adj tutto, tutta;

tutti, tutte; ogni; adv completamente; perfettamente; **– along,** per tutto il tempo; **– right,** va bene; **– the more,** tanto più; **not at –,** niente affatto

allay, a-lei´, v mitigare; calmare

allegation, a-li-gei´-shon, n accusa f

allege, a-lech´, v asserire

alleged, a-lechd´, adj presunto

allegedly, a-lech´-id-li, adv secondo quanto si dice

allegiance, a-lii´-chans, n fedeltà f

allergic, a-ler´-chik, adj allergico

allergy, a´-le-chi, n allergia f

alleviate, a-lii´-vi-eit, v alleviare

alley, al´-i, n vicolo m

alliance, a-lai´-ans, n alleanza f

allied, al´-aid, adj alleato; affine

allocate, al´-o-keit, v assegnare; stanziare

allot, a-lot´, v assegnare; spartire

allotment, a-lot´-ment, n assegnazione f; lotto di terreno m

allow, a-lau´, v permettere; concedere;

assegnare; calcolare

allowance, *a*-lau´-*a*ns, *n* (monetary) assegno *m*, indennità *f*; (rebate) sconto *m*; **to make - for,** scusare, tener conto di

alloy, al´-oi, *n* lega *f*

allude, *a*-luud´, *v* alludere

allure, *a*-liur´, *v* allettare; (tempt) sedurre

alluring, *a*-liur´-ring, *adj* allettante, seducente

allusion, *a*-luu´-shon, *n* allusione *f*

ally, al´-ai, *n* alleato *m*

ally, *a*-lai´, *v* allearsi

Almighty, ool-mai´-ti, *n* Onnipotente *m*

almond, aa´-mond, *n* mandorla *f*

almost, ool´-moust, *adv* quasi

alms, aams, *n* elemosina *f*

aloft, *a*-loft´, *adv* sopra, in alto

alone, *a*-loun´, *adv* solo

along, *a*-long´, *prep* lungo; *adv* avanti; insieme

alongside, *a*-long´-said, *prep* accanto a

aloof, *a*-luuf´, *adj* riservato; **keep –,** tenersi in disparte

aloud, *a*-laud´, *adv* ad alta voce

alphabet, al´-fa-bet, *n* alfabeto *m*

Alps, alps, *npl* Alpi *mpl*

already, ool-red´-i, *adv* già

also, ool´-sou, *adv* anche; ugualmente

altar, ool´-ta, *n* altare *m*

alter, ool´-ta, *v* mutare; modificare

alteration, ool-te-rei´-shon, *n* mutamento *m*

alternate, ool´-te-neit, *adj* alterno; **on – days,** ogni due giorni

alternative, ool-ter´-na-tiv, *adj* alternativo; *n* alternativa *f*

although, ool-Dou´, *conj* quantunque, sebbene

altitude, al´-ti-tiuud, *n* altitudine *f*, quota *f*

altogether, ool-to-geD´-a, *adv* interamente; nel complesso

aluminium, al-iu-min´-ium, *n* alluminio *m*

always, ool´-ueis, *adv* sempre

amass, *a*-mas´, *v* ammassare

amateur, am´-a-ter, *n* dilettante *m/f*

amaze, *a*-meis´, *v* stupire

amazement, *a*-meis´-ment, *n* stupore *m*

ambassador, am-bas´-a-da, *n* ambasciatore *m*

amber, am´-ba, *n* ambra *f*

ambiguity, am-bi-ghiu´-i-ti, *n* ambiguità *f*

ambiguous*, am-bi´-ghiu-os, *adj* ambiguo

ambition, am-bi´-shon, *n* ambizione *f*

ambitious*, am-bi´-shos, *adj* ambizioso

ambulance, am´-biu-*l*ans, *n* ambulanza *f*

ambush, am´-bush, *n* imboscata *f*, agguato *m*; *v* tendere un agguato

ameliorate, *a*-mii´-lio-reit, *v* migliorare

amenable to, *a*-mii´-na-bl tu, *adj* disposto a

amend, *a*-mend´, *v* (a law) emendare; (correct) correggere

amendment, *a*-mend´-ment, *n* (a law) emendamento *m*; correzione *f*

amends, *a*-mends´, **make –,** *v* farsi perdonare; indennizzare

amenities, *a*-mii´-ni-tis, *npl* attrezzature ricreative *fpl*; comodità *fpl*

America, *a*-me´-ri-ka, *n* America *f*

American, *a*-me´-ri-kan, *adj* americano

amethyst, am´-i-Zist, *n* ametista *f*

amiable, ei´-mia-bl, *adj* gentile, carino

amicable, am´-i-ka-bl, *adj* amichevole

amid(st), a-mid(st)', *prep* fra, tra, in mezzo a

amiss, a-mis', *adj* che non quadra

ammonia, a-mou´-ni-a, n ammoniaca f

ammunition, am-iu-ni´-shon, n munizioni fpl

amnesia, am-nii´-sia, n amnesia f

amnesty, am´-nis-ti, n amnistia f

among(st), a-mŏng(st)', *prep* tra, fra, in mezzo a

amorous*, am´-o-ros, *adj* amoroso

amount, a-maunt´, v ammontare; n importo m; quantità f; somma f

ample, am´-pl, *adj* ampio, vasto; abbondante

amplifier, am´-pli-fai-a, n amplificatore m

amplify, am´-pli-fai, v amplificare

amputate, am´-piu-teit, v amputare

amuck, a-mŏk´, **run –,** v correre all'impazzata; scatenarsi

amuse, a-miuus´, v divertire

amusement, a-miuus´-ment, n divertimento m, svago m

amusing*, a-miuus´-ing, *adj* divertente

an, an, *art* un, uno, una

anaemia, a-nii´-mi-a, n anemia f

anaemic, a-nii´-mik, *adj* anemico

anaesthetic, an-is-Zet´-ik, n anestetico m; **under –,** sotto anestesia

analogous, a-nal´-o-gos, *adj* analogo

analysis, a-nal´-i-sis, n analisi f; psicanalisi f

analyst, an´-a-list, n analista m/f

analyze, an´-a-lais, v analizzare

anarchy, an´-a-ki, n anarchia f

anatomy, a-na´-to-mi, n anatomia f

ancestor, an´-ses-ta, n antenato m

anchor, ang´-ka, n ancora f; v ancorare

anchorage, ang´-ka-rich, n ancoraggio m

anchovy, an´-cho-vi, n acciuga f, alice f

ancient*, ein´-shent, *adj* antico

and, and, *conj* e, ed

anecdote, an´-ik-dout, n aneddoto m

anew, a-niuu´, *adv* nuovamente, daccapo

angel, ein´-chel, n angelo m

anger, ang´-ga, n collera f, rabbia f; v far arrabbiare

angina, an-chai´-na, n angina pectoris f

angle, ang´-gl, n angolo m; punto di vista m; v pescare con la lenza

angler, ang´-gla, n pescatore con la lenza m

angry, ang´-gri, *adj* arrabbiato, in collera

anguish, ang´-guish, n angoscia f

animal, an´-i-mal, n animale m; *adj* animale

animate, an´-i-meit, v animare; ravvivare

animated, an´-i-mei-tid, *adj* animato

animation, an-i-mei´-shon, n animazione f

animosity, an-i-mo´-si-ti, n animosità f

aniseed, an´-i-siid, n anice m

ankle, ang´-kl, n caviglia f

annals, an´-als, npl annali mpl

annex, a-neks´, v annettere

annex, an´-eks, n (edificio) annesso m

annihilate, a-nai´-il-eit, v annientare

anniversary, a-ni-ver´-sa-ri, n anniversario m

annotate, an´-o-teit, v annotare

announce, a-nauns´, v annunciare

announcement, *a*-nauns´-ment, *n* annuncio *m*; (card) partecipazione *f*

announcer, *a*-nauns´-*a*, *n* annunciatore *m*, annunciatrice *f*

annoy, *a*-noi´, *v* dare fastidio a, molestare

annoying, *a*-noi´-ing, *adj* irritante

annoyance, *a*-noi´-*a*ns, *n* fastidio *m*, noia *f*

annual*, *a*n´-iu-al, *adj* annuo, annuale

annuity, *a*-niuu´-i-ti, *n* annualità *f*

annul, *a*-n$\breve{o}$l´, *v* annullare

annulment, *a*-n$\breve{o}$l´-ment, *n* annullamento *m*; abrogazione *f*

anoint, *a*-noint´, *v* ungere

anomalous*, *a*-nom´-*a*-los, *adj* anomalo

anonymous*, *a*-non´-i-mos, *adj* anonimo

anorak, a'-no-rak, *n* giacca a vento *f*

anorexia, a-no-rek´-si-a, *n* anoressia *f*

another, *a*-n$\breve{o}$´-Da, *adj* & *pron* un altro

answer, aan´-sa, *v* rispondere; *n* risposta *f*; soluzione *f*

answerable, aan´-se-ra-bl, *adj* responsabile

answering machine, aan´-se-ring ma-shiin´, *n*

segreteria telefonica *f*

ant, ant, *n* formica *f*

antagonist, an-tag´-o-nist, *n* antagonista *m/f*

antecedent, an-ti-sii´-dent, *adj* antecedente

antecedents, an-ti-sii´-dents, *npl* antecedenti *mpl*

antedate, an-ti-deit´, *v* antidatare; precedere

antediluvian, an-ti-di-luu´-vi-an, *adj* antidiluviano

antelope, an´-ti-loup, *n* antilope *f*

antenna, an-ten´-a, *n* antenna *f*

anterior, an-tier´-ri-a, *adj* anteriore

anteroom, an´-ti-ruum, *n* anticamera *f*

anthem, an´-Zem, *n* inno *m*

antibiotic, an-ti-bai-o´-tik, *adj* antibiotico; *n* antibiotico *m*

anticipate, an-tis´-i-peit, *v* anticipare; prevedere

anticipation, an-tis-i-pei´-shon, *n* previsione *f*; in –, in previsione; in anticipo

anticlimax, an-ti-klai´-maks, *n* delusione *f*

anticlockwise, an-ti-klok´-uais, *adv* & *adj* in senso antiorario

antics, an´-tiks, *npl* buffonerie *fpl*

antidote, an´-ti-dout, *n* antidoto *m*

antifreeze, an´-ti-friis, *n* antigelo *m*

antihistamine, an-ti-his´-ta-miin, *n* antistaminico *m*

antipathy, an-tip´-a-Zi, *n* antipatia *f*

antipodes, an-tip´-o-diis, *npl* antipodi *fpl*

antiquarian, an-ti-kueir´-ri-an, *n* antiquario *m*

antiquated, an´-ti-kueit-id, *adj* antiquato

antique, an-tiik´, *adj* antico; *n* pezzo d'antiquariato *m*

antiseptic, an-ti-sep´-tik, *n* antisettico *m*

antisocial, an-ti-sou´-shal, *adj* antisociale

antlers, ant´-les, *npl* corna di cervo *fpl*

anvil, an´-vil, *n* incudine *f*

anxiety, ang-sai´-i-ti, *n* ansietà *f*

anxious*, ang´-shos, *adj* ansioso; – for, desideroso di

any, en´-i, *adj* (any one) qualunque; (every) ogni; (in questions) del, dello, della, degli, delle, dei, qualche; (in negatives) nessun, nessuno, nessuna

anybody, en´-i-bo-di, *pron* chiunque; (in questions) qualcuno; (in negatives) nessuno

anyhow, en´-i-hau, *conj* comunque

anyone, e´-ni-uŏn, *pron* chiunque; (in questions) qualcuno; (in negatives) nessuno

anything, en´-i-Zing, *pron* qualunque cosa; (in questions) qualcosa; (in negatives) niente

anyway, en´-i-uei, *adv* in qualunque modo; in ogni modo; comunque

anywhere, en´-i-ueir, *adv* dovunque; (in questions) da qualche parte; (in negatives) da nessuna parte

apart, a-paart´, *adv* a parte; a distanza; a pezzi

apartheid, a-paar´-tait, *n* apartheid *m*

apartment, a-paart´-ment, *n* appartamento *m*

apartments, a-paart´-ments, *npl* stanze *fpl*

apathetic, ap-a-Zet´-ik, *adj* apatico

apathy, ap´-a-Zi, *n* apatia *f*

ape, eip, *n* scimmia *f; v* scimmiottare

aperitif, a-pe´-ri-tiif, *n* aperitivo *m*

aperture, ap´-e-cha, *n* (photo) apertura *f;* fessura *f*

apex, ei´-peks, *n* apice *m*

apologetic, a-pol´-o-che´-tik, *a* (person) che si scusa; (look, letter) di scuse

apologize, a-pol´-o-chais, *v* scusarsi

apology, a-pol´-o-chi, *n* scuse *fpl*

apoplexy, a´-po-plek-si, *n* apoplessia *f*

apostle, a-pos´-l, *n* apostolo *m*

apostrophe, a-pos´-tro-fi, *n* apostrofo *m*

apothecary, a-poZ´-i-ka-ri, *n* farmacista *m/f*

appal, a-pool´, *v* atterrire

appalling, a-pool´-ing, *adj* spaventoso, orribile

apparatus, ap-a-rei´-tos, *n* attrezzatura *f;* impianto *m;* apparato *m*

apparent*, a-pa´-rent, *adj* apparente; evidente

apparition, ap-a-ri´-shon, *n* apparizione *f*

appeal, a-piil´, *n law* appello *m;* richiesta *f; v* appellarsi; **– for,** chiedere; **– to,** (like) attrarre

appear, a-pier´, *v* apparire; (seem) sembrare

appearance, a-pier´-rans, *n*

apparizione *f;* (in public) comparsa *f;* (looks, figure) aspetto *m*

appearances, a-pier´-rans-is, *npl* apparenze *fpl*

appease, a-piis´, *v* placare, calmare; appagare

append, a-pend´, *v* allegare; apporre

appendicitis, a-pend-i-sai´-tis, *n* appendicite *f*

appendix, a-pen´-diks, *n* appendice *f*

appertain, ap-e-tein´, *v* essere pertinente

appetite, ap´-i-tait, *n* appetito *m;* desiderio *m*

appetizer, ap´-i-tais-a, *n* aperitivo *m;* stuzzichino *m*

appetizing, ap´-i-tais-ing, *adj* appetitoso

applaud, a-plood´, *v* applaudire; lodare

applause, a-ploos´, *n* applauso *m;* elogio *m*

apple, ap´-l, *n* mela *f*

apple tree, ap´-l trii, melo *m*

appliance, a-plai´-ans, *n* apparecchio *m;* (electrical) elettrodomestico *m*

applicant, ap´-li-kant, *n* candidato *m;* chi fa domanda

application, ap-li-kei´-shon, *n* (use)

applicazione f; (request) richiesta f, domanda f

apply, a-plai´, v (use) applicare; (as candidate) fare domanda, richiedere; – **to,** (turn to) rivolgersi

appoint, a-point´, v designare, nominare

appointment, a-point´-ment, n (meeting) appuntamento m; (to a post) nomina f

appointments, a-point´-ments, npl offerte di lavoro fpl

apportion, a-poor´-shon, v (money) ripartire; (blame) attribuire

apposite, ap´-o-sit, adj a proposito

appraisal, a-prei´-sal, n stima f, valutazione f; giudizio m

appraise, a-preis´, v apprezzare, valutare

appreciable, a-prii´-shi-a-bl, adj notevole

appreciate, a-prii´-shi-eit, v apprezzare; rendersi conto di; aumentare di valore

appreciation, a-prii-shi-ei´-shon, n apprezzamento m; gratitudine f

apprehend, ap´-ri-hend, v (seize) sequestrare;

arrestare; (understand) comprendere

apprehension, ap-ri-hen´-shon, n (fear) timore m; (arrest) arresto m

apprehensive*, ap-ri-hen´-siv, adj apprensivo

apprentice, a-pren´-tis, n apprendista m/f

apprenticeship, a-pren´-tis-ship, n tirocinio m, apprendistato m

apprize, a-prais´, v informare

approach, a-prouch´, v avvicinarsi; avvicinarsi; n approccio m; presa di contatto f; accesso m

approbation, ap-ro-bei´-shon, n approvazione f

appropriate, a-prou´-pri-eit, v appropriarsi; adj* adatto, appropriato

approval, a-pruu´-val, n approvazione f

approve, a-pruuv´, v approvare

approximate*, a-prok´-si-mat, adj approssimativo

apricot, ei´-pri-kot, n albicocca f

April, ei´-pril, n aprile m

apron, ei´-pron, n grembiule m

apse, aps, n abside f

apt, apt, adj adatto; dotato, capace; – **to,** incline a

aptitude, ap´-ti-tiuud, n attitudine f, tendenza f

Aquarius, ak-ueir´-ri-os, n Acquario m

aqueduct, ak´-ui-dŏkt, n acquedotto m

aqueous, ei´-kui-os, adj acquoso

aquiline, ak´-ui-lain, adj aquilino

arable, a´-ra-bl, adj arabile

arbitrary, aar´-bi-tra-ri, adj arbitrario

arbitrate, aar´-bi-treit, v arbitrare

arbitration, aar-bi-trei´-shon, n arbitraggio m; law arbitrato m

arbour, aar´-ba, n pergolato m

arc, aark, n (curved line) arco m

arcade, aar´-keid, n galleria f, portico m

arch, aarch, n (architecture) arco m

archaeologist, aar-ki-ol´-o-chist, n archeologo m

archaeology, aar-ki-ol´-o-chi, n archeologia f

archbishop, aarch-bish´-op, n arcivescovo m

archdeacon, aarch-dii´-kn, n arcidiacono m

archer, aarch´-a, n arciere m

archery, aarch´-a-ri, n tiro con l'arco m

archetype, aar´-ki-taip, n
archetipo m

architect, aar´-ki-tekt, n
architetto m

archives, aar´-kaivs, npl
archivi mpl

arctic, aark´-tik, adj artico

ardent*, aar´-dent, adj
ardente

ardour, aar´-da, n
ardore m

arduous*, aar´-diu-os, adj
arduo

area, eir-ri-a, n area f;
zona f; sfera f, campo m

arena, a-rii´-na, n arena f

argue, aar´-ghiuu, v
litigare, discutere;
sostenere, affermare

argument, aar´-ghiu-ment,
n argomento m,
motivo m; litigio m;
discussione f

Aries, eir-riis, n Ariete m

arise, a-rais´, v provenire;
presentarsi

aristocracy, a-ris-tok´-ra-
si, n aristocrazia f

aristocratic, a-ris-to-krat´-
ik, adj aristocratico

arithmetic, a-riZ´-me-tik,
n aritmetica f

ark, aark, n arca f

arm, aarm, n braccio m; v
armare

armament, aar´-ma-ment,
n armamento m

armchair, aarm´-cher, n
poltrona f

armistice, aar´-mis-tis, n
armistizio m

armour, aar´-ma, n
armatura f

armoured, aar´-med, adj
corazzato

armoured car, aar´-med
kaar, n autoblinda f

armoury, aar´-mo-ri, n
armeria f; arsenale m

armpit, aarm´-pit, n
ascella f

arms, aarms, npl armi fpl

coat of –, stemma m,
blasone m

arms race, aarms´ reis, n
corsa agli armamenti f

army, aar´-mi, n
esercito m

aromatic, a-ro-mat´-ik, adj
aromatico

around, a-raund´, adv
intorno; prep intorno a

arouse, a-raus´, v eccitare;
(awaken) svegliare

arrange, a-reinch´, v
ordinare, sistemare,
organizzare

arrangement, a-reinch´-
ment, n sistemazione f,
organizzazione f

array, a-rei´, n ordine m;
schieramento m; bella
mostra f

arrayed, a-reid´, adj
disposto; messo in
mostra

arrears, a-ries´, npl
arretrati mpl

arrest, a-rest´, v arrestare;
(development) fermare;
n arresto m

arrival, a-rai´-val, n
arrivo m

arrive, a-raiv´, v arrivare;
(aim) pervenire

arrogance, a´-ro-gans, n
arroganza f

arrogant*, a´-ro-gant, adj
arrogante

arrow, a´-rou, n freccia f

arsenal, aar´-sen-l, n
arsenale m

arsenic, aar´-sen-ik, n
arsenico m

arson, aar´-son, n
incendio doloso m

art, aart, n arte f

arterial, aar-tier´-ri-al, adj
(road) di grande traffico

artery, aar´-te-ri, n
arteria f

artful*, aart´-ful, adj
scaltro

arthritis, aarZ-rai´-tis, n
artrite f

artichoke, aar´-ti-chouk,
n carciofo m

article, aar´-ti-kl, n
articolo m

articulate, aar-tik´-iu-leit,
v articolare; adj che si
esprime chiaramente

artifice, aar´-ti-fis, n
astuzia f, artificio m

artificial*, aar-ti-fish´-al,
adj artificiale, artificioso

artillery, aar-til´-e-ri, *n*
artiglieria *f*

artisan, aar-ti-san´, *n*
artigiano *m*

artist, aar´-tist, *n* artista
m/f

artistic, aar-tis´-tik, *adj*
artistico

as, as, *conj* (manner)
come; (time) mentre;
(cause) siccome;
(although) per quanto;
(comparison) – **as** tanto
quanto, così come; –
for, in quanto a; – **if**,
come se; – **long as**,
purché; – **soon as**,
appena; – **though**, come
se; – **to**, in quanto a; –
well, egualmente; – **yet**,
finora

asbestos, as-bes´-tos, *n*
amianto *m*

ascend, a-send´, *v*
ascendere; scalare

ascent, a-sent´, *n*
ascensione *f*; salita *f*

ascertain, a-se-tein´, *v*
assicurarsi, accertare

ascribe, as-kraib´, *v*
attribuire

ash, ash, *n* cenere *f*; (tree)
frassino *m*

ashtray, ash´-trei,
portacenere *m*

ashamed, a-sheimd´, *adj*

vergognoso

ashore, a-shoor´, *adv* a
terra

Asia, ei-sha, *n* Asia *f*

Asian, ei-shan, *adj*
asiatico

aside, a-said´, *adv* in
disparte; (in a play) a
parte

ask, aask, *v* domandare;
(beg) pregare; (invite)
invitare; – **for** chiedere

askew, a-skiuu´, *adv* di
traverso

asleep, a-sliip´, *adj*
addormentato; **to be** –,
dormire; **to fall** –,
addormentarsi

asparagus, as-pa´-ra-gos, *n*
asparagi *mpl*

aspect, as´-pekt, *n* aspetto
m

aspen, as´-pn, *n* pioppo
tremulo *m*

aspersion, as-per´-shon, *n*
calunnia *f*, diffamazione
f

asphyxia, as-fik´-sia, *n*
asfissia *f*

asphyxiate, as-fik´-si-eit, *v*
asfissiare

asphyxiation, as-fik´-si-ei-
shon, *n* asfissia *f*

aspire, as-pair´, *v* ambire

aspirin, as´-prin, *n*
aspirina *f*

ass, as, *n* asino *m*

assail, a-seil´, *v* assalire

assailant, a-sei´-lant, *n*
assalitore *m*

assassinate, a-sas´-i-neit, *v*
assassinare

assault, a-soolt´, *n* assalto
m, aggressione *f*; *v*
assaltare, aggredire

assemble, a-sem´-bl, *v*
radunare; radunarsi;
mech montare

assembly, a-sem´-bli,
n assemblea *f*;
montaggio *m*

assembly line, a-sem´-bli
lain, *n* catena di
montaggio *f*

assent, a-sent´, *v* assentire;
n consenso *m*

assert, a-sert´, *v* sostenere

assertion, a-ser´-shon, *n*
asserzione *f*

assess, a-ses´, *v* valutare;
tassare

assessment, a-ses´-ment, *n*
valutazione *f*;
accertamento fiscale *m*

assets, a´-sets, *npl*
(personal) beni *mpl*;
comm attivo *m*

assiduous*, a-sid´-iu-os,
adj assiduo

assign, a-sain´, *v* assegnare

assignment, a-sain´-ment,
n incarico *m*; compito *m*

assist, a-sist´, *v* assistere

assistance, a-sist´-ans, *n*
assistenza *f*

assistant, a-sist´-ant, *n*

assistente *m/f*; (shop) commesso *m*, commessa *f*

assizes, *a-sais´*, *n* corte d'Assise *f*

associate, *a-sou´-si-eit*, *v* associare; *n* socio *m*; complice *m/f*; *adj* associato

association, *a-sou-si-ei´-shon*, *n* associazione *f*, società *f*

assorted, *a-soor´-tid*, *adj* assortito

assortment, *a-soort´-ment*, *n* assortimento *m*

assume, *a-siuum´*, *v* supporre; assumersi

assuming *a-siuum´-ing*, – **that,** *conj* supponendo che

assumption, *a-sŏmp´-shon*, *n* supposizione *f*, presupposto *m*; *relig* assunzione *f*

assurance, *a-shoo´-rans*, *n* assicurazione *f*; sicurezza di sé *f*

assure, *a-shoor´*, *v* assicurare

asterisk, *as´-te-risk*, *n* asterisco *m*

astern, *a-stern´*, *adv naut a* poppa

asthma, *as´-ma*, *n* asma *f*

astir, *a-ster´*, *adv* in moto

astonish, *as-ton´-ish*, *v* sorprendere

astound, *as-taund´*, *v* sbalordire

astray, *as-trei´*, *adv* **to go –,** smarrirsi; **to lead –,** traviare

astride, *as-traid´*, *adv* a cavalcioni

astrology, *as-trol´-o-chi*, *n* astrologia *f*

astronaut, *as´-tro´-noot*, *n* astronauta *m/f*

astronomy, *as-tron´-o-mi*, *n* astronomia *f*

astute, *as-tiut´*, *adj* astuto

astuteness, *as-tiut´-nis*, *n* scaltrezza *f*, astuzia *f*

asylum, *a-sai´-lom*, *n* rifugio *m*, asilo *m*; (mental) manicomio *m*

at, *at*, *prep* a, in, dentro, presso, da; **– once,** *adv* immediatamente; **– times,** alle volte

atheist, *ei´-Zii-ist*, *n* ateo *m*

Athens, *aZ´-ens*, *n* Atene *f*

athlete, *aZ´-liit*, *n* atleta *m/f*

athletic, *aZ-let´-ik*, *adj* atletico

atlas, *at´-las*, *n* atlante *m*

atmosphere, *at´-mo-sfier*, *n* atmosfera *f*

atom, *at´-om*, *n* atomo *m*

atonement, *a-toun´-ment*, *n* espiazione *f*

atrocious*, *a-trou´-shos*,

adj atroce

atrophy, *at´-ro-fi*, *n* atrofia *f*

attach, *a-tach´*, *v* attaccare; annettere; allegare

attachment, *a-tach´-ment*, *n* affetto *m*, attaccamento *m*

attack, *a-tak´*, *v* attaccare; aggredire; *n* attacco *m*

attain, *a-tein´*, *v* realizzare, raggiungere

attainment, *a-tein´-ment*, *n* realizzazione *f*, conseguimento *m*

attempt, *a-tempt´*, *v* provare; (risk) tentare; *n* tentativo *m*; (attack) attentato *m*

attend, *a-tend´*, *v* frequentare; (to be present) assistere a

attendance, *a-tend´-ans*, *n* presenza *f*; frequenza *f*

attendant, *a-tend´-ant*, *n* attendente *m/f*; (keeper) custode *m/f*; *adj* concomitante

attention, *a-ten´-shon*, *n* attenzione *f*

attest, *a-test´*, *v* testimoniare, attestare

attic, *at´-ik*, *n* soffitta *f*; mansarda *f*

attire, *a tair´*, *v* vestire; *n* abbigliamento *m*

attitude, *at´-i-tiuud*, *n*

atteggiamento *m*

attorney, *a-*ter´-ni, *n*
procuratore *m*; **power of
–,** procura *f*

attract, *a-*trakt´, *v* attrarre

attraction, *a-*trak´-shon, *n*
attrazione *f*

attractive, *a-*trak´-tiv, *adj*
attraente; allettante

attribute, at´-rib-iut, *n*
attributo *m*

attribute, *a-*trib´-iut, *v*
attribuire

aubergine, oo´-ber-**shiin**,
n melanzana *f*

auburn, oo´-ben, *adj* color
rame; color castano

auction, ook´-shon, *v*
vendere all'asta; *n* asta *f*,
incanto *m*

auctioneer, ook-shon-**ier**´,
n banditore *m*

audacious*, oo-dei´-shos,
adj audace

audacity, oo-das´-i-ti, *n*
audacia *f*

audible, oo' di-bl, *adj*
udibile

audience, oo´-di-ens, *n*
pubblico *m*, (radio)
ascoltatori *mpl*, (TV)
telespettatori *mpl*;
(formal hearing)
udienza *f*

audit, oo´-dit, *v* verificare;
n revisione dei conti *f*

auditor, oo dit-*a*, *n*
revisore dei conti *m*

augment, oogh-ment´, *v*
aumentare

augur, oo´-ga, *v* presagire

August, oo´-gost, *n*
agosto *m*

august, oo-göst´, *adj*
augusto

aunt, aant, *n* zia *f*

au pair, ou-per´, *n* ragazza
alla pari *f*

auspicious*, oos-pi´-shos,
adj propizio

austere*, oos-tier´, *adj*
austero

Australia, os-trei´-li-*a*, *n*
Australia *f*

Australian, os-trei´-li-an,
adj australiano

Austria, os´-tri-*a*, *n*
Austria *f*

Austrian, os´-tri-an, *adj*
austriaco

authentic, oo-Zen´-tik, *adj*
autentico

author, oo´-Za, *n* autore
m, autrice *f*

authoritative*, oo-Zo´-ri-
ta-tiv, *adj* autorevole;
autoritario

authority, oo-Zo´-ri-ti, *n*
autorità *f*

authorize, oo´-Zo-rais, *v*
autorizzare

autograph, oo´-to-graf, *n*
autografo *m*

automatic, oo-to-mat´-ik,
adj automatico

autumn, oo´-tom, *n*

autunno *m*

auxiliary, oogh-sil´-i-*a*-ri,
adj ausiliario

avail, *a-*veil´, *n* to no –,
inutilmente; – oneself
of, *v* servirsi di;
approfittare di

available, *a-*veil´-*a*-bl, *adj*
disponibile

avalanche, av´-*a*-laanch, *n*
valanga *f*

avaricious*, av-*a*-ri´-shos,
adj avaro

avenge, *a-*vench´, *v*
vendicare

avenue, av´-*e*-niuu, *n*
viale *m*

average, av´-*e*-rich, *adj*
medio; *n* media *f*

averse, *a-*vers´, *adj*
contrario (a)

aversion, *a-*ver´-shon, *n*
avversione *f*

avert, *a-*vert´, *v* evitare;
distogliere

aviary, ei´-vi-*a*-ri, *n*
uccelliera *f*

aviation, ei-vi-ei´-shon, *n*
aviazione *f*

avidity, *a-*vid´-i-ti, *n*
avidità *f*

avocado, av-*o*-kaa´-do, *n*
avocado *m*

avoid, *a-*void´, *v* evitare;
(elude) sottrarsi a

avow, *a-*vau´, *v* confessare,
dichiarare

await, *a-*ueit´, *v* aspettare

awake, *a*-ueik´, *adj* sveglio

awaken, *a*-ueik´-n, *v* svegliarsi; (arouse) destare, risvegliare

awakening, *a*-ueik´-n-ing, *n* risveglio *m*

award, *a*-uoord´, *n* premio *m*, ricompensa *f*; *law* risarcimento *m*; *v* (prize) assegnare, conferire; *law* accordare

aware, *a*-uer´, *adj* conscio; **to be – of,** rendersi conto di; essere al corrente di

awareness, *a*-uer´-niss, *n* consapevolezza *f*

away, *a*-uei´, *adv* via, fuori; **far –,** molto lontano

awe, oo, *n* rispetto *m*; timore *m*

awful*, oo´-ful, *adj* spaventoso, terribile

awhile, *a*-uail´, *adv* per un certo tempo

awkward, ook´-ued, *adj* imbarazzante; (clumsy) goffo

awkwardness, ook´-ued-nis, *n* imbarazzo *m*; goffaggine *f*

awning, oon´-ing, *n* tenda *f*

awry, *a*-rai´, *adv* & *adj* di traverso

axe, aks, *n* ascia *f*, scure *f*; *v* ridurre, annullare

axis, ak´-sis, *n* (geometry) asse *m*

axle, aks´-l, *n mech* asse *m*

azure, as´-iur, *adj* azzurro; *n* azzurro *m*

B

babble, bab´-l, v balbettare; n balbettio m

baby, bei´-bi, n bimbo m, bimba f

bachelor, bach´-i-lor, n scapolo m

back, bak, n schiena f; dorso m; v (support) sostenere; (bet) scommettere su; (car) fare marcia indietro; adv (behind) indietro; (return) di ritorno

backbone, bak´-boun, n (anatomy) spina dorsale f; fig forza f

background, bak´-graund, n sfondo m

backpack, bak´-pak, n zaino m

backseat, bak-siit´, n sedile posteriore m; fig posto secondario m

backward, bak´-uard, adj tardivo; arretrato

backwards, bak´-uards, adv indietro

bacon, bei´-kn, n pancetta f

bad*, bad, adj cattivo; brutto

badge, bach, n distintivo m

badger, bach´-ar, n tasso m; v tormentare

badminton, bad´-min-ton, n badminton m

baffle, baf´-l, v sconcertare

bag, bagh, n borsa f; sacchetto m

baggage, bagh´-ich, n bagaglio m

bagpipe, bagh´-paip, n cornamusa f

bail, beil, n cauzione f; **out on –,** in libertà su cauzione

bailiff, bei´-lif, n ufficiale giudiziario m

bait, beit, n esca f; v munire di esca

bake, beik, v cuocere al forno

baker, beik´-er, n fornaio m, fornaia f

bakery, beik´-e-ri, n panetteria f

balance, bal´-ans, n equilibrio m; (scales) bilancia f; comm saldo di conto m; v bilanciare; saldare

balance sheet, bal´-ans shiit, n bilancio m

balcony, bal´-ko-ni, n balcone m; (theatre) prima galleria f

bald*, boold, adj calvo

baldness, boold´-nis, n calvizie f

bale, beil, n balla f; v imballare; naut vuotare

baleful*, beil´-ful, adj malevolo

balk, baulk, boolk, v contrariare

ball, bool, n palla f; (golf) pallina f; (dance) ballo m

ballast, bal´-ast, n zavorra f; v zavorrare

ballet, bal´-ei, n balletto m; danza classica f

balloon, ba-luun´, n palloncino m

ballot, bal´-ot, n scrutinio m; (second ballot) ballottaggio m; v votare

ball-point, bool´-point, n penna a sfera f

balm, baam, n balsamo m

bamboo, bam-buu´, n bambù m

bamboozle, bam-buu´-sl, v abbindolare

ban, ban, n bando m, divieto m; v vietare

banana, ba-naa´-na, n banana f

band, band, n banda f

bandage, band´-ich, n benda f, fascia f

bandmaster, band´-maasta, n maestro di banda m

bandy (legged), ban´-di, adj con le gambe storte

bang, bang, n colpo m; v sbattere

banish, ban´-ish, v bandire

banister, ban´-is-ta, n ringhiera f

bank, bangk, n banca f; (river) riva f, sponda f

bank account, bangk´-a-kaunt, n conto in banca m

bank-book, bangk´-buk, n libretto di banca m

banker, bangk´-a, n banchiere m

bank-holiday, bangk-hol´-i-dei, n giorno di festa civile m

bank-note, bangk´-nout, n banconota f

bankrupt, bangk´-röpt, n fallito m; adj fallito

bankruptcy, bangk´-röp-si, n bancarotta f

banner, ban´-a, n bandiera f; striscione m

banquet, bang´-kuit, n banchetto m

banter, ban´-ta, n scherzo m; v scherzare

baptism, bap´-tis-m, n battesimo m

bar, baar, n (drinks) bar m; (metal) sbarra f; mus battuta f; law ordine degli avvocati m; v sbarrare; proibire

bar code, baar´-koud, n codice a barre m

barbarian, baar-beir´-ri-an, n barbaro m; adj barbaro

barbarity, baar-ba´-ri-ti, n barbarie f

barbecue, baar´-bi-kiu, n barbecue m

barbed, baarbd, adj spinato

barber, baar´-ba, n barbiere m

bare, beir, v spogliare; adj nudo

barefoot, beir´-fut, adj scalzo

barely, beir´-li, adv appena

bareness, beir´-nis, n nudità f

bargain, baar´-ghin, v contrattare; n occasione f

barge, baarch, n chiatta f

bark, baark, v abbaiare; n abbaiamento m; (tree) corteccia f

barley, baar´-li, n orzo m

barmaid, baar´-meid, n cameriera di bar f

barman, baar´-man, n barista m

barn, baarn, n granaio m

barometer, ba-rom´-it-a, n barometro m

baron, ba´-ron, n barone m

baroness, ba´-ron-es, n baronessa f

barracks, ba´-raks, npl caserma f

barrel, ba´-rel, n barile m; (gun) canna f

barren, ba´-ren, adj sterile; (land) arido

barricade, ba-ri-keid´, n barricata f; v barricare

barrier, ba´-ri-a, n barriera f

barrister, ba´-ris-ta, n avvocato m

barrow, ba´-rou, n

carrettino *m*
barter, baar´-ta, *v*
barattare; *n* baratto *m*
base, beis, *v* basare; *n* base
f; *adj* vile
baseball, beis´-bool, *n*
baseball *m*
baseless, beis´-lis, *adj*
senza fondamento
basement, beis´-ment, *n*
seminterrato *m*
baseness, beis´-nis, *n*
bassezza *f*
bashful*, bash´-ful, *adj*
timido
bashfulness, bash´-ful-nis,
n timidezza *f*
basic, bei-sik, *adj*
fondamentale;
elementare; **the –s,** *n*
l'essenziale *m*
basically, bei´-sik-li, *adv*
fondamentalmente
basin, bei´-sn, *n* catinella
f; (wash) lavabo *m*
basil, ba´-sil, *n* basilico *m*
basis, bei´-sis, *n* base *f*
bask, baask, *v* scaldarsi al
sole
basket, baas´-kit, *n* cesto
m, cestino *m*, cestello *m*;
canestro *m*
bass, beis, *n* (voice,
music) basso *m*
bassoon, ba-suun´, *n*
fagotto *m*
baste, beist, *v* (cookery)
inumidire; (sewing)

imbastire
bat, bat, *n* pipistrello *m*;
(sport) mazza *f*
batch, bach, *n* (bread)
infornata *f*; (articles,
etc.) mucchio *m*
bath, baaZ, *n* bagno *m*
bathroom, baaZ´-ruum *n*
stanza da bagno *f*
bathe, beiD, *v* fare i bagni
bather, bei´-Da, *n*
bagnante *m/f*
batter, bat´-a, *n* pasta da
friggere *f*
battery, bat´-a-ri, *n*
batteria *f*; (of torch,
radio) pila *f*
battle, bat´-l, *n* battaglia *f*
battleship, bat´-l-ship, *n*
corazzata *f*
bawl, bool, *v* urlare
bay, bei, *n* baia *f*; *adj*
(horse) baio; *v* latrare
bayonet, bei´-o-net, *n*
baionetta *f*
be, bii, *v* essere; esistere;
stare
beach, biich, *n* spiaggia *f*
beacon, bii´-kon, *n* faro;
segnale *m*
bead, biid, *n* perlina *f*;
(drop) goccia *f*
beagle, bii´-gl, *n*
bracchetto *m*
beak, biik, *n* becco *m*
beam, biim, *n* trave *f*;
(light) raggio *m*
beaming, bii´-ming, *adj*

raggiante
bean, biin, *n* fagiolo *m*; (of
coffee) chicco *m*
bear, bair, *n* orso *m*; *v*
(endure) sopportare;
(produce) produrre
bearable, ber´-abl, *adj*
sopportabile
bearer, ber´-a, *n* portatore
m; titolare *m/f*
bearing, ber´-ring, *n*
(behaviour) contegno
m; *mech* cuscinetto *m*
bearings, ber´-rings,
npl (location)
orientamento *m*
beard, bird, *n* barba *f*
bearded, bir´-did *adj*
barbuto
beardless, bird´-lis, *adj*
imberbe
beast, biist, *n* bestia *f*
beastly, biist´-li, *adv* & *adj*
bestiale
beat, biit, *v* battere; *n*
colpo *m*; (pulse) battito
m; *mus* battuta *f*
beautiful*, biuu´-ti-ful,
adj bello
beautify, biuu-ti-fai, *v*
abbellire
beauty, biuu´-ti, *n*
bellezza *f*
beauty spot, biuu´-ti spot,
n (mole) neo *m*;
(country) luogo
ameno *m*
beaver, bii´-va, *n*

castoro m

because, bi-kos´, *conj*
perché; **– of,** a causa di

beckon, bek´-n, *v* far
segno

become, bi-kŭm´, *v*
diventare

becoming*, bi-kŭm´-ing,
adj (conduct)
conveniente; (dress) che
sta bene

bed, bed, *n* letto *m*

bedding, bed´-ing, *n*
biancheria da letto *f*

bedpan, bed´-pan, *n*
(chamber pot) padella *f*

bedridden, bed´-rid-n, *adj*
costretto a letto

bedroom, bed´-ruum, *n*
stanza da letto *f*

bedstead, bed´-sted, *n*
lettiera *f*

bee, bii, *n* ape *f*

beech, biich, *n* faggio *m*

beef, biif, *n* carne di
manzo *f*

beehive, bii´-haiv, *n*
alveare *f*

beer, bir, *n* birra *f*

beetle, bii´-tl, *n*
coleottero *m*

beetroot, biit´-ruut, *n*
barbabietola *f*

befitting, bi-fit´-ing, *adj*
adatto

before, bi-foor´, *prep*
(time) prima di; (place)
davanti a; *adv* prima

beforehand, bi-foor´-
hand, *adv* in anticipo

befriend, bi-frend´, *v*
mostrare amicizia a

beg, begh, *v* (request, etc.)
pregare; (alms)
mendicare

beggar, beg´-a, *n*
mendicante *m/f*

begging, begh´-ing *n*
accattonaggio *m*

begin, bi-ghin´, *v*
cominciare, iniziare

beginner, bi-ghin´-a, *n*
principiante *m/f*

beginning, bi-ghin´-ing, *n*
principio *m*, inizio *m*

begrudge, bi-grŏch´, *v*
dare a malincuore

beguile, bi-gail´, *v*
incantare

behalf, be-haaf´, *n* **on –
of,** a nome di; per
conto di

behave, bi-heiv´, *v*
comportarsi

behaviour, bi-heiv´-ia, *n*
comportamento *m*

behead, bi-hed´, *v*
decapitare

behind, bi-haind´, *prep*
dietro; *adv* dietro;
indietro

behold, bi-hould´, *v*
guardare, mirare; *interj*
ecco!

being, bii´-ing, *n* esistenza
f; (human) essere *m*

belated, bi-lei´-tid, *adj* in
ritardo

belch, belch, *vulg v*
ruttare; *n* rutto *m*

belfry, bel´-fri, *n*
campanile *m*

Belgian, bel´-chan, *adj*
belga

Belgium, bel´-chum, *n*
Belgio *m*

belie, bi-lai´, *v* smentire

belief, bi-liif´, *n* credenza *f*

believable, bi-liiv´-a-bl,
adj credibile

believe, bi-liiv´, *v* credere

believer, bi-liiv´-a, *n*
credente *m/f*

belittle, bi-lit´-l, *v*
sminuire

bell, bel, *n* campana *f*;
campanello *m*;
sonaglio *m*

belligerent, bil-ich´-e-
rent, *adj* belligerante

bellow, bel´-ou, *v* muggire;
n muggito *m*

bellows, bel´-ous, *npl*
soffietto *m*

belly, bel´-i, *n* pancia *f*

belong, bi-long´, *v*
appartenere

belongings, bi-long´-ings,
npl cose *fpl*

beloved, bi-lŏv´-id, *adj*
diletto

below, bi-lou´, *prep*
sotto, al di sotto di;
adv sotto, giù

belt, belt, n cintura f; *mech* cinghia f

bemoan, bi-moun´, v lamentarsi di

bench, bench, n banco m; panchina f; *law* corte di giustizia f

bend, bend, n curva f; v curvare; piegare

beneath, bi-niiZ´, *prep* sotto; indegno di; *adv* sotto; giù

benediction, ben-i-dik´-shon, n benedizione f

benefactor, ben´-i-fak-ta, n benefattore m

beneficial*, ben-i-fi´-shal, *adj* salutare; vantaggioso

beneficiary, ben-i-fi´-sha-ri, n beneficiario m

benefit, ben´-i-fit, n beneficio m; v trarre beneficio da

benevolence, bi-nev´-o-lens, n benevolenza f

benevolent*, bi-nev´-o-lent, *adj* benevolo

benign, bi-nain´, *adj* benigno

bent, bent, *adj* piegato; n *fig* inclinazione f

bequeath, bi-kuiiZ´, v lasciare in eredità

bequest, bi-kuest´, n lascito m

bereavement, bi-riiv´-ment, n lutto m

Berlin, ber-lin´, n

Berlino f

berry, be´-ri, n bacca f

berth, berZ, n cuccetta f; *naut* ormeggio m

beseech, bi-siich´, v supplicare

beside, bi-said´, *prep* accanto a; fuori di

besides, bi-saids´, *adv* inoltre

besiege, bi-siich´, v assediare

besotted, bi-sot´-id, a infatuato

best, best, *adj* migliore; *adv* meglio

bestial, bes´-tial, *adj* bestiale

bestow, bi-stou´, v accordare, conferire

bet, bet, n scommessa f; v scommettere

betray, bi-trei´, v tradire

betrayal, bi-trei´-al, n tradimento m

betrothal, bi-trouD´-al, n fidanzamento m

better, bet´-a, *adj* migliore; *adv* meglio; v migliorare

betterment, bet´-e-ment, n miglioramento m

betting, bet´-ing, n scommesse fpl

between, bi-tuiin´, *prep* fra; *adv* in mezzo

bevel, bev´-l, v smussare

beverage, bev´-e-rich, n bevanda f

bevy, bev´-i, n brigata f

bewail, bi-ueil´, v rimpiangere

beware, bi-uer´, v guardarsi da; *interj* attenzione!

bewilder, bi-uil´-da, v sbalordire

bewilderment, bi-uil´-de-ment, n sbalordimento m

bewitch, bi-uich´, v stregare; *fig* affascinare

beyond, bi-iond´, *prep* al di là di; *adv* oltre

bias, bai´-as, n pregiudizio m

biased, bai´-ast, *adj* parziale

bible, bai´-bl, n bibbia f

bicker, bik´-a, v litigare

bickering, bik´-e-ring, n litigi mpl

bicycle, bai´-si-kl, n bicicletta f

bid, bid, n (at a sale) offerta f; v offrire; (order) comandare

bidder, bid´-a, n offerente m/f

bidding, bid´-ing, n offerte fpl

bide, baid, v aspettare

bier, bir, n feretro m

big, bigh, *adj* grande; grosso; importante

bigot, big´-ot, n fanatico m, fanatica f

bigoted, big´-ot-id, *adj*
fanatico

bike, baik, *n fam* bici *f*

bikini, bi-kii´-ni, *n*
bikini *m*

bilberry, bil´-be-ri, *n*
mirtillo *m*

bile, bail, *n* bile *f*

bilingual, bai-ling´-gual,
adj bilingue

bilious, bil´-i-os, *adj*
biliare

bill, bil, *n* conto *m*;
bolletta *f*; fattura *f*;
(poster) avviso *m*; *parl*
progetto di legge *m*;
(bird) becco *m*

billiards, bil´-iads, *npl*
biliardo *m*

billion, bi´-lion, *n*
miliardo *m*

bin, bin, *n* pattumiera *f*;
cestino dei rifiuti *m*

bind, baind, *v* legare;
(books) rilegare; (vow)
obbligare; – **up**, bendare

binding, bain´-ding, *n*
(books) rilegatura *f*; *adj*
vincolante

binoculars, bi-nok´-iu-les,
npl binocolo *m*

biography, bai-ogh´-ra-fi,
n biografia *f*

biological, bai-o-lod´-chi-
kl, *adj* biologico

biology, bai-ol´-o-chi, *n*
biologia *f*

biplane, bai´-plein, *n*

biplano *m*

birch, berch, *n* (tree)
betulla *f*; (rod) verga *f*

bird, berd, *n* uccello *m*;
–'s-eye view, vista a
volo d'uccello *f*

birth, berZ, *n* nascita *f*

birthday, berZ´-dei, *n*
compleanno *m*

birth-mark, berZ´-maark,
n voglia *f*

birthplace, berZ´-pleis, *n*
luogo di nascita *m*

birthrate, berZ´-reit, *n*
natalità *f*

biscuit, bis´-kit, *n*
biscotto *m*

bishop, bish´-op, *n*
vescovo *m*; (chess)
alfiere *m*

bit, bit, *n* pochino *m*;
(horse) morso *m*

bitch, bich, *n* cagna *f*

bite, bait, *v* mordere;
(sting) pungere; *n* morso
m; (of insect) puntura *f*

biting, bait´-ing, *adj*
mordente; (wind)
pungente

bitter*, bit´-a, *adj* amaro

bitterness, bit´-e-nis, *n*
amarezza *f*

black, blak, *n* nero *m*; *adj*
nero; (gloomy) cupo

black beetle, blak bii´-tl, *n*
scarafaggio *m*

blackberry, blak´-be-ri, *n*
mora di rovo *f*

blackbird, blak´-berd, *n*
merlo *m*

blackboard, blak´-boord,
n lavagna *f*

blackcurrant, blak´-kŏr-
ent, *n* ribes nero *m*

blacken, blak´-en, *v*
annerire; *fig* macchiare

blackleg, blak´-leg, *n*
crumiro *m*

blackmail, blak´-meil, *n*
ricatto *m*; *v* ricattare

blackmailer, blak´-meil-a,
n ricattatore *m*,
ricattatrice *f*

black market, blak maar´-
kit, *n* mercato nero *m*,
borsa nera *f*

black pudding, blak pud´-
ing, *n* sanguinaccio *m*

Black Sea, blak sii, *n* Mar
Nero *m*

blacksmith, blak´-smiZ, *n*
maniscalco *m*

blackthorn, blak´-Zoorn,
n pruno selvatico *m*

bladder, blad´-a, *n*
vescica *f*

blade, bleid, *n* lama *f*;
lametta *f*; (grass) filo
d'erba *m*; (oar) pala *f*

blame, bleim, *n* biasimo
m; *v* biasimare

blameless*, bleim´-lis, *adj*
irreprensibile

blanch, blaanch, *v*
impallidire; (cookery)
scottare

bland, bland, *adj* blando

blandishment, blan´-dish-ment, *n* lusinghe *fpl*

blank, blangk, *adj* (vacant) vacuo; (page) bianco; (shot) a salve; *n* spazio in bianco *m*

blanket, blang´-kit, *n* coperta *f*

blare, bler, *v* strombettare

blaspheme, blas-fiim´, *v* bestemmiare

blasphemy, blas´-fe-mi, *n* bestemmia *f*

blast, blaast, *v* (explode) far saltare; *n* (explosion) esplosione *f*; (gust) raffica *f*; (trumpet) squillo *m*

blatant, blei´-tant, *adj* sfacciato

blaze, bleis, *v* ardere; *n* incendio *m*

bleach, bliich, *v* candeggiare; decolorare; *n* candeggina *f*; decolorante *m*

bleak, bliik, *adj* (raw) gelido; (bare) desolato

bleat, bliit, *v* belare; *n* belato *m*

bleed, bliid, *v* sanguinare; (radiator) spurgare

bleeding, bliid´-ing, *n* emorragia *f*; *adj* sanguinante

blemish, blem´-ish, *n* macchia *f*; *v* macchiare

blend, blend, *v* mischiare; *n* miscela *f*

bless, bles, *v* benedire

blessed, blest, *adj* benedetto

blessing, bles´-ing, *n* benedizione *f*

blight, blait, *v* rovinare

blind, blaind, *adj* cieco; *v* accecare; *n* cieco *m*; (for window) avvolgibile *f*; (venetian) veneziana *f*

blind alley, blaind al´-i, *n* vicolo cieco *m*

blindfold, blaind´-fould, *v* bendare gli occhi

blindness, blaind´-nis, *n* cecità *f*

blink, blingk, *v* battere le palpebre

blinkers, bling´-kes, *n* (horse) paraocchi *m*

bliss, blis, *n* felicità *f*; beatitudine *f*

blissful, blis´-ful, *adj* beato

blister, blis´-ta, *n* vescica *f*

blithe*, blaiD, *adj* spensierato

blizzard, blis´-ad, *n* tormenta di neve *f*

bloated, blout´-id, *adj* gonfio

bloater, blout´-a, *n* aringa affumicata *f*

block, blok, *v* bloccare; *n* blocco *m*; (wood) ceppo *m*; (toy) cubo *m*; (of houses) isolato *m*

blockade, blok-eid´, *n* blocco *m*

blockage, blok´-ich, *n* ingorgo *m*; blocco *m*

blockhead, blok´-hed, *n* stupido *m*

bloke, blouk, *n fam* tipo *m*

blonde, blond, *n* bionda *f*

blood, blöd, *n* sangue *m*

blood pressure, blöd presh´-a, *n* pressione del sangue *f*

bloodhound, blöd´-haund, *n* cane segugio *m*

bloodshed, blöd´-shed, *n* spargimento di sangue *m*

bloodshot, blöd´-shot, *adj* iniettato di sangue

bloodthirsty, blöd´-Zer-sti, *adj* sanguinario

bloody, blöd´-i, *adj* sanguinante; insanguinato; sanguinoso

bloom, bluum, *v* fiorire; *n* fiore *m*; **in –,** in fiore

blossom, blos´-om, *v* fiorire; *n* fiori *mpl*

blot, blot, *v* macchiare; (dry) asciugare; *n* macchia *f*

blotch, bloch, *n* macchia *f*; chiazza *f*

blotting paper, blot´-ing pei´-pa, carta asciugante *f*

blouse, blaus, *n* blusa *f*

blow, blou, *n* pugno *m*;

colpo *m*; *v* suonare; soffiare; soffiarsi; – **up**, (tyres etc.) gonfiare; (explode) far saltare; (photo) ingrandire

blubber, blŏb´-*a*, *n* grasso di balena *m*; *v* piagnucolare

bludgeon, blŏch´-*en*, *n* randello *m*

blue, bluu, *adj* azzurro; blu; *n* azzurro *m*; blu *m*

bluebell, bluu´-bel, *n* campanella *f*

bluff, blăff, *n* bluff *m*; *v* bluffare

bluish, bluu´-ish, *adj* azzurrognolo; bluastro

blunder, blŏn´-*da*, *n* abbaglio *m*; *v* prendere un abbaglio

blunt*, blŏnt, *adj* smussato; brusco

blur, bler, *v* offuscare; *n* macchia *f*

blurt, blert, *v* lasciarsi sfuggire

blush, blŏsh, *n* rossore *m*; *v* arrossire

bluster, blŏs´-*ta*, *v* fare lo spaccone; *n* spacconate *fpl*

blustery, blŏs´-*te*-ri, *adj* tempestoso

boar, boor, *n* verro *m*; (wild) cinghiale *m*

board, boord, *n* asse *f*; tavola *f*; (directors)

consiglio di amministrazione *m*; (food) vitto *m*; *v* chiudere con assi

boarding house, boor´-ding haus, *n* pensione *f*

boarding school, boor´-ding skuul, *n* collegio *m*

boarder, boor´-da, *n* pensionante *m/f*

boast, boust, *v* vantarsi; *n* vanteria *f*

boaster, bous´-ta, *n* spaccone *m*

boat, bout, *n* barca *f*

boat-hook, bout´-huk, *n* alighiero *m*

boatswain, bou´-sn, *n* nostromo *m*

bob, bob, *v* andare su e giù, oscillare

bobbin, bob´-in, *n* rocchetto *m*; spoletta *f*

bodice, bod´-is, *n* corpino *m*

bodily, bod´-i-li, *adj* corporale; *adv* di peso

body, bod´-i, *n* corpo *m*; (corpse) cadavere *m*; (vehicle) carrozzeria *f*

bodyguard, bod´-i-gaard, *n* guardia del corpo *f*

bog, bogh, *n* pantano *m*

bogey, bou´-ghi, *n* (children's) uomo nero *m*

bogus, bou´-gus, *adj* fasullo

boil, boil, *v* bollire; *n med* foruncolo *m*

boiler, boil´-*a*, *n* caldaia *f*

boisterous, bois´-*te*-ros, *adj* impetuoso; turbolento

bold*, bould, *adj* audace, ardito

boldness, bould´-nis, *n* audacia *f*

bolster, boul´-sta, *n* capezzale *m*; – **up**, *v* sostenere

bolt, boult, *v* chiudere col catenaccio; (horse) imbizzarrirsi; *n* catenaccio *m*; (lightning) fulmine *m*

bomb, bom, *n* bomba *f*; *v* bombardare

bombard, bom-baard´, *v* bombardare

bombastic, bom-bas´-tik, *adj* ampolloso

bond, bond, *n* (tie) legame *m*; (obligation) impegno *m*; (stock) buono del tesoro *m*, obbligazione *f*; **in –**, (customs) in attesa di sdoganamento

bondage, bon´-dich, *n* servitù *f*

bone, boun, *n* osso *m*; (fish) spina di pesce *f*; *v* disossare; (fish) diliscare

bonfire, bon´-fair, *n* falò *m*

bonnet, bon´-it, n cuffia f; (car) cofano m

bonus, bou´-nus, n gratifica f

bony, bou´-ni, adj ossuto

book, buk, n libro m; v prenotare, riservare

bookbinder, buk´-baind-a, n rilegatore m

book-case, buk´-keis, n libreria f

booking-office, buk´-ing-of-is, n biglietteria f

book-keeper, buk´-kiip-a, n contabile m/f

book-keeping, buk´-kiip-ing, n contabilità f

book-mark, buk´-maark, n segnalibro m

bookseller, buk´-sel-a, n libraio m

bookshop, buk´-shop, n libreria f

bookstall, buk´-stool, n edicola f, chiosco di giornali m

bookworm, buk´-uerm, n fig topo di biblioteca m

boom, buum, n comm boom m; (noise) rombo m; v (trade) andare a gonfie vele; (noise) rimbombare

boon, buun, n benedizione f, manna f

boor, boor, n zotico m

boorish*, boor´-rish, adj zotico

boost, buust, v incrementare; n spinta f

boot, buut, n stivale m

booth, buuD, n cabina f

booty, buu´-ti, n bottino m

booze, buus, n fam alcolici mpl

border, boor´-da, n bordo m; (frontier) confine m; v costeggiare; confinare

bordering, boor´-de-ring, adj confinante; fig vicino

bore, boor, v perforare; (weary) annoiare; n (gun) calibro m; (person) noioso m, noiosa f

born, boorn, adj nato

borough, bŏ´-ra, n circoscrizione amministrativa f

borrow, bo´-rou, v prendere in prestito

bosom, bu´-som, n seno m

botanist, bot´-a-nist, n botanico m

botany, bot´-a-ni, n botanica f

both, bouZ, adj ambedue, entrambi

bother, boD´-a, v seccare; n seccatura f

bottle, bot´-l, n bottiglia f; v imbottigliare

bottom, bot´-om, n fondo m

bottomless, bot´-om-lis, adj senza fondo

bough, bau, n ramo m

bounce, bauns, v rimbalzare; n rimbalzo m

bound, baund, v limitare; (jump) saltare; n (jump) balzo m; **– for,** adj diretto a; **– to,** (obliged) tenuto a

boundary, baun´-da-ri, n confine m

bountiful*, baun´-ti-ful, adj abbondante

bounty, baun´-ti, n liberalità f; (reward) taglia f

bouquet, bu-kei´, n bouquet m

bout, baut, n attacco m, accesso m

bow, bou, n (archery) arco m; (violin) archetto m; (tie, knot) fiocco m

bow, bau, v inchinarsi; n inchino m; (ship) prua f

bowels, bau´-els, npl intestino m; viscere fpl

bowl, boul, n scodella f; bacinella f; v (cricket) lanciare la palla

bowling, bou´-ling, n bowling m

box, boks, v (fight) fare pugilato; n scatola f; (chest) cassa f; (theatre) palco m; **– on the ears,** scapaccione m

boxer, bok´-sa, n pugile m

boxing, bok´-sing, n pugilato m

Boxing Day, bok´-sing dei, il giorno di Santo Stefano m

boy, boi, n ragazzo m

boycott, boi´-kot, v boicottare; n boicottaggio m

boyfriend, boi´-frend, n ragazzo m

bra, braa, n reggiseno m

brace, breis, v rinforzare; n apparecchio ortodontico m; (two) paio m

bracelet, breis´-lit, n braccialetto m

braces, brei´-sis, npl bretelle fpl

bracing, brei´-sing, adj tonificante

bracken, brak´-n, n felce f

bracket, brak´-it, n mensola f; (parenthesis) parentesi f

brackish, brak´-ish, adj salmastro

brag, bragh, v vantarsi

braggart, brag´-at, n spaccone m

braid, breid, n treccia f; (dress) guarnizione f; v intrecciare

brain, brein, n cervello m

braise, breis, v brasare

brake, breik, n freno m; v frenare

bramble, bram´-bl, n rovo m

bran, bran, n crusca f

branch, braanch, n ramo m; comm filiale f; – off, v ramificarsi

brand, brand, n marca f; (on cattle) marchio m; v marchiare

brandish, bran´-dish, v brandire

brand-new, brand-niuu´, adj nuovo di zecca

brandy, bran´-di, n acquavite f

brass, braas, n ottone m

bravado, bra-vaa´-dou, n spavalderia f

brave*, breiv, adj valoroso

bravery, breiv´-e-ri, n valore m

bravo! braa-vou´, interj bravo!

brawl, brool, v azzuffarsi; n rissa f

brawn, broon, n sopressata f; muscoli mpl

brawny, broo´-ni, adj muscoloso

bray, brei, v (donkey) ragliare

brazen, brei´-sen, adj sfacciato

brazier, brei´-sia, n braciere m

Brazil, bra-sil´, n Brasile m

Brazilian, bra-si´-lian, adj brasiliano

brazil-nut, bra-sil´-nŏt, n noce del Brasile f

breach, briich, n rottura f; infrazione f; abuso m

bread, bred, n pane m

breadth, bredZ, n larghezza f

break, breik, v rompere; (the law) violare; n rottura f; (pause) pausa f; (school) ricreazione f

breakage, breik´-ich, n danni mpl

breakdown, breik´-daun, n interruzione f; (health) esaurimento m; mech panne f

breakers, breik´-es, npl (wave) cavalloni mpl

breakfast, brek´-fast, v far colazione; n prima colazione f

breakwater, breik´-uoo-ta, n frangiflutti m

bream, briim, n reina f

breast, brest, n petto m; seno m

breastbone, brest´-boun, n sterno m

breast-stroke, brest´-strouk, n nuoto a rana m

breath, breZ, n respiro m; fiato m

breathe, briiD, v respirare

breathless, breZ´-lis, adj senza fiato

breech, briich, n (gun) culatta f

breeches, briich´-is, *npl* calzoni *mpl*

breed, briid, *v* produrre; riprodursi; *n* razza *f*

breeder, brii´-da, *n* allevatore *m*

breeding, brii´-ding, *n* educazione *f*; (stock) allevamento *m*

breeze, briis, *n* brezza *f*

breezy, brii´-si, *adj* ventoso

brevity, brev´-i-ti, *n* brevità *f*

brew, bruu, *v* fabbricar birra

brewer, bruu´-a, *n* birraio *m*

brewery, bruu´-e-ri, *n* fabbrica di birra *f*

briar, brai´-a, *n* (wood) radica *f*; (bramble) rovo *m*

bribe, braib, *v* corrompere; *n* bustarella *f*

bribery, brai´-be-ri, *n* corruzione *f*

brick, brik, *n* mattone *m*

bricklayer, brik´-lei-a, *n* muratore *m*

bridal, brai´-dl, *adj* nuziale

bride, braid, *n* sposa *f*

bridegroom, braid´-gruum, *n* sposo *m*

bridesmaid, braids´-meid, *n* damigella d'onore *f*

bridge, brich, *n* ponte *m*; *v* gettare un ponte su

bridle, brai´-dl, *n* briglia *f*; *v* imbrigliare

brief, briif, *adj** breve; *v* dare istruzioni a; *n law* causa *f*

briefcase, briif´-keis, *n* valigetta ventiquattr' ore *f*

brigade, bri-gheid´, *n* brigata *f*

bright*, brait, *adj* luminoso; sereno; (lively) vivace; (clever) intelligente

brighten, brait´-n, *v* rischiarare; (enliven) rallegrare

brightness, brait´-nis, *n* luminosità *f*; vivacità *f*

brill, bril, *n* (fish) rombo *m*

brilliancy, bril´-ian-si, *n* splendore *m*

brilliant*, bril´-iant, *adj* brillante

brim, brim, *n* orlo *m*; (hat) falda *f*; – **over,** *v* traboccare

brimstone, brim´-stoun, *n* zolfo *m*

brine, brain, *n* salamoia *f*

bring, bring, *v* portare, recare; – **forward,** (accounts) riportare; – **in,** (produce) produrre; – **up,** (educate) allevare

brink, bringk, *n* orlo *m*

brisk*, brisk, *adj* vivace; vispo

brisket, bris´-kit, *n* punta di petto *f*

briskness, brisk´-nis, *n* vivacità *f*

bristle, bris´-l, *n* setola *f*; *v* rizzarsi

bristly, bris´-li, *adj* ispido

Britain, bri´-tn, *n* Gran Bretagna *f*

British, bri´-tish, *adj* britannico

brittle, brit´-l, *adj* fragile

brittleness, brit´-l-nis, *n* fragilità *f*

broach, brouch, *v* affrontare

broad*, brood, *adj* largo; (accent) marcato

broadcast, brood´-kaast, *n* (radio, TV) trasmissione *f*; *v* trasmettere

brocade, bro-keid´, *n* broccato *m*

broccoli, brok´-o-li, *n* broccolo *m*

brochure, broush´-a, *n* dépliant *m*

brogue, brough, *n* accento *m*; scarpone *m*

broil, broil, *n* (quarrel) rissa *f*

broken, brou´-kn, *adj* rotto; (language) stentato

broker, brou-ka, *n* intermediario *m*

brokerage, brou´-ke-rich,

n intermediazione *f*

bromide, brou´-maid, *n*
bromuro *m*

bronchitis, brong-kai´-tis,
n bronchite *f*

bronze, brons, *n* bronzo *m*;
v bronzare; (tan)
abbronzarsi

brooch, brouch, *n* spilla *f*

brood, bruud, *n* covata *f*; *v*
covare

brook, bruk, *n* ruscello *m*

broom, bruum, *n* scopa *f*;
(plant) ginestra *f*

broth, broZ, *n* brodo *m*

brothel, broZ´-l,
bordello *m*

brother, brŏ´-Da, *n*
fratello *m*

brother-in-law, brŏ´-De-
rin-loo, *n* cognato *m*

brotherly, brŏ´-De-li, *adj*
fraterno

brow, brau, *n* sopracciglio
m; *fig* fronte *f*

browbeat, brau´-biit, *v*
intimidire

brown, braun, *adj*
marrone; *n* marrone *m*; *v*
abbrunire; (cookery)
rosolare

brownish, brau´-nish, *adj*
marroncino

browse, braus, *v* curiosare
qua e là

bruise, bruus, *n* livido *m*;
ammaccatura *f*; *v* farsi
un livido; ammaccare

brunette, bru-net´, *n*
brunetta *f*

brunt, brŏnt, *n* urto *m*

brush, brŏsh, *n* spazzola *f*;
(paint) pennello *m*; *v*
spazzolare; spennellare;
(sweep) spazzare

brushwood, brŏsh´-uud, *n*
sottobosco *m*

brusque, brusk, *adj* brusco

Brussels, brŏs-ls, *n*
Bruxelles *f*

Brussels sprouts, brŏs-ls-
sprauts´, *npl* cavolini di
Bruxelles *mpl*

brutal*, bruu´-tl, *adj*
brutale

brutality, bru-tal´-i-ti, *n*
brutalità *f*

brutalize, bruu´-tal-ais, *v*
abbrutire; brutalizzare

brute, bruut, *n* bruto *m*

bubble, bŏb´-l, *n* bolla *f*; *v*
ribollire

buck, bŏk, *n* (deer) daino
m; *adj* maschio

bucket, bŏk´-it, *n*
secchio *m*

buckle, bŏk´-l, *n* fibbia *f*; *v*
affibbiare, allacciare

buckskin, bŏk´-skin, *n*
pelle di daino *f*

buckwheat, bŏk´-uiit, *n*
grano saraceno *m*

bud, bŏd, *n* bocciolo *m*;
gemma *f*; *v* sbocciare;
germogliare

budge, bŏch, *v* muoversi

budget, bŏch´-it, *n*
bilancio *m*

buff, bŏf, *adj* color
camoscio; *v* lucidare

buffalo, bŏf´-a-lou, *n*
buffalo *m*

buffer, bŏf´-a, *n* (railway)
respingente *m*

buffet, bu-fei, *n* buffet *m*

buffet, bŏf´-it, *v*
sballottare

buffoon, bu-fuun´, *n*
buffone *m*

bug, bŏgh, *n* cimice *f*

bugbear, bŏg´-ber, *n*
spauracchio *m*

buggy, bŏ´-ghi, *n*
passeggino *m*

bugle, biuu´-gl, *n*
cornetta *f*

build, bild, *v* costruire

builder, bil´-da, *n*
costruttore edile *m*

building, bil´-ding, *n*
edificio *m*, palazzo *m*

bulb, bŏlb, *n* bulbo *m*;
(lamp) lampadina *f*

bulge, bŏlch, *v* gonfiare; *n*
rigonfiamento *m*

bulk, bŏlk, *n* volume *m*; **in
–,** in grande quantità

bulky, bŏl´-ki, *adj*
voluminoso

bull, bul, *n* toro *m*; (stock-
exchange) rialzista *m/f*;
–'s eye, (target) centro
del bersaglio

bulldog, bul´-dogh, *n*

bulldog *m*

bulldozer, bul´-dous-*a*, *n*
bulldozer *m*

bullet, bul´-it, *n* proiettile
m, pallottola *f*

bulletin, bul´-i-tin, *n*
bollettino *m*

bullfinch, bul´-finch, *n*
ciuffolotto *m*

bullion, bul´-ion, *n* oro in
lingotti *m*

bullock, bul´-ok, *n*
manzo *m*

bully, bul´-i, *n* prepotente
m/f; *v* fare il prepotente
con

bulrush, bul´-rŏsh, *n*
giunco *m*

bump, bŏmp, *n* colpo *m*,
botta *f*; (swelling)
bernoccolo *m*; *v* urtare,
sbattere

bumper, bŏm´-pa, *n*
paraurti *m*

bumpkin, bŏmp´-kin, *n*
buzzurro *m*

bumptious, bŏmp´-shos,
adj arrogante

bun, bŏn, *n* panino *m*;
(hair) chignon *m*

bunch, bŏnch, *v*
ammucchiare; *n* mazzo
m; (bananas) casco *m*;
(people) gruppo *m*;
– of grapes, grappolo
d'uva *m*

bundle, bŏn´-dl, *n* fagotto
m; fascio *m*; (of wood)

fascina *f*; *v* fare un
fascio di

bung, bŏng, *n* tappo *m*

bungalow, bŏng´-ga-lou, *n*
bungalow *m*

bungle, bŏng´-gl, *v* fare
pasticci

bungler, bŏng´-gla, *n*
pasticcione *m*,
pasticciona *f*

bunion, bŏn´-ion, *n* callo
al piede *m*

bunk, bŏnk, *n* cuccetta *f*

bunk bed, bŏnk bed, *n*
letto a castello *m*

bunker, bŏng´-ka, *n* (coal)
carbonaia *f*

bunkum, bŏng´-kom, *n*
sciocchezze *fpl*

bunny, bŏn-i, *n*
coniglietto *m*

buoy, boi, *n* boa *f*

buoyancy, boi´-an-si, *n*
galleggiabilità *f*

buoyant, boi´-ant, *adj*
galleggiante; di
buonumore

burden, ber´-dn, *n* carico
m; peso *m*; *v* caricare;
opprimere

burdensome, ber´-dn-som,
adj pesante

bureau, biu´-rou, *n* ufficio
m; scrittoio *m*

bureaucracy, biu-ro´-kra-
si, *n* burocrazia *f*

burger, ber´-gha, *n*
hamburger *m*

burglar, ber´-gla, *n*
ladro *m*

burglary, ber´-gla-ri, *n*
furto *m*

burial, be´-ri-al, *n*
seppellimento *m*

burial-ground, be´-ri-al-
graund, *n* cimitero *m*

burlesque, ber-lesk´, *n*
parodia *f*

burly, ber´-li, *adj* robusto

burn, bern, *v* bruciare;
(arson) incendiare; *n*
bruciatura *f*; *med*
ustione *f*

burner, ber´-na, *n* becco a
gas *m*

burnish, ber´-nish, *v*
brunire

burrow, bŏ´-rou, *v* scavare
una tana; *n* tana *f*

bursar, ber´-sa, *n* (school)
economo *m*

burst, berst, *v* scoppiare; *n*
scoppio *m*

bury, be´-ri, *v* seppellire;
(conceal) sotterrare

bus, bŏs, *n* autobus *m*

bush, bush, *n* cespuglio *m*

bushel, bush´-l, *n* staio *m*

bushy, bush-i, *adj* folto

business, bis´-nis, *n* affari
mpl; impresa *f*

business-like, bis´-nis-
laik, *adj* pratico;
efficiente

businessman, bis´-nis-
man, *n* uomo d'affari,

imprenditore *m*

businesswoman, bis´-nis-uu-man, *n* imprenditrice *f*

busker, bŏs´-ka, *n* suonatore ambulante *m*

bust, bŏst, *n* busto *m*

bustle, bŭs´-l, *n* trambusto *m*; *v* affaccendarsi

bus stop, bŏs' stop, *n* fermata d'autobus *f*

busy, bis´-i, *adj* occupato; affaccendato; (place) movimentato; *v* – **oneself,** affaccendarsi

busybody, bis´-i-bod-i, *n* ficcanaso *m/f*

but, bŏt, *conj* & *prep* ma; *adv* solo, solamente

butcher, buch´-a, *n* macellaio *m*; *v* macellare

butler, bŏt´-la, *n* maggiordomo *m*

butt, bŏt, *n* (gun) calcio *m*; (cask) tino *m*; *v* dare una testata a

butter, bŏt´-a, *n* burro *m*; *v* imburrare

buttercup, bŏt´-e-kŏp, *n* ranuncolo *m*

butter-dish, bŏt´-e-dish, *n* burriera *f*

butterfly, bŏt´-e-flai, *n* farfalla *f*

buttock, bŏt´-ok, *n* natica *f*

button, bŏt´-n, *n* bottone *m*; *v* abbottonare

button-hole, bŏt´-n-houl, *n* occhiello *m*

buttress, bŏt´-ris, *n* contrafforte *m*; *v* puntellare

butts, bŏts, *npl* poligono di tiro *m*

buxom, bŏk´-som, *adj* (woman) formosa

buy, bai, *v* comprare

buyer, bai´-a, *n* compratore *m*

buzz, bŏs, *n* ronzio *m*; brusio *m*; *v* ronzare

buzzard, bŏs´-ad, *n* poiana *f*

buzzer, bŏs-a, *n* cicalino *m*; sirena *f*

by, bai, *prep* da; per; di; accanto a

bye, bai, *interj* ciao!, arrivederci!

by-law, bai´-loo, *n* ordinanza locale *f*

bystander, bai´-stan-da, *n* spettatore *m*

byway, bai´-uei, *n* strada secondaria *f*

byword, bai´-uerd, *n* detto comune *m*; – **for** sinonimo di

cab, kab, n taxi m

cabbage, kab´-ich, n cavolo m

cabin, kab´-in, n cabina f; capanna f

cabinet, kab´-in-it, n consiglio dei ministri m; armadietto m

cabinet-maker, kab´-in-it-meik-a, n ebanista m

cable, kei´-bl, n cavo m; v telegrafare

cable television, kei´-bl te´-li-vish-on, n televisione via cavo f

cackle, kak´-l, v ridacchiare

caddy, ka´-di, n scatola da tè f

cadge, kach, v scroccare

café, ka´-fei, n caffè m, bar m

cafeteria, ka-fe-tie´-ri-a, n bar self-service m

cage, keich, n gabbia f; v ingabbiare

cajole, ka-choul´, v lusingare

cake, keik, n torta f

calculate, kal´-kiu-leit, v calcolare

calculator, kal´-kiu-lei-ta, n calcolatrice f

calendar, kal´-en-da, n calendario m

calf, kaaf, n vitello m; polpaccio m

call, kool, v chiamare; (name) chiamarsi; n chiamata f

callous*, kal´-os, adj insensibile

calm, kaam, n calma f; adj* calmo; v calmare

calmness, kaam´-nis, n calma f

calorie, ka´-lo-ri, n caloria f

camcorder, kam´-koor-da, n camcorder f

camel, kam´-l, n cammello m

cameo, kam´-i-ou, n cammeo m

camera, kam´-e-ra, n macchina fotografica f

camisole, kam´-i-soul, n camicetta f

camomile, kam´-o-mail, n camomilla f

camouflage, kam´-u-flaash, n mimetizzazione f

camp, kamp, v accamparsi; n campeggio m; accampamento m

camp bed, kamp´-bed, n brandina f

campaign, kam-pein´, n campagna f

camping, kam´-ping, n campeggio

campsite, kamp´-sait, n campeggio m, camping m

campus, kam´-pus, n campus m

can, kan, n scatoletta f, lattina f

can, kan, v (to be able) potere; (to know) sapere

Canada, ka´-na-da, n

Canada m

Canadian, ka-nei´-di-an, adj canadese

canal, ka-nal´, n canale m

canary, ka-ner´-ri, n canarino m

cancel, kan´-sl, v cancellare

Cancer kan´-sa, n Cancro m

cancer, kan´-sa, n cancro m

candid*, kan´-did, adj franco

candidate, kan´-di-dat, n candidato m

candied, kan´-did, adj candito

candle, kan´-dl, n candela f

candlestick, kan´-dl-stik, n candeliere m

candour, kan´-da, n candore m

candy, kan´-di, n dolciumi mpl

candyfloss, kan´-di-flos, n zucchero filato m

cane, kein, n bastone da passeggio m; bacchetta f; v bacchettare

canine, kei´-nain, adj canino

cannabis, kan´-a-bis, n canapa indiana f

cannibal, kan´-i-bl, n cannibale m/f

cannon, kan´-on, n

cannone m

canoe, ka-nuu´, n canoa f

can opener, kan´-oup-na, n apriscatole m

canopy, kan´-o-pi, n baldacchino m

cantankerous, kan-tang´-ke-ros, adj bisbetico

canteen, kan-tiin´, n mensa f

canvas, kan´-vas, n tela f

canvass, kan´-vas, v fare propaganda elettorale

cap, kap, n berretto m; tappo m; cappuccio m

capable, kei´-pa-bl, adj capace

capacity, ka-pa´-si-ti, n capacità f; capienza f

cape, keip, n mantello m

caper, kei´-pa, n cappero m

capital, kap´-i-tl, n (money) capitale m; (city) capitale f; (letter) lettera maiuscola f

capitalism, kap´-i-ta-lis-m, n capitalismo m

Capricorn, kap´-ri-koorn, n Capricorno m

capsize, kap-sais´, v capovolgere

capsule, kap´-siuul, n capsula f

captain, kap´-tin, n capitano m

captive, kap´-tiv, adj prigioniero

captivity, kap-tiv´-i-ti, n prigionia f; cattività f

capture, kap´-cha, n cattura f; v catturare

car, kaar, n auto f; vagone m

caramel, ka´-ra-mel, n caramello m

caravan, ka´-ra-van, n roulotte f

carbon, kaar´-bon, n carbonio m

carbon paper, kaar´-bon pei´-pa, n carta carbone f

carburettor, kaar-ba-ret´-a, n carburatore m

carcass, kaar´-kas, n carcassa f

card, kaard, n biglietto da visita m; (playing) carta f

cardboard, kaard´-boord, n cartone m

cardboard box, kaard´-boord boks, n scatola di cartone f

cardigan, kaar´-di-gan, n cardigan m

cardinal, kaar´-di-nl, n cardinale m

care, ker, n attenzione f; (anxiety) preoccupazione f; **take –!** interj attenzion!; **to take – of,** v badare a

career, ka-riir´, n carriera f

careful*, ker´-ful, adj

attento
careless*, ker´-lis, *adj*
negligente; disattento
carelessness, ker´-lis-nis,
n negligenza *f*
caress, ka-res´, *n* carezza *f*;
v accarezzare
caretaker, ker´-tei-ka, *n*
custode *m/f*
car ferry, kaar´-fe-ri, *n*
traghetto *m*
cargo, kaar´-gou, *n*
carico *m*
car hire, kaar´-hair, *n*
autonoleggio *m*
caricature, ka-ri-ka-
chiuur, *n* caricatura *f*
carnage, kaar´-nich, *n*
carneficina *f*
carnal*, kaar´-nl, *adj*
·carnale
carnation, kaar-nei´-shon,
n garofano *m*
carnival, kaar´-ni-vl, *n*
carnevale *m*
carol, ka´-rol, *n* canto di
Natale *m*
carp, kaarp, *n* carpa *f*
car park, kaar´-paark, *n*
parcheggio *m*
carpenter, kaar´-pen-ta, *n*
falegname *m*
carpet, kaar´-pit, *n*
tappeto *m*; moquette *f*
carriage, ka´-rich, *n*
vettura *f*
carrier bag, ka´-ri-a bagh,
n sacchetto *m*, busta di

plastica *f*
carrot, ka´-rot, *n* carota *f*
carry, ka´-ri, *v* portare; –
on, *fig* continuare
cart, kaart, *n* carretto *m*
carton, kaar´-ton, *n* (milk
etc.) cartone *m*;
(cigarettes) stecca *f*
cartoon, kaar-tuun´, *n*
fumetto *m*; cartone
animato *m*
cartridge, kaar´-trich, *n*
cartuccia *f*
carve, kaarv, *v* intagliare;
(meat) tagliare
carving, kaar´-ving, *n*
intaglio *m*
car wash, kaar´-uosh, *n*
autolavaggio *m*
cascade, kas-keid´, *n*
cascata *f*
case, keis, *n* caso *m*;
scatola *f*; astuccio *m*;
valigia *f*; *law* causa *f*; **in
–**, in caso
casement, keis´-ment, *n*
finestra *f*
cash, kash, *n* denaro *m*;
(ready money) contanti
mpl; *v* incassare
cash-book, kash´-buk, *n*
libro di cassa *m*
cash card, kash´-kaard, *n*
carta per prelievi
automatici *f*
cash dispenser, kash dis-
pen´-sa, *n* sportello
automatico *m*

cashier, kash´-ir, *n*
cassiere *m*, cassiera *f*
cashmere, kash´-mir, *n*
cachemire *m*
cask, kaask, *n* barile *m*
casket, kaas´-kit, *n*
cofanetto *m*
cassette, ka-set´, *n*
cassetta *f*
cassette player, ka-set'
plei´-a, *n* riproduttore a
cassetta *m*
cast, kaast, *n* (theatre)
cast *m*; (plaster)
ingessatura *f*; *v* gettare
caste, kaast, *n* casta *f*
cast iron, kaast ai´-on, *n*
ghisa *f*
castle, kaa´-sl, *n* castello
m; (chess) torre *f*
castor, kaas´-ta, *n* rotella *f*
castor oil, kaas´-to-roil, *n*
olio di ricino *m*
casual*, kash´-u-al, *adj*
casuale
casualties, kash´-u-al-tis,
npl vittime *fpl*
casualty, kash´-u-al-ti, *n*
pronto soccorso *m*
cat, kat, *n* gatto *m*
catalogue, kat´-o-logh, *n*
catalogo *m*; *v* catalogare
catarrh, ka-taar´, *n*
catarro *m*
catastrophe, ka-tas´-tro-fi,
n catastrofe *f*
catch, kach, *v* prendere;
afferrare; – **up**,

raggiungere; n presa f; gancio m

catching, kach´-ing, *adj* contagioso

catchword, kach´-uerd, n slogan m

category, kat´-i-go-ri, n categoria f

cater, kei´-ta, v provvedere; (food) provvedere alla ristorazione

catering, kei´-te-ring, n ristorazione f

caterpillar, kat´-e-pil-a, n bruco m

cathedral, ka-Zii´-dral, n cattedrale f, duomo m

catholic, kaZ´-o-lik, n cattolico m; *adj* cattolico

cattle, kat´-l, n bestiame m

cauliflower, ko´-li-flau-a, n cavolfiore m

cause, koos, n causa f; v causare

caustic, koos´-tik, *adj* caustico

cauterize, koo´-te-rais, v cauterizzare

caution, koo´-shon, n cautela f; diffida f; v diffidare

cautious*, koo´-shos, *adj* cauto

cavalier, kav-a-lir´, *adj* brusco, sbrigativo

cavalry, kav´-l-ri, n cavalleria f

cave, keiv, n caverna f

caviar, kav´-iaar, n caviale m

cavity, kav´-i-ti, n cavità f; (tooth) carie f

caw, koo, v gracchiare

cayenne pepper, kei-en' pep´-a, n pepe di Caienna m

CD, sii-dii´, n CD m

CD player, sii-dii' plei´-a, n lettore di CD m

CD ROM, sii-dii-rom´, n CD-rom m

cease, siis, v cessare

ceasefire, siis´-fair, n cessate il fuoco m

ceaseless*, siis´-lis, *adj* incessante

cedar, sii´-da, n cedro m

ceiling, sii´-ling, n soffitto m

celebrate, sel´-i-breit, v celebrare

celebrated, sel´-i-breit-id, *adj* celebre

celebration, sel-i-brei´-shon, n celebrazione f; festeggiamento m

celery, sel´-e-ri, n sedano m

cell, sel, n cella f; cellula f

cellar, sel´-a, n cantina f

cement, si-ment´, n cemento m; v cementare

cemetery, sem´-it-ri, n cimitero m

censor, sen´-sa, n

censore m

censorship, sen´-so-ship, n censura f

census, sen-sus, n censimento m

cent, sent, n (coin) centesimo m

centenary, sen-tii-ne-ri, n centenario m

centigrade, sen´-ti-greid, *adj* centigrado

centimetre, sen´-ti-mii-ta, n centimetro m

central, sen´-tral, *adj* centrale

central heating, sen´-tral hii´-ting, n riscaldamento autonomo m

centralize, sen´-tral-ais, v centralizzare

centre, sen´-ta, n centro m

century, sen´-chu-ri, n secolo m

ceramics, se-ram´-iks, n ceramica f

cereal, siir´-ri-al, n cereale m

ceremony, se´-ri-mo-ni, n cerimonia f

certain*, ser´-tan, *adj* certo

certainty, ser´-tan-ti, n certezza f

certificate, ser-tif´-i-kat, n certificato m; diploma m

certify, ser´-ti-fai, v certificare, attestare

chain, chein, n catena f; – **up,** v incatenare

chair, cher, n sedia f; poltrona f; (university) cattedra f

chairman, cher´-man, n presidente m

chalk, chook, n gesso m

challenge, chal´-inch, n sfida f; v sfidare

chambermaid, cheim´-be-meid, n cameriera f

chambers, cheim´-bes, npl (office) studio legale m

chamois, sham´-uŏ, n camoscio m

champagne, sham-pein´, n champagne m

champion, cham´-pion, n campione m, campionessa f

championship, cham´-pion-ship, n campionato m

chance, chaans, n caso m; occasione f; possibilità f; adj casuale; v rischiare

chancellor, chaan´-se-la, n cancelliere m

chandelier, shan-di-lir´, n lampadario m

change, cheinch, n spiccioli mpl; resto m; cambiamento m; v cambiare

changeable, chein´-cha-bl, adj variabile

changing room, chein´-

ching ruum, n camerino m; spogliatoio m

channel, chan´-l, n canale m; **the English –,** la Manica f

chant, chaant, n canto m

chaos, kei´-os, n caos m

chaotic, kei-ot´-ik, adj caotico

chap, chap, n screpolatura f; (fellow) tipo m; v screpolare

chapel, chap´-l, n cappella f

chaplain, chap´-lin, n cappellano m

chapter, chap´-ta, n capitolo m

char, chaar, v carbonizzare

character, kar´-ik-ta, n carattere m; personaggio m

characteristic, kar´-ik-te-ris-tik, adj caratteristico

charcoal, chaar´-koul, n carbone di legna m; carboncino m

charge, chaarch, n tariffa f; accusa f; carica f; v chiedere; accusare; caricare; **to be in – of,** essere responsabile di

charitable, cha´-ri-ta-bl, adj caritatevole

charity, cha´-ri-ti, n carità f; opera pia f

charm, chaarm, n fascino m; v affascinare;

incantare

charming*, chaar´-ming, adj affascinante

chart, chaart, n carta nautica f

charter, chaar´-ta, v noleggiare

charter flight, chaar´-ta flait, n volo charter m

chase, cheis, n caccia f; v cacciare; (pursue) inseguire

chasm, kas-m, n abisso m

chastity, chas´-ti-ti, n castità f

chat, chat, n chiacchierata f; v chiacchierare

chatter, chat´-a, n ciance fpl; v cianciare; (teeth) battere i denti

chatter-box, chat´-a-boks, n chiacchierone m, chiacchierona f

chauffeur, shou-fer´, n chauffeur m, autista m

cheap*, chiip, adj a buon mercato

cheat, chiit, v imbrogliare

cheating, chii´-ting, n imbrogli mpl

check, chek, n controllo m; (restraint) freno m; (chess) scacco m; (pattern) quadretto m; v controllare; (restrain) frenare

check-in, chek´-in, n accettazione bagagli f

checkmate, chek-meit´, n scacco matto m; v dare scacco matto

checkout, chek´-aut, n (supermarket) cassa f

cheek, chiik, n guancia f; sfacciataggine f

cheer, chir, v rallegrare

cheerful*, chir´-ful, adj allegro

cheers, chirs, interj cin cin!

cheese, chiis, n formaggio m

chef, shef, n chef m

chemical, kem´-i-kl, n prodotto chimico m; adj* chimico

chemist, kem´-ist, n (scientist) chimico m; (pharmacist) farmacista m/f

chemistry, kem´-ist-ri, n chimica f

cheque, chek, n assegno m

chequebook, chek´-buk, n libretto degli assegni m

cheque card, chek´-kaard, n carta assegni f

cherish, che´-rish, v amare

cherry, che´-ri, n ciliegia f

cherub, che´-rub, n cherubino m

chess, ches, n scacchi mpl

chest, chest, n petto m; (box) cassa f

chestnut, ches´-nŏt, n castagna f

chest of drawers, chest´-ov-droos, n cassettone m

chew, chu, v masticare

chewing gum, chu´-ing-gŏm, n gomma da masticare f

chick, chik, n pulcino m

chicken, chik´-in, n pollo m

chickenpox, chik´-in-poks, n varicella f

chief, chiif, n capo m; adj principale

chiefly, chiif´-li, adv principalmente

chilblain, chil´-blein, n gelone m

child, chaild, n bambino m, bambina f

childbirth, chaild´-berZ, n parto m

childish*, chail-dish, adj puerile

chill, chil, n colpo d'aria m; v raffreddare

chilli, chil´-i, n peperoncino m

chilly, chil´-i, adj freddo

chime, chaim, n rintocco m; v suonare

chimney, chim´-ni, n camino m

chimney sweep, chim´-ni suiip, n spazzacamino m

chin, chin, n mento m

china, chai´-na, n porcellana f

China, chai´-na, n Cina f

Chinese, chai-niis´, adj cinese

chink, chingk, n crepaccio m; tintinnio m

chip, chip, n patata fritta f; scheggia f; v scheggiare

chiropodist, ki-rop´-o-dist, n pedicure m/f

chirp, cherp, n cinguettio m; v cinguettare

chisel, chis´-l, n scalpello m

chivalrous, shiv´-l-ros, adj cavalleresco

chive, chaiv, n erba cipollina f

chlorine, kloo´-riin, n cloro m

chloroform, klo´-ro-foorm, n cloroformio m

chocolate, chok´-o-lat, n cioccolata f; cioccolato m

choice, chois, n scelta f; adj scelto

choir, kuair, n coro m

choke, chouk, v soffocare

cholera, kol´-e-ra, n colera m

choose, chuus, v scegliere

chop, chop, n costoletta f; v spaccare; tagliare

chopsticks, chop´-stiks, npl bacchette cinesi fpl

choral, koo´-ral, adj corale

chord, koord, n mus

accordo *m*

chorus, koo´-rus, *n* coro *m*; ritornello *m*

Christ, kraist, *n* Cristo *m*

christen, kris´-n, *v* battezzare

christening, kris´-ning, *n* battesimo *m*

Christmas, kris´-mas, *n* Natale *m*

Christmas tree, kris´-mas trii, *n* albero di Natale *m*

chronic, kron´-ik, *adj* cronico

chronicle, kron´-ik-l, *n* cronaca *f*

chrysanthemum, kri-san´-Ze-mum, *n* crisantemo *m*

chubby, chŏb´-i, *adj* paffuto

chuck, chŏk, *v* buttare

chuckle, chŏk´-l, *n* risatina *f*; *v* ridacchiare

chum, chŏm, *n* compagno *m*

chunk, chŏngk, *n* grossa fetta *f*

church, cherch, *n* chiesa *f*

churchyard, cherch´-iaard, *n* camposanto *m*

churlish, cher´-lish, *adj* sgarbato

cider, sai´-da, *n* sidro *m*

cigar, si-gaar´, *n* sigaro *m*

cigarette, sig-a-ret´, *n* sigaretta *f*

cinder, sin´-da, *n* brace *f*

cinema, si´-ni-ma, *n* cinema *m*

cinnamon, si´-na-mon, *n* cannella *f*

circle, ser´-kl, *n* cerchio *m*; (in theatre) galleria *f*; *v* cerchiare

circuit, ser´-kit, *n* circuito *m*

circuitous*, ser-kiu´-it-os, *adj* indiretto

circular, ser´-kiu-la, *n* circolare *f*; *adj* circolare

circulate, ser´-kiu-leit, *v* circolare

circumcise, ser´-kum-sais, *v* circoncidere

circumference, ser-kŏm´-fe-rens, *n* circonferenza *f*

circumflex, ser´-kum-fleks, *adj* circonflesso

circumscribe, ser´-kum-skraib, *v* circoscrivere

circumspect, ser´-kum-spekt, *adj* circospetto

circumstance, ser´-kum-stans, *n* circostanza *f*

circumvent, ser-kum-vent´, *v* aggirare

circus, ser´-kus, *n* circo *m*; (place) piazza rotonda *f*

cistern, sis´-ten, *n* cisterna *f*

citizen, sit´-i-sen, *n* cittadino *m*

citizenship, sit´-i-sen-ship, *n* cittadinanza *f*

city, sit´-i, *n* città *f*

civil, siv´-il, *adj* civile

civilian, siv-il´-ian, *n* borghese *m/f*; civile *m/f*

civilization, siv-il-ai-sei´-shon, *n* civiltà *f*

claim, kleim, *n* rivendicazione *f*; (demand) pretesa *f*; *v* rivendicare; pretendere

clamber, klam´-ba, *v* arrampicarsi

clamour, klam´-a, *n* clamore *m*

clamp, klamp, *n* morsetto *m*; *v* stringere con un morsetto

clan, klan, *n* clan *m*

clandestine, klan-des´-tin, *adj* clandestino

clap, klap, *v* applaudire; *n* battimano *m*; (thunder) colpo *m*

clapping, klap´-ing, *n* applauso *m*

claret, kla´-rit, *n* vino rosso di Bordeaux *m*

clarify, kla´-ri-fai, *v* chiarificare

clarinet, kla-ri-net´, *n* clarinetto *m*

clash, klash, *n* scontro *m*; *v* scontrarsi

clasp, klaasp, *v* stringere; *n* (catch) fermaglio *m*

class, klaas, *n* classe *f*; *v* classificare

classify, klas´-i-fai, *v* classificare

clatter, klat´-a, n strepitio m; v strepitare

clause, kloos, n clausola f

claw, kloo, n artiglio m; (lobster etc.) pinza f; v graffiare

clay, klei, n creta f

clean, kliin, v pulire; adj* pulito

cleaner, klii´-na, n addetto alle pulizie m; donna delle pulizie f

cleaning, klii´-ning, n pulizia f

cleanliness, klen´-li-nis, n pulizia f

cleanse, klens, v pulire; purificare

clear, klir, adj* chiaro; libero; v sgombrare; (table) sparecchiare; (sky) schiarirsi

cleaver, klii-va, n mannaia f

cleft, kleft, n fenditura f

clench, klench, v serrare

clergy, kler´-chi, n clero m

clergyman, kler´-chi-man, n sacerdote m

clerical, kle´-ri-kl, adj d'ufficio; relig clericale

clerk, klaark, n impiegato m, impiegata f

clever*, klev´-a, adj intelligente; abile

client, klai´-ent, n cliente m/f

clientele, klii-on-tel´, n clientela f

cliff, klif, n scogliera f

climate, klai´-mit, n clima m

climax, klai´-maks, n culmine m

climb, klaim, n salita f; scalata f; v salire; scalare; arrampicarsi

climber, klai´-ma, n alpinista m/f

clinch, klinch, v concludere

cling, kling, v aggrapparsi

clinic, kli´-nik, n clinica f

clink, klingk, n tintinnio m; v tintinnare

clip, klip, n forcina f; graffetta f; v tagliare

cloak, klouk, n mantello m

cloak-room, klouk´-ruum, n guardaroba m

clock, klok, n orologio m

clog, klogh, n zoccolo m; – up, v intasarsi

cloister, klois´-ta, n chiostro m

clone, kloun, n clone m; v clonare

close, klous, v chiudere; adj vicino; (weather) afoso

closely, klous´-li, adv da vicino, attentamente; strettamente

closet, klos´-it, n armadio m

closure, klou´-sha, n chiusura f

clot, klot, n grumo m; v coagularsi

cloth, kloZ, n tessuto m

clothe, klouD, v vestire

clothes, klouDs, npl vestiti mpl

clothing, klou´-Ding, n abbigliamento m

cloud, klaud, n nuvola f; v offuscarsi

cloudy, klau´-di, adj nuvoloso; fig torbido

clout, klaut, n scapaccione m

clove, klouv, n chiodo di garofano m; (garlic) spicchio m

clover, klou´-va, n trifoglio m

clown, klaun, n pagliaccio m

club, klöb, n club m; mazza f

cluck, klök, v chiocciare

clue, kluu, n indizio m; (crossword) definizione f

clump, klömp, n (grass) ciuffo m; (trees etc.) gruppo m

clumsiness, klöm´-si-nis, n goffaggine f

clumsy, klöm´-si, adj goffo

cluster, klös´-ta, n (grapes) grappolo m; (group) gruppo m

clutch, klöch, n stretta f;

(car) frizione f; v afferrare

coach, kouch, n pullman m; (sport) allenatore m; v allenare

coagulate, kou-agh´-iu-leit, v coagulare

coal, koul, n carbone m

coalition, kou-a-li´-shon, n coalizione f

coal mine, koul´-main, n miniera di carbone f

coarse*, koors, adj grosso; volgare

coarseness, koors´-nis, n grossezza f; ruvidezza f; volgarità f

coast, koust, n costa f

coastguard, koust´-gaard, n guardacoste m; guardia costiera f

coat, kout, n cappotto m; (animal) pelo m; (paint) mano f

coating, kou´-ting, n rivestimento m

coax, kouks, v blandire

cobbler, kob´-la, n calzolaio m

cobweb, kob´-ueb, n ragnatela f

cocaine, kou-kein´, n cocaina f

cock, kok, n gallo m

cockerel, kok´-e-rel, n galletto m

cockle, kok´-l, n vongola f

cockroach, kok´-rouch, n

scarafaggio m

cocoa, kou´-kou, n cacao m

coconut, kou´-ko-nŏt, n noce di cocco f

cocoon, ko-kuun´, n bozzolo m

cod, kod, n merluzzo m

code, koud, n codice m

cod-liver oil, kod´-li-va-roil, n olio di fegato di merluzzo m

coerce, kou-ers´, v costringere

coffee, kof´-i, n caffè m

coffeepot, kof´-i-pot, n caffettiera f

coffee table, kof´-i tei´-bl, n tavolino m

coffin, kof´-in, n bara f

cog, kogh, n dente f

cognac, kon´-iak, n cognac m

cogwheel, kogh´-uiil, n ruota dentata f

coherence, kou-hir´-rens, n coerenza f

coherent*, kou-hir´-rent, adj coerente

cohesion, kou-hii´-shon, n coesione f

cohesive*, kou-hii´-siv, adj coesivo

coil, koil, n rotolo m; bobina f

coin, koin, n moneta f; v coniare

coincide, kou-in-said´, v

coincidere

coincidence, kou-in´-si-dens, n coincidenza f

Coke, kouk, ® n coca f

colander, kol´-en-da, n colino m

cold, kould, n freddo m; raffreddore m; adj freddo

colic, kol´-ik, n colica f

collaborate, ko-lab´-o-reit, v collaborare

collapse, ko-laps´, n crollo m; v crollare

collar, kol´-a, n colletto m; (dog) collare m

collarbone, kol´-a-boun, n clavicola f

collateral, ko-lat´-e-ral, n garanzia f

colleague, kol´-iigh, n collega m f

collect, ko-lekt´, v raccogliere; ritirare, andare a prendere; radunarsi

collected, ko-lek´-tid, adj padrone di sé

collection, ko-lek´-shon, n raccolta f; collezione f; colletta f

collective*, ko-lek´-tiv, adj collettivo

collector, ko-lek´-ta, n collezionista m/f; (revenue) esattore m

college, kol´-ich, n college m; istituto superiore m

collide, ko-laid´, v

scontrarsi

collier, kol´-ie, n
minatore m

colliery, kol´-ie-ri, n
miniera di carbone f

collision, ko-li´-shon, n
collisione f

colloquial, ko-lou´-kui-al,
adj familiare

collusion, ko-luu´-shon, n
collusione f

colon, kou´-lon, n due
punti mpl

colonel, ker´-nl, n
colonnello m

colonial, ko-lou´-ni-al, adj
coloniale

colony, kol´-o-ni, n
colonia f

colossal, ko-los´-l, adj
colossale

colour, kŏl´-a, n colore m;
v colorare

colourful, kŏl´-o-ful, adj
dai colori vivaci

colouring, kŏl´-o-ring, n
colorante m

colt, koult, n puledro m

column, kol´-om, n
colonna f; rubrica f

coma, kou´-ma, n coma m

comb, koum, n pettine m;
v pettinare

combat, kom´-bat, n
combattimento m; v
combattere

combination, kom-bi-
nei´-shon, n

combinazione f

combine, kom-bain´, v
combinare

come, kŏm, v venire; –
down, scendere; – **in,**
entrare; – **off,** staccarsi;
– **out,** uscire; – **up,** salire

comedian, ko-mii´-di-an,
n comico m

comedy, kom´-i-di, n
commedia f

comet, kom´-it, n
cometa f

comfort, kŏm´-fot, n
benessere m; comodità f;
v consolare, confortare

comfortable, kŏm´-fo-ta-
bl, adj comodo

comfortably, kŏm´-fo-ta-
bli, adv comodamente;
agiatamente

comic, kom´-ik, adj
comico; n fumetto m

coming, kŏm´-ing, adj
prossimo; n venuta f

comma, kom´-a, n virgola
f

command, ko-maand´, n
ordine m; (knowledge)
padronanza f; v ordinare

commander, ko-maand´-a,
n comandante m

commandment, ko-
maand´-ment, n
comandamento m

commemorate, ko-mem´-
o-reit, v commemorare

commence, ko-mens´, v

cominciare

commencement, ko-
mens´-ment, n
principio m

commend, ko-mend´, v
raccomandare; (praise)
lodare

commendation, ko-men-
dei´-shon, n elogio m

comment, kom´-ent, n
commento m; v
commentare

commerce, kom´-ers, n
commercio m

commercial, ko-mer´-shal,
adj commerciale

commiserate, ko-mis´-e-
reit, v commiserare

commission, ko-mish´-on,
v commissionare; n
(percentage)
commissione f

commit, ko-mit´, v (crime,
fault) commettere;
(bind) impegnarsi

commitment, ko-mit´-
ment, n impegno m;
dedizione f

committee, ko-mit´-i, n
comitato m

commodity, ko-mod´-i-ti,
n prodotto m, articolo m

common, kom´-on, adj*
(usual) comune;
(vulgar) volgare; n
terreno municipale m

commonplace, kom´-on-
pleis, adj banale; trito

Commons, kom´-ons, *npl* (House of —) Camera dei Comuni *f*

commonwealth, kom´-on-uelZ, *n* commonwealth *m*

commotion, ko-mou´-shon, *n* confusione *f*

communicate, ko-miuu´-ni-keit, *v* comunicare

communication, ko-miuu-ni-kei´-shon, *n* comunicazione *f*

Communion, ko-miuu´-nion, *n relig* comunione *f*

community, ko-miuu´-ni-ti, *n* comunità *f*

commute, ko-miuut, *v* fare il pendolare

commuter, ko-miuut´-a, *n* pendolare *m/f*

compact*, kom-pakt´, *adj* compatto

companion, kom-pan´-ion, *n* compagno *m*

companionship, kom-pan´-ion-ship, *n* compagnia *f*

company, kom´-pa-ni, *n* compagnia *f*; società *f*

comparative*, kom-pa´-ra-tiv, *adj* comparativo

compare, kom-per´, *v* paragonare

comparison, kom-pa´-ri-sn, *n* paragone *m*

compartment, kom-paart´-ment, *n* scompartimento *m*

compass, köm´-pas, *n* bussola *f*

compasses, köm´-pas-is, *npl* compasso *m*

compassionate*, kom-pa´-sho-nat, *adj* compassionevole

compatible, kom-pa´-ti-bl, *adj* compatibile

compel, kom-pel´, *v* costringere

compelling, kom-pel´-ing, *adj* convincente

compensate, kom´-pen-seit, *v* compensare

compensation, kom-pen-sei´-shon, *n* compensazione *f*; risarcimento *m*

compete, kom-piit´, *v* concorrere

competent, kom´-pi-tent, *adj* competente

competition, kom-pi-tish´-n, *n* concorrenza *f*; (games etc.) gara *f*; concorso *m*

competitive, kom-pe´-ti-tiv, *adj* concorrenziale; agonistico

competitor, kom-pet´-i-ta, *n* concorrente *m/f*

compile, kom-pail´, *v* compilare

complacent, kom-plei´-sent, *adj* compiaciuto

complain, kom-plein´, *v* lagnarsi; reclamare

complaint, kom-pleint´, *n* lagnanza *f*; reclamo *m*

complement, kom´-pli-ment, *n* complemento *m*

complete, kom-pliit´, *v* completare; *adj* completo

completion, kom-plii´-shon, *n* completamento *m*

complex, kom´-pleks, *adj* complesso

complexion, kom-plek´-shon, *n* carnagione *f*

compliance, kom-plai´-ans, *n* accordo *m*

complicate, kom´-pli-keit, *v* complicare

compliment, kom´-pli-ment, *n* complimento *m*

comply with, kom-plai´ uiD, *v* conformarsi a

component, kom-pou´-nent, *n* componente *m*

compose, kom-pous´, *v* comporre

composer, kom-pou´-sa, *n* compositore *m*

composite, kom´-po-sit, *adj* composto

composition, kom-po-si´-shon, *n* composizione *f*

composure, kom-pou´-sha, *n* calma *f*

compound, kom´-paund, *n* composto *m*; (enclosure) recinto *m*;

adj composto

comprehend, kom-pri-hend´, *v* comprendere, capire

comprehension, kom-pri-hen´-shon, *n* comprensione *f*

compress, kom´-pres, *n* compressa *f*; *v* comprimere

comprise, kom-prais´, *v* comprendere

compromise, kom´-pro-mais, *n* compromesso *m*; *v* compromettere

compulsion, kom-pŏl´-shon, *n* costrizione *f*

compulsory, kom-pŏl´-so-ri, *adj* obbligatorio

computer, kom-piuu´-ta, *n* computer *m*

comrade, kom´-reid, *n* compagno *m*

con, kon, *v* truffare; *n* truffa *f*

conceal, kon-siil´, *v* nascondere

concede, kon-siid´, *v* concedere, ammettere

conceit, kon-siit´, *n* presunzione *f*

conceited*, kon-sii´-tid, *adj* presuntuoso

conceive, kon-siiv´, *v* concepire

concentrate, kon´-sen-treit, *v* concentrare

concentration camp, ko-sen-trei´-shon kamp, *n* campo di concentramento *m*

concept, kon´-sept, *n* concetto *m*

concern, kon-sern´, *n* affare *m*; azienda *f*; preoccupazione *f*; *v* riguardare

concerned, kon-sernd´, *adj* preoccupato

concerning, kon-ser´-ning, *prep* riguardo a

concert, kon´-set, *n* concerto *m*

concession, kon-sesh´-n, *n* concessione *f*; riduzione *f*

conciliate, kon-sil´-i-eit, *v* conciliare

concise*, kon-sais´, *adj* conciso

conclude, kon-kluud´, *v* concludere

conclusion, kon-kluu´-shon, *n* conclusione *f*

conclusive*, kon-kluu´-siv, *adj* conclusivo

concoct, kon-kokt´, *v* elaborare; preparare

concord, kon´-koord, *n* concordia *f*

concrete, kon´-kriit, *n* calcestruzzo *m*; *adj* concreto

concurrence, kon-kŏ´-rens, *n* concorso *m*

concussion, kon-kŏsh´-n, *n* commozione cerebrale *f*

condemn, kon-dem´, *v* condannare

condense, kon-dens´, *v* condensare

condescending, kon-di-sen´-ding, *adj* sussiegoso

condiment, kon´-di-ment, *n* condimento *m*

condition, kon-di´-shon, *n* condizione *f*; malattia *f*

conditional*, kon-di´-shon-al, *adj* condizionale

conditioner, kon-di-shon-a, *n* (hair) balsamo *m*; (fabric) ammorbidente *m*

condolences, kon-dou´-len-sis, *npl* condoglianze *fpl*

condom, kon´-dom, *n* preservativo *m*

condone, kon-doun´, *v* condonare

conducive, kon-diuu´-siv, *adj* favorevole

conduct, kon´-dŏkt, *n* condotta *f*

conduct, kon-dŏkt´, *v* condurre; *mus* dirigere

conductor, kon-dŏkt´-a, *n* (bus) controllore *m*; *mus* direttore d'orchestra *m*

cone, koun, *n* cono *m*; pigna *f*

confectioner, kon-fek´-sho-na, *n* pasticciere *m*;

(shop) pasticceria f

confectionery, kon-fek´-sho-ne-ri, n dolciumi mpl

confederation, kon-fed-e-rei´-shon, n confederazione f

confer, kon-fer´, v conferire

conference, kon´-fe-rens, n conferenza f; congresso m

confess, kon-fes´, v confessare

confession, kon-fesh´-n, n confessione f

confide, kon-faid´, v confidare

confidence, kon´-fi-dens, n confidenza f

confident*, kon´-fi-dent, adj sicuro

confidential*, kon-fi-den´-shal, adj riservato, confidenziale

confine, kon-fain´, v limitare; (lock-up) rinchiudere

confinement, kon-fain´-ment, n reclusione f

confirm, kon-ferm´, v confermare; cresimare

confirmation, kon-fe-mei´-shon, n conferma f; relig cresima f

confiscate, kon´-fis-keit, v confiscare

conflict, kon´-flikt, n

conflitto m; v essere in conflitto

conflicting, kon-flik´-ting, adj contraddittorio

conform, kon-foorm´, v conformarsi

conformable, kon-foor´-ma-bl, adj conforme

confound, kon-faund´, v confondere

confront, kon-frònt´, v affrontare

confuse, kon-fiuus´, v confondere

confusing, kon-fiuu´-sing, adj confuso; ambiguo

confusion, kon-fiuu´-shon, n confusione f

confute, kon-fiuut´, v confutare

congeal, kon-chiil´, v coagularsi

congenial, kon-chii´-ni-al, adj simpatico

congenital, kon-chen´-i-tl, adj congenito

congested, kon-ches´-tid, adj congestionato

congestion, kon-ches´-chon, n congestione f

congratulate, kon-grat´-iu-leit, v congratularsi con

congratulations, kon-gratiu-lei´-shons, npl auguri mpl; congratulazioni fpl

congregate, kong´-gri-gheit, v congregarsi

congregation, kong-gri-ghei´-shon, n congregazione f

congress, kong´-gres, n congresso m

conjecture, kon-chek´-cha, n congettura f

conjunction, kon-chŏngk´-shon, n congiunzione f

conjure, kŏn´-cha, v fare giochi di prestigio

conjurer, kŏn´-chu-ra, n prestigiatore m

connect, ko-nekt´, v connèttere, collegare; allacciare, installare

connection, ko-nek-shon, n nesso m; collegamento m; (train etc.) coincidenza f

connive at, ko-naiv´, v essere connivente in

connoisseur, ko-no-ser´, n conoscitore m

conquer, kong´-ka, v conquistare; vincere

conqueror, kong´-ke-ra, n conquistatore m

conquest, kong´-kuest, n conquista f

conscience, kon´-shens, n coscienza f

conscientious*, kon-shi-en´-shos, adj coscienzioso

conscious*, kon´-shos, adj conscio; cosciente

consciousness, kon´-shos-nis, n conoscenza f; coscienza f

conscript, kon´-skript, n coscritto m

consecrate, kon´-si-kreit, v consacrare

consecutive*, kon-sek´-iu-tiv, adj consecutivo

consent, kon-sent´, n consenso m; v acconsentire

consequence, kon´-si-kuens, n conseguenza f

consequential, kon-si-kuen´-shal, adj conseguente; importante

consequently, kon´-si-kuent-li, adv di conseguenza

conservative, kon-ser´-va-tiv, adj conservatore

conservatory, kon-ser´-va-to-ri, n serra f

conserve, kon-serv´, v conservare; n conserva f

consider, kon-sid´-a, v considerare

considerable, kon-sid´-e-ra-bl, adj considerevole

considerate, kon-sid´-e-rat, adj riguardoso

consideration, kon-sid-e-rei´-shon, n considerazione f

considering, kon-sid´-e-ring, prep considerato

consign, kon-sain´, v consegnare

consignment, kon-sain´-ment, n consegna f

consist (of), kon-sist´, v constare di

consistency, kon-sis´-ten-si, n consistenza f; coerenza f

consistent*, kon-sis´-tent, adj consistente; coerente

consolation, kon-so-lei´-shon, n consolazione f

console, kon-soul´, v consolare

consolidate, kon-sol´-i-deit, v consolidare

consonant, kon´-so-nant, n consonante f

consort, kon-soort´, v frequentare

conspicuous*, kon-spik´-iu-os, adj evidente; vistoso

conspiracy, kon-spi´-ra-si, n cospirazione f

conspirator, kon-spi´-ra-ta, n cospiratore m

conspire, kon-spair´, v cospirare

constable, kon´-sta-bl, n agente di polizia m

constabulary, kon-stab´-iu-la-ri, n polizia f

constancy, kon´-stan-si, n costanza f

constant*, kon´-stant, adj costante

constipation, kon-sti-pei´-shon, n stitichezza f

constituency, kon-stit´-iu-en-si, n collegio elettorale m

constituent, kon-stit´-iu-ent, n elettore m

constitute, kon´-sti-tiuut, v costituire

constitution, kon-sti-tiuu´-shon, n costituzione f

constrain, kon-strein´, v costringere

constraint, kon-streint´, n costrizione f

constriction, kon-strik´-shon, n costrizione f

construct, kon-strökt´, v costruire

construction, kon-strök´-shon, n costruzione f

construe, kon´-struu, v interpretare

consul, kon´-sul, n console m

consulate, kon´-siu-lat, n consolato m

consult, kon-sölt´, v consultare

consultation, kon-sul-tei´-shon, n consulto m

consume, kon-siuum´, v consumare

consumer, kon-siuu´-ma, n consumatore m

consummate, kon´-som-eit, v consumare

consumption, kon-sŏmp´-shon, n consumo m

contact, kon´-takt, n contatto m; (person) conoscenza f

contagious, kon-tei´-chos, adj contagioso

contain, kon-tein´, v contenere

contaminate, kon-tam´-i-neit, v contaminare

contemplate, kon´-tem-pleit, v contemplare

contemporary, kon-tem´-po-ra-ri, adj contemporaneo; n coetaneo m

contempt, kon-tempt´, n disprezzo m

contemptible, kon-temp´-ti-bl, adj spregevole

contend, kon-tend´, v combattere; (maintain) sostenere

content, kon-tent´, adj contento; v accontentare

content, kon´-tent, n contenuto m

contention, kon-ten´-shon, n contesa f; affermazione f

contentment, kon-tent´-ment, n contentezza f

contents, kon´-tents, npl contenuto m; (book) indice m

contest, kon-test´, v contestare

contest, kon´-test, n concorso m

context, kon´-tekst, n contesto m

continent, kon´-ti-nent, n continente m

continental, kon-ti-nen´-tl, adj continentale

contingency, kon-tin´-chen-si, n eventualità f

continual*, kon-tin´-iu-al, adj continuo

continuation, kon-tin-iu-ei´-shon, n continuazione f

continue, kon-tin´-iuu, v continuare

continuous*, kon-tin´-iu-os, adj continuo

contortion, kon-toor´-shon, n contorsione f

contraband, kon´-tra-band, n contrabbando m

contraceptive, kon-tra-sep´-tiv, adj anticoncezionale

contract, kon-trakt´, v contrarre; contrarsi

contract, kon´-trakt, n contratto m

contraction, kon-trak´-shon, n contrazione f

contractor, kon-trak´-ta, n imprenditore m

contradict, kon-tra-dikt´, v contraddire

contradiction, kon-tra-dik´-shon, n contraddizione f

contrary, kon´-tra-ri, n contrario m; adj contrario

contrast, kon´-traast, n contrasto m

contrast, kon-traast´, v contrastare

contravene, kon-tra-viin´, v contravvenire

contravention, kon-tra-ven´-shon, n contravvenzione f

contribute, kon-trib´-iut, v contribuire

contribution, kon-trib-iuu´-shon, n contributo m

contrite, kon´-trait, adj mortificato

contrivance, kon-trai´-vens, n espediente m

contrive, kon-traiv´, v inventare; trovare

control, kon-troul´, v controllare; n controllo m; comando m

controller, kon-troul´-a, n controllore m

controversial, kon-tro-ver´-shal, adj controverso; polemico

controversy, kon´-tro-ver-si, n controversia f; polemica

conundrum, ko-nŏn´-drom, n enigma m

convalescence, kon-va-les´-ens, n convalescenza f

convalescent, kon-va-les´-ent, adj convalescente

convenience, kon-vii´-ni-ens, n comodità f

convenient*, kon-vii´-ni-ent, adj conveniente; comodo

convent, kon´-vent, n convento m

convention, kon-ven´-shon, n convenzione f; convegno m

converge, kon-verch´, v convergere

conversant with, kon´-ver-sant uiD, adj pratico di

conversation, kon-ve-sei´-shon, n conversazione f

converse, kon-vers´, v conversare

conversion, kon-ver´-shon, n conversione f

convert, kon-vert´, v convertire

convert, kon´-vert, n convertito m

convex, kon´-veks, adj convesso

convey, kon-vei´, v trasportare; comunicare

conveyance, kon-vei´-ans, n trasporto m; mezzo di trasporto m

convict, kon´-vikt, n carcerato m; v condannare

conviction, kon-vik´-shon, n condanna f; (belief) convinzione f

convince, kon-vins´, v convincere

convincing, kon-vin´-sing, adj convincente

convivial, kon-vi´-vi-al, adj gioviale

convoy, kon´-voi, n convoglio m

convulse, kon-vŏls´, v contorcersi

convulsion, kon-vŏl´-shon, n convulsione f

coo, kuu, v tubare

cook, kuk, n cuoco m, cuoca f; v cucinare; cuocere

cooker, kuk´-a, n (stove) cucina f

cookery, kuk´-e-ri, n cucina f

cool, kuul, adj fresco; calmo; v raffreddare; rinfrescare

coolness, kuul´-nis, n freschezza f; sangue freddo m

coop, kuup, n stia f; – up, v ingabbiare

cooperate, kou-op´-e-reit, v cooperare

cooperative, kou-op´-e-ra-tiv, n cooperativa f

cope with, koup uiD, v far fronte a, affrontare

copious*, kou´-pi-os, adj copioso

copper, kop´-a, n rame m; monetina f; adj di rame

coppice, kop´-is, n bosco ceduo m

copy, kop´-i, n copia f; v copiare

copybook, kop´-i-buk, n quaderno m

copyright, kop´-i-rait, n diritto d'autore m

coquetry, kok´-it-ri, n civetteria f

coral, ko´-ral, n corallo m

cord, koord, n corda f; filo m

cordial*, koor´-di-al, adj cordiale

corduroy, koor´-diu-roi, n velluto a coste m

core, koor, n torsolo m; fig cuore m

cork, koork, n sughero m; (bottle) turacciolo m; v tappare

corkscrew, koork´-skruu, n cavatappi m

cormorant, koor´-mo-rant, n cormorano m

corn, koorn, n grano m; (foot) callo m

corned beef, koornd-biif´, n carne di manzo in scatola f

corner, koor´-na, n angolo m; calcio d'angolo m; v

mettere con le spalle al
muro

cornflakes, koorn´-fleiks,
npl fiocchi di granturco
mpl

cornflour, koorn´-flau-a, n
farina di granturco f

cornflower, koorn´-flau-a,
n fiordaliso m

coronation, ko-ro-nei´-
shon, n incoronazione f

coroner, ko´-ro-na, n
magistrato inquirente m

coronet, ko´-ro-net, n
diadema m

corporal, koor´-po-ral, n
caporale m; adj
corporale

corporation, koor-po-rei´-
shon, n società f; (city)
consiglio comunale m

corps, koor, n corpo m

corpse, koorps, n
cadavere m

corpulent, koor´-piu-lent,
adj corpulento

corpuscle, koor´-pŏs-l, n
corpuscolo m

correct, ko-rekt´, adj*
corretto; esatto; v
correggere

corrective, ko-rek´-tiv, adj
correttivo

correctness, ko-rekt´-nis,
n correttezza f

correspond, ko-ris-pond´,
v corrispondere

correspondence, ko-ris-

pon´-dens, n
corrispondenza f

correspondent, ko-ris-
pon´-dent, n
corrispondente m/f

corridor, ko´-ri-door, n
corridoio m

corroborate, ko-rob´-o-
reit, v corroborare

corroboration, ko-rob-o-
rei´-shon, n
corroborazione f

corrode, ko-roud´, v
corrodere

corrosive, ko-rou´-siv, adj
corrosivo

corrugated, ko´-ru-ghei-
tid, adj ondulato

corrugated iron, ko´-ru-
ghei-tid ai-´on, n
lamiera ondulata f

corrupt, ko-rŏpt´, v
corrompere; adj*
corrotto

corruption, ko-rŏp´-shon,
n corruzione f

corset, koor´-sit, n
busto m

cost, kost, n prezzo m;
costo m; v costare

costly, kost´-li, adj costoso

cost-of-living, kost ov li´-
ving, n costo della
vita m

costs, kosts, n npl spese fpl

costume, kos´-tiuum, n
costume m

cosy, kou´-si, adj

confortevole;
accogliente; n
copriteiera m

cot, kot, n culla f

cottage, kot´-ich, n
cottage m

cotton, kot´-n, n cotone m

cotton wool, kot´-n-uul, n
bambagia f; cotone
idrofilo m

couch, kauch, n divano m

cough, kof, n tosse f; v
tossire

council, kaun´-sil, n
consiglio m; (city)
consiglio comunale m

council estate, kaun´-sil
is-teit´, n complesso di
case popolari m

council flat, kaun´-sil flat,
n casa popolare f

councillor, kaun´-sil-a, n
consigliere m

counsel, kaun´-sl, v
consigliare; n law
avvocato m

count, kaunt, v contare; n
conteggio m

countdown, kaunt´-daun,
n conto alla rovescia m

counter, kaun´-ta, n
banco m; adv contro

counteract, kaun-te-rakt´,
v neutralizzare

counterbalance, kaun-te-
bal´-ans, v
controbilanciare

counterfeit, kaun´-te-fit, n

(ship) rotta f; (meals) piatto m; **of –**, adv naturalmente

counterfoil, kaun´-te-foil, n matrice f

counterpart, kaun´-te-paart, n omologo; duplicato m

countersign, kaun´-te-sain, v controfirmare

countless, kaunt´-lis, adj innumerevole

country, kŏn´-tri, n (rural) campagna f; (state) paese m

countryman, kŏn´-tri-man, n campagnolo m; (compatriot) compatriota m

county, kaun´-ti, n contea f

coup, kuu, n colpo di stato m

couple, kŏp´-l, n coppia f; (pair) paio m; v accoppiare; (wagons) attaccare

coupon, kuu´-pon, n buono m, coupon m

courage, kŏ´-rich, n coraggio m

courageous*, ko-rei´-chos, adj coraggioso

courgette, kuur-chet´, n zucchina f

courier, ku´-ri-a, n corriere m; tour leader m/f

course, koors, n corso m;

court, koort, v corteggiare; n (royal) corte f; law tribunale m

courteous*, ker´-ti-os, adj cortese

courtesy, ker´-ti-si, n cortesia f

courtier, koor´-ti-a, n cortigiano m

court martial, koort maar´-shal, n corte marziale f

courtship, koort´-ship, n corteggiamento m

courtyard, koort´-iaard, n cortile m

cousin, kŏs´-in, n cugino m, cugina f

cove, kouv, n cala f

covenant, kŏv´-e-nant, n patto m

cover, kŏv´-a, n copertina f; coperchio m; riparo m; v coprire

cover charge, kŏv´-a chaarch, n (restaurant) coperto m

covet, kŏv´-it, v bramare

cow, kau, n vacca f

coward, kau´-ad, n vigliacco m

cowardice, kau´-a-dis, n vigliaccheria f

cowardly, kau´-ad-li, adj vigliacco

cowboy, kau´-boi, n cowboy m

cower, kau´-a, v rannicchiarsi

cowl, kaul, n cappuccio m

cowslip, kau´-slip, n primula f

coxswain, kok´-sn, n nocchiere m

coy*, koi, adj modesto

crab, krab, n granchio m

crab apple, krab´-ap-l, n mela selvatica f

crack, krak, v scricchiolare; (whip) schioccare; (glass) incrinarsi; (nut) schiacciare; n incrinatura f; crepa f; crepitio m; (drug) crack m

cracker, krak´-a, n cracker m; petardo m

crackle, krak´-l, v crepitare

cradle, krei´-dl, n culla f

craft, kraaft, n (trade) mestiere m; naut bastimento m; (cunning) astuzia f

craftsman, kraafts´-man, n artigiano m

crafty, kraaf´-ti, adj astuto

crag, kragh, n roccia f

cram, kram, v stipare; fare una sgobbata finale

cramp, kramp, n crampo m

cranberry, kran´-be-ri, n mirtillo m

crane, krein, n gru f

crank, krangk, n manovella f

crankshaft, krangk´-shaaft, n albero a gomiti m

crash, krash, v schiantarsi; scontrarsi; rompere; n scontro m; crollo m

crate, kreit, n cassa f

crater, kreit´-a, n cratere m

crave for, kreiv foor, v desiderare ardentemente

craving, krei´-ving, n voglia f

crawl, krool, v strisciare; n (swimming) crawl m

crayfish, krei´-fish, n gambero m

crayon, krei´-on, n pastello m

craze, kreis, n mania f

crazy, krei´-si, adj pazzo, matto

creak, kriik, v scricchiolare

cream, kriim, n crema f; panna f

creamy, krii´-mi, adj cremoso

crease, kriis, v spiegazzare; n piega f

create, kri-eit´, v creare

creation, kri-ei´-shon, n creazione f

creature, krii´-cha, n creatura f

crèche, kresh, n asilo nido m

credentials, kri-den´-shals, npl credenziali fpl

credible, kred´-i-bl, adj credibile

credit, kred´-it, n credito m; v accreditare

credit card, kred´-it kaard, n carta di credito f

creditor, kred´-i-ta, n creditore m

credulous*, kred´-iu-los, adj credulo

creed, kriid, n credo m; dottrina f

creek, kriik, n fiumiciattolo m

creep, kriip, v strisciare

creeper, krii´-pa, n (plant) rampicante m

cremate, kri-meit´, v cremare

cremation, kri-mei´-shon, n cremazione f

crematorium, kre´-ma-too-ri-um, n crematorio m

creole, krii´-oul, adj creolo

crescent, kres´-ent, n mezzaluna f

cress, kres, n crescione m

crest, krest, n cresta f

crestfallen, krest´-fool-en, adj abbattuto

crevice, krev´-is, n crepa f

crew, kruu, n equipaggio m

crib, krib, n culla f

crick, krik, n torcicollo m

cricket, krik´-it, n grillo m; (game) cricket m

crime, kraim, n delitto m

criminal, krim´-i-nal, n criminale m/f; adj* criminale

criminal record, krim´-i-nal rek´-oord, n menzione nel casellario giudiziale f

crimson, krim´-son, adj cremisi

cringe, krinch, v vergognarsi

crinkle, kring´-kl, v sgualcire

cripple, krip´-l, n zoppo m

crisis, krai´-sis, n crisi f

crisp, krisp, adj croccante; n patatina f

criterion, krai-tir´-ri-on, n criterio m

critic, kri´-tik, n critico m

critical*, krit´-i-kal, adj critico

criticism, krit´-i-sism, n critica f

criticize, krit´-i-sais, v criticare

croak, krouk, v (frog) gracidare; (crow) gracchiare

crochet, krou´-shei, v lavorare all'uncinetto; n

uncinetto *m*

crockery, krok´-e-ri, *n*
vasellame *m*

crocodile, krok´-o-dail, *n*
coccodrillo *m*

crocus, krou´-kus, *n*
croco *m*

crook, kruk, *n* truffatore *m*

crooked*, kru´-kid, *adj*
curvo; (nose) adunco; *fig*
disonesto

crop, krop, *n* raccolto *m*; *v*
(hair) rapare

cross, kros, *n* croce *f*;
incrocio *m*; *adj*
arrabbiato; *v*
attraversare; sbarrare;
incrociare; – out,
cancellare

crossbar, kros´-baar, *n*
traversa *f*

cross-country, kros-kŏn´-
tri, *adj* campestre

crossing, kros´-ing, *n*
passaggio *m*

crossroad, kros´-roud, *n*
incrocio *m*

crossword, kros´-uerd, *n*
cruciverba *m*

crotchet, krot´-shit, *n mus*
semiminima *f*

crouch, krauch, *v*
rannicchiarsi

crow, krou, *n* cornacchia
f; *v* (cock) cantare

crowbar, krou´-baar, *n*
piede di porco *m*

crowd, kraud, *n* folla *f*; *v*

affollare

crown, kraun, *v*
incoronare; *n* corona *f*

crucial, kruu´-shal, *adj*
cruciale

crucifix, kruu´-si-fiks, *n*
crocifisso *m*

crucify, kruu´-si-fai, *v*
crocifiggere

crude*, kruud, *adj* rozzo

cruel*, kruu´-el, *adj*
crudele

cruelty, kruu´-el-ti, *n*
crudeltà *f*

cruise, kruus, *n* crociera *f*;
v viaggiare a velocità di
crociera

cruiser, kruu´-sa, *n*
incrociatore *m*

crumb, krŏm, *n* mollica *f*;
briciola *f*

crumble, krŏm´-bl, *v*
sbriciolarsi

crumple, krŏm´-pl, *v*
sgualcire

crunch, krŏnch, *v*
sgranocchiare;
scricchiolare

crush, krŏsh, *n* ressa *f*;
cotta *f*; *v* (grapes, olives)
spremere; (pound)
schiacciare

crust, krŏst, *n* crosta *f*

crusty, krŏs´-ti, *adj* ben
cotto

crutch, krŏch, *n* gruccia *f*

cry, krai, *n* grido *m*; *v*
(call) gridare; (weep)

piangere

cryptic, krip´-tik, *adj*
sibillino

crystal, kris´-tl, *n*
cristallo *m*

cub, kŏb, *n* (lion)
leoncino *m*; (bear)
orsacchiotto *m*; (wolf)
lupetto *m*

cube, kiuub, *n* cubo *m*

cubic, kiuu´-bik, *adj*
cubico; cubo

cubicle, kiuu´-bi-kl, *n*
cabina *f*

cuckoo, ku´-kuu, *n*
cuculo *m*

cucumber, kiuu´-kŏm-ba,
n cetriolo *m*

cuddle, kŏd´-l, *v* coccolare

cudgel, kŏch´-el, *n*
randello *m*; *v* bastonare

cue, kiuu, *n* imbeccata *f*;
(billiards) stecca *f*

cuff, kŏf, *n* polsino *m*

cufflinks, kŏf´-lingks, *n*
gemelli *mpl*

culinary, kŏl´-i-na-ri, *adj*
culinario

culminate, kŏl´-mi-neit, *v*
culminare

culpable, kŏl´-pa-bl, *adj*
colpevole

culprit, kŏl´-prit, *n*
colpevole *m/f*

cult, kŏlt, *n* culto *m*

cultivate, kŏl´-ti-veit, *v*
coltivare

culture, kŏl´-cha, *n*

cultura f

cumbersome, kŏm´-be-som, *adj* ingombrante

cunning, kŏn´-ing, *adj* astuto; *n* astuzia f

cup, kŏp, *n* tazza f; coppa f

cupboard, kŏb´-ad, *n* armadio m

curate, kiuur´-rit, *n* curato m

curator, kiuur-reit´-a, *n* direttore di museo m

curb, kerb, *n* freno m; orlo del marciapiede m; *v* frenare

curd, kerd, *n* latte cagliato m

curdle, ker-dl, *v* cagliare

cure, kiuur, *n* cura f; *v* curare; affumicare

curfew, ker´-fiuu, *n* coprifuoco m

curiosity, kiuur-ri-os´-i-ti, *n* curiosità f

curious*, kiuur´-ri-os, *adj* (inquisitive) curioso; (peculiar) strano

curl, kerl, *n* riccio m; *v* arricciare

curler, ker´-la, *n* bigodino m

curly, ker´-li, *adj* riccio

currant, kŏ´-rant, *n* uva passa f

currency, kŏ´-ren-si, *n* valuta f, moneta f

current, kŏ´-rent, *n* corrente f; *adj* corrente

current account, kŏ´-rent a-kaunt´, *n* conto corrente m

current affairs, kŏ´-rent a-fers, *npl* attualità f

curse, kers, *n* maledizione f; *v* maledire

cursory, ker´-so-ri, *adj* frettoloso

curt*, kert, *adj* brusco, secco

curtail, ker-teil´, *v* accorciare; ridurre

curtailment, ker-teil´-ment, *n* riduzione f

curtain, ker´-tan, *n* tenda f; sipario m

curtsy, kert´-si, *n* inchino m, riverenza f; *v* fare la riverenza

curve, kerv, *n* curva f; *v* curvarsi

cushion, kush´-on, *n* cuscino m

custard, kŏs´-tad, *n* crema pasticcera f

custody, kŏs´-to-di, *n* prigione f; (care) tutela f

custom, kŏs´-tom, *n* costume m, consuetudine f; (trade) clientela f

customer, kŏs´-tom-a, *n* cliente m/f

customs, kŏs´-toms, *n* dogana f

cut, kŏt, *n* taglio m; riduzione f; *v* tagliare;

ridurre; – **off,** tagliare fuori

cute, kiuut, *adj* carino

cuticle, kiuu´-ti-kl, *n* pellicina f

cutlery, kŏt´-le-ri, *n* posate fpl

cutlet, kŏt´-let, *n* costoletta f

cutting, kŏt´-ing, *n* ritaglio m

cuttlefish, kŏt´-l-fish, *n* seppia f

cyclamen, sik´-la-men, *n* ciclamino m

cycle, sai´-kl, *n* bicicletta f; (time) ciclo m; *v* andare in bicicletta

cylinder, sil´-in-da, *n* cilindro m

cynical*, sin´-i-kl, *adj* cinico

cypress, sai´-pres, *n* cipresso m

cystitis, sis-tai´-tis, *n* cistite f

dabble, da´-bl, – **in**, v
occuparsi di

dabbler, dab´-la, n
dilettante m/f

daffodil, daf´-o-dil, n
giunchiglia f

dagger, dag´-a, n
pugnale m

dahlia, dei´-li-a, n dalia f

daily, dei´-li, adj
quotidiano, giornaliero;
adv ogni giorno

dainty, dein´-ti, adj
delicato; elegante

dairy, der´-ri, n latteria f;
adj caseario

daisy, dei´-si, n
margherita f

dale, deil, n valle f

dally, dal´-i, v perder
tempo

dam, dam, n diga f; v

sbarrare

damage, dam´-ich, n
danno m; v danneggiare

damask, dam´-ask, n
damasco m; adj
damascato

damn, dam, v maledire;
interj accidenti!

damnation, dam-nei´-
shon, n dannazione f

damp, damp, n umidità f;
adj umido

dance, daans, n danza f,
ballo m; v danzare,
ballare

dancer, daan´-sa, n
ballerino m, ballerina f

dancing, daan´-sing, n
danza f, ballo m

dandelion, dan´-di-lai-on,
n dente di leone m

dandruff, dan´-drof, n

forfora f

Dane, dein, n Danese m/f

danger, dein´-cha, n
pericolo m

dangerous*, dein´-che-ros,
adj pericoloso

dangle, dang´-gl, v
dondolare

Danish, dei-nish, adj
danese

Danube, dan´-iuub, n
Danubio m

dapper, dap´-a, adj lindo

dare, der, v osare

daring*, der´-ring, adj
audace

dark, daark, adj scuro;
buio; fosco

darken, daark´-n, v
scurire; oscurarsi

darkness, daark´-nis, n
oscurità f; buio m

darling, daar´-ling, n
tesoro m; adj caro

darn, daarn, v
rammendare

dart, daart, n freccetta;
(sewing) pince f; v
sfrecciare

dash, dash, n lineetta f; v
(throw) lanciare; (rush)
precipitarsi

dashboard, dash´-boord, n
cruscotto m

dashing*, dash´-ing, adj
brillante

dastardly, daas´-tad-li, adj
codardo

data, dei´-ta, *npl* dati *mpl*

date, deit, *n* data *f*;
appuntamento *m*;
dattero *m*; *v* datare;
uscire con

daughter, doo´-ta, *n*
figlia *f*

daughter-in-law, doo´-ta-rin-loo, *n* nuora *f*

dawdle, doo´-dl, *v*
gironzolare

dawn, doon, *n* alba *f*; *v*
albeggiare

day, dei, *n* giorno *m*;
giornata *f*

daybreak, dei´-breik, *n*
spuntar del giorno *m*

daydream, dei´-driim, *v*
sognare ad occhi aperti

daylight, dei´-lait, *n* luce
del giorno *f*

dazzle, das´-l, *v* abbagliare

deacon, dii´-kn, *n*
diacono *m*

dead, ded, *adj* morto

deaden, ded´-n, *v* attutire

deadlock, ded´-lok, *n*
impasse *f*

deadly, ded´-li, *adj* mortale

deaf, def, *adj* sordo

deafen, def´-n, *v* assordare

deafness, def´-nis, *n*
sordità *f*

deal, diil, *n* affare *m*;
accordo *m*; *v* (trade)
commerciare; (cards)
dare; – with, trattare di;
trattare con

dealer, dii´-la, *n*
commerciante *m/f*

dean, diin, *n* decano *m*;
preside *m/f*

dear, dir, *adj* caro

dearly, dir´-li, *adv* molto;
caro

death, deZ, *n* morte *f*

debar, di-baar´, *v*
escludere

debase, di-beis´, *v*
degradare

debate, di-beit´, *n*
dibattito *m*; *v* dibattere

debauchery, di-boo´-che-ri, *n* dissolutezza *f*

debit, deb´-it, *n* debito *m*;
v addebitare

debt, det, *n* debito *m*

debtor, det´-a, *n*
debitore *m*

decade, dek´-eid, *n*
decennio *m*

decadence, dek´-a-dens, *n*
decadenza *f*

decaffeinated, dii-ka´-fi-nei-ted, *adj* decaffeinato

decamp, di-kamp´, *v*
filarsela

decant, di-kant´, *v*
travasare

decanter, di-kan´-ta, *n*
caraffa *f*

decapitate, di-kap´-i-teit,
v decapitare

decay, di-kei´, *n*
decadimento *m*; carie *f*;
v decomporsi; cariarsi

decease, di-siis´, *n*
decesso *m*

deceased, di-siist´, *adj*
defunto

deceit, di-siit´, *n*
inganno *m*

deceitful*, di-siit´-ful, *adj*
falso

deceive, di-siiv´, *v*
ingannare

December, di-sem´-ba, *n*
dicembre *m*

decency, dii´-sen-si, *n*
decenza *f*

decent*, dii´-sent, *adj*
decente; (nice) onesto

deception, di-sep´-shon, *n*
inganno *m*

deceptive, di-sep´-tiv, *adj*
ingannevole

decide, di-said´, *v* decidere

decided*, di-sai´-did, *adj*
deciso

decimal, des´-i-mal, *adj*
decimale; *n* decimale *m*

decipher, di-sai´-fa, *v*
decifrare

decision, di-si´-shon, *n*
decisione *f*

decisive*, di-sai´-siv, *adj*
decisivo

deck, dek, *n naut* ponte di
coperta *m*; (cards) mazzo
m; *v* abbellire

deckchair, dek´-cher, *n*
sedia a sdraio *f*

declaration, dek-la-rei´-shon, *n* dichiarazione *f*

declare, di-kler´, v
dichiarare

decline, di-klain´, n
declino m; v declinare;
rifiutare

decompose, dii-kom-
pous´, v decomporre

decorate, dek´-o-reit, v
decorare; tinteggiare e
tappezzare

decoration, dek-o-rei´-
shon, n decorazione f

decorous*, dek´-o-ros, adj
decoroso

decoy, dii´-koi, n esca f;
uccello da richiamo m

decrease, dii´-kriis, n
diminuzione f

decrease, di-kriis´, v
diminuire

decree, di-krii´, n decreto
m; v decretare

dedicate, ded´-i-keit, v
dedicare

deduce, di-diuus´, v
dedurre

deduct, di-dökt´, v
sottrarre

deduction, di-dök´-shon,
n deduzione f

deed, diid, n azione f, atto
m; law atto m

deem, diim, v stimare

deep*, diip, adj profondo

deepen, diip´-n, v
approfondire;
approfondirsi

deer, dir, n daino m; (red)

cervo m

deface, di-feis´, v
deturpare

defamation, def-a-mei´-
shon, n diffamazione f

defame, di-feim´, v
diffamare

default, di-foolt´, n
contumacia f

defeat, di-fiit´, n sconfitta
f; v sconfiggere

defect, dii´-fekt, n difetto
m

defective*, di-fek´-tiv, adj
difettoso

defence, di-fens´, n
difesa f

defenceless, di-fens´-lis,
adj indifeso

defend, di-fend´, v
difendere

defendant, di-fen´-dant, n
imputato m

defender, di-fen´-da, n
difensore m

defensible, di-fen´-si-bl,
adj scusabile

defensive, di-fen´-siv, n
difensiva f

defer, di-fer´, v differire,
rinviare

deferential*, def-e-ren´-
shal, adj rispettoso

defiance, di-fai´-ans, n
sfida f

defiant, di-fai´-ant, adj di
sfida

deficiency, di-fish´-en-si, n

carenza f

deficient, di-fish´-ent, adj
carente

deficit, def´-i-sit, n deficit
m, disavanzo m

define, di-fain´, v definire

definite*, def´-i-nit, adj
deciso; definito;
(article) determinativo

definition, def-i-ni´-shon,
n definizione f

deflect, di-flekt´, v deviare

deflection, di-flek´-shon,
n deviazione f

deform, di-foorm´, v
deformare

defraud, di-frood´, v
defraudare

defray, di-frei´, v pagare

defrost, di-frost´, v
sbrinare; scongelare

deft*, deft, adj abile

defunct, di-föngkt´, adj
morto e sepolto

defy, di-fai´, v sfidare

degenerate, di-chen´-e-ret,
adj degenere; v
degenerare

degradation, deg-ra-dei´-
shon, n degradazione f

degrade, di-greid´, v
degradare

degree, di-grii´, n grado m;
laurea f

dehydrated, dii´-hai-drei-
tid, adj disidratato

deign, dein, v degnare

dejected, di-chek´-tid, adj

abbattuto

dejection, di-chek´-shon, n abbattimento m

delay, di-lei´, n ritardo m; v tardare

delectable, di-lek´-ta-bl, adj delizioso

delegate, del´-i-gheit, n delegato m; v delegare

delete, di-liit´, v cancellare

deleterious, di-li-tir´-ri-os, adj deleterio

deletion, de-lii´-shon, n cancellazione f

deliberate, di-lib´-e-reit, v deliberare

deliberate, di-lib´-e-rat, adj* intenzionale

delicacy, del´-i-ka-si, n delicatezza f; (food) leccornia f

delicate*, del´-i-kat, adj delicato

delicious*, di-lish´-os, adj delizioso

delight, de-lait´, n piacere m; v dilettare

delightful*, de-lait´-ful, adj incantevole

delineate, di-lin´-i-eit, v delineare

delinquent, di-ling´-kuent, n delinquente m/f

delirious, di-li´-ri-os, to be –, v delirare

delirium, di-li´-ri-om, n delirio m

deliver, di-li´-va, v (goods) consegnare; (letters) distribuire; (speech) fare

delivery, di-li´-ve-ri, n (goods) consegna f; (letters) distribuzione f

delude, di-luud´, v illudere

delusion, di-luu´-shon, n illusione f

delve, delv, v scavare; approfondire

demand, di-maand´, n domanda f; v domandare

demean, di-miin´, v – oneself, abbassarsi

demeanour, di-mii´-na, n contegno m

demented, di-men´-tid, adj demente

demise, di-mais´, n decesso m

democracy, di-mok´-ra-si, n democrazia f

democrat, dem´-o-krat, n democratico m

democratic, dem-o-krat´-ik, adj democratico

demolish, di-mol´-ish, v demolire

demon, dii´-mon, n demonio m

demonstrate, dem´-on-streit, v dimostrare; manifestare

demoralize, di-mo´-ra-lais, v demoralizzare

demote, di-mout´, v degradare

demur, di-mer´, v esitare

demure*, di´-miuur, adj contegnoso

den, den, n covo m; tana f

denial, di-nai´-al, n negazione f; rifiuto m

denim, den´-im n tessuto jeans m

denizen, den´-i-sen, n abitante m/f

Denmark, den´-maark, n Danimarca f

denomination, di-nom-i-nei´-shon, n confessione f; valore m

denote, di-nout´, v denotare

denounce, di-nauns´, v denunciare

dense*, dens, adj denso; ottuso

density, den´-si-ti, n densità f

dent, dent, n ammaccatura f; (notch) tacca f; v ammaccare

dental, den-tal, adj dentale

dentist, den´-tist, n dentista m/f

dentistry, den´-tist-ri, n odontoiatria f

dentures, den´-chus, npl dentiera f

denude, di-niuud´, v spogliare

deny, di-nai´, v negare;
smentire; (deprive)
privarsi

deodorant, dii-ou´-do-
rant, n deodorante m

deodorize, dii-ou´-do-rais,
v deodorare

depart, di-paart´, v partire

department, di-paart´-
ment, n reparto m;
dipartimento m;
ministero m

department store, di-
paart´-ment stoor, n
grande magazzino m

departure, di-paar´-cha, n
partenza f

depend, di-pend´, v
dipendere; – **upon,**
contare su

dependant, di-pen´-dant,
n persona a carico f

depict, di-pikt´, v
dipingere, descrivere

deplete, di-pliit´, v
esaurire

depletion, di-plii´-shon, n
esaurimento m

deplore, di-ploor´, v
deplorare

deport, di-poort´, v
deportare

deportment, di-poort´-
ment, n portamento m

depose, di-pous´, v
deporre

deposit, di-pos´-it, n
deposito m; cauzione f; v
depositare

depositor, di-pos´-i-ta, n
depositante m

depository, di-pos´-i-to-ri,
n deposito m

depot, dep´-ou, n deposito
m; stazione ferroviaria f

deprecate, dep´-ri-keit, v
deprecare

depreciate, di-prii´-shi-eit,
v deprezzare

depress, di-pres´, v
deprimere

depression, di-pre´-shon,
n depressione f

deprivation, dep-ri-vei´-
shon, n privazione f

deprive, di-praiv´, v
privare

depth, depZ, n
profondità f

deputy, dep´-iu-ti, n vice
m/f; supplente m/f

derailment, di-reil´-ment,
n deragliamento m

deranged, di-reinchd´, adj
squilibrato

derelict, de´-ri-likt, adj in
rovina

deride, di-raid´, v deridere

derisive*, di-rai´-siv, adj
derisivo

derive, di-raiv´, v
derivare; dedurre

derogatory, di-ro´-ga-to-ri,
adj spregiativo

descend, di-send´, v
discendere

descendant, di-sen´-dant,
n discendente m/f

descent, di-sent´, n discesa
f; origine f

describe, dis-kraib´, v
descrivere

description, dis-krip´-
shon, n descrizione f;
specie f

desecrate, des´-i-kreit, v
profanare

desert, des´-et, n
deserto m

desert, di-sert´, v disertare

deserter, di-ser´-ta, n
disertore m

desertion, di-ser´-shon, n
diserzione f

deserve, di-serv´, v
meritare

deserving, di-ser´-ving, adj
meritevole

design, di-sain´, v
disegnare; n disegno m;
(pattern) motivo m

designate, des´-igh-neit, v
designare

designer, di-sai´-na, n
disegnatore m; stilista
m/f

designing, di-sai´-ning, adj
intrigante

desirable, di-sai´-ra-bl, adj
desiderabile

desire, di-sair´, n desiderio
m; (craving) voglia f; v
desiderare

desirous, di-sair´-ros, adj

desideroso

desist, di-sist´, v desistere

desk, desk, n scrivania f; banco m

desolate*, des´-o-lat, adj desolato

despair, di-sper´, n disperazione f; v disperare

desperate*, des´-pe-rat, adj disperato

despicable, dis-pi´-ka-bl, adj disprezzabile

despise, di-spais´, v disprezzare

despite, di-spait´, prep a dispetto di; malgrado

despondent, di-spon´-dent, adj scoraggiato

despot, des´-pot, n despota m

dessert, di-sert´, n dessert m

destination, des-ti-nei´-shon, n destinazione f

destine, des´-tin, v destinare

destiny, des´-ti-ni, n destino m

destitute, des´-ti-tiuut, adj indigente

destitution, des-ti-tiuu´-shon, n indigenza f

destroy, di-stroi´, v distruggere

destruction, dis-trök´-shon, n distruzione f

destructive, dis-trök´-tiv,

---

adj distruttivo

desultory, des´-ul-tri, adj sconnesso; saltuario

detach, di-tach´, v staccare; distaccare

detachable, di-tach´-a-bl, adj staccabile

detail, dii´-teil, n dettaglio m, particolare m

detail, di-teil´, v dettagliare, particolareggiare

detain, di-tein´, v trattenere; (prison) tenere in prigione

detect, di-tekt´, v scorgere; notare

detective, di-tek´-tiv, n investigatore m

detention, di-ten´-shon, n detenzione f

deter, di-ter´, v dissuadere

detergent, di-ter´-chent, n detersivo m

deteriorate, di-tir´-ri-o-reit, v deteriorare

determine, di-ter´-min, v determinare

detest, di-test´, v detestare

dethrone, di-Zroun´, v detronizzare

detonation, det-o-nei´-shon, n detonazione f

detour, dii´-tuur, n deviazione f

detract, di-trakt´, v denigrare; (value) detrarre

---

detrimental*, det-ri-men´-tl, adj nocivo

deuce, diuus, n (tennis) parità f

devastate, dev´-as-teit, v devastare

develop, di-vel´-op, v sviluppare

development, di-vel´-op-ment, n sviluppo m

deviate, dii´-vi-eit, v deviare

device, di-vais´, n congegno m; stratagemma m

devil, dev´-l, n diavolo m

devious, dii´-vi-os, adj subdolo

devise, di-vais´, v ideare; law legare

devoid, di-void´, adj privo

devote, di-vout´, v dedicare; – oneself, consacrarsi

devour, di-vaur´, v divorare

devout*, di-vaut´, adj devoto

dew, diuu, n rugiada f

dexterous*, deks´-tros, adj destro, abile

diabetes, dai-a-bii´-tis, n diabete m

diabolical*, dai-a-bol´-i-kl, adj infernale

diagnose, dai´-agh-nous, v fare la diagnosi

diagonal, dai-agh´-o-nal,

adj diagonale

diagram, dai´-*a*-gram, *n*
diagramma *m*

dial, dai´-*al*, *n* quadrante
m; *v* (telephone
number) fare

dialect, dai´-*a*-lekt, *n*
dialetto *m*

dialogue, dai´-*a*-logh, *n*
dialogo *m*

diameter, dai-am´-i-*ta*, *n*
diametro *m*

diamond, dai´-*a*-mond, *n*
diamante *m*; (cards)
quadri *mpl*

diarrhœa, dai-a-rii´-*a*, *n*
diarrea *f*

diary, dai´-*a*-ri, *n* diario *m*;
(pocket) agenda *f*

dice, dais, *n* dadi *mpl*

dictate, dik´-teit, *v* dettare

dictator, dik-tei´-*ta*, *n*
dittatore *m*

dictionary, dik´-sho-na-ri,
n dizionario *m*

die, dai, *v* morire

diesel, dii´-sel, *n* (car)
diesel *m*; (fuel)
gasolio *m*

diet, dai´-et, *n* dieta *f*; *v*
stare a dieta

differ, dif´-*a*, *v* differire;
dissentire

difference, dif´-*e*-rens, *n*
differenza *f*

different*, dif´-*e*-rent, *adj*
differente

difficult, dif´-i-kelt, *adj*

difficile

difficulty, dif´-i-kel-ti, *n*
difficoltà *f*

diffident, dif´-i-dent, *adj*
timido

diffuse, dif-iuus´, *adj*
diffuso; *v* diffondere

dig, digh, *v* scavare; **– up,**
sradicare

digest, di-chest´, *v* digerire

digestion, di-ches´-chon,
n digestione *f*

dignified, digh´-ni-faid,
adj dignitoso

dignitary, digh´-ni-*ta*-ri, *n*
dignitario *m*

dignity, digh´-ni-ti, *n*
dignità *f*

digression, dai-gresh´-on,
n digressione *f*

dike, daik, *n* diga *f*

dilapidated, di-lap´-i-dei-
tid, *adj* devastato

dilapidation, di-lap-i-dei´-
shon, *n* sfacelo

dilate, dai-leit´, *v* dilatare

dilatory, dil´-*a*-to-ri, *adj*
dilatorio; tardo

dilemma, dai-lem´-*a*, *n*
dilemma *m*

diligence, dil´-i-*ch*ens, *n*
diligenza *f*

diligent*, dil´-i-*ch*ent, *adj*
diligente

dilute, di-luut´, *v* diluire

dim, dim, *adj* fosco; *v*
(darken) oscurarsi

dimension, dai-men´-

shon, *n* dimensione *f*

diminish, di-min´-ish, *v*
diminuire

dimple, dim´-*pl*, *n*
fossetta *f*

din, din, *n* baccano *m*

dine, dain, *v* pranzare;
cenare

dinghy, ding´-gi, *n*
gommone *m*

dingy, din´-*ch*i, *adj*
squallido

dining car, dai´-ning kaar,
n vagone ristorante *m*

dining room, dai´-ning
ruum, *n* sala da pranzo *f*

dinner, din´-*a*, *n* pranzo *m*;
cena *f*

dip, dip, *n* cunetta *f*; tuffo
m; *v* abbassarsi;
immergere

diphtheria, dif-Ziir´-ri-*a*, *n*
difterite *f*

diplomacy, di-plou´-*ma*-si,
n diplomazia *f*

dire, dair, *adj* terribile;
tremendo

direct, di-rekt´, *adj**
diretto; *v* dirigere;
(address) indirizzare

direction, di-rek´-shon, *n*
direzione *f*

directly, di-rekt´-li, *adv*
subito

director, di-rek´-*ta*, *n*
direttore *m*; regista *m/f*

directory, di-rek´-to-ri, *n*
elenco *m*

dirt, dert, n sporcizia f; (earth) terra f

dirty, der´-ti, adj sporco

disability, dis-a-bil´-i-ti, n invalidità f; handicap m

disable, dis-ei´-bel, v rendere invalido

disabled, dis-ei´-beld, adj invalido; handicappato

disabuse, dis-a-biuus´, v disingannare

disadvantage, dis-ad-vaan´-tich, n svantaggio m

disagree, dis-a-grii´, v dissentire

disagreeable, dis-a-grii´-a-bl, adj sgradevole

disallow, dis-a-lau´, v respingere; annullare

disappear, dis-a-pir´, v sparire

disappearance, dis-a-pir´-rans, n scomparsa f

disappoint, dis-a-point´, v deludere

disappointment, dis-a-point´-ment, n delusione f

disapprove, dis-a-pruuv´, v disapprovare

disarm, dis-aarm´, v disarmare

disaster, dis-aas´-ta, n disastro m

disastrous*, dis-aas´-tros, adj disastroso

disbelief, dis-bi-liif´, n

incredulità f

disburse, dis-bers´, v sborsare

disc, disk, n disco m

discard, dis-kaard´, v scartare; sbarazzarsi di

discern, di-sern´, v discernere, distinguere

discerning, di-ser´-ning, adj esperto; oculato

discharge, dis´-chaarch, n (dismissal) licenziamento m; (electricity, gun) scarica f; mil congedo m; med secrezione f

discharge, dis-chaarch´, v (load) scaricare; (duties) adempire; mil congedare; (patient) dimettere

disciple, dis-ai´-pl, n discepolo m

discipline, dis´-i-plin, n disciplina f

disc jockey, disk´-cho-ki, n disc jokey m/f

disclaim, dis-kleim´, v negare; smentire

disclose, dis-klous´, v rivelare

disclosure, dis-klou´-sha, n rivelazione f

disco, dis´-kou, n discoteca f

discolour, dis-kŏl´-a, v scolorire

discomfort, dis-kŏm´-fot,

n scomodità f; disagio m

disconnect, dis-ko-nekt´, v staccare

discontent, dis-kon´-tent, n scontentezza f; malcontento m

discontented, dis-kon-ten´-tid, adj scontento

discontinue, dis-kon-tin´-iuu, v (cease) cessare; comm mettere fuori produzione

discord, dis-koord´, n disaccordo m

discount, dis´-kaunt, n sconto m; at a –, scontato

discount, dis-kaunt´, v scontare

discourage, dis-kŏ´-rich, v scoraggiare

discourse, dis´-koors, n dissertazione f

discourteous*, dis-kŏr´-ti-os, adj scortese

discover, dis-kŏv´-a, v scoprire

discovery, dis-kŏv´-e-ri, n scoperta f

discredit, dis-kre´-dit, v screditare; n discredito m

discreet*, dis-kriit´, adj discreto

discrepancy, dis-krep´-an-si, n discrepanza f

discriminate, dis-krim´-i-neit, v distinguere; fare

discriminazioni

discuss, dis-kŏs´, *v*
discutere

discussion, dis-kŏsh´-n, *n*
discussione *f*

disdain, dis-dein´, *n*
sdegno *m; v* sdegnare

disdainful*, dis-dein´-ful,
adj sdegnoso

disease, di-siis´, *n*
malattia *f*

diseased, di-siisd´, *adj*
ammalato

disembark, dis-im-baark´,
v sbarcare

disengaged, dis-in-
gheichd´, *adj* libero

disentangle, dis-in-tang´-
gl, *v* sbrogliare;
districarsi

disfavour, dis-fei´-va, *n*
disgrazia *f*

disfigure, dis-fi´-gha, *v*
sfigurare

disgrace, dis-greis´, *n*
vergogna *f*; disgrazia *f*; *v*
disonorare

disguise, dis-gais´, *n*
travestimento *m; v*
travestire; (camouflage)
mascherare

disgust, dis-gŏst´, *n*
disgusto *m; v* disgustare

dish, dish, *n* piatto *m*;
(meals) pietanza *f; – up,*
v servire

dishcloth, dish´-kloZ, *n*
strofinaccio *m*

dishearten, dis-haar´-tn, *v*
scoraggiare

dishevelled, di-shev´-eld,
adj scarmigliato

dishonest*, dis-on´-ist, *adj*
disonesto

dishonour, dis-on´-a, *n*
disonore *m; v* disonorare

dishwasher, dish´-uosh´-a,
n lavastoviglie *f*

disillusion, dis-i-luu´-
shon, *v* disilludere

disinclination, dis-in-klin-
ei´-shon, *n* avversione *f*

disinfect, dis-in-fekt´, *v*
disinfettare

disinherit, dis-in-he´-rit, *v*
diseredare

disjointed, dis-choin´-tid,
adj sconnesso

disk, disk, *n* disco *m*

dislike, dis-laik´, *n*
avversione *f*, antipatia *f*;
v non amare

dislocate, dis´-lo-keit, *v*
slogare

disloyal, dis-loi´-al, *adj*
sleale

dismal*, dis´-mal, *adj*
triste, cupo

dismay, dis-mei´, *n*
sgomento *m; v*
sgomentare

dismiss, dis-mis´, *v*
licenziare; congedare;
scartare

dismissal, dis-mi´-sl, *n*
licenziamento *m*

dismount, dis-maunt´, *v*
smontare

disobedient*, dis-o-bii´-
di-ent, *adj* disubbidiente

disobey, dis-o-bei´, *v*
disubbidire

disorder, dis-oor´-da, *n*
disordine *m; med*
disturbo *m*

disorientated, dis-oor´-ri-
en-tei-tid, *adj*
disorientato

disown, dis-oun´, *v*
sconfessare

disparage, dis-pa´-rich, *v*
denigrare

dispatch, dis-pach´, *n*
spedizione *f*; invio *m; v*
spedire; inviare

dispel, dis-pel´, *v*
scacciare; dissipare

dispensary, dis-pen´-sa-ri,
n dispensario *m*

dispensation, dis-pen-sei´-
shon, *n* dispensa *f*

disperse, dis-pers´, *v*
disperdere; disperdersi

display, dis-plei´, *n* mostra
f; display *m; v* esporre

displease, dis-pliis´, *v*
dispiacere

displeasure, dis-plesh´-a,
n dispiacere *m*

disposable, dis-pou´-sa-bl,
adj usa e getta

disposable nappy, dis-
pou´-sa-bl na´-pi, *n*
pannolino *m*

disposal, dis-pou´-*sal*, n
disposizione f;
smaltimento m

dispose, dis-pous´, v
disporre; – **of,** sbarazzarsi
di

disposed, dis-pousd´, adj
disposto

disprove, dis-pruuv´, v
confutare

disputable, dis-piu´-ta-bl,
adj discutibile

dispute, dis-piuut´, n
disputa f, controversia f;
v discutere

disqualify, dis-kuo´-li-fai,
v squalificare

disquiet, dis-kuai´-et, n
inquietudine f

disregard, dis-ri-gaard´, n
indifferenza f;
inosservanza f; v
trascurare

disrepute, dis-ri-piuut´, n
discredito m

disrespect, dis-ri-spekt´, n
irriverenza f

disrespectful, dis-ri-
spekt´-ful, adj irriverente

disrupt, dis-röpt, v
disturbare;
scombussolare

dissatisfied, dis-sat´-is-
faid, adj insoddisfatto

dissect, di-sekt´, v
analizzare; med sezionare

dissent, di-sent´, v
dissentire; n dissenso m

dissimilar, di-sim´-i-la, adj
dissimile

dissipate, dis´-i-peit, v
dissipare

dissociate, di-sou´-si-eit, v
dissociare

dissolute*, dis´-o-luut, adj
dissoluto

dissolve, di-solv´, v
dissolvere

dissuade, dis-ueid´, v
dissuadere

distance, dis´-tans, n
distanza f

distant*, dis´-tant, adj
distante

distaste, dis-teist´, n
ripugnanza f

distasteful, dis-teist´-ful,
adj ripugnante

distemper, dis-tem´-pa, n
(paint) tempera f; (dog)
cimurro m

distend, dis-tend´, v
dilatare

distil, dis-til´, v distillare

distinct*, dis-tingkt´, adj
distinto

distinction, dis-tingk´-
shon, n distinzione f

distinguish, dis-ting´-
guish, v distinguere

distort, dis-toort´, v
distorcere

distract, dis-trakt´, v
distrarre

distraction, dis-trak´-
shon, n distrazione f

distress, dis-tres´, n
angoscia f; naut pericolo
m; v addolorare

distressing, dis-tres´-ing,
adj doloroso

distribute, dis-trib´-iuut, v
distribuire

district, dis´-trikt, n
distretto m

distrust, dis-tröst´, n
diffidenza f; v diffidare

disturb, dis-terb´, v
disturbare

disturbance, dis-ter´-bans,
n disturbo m; (mob)
disordini mpl

disuse, dis-iuus´, n
disuso m

ditch, dich, n fosso m

ditto, dit´-o, adv idem

dive, daiv, n tuffo m; v
tuffarsi

diver, daiv´-a, n tuffatore
m; palombaro m

diverge, dai-verch´, v
divergere

diverse, dai-vers´, adj
diverso

diversion, dai-ver´-shon,
n deviazione f;
distrazione f

divert, dai-vert´, v
divergere

divide, di-vaid´, v
dividere; (distribute)
spartire

divine*, di-vain´, adj
divino

diving board, dai´-ving
boord, n trampolino m

division, di-vi´-shon, n
divisione f; (football)
serie f

divorce, di-voors´, n
divorzio m; v divorziare

divulge, dai-vŏlch´, v
divulgare

DIY, dii-ai-uai, n fai da te
m; bricolage m

dizzy, dis´-i, adj
vertiginoso; stordito

do, duu, v fare; (be
enough) essere
abbastanza

docile, dou´-sail, adj docile

dock, dok, n bacino m;
banco degli imputati m

dockyard, dok´-iaard, n
cantiere navale m

doctor, dok´-ta, n dottore
m; medico m; v
adulterare

doctrine, dok´-trin, n
dottrina f

document, dok´-iu-ment,
n documento m

dodge, doch, v schivare

dog, dogh, n cane m

dogged*, dogh´-id, adj
ostinato

dole, doul, n sussidio di
disoccupazione m; v
distribuire

doleful*, doul´-ful, adj
afflitto

doll, dol, n bambola f

dollar, do´-la, n dollaro m

Dolomites, do´-lo-maits,
npl Dolomiti fpl

dolphin, dol´-fin, n
delfino m

dome, doum, n cupola f

domestic, do-mes´-tik, adj
domestico; (flight)
nazionale

domesticated, do-mes´-ti-
kei-tid, adj
addomesticato

domicile, dom´-i-sail, n
domicilio m

dominate, dom´-i-neit, v
dominare

domineer, dom-i-niir´, v
tiranneggiare

domino, dom´-i-nou, n
domino m

donate, dou-neit´, v
donare

donation, dou-nei´-shon,
n donazione f

donkey, dong´-ki, n
asino m

donor, dou´-na, n
donatore m, donatrice f

doom, duum, n rovina f; v
condannare

doomsday, duums´-dei, n
giorno del giudizio m

door, door, n porta f

doorbell, door´-bel, n
campanello m

doorkeeper, door´-kiip-a,
n portinaio m

doormat, door´-mat, n
zerbino m

dormitory, door´-mi-to-ri,
n dormitorio m

dose, dous, n dose f

dot, dot, n punto m; v
mettere i puntini

double, dŏb´-l, adj & adv
doppio; n doppio m;
sosia m/f; v raddoppiare

doubt, daut, n dubbio m; v
dubitare

doubtful*, daut´-ful, adj
dubbioso

douche, duush, n
irrigazione f

dough, dou, n pasta f

dove, dŏv, n colomba f

down, daun, adv & prep
giù; in fondo; n
piumino m

downcast, daun´-kaast, adj
abbattuto

downfall, daun´-fool, n
caduta f; rovina f

downhill, daun´-hil, adj &
adv in discesa

downpour, daun´-poor, n
acquazzone m

downstairs, daun-sters´,
adv di sotto; adj al piano
di sotto

downwards, daun´-ueds,
adv in giù

dowry, dau´-ri, n dote f

doze, dous, n v
sonnecchiare

dozen, dŏs´-n, n dozzina f

drab, drab, adj tetro, grigio

draft, draaft, n cambiale f; abbozzo m; brutta copia f; v redigere

drag, dragh, v trascinare; dragare; n noia f

dragon, drag´-on, n drago m

dragonfly, drag´-on-flai, n libellula f

drain, drein, n fogna f; canale di scolo m; v prosciugare

drainage, drein´-ich, n fognatura f

drake, dreik, n anatra maschio f

drama, draam´-a, n dramma m

dramatic, dra-mat´-ik, adj drammatico

drastic, dras´-tik, adj drastico

draught, draaft, n corrente d'aria f; sorso m

draughtboard, draaft´-boord, n scacchiera f

draughts, draafts, npl (gioco della) dama f

draughtsman, draafts´-man, n disegnatore m

draw, droo, n (lottery) estrazione f; (game) pareggio m; v (pull) tirare; (sketch) disegnare; (money) ritirare

drawback, droo´-bak, n svantaggio m

drawer, droo´-a, n cassetto m

drawing, droo´-ing, n disegno m

drawl, drool, n cadenza strascicata f

dread, dred, n paura f; v aver paura di

dreadful*, dred´-ful, adj spaventoso

dream, driim, n sogno m; v sognare

dreary, drir´-ri, adj tetro; monotono

dredge, drech, v dragare

dregs, dreghs, npl feccia f

drench, drench, v inzuppare

dress, dres, n vestito m; v vestire; vestirsi; (wounds) fasciare

dressing, dres´-ing, n med fasciatura f; (cooking) condimento m

dressing gown, dres´-ing-gaun, n veste da camera f

dressing room, dres´-ing-ruum, n camerino m; spogliatoio m

dressmaker, dres´-meik-a, n sarta f

dribble, drib´-l, v (drop) sgocciolare; (saliva) sbavare

drift, drift, n (current) direzione f; (snow etc.) cumulo m; (meaning) senso m; v andare alla deriva

drill, dril, v mil fare esercitazioni; (bore) forare; n mil esercitazione f; (tool) trapano m

drink, dringk, n bibita f; bevanda f; v bere

drip, drip, n goccia f; v gocciolare

dripping, drip´-ing, n grasso dell'arrosto m

drive, draiv, n (outing) giro in macchina m; (approach) vialetto d'accesso m; v guidare

driver, drai´-va, n conducente m/f; autista m/f

driving licence, drai´-ving lai´-sens, n patente f

drizzle, dris´-l, n pioggerella f

droll, droul, adj comico

drone, droun, n fuco m; v ronzare

droop, druup, v chinarsi; (plants) appassire

drop, drop, n goccia f; caduta f; v cadere; calare; (let fall) lasciar cadere

drought, draut, n siccità f

drove, drouv, n (cattle) mandria f

drown, draun, v annegare, affogare

drowsy, drau´-si, *adj*
sonnolento

drudgery, drŏch´-e-ri, *n*
lavoro faticoso *m*

drug, drŏgh, *n* medicinale
m; droga *f*; *v* narcotizzare

drum, drŏm, *n* tamburo *m*;
v tamburellare

drummer, drŏm´-a, *n*
batterista *m*

drums, drŏms, *n* batteria *f*

drunk, drŏngk, *adj* ubriaco

drunkard, drŏng´-kad, *n*
ubriacone *m*

drunkenness, drŏng´-ken-
nis, *n* ubriachezza *f*

dry, drai, *adj** secco;
asciutto; *v* seccare;
asciugare

dry-cleaner's, drai-klii´-
nes, *n* lavasecco *m*

dryness, drai´-nis, *n*
siccità *f*

dual carriageway, diu-al-
ka´-rich-uei, *n* strada a
doppia carreggiata *f*

dubious*, diuu´-bi-os, *adj*
dubbio

duck, dŏk, *n* anatra *f*; *v*
abbassare la testa

due, diuu, *n* dovuto *m*; *adj*
dovuto

duel, diu´-el, *n* duello *m*; *v*
battersi in duello

dues, diuus, *npl* diritti *mpl*

duet, diu-et´, *n* duetto *m*

duke, diuuk, *n* duca *m*

dull, dŏl, *adj* (mind)

ottuso; (weather) triste;
(sounds) sordo;
(colours) spento

duly, diuu´-li, *adv*
debitamente

dumb, dŏm, *adj* muto

dumbfound, dŏm-faund´,
v sbigottire

dummy, dŏm´-i, *n*
manichino *m*;
tettarella *f*

dump, dŏmp, *n* discarica *f*

dumping, dŏm´-ping, *n*
scarico *m*

dung, dŏng, *n* sterco *m*

dungeon, dŏn´-chen, *n*
segreta *f*

dupe, diuup, *n* babbeo *m*;
v abbindolare

duplicate, diuu´-pli-kat, *n*
duplicato *m*; *adj*
duplicato

duplicate, diuu´-pli-keit, *v*
duplicare

durable, diur´-ra-bl, *adj*
durevole

duration, diur-rei´-shon, *n*
durata *f*

during, diur´-ring, *prep*
durante

dusk, dŏsk, *n*
crepuscolo *m*

dusky, dŏs´-ki, *adj* scuro

dust, dŏst, *n* polvere *f*; *v*
spolverare

dustbin, dŏst´-bin, *n*
bidone della
spazzatura *m*

duster, dŏs´-ta, *n*
strofinaccio *m*

dustman, dŏst´-man, *n*
netturbino *m*

Dutch, dŏch, *adj* olandese

dutiful*, diu´-ti-ful, *adj*
rispettoso

duty, diu´-ti, *n* dovere *m*;
(tax) diritto *m*, dazio *m*;
(officials) funzione *f*

duvet, diuu´-vei, *n*
piumone *m*

dwarf, duoorf, *n* nano *m*;
v rimpicciolire

dwell, duel, *v* dimorare; –
upon, insistere

dweller, duel´-a, *n*
abitante *m/f*

dwelling, duel´-ing, *n*
dimora *f*

dwindle, duin´-dl, *v*
diminuire

dye, dai, *n* tintura *f*; *v*
tingere

dynamic, dai-na´-mik, *adj*
dinamico

dynamite, dai´-na-mait, *n*
dinamite *f*

dynamo, dai´-na-mou, *n*
dinamo *f*

dysentery, dis´-n-tri, *n*
dissenteria *f*

dyslexia, dis-lek´-si-a, *n*
dislessia *f*

E

each, iich, *adj* ciascuno, ciascuna; ogni; *pron* ognuno, ognuna; – **other,** l'un l'altro, l'un l'altra

eager*, ii´-ga, *adj* (keen) desideroso; (desire) ardente

eagerness, ii´-ghe-nis, *n* desiderio *m*

eagle, ii´-gl, *n* aquila *f*

ear, ir, *n* orecchio *m*; (corn) spiga *f*

earl, erl, *n* conte *m*

early, er´-li, *adv* presto; in anticipo; *adj* primo; prematuro

earn, ern, *v* guadagnare; meritare

earnest*, er´-nist, *adj* serio

earnings, er´-nings, *npl* guadagni *mpl*

earphones, ir´-founs, *npl* cuffie *fpl*

earring, ir´-ring, *n* orecchino *m*

earth, erZ, *n* terra *f*; *v* (electricity) collegare a terra

earthenware, erZ´-en-uer, *n* terracotta *f*

earthly, erZ´-li, *adj* terreno; terrestre

earthquake, erZ´-kueik, *n* terremoto *m*

earwig, ir´-uigh, *n* (insect) forbicina *f*

ease, iis, *n* (comfort) agio *m*; (facility) facilità *f*; *v* alleviare; facilitare; **at one's –,** a proprio agio

easel, ii´-sl, *n* cavalletto *m*

easily, ii´-si-li, *adv* facilmente

east, iist, *n* est *m*, oriente *m*

Easter, iis´-ta, *n* Pasqua *f*

easterly, iis´-te-li, *adj* dell'est; verso est

eastern, iis´-ten, *adj* orientale

easy, ii´-si, *adj* facile

eat, iit, *v* mangiare; (corrode) corrodere

eatable, ii´-ta-bl, *adj* mangiabile; commestibile

eavesdrop, iivs´-drop, *v* origliare

ebb, eb, *n* riflusso *m*; *v* rifluire

ebony, eb-o-ni, *n* ebano *m*

eccentric, ek-sen´-trik, *adj* eccentrico

echo, ek´-ou, *n* eco *m*; *v* far eco

eclipse, i-klips´, *n* eclissi *f*; *v* eclissare

economic, ii-ko-nom´-ik, *adj* economico; (profitable) redditizio

economical*, ii-ko-nom´-i-kal, *adj* economico; (person) parsimonioso

economize, i-kon´-o-mais, *v* economizzare

economy, i-kon´-o-mi, *n* economia *f*

ecstasy, ek´-sta-si, *n* estasi *f*

eddy, ed´-i, *n* mulinello *m*; gorgo *m*

edge, ech, n (knife) filo m; (brink) orlo m; v (border) orlare

edible, ed´-i-bl, adj commestibile

edify, ed´-i-fai, v edificare

edit, ed´-it, v dirigere; curare; editare

edition, ed-i´-shon, n edizione f

editor, ed´-i-ta, n redattore m, redattrice f; curatore m, curatrice f

editorial, ed-i-toor´-ri-al, adj editoriale; redazionale; n articolo di fondo m

educate, ed´-iu-keit, v istruire; (rear) educare

education, ed-iu-kei´-shon, n istruzione f; insegnamento m

eel, iil, n anguilla f

effect, if-ekt´, n effetto m; v effettuare

effective*, if-ek´-tiv, adj effettivo

effectual*, if-ek´-tiu-al, adj efficace

effeminate, if-em´-i-nat, adj effeminato

effervescent, ef-e-ves´-ent, adj effervescente

efficacious*, ef-i-kei´-shos, adj efficace

efficiency, if-ish´-en-si, n efficienza f

efficient, if-ish´-ent, adj (person) efficiente

effort, ef´-et, n sforzo m

effrontery, if-rŏn´-te-ri, n sfrontatezza f

effusive*, if-iu´-siv, adj espansivo

egg, egh, n uovo m

egg cup, egh´-kŏp, n portauovo m

egg white, egh´-uait, n albume m

egotism, eg´-o-tism, n egoismo m

Egypt, ii´-chipt, n Egitto m

eiderdown, ai´-de-daun, n (quilt) piumino m

eight, eit, adj otto

eighteen, ei-tiin´, adj diciotto

eighteenth, ei-tiinZ´, adj diciottesimo; (date) diciotto

eighth, eitZ, adj ottavo; (date) otto

eightieth, ei´-ti-eZ, adj ottantesimo

eighty, ei´-ti, adj ottanta

Eire, er´-re, n Irlanda f

either, ai´-Da, pron l'uno o l'altro; adj l'uno o l'altro; entrambi; conj o… o…né… né…; adv neanche

eject, i-chekt´, v espellere

elaborate, i-lab´-o-reit, v elaborare; adj elaborato; (detailed) complicato

elapse, i-laps´, v trascorrere

elastic, i-las´-tik, n elastico m; adj elastico

elate, i-leit´, v esaltare

elbow, el´-bou, n gomito m; v sgomitare

elder, el´-da, adj maggiore; n (tree) sambuco m

elderly, el´-de-li, adj anziano

eldest, el´-dist, adj maggiore

elect, i-lekt´, v eleggere; adj designato

election, i-lek´-shon, n elezione f

electric(al), i-lek´-trik(-l), adj elettrico

electrician, e-lik-trish´-an, n elettricista m

electricity, e-lik-tri´-si-ti, n elettricità f

electrify, i-lek´-tri-fai, v elettrificare

elegance, el´-i-gans, n eleganza f

elegant*, el´-i-gant, adj elegante

element, el´-i-ment, n elemento m; (of kettle) resistenza f

elementary, el-i-men´-ta-ri, adj elementare

elephant, el´-i-fant, n elefante m

electrocute, i-lek-tro´-kiut, v fulminare

electronic, e-lik-tron´-ik, *adj* elettronico

elevate, el´-i-veit, *v* elevare

eleven, i-lev´-en, *adj* undici

eleventh, i-lev´-enZ, *adj* undicesimo; (date) undici

elf, elf, *n* folletto *m*

elicit, i-lis´-it, *v* ottenere; strappare

eligible, el´-i-chi-bl, *adj* idoneo

eliminate, i-lim´-i-neit, *v* eliminare

élite, i-liit´, *n* élite *f*

elk, elk, *n* alce *m*

elm, elm, *n* olmo *m*

elongate, ii-long´-gheit, *v* allungare

elope, i-loup´, *v* scappare

elopement, i-loup´-ment, *n* fuga d'amore *f*

eloquent*, el´-o-kuent, *adj* eloquente

else, els, *adv* altro; altrimenti

elsewhere, els´-uer, *adv* altrove

elucidate, i-luu´-si-deit, *v* delucidare

elude, i-luud´, *v* eludere

elusive, i-luu´-siv, *adj* inafferrabile

emaciated, i-mei´-si-ei-tid, *adj* emaciato

e-mail, ii´-meil, *n* posta

elettronica *f*

emanate, em´-a-neit, *v* emanare

emancipate, i-man´-si-peit, *v* emancipare

embalm, im-baam´, *v* imbalsamare

embankment, im-bangk´-ment, *n* banchina *f*; (railway, road) scarpata *f*

embark, im-baark´, *v* imbarcare

embarrass, im-ba´-ras, *v* imbarazzare

embarrassment, im-ba´-ras-ment, *n* imbarazzo *m*

embassy, em´-ba-si, *n* ambasciata *f*

embellish, im-bel´-ish, *v* abbellire

embers, em´-bes, *npl* braci *fpl*

embezzle, im-bes´-l, *v* appropriarsi indebitamente di

embitter, im-bit´-a, *v* inasprire

embody, im-bod´-i, *v* comprendere; personificare

embolden, im-boul´-dn, *v* incitare

embrace, im-breis´, *v* abbracciare

embroider, im-broi´-da, *v* ricamare

embroidery, im-broi´-de-ri, *n* ricamo *m*

embroil, im-broil´, *v* coinvolgere

emerald, em´-e-rald, *n* smeraldo *m*

emerge, i-merch´, *v* emergere

emergency, i-mer´-chen-si, *n* emergenza *f*

emetic, i-met´-ik, *n* emetico *m*

emigrant, em´-i-grant, *n* emigrante *m/f*

emigrate, em´-i-greit, *v* emigrare

eminence, em´-in-ens, *n* eminenza *f*

eminent*, em´-in-ent, *adj* eminente

emissary, em´-is-a-ri, *n* emissario *m*

emit, i-mit´, *v* emettere

emotion, i-mou´-shon, *n* emozione *f*

emotional, i-mou´-shon-l, *adj* emotivo; commovente

emperor, em´-pe-ra, *n* imperatore *m*

emphasis, em´-fa-sis, *n* enfasi *f*

emphasize, em´-fa-sais, *v* accentuare; sottolineare

emphatic, im-fat´-ik, *adj* enfatico

empire, im´-per, *n* impero *m*

employ, im-ploi´, *v* impiegare

employee, im-ploi´-ii, n dipendente m/f

employer, im-ploi´-a, n datore di lavoro m

employment, im-ploi´-ment, n impiego m

empower, im-pau´-a, v autorizzare

empress, em´-pris, n imperatrice f

empty, emp´-ti, adj vuoto

emulate, em´-iu-leit, v emulare

enable, in-ei´-bl, v permettere

enact, in-akt´, v promulgare; (theatre) rappresentare

enamel, in-am´-l, n smalto m; v smaltare

enamoured, in-am´-ed, adj innamorato

encamp, in-kamp´, v accamparsi

enchant, in-chaant´, v incantare

enchantment, in-chaant´-ment, n incanto m

encircle, in-ser´-kl, v circondare

enclose, in-klous´, v allegare

enclosure, in-klou´-sha, n (letter) allegato m; (fence) recinto m

encompass, in-kŏm´-pas, v comprendere

encore, ong-koor´,

interj bis!

encounter, in-kaun´-ta, n incontro m; v incontrare

encourage, in-kŏ´-rich, v incoraggiare

encroachment, in-krouch´-ment, n violazione f

encumber, in-kŏm´-ba, v ingombrare; (property) gravare

encumbrance, in-kŏm´-brans, n (burden) peso m

encyclopædia, in-sai-klo-pii´-di-a, n enciclopedia f

end, end, n fine f; (aim) fine m; v finire

endanger, in-dein´-cha, v mettere in pericolo

endear, in-dir´, v render caro

endearment, in-dir´-ment, n tenerezza f

endeavour, in-dev´-a, n sforzo m; v sforzarsi

endive, en´-div, n indivia f

endless*, end´-lis, adj senza fine; infinito

endorse, in-doors´, v girare; (approve) appoggiare

endorsement, in-doors´-ment, n girata f; (approval) appoggio m

endow, in-dau´, v dotare

endurance, in-diur´-rans,

n tolleranza f

endure, in-diur´, v sopportare

enema, en´-i-ma, n clistere m

enemy, en´-i-mi, n nemico m

energetic, en-e-chet´-ik, adj energico

energy, en´-e-chi, n energia f

enervate, en´-e-veit, v snervare

enforce, in-fors´, v rafforzare; far rispettare

engage, in-gheich´, v occupare; (employ) assumere; (reserve) riservare; (enemy) attaccare; (bind) impegnarsi

engaged, in-gheichd´, adj occupato; fidanzato

engagement, in-gheich´-ment, n impegno m; fidanzamento m

engaging, in-ghei´-ching, adj attraente

engender, in-chen´-da, v generare

engine, en´-chin, n motore m; locomotiva f

engineer, en-chi-nir´, n ingegnere m; tecnico m

engineering, en-chi-nir´-ring, n ingegneria f

England, ing´-ghland, n Inghilterra f

English, ing´-ghlish, adj
inglese; n (language)
inglese m

engrave, in-greiv´, v
intagliare

engrossed, in-grousd´, adj
assorto

engulf, in-gŏlf´, v
inghiottire

enhance, in-haans´, v
aumentare; far risaltare

enjoy, in-choi´, v (like)
godere; – oneself,
divertirsi

enjoyment, in-choi´-
ment, n piacere m

enlarge, in-laarch´, v
ingrandire

enlargement, in-
laarch´-ment, n
ingrandimento m

enlighten, in-lai´-tn, v
illuminare, dare
chiarimenti

enlist, in-list´, v arruolare

enliven, in-lai´-ven, v
rallegrare

enmity, en´-mi-ti, n
inimicizia f

ennoble, i-nou´-bl, v
nobilitare

enormous*, i-noor´-mos,
adj enorme

enough, i-nŏf´, adv
abbastanza

enquire, in-kuair´, (see
inquire)

enrage, in-reich´, v far
arrabbiare

enrapture, in-rap´-cha, v
estasiare

enrich, in-rich´, v
arricchire

enrol, in-roul´, v iscrivere;
iscriversi

ensign, en´-sain, n
bandiera f; insegna f

enslave, in-sleiv´, v
rendere schiavo

ensnare, in-sner´, v
prendere in trappola

ensue, in-siuu´, v derivare

entail, in-teil´, v
comportare

entangle, in-tang´-gl, v
impigliare

enter, en´-ta, v entrare;
partecipare a

enterprise, en´-te-prais, n
impresa f

entertain, en-te-tein´, v
intrattenere; considerare

entertainment, en-te-
tein´-ment, n spettacolo
m; trattenimento m

enthusiasm, in-Ziuu´-si-
asm, n entusiasmo m

entice, in-tais´, v allettare

entire*, in-tair´, adj intero

entitle, in-tai´-tl, v dar
diritto a; intitolare

entrance, en´-trans, n
entrata f; ingresso m

entrance, in-traans´, v
incantare

entreat, in-triit´, v

supplicare

entrench, in-trench´, v
trincerarsi

entrepreneur, on-tre-pre-
ner´, n imprenditore m

entrust, in-trŏst´, v
affidare

entry, en´-tri, n
ingresso m; (record)
registrazione f

entwine, in-tuain´, v
intrecciare

enumerate, i-niuu´-me-
reit, v enumerare

envelop, in-vel´-op, v
avvolgere

envelope, en´-ve-loup, n
busta f

envious*, en´-vi-os, adj
invidioso

environment, in-vair´-
ron-ment, n ambiente m

environs, in-vair´-rons,
npl dintorni mpl

envoy, en´-voi, n inviato
m

envy, en´-vi, n invidia f; v
invidiare

epidemic, ep-i-dem´-ik, n
epidemia f

epilepsy, ep´-i-lep-si, n
epilessia f

episode, ep´-i-soud, n
episodio m

epoch, ii´-pok, n epoca f

equal, ii´-kual, adj*
uguale; n pari m/f; v
uguagliare

equality, i-kuol´-i-ti, n
uguaglianza f

equalize, ii´-kua-lais, v
pareggiare

equator, i-kuei´-ta, n
equatore m

equilibrium, ii-kui-lib´-ri-
um, n equilibrio m

equip, i-kuip´, v
equipaggiare; attrezzare

equitable, ek´-ui-ta-bl, adj
(just) giusto; (fair) equo

equity, ek´-ui-ti, n equità f

equivalent, i-kui´-va-lent,
adj equivalente

era, ir´-ra, n era f

eradicate, i-rad´-i-keit, v
sradicare

erase, i-reis´, v cancellare

eraser, i-reis´-a, n gomma
da cancellare f

erect, i-rekt´, v erigere; adj
eretto

ermine, er´-min, n
ermellino m

erode, i´-roud, v erodere

erotic, i´-ro-tik, adj
erotico

err, er, v errare

errand, e´-rand, n
commissione f

erratic, i-rat´-ik, adj
imprevedibile

erroneous*, i-rou´-ni-os,
adj erroneo

error, e´-ra, n errore m

eruption, i-rŏp´-shon, n
eruzione f

escalate, es´-ka-leit, v
intensificarsi

escalator, es-ka-lei´-ta, n
scala mobile f

escape, is-keip´, v
scampare; n fuga f

escort, es´-koort, n scorta f

escort, is-koort´, v
scortare

especially, is-pesh´-al-i,
adv specialmente

espionage, es´-pio-naash,
n spionaggio m

essay, es´-ei, n saggio m

essence, es´-ens, n
essenza f

essential*, i-sen´-shal, adj
essenziale

establish, is-tab´-lish, v
fondare; stabilire

establishment, is-tab´-
lish-ment, n istituzione f

estate, is-teit´, n proprietà
f; (housing) complesso
edilizio m

estate agency, is-teit´ ei´-
chen-si, n agenzia
immobiliare f

esteem, is-tiim´, n stima f;
v stimare

estimate, es´-ti-mat, n
stima f; preventivo m

estimate, es´-ti-meit, v
stimare

estranged, is-treinchd´, adj
separato

etching, ech´-ing, n
acquaforte f

eternal*, i-ter´-nal, adj
eterno

eternity, i-ter´-ni-ti, n
eternità f

ether, ii´-Za, n etere m

ethical, eZ´-i-kal, adj etico

ethics, eZ´-iks, n etica f;
npl morale f

Europe, iuur´-rop, n
Europa f

European, iuur-ro-pii´-an,
adj europeo

evacuate, i-vak´-iu-eit, v
evacuare

evade, i-veid´, v evadere

evaporate, i-vap´-o-reit, v
evaporare

evasive*, i-vei´-siv, adj
evasivo

eve, iiv, n vigilia f

even, ii´-ven, adj regolare;
costante; (numbers)
pari; adv perfino; anche

evening, iiv´-ning, n sera f

event, i-vent´, n
avvenimento m

eventful, i-vent´-ful, adj
pieno di avvenimenti,
movimentato

eventually, i-ven´-tiu-al-i,
adv finalmente

ever, ev´-a, adv sempre;
(at any time) mai

everlasting*, ev-e-laas´-
ting, adj eterno

evermore, ev´-e-moor, adv
sempre

every, ev´-ri, adj ogni;

tutti, tutte

everybody, ev´-ri-bod-i, *pron* ognuno; tutti, tutte

everyone, ev´-ri-uŏn, *pron* ognuno; tutti, tutte

everything, ev´-ri-Zing, *pron* tutto, ogni cosa

everywhere, ev´-ri-uer, *adv* dappertutto

evict, i-vikt´, *v* sfrattare

eviction, i-vik´-shon, *n* sfratto *m*

evidence, ev´-i-dens, *n* (proof) prova *f*; (testimony) testimonianza *f*

evident*, ev´-i-dent, *adj* evidente

evil, ii´-vil, *n* male *m*; *adj* malvagio

evince, i-vins´, *v* manifestare

evoke, i-vouk´, *v* evocare

evolution, ii-vo-luu´-shon, *n* evoluzione *f*

evolve, i-volv´, *v* evolversi

ewe, iuu, *n* pecora *f*

exact, igh-sakt´, *adj** esatto; *v* esigere

exacting, igh-sak´-ting, *adj* esigente

exaggerate, igh-sach´-e-reit, *v* esagerare

exaggeration, igh-sach-e-rei´-shon, *n* esagerazione *f*

exalt, igh-soolt´, *v* esaltare

examination, igh-sam-i-

nei´-shon, *n* esame *m*; (search) ispezione *f*; (legal) interrogatorio *m*

examine, igh-sam´-in, *v* esaminare; interrogare

example, igh-saam´-pl, *n* esempio *m*

exasperate, igh-saas´-pe-reit, *v* esasperare

excavate, eks´-ka-veit, *v* scavare

exceed, ik-siid´, *v* superare

exceedingly, ik-sii´-ding-li, *adv* straordinariamente

excel, ik-sel´, *v* eccellere

excellent*, ek´-se-lent, *adj* eccellente

except, ik´-sept, *prep* eccetto; *v* eccettuare

exception, ik-sep´-shon, *n* eccezione *f*; **take –,** *v* obiettare

exceptional*, ik-sep´-shon-al, *adj* eccezionale

excerpt, ek´-serpt, *n* estratto *m*; brano *m*

excess, ik-ses´, *n* eccesso *m*

excessive*, ik-ses´-iv, *adj* eccessivo

exchange, iks-cheinch´, *n* cambio *m*; (telephone) centralino *m*

exchequer, iks-chek´-a, *n* ministero delle finanze *m*

excise, ek´-sais, *n* dazio *m*

excitable, ik-sait´-a-bl, *adj* eccitabile

excite, ik-sait´, *v* eccitare

excitement, ik-sait´-ment, *n* eccitazione *f*

exciting, ik-sai´-ting, *adj* eccitante

exclaim, iks-kleim´, *v* esclamare

exclamation, eks-kla-mei´-shon, *n* esclamazione *f*

exclamation mark, eks-kla-mei´-shon maark, *n* punto esclamativo *m*

exclude, iks-kluud´, *v* escludere

exclusive*, iks-kluu´-siv, *adj* esclusivo

excruciating, iks-kruu´-shi-ei-ting, *adj* atroce

exculpate, eks´-kŏl-peit, *v* scagionare

excursion, iks-ker´-shon, *n* gita *f*

excuse, iks-kiuus´, *v* scusare; *n* scusa *f*

execute, ek´-si-kiuut, *v* (perform) eseguire; (put to death) giustiziare

executioner, ek-si-kiuu´-shon-a, *n* boia *m*

exempt, igh-sempt´, *v* esentare; *adj* esentato

exemption, igh-semp´-shon, *n* esenzione *f*

exercise, eks´-e-sais, *n* esercizio *m*; moto *m*; *v*

esercitarsi; fare del moto

exert, igh-*sert*´, *v* sforzarsi

exertion, igh-*ser*´-shon, *n* sforzo *m*

exhale, eks-*heil*´, *v* espirare

exhaust, igh-*soost*´, *v* esaurire; *n* (tubo di) scappamento *m*

exhaustive*, igh-*soost*´-iv, *adj* esauriente

exhibit, igh-*sib*´-it, *n* oggetto esposto *m; law* reperto *m; v* mostrare; esporre

exhibition, eks-i-*bish*´-on, *n* esposizione *f;* mostra *f*

exhilarating, igh-*sil*´-a-rei-ting, *adj* tonificante

exhort, igh-*soort*´, *v* esortare

exile, ek´-sail, *n* esilio *m;* (person) esule *m; v* esiliare

exist, igh-*sist*´, *v* esistere

existence, igh-*sis*´-tens, *n* esistenza *f*

exit, ek´-sit, *n* uscita *f; v* uscire

exodus, ek´-so-dus, *n* esodo *m*

exonerate, igh-*son*´-e-reit, *v* discolpare

exorbitant*, igh-*soor*´-bi-tant, *adj* esorbitante

exotic, igh-*sot*´-ik, *adj* esotico

expand, iks-*pand*´, *v*

espandere; ampliare

expansion, iks-*pan*´-shon, *n* espansione *f*

expect, iks-*pekt*´, *v* aspettare; (believe) supporre

expectation, eks-pek-*tei*´-shon, *n* aspettativa *f*

expectorate, iks-*pek*´-to-reit, *v* espettorare

expedient, iks-*pii*´-di-ent, *n* espediente *m*

expedite, eks´-pi-dait, *v* affrettare, accelerare

expedition, eks-pi-*di*´-shon, *n* spedizione *f*

expel, iks-*pel*´, *v* espellere

expend, iks´-pend, *v* spendere; (use up) consumare

expenditure, iks-*pen*´-di-cha, *n* spesa *f*

expense, iks-*pens*´, *n* spesa *f*

expensive*, iks-*pen*´-siv, *adj* costoso

experience, iks-*pir*´-ri-ens, *n* esperienza *f; v* provare

experiment, iks-*pe*´-ri-ment, *n* esperimento *m; v* sperimentare

expert, eks-*pert*´, *n* perito *m,* esperto *m; adj* esperto

expire, iks-*pair*´, *v* (time) scadere; (to die) spirare

explain, iks-*plein*´, *v* spiegare

explanation, eks-pla-*nei*´-

shon, *n* spiegazione *f*

explicit*, iks-*plis*´-it, *adj* esplicito

explode, iks-*ploud*´, *v* esplodere

exploit, eks-*ploit*´, *n* impresa *f; v* sfruttare

explore, iks-*ploor*´, *v* esplorare

explosion, iks-*plou*´-shon, *n* esplosione *f*

explosive*, iks-*plou*´-siv, *adj* esplosivo; *n* esplosivo *m*

export, iks-*poort*´, *v* esportare

export, eks´-poort, *n* esportazione *f*

expose, iks-*pous*´, *v* esporre; (disclose) smascherare

exposure, iks-*pou*´-sha, *n* esposizione *f;* assideramento *m*

expound, iks-*paund*´, *v* spiegare

express, iks-*pres*´, *n* espresso *m; adj** espresso

expression, iks-*presh*´-on, *n* espressione *f*

expulsion, iks-*pöl*´-shon, *n* espulsione *f*

exquisite*, iks-*kui*´-sit, *adj* squisito

extend, iks-*tend*´, *v* prorogare; estendere; ampliare

extension, iks-*ten*´-shon,

n (contract) proroga *f*; (wire) prolunga *f*; (telephone) interno *m*

extensive*, iks-ten´-siv, *adj* vasto

extent, iks-tent´, *n* estensione *f*

extenuating, iks-ten´-iu-ei-ting, *adj* attenuante

exterior, iks-tiir´-ri-a, *n* esteriore *m*, esterno *m*; *adj** esterno, esteriore

exterminate, iks-ter´-mi-neit, *v* sterminare

external, iks-ter´-nal, *adj* esterno

extinct, iks-tingkt´, *adj* estinto

extinguish, iks-ting´-guish, *v* estinguere; spegnere

extort, iks-toort´, *v* estorcere; strappare

extortion, iks-toor´-shon, *n* estorsione *f*

extra, eks´-tra, *n* extra *m*; *adj* extra

extract, iks-trakt´, *v* estrarre

extract, eks´-trakt, *n* estratto *m*; brano *m*

extraordinary, iks-troor´-di-na-ri, *adj* straordinario

extravagant*, iks-trav´-a-gant, *adj* stravagante; costoso; (exaggerated) esagerato

extreme*, iks-triim´, *adj* estremo

extrovert, eks´-tro-vert, *n* estroverso *m*

eye, ai, *n* occhio *m*

eyeball, ai´-bool, *n* bulbo oculare *m*

eyebrow, ai´-brau, *n* sopracciglio *m*

eyelash, ai´-lash, *n* ciglio *m*

eyelet, ai´-lit, *n* occhiello *m*

eyelid, ai´-lid, *n* palpebra *f*

eyesight, ai´-sait, *n* vista *f*

eyewitness, ai´-uit´-nis, *n* testimone oculare *m/f*

fable, fei´-bl, n favola f
fabric, fab´-rik, n tessuto m, stoffa f
fabrication, fab-ri-kei´-shon, n fabbricazione f
fabulous*, fab´-iu-los, adj favoloso
facade, fa-saad´, n facciata f
face, feis, n faccia f; (clock) quadrante m; v affrontare
facetious*, fa-sii´-shos, adj faceto
facilitate, fa-sil´-i-teit, v facilitare
facilities, fa-sil´-i-tis, npl attrezzature fpl; agevolazioni fpl
facsimile, fak-sim´-i-li, n facsimile m
fact, fakt, n fatto m

factory, fak´-to-ri, n fabbrica f
faculty, fak´-ul-ti, n facoltà f
fade, feid, v affievolirsi; (colour) scolorire
fail, feil, v (omit) mancare; (miscarry) fallire; (exam) essere respinto; without –, certamente
failure, feil´-ia, n fallimento m; fiasco m
faint, feint, v svenire; adj* debole; vago; n svenimento m
fair, fer, n fiera f; adj* bello; (just) giusto; (hair) biondo
fairness, fer´-nis, n bellezza f; giustizia f
fairy, fer´-ri, n fata f

fairy tale, fer´-ri-teil, n favola f
faith, feiZ, n fede f
faithful*, feiZ´-ful, adj fedele
faithless, feiZ´-lis, adj infedele
falcon, fool´-kn, n falco m
fall, fool, n caduta f; v cadere
false*, fols, adj falso
falsehood, fols´-hud, n falsità f
falsification, fol-si-fi-kei´-shon, n falsificazione f
falsify, fol´-si-fai, v falsificare
falter, fol´-ta, v esitare
fame, feim, n fama f
famed, feimd, adj famoso
familiar*, fa-mil´-ia, adj familiare
family, fam´-i-li, n famiglia f
famine, fam´-in, n carestia f
famished, fam´-isht, adj affamato
famous*, fei´-mos, adj famoso
fan, fan, n ventaglio m; ventilatore m; fan m/f; v sventolare
fanatic, fa-nat´-ik, n fanatico m; adj fanatico
fancy, fan´-si, n fantasia f; (desire) capriccio m; v immaginare; avere

voglia di

fancy dress, fan´-si dres, n costume m, maschera f

fang, fang, n zanna f; (snake) dente m

fantastic, fan-tas´-tik, adj fantastico

fantasy, fan´-ta-si, n fantasia f

far, faar, adj & adv lontano

farce, faars, n farsa f

fare, fer, n (bus, train) tariffa f; (taxi) prezzo della corsa m

farewell, fer-uel´, interj addio!

farm, faarm, n fattoria f; v coltivare

farmer, faar´-ma, n agricoltore m

farther, faar´-Da, adv più lontano

fascinate, fas´-i-neit, v affascinare

fashion, fash´-on, n moda f; v foggiare; **out of –,** fuorimoda

fashionable, fash´-on-a-bl, adj di moda; alla moda

fast, faast, adj rapido; (firm, fixed, tight) saldo; (colour) resistente; n digiuno m; v digiunare

fasten, faas´-n, v abbottonare; fissare; (close) chiudere

fast food, faast´-fuud, n

fastidious*, fas-tid´-i-os, adj schizzinoso

fat, fat, n grasso m; adj grasso

fatal*, fei´-tl, adj fatale

fatality, fa-tal´-i-ti, n fatalità f

fate, feit, n fato m

fated, fei´-tid, adj destinato

father, faa´-Da, n padre m

father-in-law, faa´-De-rin-loo, n suocero m

fatherly, faa´-De-li, adj paterno

fathom, faD´-om, v sondare

fatigue, fa-tiigh´, n stanchezza f; v affaticare

fatten, fat´-n, v ingrassare

fault, foolt, n difetto m; colpa f; (tennis) fallo m

faultless*, folt´-lis, adj senza difetto

faulty, fol´-ti, adj difettoso

favour, fei´-va, n favore m; v favorire

favourable, fei´-vo-ra-bl, adj favorevole

favourite, fei´-vo-rit, n favorito m; adj favorito

fawn, foon, n daino m; adj fulvo

fax, faks, n fax m; v faxare

fear, fir, n paura f; v temere

fearful*, fir´-ful, adj

terribile

fearless*, fir´-lis, adj intrepido

feasible, fii´-si-bl, adj fattibile

feast, fiist, n banchetto m; v festeggiare

feat, fiit, n impresa f

feather, feD´-a, n penna f; piuma f

feature, fii´-cha, n caratteristica f; v figurare; avere come protagonista

features, fii´-chus, npl (face) lineamenti mpl

February, feb´-ru-a-ri, n febbraio m

federal, fed´-e-ral, adj federale

federation, fed-e-rei´-shon, n federazione f

fed up, fed-ŏp´, adj stufo

fee, fii, n onorario m; (school) tassa scolastica f; (club) quota d'iscrizione f

feeble, fii´-bl, adj debole

feed, fiid, v nutrire; n mangime m

feel, fiil, v sentire; (touch) tastare; n tatto m

feeler, fii´-la, n (insects) antenna f

feeling, fii´-ling, n sentimento m

feign, fein, v fingere

feint, feint, n finta f

fell, fel, *v* abbattere

fellow, fel´-ou, *n* membro *m*; *fam* tipo *m*

fellowship, fel´-ou-ship, *n* associazione *f*

felony, fel´-o-ni, *n* crimine *m*

felt, felt, *n* feltro *m*

female, fii´-meil, *adj* femminile; *n* femmina *f*

feminine, fem´-i-nin, *adj* femminile

feminist, fem´-i-nist, *n* femminista *f*

fence, fens, *n* steccato *m*; *v* recingere; tirare di scherma

fencing, fen´-sing, *n* scherma *f*

ferment, fe-ment´, *v* fermentare

fern, fern, *n* felce *f*

ferocious*, fi-rou´-shos, *adj* feroce

ferret, fe´-rit, *n* furetto *m*

ferry, fe´-ri, *n* traghetto *m*; *v* traghettare

fertile, fer´-tail, *adj* fertile

fertilize, fer´-ti-lais, *v* fertilizzare

fervent*, fer´-vent, *adj* fervido

fester, fes´-ta, *v* suppurare

festival, fes´-ti-vl, *n* festa *f*; festival *m*

festive, fes´-tiv, *adj* festivo

festoon, fes-tuun´, *v* inghirlandare

fetch, fech, *v* portare; (call for) andare a cercare

fetter, fet´-a, *v* incatenare

fetters, fet´es, *npl* catene *fpl*

feud, fiuud, *n* faida *f*

feudal, fiuu´-dl, *adj* feudale

fever, fii´-va, *n* febbre *f*

feverish, fii´-ve-rish, *adj* febbricitante

few, fiuu, *adj* pochi; **a –,** alcuni, alcune

fibre, fai´-ba, *n* fibra *f*

fickle, fik´-l, *adj* incostante

fiction, fik´-shon, *n* finzione *f*; narrativa *f*

fictitious*, fik-ti´-shos, *adj* fittizio

fidelity, fi-del´-i-ti, *n* fedeltà *f*

fidget, fich´-it, *v* agitarsi

fidgety, fich´-it-i, *adj* irrequieto

field, fiild, *n* campo *m*

flendish, fiin´-dish, *adj* diabolico

fierce, firs, *adj* feroce

fiery, fair´-ri, *adj* ardente; (temper) focoso

fifteen, fif-tiin´, *adj* quindici

fifteenth, fif-tiinZ´, *adj* quindicesimo; (date) quindici

fifth, fifZ, *adj* quinto

fiftieth, fif´-ti-eZ, *adj* cinquantesimo

fifty, fif´-ti, *adj* cinquanta

fig, figh, *n* fico *m*

fight, fait, *n* lotta *f*; combattimento *m*; *v* lottare contro; combattere

figure, fi´-ga, *n* figura *f*; (number) cifra *f*; *v* figurare

filch, filch, *v* sgraffignare

file, fail, *n* (tool) lima *f*; *mil* fila *f*; (office) dossier *m*; *comp* file *m*; *v* limare; (letters etc.) classificare

filigree, fil´-i-grii, *n* filigrana *f*

fill, fil, *v* riempire; (teeth) otturare

fillet, fil´-it, *n* filetto *m*

filly, fil´-i, *n* puledra *f*

film, film, *v* filmare; *n* pellicola *f*; film *m*

filter, fil´-ta, *n* filtro *m*; *v* filtrare

filth, filZ, *n* sporcizia *f*

filthy, fil´-Zi, *adj* sporco

fin, fin, *n* pinna *f*

final*, fai´-nal, *adj* decisivo; (last) finale

finalize, fai´-nal-ais, *v* mettere a punto

finance, fi-nans´, *v* finanziare

finance, fai´-nans, *n* finanza *f*

financial, fi-nan´-shal, *adj* finanziario

finch, finch, n
fringuello m

find, faind, v trovare;
ritrovare; n trovata f;
scoperta f

fine, fain, n ammenda f;
multa f; adj* bello; fino;
v multare

finger, fing´-ga, n dito m; v
toccare

finish, fin´-ish, v finire;
(cease) terminare; n fine
f; (goods) finitura f

fir, fer, n abete m

fir cone, fer´-koun, n
pigna f

fire, fair, v sparare; n
fuoco m; incendio m

fire alarm, fair´-ra-laarm,
n allarme antincendio m

fire brigade, fair´-bri-
gheid, n (corpo dei)
vigili del fuoco mpl,
pompieri mpl

fire engine, fair´-ren-chin,
n autopompa f

fire escape, fair´-ris-keip,
n scala di sicurezza f

fire exit, fair´-rek-sit, n
uscita di sicurezza f

firefly, fair´-flai, n
lucciola f

fireman, fair´-man, n
pompiere m

fireplace, fair´-pleis, n
caminetto m

fireproof, fair´-pruuf, adj
resistente al fuoco

fireworks, fair´-uerks, npl
fuochi d'artificio mpl

firm, ferm, n ditta f,
azienda f; adj fermo,
risoluto

first, ferst, adj primo; adv
prima; per prima cosa

first aid, ferst-eid´, n
pronto soccorso m

fish, fish, n pesce m; v
pescare

fishbone, fish´-boun, n
lisca f, spina di pesce f

fisherman, fish´-e-man, n
pescatore m

fishing, fish´-ing, n pesca f

fishing rod, fish´-ing rod,
n canna da pesca f

fishmonger, fish´-mŏng-
ga, n pescivendolo m

fist, fist, n pugno m

fistula, fis´-tiu-la, n
fistola f

fit, fit, n attacco m;
convulsione f; adj
adatto; v andare bene;
(clothes) stare bene

fittings, fit´-ings, npl
accessori mpl

five, faiv, adj cinque

fix, fiks, v fissare;
riparare; preparare; n fig
pasticcio m

fixture, fiks´-cha, n
infisso m

fizzy, fi´-si, adj frizzante

flabby, flab´-i, adj flaccido

flag, flagh, n bandiera f

flagon, flagh´-on, n
fiasco m

flagpole, flagh´-poul, n
pennone m

flagship, flagh´-ship, n
nave ammiraglia f

flagrant*, flei´-grant, adj
flagrante

flake, fleik, n scaglia f;
(snow) fiocco m

flaky, flei´-ki, adj
squamoso

flame, fleim, n fiamma f

flaming, flei´-ming, adj
fiammeggiante

flank, flangk, n fianco m;
v fiancheggiare

flannel, flan´-l, n flanella f

flap, flap, n (table etc.)
ribalta f; (pocket) falda
f; v (wings) battere le ali

flare, fler, n bagliore m; v
fiammeggiare

flash, flash, v lampeggiare;
n lampo m

flashlight, flash´-lait, n
torcia tascabile f

flashy, flash´-i, adj vistoso

flask, flaask, n fiaschetta f

flat, flat, adj* piatto,
piano; (market) debole;
(drink) sgassato; n
appartamento m;
(music) bemolle m

flatten, flat´-n, v
appiattire; livellare

flatter, flat´-a, v lusingare

flattering, flat´-e-ring, adj

lusinghiero

flattery, flat´-e-ri, n lusinghe *fpl*

flavour, flei´-va, *v* condire; n sapore m; gusto m

flaw, floo, n difetto m

flax, flaks, n lino m

flea, flii, n pulce f

flee, flii, *v* fuggire

fleece, fliis, n vello m; *v fig* spogliare

fleet, fliit, n flotta f

flesh, flesh, n carne f

flexible, flek´-si-bl, *adj* flessibile

flicker, flik´-a, n tremolio m; *v* tremolare

flight, flait, n volo m; fuga f; (stairs) scalinata f

flimsy, flim´-si, *adj* leggero

flinch, flinch, *v* trasalire

fling, fling, *v* scagliare

flint, flint, n selce f; (fire) pietra focaia f

flippant*, flip´-ant, *adj* petulante; irriverente

flirt, flert, n civetta f; *v* civettare

float, flout, n galleggiante m; (procession) carro m; *v* (ship) galleggiare; (a company) lanciare

flock, flok, n (cattle) gregge m; (birds) stormo m; *v* adunarsi

flog, flogh, *v* sferzare, frustare

flood, flöd, n inondazione f; *v* inondare

floor, floor, n pavimento m; (storey) piano m; *v* atterrare

floppy disk, flo´-pi disk, n floppy disk m

florid*, flo´-rid, *adj* florido

florist, flo´-rist, n fiorista m/f

floss, flos, n (dental) filo interdentale m; *v* usare il filo interdentale

flour, flau´-a, n farina f

flourish, flö´-rish, n (pen) svolazzo m; *v* fiorire; prosperare

flout, flaut, *v* beffarsi di

flow, flou, n corrente f; circolazione f; flusso m; *v* scorrere

flower, flau´-a, n fiore m; *v* fiorire

flu, fluu, n influenza f

fluctuate, flök´-tiu-eit, *v* fluttuare

fluency, fluu´-en-si, n scioltezza f

fluent*, fluu´-ent, *adj* corrente

fluffy, flöf´-i, *adj* lanuginoso; (toy) di peluche; (jumper) morbido e peloso

fluid, fluu´-id, n fluido m; *adj* fluido

fluke, fluuk, n (chance) colpo di fortuna m

flurry, flö´-ri, n trambusto m

flush, flösh, n rossore m; *v* arrossire; tirare lo sciacquone; *adj* a livello di

fluster, flös´-ta, n agitazione f; *v* agitarsi

flute, fluut, n flauto m

flutter, flöt´-a, n battito m; *v* palpitare; battere le ali

fly, flai, *v* volare; (aircraft) pilotare; (flag) sventolare; n mosca f

foal, foul, n puledro m

foam, foum, n schiuma f; (rubber) gommapiuma f; *v* schiumare

focus, fou´-kus, n fuoco m; *v* (optics) centrare; (camera) mettere a fuoco

fodder, fod´-a, n foraggio m

foe, fou, n nemico m

fog, fogh, n nebbia f

foggy, fo´-ghi, *adj* nebbioso

foil, foil, n lamina di metallo f; (kitchen) carta stagnola f; (fencing) fioretto m; *v* sventare

foist, foist, *v* spacciare

fold, fould, n piega f; ovile m; *v* piegare; (arms) incrociare

foliage, fou´-li-ich, *n*
fogliame *m*

folk, fouk, *n* gente *f*

follow, fol´-ou, *v* seguire

follower, fol´-ou-a, *n*
seguace *m*; discepolo *m*

folly, fol´-i, *n* follia *f*

fond*, fond, *adj*
affettuoso; **to be – of,** *v*
amare

fondle, fon´-dl, *v* carezzare

fondness, fond´-nis, *n*
affetto *m*

font, font, *n* fonte *f*

food, fuud, *n* cibo *m*;
(plants) fertilizzante *m*

food processor, fuud
prou´-ses-a, *n* robot da
cucina *m*

fool, fuul, *n* sciocco *m*; *v*
ingannare

foolhardy, fuul´-haar-di,
adj avventato

foolish*, fuul´-ish, *adj*
sciocco

foot, fut, *n* piede *m*

football, fut´-bool, *n*
pallone *m*; (game)
calcio *m*

footballer, fut´-bool-a, *n*
calciatore *m*

footpath, fut´-paaZ, *n*
sentiero *m*; (pavement)
marciapiede *m*

footprint, fut´-print, *n*
orma *f*, impronta *f*

footstep, fut´-step, *n*
passo *m*

footstool, fut´-stuul, *n*
poggiapiedi *m*

for, foor, *prep* per; *conj*
poiché

forage, fo´-rich, *v* andare
in cerca di

forbear, fo-ber´, *v*
astenersi

forbearance, fo-ber´-rans,
n tolleranza *f*

forbearing, fo-ber´-ring,
adj tollerante

forbid, fo-bid´, *v* proibire,
vietare

force, foors, *n* forza *f*;
violenza *f*; *v* forzare

forceful, foors´-ful, *adj*
forte

forceps, foor´-seps, *npl*
forcipe *m*

forcible, foor´-si-bl, *adj*
vigoroso

ford, foord, *n* guado *m*; *v*
guadare

fore, foor, *adj* anteriore; *n*
davanti *m*

forearm, foor´-raarm, *n*
avambraccio *m*

forebode, fo-boud´, *v*
presagire

foreboding, fo-bou´-ding,
n presagio *m*

forecast, foor´-kaast, *v*
prevedere; *n* previsione *f*

foreclose, fo-klous´, *v*
pignorare

forefathers, foor´-faa-Des,
npl antenati *mpl*

forefinger, foor´-fing-ga, *n*
indice *m*

forego, fo-gou´, *v*
rinunciare a

foregoing, foor´-gou-ing,
adj precedente

foregone, foor´-gon, *adj*
scontato

foreground, foor´-graund,
n primo piano *m*

forehead, foor´-hed, *n*
fronte *f*

foreign, fo´-rin, *adj*
straniero

foreigner, fo´-ti-na, *n*
straniero *m*

foreman, foor´-man, *n*
caposquadra *m*

foremost, foor´-moust, *adj*
principale

forerunner, foor-rŏn´-a, *n*
precursore *m*

foresee, fo-sii´, *v*
prevedere

foresight, foor´-sait, *n*
previdenza *f*

forest, fo´-rist, *n* foresta *f*

forestall, fo-stool´, *v*
prevenire

forester, fo´-ris-ta, *n*
guardia forestale *f*

foretaste, foor´-teist, *n*
pregustazione *f*

foretell, fo-tel´, *v* predire

forethought, foor´-Zoot, *n*
previdenza *f*

forewarn, fo-uoorn´, *v*
avvertire

forfeit, foor´-fit, v perdere; n confisca f; (in games) penitenza f

forge, foorch, n fucina f; v forgiare; (falsify) falsificare

forger, foorch´-a, n falsario m

forgery, foorch´-e-ri, n falsificazione f; falso m

forget, fo-ghet´, v dimenticare

forgetful, fo-ghet´-ful, adj dimentico; di scarsa memoria

forgetfulness, fo-ghet´-ful-nis, n dimenticanza f

forget-me-not, fo-ghet´-mi-not, v nontiscordardimé m

forgive, fo-ghiv´, v perdonare

forgiveness, fo-ghiv´-nis, n perdono m

forgo, fo-gou´, v rinunciare a

fork, foork, n forchetta f; (road) biforcazione f; v biforcarsi

forlorn, fo-loorn´, adj abbandonato; disperato

form, foorm, n (shape) forma f; (to fill up) modulo m; (class) classe f; v formare; formarsi

formal*, foor´-mal, adj formale

formality, fo-mal´-i-ti, n

formalità f

formation, foor-mei´-shon, n formazione f

former, foor´-ma, adj vecchio; ex; pron primo; quello

formerly, foor´-me-li, adv una volta, in passato

forsake, fo-seik´, v abbandonare

fort, foort, n forte m

forth, foorZ, adv avanti

forthcoming, foorZ-kŏm´-ing, adj prossimo

forthwith, foorZ-uiD´, adv immediatamente

fortieth, foor´-ti-eZ, adj quarantesimo

fortification, foor-ti-fi-kei´-shon, n fortificazione f

fortify, foor´-ti-fai, v fortificare

fortnight, foort´-nait, n quindici giorni mpl, due settimane fpl

fortress, foor´-tris, n fortezza f

fortuitous*, fo-tiuu´-i-tos, adj fortuito

fortunate*, foor´-tiu-nit, adj fortunato

fortune, foor´-tiuun, n fortuna f

forty, foor´-ti, adj quaranta

forward, foor´-uad, adv avanti; v spedire

forwardness, foor´-uad-nis, n precocità f; insolenza f

fossil, fos´-l, n fossile m

foster, fos´-ta, v nutrire; incoraggiare

foster parents, fos´-te-per-rents, npl genitori adottivi mpl

foul, faul, adj cattivo; brutto; osceno; n fallo m; v sporcare

found, faund, v fondare

foundation, faun-dei´-shon, n fondamento m; fondazione f

founder, faun´-da, n fondatore m

foundling, faund´-ling, n trovatello m

foundry, faun´-dri, n fonderia f

fountain, faun´-tin, n fontana f

fountain pen, faun´-tin pen, n penna stilografica f

four, foor, adj quattro

fourteen, foor-tiin´, adj quattordici

fourteenth, foor-tiinZ´, adj quattordicesimo; (date) quattordici

fourth, foorZ, adj quarto; (date) quattro

fourthly, foorZ´-li, adv in quarto luogo

fowl, faul, n pollame m

fox, foks, n volpe f

fraction, frak´-shon, n frazione f

fracture, frak´-cha, n frattura f; v fratturare

fragile, frach´-ail, adj fragile

fragment, fragh´-ment, n frammento m

fragrance, frei´-grans, n fragranza f

fragrant*, frei´-grant, adj fragrante

frail, freil, adj fragile; (health) debole

frame, freim, n struttura f; (picture) cornice f; v incorniciare

framework, freim´-uerk, n struttura f; (panelling etc.) intelaiatura f

France, fraans, n Francia f

franchise, fran´-chais, n concessione f

frank, frangk, adj franco

frankness, frangk´-nis, n franchezza f

frantic, fran´-tik, adj frenetico

fraternal*, fra-ter´-nal, adj fraterno

fraud, frood, n frode f

fraudulent*, froo´-diu-lent, adj fraudolento

fray, frei, v logorarsi; n (scuffle) rissa f

freak, friik, n avvenimento

eccezionale m; fenomeno da baraccone m

freakish, friik´-ish, adj bizzarro

freckle, frek´-l, n lentiggine f; v coprirsi di lentiggini

free, frii, v liberare; adj* libero; gratis

freedom, frii´-dom, n libertà f

freemason, frii´-mei-son, n massone m

freeze, friis, v gelare; congelare

freezer, frii´-sa, n congelatore m; freezer m

freezing, frii´-sing, adj gelido

freight, freit, n carico m; (cost) nolo m

French, french, adj francese; n (language) francese m

frenzy, fren´-si, n frenesia f

frequency, frii´-kuen-si, n frequenza f

frequent*, frii´-kuent, adj frequente

frequent, fri-kuent´, v frequentare

fresh*, fresh, adj fresco

freshness, fresh´-nis, n freschezza f

fret, fret, v agitarsi

fretful*, fret´-ful, adj

irrequieto

friar, frai´-a, n frate m

friction, frik´-shon, n attrito m; (massage) frizione f

Friday, frai´-di, n venerdì m

fridge, frich, n frigo m, frigorifero m

friend, frend, n amico m

friendly, frend´-li, adj amichevole

friendship, frend´-ship, n amicizia f

fright, frait, n spavento m

frightful*, frait´-ful, adj pauroso

frighten, frait´-n, v spaventare

frightening, frait´-ning, adj spaventoso

frigid*, frich´-id, adj frigido

frill, fril, n balza f; v increspare

fringe, frinch, n frangia f; (edge) orlo m; v orlare

frisky, fris´-ki, adj vivace

fritter, frit´-a, n frittella f; – away, v sciupare

frivolous*, friv´-o-los, adj frivolo

frizzle, fris´-l, v sfrigolare

fro, frou, to and –, adv avanti e indietro

frock, frok, n vestito m

frog, frogh, n rana f; (small) ranocchia f

frolic, frol´-ik, *v* saltellare

from, from, *prep* da

front, frŏnt, *n* davanti *m*; (book) copertina *f*; (building) facciata *f*; **in –,** davanti

frontier, frŏn´-tir, *n* frontiera *f*

frost, frost, *n* gelo *m*

frostbitten, frost´-bit-n, *adj* congelato

frosty, fros´-ti, *adj* glaciale

froth, froZ, *n* spuma *f*; *v* schiumare

frown, fraun, *n* cipiglio *m*; *v* aggrottare le sopracciglia

frugal*, fruu´-gal, *adj* frugale

fruit, fruut, *n* frutto *m*; frutta *f*

fruiterer, fruu´-te-ra, *n* fruttivendolo *m*

fruitful, fruut´-ful, *adj* fruttuoso

fruitless*, fruut´-lis, *adj* infruttuoso

frustrate, frŏs-treit´, *v* frustrare

fry, frai, *v* friggere

frying pan, frai´-ing pan, *n* padella *f*

fuchsia, fiuu´-sha, *n* fucsia *f*; (colour) fucsia *m*

fuel, fiu´-el, *n* combustibile *m*; carburante *m*

fugitive, fiuu´-chi-tiv, *n*

fuggiasco *m*

fugue, fiuugh, *n mus* fuga *f*

fulcrum, ful´-krom, *n* fulcro *m*

fulfil, ful-fil´, *v* compiere; (promise) mantenere; (dream, wish) realizzare

fulfilment, ful-fil´-ment, *n* compimento *m*; realizzazione *f*; soddisfazione *f*

full, ful, *adj* pieno

fume, fiuum, *n* esalazione *f*; *v* (rage) essere furioso

fumigate, fiuu´-mi-geit, *v* fumigare

fun, fŏn, *n* divertimento *m*; (joke) scherzo *m*

function, fŏngk´-shon, *n* funzione *f*; *v* funzionare

functionary, fŏngk´-sho-na-ri, *n* funzionario *m*

fund, fŏnd, *n* fondo *m*

fundamental*, fŏn-da-men´-tl, *adj* fondamentale

funds, fŏnds, *npl* (money) fondi *mpl*

funeral, fiuu´-ne-ral, *n* funerale *m*

funfair, fŏn´-fer, *n* luna park *m*

funnel, fŏn´-l, *n* imbuto *m*

funny, fŏn´-i, *adj* divertente; (person) buffo; (peculiar) strano

fur, fer, *n* pelliccia *f*

furious*, fiuur´-ri-os, *adj*

furioso

furlough, fer´-lou, *n* licenza *f*

furnace, fer´-nis, *n* fornace *f*

furnish, fer´-nish, *v* ammobiliare; arredare

furniture, fer´-ni-cha, *n* mobilia *f*; mobili *mpl*

furrier, fŏ´-ri-a, *n* pellicciaio *m*

furrow, fŏ´-rou, *n* solco *m*; *v* solcare

further, fer´-Da, *adj* più lontano; altro; *adv* di più; più lontano; *v* promuovere

further education, fer-Der-red-iu-kei´-shon, *n* corsi di formazione *mpl*

furtive*, fer´-tiv, *adj* furtivo

fury, fiur´-ri, *n* furia *f*

fuse, fiuus, *n* miccia *f*; fusibile *m*; valvola *f*; *v* fondersi; far saltare

fuss, fŏs, *n* storie *fpl*; *v* fare storie

fussy, fŏs´-i, *adj* esigente; pignolo

fusty, fŏs´-ti, *adj* stantio

future, fiuu´-cha, *n* futuro *m*; *adj* futuro

giocatore d'azzardo m

game, gheim, n gioco m;
partita f; (animals)
selvaggina f

gammon, gam´-on, n
prosciutto m

gamut, gam´-ut, n
gamma f

gander, gan´-da, n oca
maschio f

gang, gang, n banda f;
(friends) comitiva f

gangster, gang´-sta, n
gangster m

gangway, gang´-uei, n
(passage) corridoio m;
(ship's) passerella

gap, gap, n spazio vuoto m;
lacuna f

gape, gheip, v restare a
bocca aperta

garage, ga-raach, n garage
m; stazione di servizio f

garbage, gaar´-bich, n
rifiuti mpl

garden, gaar-dn, n
giardino m; (kitchen)
orto m

gardener, gaard´-na, n
giardiniere m

gardening, gaard´-ning, n
giardinaggio m

gargle, gaar´-gl, v fare
gargarismi

garish, gher´-rish, adj
vistoso

garland, gaar´-land, n
ghirlanda f

gable, ghei´-bl, n
frontone m

gadfly, gad´-flai, n
tafano m

gaff, gaf, n rampone m

gag, gagh, n bavaglio m;
(joke) battuta f; v
imbavagliare

gaiety, ghei´-e-ti, n
gaiezza f

gaily, ghei´-li, adv
gaiamente

gain, ghein, n guadagno
m; v ottenere; (watch)
andare avanti

gait, gheit, n andatura f;
passo m

gaiter, ghei´-ta, n ghetta f

galaxy, gal´-ak-si, n
galassia f

gale, gheil, n bufera f;
burrasca f

gallant*, gal´-ant, adj
galante; (heroic) prode

gallantry, gal´-ant-ri, n
(courage) prodezza f;
(manners) galanteria f

gallery, gal´-e-ri, n galleria
f; loggione m

galling, gool´-ing, adj
seccante

gallon, gal´-on, n
gallone m

gallop, gal´-op, n galoppo
m; v galoppare

gallows, gal´-ous, npl
patibolo m

galore, ga-loor´, adv in
abbondanza

galoshes, ga-losh´-is, npl
galosce fpl

gamble, gam´-bl, v giocare
d'azzardo; n azzardo m

gambler, gam´-bla, n

garlic, gaar´-lik, n aglio m

garment, gaar´-ment, n indumento m

garnish, gaar´-nish, n guarnizione f; v guarnire

garret, ga´-rit, n soffitta f

garrison, ga´-ri-son, n guarnigione f

garrulous, ga´-riu-los, adj ciarliero

garter, gaar´-ta, n giarrettiera f

gas, gas, n gas m

gas cylinder, gas sil´-in-da, n bombola del gas f

gaseous, ghei´-si-os, adj gassoso

gas fire, gas´-fair, n stufa a gas f

gash, gash, n sfregio m; v sfregiare

gas mask, gas´-maask, n maschera antigas f

gasp, gaasp, n anelito m; v ansimare

gastric, gas´-trik, adj gastrico

gate, gheit, n cancello m; (airport) uscita f

gather, gaD´-a, v raccogliere; (people) riunirsi

gathering, gaD´-e-ring, n riunione f

gaudy, goo´-di, adj vistoso

gauge, gheich, n indicatore m; v misurare; fig stimare

gaunt, goont, adj smunto

gauntlet, goont´-lit, n guanto lungo m

gauze, goos, n garza f

gawky, goo´-ki, adj goffo

gay, ghei, adj gay; n gay m/f

gaze, gheis, v guardare fisso; n sguardo fisso m

gazelle, ga-sel´, n gazzella f

gazette, ga-set´, n gazzetta f

gear, ghir, n mech ingranaggio m; (car) marcia f

gearbox, ghir´-boks, n scatola del cambio f

gelatine, chel´-a-tin, n gelatina f

gem, chem, n gemma f

Gemini, chem´-in-ai, n Gemelli mpl

gender, chen´-da, n genere m ,

general, chen´-e-ral, n generale m; adj generale

generalize, chen´-e-ra-lais, v generalizzare

generally, chen´-e-ra-li, adv generalmente

generate, chen´-e-reit, v generare

generation, chen´-e-rei-shon, n generazione f

generosity, chen-e-ros´-i-ti, n generosità f

generous*, chen´-e-ros, adj generoso

genetic, chi-ne´-tik, adj genetico

Geneva, chi-nii´-va, n Ginevra f

genial*, chii´-ni-al, adj (kindly) cordiale

genitals, chen´-i-tals, npl genitali mpl

genitive, chen´-i-tiv, n genitivo m

genius, chii´-ni-os, n genio m

Genoa, che´-nou-a, n Genova f

genteel, chen-tiil´, adj distinto

gentle, chen´-tl, adj dolce; delicato

gentleman, chen´-tl-man, n gentiluomo m

gentleness, chen´-tl-nis, n dolcezza f; delicatezza f

gently, chent´-li, adv dolcemente; delicatamente

gents, chents, n bagno degli uomini m

genuine*, chen´-iu-in, adj genuino

geography, chiogh´-ra-fi, n geografia f

geology, chi-ol´-o-chi, n geologia f

geometry, chi-om´-e-tri, n geometria f

geranium, chi-rei´-ni-um, n geranio m

germ, cherm, n germe m;

microbo m

German, cher´-man, *adj*
tedesco; *n* (language)
tedesco m

Germany, cher´-ma-ni, *n*
Germania f

gesticulate, ches-tik´-iu-
leit, *v* gesticolare

gesture, ches´-cha, *n*
gesto m

get, ghet, *v* (obtain)
procurare, ottenere;
(earn) guadagnare;
(fetch) andare a
prendere; (induce)
indurre; (reach)
arrivare; (become)
diventare; – **back,**
(receive back)
ricuperare; – **down,**
(descend) scendere; –
in, entrare; (home)
rincasare; – **off,** (alight)
scendere da; (free)
liberarsi; – **on,** salire su;
(progress) andare; – **out,**
uscire; – **up,** alzarsi

geyser, ghii´-sa, *n* geyser
m

ghastly, gaast´-li, *adj*
orrendo

gherkin, gher´-kin, *n*
cetriolino m

ghost, goust, *n* spettro m,
fantasma m

ghostly, goust´-li, *adj*
spettrale

giant, chai´-ant, *n*

gigante m

gibberish, chib´-e-rish, *n*
parole sconnesse *fpl*

gibbet, chib´-it, *n* patibolo
m

giblets, chib´-lits, *npl*
frattaglie *fpl*

Gibraltar, chib-rol´-ta, *n*
Gibilterra f

giddiness, ghid´-i-nis, *n*
vertigini *fpl*

giddy, ghid´-i, *adj* stordito;
vertiginoso

gift, ghift, *n* dono m

gifted, ghif´-tid, *adj* dotato

gigantic, chai-gan´-tik, *adj*
gigantesco

giggle, ghigh´-l, *n* risolino
sciocco; *v* ridere
scioccamente

gild, ghild, *v* dorare

gills, ghils, *npl* branchie
fpl

gilt, ghilt, *adj* dorato; *n*
doratura f

gimlet, ghim´-lit, *n*
succhiello m

gin, chin, *n* gin m

ginger, chin´-cha, *n*
zenzero m

gingerbread, chin´-cha-
bred, *n* pan pepato m

giraffe, chi-raaf´, *n* giraffa
f

girder, gher´-da, *n* trave f

girdle, gher´-dl, *n* guaina f

girl, gherl, *n* ragazza f

girlfriend, gherl´-frend, *n*

amica f; ragazza f

girth, gherZ, *n*
circonferenza f

gist, chist, *n* succo m,
nocciolo m

give, ghiv, *v* dare; – **back,**
restituire; – **in,** cedere; –
up, rinunciare a;
(oneself) arrendersi

giver, ghiv´-a, *n*
donatore m

glacier, ghla´-si-a, *n*
ghiacciaio m

glad*, ghlad, *adj* lieto;
contento

gladden, ghlad´-n, *v*
allietare; rallegrare

glade, ghleid, *n* radura f

glamorous, ghla´-mo-tos,
adj affascinante;
brillante

glamour, ghla´-ma, *n*
fascino m

glance, ghlaans, *n*
occhiata f; – **at,** *v* dare
uno sguardo a; – **off,**
rimbalzare su

gland, ghland, *n*
ghiandola f

glare, ghler, *n* bagliore m;
(stare) sguardo furioso
m; *v* abbagliare; (stare)
guardare fisso

glaring*, ghler´-ring, *adj*
abbagliante; lampante

glass, ghlaas, *n* vetro m;
(tumbler) bicchiere m

glasses, ghlaas´-is, *npl*

occhiali *mpl*

glasshouse, ghlaas´-haus, *n* serra *f*

glassy, ghlaa´-si, *adj* vitreo

glaze, ghleis, *n* smalto *m*; *v* smaltare

glazier, ghlei´-si-a, *n* vetraio *m*

gleam, ghliim, *n* barlume *m*; luccichio *m*; *v* luccicare; brillare

glean, ghliin, *v* racimolare

glee, ghlii, *n* gioia *f*

glen, ghlen, *n* valletta *f*

glib*, ghlib, *adj* disinvolto; dalla parola facile

glide, ghlaid, *v* scivolare; planare

glider, ghlai´-da, *n* aliante *m*

glimmer, ghlim´-a, *n* barlume *m*; *v* baluginare

glimpse, ghlimps, *n* occhiata *f*; *v* intravedere

glint, ghlint, *n* scintillio *m*; *v* scintillare

glisten, ghlis´-n, *v* brillare

glitter, ghlit´-a, *n* sfavillio *m*; *v* sfavillare; luccicare

gloat, ghlout, *v* gongolare

global, ghlou´-bl, *adj* globale

global warming, ghlou´-bl uoor´-ming, *n* riscaldamento dell'atmosfera terrestre *m*

globe, ghloub, *n* globo *m*;

sfera *f*; mappamondo *m*

gloom, ghluum, *n* oscurità *f*; (dismal) tristezza *f*

gloomy, ghluu´-mi, *adj* oscuro; (person) triste

glorify, ghlo´-ri-fai, *v* esaltare

glorious*, ghlo´-ri-os, *adj* magnifico

glory, ghlo´-ri, *n* gloria *f*; – **in,** *v* gloriarsi di

gloss, ghlos, *n* lucentezza *f*; vernice lucida *f*; – **over,** *v* sorvolare

glossy, ghlos´-i, *adj* lucido

glove, ghlöv, *n* guanto *m*

glow, ghlou, *n* bagliore *m*; *v* ardere; arrossire

glue, ghluu, *n* colla *f*; *v* incollare

glum, ghlöm, *adj* cupo

glut, ghlöt, *n* sovrabbondanza *f*; *v* saturare

glutton, ghlöt´-n, *n* ghiottone *m*

gnarled, naarld, *adj* nodoso

gnash, nash, *v* digrignare

gnat, nat, *n* moscerino *m*

gnaw, noo, *v* rodere

go, gou, *v* andare; – **away,** andare via; (journey) partire; – **back,** ritornare, – **down,** scendere; (sun) tramontare; – **for,** andare a prendere;

(attack) lanciarsi contro; – **off,** (depart) partire; (food) andare a male; (guns) sparare; – **out,** uscire; spegnersi; – **up,** salire; – **without,** far a meno di

goad, goud, *v* pungolare

goal, goul, *n* (football) porta *f*; (score) gol *m*, rete *f*; (object) meta *f*

goalkeeper, goul-kii´-pa, *n* portiere *m*

goat, gout, *n* capra *f*

gobble, gob´-l, *v* tranguiare

goblet, gob´-lit, *n* coppa *f*; calice *m*

goblin, gob´-lin, *n* folletto *m*

God, god, *n* Dio *m*

god, god, *n* dio *m*; idolo *m*

godchild, god´-chaild, *n* figlioccio *m*, figlioccia *f*

goddess, god´-is, *n* dea *f*

godfather, god´-faa´-Da, *n* padrino *m*

godmother, god´-mö´-Da, *n* madrina *f*

goggles, gogh´-ls, *npl* occhiali di protezione *mpl*

gold, gould, *n* oro *m*

golden, goul´-dn, *adj* d'oro; dorato

goldfish, gould´-fish, *n* pesciolino rosso *m*

goldsmith, gould´-smiZ,

orefice *m*, orafo *m*

golf, golf, *n* golf *m*

golf course, golf´-koors, *n* campo da golf *m*

golfer, golf´-*a*, *n* golfista *m/f*

gong, gong, *n* gong *m*

good, gud, *adj* buono; *n* bene *m*; (use) vantaggio *m*; – **morning!, – day!, – afternoon!,** buon giorno!; – **evening!** buona sera!; – **night!** buona notte!

goodbye, gud-bai´, *interj* arrivederci!

Good Friday, gud frai´-di, *n* venerdì santo *m*

good-looking, gud-luk´-ing, *adj* bello

good-natured, gud-nei´-chud, *adj* buono

goodness, gud´-nis, *n* bontà *f*

goods, guds, *npl* merci *fpl*

good-will, gud´-uil, *n* buona volontà *f*

goose, guus, *n* oca *f*

gooseberry, gus´-be-ri, *n* uva spina *f*

goosepimples, guus´-pimpls, *n* pelle d'oca *f*

gore, goor, *n* (blood) sangue *m*; *v* incornare

gorge, goorch, *n* (ravine) gola *f*; *v* (feed) ingozzare

gorgeous*, goor´-chos, *adj* magnifico; fantastico

gorilla, go-ril´-*a*, *n* gorilla *m*

gory, goor´-ri, *adj* sanguinoso

gospel, gos´-pl, *n* vangelo *m*

gossamer, gos´-a-ma, *n* mussolina *f*

gossip, gos´-ip, *v* spettegolare; *n* pettegolezzi *mpl*; pettegolo *m*, pettegola *f*

gouge, gauch, *v* scavare; strappare

gout, gaut, *n* gotta *f*

govern, gŏv´-en, *v* governare

governess, gŏv´-e-nis, *n* governante *f*

government, gŏv´-en-ment, *n* governo *m*

governor, gŏv´-e-na, *n* governatore *m*

gown, gaun, *n* abito *m*; (official) toga *f*

grab, grab, *v* afferrare; impadronirsi di

grace, greis, *n* grazia *f*

graceful*, greis´-ful, *adj* aggraziato

graceless, greis´-lis, *adj* sgarbato

gracious*, grei´-shos, *adj* grazioso

gradation, gra-dei´-shon, *n* gradazione *f*

grade, greid, *n* grado *m*; categoria *f*; voto *m*; *v*

classificare; graduare

gradient, grei´-di-ent, *n* pendenza *f*

gradual*, grad´-iu-al, *adj* graduale

graduate, grad´-iu-eit, *v* graduare; (university) laurearsi

graduate, grad´-iu-at, *n* laureato *m*, laureata *f*

graft, graaft, *n* innesto *m*; *fig* corruzione *f*; *v* innestare

grain, grein, *n* (cereal) grano *m*; (sand) granellino *m*; (wood) venatura *f*

grammar, gram´-a, *n* grammatica *f*

gram(me), gram, *n* grammo *m*

granary, gran´-a-ri, *n* granaio *m*

grand*, grand, *adj* splendido; imponente

grandchild, grand´-chaild, *n* nipote *m/f*

granddaughter, grand´-doo-ta, *n* nipote *f*

grandfather, grand´-faa-Da, *n* nonno *m*

grandmother, grand´-mŏ-Da, *n* nonna *f*

grandson, grand´-sŏn, *n* nipote *m*

grant, graant, *n* sovvenzione *f*; (university) borsa di studio f; v concedere

grape, greip, n uva f

grapefruit, greip´-fruut, n pompelmo m

graph, graaf, n grafico m

graphic, gra´-fik, adj grafico; (description) vivido

graphics, gra´-fiks, n grafica f

grapple, grap´-l, v: – **with,** essere alle prese con

grasp, graasp, n presa f; v afferrare

grass, graas, n erba f

grasshopper, graas´-hop-a, n cavalletta f

grassy, graa´-si, adj erboso

grate, greit, v grattugiare; (brakes, wheels etc.) stridere; n griglia f

grateful*, greit´-ful, adj grato, riconoscente

gratefulness, greit´-ful-nis, n gratitudine f

grater, grei´-ta, n grattugia f

gratification, grat-i-fi-kei´-shon, n gratificazione f

gratify, grat´-i-fai, v gratificare

gratifying, grat´-i-fai-ing, adj soddisfacente

grating, grei´-ting, n griglia f; adj (noise) stridulo

gratis, grei´-tis, adv gratis

gratitude, grat´-i-tiuud, n gratitudine f

gratuitous*, gra-tiuu´-i-tos, adj gratuito

gratuity, gra-tiuu´-i-ti, n gratifica f; (tip) mancia f

grave, greiv, n fossa f; adj* grave, serio

gravedigger, greiv´-di-ga, n becchino m

gravestone, greiv´-stoun, n lapide f

graveyard, greiv´-iaard, n camposanto m

gravel, grav´-l, n ghiaia f

gravitate, grav´-i-teit, v gravitare

gravity, grav´-i-ti, n gravità f

gravy, grei´-vi, n sugo dell'arrosto m

graze, greis, v (feed) pascere; (slight rub) sfiorare

grease, griis, n grasso m; unto m; v ingrassare, lubrificare; ungere

greasy, grii´-si, adj grasso, unto; (surface) sdrucciolevole

great*, greit, adj grande; magnifico

Great Britain, greit bri´-tn, n Gran Bretagna f

greatness, greit´-nis, n grandezza f

Greece, griis, n Grecia f

greed, griid, n ingordigia f;

avidità f

greedily, grii´-di-li adv ingordamente; avidamente

greedy, grii´-di, adj ingordo; avido

Greek, griik, adj greco; n (language) greco m

green, griin, n verde m; adj verde; v verdeggiare

greengage, griin´-gheich, n susina f

greengrocer, griin´-grou-sa, n fruttivendolo m

greenhouse, griin´-haus, n serra f

greenish, grii´-nish, adj verdastro

greens, griins, npl verdura f

greet, griit, v salutare

greeting, grii´-ting, n saluto m

grenade, gre-neid´, n granata f

grey, grei, adj grigio

greyhound, grei´-haund, n levriero m

grief, griif, n dolore m

grievance, grii´-vans, n lagnanza f

grieve, griiv, v addolorare; piangere qualcuno

grievous*, grii´-vos, adj penoso; grave; – **bodily harm,** n lesione personale f

grill, gril, n griglia f; grill

m; *v* cuocere alla griglia

grim*, grim, *adj* orribile; brutto

grimace, gri-meis´, *n* smorfia *f*

grime, graim, *n* sudiciume *m*

grin, grin, *n* smorfia *f*; *v* ridere sardonicamente

grind, graind, *v* tritare, macinare; (sharpen) arrotare

grinder, grain´-da, *n* macinino *m*; affilacoltelli *m*

grip, grip, *n* stretta *f*; *v* stringere

gripping, grip´-ing, *adj* avvincente

grisly, gris´-li, *adj* orribile

grit, grit, *n* ghiaia *f*; sassolino *m*; bruscolino *m*

groan, groun, *n* gemito *m*; *v* gemere

grocer, grou´-sa, *n* negoziante di generi alimentari *m/f*

groceries, grou´-sa-ris, *npl* generi alimentari *mpl*

grog, grogh, *n* ponce *m*

groggy, grogh´-i, *adj* barcollante

groin, groin, *n* inguine *m*

groom, gruum, *n* stalliere *m*; sposo *m*

groove, gruuv, *n* solco *m*

grope, group, *v* brancolare

gross*, grous, *adj* (thick, coarse) grossolano; (profit, income) lordo

ground, graund, *n* suolo *m*; terreno *m*; (sport) campo *m*; *v* (ship) arenarsi

ground floor, graund flor´, *n* pianterreno *m*

groundless*, graund´-lis, *adj* infondato

grounds, graunds, *npl* (park) giardini *mpl*; (reasons) motivi *mpl*

group, gruup, *n* gruppo *m*; *v* raggruppare

grouse, graus, *n* gallo cedrone *m*; *v fig* brontolare

grovel, grov´-l, *v* strisciare

grow, grou, *v* crescere; coltivare

grower, grou´-a, *n* coltivatore *m*

grown-up, groun´-öp, *adj* adulto

growl, graul, *n* ringhio *m*; *v* ringhiare

growth, grouZ, *n* tumore *m*; crescita *f*

grub, gröb, *n* bruco *m*

grudge, gröch, *n* rancore *m*; *v* invidiare; dare a malincuore

gruesome, gruu´-som, *adj* orripilante

gruff, gröf, *adj* arcigno

grumble, gröm´-bl, *v*

borbottare

grunt, grönt, *v* grugnire; *n* grugnito *m*

guarantee, ga-ran-tii´, *n* garanzia *f*; *v* garantire

guard, gaard, *n* guardia *f*; (railway) capotreno *m*; *v* fare la guardia a; proteggere

guarded, gaar´-did, *adj* circospetto

guardian, gaar´-di-an, *n* custode *m*; tutore *m*

guess, ghes, *v* indovinare

guesswork, ghes´-uerk, *n* supposizione *f*

guest, ghest, *n* ospite *m/f*; cliente *m/f*

guesthouse, ghest´-haus, *n* pensione *f*

guest room, ghest´-ruum, *n* stanza degli ospiti *f*

guidance, gai´-dens, *n* guida *f*

guide, gaid, *v* guidare; *n* guida *f*

guild, ghild, *n* corporazione *f*

guile, gail, *n* astuzia *f*

guilt, ghilt, *n* colpa *f*

guilty, ghil´-ti, *adj* colpevole

guinea pig, ghin´-i-pigh, *n* porcellino d'India *m*; cavia *f*

guise, gais, *n* guisa *f*

guitar, ghi´-taar, *n* chitarra *f*

gulf, gŭlf, n golfo m;
abisso m

gull, gŭl, n gabbiano m

gullet, gŭl´-it, n gargarozzo
m

gulp, gŭlp, v inghiottire; n
sorso m; boccone m

gum, gŭm, n gomma f;
incollare

gums, gŭms, npl gengive
fpl

gun, gŭn, n fucile m;
pistola f

gurgle, gher´-gl, v
gorgogliare; n gorgoglio
m

gush, gŭsh, n getto m; v
sgorgare

gust, gŭst, n raffica f

gut, gŭt, n intestino m

gutter, gŭt´-a, n cunetta f;
(roof) grondaia f

guy, gai, n (person) tipo m

gym, chim, n palestra f

gymnast, chim´-nast, n
ginnasta m/f

gymnastics, chim-nas´-
tiks, n ginnastica f

gypsy, chip´-si, n zingaro
m, zingara f; adj gitano

H

haberdashery, hab´-e-dash-e-ri, n merceria f

habit, hab´-it, n abitudine f; tonaca f

habitable, hab´-it-a-bl, adj abitabile

habitual*, ha-bit´-iu-al, adj abituale

hack, hak, v fare a pezzi

hackneyed, hak´-nid, adj banale

haddock, had´-ok, n eglefino m

haggard*, hagh´-ad, adj smunto

haggle, hagh´-l, v mercanteggiare

Hague, heigh, n The –, L'Aja f

hail, heil, n grandine f; v grandinare; (call) chiamare

hair, her, n capelli mpl; (animal) pelo m

hairbrush, her´-brŏsh, n spazzola per capelli f

hairdresser, her´-dres-a, n parrucchiere m, parrucchiera f

hair-dryer, her´-drai-a, n asciugacapelli m

hairpin, her´-pin, n forcina f

hairspray, her´-sprei, n lacca per capelli f

hairy, her´-ri, adj peloso

hake, heik, n nasello m

half, haaf, n metà f; adj mezzo

halibut, hal´-i-but, n halibut m, ipoglosso m

hall, hool, n sala f; (entry) ingresso m

hallucination, ha-lu-si-nei´-shon, n allucinazione f

halt, hoolt, n fermata f; v fermare, fermarsi

halter, hol´-ta, n cavezza f

halve, haav, v dimezzare

ham, ham, n prosciutto m

hamburger, ham´-ber-gha, n hamburger m

hamlet, ham´-lit, n borgo m

hammer, ham´-a, n martello m; v martellare

hammock, ham´-ok, n amaca f

hamper, ham´-pa, n cesta f; v ostacolare

hand, hand, n mano f; (clock) lancetta f; v dare; **on the one –,** da un lato; **on the other –,** dall'altro (lato)

handbag, hand´-bagh, n borsa f, borsetta f

handbook, hand´-buk, n manuale m

handcuffs, hand´-kŏfs, npl manette fpl

handful, hand´-ful, n manciata f

handicapped, han-di´-kapt, adj handicappato, portatore di handicap

handkerchief, hang´-ke-chiif, n fazzoletto m

handle, han´-dl, n manico m; (knob) maniglia f; v maneggiare

hand-luggage, hand´-lŏgh-ich, n bagaglio a mano m

handmade, hand´-meid, adj fatto a mano

handrail, hand´-reil, n corrimano m

handshake, hand´-sheik, n stretta di mano f

handsome*, han´-som, adj bello

handwriting, hand´-raiting, n scrittura f, calligrafia f

handy, han´-di, adj comodo; a portata di mano; abile

hang, hang, v appendere; impiccare; – **up,** appendere; riagganciare

hangar, hang´-a, n hangar m

hang-gliding, hang´-ghlaiding, n volo col deltaplano m

hangover, hang´-ou-va, n postumi della sbornia mpl

hanker, hang-ka, v bramare

happen, hap´-n, v succedere, accadere, capitare

happily, hap´-i-li, adv felicemente; con gioia

happiness, hap´-i-nis, n felicità f

happy, hap´-i, adj contento, felice; allegro

harass, ha´-ras, v tormentare

harassment, ha´-ras-ment, n molestia f

harbour, haar´-ba, n porto m; v nutrire

hard, haard, adj duro; difficile; adv (work) sodo; (push) forte

hardback, haard´-bak, n edizione rilegata f

hard disk, haard disk, n comp disco rigido m, hard disk m

hard drug, haard drŏgh, n droga pesante f

harden, haar´-den, v indurire

hardly, haard´-li, adv appena

hardship, haard´-ship, n privazioni fpl; sofferenze fpl

hardware, haard´-uer, n hardware m; (tools) ferramenta fpl

hardy, haar´-di, adj robusto

hare, her, n lepre f

harelip, her-lip´, n labbro leporino m

harm, haarm, n male m; danno m; v far male a

harmful, haarm´-ful, adj dannoso, nocivo

harmless, haarm´-lis, adj innocuo

harmonious, haar-mou´-ni-os, adj armonioso

harmonize, haar´-mon-ais, v armonizzare

harness, haar´-nis, n bardatura f; v bardare; (forces) utilizzare

harp, haarp, n arpa f

harpoon, haar-puun´, n arpione m; v arpionare

harrowing, ha´-rou-ing, adj straziante

harsh, haarsh, adj duro; severo; stridente

harvest, haar´-vist, n raccolto m; v raccogliere; mietere

hassle, has-l, n seccatura f; v seccare

haste, heist, n fretta f

hasten, hei´-sn, v affrettare

hastily, heis´-ti-li, adv affrettatamente

hat, hat, n cappello m

hatch, hach, v covare; boccaporto m

hatchback, hach´-bak, n auto con portellone posteriore f

hatchet, hach´-it, n accetta f

hate, heit, n odio m; v odiare

hateful*, heit´-ful, adj odioso

hatred, hei´-trid, n odio m

haughtiness, hoo´-ti-nis,

n alterigia *f*

haughty, hoo´-ti, *adj*
altero

haul, hool, *v* tirare; *n*
tirata *f*; (catch) retata *f*

haunch, hoonch, *n* anca *f*;
(meat) coscia *f*

haunt, hoont, *v*
perseguitare;
frequentare; *n* ritrovo *m*;
(animals) tana *f*

have, hav, *v* avere; (cause)
fare

haven, hei´-ven, *n*
rifugio *m*

haversack, hav´-e-sak, *n*
bisaccia *f*

havoc, hav´-ok, *n* caos *m*

hawk, hook, *n* falco *m*

hawker, hoo´-ka, *n*
venditore ambulante *m*

hawthorn, hoo´-Zoorn, *n*
biancospino *m*

hay, hei, *n* fieno *m*

hayfever, hei´-fii-va, *n*
raffreddore da fieno *m*

hazard, has´-ed, *n* rischio
m; *v* rischiare

hazardous*, has´-ed-os,
adj rischioso

haze, heis, *n* foschia *f*

hazel, he´-sl, *n* nocciolo
m; *adj* castano

hazelnut, he´-sl-nŏt, *n*
nocciola *f*

hazy, hei´-si, *adj* fosco;
offuscato

he, hii, *pron* lui, egli

head, hed, *n* testa *f*;
capo *m*

headache, hed´-eik, *n* mal
di testa *m*

heading, hed´-ing, *n* titolo
m; intestazione *f*

headline, hed´-lain, *n*
titolo *m*

headlong, hed´-long, *adv* a
capofitto

headmaster, hed-maas´-ta,
n direttore didattico *m*;
preside *m*

headphones, hed´-founs,
npl cuffie *fpl*

headquarters, hed´-kuoor-
tes, *n* sede centrale *f*; *mil*
quartier generale *m*

headroom, hed´-ruum, *n*
altezza massima *f*

headstrong, hed´-strong,
adj caparbio

heady, hed´-i, *adj*
inebriante

heal, hiil, *v* guarire

healing, hii´-ling, *adj*
curativo; *n* guarigione *f*

health, helZ, *n* salute *f*

healthy, hel´-Zi, *adj* sano;
salutare

heap, hiip, *n* mucchio *m*; *v*
ammucchiare

hear, hir, *v* sentire

hearing, hir´-ring, *n* udito
m; (court) udienza *f*

hearing aid, hir´-ring eid,
n apparecchio
acustico *m*

hearsay, hir´-sei, *n* diceria
f, sentito dire *m*

hearse, hers, *n* carro
funebre *m*

heart, haart, *n* cuore *m*

heartbroken, haart´-
brouk-n, *adj* affranto

heartburn, haart´-bern, *n*
acidità di stomaco *f*

heartily, haart´-i-li, *adv* di
cuore

heartless, haart´-lis, *adj*
spietato

hearth, haarZ, *n* focolare
m

hearty, haar´-ti, *adj*
caloroso; robusto;
vigoroso

heat, hiit, *n* calore *m*; *v*
scaldare

heater, hii´-ta, *n*
termosifone *m*

heating, hii´-ting, *n*
riscaldamento *m*

heath, hiiZ, *n* landa *f*

heathen, hii´-Den, *n*
pagano *m*

heather, heD´-a, *n* erica *f*

heat-stroke, hiit´-strouk,
n colpo di calore *m*

heatwave, hiit´-ueiv, *n*
ondata di caldo *f*

heave, hiiv, *v* sollevare;
spingere; tirare

heaven, hev´-en, *n* cielo
m, paradiso *m*

heavenly, hev´-en-li, *adj*
celeste, divino

heavily, hev´-i-li, *adv*
(smoke, drink) molto;
(rain, snow) forte

heavy, hev´-i, *adj* pesante

hedge, hech, *n* siepe *f*

hedgehog, hech´-hogh, *n*
riccio *m*

heedless, hiid´-lis, *adj*
avventato

heel, hiil, *n* tallone *m*,
calcagno *m*; (shoe)
tacco *m*

hefty, hef´-ti, *adj* pesante

heifer, hef´-a, *n* giovenca *f*

height, hait, *n* altezza *f*;
apice *m*

heighten, hai´-ten, *v*
alzare; *fig* esaltare

heinous*, hei´-nos, *adj*
nefando

heir, er, *n* erede *m*

heiress, er-res, *n* erede *f*

heirloom, er´-luum, *n*
ricordo di famiglia *m*

helicopter, hel´-i-kop-ta,
n elicottero *m*

hell, hel, *n* inferno *m*

hellish, hel´-ish, *adj*
infernale

hello, hel-ou´, *interj* ciao!;
salve!; (telephone)
pronto?

helm, helm, *n* timone *m*

helmet, hel´-mit, *n* casco
m; elmetto *m*

help, help, *n* aiuto *m*;
aiutante *m/f*; *v* aiutare;
contribuire; servire

helper, hel´-pa, *n* aiutante
m/f

helpful*, help´-ful, *adj*
utile

helpless*, help´-lis, *adj*
impotente; indifeso

hem, hem, *n* orlo *m*; *v*
orlare; **– in,** cingere

hemp, hemp, *n* canapa *f*

hen, hen, *n* gallina *f*

hence, hens, *adv* per cui

her, her, *pron* lei; le; la; *adj*
suo, sua, suoi, sue

herb, herb, *n* erba *f*

herd, herd, *n* mandria *f*;
branco *m*

herdsman, herds´-man, *n*
mandriano *m*

here, hir, *adv* qui, qua

hereditary, hi-red´-i-ta-ri,
adj ereditario

heresy, he´-ri-si, *n* eresia *f*

heretic, he´-ri-tik, *n*
eretico *m*

heritage, he´-ri-titch, *n*
patrimonio *m*, eredità *f*

hermetic, her-met´-ik, *adj*
ermetico

hermit, her´-mit, *n*
eremita *m/f*

hernia, her´-ni-a, *n* ernia *f*

hero, hir´-rou, *n* eroe *m*

heroic, hi-rou´-ik, *adj*
eroico

heroin, he´-rou-in, *n*
(drug) eroina *f*

heroine, he´-rou-in, *n*
eroina *f*

heroism, he´-rou-ism, *n*
eroismo *m*

herring, he´-ring, *n*
aringa *f*

hers, hers, *pron* il suo, la
sua, i suoi, le sue; **a
friend of –,** un suo
amico

herself, her-self´, *pron refl*
si; se stessa

hesitate, hes´-i-teit, *v*
esitare

hesitation, hes-i-tei´-
shon, *n* esitazione *f*

heterosexual, he-te-rou-
sek´-siu-al, *adj*
eterosessuale; *n*
eterosessuale *m/f*

hiccough, hik´-ŏp, *n*
singhiozzo *m*

hide, haid, *n* pelle *f*; cuoio
m; *v* nascondere

hide-and-seek, haid´-en-
siik, *n* nascondino *m*

hideous*, hid´-i-os, *adj*
orrendo

hiding, hai´-ding, *n*
(beating) botte *fpl*

hiding place, hai´-ding
pleis, *n* nascondiglio *m*

hi-fi, hai´-fai, *n* stereo *m*

high, hai, *adj* alto

high chair, hai´-cher, *n*
seggiolone *m*

highway, hai´-uei, *n*
superstrada *f*

hijack, hai´-chak, *v*
dirottare

hilarious, hi-ler´-ri-os, *adj*
spassoso

hilarity, hi-la´-ri-ti, *n*
ilarità *f*

hill, hil, *n* collina *f*

hilly, hil´-i, *adj* collinoso

hilt, hilt, *n* impugnatura *f*

him, him, *pron* lui; gli; lo

himself, him-self´, *pron
refl* si; se stesso

hind, haind, *adj* posteriore

hinder, hin´-da, *v*
impedire

hindrance, hin´-drans, *n*
impedimento *m*

hinge, hinch, *n* cardine *m*

hint, hint, *n* cenno *m*;
allusione *f*; *v* accennare;
alludere

hip, hip, *n* anca *f*

hippo, hip´-ou, *n*
ippopotamo *m*

hire, hair, *v* noleggiare; *n*
nolo *m*; noleggio *m*

his, his, *pron* il suo, la sua,
i suoi, le sue; *adj* suo,
sua, suoi, sue; **a friend
of –,** un suo amico

hiss, his, *v* sibilare; *n*
sibilo *m*

historian, his-toor´-ri-an,
n storico *m*

historic(al), his-to´-rik(-
al), *adj* storico

history, his´-to-ri, *n*
storia *f*

hit, hit, *n* colpo *m*;
successo *m*; *v* colpire

hitch, hich, *n* intoppo *m*;
v tirare su; attaccare

hitchhike, hich´-haik, *v*
fare l'autostop

hitchhiker, hich´-haik-a,
n autostoppista *m/f*

hi-tech, hai-tek´, *adj* hi-
tech

hive, haiv, *n* alveare *m*

hoarse*, hoors, *adj* rauco

hoax, houks, *n* burla *f*

hobby, hob´-i, *n* hobby *m*

hockey, hok´-i, *n* hockey
m

hoe, hou, *n* zappa *f*; *v*
zappare

hog, hogh, *n* maiale *m*

hoist, hoist, *v* issare

hold, hould, *n* presa *f*;
stiva *f*; *v* tenere;
contenere; possedere; **–
back,** trattenere; **– on,** *v*
aspettare; resistere

holder, houl´-da, *n*
possessore *m*; titolare
m/f; contenitore *m*

hole, houl, *n* buco *m*

holiday, hol´-i-dei, *n*
giorno di vacanza *m*;
(bank holiday) giorno
festivo *m*

holidays, hol´-i-deis, *npl*
vacanze *fpl*; ferie *fpl*

holiness, houl´-i-nis, *n*
santità *f*

Holland, hol´-and, *n*
Olanda *f*

hollow, hol´-ou, *n* cavità *f*;

adj cavo; vuoto; *v*
scavare

holly, hol´-i, *n*
agrifoglio *m*

holocaust, hol´-o-koost, *n*
olocausto *m*

holy, hou´-li, *adj* santo

homage, hom´-ich, *n*
omaggio *m*

home, houm, *n* casa *f*;
patria *f*; **at –,** a casa

homeless, houm´-lis, *adj*
senzatetto

homely, houm´-li, *adj*
accogliente; alla buona

home-made, houm´-meid,
adj fatto in casa;
casalingo

homesick, houm´-sik, *adj*
to be –, avere nostalgia

homicide, hom´-i-said, *n*
omicidio *m*

homosexual, hom-ou-
sek´-siu-al, *adj*
omosessuale; *n*
omosessuale *m/f*

honest*, on´-ist, *adj*
onesto

honesty, on´-is-ti, *n*
onestà *f*

honey, hŏn´-i, *n* miele *m*

honeymoon, hŏn´-i-
muun, *n* luna di miele *f*

honeysuckle, hŏn´-i-sŏk-
l, *n* caprifoglio *m*

honorary, on´-o-ta-ri, *adj*
onorario

honour, on´-a, *n* onore *m*;

v onorare

honourable, on´-*e-ra*-bl, *adj* onorevole

hood, hud, *n* cappuccio *m*; cappa *f*; capote *f*

hoof, huuf, *n* zoccolo *m*

hook, huk, *n* gancio *m*; amo *m*; *v* agganciare

hooligan, huu´-li-*gan*, *n* teppista *m*

hoop, huup, *n* cerchio *m*

hoot, huut, *v* ululare; suonare il clacson

hoover®, huuv´-*a*, *n* aspirapolvere *m*; *v* passare l'aspirapolvere

hop, hop, *n* luppolo *m*; *v* saltellare; saltare

hope, houp, *n* speranza *f*; *v* sperare

hopeful*, houp´-ful, *adj* pieno di speranze

hopeless*, houp´-lis, *adj* disperato; senza speranza

horizon, ho-rai-*son*, *n* orizzonte *m*

horizontal, ho-ri-son´-*tal*, *adj* orizzontale

hormone, hoor´-moun, *n* ormone *m*

horn, hoorn, *n* corno *m*; clacson *m*

hornet, hoor´-nit, *n* calabrone *m*

horoscope, ho´-ro-skoup, *n* oroscopo *m*

horrible, ho´-ri-bl, *adj* orrido

horrid, ho´-rid, *adj* orrendo

horrify, ho´-ri-fai, *v* inorridire

horror, ho´-ra, *n* orrore *m*

horse, hoors, *n* cavallo *m*

horseback, hoors´-bak, **on –,** *adv* a cavallo

horsepower, hoors´-pau-a, *n* cavalli vapore *mpl*

horseradish, hoors´-rad-ish, *n* rafano *m*

horseshoe, hoors´-shuu, *n* ferro di cavallo *m*

hose, hous, *n* tubo di gomma *m*

hosiery, hou´-sie-ri, *n* maglieria *f*

hospitable, hos-pi´-ta-bl, *adj* ospitale

hospital, hos´-pi-tl, *n* ospedale *m*

hospitality, hos-pi-ta´-li-ti, *n* ospitalità *f*

host, houst, *n* ospite *m*

hostage, hos´-tich, *n* ostaggio *m*

hostel, hos´-tl, *n* ostello *m*

hostess, hous´-tes, *n* ospite *m*; hostess *f*

hostile, hos´-tail, *adj* ostile

hot*, hot, *adj* caldo; piccante

hotel, hou-tel´, *n* albergo *m*

hothouse, hot´-haus, *n* serra *f*

hot-water bottle, hot-

uoo´-ta bot´-l, *n* borsa dell'acqua calda *f*

hound, haund, *n* segugio *m*; *v* perseguitare

hour, au-a, *n* ora *f*

hourly, au´-e-li, *adv* ogni ora; *adj* all'ora

house, haus, *n* casa *f*

household, haus´-hould, *n* famiglia *f*

housekeeper, haus´-kii-pa, *n* governante *f*

House of Commons, haus-ov-kom´-ons, *n* Camera dei Comuni *f*

housewife, haus´-uaif, *n* casalinga *f*

hovel, hov´-l, *n* tugurio *m*

hover, hov´-a, *v* sorvolare

how, hau, *adv* come; **– far is it?,** quanto è lontano?; **– much?,** quanto? quanta?; **– many?,** quanti? quante?

however, hau-ev´-a, *conj* tuttavia

howl, haul, *v* ululare

hub, hŏb, *n* mozzo *m*; *fig* fulcro *m*

huddle, hŏd´-l, *v* raggomitolarsi

hue, hiuu, *n* tinta *f*

hue and cry, hiuu-en-krai´, *n* clamore *m*

hug, hŏgh, *v* abbracciare; *n* abbraccio *m*

huge, hiuuch, *adj* enorme, immenso

hull, hŏl, n scafo m

hum, hŏm, v canticchiare

human*, hiuu´-man, adj umano; n essere umano m

humane*, hiu-mein´, adj umanitario

humanity, hiu-man´-i-ti, n umanità f

humble, hŏm´-bl, adj umile; v umiliare

humid, hiuu´-mid, adj umido

humidity, hiu-mid´-i-ti, n umidità f

humiliate, hiu-mil´-i-eit, v umiliare

humiliation, hiu-mi-li-ei´-shon, n umiliazione f

humorous, hiuu´-mo-ros, adj umoristico; spiritoso

humour, hiuu´-ma, n umorismo m; v compiacere

hunch, hŏnch, n gobba f

hunchback, hŏnch´-bak, n gobbo m

hundred, hŏn´-drid, adj cento

hundredth, hŏn´-dredZ, adj centesimo

hunger, hŏng´-ga, n fame f

hungry, hŏng´-gri, adj affamato

hunt, hŏnt, n caccia f; v cacciare

hunter, hŏn-ta, n cacciatore m

hurdle, her´-dl, n ostacolo m

hurl, herl, v scagliare

hurricane, hŏ´-ri-kan, n uragano m

hurry, hŏ´-ri, n fretta f; v affrettare

hurt, hert, v far male; ferire

hurtful*, hert´-ful, adj che ferisce

husband, hŏs´-band, n marito m

hush! hŏsh, interj zitto! – **up,** v mettere a tacere

husky, hŏs´-ki, adj roco

hustle, hŏs´-l, v spingere

hut, hŏt, n capanna f

hutch, hŏch, n (rabbit) conigliera f

hyacinth, hai´-a-sinZ, n giacinto m

hydrant, hai´-drant, n idrante m

hydraulic, hai-dro´-lik, adj idraulico

hydrogen, hai´-dro-chen, n idrogeno m

hygiene, hai´-chiin, n igiene f

hygienic, hai-chii´-nik, adj igienico

hymn, him, n inno m

hype, haip, n pubblicità f

hyphen, hai´-fen, n lineetta f, trattino m

hypnotize, hip´-no-tais, v ipnotizzare

hypocrisy, hi-po´-kri-si, n ipocrisia f

hypocrite, hip´-o-krit, n ipocrita m/f

hypothermia, haip-ou-Zer´-mi-a, n ipotermia f

hysterical, his-te´-ri-kl, adj isterico

I, ai, *pron* io

ice, ais, *n* ghiaccio *m*

iceberg, ais´-bergh, *n* iceberg *m*

icebound, ais´-baund, *adj* bloccato dal ghiaccio

ice cream, ais-criim´, *n* gelato *m*

ice hockey, ais´-ho-ki, *n* hockey su ghiaccio *m*

ice lolly, ais lo´-li, *n* (sorbet) ghiacciolo *m*

ice rink, ais´-rink, *n* pista di pattinaggio su ghiaccio *f*

ice skating, ais´-skei-ting, *n* pattinaggio su ghiaccio *m*

icicle, ai´-si-kl, *n* ghiacciolo *m*

icing, ai´-sing, *n* glassa *f*

icing sugar, ai´-sing shu´-ga, *n* zucchero a velo *m*

icy, ai´-si, *adj* gelido; ghiacciato

idea, ai-di´-a, *n* idea *f*

ideal, ai-di´-al, *n* ideale *m*; *adj* ideale

idealize, ai-di´-a-lais, *v* idealizzare

identical*, ai-den´-ti-kl, *adj* identico

identify, ai-den´-ti-fai, *v* identificare

identity, ai-den´-ti-ti, *n* identità *f*

idiom, id´-i-om, *n* espressione idiomatica *f*

idiot, id´-i-ot, *n* idiota *m/f*

idiotic, id-i-ot´-ik, *adj* idiota

idle, ai´-dl, *adj* pigro; ozioso; inattivo; *v* oziare; (engine) girare al

minimo

idleness, aidl´-nis, *n* ozio *m*

idler, aid´-la, *n* poltrone *m*, fannullone *m*

idol, ai´-dl, *n* idolo *m*

idolize, ai´-dol-ais, *v* idolatrare

idyll, is´-il, *n* idillio *m*

idyllic, i´-dil-ik, *adj* idilliaco

if, if, *conj* se; **even –**, anche se

ignite, igh-nait´, *v* accendere; accendersi

ignition, igh-ni´-shon, *n* accensione *f*

ignoble, igh-nou´-bl, *adj* ignobile

ignominious, igh-no-min´-i-os, *adj* ignominioso

ignominy, igh´-no-min-i, *n* ignominia *f*

ignorance, igh´-no-rans, *n* ignoranza *f*

ignorant, igh´-no-rant, *adj* ignorante

ignore, igh-noor´, *v* ignorare

ill, il, *adj* malato; **be –**, essere ammalato; (sick) star male

illness, il´-nis, *n* malattia *f*

illegal*, i-lii´-gl, *adj* illegale

illegible, il-lech´-i-bl, *adj* illeggibile

illegitimate*, i-li-chit´-i-mat, *adj* illegittimo

illiterate, i-lit´-e-ret, *adj* analfabeta

illogical*, i-loch´-i-kl, *adj* illogico

illuminate, i-luu´-mi-neit, *v* illuminare

illumination, i-luu-mi-nei´-shon, *n* illuminazione *f*

illusion, i-luu´-shon, *n* illusione *f*

illusory, i-luu´-so-ri, *adj* illusorio

illustrate, il´-us-treit, *v* illustrare

illustration, il-us-trei´-shon, *n* illustrazione *f*

illustrious*, i-lŏs´-tri-os, *adj* illustre

image, im´-ich, *n* immagine *f*

imaginary, i-mach´-in-a-ri, *adj* immaginario

imagination, i-mach-in-ei´-shon, *n* immaginazione *f*

imagine, i-mach´-in, *v* immaginarsi

imbecile, im´-bi-siil, *n* imbecille *m/f*

imbue, im-biuu´, *v* permeare

imitate, im´-i-teit, *v* imitare

immaculate*, i-mak´-iu-let, *adj* immacolato

immaterial*, i-ma-tiir´-ri-al, *adj* immateriale

immature, i-ma-tiuur´, *adj* immaturo

immeasurable, i-mesh´-u-ra-bl, *adj* incommensurabile

immediate*, i-mii´-di-et, *adj* immediato

immense*, i-mens´, *adj* immenso

immensity, i-mens´-i-ti, *n* immensità *f*

immerse, i-mers´, *v* immergere

immigrant, im´-i-grant, *n* immigrante *m/f*

immigrate, im´-i-greit, *v* immigrare

immigration, im-i-grei´-shon, *n* immigrazione *f*

imminent, im´-i-nent, *adj* imminente

immoderate, i-mod´-e-rat, *adj* smodato

immodest*, i-mod´-ist, *adj* immodesto; indecente

immoral*, i-mo´-ral, *adj* immorale

immortal*, i-moor´-tal, *adj* immortale

immortalize, i-moor´-tal-ais, *v* immortalare

immovable, i-muu´-va-bl, *adj* irremovibile

immune, i-miuun´, *adj* immune

immunity, i-miuu´-ni-ti, *n* immunità *f*

imp, imp, *n* folletto *m*; (little rascal) demonietto *m*

impact, im´-pakt, *n* impatto *m*; scontro *m*

impair, im-per´, *v* danneggiare; deteriorare; diminuire

impale, im-peil´, *v* impalare

impart, im-paart´, *v* impartire; comunicare

impartial*, im-paar´-shal, *adj* imparziale

impassable, im-paas´-a-bl, *adj* intransitabile, impraticabile

impassive, im-pas´-iv, *adj* impassibile

impatience, im-pei´-shens, *n* impazienza *f*

impatient, im-pei´-shent, *adj* impaziente

impeach, im-piich´, *v* mettere in stato d'accusa; attaccare

impeachment, im-piich´-ment, *n* accusa *f*

impecunious, im-pi-kiuu´-ni-os, *adj* indigente

impede, im-piid´, *v* impedire

impediment, im-ped´-i-ment, *n* impedimento *m*

impel, im-pel´, *v* costringere

impending, im-pen´-ding, *adj* imminente

imperative, im-pe´-ra-tiv, *n gram* imperativo *m*; *adj* imperativo; indispensabile

imperfect, im-per´-fikt, *n* imperfetto *m*; *adj* imperfetto; difettoso

imperfection, im-pe-fek´-shon, *n* imperfezione *f*

imperial, im-pir´-ri-al, *adj* imperiale

imperil, im-pe´-ril, *v* mettere in pericolo

impersonate, im-per´-son-eit, *v* impersonare

impertinence, im-per´-ti-nens, *n* impertinenza *f*

impertinent, im-per´-ti-nent, *adj* impertinente

impervious, im-per´-vi-os, *adj* impervio

impetuous, im-pet´-iu-os, *adj* impetuoso

impetus, im´-pi-tus, *n* impeto *m*

implant, im-plaant´, *v* innestare; inculcare

implement, im´-pli-ment, *n* attrezzo *m*; utensile *m*

implicate, im´-pli-keit, *v* implicare

implicit, im-plis´-it, *adj* implicito

implore, im-ploor´, *v* implorare

imply, im-plai´, *v* implicare; (suggest) insinuare

impolite, im-po-lait´, *adj* scortese

import, im´-poort, *n* importazione *f*

import, im-poort´, *v* importare

importance, im-poor´-tans, *n* importanza *f*

important, im-poor´-tant, *adj* importante

importer, im-poor´-ta, *n* importatore *m*

impose, im-pous´, *v* imporre; – **upon**, abusare di

imposing, im-pou´-sing, *adj* imponente

imposition, im-po-si´-shon, *n* imposizione *f*

impossibility, im-pos-i-bil´-i-ti, *n* impossibilità *f*

impossible, im-pos´-i-bl, *adj* impossibile

impostor, im-pos´-ta, *n* impostore *m*

impotent, im´-po-tent, *adj* impotente

impound, im-paund´, *v* sequestrare, confiscare

impoverish, im-pov´-e-rish, *v* impoverire

impracticable, im-prak´-ti-ka-bl, *adj* impraticabile

imprecation, im-pri-kei´-shon, *n* imprecazione *f*

impregnable, im-pregh´-na-bl, *adj* inespugnabile

impregnate, im´-pregh-neit, *v* impregnare

impress, im-pres´, *v* fare un'impressione; *n* impressione *f*

impression, im-pre´-shon, *n* impressione *f*

impressive, im-pres´-iv, *adj* impressionante

imprint, im´-print, *n* sigla editoriale *f*

imprint, im-print´, *v* stampare

imprison, im-pris´-n, *v* imprigionare

imprisonment, im-pris´-n-ment, *n* reclusione *f*

improbable, im-prob´-a-bl, *adj* improbabile

improper, im-prop´-a, *adj* improprio; sconveniente

impropriety, im-pro-prai´-i-ti, *n* sconvenienza *f*

improve, im-pruuv´, *v* migliorare

improvement, im-pruuv´-ment, *n* miglioramento *m*; miglioria *f*

improvise, im´-pro-vais, *v* improvvisare

impudence, im´-piu-dens, *n* impudenza *f*

impudent, im´-piu-dent, *adj* impudente

impulse, im´-pöls, *n* impulso *m*

impulsive, im-pŏl´-siv, *adj*
impulsivo

impure, im-piuur´, *adj*
impuro

impurity, im-piuur´-ri-ti,
n impurità *f*

impute, im-piut´, *v*
imputare

in, in, *prep* a; in; *adv*
dentro

inability, in-*a*-bil´-i-ti, *n*
incapacità *f*

inaccessible, in-ak-ses´-i-
bl, *adj* inaccessibile

inaccuracy, in-ak´-iu-ra-
si, *n* inesattezza *f*

inaccurate*, in-ak´-iu-rat,
adj inaccurato; inesatto

inadequate, in-ad´-i-kuat,
adj inadeguato;
insufficiente

inadvertently, in-ad-ver´-
tent-li, *adv*
inavvertitamente

inane, i-nein´, *adj* sciocco

inanimate, in-nan´-i-mat,
adj inanimato

inapt, i-napt´, *adj* poco
appropriato

inasmuch as, i-n*a*s-mŏch´
as, *conj* in quanto;
poiché

inaudible, i-noo´-di-bl, *adj*
appena percettibile

inaugurate, i-noo´-ghiu-
reit, *v* inaugurare

inborn, in´-boorn, *adj*
innato; congenito

inbred, in-bred´, *adj*
innato; congenito

incalculable, in-kal´-kiu-
la-bl, *adj* incalcolabile

incapable, in-kei´-pa-bl,
adj incapace

incapacitate, in-ka-pas´-i-
teit, *v* inabilitare

incapacity, in-ka-pas´-i-ti,
n incapacità *f*; *law*
inabilitazione *f*

incarnation, in-kaar-nei´-
shon, *n* incarnazione *f*

incautious*, in-koo´-shos,
adj incauto

incense, in´-sens, *n*
incenso *m*

incense, in-sens´, *v* fare
infuriare

incentive, in-sen´-tiv, *n*
incentivo *m*

incessant*, in-ses´-ant, *adj*
incessante

inch, inch, *n* pollice *m* (=
2,54 cm)

incident, in´-si-dent, *n*
incidente *m*

incidental*, in-si-den´-tl,
adj fortuito; secondario

incision, in-si´-shon, *n*
incisione *f*

incite, in-sait´, *v* incitare

incivility, in-si-vil´-i-ti, *n*
inciviltà *f*

inclination, in-kli-nei´-
shon, *n* inclinazione *f*

incline, in-klain´, *n*
(slope) pendio *m*; *v*

inclinare; inclinarsi

include, in-kluud´, *v*
includere

inclusive, in-kluu´-siv, *adj*
incluso

incoherent, in-ko-hiir´-
rent, *adj* incoerente

income, in´-kom, *n*
reddito *m*

income tax, in´-kom taks,
n imposta sul reddito *f*

incoming, in´-kŏm-ing,
adj in arrivo; (new)
entrante

incomparable, in-kom´-
pa-ra-bl, *adj*
incomparabile

incompatible, in-kom-
pat´-i-bl, *adj*
incompatibile

incompetent, in-kom´-pi-
tent, *adj* incompetente

incomplete*, in-kom-
pliit´, *adj* incompleto

incomprehensible, in-
kom-pri-hen´-si-bl, *adj*
incomprensibile

inconceivable, in-kon-sii´-
va-bl, *adj* inconcepibile

inconclusive*, in-kon-
kluu´-siv, *adj*
inconcludente

incongruous, in-kong´-
gru-os, *adj* incongruo

inconsiderable, in-kon-
si´-de-ra-bl, *adj*
inconsiderabile

inconsiderate, in-kon-si´-

de-ret, *adj* senza
riguardo, sconsiderato

inconsistent, in-kon-sis´-
tent, *adj* incoerente

inconsolable, in-kon-
soul´-a-bl, *adj*
inconsolabile

inconstant*, in-kon´-
stant, *adj* incostante

inconvenience, in-kon-
vii´-ni-ens, *v* disturbare,
incomodare; *n* disturbo
m; inconveniente *m*

inconvenient, in-kon-vii´-
ni-ent, *adj* scomodo

incorporate, in-koor´-po-
reit, *v* incorporare

incorrect*, in-ko-rekt´, *adj*
scorretto; inesatto

incorrigible, in-ko´-ri-chi-
bl, *adj* incorreggibile

increase, in-kriis´, *v*
aumentare; *n*
aumento *m*

incredible, in-kred´-i-bl,
adj incredibile

incredulous, in-kred´-iu-
los, *adj* incredulo

incriminate, in-krim´-i-
neit, *v* incriminare

inculcate, in´-kŏl-keit, *v*
inculcare

incur, in-ker´, *v* incorrere

incurable, in-kiur´-ra-bl,
adj incurabile

indebted, in-det´-id, *adj*
obbligato

indecent, in-dii´-sent, *adj*

indecente

indecision, in-di-si´-shon,
n indecisione *f*

indecisive*, in-di-sai´-siv,
adj indeciso

indecorous, in-dek´-o-ros,
adj indecoroso

indeed, in-diid´, *adv*
infatti; davvero

indefensible, in-di-fen´-si-
bl, *adj* insostenibile;
ingiustificabile

indefinite, in-def´-i-nit,
adj indefinito

indelible, in-del´-i-bl, *adj*
indelebile

indelicate, in-del´-i-kat,
adj indelicato

indemnify, in-dem´-ni-fai,
v indennizzare

indemnity, in-dem´-ni-ti,
n indennità *f*

independence, in-di-pen´-
dens, *n* indipendenza *f*

independent, in-di-pen´-
dent, *adj* indipendente

indescribable, in-dis-
krai´-ba-bl, *adj*
indescrivibile

indestructible, in-dis-
trŏk´-ti-bl, *adj*
indistruttibile

index, in´-deks, *n*
indice *m*

index finger in´-deks
fing´-ga, *n* indice *m*

India, in´-di-a, *n* India *f*

Indian, in´-di-an, *adj*

indiano

indicate, in´-di-keit, *v*
indicare

indication, in-di-kei´-
shon, *n* indicazione *f*

indicator, in´-di-kei-ta, *n*
indicatore *m*

indict, in-dait´, *v*
incriminare

indifference, in-dif´-e-
rens, *n* indifferenza *f*

indifferent*, in-dif´-e-
rent, *adj* indifferente;
mediocre

indigestible, in-di-ches´-
ti-bl, *adj* indigesto

indigestion, in-di-ches´-
chon, *n* acidità di
stomaco *f*

indignant*, in-digh´-nant,
adj indignato

indignity, in-digh´-ni-ti, *n*
umiliazione *f*

indigo, in´-di-gou, *n*
indaco *m*

indirect*, in-dai-rekt´, *adj*
indiretto

indiscreet*, in-dis-kriit´,
adj indiscreto

indiscriminate*, in-dis-
krim´-i-nat, *adj*
indiscriminato

indispensable, in-dis-
pen´-sa-bl, *adj*
indispensabile

indisposed, in-dis-pousd´,
adj indisposto

indisposition, in-dis-po-

sish´-on, n
indisposizione f

indisputable, in-dis-piu´-
ta-bl, *adj* indiscutibile

indistinct*, in-dis-tingkt´,
adj indistinto; confuso

indistinguishable, in-dis-
ting-gui´-sha-bl, *adj*
indistinguibile

individual, in-di-vid´-iu-
al, *adj* individuale;
personale; n individuo m

indolent, in´-do-lent, *adj*
indolente

indoors, in-doors´, *adv* in
casa; al coperto;
all'interno

induce, in-diuus´, *v*
persuadere

inducement, in-diuus´-
ment, n incentivo m

indulge, in-dŏlch´, *v*
accontentare; soddisfare

indulgent*, in-dŏl´-chent,
adj indulgente

industrial, in-dŏs´-tri-al,
adj industriale

industrious*, in-dŏs´-tri-
os, *adj* industrioso;
diligente

industry, in´-dus-tri, n
industria f

inebriated, in-ii´-bri-ei-
tid, *adj* ubriaco

ineffective, in-i-fek´-tiv,
adj inefficace

inefficient, in-i-fish´-ent,
adj inefficiente; (person)
incapace

inept, i-nept´, *adj* inetto

inequality, in-i-kuol´-i-ti,
n ineguaglianza f;
disuguaglianza f

inert, in-ert´, *adj* inerte

inestimable, in-es´-ti-ma-
bl, *adj* inestimabile

inevitable, in-ev´-i-ta-bl,
adj inevitabile

inexact, in-igh-sakt´, *adj*
inesatto

inexcusable, in-iks-kiuu´-
sa-bl, *adj* imperdonabile

inexhaustible, in-igh-
soos´-ti-bl, *adj*
inesauribile

inexpensive*, in-iks-pen´-
siv, *adj* economico, poco
costoso

inexperience, in-iks-pir´-
ri-ens, n inesperienza f

inexperienced, in-iks-pir´-
ri-enst, *adj* inesperto

inexplicable, in-iks-plik´-
a-bl, *adj* inesplicabile

inexpressible, in-iks-
pres´-i-bl, *adj*
inesprimibile

infallible, in-fal´-i-bl, *adj*
infallibile

infamous*, in´-fa-mos, *adj*
famigerato

infamy, in-fa-mi, n
infamia f

infancy, in´-fan-si, n
infanzia f

infant, in´-fant, n

bambino m; *law*
minorenne m/f

infantry, in´-fan-tri, n
fanteria f

infatuation, in-fat-iu-ei´-
shon, n infatuazione f

infect, in-fekt´, *v* infettare

infection, in-fek´-shon, n
infezione f

infectious, in-fek´-shos,
adj contagioso, infettivo

infer, in-fer´, *v* dedurre

inference, in´-fe-rens, n
deduzione f

inferior, in-fir´-ri-a, *adj*
inferiore

infernal, in-fer´-nal, *adj*
infernale

infest, in-fest´, *v* infestare

infinite*, in´-fi-nit, *adj*
infinito

infirm, in-ferm´, *adj*
infermo

infirmary, in-ferm´-a-ri, n
infermeria f

inflame, in-fleim´, *v*
infiammare

inflammable, in-flam´-a-
bl, *adj* infiammabile

inflammation, in-fla-mei´-
shon, n infiammazione f

inflate, in-fleit´, *v* gonfiare;
(prices) aumentare

inflexible, in-flek´-si-bl,
adj inflessibile

inflict, in-flikt´, *v*
infliggere

inflow, in´-flou, n

afflusso m

influence, in´-flu-ens, n influenza f; v influire; influenzare

influential, in-flu-en´-shal, adj influente

influenza, in-flu-en´-sa, n influenza f

influx, in´-flŏks, n afflusso m; flusso m

inform, in-foorm´, v informare; avvisare

informal*, in-foor´-mal, adj informale; non formale; non ufficiale

information, in-fo-mei´-shon, n informazioni fpl

infrequent, in-frii´-kuent, adj raro, non comune

infringe, in-frinch´, v infrangere, violare

infringement, in-frinch´-ment, n infrazione f, violazione f

infuriate, in-fiur´-ri-eit, v rendere furioso

infuse, in-fiuus´, v infondere; (tea etc.) mettere in infusione

ingenious*, in-chii´-ni-os, adj ingegnoso

ingenuity, in-chin-iuu´-i-ti, n ingegnosità f

ingot, in´-got, n lingotto m

ingrained, in-greind´, adj incrostato; inveterato

ingratiate, in-grei´-shi-eit,

v ingraziarsi

ingratitude, in-grat´-i-tiuud, n ingratitudine f

ingredient, in-grii´-di-ent, n ingrediente m

ingrowing, in´-grou-ing, adj incarnito

inhabit, in-hab´-it, v abitare; vivere in

inhabitable, in-hab´-it-a-bl, adj abitabile

inhabitant, in-hab´-it-ant, n abitante m/f

inhale, in-heil´, v inalare; aspirare; inspirare

inherent*, in-hir´-rent, adj inerente

inherit, in-he´-rit, v ereditare

inheritance, in-he´-rit-ans, n eredità f

inhospitable, in-hos-pi´-ta-bl, adj inospitale

inhuman, in-hiuu´-man, adj disumano; inumano

iniquitous, in-ik´-ui-tos, adj iniquo

initial, in-ish´-al, n iniziale f; adj* iniziale

initiate, in-ish´-i-eit, v iniziare

initiative, in-ish´-a-tiv, n iniziativa f

inject, in-chekt´, v iniettare

injection, in-chek´-shon, n iniezione f

injunction, in-chŏngk´-

shon, n ingiunzione f

injure, in´-cha, v ferire; nuocere a

injurious*, in-chur´-ri-os, adj nocivo

injury, in´-chu-ri, n ferita f, lesione f; danno m

injury time, in´-chu-ri taim, n minuti di recupero mpl

injustice, in-chŏs´-tis, n ingiustizia f

ink, ingk, n inchiostro m

ink-jet printer, ingk´-chet prin´-ta, n stampante a getto d'inchiostro f

inlaid, in-leid´, adj intarsiato

inland, in´-land, adj interno; adv all'interno

in-laws, in´-loos, npl suoceri mpl

inlet, in´-let, n insenatura f

inmate, in´-meit, n carcerato m; degente m/f

inmost, in´-moust, adj il più profondo; il più intimo

inn, in, n locanda f

innate, i´-neit, adj innato

inner, in´-a, adj interno; intimo

innocent*, i´-no-sent, adj innocente

innocuous, i-nok´-iu-os, adj innocuo

innovation, i-no-vei´-

shon, n innovazione f

innumerable, i-niu´-me-ra-bl, *adj* innumerevole

inoculate, i-nok´-iu-leit, *v* inoculare

inoffensive, i-no-fen´-siv, *adj* inoffensivo

inopportune, in-op´-o-tiuun, *adj* inopportuno

input, in´-put, *n* input *m*

inquest, ing´-kuest, *n* inchiesta giudiziaria f

inquire, ing-kuair´, *v* informarsi; domandare

inquiry, ing-kuair´-ri, *n* richiesta di informazioni f; indagine f; inchiesta f

inquisition, ing-kui-sish´-on, *n* inquisizione f

inquisitive*, ing-kui´-sit-iv, *adj* curioso, indiscreto

insane*, in-sein´, *adj* pazzo, folle

insanity, in-san´-i-ti, *n* follia f

insatiable, in-sei´-sha-bl, *adj* insaziabile

inscribe, in-skraib´, *v* scrivere

inscription, in-skrip´-shon, *n* iscrizione f; dedica f

insect, in´-sekt, *n* insetto *m*

insecure, in-si-kiur´, *adj* insicuro; malsicuro

insensible, in-sen´-si-bl, *adj* insensibile;

(unconscious) svenuto

inseparable, in-sep´-a-ra-bl, *adj* inseparabile

insert, in-sert´, *v* inserire

insertion, in-ser´-shon, *n* inserzione f

inside, in-said´, *adv* dentro; *adj* interno; *n* interno *m*

insidious, in-sid´-i-os, *adj* insidioso

insight, in´-sait, *n* intuito *m*; perspicacia f

insignificant, in-sigh-nif´-i-kant, *adj* insignificante

insincere, in-sin-sir´, *adj* insincero

insinuate, in-sin´-iu-eit, *v* insinuare

insipid, in-sip´-id, *adj* insipido

insist (on), in-sist´, *v* insistere

insolence, in´-so-lens, *n* insolenza f

insolent, in´-so-lent, *adj* insolente

insolvent, in-sol´-vent, *adj* insolvente

inspect, in-spekt´, *v* ispezionare

inspection, in-spek´-shon, *n* ispezione f

inspector, in-spek´-ta, *n* ispettore *m*; (on bus) controllore *m*

inspiration, in-spi-rei´-shon, *n* spirazione f

inspire, in-spair´, *v* spirare

install, in-stool´, *v* installare

installation, in-sta-lei´-shon, *n* installazione f

instalment, in-stool´-ment, *n* rata f; **pay in –s,** *v* pagare a rate

instance, in´-stans, *n* esempio *m*, caso *m*

instant, in´-stant, *n* istante *m*; *adj** immediato; (coffee) istantaneo

instead, in-sted´, *prep* invece; **– of,** *adv* invece di

instep, in´-step, *n* collo del piede *m*

instigate, in´-sti-gheit, *v* istigare

instil, in-stil´, *v* inculcare

instinct, in´-stingkt, *n* istinto *m*

institute, in´-sti-tiuut, *n* istituto *m*

instruct, in´-strŏkt, *v* istruire; (order) dare istruzioni

instruction, in-strŏk´-shon, *n* istruzione f

instrument, in´-stru-ment, *n* strumento *m*

insubordination, in-su-boor-di-nei´-shon, *n* insubordinazione f

insufferable, in-sŏf´-e-ra-bl, *adj* insopportabile

insufficient*, in-suf-ish´-ent, *adj* insufficiente

insulate, in´-siu-leit, *v* isolare

insulation, in-siu-lei´-shon, *n* isolamento *m*

insulin, in´-siu-lin, *n* insulina *f*

insult, in-sŏlt´, *v* insultare

insult, in´-sŏlt, *n* insulto *m*

insurance, in-shoo´-rans, *n* assicurazione *f*

insure, in-shoor´, *v* assicurare

insurrection, in-se-rek´-shon, *n* insurrezione *f*

intact, in-takt´, *adj* intatto

intellect, in´-til-ekt, *n* intelletto *m*

intelligence, in-tel´-i-chens, *n* intelligenza *f*

intelligent, in-tel´-i-chent, *adj* intelligente

intemperate, in-tem´-pe-rat, *adj* intemperante; smoderato

intend, in-tend´, *v* avere l'intenzione, volere

intense*, in-tens´, *adj* intenso

intensive care, in-ten´-siv ker, *n* rianimazione *f*

intent, in-tent´, *n* intenzione *f*; *adj* intento

intention, in-ten´-shon, *n* intenzione *f*

intentional*, in-ten´-

shon-al, *adj* intenzionale, fatto apposta

inter, in-ter´, *v* sotterrare

intercept, in-te-sept´, *v* intercettare

interchange, in-te-cheinch´, *v* scambiare

intercourse, in´-te-koors, *n* rapporto *m*

interdict, in-te-dikt´, *v* interdire

interest, in´-te-rest, *n* interesse *m*

interesting, in´-te-res-ting, *adj* interessante

interfere, in-te-fir´, *v* intromettersi

interference, in-te-fir´-rens, *n* intromissione *f*; (radio) interferenza *f*

interior, in-tiir´-ri-a, *adj* interiore, interno; *n* interno *m*

interlace, in-te-leis´, *v* intrecciare

interloper, in-te-lou´-pa, *n* intruso *m*

interlude, in´-te-luud, *n* intermezzo *m*

intermediate, in-te-mii´-di-at, *adj* intermediario

interment, in-ter´-ment, *n* sepoltura *f*

intermingle, in-te-ming´-gl, *v* mescolare

intermission, in-te-mish´-on, *n* interruzione *f*

intermittent*, in-te-mit´-ent, *adj* intermittente

intern, in-tern´, *v* internare

internal*, in-ter´-nal, *adj* interno

international, in-te-nash´-nal, *adj* internazionale

Internet, in´-te-net, *n* Internet *f*

interpret, in-ter´-prit, *v* interpretare

interpreter, in-ter´-prit-a, *n* interprete *m/f*

interrogate, in-te´-ro-gheit, *v* interrogare

interrupt, in-te-rŏpt´, *v* interrompere

interval, in´-te-val, *n* intervallo *m*

intervene, in-te-viin´, *v* intervenire

intervention, in-te-ven´-shon, *n* intervento *m*

interview, in´-te-viuu, *n* intervista *f*; (for job) colloquio *m*; *v* intervistare

interviewer, in´-te-viu-a, *n* intervistatore *m*, intervistatrice *f*

intestate, in-tes´-tet, *adj* intestato

intestine, in-tes´-tin, *n* intestino *m*

intimacy, in´-ti-ma-si, *n* intimità *f*

intimate*, in´-ti-mat, *adj*

intimo
intimate, in´-ti-meit, v
  lasciar capire
intimation, in-ti-mei´-
  shon, n accenno m
intimidate, in-tim´-i-deit,
  v intimidire
into, in´-tu, prep in,
  dentro
intolerable, in-tol´-e-ra-bl,
  adj intollerabile
intoxicate, in-tok´-si-keit,
  v ubriacare; inebriare
intrepid*, in-trep´-id, adj
  intrepido
intricate*, in´-tri-kat, adj
  intricato
intrigue, in´-triigh, n
  intrigo m; v intrigare
intriguing, in-trii´-ghing,
  adj intrigante
intrinsic, in-trin´-sik, adj
  intrinseco
introduce, in-tro-dius´, v
  introdurre; presentare
introductory, in-tro-dŏk´-
  to-ri, adj introduttivo;
  (offer) di lancio
intrude, in-truud´, v
  disturbare
intruder, in-truu´-da, n
  intruso m
intuition, in-tiu-ish´-on, n
  intuito m
inundate, in-un-deit´, v
  inondare
inure, in-iur´, v assuefare
invade, in-veid´, v

invadere
invader, in-veid´-a, n
  invasore m
invalid, in´-va-lid, n
  invalido m; infermo m
invalid, in-val´-id, adj
  invalido, non valido
invaluable, in-val´-iu-a-bl,
  adj inestimabile
invariable, in-ver´-ri-a-bl,
  adj invariabile
invasion, in-vei´-shon, n
  invasione f
invent, in-vent´, v
  inventare
invention, in-ven´-shon, n
  invenzione f
inventor, in-ven´-ta, n
  inventore m
inventory, in´-ven-tri, n
  inventario m
invert, in-vert´, v invertire
invest, in-vest´, v
  investire
investigate, in-ves´-ti-
  gheit, v investigare
investigation, in-ves-ti-
  ghei´-shon, n indagine f
investment, in-vest´-
  ment, n investimento m
investor, in-ves´-ta, n
  investitore m
inveterate*, in-vet´-e-rat,
  adj inveterato
invigorate, in-vi´-go-reit,
  v invigorire
invincible, in-vin´-si-bl,
  adj invincibile

invisible, in-vis´-i-bl, adj
  invisibile
invitation, in-vi-tei´-shon,
  n invito m
invite, in-vait´, v invitare
invoice, in´-vois, n fattura
  f; v fatturare
invoke, in-vouk´, v
  invocare
involuntary, in-vol´-un-
  ta-ri, adj involontario
involve, in-volv´, v
  coinvolgere; comportere
inward, in´-uad, adj
  interiore, intimo
iodine, ai´-o-diin, n
  iodio m
Ireland, air´-land, n
  Irlanda f
iris, air´-ris, n (flower)
  giaggiolo m; (eye) iride f
Irish, air´-rish, adj
  irlandese
irksome*, erk´-som, adj
  tedioso
iron, ai´-on, v stirare; n
  ferro m; ferro da stiro m
ironic(al)*, ai-ron´-i-k(-
  l), adj ironico
ironmonger, ai´-on-mŏng-
  ga, n negoziante di
  ferramenta m/f
irony, ai´-ron-i, n ironia f
irreconcilable, i-rek-on-
  sai´-la-bl, adj
  irreconciliabile
irregular*, i-re´-ghiu-la,
  adj irregolare

irrelevant, i-rel´-i-vant,
adj non pertinente

irreproachable, i-ri-
prouch´-a-bl, *adj*
irreprensibile

irresistible, i-ri-sis´-ti-bl,
adj irresistibile

irrespective of, i-ri-spek´-
tiv ov, *prep* a prescindere
da

irresponsible, i-ri-spon´-
si-bl, *adj* irresponsabile

irretrievable, i-ri-trii´-va-
bl, *adj* irrecuperabile;
irreparabile

irreverent*, i-rev´-e-rent,
adj irriverente

irrigate, i´-ri-gheit, *v*
irrigare

irritable, i´-ri-ta-bl, *adj*
irritabile

irritate, i´-ri-teit, *v* irritare

Islam, is´-laam, *n* Islam *m*

Islamic, is-lam´-ik, *adj*
islamico

island, ai´-land, *n* isola *f*

islander, ai´-lan-da, *n*
isolano *m*

isolate, ai´-sol-eit, *v*
isolare

isolation, ai-so-lei´-shon,
n isolamento *m*

issue, i´-shuu, *v* emettere;
pubblicare; *n* questione
f; emissione *f*; numero *m*

isthmus, is´-mos, *n*
istmo *m*

it, it, *pron* esso, essa; lo, la;
gli, le

Italian, i-tal´-ian, *adj*
italiano; *n* (language)
italiano *m*

italic, i-tal´-ik, *n* (type)
caratteri corsivi *mpl*

Italy, i´-ta-li, *n* Italia *f*

itch, ich, *v* prudere; *n*
prurito *m*

item, ai´-tem, *n* articolo
m; (accounts) voce *f*

itinerant, ai-tin´-e-rant,
adj ambulante;
itinerante; girovago

its, its, *adj* il suo, la sua; i
suoi, le sue

itself, it-self´, *pron*
(reflexive) si; esso
stesso, essa stessa; **by –,**
da sé

ivory, ai´-ve-ri, *n* avorio *m*

ivy, ai´-vi, *n* edera *f*

jabber, chab´-a, v ciarlare

jack, chak, n mech cric m

jackal, chak´-l, n
sciacallo m

jacket, chak´-ot, n giacca
f; (of book)
sopraccopertina f

jackpot, chak´-pot, n
montepremi m

jade, cheid, n giada f

jaded, chei´-did, adj
spossato

jagged, cha´-ghid, adj
dentellato; frastagliato

jail, cheil, n carcere m; v
incarcerare

jailor, chei´-la, n
carceriere m

jam, chaam, n marmellata
f; (traffic) ingorgo m;
v ostruire; (block)
bloccare

jangle, chang´-gl, n
tintinnio m; v tintinnare

January, chan´-iu-a-ri, n
gennaio m

Japan, cha-pan´, n
Giappone m

Japanese, cha-pa-niis´, adj
giapponese; n
(language) giapponese

jar, chaar, n vasetto m;
(shock) scossone m; v
(annoy) infastidire

jargon, chaar´-gon, n
gergo m

jaundice, choon´-dis, n
itterizia f

jaundiced, choon´-dist adj
med itterico; fig cinico

javelin, cha´-ve-lin, n
giavellotto m

jaw, choo, n mascella f

jealous*, chel´-os, adj
geloso

jealousy, chel´-o-si, n
gelosia f

jeans, chiins, npl jeans mpl

jeer, chir, v schernire; n
scherno m

jelly, chel´-i, n gelatina f

jellyfish, chel´-i-fish, n
medusa f

jeopardize, chep´-e-dais, v
rischiare

jeopardy, chep´-e-di, n
rischio m

jerk, cherk, v procedere a
sobbalzi; n sobbalzo m

jersey, cher´-si, n maglia f

jest, chest, v scherzare; n
scherzo m

jester, ches´-ta, n buffone
di corte

jet, chet, n (aircraft) jet
m; (liquid) getto m;
(mineral) giaietto m

jettison, chet´-i-son, v
gettar a mare

jetty, chet´-i, n molo m

jewel, chuu´-el, n
gioiello m

jeweller, chuu´-el-a, n
gioielliere m

jewellery, chuu´-el-ri, n gioielli mpl

Jewish, chuu´-ish, adj ebreo

jigsaw, chig´-soo, n puzzle m

jilt, chilt, v piantare in asso, abbandonare

job, chob, n lavoro m

jockey, chok´-i, n fantino m

jocular, chok´-iu-la, adj gioviale

jog, chog, v fare jogging

join, choin, v unire, unirsi; (political party) iscriversi; (club) diventare socio; – **in,** partecipare a

joiner, choi´-na, n falegname m

joint, choint, n giuntura f; (meat) taglio m; (roast) arrosto m; (anatomy) articolazione f

jointly, choint´-li, adv congiuntamente

joke, chook, n scherzo m; v scherzare

joker, choo´-ka, n burlone m; (cards) jolly m

jolly, chol´-i, adj allegro

jolt, choult, n sobbalzo m; v sobbalzare

jostle, chos´-l, v spintonare

journal, cher´-nal, n giornale m

journalism, cher´-na-lism, n giornalismo m

journalist, cher´-na-list, n giornalista m/f

journey, cher´-ni, n viaggio m; v viaggiare

jovial*, chou´-vi-al, adj gioviale

joy, choi, n gioia f

joyful*, choi´-ful, adj lieto, gioioso

jubilant, chuu´-bi-lant, adj giubilante

jubilee, chuu´-bi-lii, n giubileo m

judge, chŏch, n giudice m; conoscitore m; v giudicare

judgment, chŏch´-ment, n giudizio m; sentenza f

judicial, chu-dish´-al, adj giudiziario

judicious*, chu-dish´-os, adj giudizioso

jug, chŏgh, n brocca f, caraffa f

juggle, chŏgh´-l, v fare il giocoliere

juggler, chŏgh´-la, n giocoliere m

juice, chuus, n succo m; (meat) sugo m

juicy, chuu´-si, adj succoso; sugoso

July, chu-lai´, n luglio m

jumble, chŏm´-bl, v mescolare; n miscuglio m

jump, chŏmp, n salto m; v saltare

jumper, chŏm´-pa, n maglione m; saltatore m, saltatrice f

junction, chŏngk´-shon, n (road) crocevia m; (railway) stazione di smistamento f

juncture, chŏngk´-cha, n (period) congiuntura f

June, chuun, n giugno m

jungle, chŏng´-gl, n giungla f

junior, chuu´-ni-a, adj più giovane; subalterno

juniper, chuu´-ni-pa, n ginepro m

jurisdiction, chur-ris-dik´-shon, n giurisdizione f

juror, chur´-ra, n giurato m

jury, chur´-ri, n giuria f

just, chŏst, adj (fair) giusto; adv (exactly) proprio; (only) soltanto; (barely) appena

justice, chŏst´-is, n giustizia f

justification, chŏs-ti-fi-kei´-shon, n giustificazione f

justify, chŏst´-i-fai, v giustificare

jut (out), chŏt (aut), v sporgere

juvenile, chuu´-ve-nail, adj minorile; infantile

K

kangaroo, kang-ga-**ruu´,** n
  canguro m
kebab, ki-bab´, n spiedino
  di carne e verdure m
keel, kiil, n chiglia f
keen*, kiin, adj entusiasta;
  (intelligence) acuto
keenness, kiin´-nis, n
  entusiasmo m; (mind)
  acutezza f
keep, kiip, n
  mantenimento m; v
  (retain) tenere;
  (support) mantenere;
  (preserve) conservare; –
  back, trattenere; – **off,**
  tener lontano; – **up,**
  mantenere
keeper, kii´-pa, n
  guardiano m
keepsake, kiip´-seik, n
  ricordo m

keg, kegh, n barile m
kennel, ken´-l, n canile m
kerb, kerb, n orlo del
  marciapiede m
kernel, ker´-nel, n (nut)
  gheriglio m
kettle, ket´-l, n
  bollitore m
kettledrum, ket´-l-dröm,
  n mus timpano m
key, kii, n chiave f;
  (piano, typewriter)
  tasto m
keyboard, kii´-boord, n
  tastiera f
keyhole, kii´-houl, n buco
  della serratura m
kick, kik, n calcio m; v
  dare calci; (horse)
  scalciare
kid, kid, n capretto m; fig
  bambino m, bambina f

kidnap, kid´-nap, v rapire
kidney, kid´-ni, n rene m;
  (cookery) rognone m
kill, kil, v uccidere
kiln, kiln, n fornace f
kilo, kii´-lou, n chilo m
kin, kin, n parente m/f
kind, kaind, n specie f,
  genere m; adj* buono,
  gentile
kindness, kaind´-nis, n
  gentilezza f
kindle, kin´-dl, v
  accendere
king, king, n re m
kingdom, king´-dom, n
  regno m
kiosk, kii´-osk, n
  chiosco m
kipper, kip´-a, n aringa
  affumicata f
kiss, kis, n bacio m; v
  baciare
kit, kit, n
  equipaggiamento m,
  attrezzatura f
kitchen, kit´-shin, n
  cucina f
kite, kait, n aquilone m;
  (bird) nibbio m
kitten, kit´-n, n gattino m
knack, nak, n abilità f
knave, neiv, n (cards)
  fante m
knead, niid, v impastare
knee, nii, n ginocchio m
kneecap, nii´-kap, n
  rotula f

kneel, niil, *v* inginocchiarsi

knell, nel, *n* rintocco funebre *m*

knickers, nik´-es, *npl* mutandine da donna *fpl*

knife, naif, *n* coltello *m*

knight, nait, *n* cavaliere *m*

knit, nit, *v* lavorare a maglia

knitting, nit´-ing, *n* lavoro a maglia *m*

knob, nob, *n* pomello *m*; (on radio, TV) manopola *f*

knock, nok, *n* colpo *m*; *v* colpire; bussare; – **against,** urtare contro; – **down,** gettare a terra

knocker, nok´-a, *n* (door) battente *m*

knot, not, *n* nodo *m*; *v* annodare

knotty, not´-i, *adj* nodoso

know, nou, *v* sapere; conoscere

knowledge, nol´-ich, *n* conoscenza *f*; sapere *m*

known, noun, *adj* conosciuto

knuckle, nŏk´-l, *n* nocca *f*

label, lei´-bl, n etichetta f;
v etichettare

laboratory, lab´-o-ra-to-ri,
n laboratorio m

laborious*, la-boor´-ri-os,
adj laborioso

Labour, lei´-ba, n il
partito laburista m

labour, lei´-ba, n fatica f;
manodopera f; med
doglie fpl; v lavorare;
affaticarsi

labourer, lei´-be-ra,
n manovale m;
bracciante m

lace, leis, n merletto m,
pizzo m; (shoe) laccio m;
v allacciare

lacerate, las´-e-reit, v
lacerare

lack, lak, n (shortage)
mancanza f; v mancare

lacquer, lak´-a, n lacca f

lad, lad, n ragazzo m

ladder, lad´-a, n scala f;
smagliatura f

ladle, leid´-l, n mestolo m

lady, lei´-di, n signora f

ladybird, lei´-di-berd, n
coccinella f

lag, lagh, v trascinarsi; –
behind, restare indietro

lagoon, la-guun´, n laguna
f

lair, ler, n covo m

lake, leik, n lago m

lamb, lam, n agnello m

lame*, leim, adj zoppo;
zoppicante

lament, la-ment´, v
lamentarsi; n lamento m

lamp, lamp, n lampada f;
(street) lampione m

lance, laans, n lancia f; v

med incidere

land, land, n terra f;
(property) terreno m; v
sbarcare

landing, lan´-ding, n
atterraggio m; (stairs)
pianerottolo m

landlady, land´-lei-di, n
padrona di casa f; (pub)
proprietaria f

landlord, land´-loord, n
padrone di casa m; (pub)
proprietario m

landmark, land´-maark, n
punto di riferimento m;
fig pietra miliare f

landscape, land´-skeip, n
paesaggio m

landslide, land´-slaid, n
frana f

lane, lein, n sentiero m;
corsia f

language, lang´-guich, n
lingua f; linguaggio m

languid*, lang´-guid, adj
languido

languish, lang´-guish, v
languire

lanky, lang´-ki, adj
mingherlino

lantern, lan´-ten, n
lanterna f

lap, lap, n grembo m;
(sport) giro m; v (drink)
leccare

lapel, la-pel´, n risvolto m

lapse, laps, n mancanza f;
(time) lasso di tempo m;

v trascorrere

larceny, laar´-se-ni, *n* furto *m*

lard, laard, *n* strutto *m*

larder, laar´-da, *n* dispensa *f*

large*, laarch, *adj* grande; grosso; considerevole

lark, laark, *n* allodola *f*; *fam* scherzo *m*

laser, lei´-sa, *n* laser *m*

lash, lash, *n* (whip) frustata *f*; (eye) ciglio *m*; *v* frustare

last, laast, *v* durare; *adj** ultimo; scorso

lasting*, laas´-ting, *adj* duraturo

latch, lach, *n* chiavistello *m*

late, leit, *adj* tardi; (belated) in ritardo; (formerly) ex; (deceased) defunto

lately, leit´-li, *adv* ultimamente

latent, lei´-tent, *adj* latente

lathe, leiD, *n* tornio *m*

lather, laa´-Da, *n* schiuma *f*; *v* insaponare

latitude, lat´-i-tiuud, *n* latitudine *f*

latter, lat´-a, *adj* ultimo; secondo; *pron* ultimo; questo

latterly, lat´-e-li, *adv* negli ultimi tempi

lattice, lat´-is, *n* graticcio *m*

laudable, loo´-da-bl, *adj* lodevole

laugh, laaf, *n* risata *f*; *v* ridere; – **at,** ridere di

laughable, laaf´-a-bl *adj* ridicolo

laughing stock, laaf´-ing stok, *n* zimbello *m*

laughter, laaf´-ta, *n* riso *m*; risata *f*

launch, loonch, *n* lancio *m*; *naut* varo *m*; *v* lanciare; *naut* varare

launderette, loon-dret´, *n* lavanderia automatica *f*

laundry, loon´-dri, *n* lavanderia *f*; bucato *m*

laurel, lo´-rel, *n* alloro *m*

lavatory, lav´-a-to-ri, *n* gabinetto *m*

lavender, lav´-en-da, *n* lavanda *f*

lavish*, lav´-ish, *adj* prodigo; sontuoso

law, loo, *n* legge *f*

lawful*, loo´-ful, *adj* legale

lawn, loon, *n* prato all'inglese *m*

lawn-mower, loon´-mou-a, *n* tagliaerba *m*

lawsuit, loo´-suut, *n* processo *m*, causa *f*

lawyer, loo´-ia, *n* avvocato *m*

lax*, laks, *adj* permissivo; lassista

laxative, lak´-sa-tiv, *n* lassativo *m*

lay, lei, *v* mettere, porre; (table) apparecchiare; (hen) fare le uova

layer, lei´-a, *n* strato *m*

layman, lei´-man, *n* laico *m*

laziness, lei´-si-nis, *n* pigrizia *f*

lazy, lei´-si, *adj* pigro

lead, led, *n* piombo *m*; (pencil) mina *f*

lead, liid, *v* condurre; guidare

leading, lii´-ding, *adj* primo; principale

leader, lii´-da, *n* capo *m*; leader *m/f*; (article) articolo di fondo *m*

leadership, lii´-de-ship, *n* guida *f*; comando *m*

leaf, liif, *n* foglia *f*

leaflet, liif´-lit, *n* volantino *m*; dépliant *m*

leafy, lii´-fi, *adj* (tree) frondoso

league, liigh, *n* lega *f*; campionato *m*

leak, liik, *v* perdere; trapelare; colare; (boat) far acqua; *n* fuga *f*; perdita *f*; infiltrazione *f*

lean, liin, *adj* magro; – **against,** *v* appoggiarsi contro; – **on,** appoggiarsi a; – **out,**

sporgersi

leap, liip, v balzare; n balzo m

leap year, liip´-iir, n anno bisestile m

learn, lern, v imparare; (news) apprendere

learner, ler´-na, n apprendista m/f; principiante m/f

learning, ler´-ning, n cultura f; sapere m

lease, liis, n contratto d'affitto m; v affittare

leash, liish, n guinzaglio m

least, liist, adj il minimo, il più piccolo; adv meno; **at –,** almeno

leather, leD´-a, n cuoio m; pelle f

leave, liiv, n congedo m, licenza f; v partire; lasciare; **– behind,** lasciare; dimenticare; **– off,** smettere; **– out,** tralasciare

lecture, lek´-cha, n lezione f; conferenza f; v fare lezioni; fare conferenze

lecturer, lek´-chu-ra, n docente m/f; conferenziere m

ledge, lech, n (window) davanzale m

ledger, lech´-a, n libro mastro m

leech, liich, n sanguisuga f

leek, liik, n porro m

left, left, adv a sinistra; adj sinistro; n sinistra f

left-handed, left-han´-did, adj mancino

leftovers, left´-ou-ves, npl avanzi mpl

leg, legh, n gamba f; zampa f; (cookery) coscia f; (journey) tappa f; (sport) girone m

legacy, leg´-a-si, n eredità f

legal, lii´-gal, adj legale

legalize, lii´ga-lais, v legalizzare

legend, lech´-ind, n leggenda f

leggings, legh´-ings, npl pantacollant mpl

legible, lech´-i-bl, adj leggibile

legion, lii´-chon, n legione f

legislate, lech´-is-leit, v legislare

legislation, lech-is-lei´-shon, n legislazione f

legitimacy, lech-it´-i-ma-si, n legittimità f

legitimate, lech-it´-i-mat, v legittimare

leisure, lesh´-a, n tempo libero m

leisure centre, lesh´-a sen´-ta, n centro ricreativo e sportivo m

leisurely, lesh´-u-li, adv con comodo

lemon, lem´-on, n limone m

lemonade, lem-on-eid´, n limonata f

lend, lend, v prestare

length, lengZ, n lunghezza f; (time) durata f

lengthen, leng´-Zen, v allungare; prolungare

lengthways, lengZ´-ueis, adv in lunghezza

lengthy, leng´-Zi, adj molto lungo

leniency, lii´-ni-en-si, n clemenza f; mitezza f

lenient*, lii´-ni-ent, adj clemente; mite

lens, lens, n lente f

Lent, lent, n Quaresima f

lentil, len´-til, n lenticchia f

Leo, lii´-ou, n Leone m

leopard, lep´-ad, n leopardo m

leper, lep´-a, n lebbroso m

leprosy, lep´-ro-si, n lebbra f

leprous, lep´-ros, adj lebbroso

lesbian, les´-bi-an, n lesbica f

less, les, adv meno, di meno; pron meno; adj meno; minore

lessen, les´-n, v diminuire

lesson, les´-n, n lezione f

let, let, v lasciare; (house etc.) affittare

lethal, lii´-Zal, *adj* letale

letter, let´-*a*, *n* lettera *f*

letterbox, let´-*a*-boks, *n* buca delle lettere *f*

lettuce, let´-is, *n* lattuga *f*

level, lev´-l, *adj* piatto, piano; *v* livellare; *n* livello *m*

level crossing, lev´-l kros´-ing, *n* passaggio a livello *m*

lever, lii´-va, *n* leva *f*

levity, lev´-i-ti, *n* leggerezza *f*

levy, lev´-i, *v* (taxes) imporre; *n* imposta *f*

lewd*, liuud, *adj* osceno

lewdness, liuud´-nis, *n* oscenità *f*

liability, lai-*a*-bil´-i-ti, *n* responsabilità *f*; (legal) rischio *m*; *comm* debito *m*

liable, lai´-*a*-bl, *adj* responsabile; – **to,** (inclined) soggetto a

liar, lai´-a, *n* bugiardo *m*

libel, lai´-bl, *n* diffamazione *f*

libellous, lai´-bel-os, *adj* diffamatorio

liberal, lib´-e-ral, *adj* liberale

liberate, lib´-e-reit, *v* liberare

liberty, lib´-e-ti, *n* libertà *f*

Libra, lii-bra, *n* Bilancia *f*

librarian, lai-brer´-ri-an, *n* bibliotecario *m*, bibliotecaria *f*

library, lai´-bre-ri, *n* biblioteca *f*

licence, lai´-sens, *n* licenza *f*, permesso *m*, autorizzazione *f*

license, lai´-sens, *n* autorizzare

lichen, lai´-ken, *n* lichene *m*

lick, lik, *v* leccare

lid, lid, *n* coperchio *m*

lie, lai, *n* bugia *f*; *v* dire bugie

lie, lai, *v* giacere; trovarsi; – **about,** essere in giro; – **down,** sdraiarsi

lieutenant, lef-ten´-ant, *n* tenente *m*

life, laif, *n* vita *f*

lifebelt, laif´-belt, *n* salvagente *m*

lifeboat, laif´-bout, *n* scialuppa di salvataggio *f*

lifeguard, laif´-gaard, *n* bagnino *m*

life insurance, laif' in-shoor´-rans, *n* assicurazione sulla vita *f*

life jacket, laif' chak´-it, *n* giubbotto salvagente *m*

lifeless, laif´-lis, *adj* senza vita

life-size, laif´-sais, *adj* a grandezza naturale

lifetime, laif´-taim, *n* vita *f*; **in my –,** in vita mia

lift, lift, *n* ascensore *m*; *v* sollevare, alzare; revocare

light, lait, *n* luce *f*; *adj** chiaro; leggero; *v* accendere; illuminare

lighten, lait´-n, *v* rischiarare; (weight) alleggerire

lighter, lai´-ta, *n* accendino *m*

lighthouse, lait´-haus, *n* faro *m*

lighting, lai´-ting, *n* illuminazione *f*

lightness, lait´-nis, *n* leggerezza *f*

lightning, lait´-ning, *n* fulmine *m*

lightning conductor, lait´-ning kon-dǒk´-ta, *n* parafulmine *m*

like, laik, *prep* come; *v* piacere; *adv* simile; uguale

likelihood, laik´-li-hud, *n* probabilità *f*

likely, laik´-li, *adj* probabile; *adv* probabilmente

likeness, laik´-nis, *n* rassomiglianza *f*

likewise, laik´-uais, *adv* allo stesso modo

liking, lai´-king, *n* gusto *m*; inclinazione *f*; (person) simpatia *f*

lilac, lai´-lak, *n* (flower)

lillà m; (colour) lilla m

lily, lil´-i, n giglio m

limb, lim, n (anatomy) arto m

lime, laim, n calce f; (fruit) limetta f; (tree) tiglio m

limelight, laim´-lait, n luci della ribalta fpl

limit, lim´-it, n limite m; v limitare

limited, lim´-it-id, adj limitato; **Ltd. Co.,** n società a responsabilità limitata f

limp, limp, v zoppicare; adj (soft) floscio

limpet, lim´-pit, n patella f

line, lain, n linea f; (fishing) lenza f; (rope) corda f; (wrinkle) ruga f; v foderare; mettere in fila

lineage, lin´-i-ich, n lignaggio m

linen, lin´-in, n lino m; biancheria f

liner, lain´-a, n transatlantico m

linger, ling´-ga, v indugiare

lingering, ling´-ge-ring, adj persistente

linguist, ling´-guist, n linguista m/f

lining, lain´-ing, n fodera f

link, lingk, v unire; collegare; n anello m; fig

legame m

linoleum, lin-ou´-li-am, n linoleum m

linseed, lin´-siid, n semi di lino mpl

lint, lint, n garza f

lion, lai´-on, n leone m

lioness, lai´-on-es, n leonessa f

lip, lip, n labbro m

lipstick, lip´-stik, n rossetto m

liquefy, lik´-ui-fai, v liquefare; liquefarsi

liqueur, li-ker´, n liquore m

liquid, lik´-uid, n liquido m; adj liquido

liquidate, lik´-ui-deit, v liquidare

liquidation, lik-ui-dei´-shon, n liquidazione f

liquidize, lik´-ui-dais, v passare al frullatore

liquidizer, lik´-ui-dai-sa, n frullatore a brocca m

liquor, lik´-a, n (alcoholic drink) liquore m

liquorice, lik´-o-ris, n liquorizia f

Lisbon, lis´-bon, n Lisbona f

lisp, lisp, v parlare con la 's' blesa

list, list, n lista f; elenco m; v fare una lista; elencare

listen, lis´-n, v ascoltare

listener, lis´-na, n ascoltatore m, ascoltatrice f

literal, lit´-e-ral, adj letterale

literally, lit´-e-ra-li, adv letteralmente

literary, lit´-e-ra-ri, adj letterario

literature, lit´-e-ra-cha, n letteratura f

litigate, lit´-i-gheit, v essere in causa

litigation, lit-i-ghei´-shon, n causa giudiziaria f

litre, lii-ta, n litro m

litter, lit´-a, n (dirt) rifiuti mpl; (animals) figliata f; v coprire di rifiuti

little, lit´-l, adj (size) piccolo; (time, quantity) poco; adv poco

little finger, lit´-l fing´-ga, n mignolo m

live, liv, v vivere; (reside) abitare

live, laiv, adj vivo; (performance) dal vivo; (broadcast) in diretta; (wire) ad alta tensione

lively, laiv´-li, adj vivace

liver, liv´-a, n fegato m

livery, liv´-e-ri, n livrea f

livid, liv´-id, adj livido; (rage) furibondo

living, liv´-ing, n vita f; adj vivo, vivente

living room, liv´-ing

ruum, n soggiorno m

lizard, lis´-ad, n lucertola f

load, loud, v caricare; n carico m

loaf, louf, v (about) bighellonare; n (bread) pane m, pagnotta f

loafer, lou´-fa, n bighellone m

loan, loun, v prestare; n prestito m; **on –,** adv in prestito

loathe, louD, v detestare

loathing, lou´-Ding, n avversione f

loathsome, louD´-som, adj detestabile

lobe, loub, n (ear) lobo m

lobster, lob´-sta, n aragosta f

local, lou´-kl, adj locale

locate, lou-keit´, v localizzare

location, lou-kei´-shon, n posizione f; (cinema) esterni mpl; **shot on –,** girato in esterni

lock, lok, n serratura f; (canal) chiusa f; (hair) ciocca f; v chiudere a chiave; **– in,** rinchiudere; **– out,** chiudere fuori; **– up,** v chiudere; (imprison) rinchiudere

locker, lok´-a, n armadietto m

locksmith, lok´-smiZ, n

fabbro ferraio m

locomotive, lou-ko-mou´-tiv, n locomotiva f

locum, lou´-kum, n medico sostituto m

locust, lou´-kust, n locusta f

lodge, loch, n portineria f; guardiola f; (masonic) loggia f; v alloggiare

lodger, loch´-a, n inquilino m

lodging, loch´-ing, n alloggio m

loft, loft, n soffitta f

log, logh, n (wood) ceppo m

logbook, logh´-buk, n giornale di bordo m

logic, loch´-ik, n logica f

logical*, loch´-i-kl, adj logico

loin, loin, n (meat) lombata f

loiter, loi´-ta, v girovagare

loiterer, loi´-te-ra, n fannullone m

loll, lol, v ciondolare

lollipop, lol´-i-pop, n lecca lecca m

London, lŏn´-don, n Londra f

loneliness, loun´-li-nis, n solitudine f

lonely, loun´-li, adj solo; solitario, isolato

long, long, adj lungo; adv a lungo; **– for,** v desiderare

longing, long´-ing, n desiderio m

longitude, long´-i-tiuud, n longitudine f

long jump, long´-chŏmp, n salto in lungo m

long-life, long´-laif, adj (milk) a lunga conservazione; (batteries) di lunga durata

long-term, long´-term, adj a lungo termine

loo, luu, n fam gabinetto m

look, luk, n sguardo m; aspetto m; v guardare; (appear) sembrare; **– after,** badare a; **– at,** guardare; **– for,** v cercare; **– out,** v guardare fuori; n vedetta f; interj attenzione! **be on the – out,** v stare di vedetta

loom, luum, n telaio m; v apparire in lontananza

loop, luup, n cappio m

loophole, luup´-houl, n scappatoia f

loose, luus, adj sciolto; allentato; ampio; dissoluto

loosen, luus´-n, v sciogliere; allentare

loot, luut, v saccheggiare; n bottino m

lop, lop, v recidere

loquacious, lo-kuei´-shos, *adj* loquace

Lord (the), loord, *n* Signore *m*

lord, loord, *n* (peer) lord *m*

lorry, lo´-ri, *n* camion *m*

lose, luus, *v* perdere

loser, luu´-sa, *n* perdente *m/f*

loss, los, *n* perdita *f*

lost property, lost prop´-e-ti, *n* oggetti smarriti *mpl*; **– office,** ufficio oggetti smarriti

lot, lot, *n* (auction) lotto *m*; **a –,** molto; **a – of,** una gran quantità di; **the –,** tutto

lotion, lou´-shon, *n* lozione *f*

lottery, lot´-e-ri, *n* lotteria *f*

loud*, laud, *adj* alto; (colours) vistoso; *adv* forte

loudspeaker, laud-spii´-ka, *n* altoparlante *m*

lounge, launch, *n* salotto *m*; sala d'attesa *f*; *v* poltrire

louse, laus, *n* pidocchio *m*

lout, laut, *n* giovinastro *m*

love, löv, *n* amore *m*; *v* amare

loveliness, löv´-li-nis, *n* grazia *f*

lovely, löv´-li, *adj* bello; buono

lover, löv´-a, *n* amante *m/f*; innamorato *m*, innamorata *f*

low, lou, *adj** basso; *adv* in basso

lower, lou´-a, *v* abbassare

lowland, lou´-land, *n* pianura *f*

loyal, loi´-al, *adj* leale

loyalty, loi´-al-ti, *n* lealtà *f*

lozenge, los´-inch, *n* pastiglia *f*

lubricate, luu´-bri-keit, *v* lubrificare

lucid*, luu´-sid, *adj* lucido

luck, lök, *n* sorte *f*; fortuna *f*

luckily, lök´-i-li, *adv* fortunatamente

lucky, lök´-i, *adj* fortunato; (charm) che porta fortuna

ludicrous, luu´-di-kros, *adj* ridicolo

luggage, lögh´-ich, *n* bagagli *mpl*

lukewarm, luuk´-uoorm, *adj* tiepido

lull, löl, *v* ninnare; *n* (pause) pausa *f*

lullaby, löl´-a-bai, *n* ninnananna *f*

lumbago, löm-bei´-gou, *n* lombaggine *f*

luminous*, luu´-mi-nos, *adj* luminoso

lump, lömp, *n* pezzo *m*; (in sauce) grumo *m*; (throat) nodo *m*; (sugar) zolletta *f*

lumpy, löm´-pi, *adj* grumoso

lunacy, luu´-na-si, *n* demenza *f*

lunar, luu´-na, *adj* lunare

lunatic, luu´-na-tik, *n* pazzo *m*, pazza *f*

lunch, lönch, *n* pranzo *m*

lung, löng, *n* polmone *m*

lurch, lerch, *v* traballare; **leave in the –,** piantare in asso

lure, liur, *v* allettare; *n* allettamento *m*

lurid, liur´-rid, *adj* (colours) sgargiante; (details) scioccante

lurk, lerk, *v* stare in agguato

luscious, lö´-shos, *adj* succulento

lust, löst, *n* libidine *f*; *v* desiderare

lustre, lös´-ta, *n* splendore *m*

lute, luut, *n* liuto *m*

luxurious*, lök-shur´-ri-os, *adj* lussuoso

luxury, lök´-she-ri, *n* lusso *m*

lymph, limf, *n* linfa *f*

lynch, linch, *v* linciare

lyrics, li´-riks, *npl* parole *fpl*

macaroni, mak-*a*-rou´-ni,
n maccheroni *mpl*

macaroon, mak-*a*-ruun´, n
amaretto *m*

mace, meis, n mazza *f*

machine, m*a*-shiin´, n
macchina *f*

machinery, m*a*-shiin´-*e*-ri,
n macchinario *m*

machine gun, m*a*-shiin'
gŏn, n mitragliatrice *f*

machinist, m*a*-shiin´-ist, n
macchinista *m/f*

mackerel, mak´-*e*-rel, n
sgombro *m*

mackintosh, mak´-in-
tosh, n impermeabile *m*

mad, mad, *adj* pazzo

madam, mad´-*a*m, n
signora *f*

madly, mad´-li, *adv*
pazzamente

madman, mad´-m*a*n, n
pazzo *m*

madness, mad´-nis, n
pazzia *f*

magazine, ma-g*a*-siin´, n
rivista *f*

maggot, magh´-ot, n
verme *m*

magic, mach´-ik, n magia
f; *adj* magico

magistrate, mach´-is-treit,
n magistrato *m*

magnanimity, magh-n*a*-
nim´-i-ti, n
magnanimità *f*

magnanimous*, magh-
nan´-i-mos, *adj*
magnanimo

magnesia, magh-nii´-sha,
n magnesia *f*

magnesium, magh-nii´-si-
am, n magnesio *m*

magnet, magh´-nit, n
magnete *m*, calamita *f*

magnetic, magh-net´-ik,
adj magnetico

magnetism, magh´-nit-
ism, n magnetismo *m*

magnetize, magh´-nit-ais,
v magnetizzare

magnificent*, magh-nif-
i-sent, *adj* magnifico

magnify, magh´-ni-fai, *v*
ingrandire

magnifying glass, magh´-
ni-fai-ing ghlaas, n lente
d'ingrandimento *f*

magnitude, magh´-ni-
tiuud, n (size)
grandezza *f*

magpie, magh´-pai, n
gazza *f*

mahogany, m*a*-ho´-g*a*-ni,
n mogano *m*

maid, meid, n domestica *f*

maiden, meid´-n, n
fanciulla *f*

mail, meil, n posta *f*; *v*
spedire per posta

maim, meim, *v* mutilare

main, mein, *adj**
principale; n (water, gas)
conduttura principale *f*;
(electricity) linea
principale *f*

mainland, mein´-l*a*nd, n
continente *m*

mainstream, mein´-striim,
n corrente principale *f*

maintain, mein-tein´, *v*

mantenere

maintenance, mein´-te-nans, n manutenzione f; *law* mantenimento m

maize, meis, n granturco m, mais m

majestic, ma-ches´-tik, *adj* maestoso

majesty, ma´-chis-ti, n maestà f

major, mei-cha, n maggiore m; (age) maggiorenne m/f; *adj* maggiore

majority, ma-cho´-ri-ti, n maggioranza f; (of age) maggiorità f

make, meik, n fabbricazione f; v fare; (manufacture) fabbricare

maker, mei´-ka, n fabbricante m

makeshift, meik´-shift, *adj* improvvisato, di fortuna

make-up, meik´-ŏp, n (face) trucco m; v truccarsi

making, mei´-king, n creazione f

malaria, ma-ler´-ri-a, n malaria f

male, meil, *adj* maschio; maschile; n maschio m

malevolent, ma-lev´-o-lent, *adj* malevolo

malice, mal´-is, n malevolenza f

malicious*, ma-lish´-os, *adj* malevolo

malign, ma-lain´, v malignare, calunniare

malignant*, ma-ligh´-nant, *adj* maligno

mallet, mal´-it, n maglio m

malnutrition, mal-niuu-trish´-on, n denutrizione f

malt, moolt, n malto m

maltreat, mal-triit´, v maltrattare

mammal, mam´-el, n mammifero m

man, maan, n uomo m; v equipaggiare

manage, man´-ich, v (business) gestire; (accomplish) farcela

management, man´-ich-ment, n, amministrazione f, direzione f

manager, man´-ich-a, n direttore m, direttrice f; gestore m; manager m/f

mandate, man´-deit, n mandato m

mandoline, man-do-lin´, n mandolino m

mane, mein, n criniera f

manger, mein´-cha, n mangiatoia f

mangle, mang´-gl, v straziare

mania, mei´-ni-a, n

mania f

maniac, mei´-ni-ak, n maniaco m

manicure, man´-i-kiur, n manicure f

manifest, man´-i-fest, *adj* manifesto; v manifestare

manifold, man´-i-fould, *adj* molteplice

manipulate, ma-nip´-iu-leit, v manipolare

mankind, man-kaind´, n umanità f

manly, man´-li, *adj* virile

manner, man´-a, n maniera f; modo m; genere m

manners, man´-es, npl maniere fpl, modi mpl

manœuvre, ma-nuu´-va, n manovra f; v manovrare

manor, man´-a, n maniero m

mansion, man´-shon, n casa signorile f

manslaughter, man´-sloo-ta, n omicidio preterintenzionale m

mantelpiece, man´-tl-piis, n mensola del caminetto f

manual, man´-iu-al, n (handbook) manuale m; *adj* manuale

manufacture, man-iu-fak´-cha, n manifattura f

manufacturer, man-iu-

fak´-chu-ra, n
fabbricante m

manure, ma-niur´, n
concime m; v concimare

manuscript, man´-iu-
skript, n manoscritto m

many, men´-i, adj & pron
molti, molte

map, map, n carta
geografica f; (town)
pianta f; v tracciare il
piano di

maple, mei´-pl, n acero m

mar, maar, v guastare;
turbare

marble, maar´-bl, n
marmo m; (toy) bilia f

March, maarch, n
marzo m

march, maarch, v
marciare; n marcia f

mare, mer, n giumenta f

margarine, maar-cha-
riin´, n margarina f

margin, maar´-chin, n
margine m

marginal, maar-chi´-nal,
adj marginale

marigold, ma´-ri-gould, n
calendula f

marine, ma-riin´, n
marine m; adj marino

mariner, ma´-ri-na, n
marinaio m

maritime, ma´-ri-taim, adj
marittimo

mark, maark, n segno m;
macchia f; voto m; v

segnare; macchiare; dare
il voto a

market, maar´-kit, n
mercato m; v mettere sul
mercato

marmalade, maar´-ma-
leid, n marmellata
d'arance f

marmot, maar´-mot, n
marmotta f

maroon, ma-ruun´, adj
bordeaux; v
abbandonare

marquee, maar-kii´, n
(tent) padiglione m

marriage, ma´-rich, n
matrimonio m; (feast)
nozze fpl

married, ma´-rid, adj
sposato

marrow, ma´-rou, n
midollo m; (vegetable)
zucca f

marry, ma´-ri, v sposare,
sposarsi

Marseilles, maar-sei´, n
Marsiglia f

marsh, maarsh, n palude f

marshal, maar´-shal, n
maresciallo m

marten, maar´-tin, n
martora f

martial, maar´-shal, adj
marziale

martyr, maar´-ta, n
martire m/f

martyrdom, maar´-te-
dom, n martirio m

marvel, maar´-vl, v
meravigliarsi; n
meraviglia f

marvellous*, maar´-vel-os,
adj meraviglioso

marzipan, maar´-zi-pan, n
marzapane m

masculine, mas´-kiu-lin,
adj maschile; mascolino

mash, mash, v schiacciare

mashed potatoes, masht
po-tei´-tous, n purè di
patate m

mask, maask, v
mascherare; n
maschera f

mason, mei´-son, n
scalpellino m

masonic, ma-son´-ik, adj
massonico

masonry, mei´-son-ri, n
muratura f; massoneria f

masquerade, mas-ke-reid´,
v travestirsi; n
mascherata f

mass, mas, n massa f; relig
messa f; v ammassarsi

massacre, mas´-a-ka, n
massacro m; v
massacrare

massage, ma-saach´, n
massaggio m; v
massaggiare

massive*, mas´-iv, adj
massiccio; enorme

mast, maast, n naut
albero m

master, maas´-ta, v

dominare; domare; imparare a fondo; n padrone m; (teacher) maestro m

masterly, maas´-te-li, adj da maestro

masterpiece, maas´-te-piis, n capolavoro m

masticate, mas´-ti-keit, v masticare

mastiff, mas´-tif, n mastino m

mat, mat, n stuoia f; (door) zerbino m; (bath) tappetino m; (table) tovaglietta all'americana f

match, mach, n fiammifero m; (contest) partita f; v (colours etc.) intonare

matchless, mach´-lis, adj senza pari

mate, meit, v accoppiarsi; n amico m

material, ma-tir´-ri-al, n materiale m; stoffa f

materialize, ma-tir´-ri-al-ais, v materializzarsi

maternal*, ma-ter´-nal, adj materno

mathematics, maZ-i-mat´-iks, n matematica f

matrimony, mat´-ri-mo-ni, n matrimonio m

matron, mei´-tron, n (hospital) capoinfermiera f

matter, mat´-a, n materia f, sostanza f; questione f

matting, mat´-ing, n stuoia f

mattress, mat´-ris, n materasso m

mature, ma-tiur´, adj maturo; (cheese) stagionato; v maturare

maturity, ma-tiur´-ri-ti, n maturità f

maul, mool, v dilaniare, sbranare

mauve, mouv, adj malva

maxim, mak´-sim, n massima f

maximum, mak´-si-mum, n massimo m; adj massimo

May, mei, n maggio m

may, mei, v essere permesso; essere possibile

maybe, mei´-bii, adv forse

mayor, mei´-a, n sindaco m

maze, meis, n labirinto m

me, mii, pron mi, me

meadow, med´-ou, n prato m

meagre, mii´-ga, adj magro, meschino

meal, miil, n pasto m; farina f

mean, miin, v voler dire; (signify) significare; adj meschino; (poor) misero

meaning, mii´-ning, n

significato m; senso m

meaningful, mii´-ning-ful, adj significativo

meaningless, mii´-ning-les, adj senza senso

means, miins, npl mezzi mpl

meanwhile, miin´-uail, adv frattanto

measles, miis´-ls, npl morbillo m

measure, mesh´-a, v misurare; n misura f; (stick, tape) metro m

measurement, mesh´-e-ment, n misura f

meat, miit, n carne f

mechanic, mi-kan´-ik, n meccanico m

mechanical, mi-kan´-ik-l, adj meccanico

mechanics, mi-kan´-iks, n meccanica f

mechanism, mek´-a-nism, n meccanismo m

medal, med´-l, n medaglia f

meddle, med´-l, v immischiarsi

mediate, mii´-di-eit, v fare da mediatore

medical, med´-i-kl, adj medico

medication, med-i-kei´-shon, n medicinali mpl, farmaci mpl

medicine, med´-i-sin, n medicina f

medieval, med-ii´-val, *adj*
medievale

mediocre, mii´-di-ou-ka,
adj mediocre

meditate, med´-i-teit, *v*
meditare

Mediterranean, med-i-te-
rei´-ni-an, *adj*
mediterraneo; **the –,** *n* il
Mediterraneo *m*

medium, mii´-di-um, *n*
mezzo *m*; *adj* medio

meek*, miik, *adj*
mansueto

meet, miit, *v* incontrare;
incontrarsi; fare la
conoscenza di

meeting, mii´-ting, *n*
incontro *m*; riunione *f*

melancholy, mel´-an-kol-
i, *n* melanconia *f*; *adj*
melanconico

mellow, mel´-ou, *adj*
maturo; dolce

melodious*, mi-lou´-di-os,
adj melodioso

melody, mel´-o-di, *n*
melodia *f*

melon, mel´-on, *n*
melone *m*

melt, melt, *v* fondere

member, mem´-ba, *n*
membro *m*; (club) socio
m; (parliament)
deputato *m*

membership, mem-be-
ship, *n* iscrizione *f*

memo, mem´-ou, *n*

comunicazione di
servizio *f*

memoirs, mem´-uaars, *npl*
memorie *fpl*

memorandum, mem-o-
ran´-dom, *n*
memorandum *m*

memorial, mi-moo´-ri-al,
n monumento
commemorativo *m*

memorize, mem´-o-rais, *v*
memorizzare

memory, mem´-o-ri, *n*
memoria *f*

menace, men´-is, *n*
minaccia *f*; *v* minacciare

menagerie, mi-nach´-e-ri,
n serraglio *m*

mend, mend, *v* riparare;
(sew) rammendare

menial, mii´-ni-al, *adj*
servile, umile

meningitis, men-in-chai´-
tis, *n* meningite *f*

menopause, men´-o-poos,
n menopausa *f*

mental, men´-tl, *adj*
mentale

mention, men´-shon, *v*
menzionare

menu, men´-iu, *n* menù *m*

mercantile, mer´-kan-tail,
adj mercantile

merchandise, mer´-chan-
dais, *n* merce *f*

merchant, mer´-chant, *n*
mercante *m*,
commerciante *m/f*

merciful*, mer´-si-ful, *adj*
misericordioso

mercury, mer´-kiu-ri, *n*
mercurio *m*

mercy, mer´-si, *n*
misericordia *f*

mere, mir, *adj** puro;
semplice

merge, merch, *v* fondere;
fondersi; assorbire

meridian, mi-ri´-di-an, *n*
meridiano *m*

merit, me´-rit, *v* meritare;
n merito *m*

meritorious*, me-ri-too´-
ri-os, *adj* meritorio

mermaid, mer´-meid, *n*
sirena *f*

merriment, me´-ri-ment,
n allegria *f*

merry, me´-ri, *adj* allegro,
gioioso

mesh, mesh, *n* maglia *f*

mesmerize, mes´-me-rais,
v ipnotizzare

mess, mes, *n* disordine *m*;
sporcizia *f*; pasticcio *m*;
– up, *v* rovinare

message, mes´-ich, *n*
messaggio *m*

messenger, mes´-in-cha, *n*
messaggero *m*

messy, me´-si, *adj*
disordinato; sporco

metal, met´-l, *n* metallo *m*

metallic, mi-tal´-ik, *adj*
metallico

meteor, mii´-ti-oor, *n*

meteora f

meter, mii´-ta, n
contatore m

method, meZ´-od, n
metodo m

methylated spirits, meZ´-
i-lei-tid spi´-rits, npl
alcol denaturato m

metre, mii´-ta, n metro m

metric, met´-rik, adj
metrico

metropolis, mi-trop´-o-lis,
n metropoli f

Mexico, mek´-si-kou, n
Messico m

microphone, mai´-kro-
foun, n microfono m

microscope, mai´-kro-
skoup, n microscopio m

microwave, mai´-krou-
ueiv, n microonda f;
(oven) forno a
microonde m

midday, mid-dei´, n
mezzogiorno m

middle, mid´-l, n mezzo m;
centro m; adj di mezzo

middleman, mid´-l-man, n
intermediario m

midge, mich, n
moscerino m

midget, mich´-it, n nano
m, nana f

midnight, mid´-nait, n
mezzanotte f

midst, midst, prep mezzo

midwife, mid´-uaif, n
ostetrica f

might, mait, n potere m

mighty, mai´-ti, adj
potente

migraine, mii´-grein, n
emicrania f

migrate, mai´-greit, v
emigrare

Milan, mi-lan´, n Milano f

mild*, maild, adj mite;
(not strong) leggero

mildew, mil´-diuu, n
muffa f

mile, mail, n miglio m (=
1,6 km)

milestone, mail´-stoun, n
pietra miliare f

military, mil´-i-ta-ri, adj
militare; **the –,** n
l'esercito m

milk, milk, n latte m

milk shake, milk´-sheik, n
frappé m

milky, milk´-i, adj di latte

Milky Way, milk´-i uei, n
Via Lattea f

mill, mil, n mulino m;
macinino m; fabbrica f

miller, mil´-a, n
mugnaio m

milliner, mil´-i-na, n
modista f

million, mil´-ion, n
milione m

millionaire, mil´-ion-er, n
milionario m;
miliardario m

mimic, mim´-ik, v imitare

mince, mins, v tritare; n

carne tritata f

mincemeat, mins´-miit, n
frutta secca e candita
per pasticceria f

mind, maind, n mente f;
opinione f; v fare
attenzione a; (look
after) badare a; (object
to) importare

mine, main, pron il mio, la
mia; i miei, le mie

mine, main, n (pit)
miniera f; (explosive)
mina f

miner, main´-a, n
minatore m

mineral, min´-e-ral, n
minerale m

mineral water, min´-e-ral
uoo´-ta, n acqua
minerale f

mingle, ming´-gl, v
mischiare

miniature, min´-i-cha, n
miniatura f

minimize, min´-i-mais, v
ridurre al minimo

minimum, min´-i-mum, n
minimo m; adj minimo

minister, min´-is-ta, n
(politics) ministro m;
relig pastore m; v
assistere

ministry, min´-is-tri, n
ministero m

mink, mink, n visone m

minor, mai´-na, n minore
m/f, minorenne m/f; adj

piccolo

minority, mi-no´-ri-ti, n
minoranza f

minstrel, mins´-trel, n
menestrello m

mint, mint, n (coin) zecca
f; (plant) menta f; v
batter moneta

minuet, min-iu-et´, n
minuetto m

minus, mai´-nus, n meno
m; prep meno; senza

minute, min´-it, n
minuto m

minute*, mai-niuut´, adj
minuscolo; (precise)
minuzioso

miracle, mi´-ri-kl, n
miracolo m

miraculous*, mi-rak´-iu-
los, adj miracoloso

mirage, mi-raash´, n
miraggio m

mirror, mir´-a, n specchio
m; v riflettere

mirth, merZ, n gaiezza f

misadventure, mis-ad-
ven´-cha, n sfortuna f

misapprehension, mis-apri-
hen´-shon, n
malinteso m

misappropriate, mis-aprou´-
pri-eit, v
appropriarsi
indebitamente di

misbehave, mis-bi-heiv´, v
comportarsi male

miscarriage, mis´-ka-rich,

n (birth) aborto
spontaneo m; (justice)
errore giudiziario m

miscarry, mis-ka´-ri, v med
abortire; fallire

miscellaneous*, mis-e-
lei´-ni-os, adj vario;
misto

mischief, mis´-chif, n
malizia f; birichinata f

mischievous*, mis´-chiv-
os, adj malizioso;
birichino

misconduct, mis-kon´-
dŏkt, n comportamento
scorretto m

misconstruction, mis-
kon-strŏk´-shon, n
interpretazione errata f

miscount, mis-kaunt´, v
calcolare male

misdemeanour, mis-di-
mii´-na, n law
infrazione f

misdirect, mis-di-rekt´, v
dare indicazioni
sbagliate

miser, mai´-sa, n avaro m

miserly, mai´-se-li, adj
avaro

miserable, mis´-e-ra-bl,
adj infelice; miserabile

misery, mis´-e-ri, n
miseria f

misfit, mis´-fit, n
disadattato m

misfortune, mis-foor´-
tiuun, n sfortuna f

n (birth) aborto

misgiving, mis-ghiv´-ing,
n timore m

misguided, mis-gai´-did,
adj poco giudizioso

mishap, mis´-hap, n
incidente m;
contrattempo m

misinform, mis-in-foorm´,
v informare male

misjudge, mis-chŏch´, v
calcolare male

mislay, mis-lei´, v smarrire

mislead, mis-liid´, v
sviare; (fraud) ingannare

mismanage, mis-man´-ich,
v gestire male

misplace, mis-pleis´, v
smarrire

misprint, mis´-print, n
errore di stampa m,
refuso m

mispronounce, mis-pro-
nauns´, v pronunciare
male

misrepresent, mis-rep-ri-
sent´, v travisare

miss, mis, v (train etc.)
perdere; (feel lack of)
sentire la mancanza di;
(shots) mancare il
bersaglio

Miss, mis, n signorina f

missile, mis´-ail, n
proiettile m

missing, mis´-ing, adj
smarrito; scomparso;
mancante

missing person, mis´-ing

per'-son, n disperso m

mission, mish'-on, n
missione f

missionary, mish'-on-a-ri,
n missionario m

mist, mist, n nebbia f,
bruma f

mistake, mis-teik', n
errore m, sbaglio m; v
sbagliare

mistaken, mis-tei'-kn, adj
sbagliato

Mister (Mr.), mis'-ta, n
signore m

mistletoe, mis'-el-tou, n
vischio m

mistress, mis'-tris, n
(house) padrona f;
(school) maestra f;
(lover) amante f

mistrust, mis-tröst',
v diffidare di; n
diffidenza f

misty, mis'-ti, adj
nebbioso, brumoso

misunderstand, mis-
ön-de-stand', v
fraintendere, capire
male

misunderstanding, mis-
ön-de-stan'-ding, n
malinteso m

misuse, mis-iuus', v usare
male; abusare di

mitigate, mit'-i-gheit, v
mitigare

mix, miks, v mescolare

mixed, mikst, adj misto

mixture, miks'-cha, n
mistura f

moan, moun, v gemere; n
gemito m

mob, mob, v accalcarsi
intorno; n calca f

mobile, mou'-bail, adj
mobile; n (telephone)
telefonino m

mobilize, mou'-bi-lais, v
mobilitare

mock, mok, v beffarsi; –
at, farsi beffe di

mockery, mok'-e-ri, n
beffeggiamento m

mockingly, mok'-ing-li,
adv beffardamente

mode, moud, n modo m,
maniera f

model, mod'-l, n modello
m; (person) modello m,
modella f; v modellare

moderate, mod'-e-reit, v
moderare

moderate, mod'-e-rat, adj*
moderato

moderation, mod-e-rei'-
shon, n moderazione f

modern, mod'-en, adj
moderno

modest*, mod'-ist, adj
modesto

modify, mod'-i-fai, v
modificare

moist, moist, adj umido

moisten, mois'-n, v
inumidire

moisture, mois'-cha, n

umidità f

mole, moul, n talpa f;
neo m

molest, mo-lest', v
molestare

molten, moul'-ten, adj
fuso

moment, mou'-ment, n
momento m

momentous, mo-men'-tos,
adj solenne

momentum, mo-men'-
tom, n impulso m

monarch, mon'-ak, n
monarca m

monarchy, mon'-a-ki, n
monarchia f

monastery, mon'-as-tri, n
monastero m

Monday, mön'-di, n
lunedì m

monetary, mön'-i-ta-ri, adj
monetario

money, mön'-i, n denaro
m; soldi mpl

mongrel, möng'-grel, n
(dog) bastardino m

monk, möngk, n
monaco m

monkey, möng'-ki, n
scimmia f

monocle, mon'-o-kl, n
monocolo m

monogram, mon'-o-gram,
n monogramma m

monoplane, mon'-ou-
plein, n monoplano m

monopolize, mo-nop'-olais, *v* monopolizzare

monopoly, mo-nop´-o-li, *n* monopolio *m*

monotonous*, mon-ot´-o-nos, *adj* monotono

monster, mon´-sta, *n* mostro *m*

monstrous*, mon´-stros, *adj* mostruoso

month, mŏnZ, *n* mese *m*

monthly, mŏnZ´-li, *adj* mensile; *adv* al mese

monument, mon´-iument, *n* monumento *m*

mood, muud, *n* umore *m*

moody, muud´-i, *adj* lunatico

moon, muun, *n* luna *f*

moonlight, muun´-lait, *n* chiaro di luna *m*

moor, moor, *n* (heath) brughiera *f; v* (ship) ormeggiare

mop, mop, *n* spazzolone per pavimenti *m; v* lavare i pavimenti

mope, moup, *v* essere depresso

moral, mo´-ral, *n* morale *f*

moratorium, mo-ra-toor´-ri-um, *n* moratoria *f*

morbid*, moor´-bid, *adj* morboso

more, moor, *adj & pron* più; ancora; *adv* di più; **once –,** ancora una volta

moreover, moor-ou´-va,

adv inoltre

morning, moor´-ning, *n* mattino *m*, mattina *f*; mattinata *f*

morose, mo-rous´, *adj* mesto

morphine*, moor´-fiin, *n* morfina *f*

morsel, moor´-sel, *n* boccone *m*

mortal, moor´-tl, *n* mortale *m; adj* mortale; fatale

mortality, moor-tal´-i-ti, *n* mortalità *f*

mortar, moor´-ta, *n* mortaio *m*; malta *f*

mortgage, moor´-ghich, *n* ipoteca *f*; mutuo *m*

mortification, moor-ti-fi-kei´-shon, *n* mortificazione *f*

mortuary, moor´-tiu-a-ri, *n* camera mortuaria *f*

mosaic, mou´-sei-ik, *n* mosaico *m*

mosque, mosk, *n* moschea *f*

mosquito, mos-kii´-tou, *n* zanzara *f*

moss, mos, *n* muschio *m*

most, moust, *adj* più; la maggior parte di; *pron* la maggior parte; *adv* di più; (very) molto

mostly, moust´-li, *adv* per lo più

moth, moZ, *n* falena *f*;

tarma *f*

mother, mŏD´-a, *n* madre *f*

mother-in-law, mŏD´-e-rin-loo, *n* suocera *f*

motherly, mŏD´-e-li, *adj* materno

mother tongue, mŏD´-a tŏng, *n* madrelingua *f*

motion, mou´-shon, *n* moto *m*, movimento *m*

motionless, mou´-shon-lis, *adj* immobile

motive, mou´-tiv, *n* motivo *m*

motor, mou´-ta, *n* motore *m*

motorbike, mou´-to-baik, *n* moto *f*

motorcycle, mou´-to-sai-kl, *n* motocicletta *f*

motorist, mou´-to-rist, *n* automobilista *m/f*

mottled, mot´-ld, *adj* screziato

motto, mot´-ou, *n* motto *m*

mould, mould, *n* forma *f*, stampo *m*; (mildew) muffa *f; v* modellare

mouldy, moul´-di, *adj* ammuffito

moult, moult, *v* fare la muta

mound, maund, *n* monticello di terra *m*

mount, maunt, *n* monte *m; v* montare

mountain, maun´-tin, n
montagna f

mountain bike, maun´-
tin-baik, n mountain
bike f

mountaineering, maun-ti-
nir´-ring, n alpinismo m

mourn, moorn, v
lamentare; piangere

mourning, moor´-ning, n
lutto m

mouse, maus, n topo m

mousetrap, maus´-trap, n
trappola per topi f

mousse, muus, n spuma f

moustache, mus-taash´, n
baffi mpl

mouth, mauZ, n bocca f

mouthful, mauZ´-ful, n
boccone m; sorsata f

mouthpiece, mauZ´-piis,
n imboccatura f,
bocchino m

movable, muu´-va-bl, adj
mobile

move, muuv, v muovere;
(removal) traslocare; n
mossa f; (removal)
trasloco m

movement, muuv´-ment,
n movimento m

movie, muu´-vi, n film m

mow, mou, v falciare

mower, mou´-a, n
tagliaerba m

much, mŏch, adj & pron
molto; adv molto; **how
–?** quanto?

mud, mŏd, n fango m

muddle, mŏd´-l, n
pasticcio m; disordine m

muddy, mŏd´-i, adj
fangoso

mudguard, mŏd´-gaard, n
parafango m

muffle, mŏf´-l, v
imbacuccare; (sound)
attutire

muffler, mŏf´-la, n
sciarpa f

mug, mŏgh, n tazza f;
boccale m

mulberry, mŏl´-be-ri, n
mora di gelso f; (tree)
gelso m

mule, miuul, n mulo m

multifarious, mŏl-ti-fer´-
ri-os, adj molteplice

multiplication, mŏl-ti-pli-
kei´-shon, n
moltiplicazione f

multiply, mŏl´-ti-plai, v
moltiplicare

multitude, mŏl-ti-tiuud,
n moltitudine f

mumble, mŏm´-bl, v
mormorare

mummy, mŏm´-i, n
mummia f; fam mamma

mumps, mŏmps, npl
orecchioni mpl

munch, mŏnch, v
sgranocchiare

municipal, miu-nis´-i-pal,
adj municipale

munificent, miu-nif´-i-

sent, adj munifico

munition, miu-nish´-on, n
munizione f

murder, mer´-da, n
omicidio m; v
assassinare

murderer, mer´-de-ra, n
assassino m; omicida m/f

murky, mer´-ki, adj fosco,
tenebroso

murmur, mer´-ma, n
mormorio m; v
mormorare

muscle, mŏs´-l, n
muscolo m

muse, miuus, v meditare;
n musa f

museum, miu-sii´-om, n
museo m

mushroom, mŏsh´-rum, n
fungo m

music, miuu´-sik, n
musica f

musical, miuu´-si-kl, adj
musicale

musician, miu-sish´-an, n
musicista m/f

musk, mŏsk, n muschio m

Muslim, mus´-lim, adj
musulmano; n
musulmano m

mussel, mŏs´-l, n cozza f

must, mŏst, v dovere

mustard, mŏs´-tad, n
senape f

muster, mŏs´-ta, v
radunare

musty, mŏs´-ti, adj

ammuffito; (smell) di
muffa

mute, miuut, *adj* muto; *n*
muto *m*

mutilate, miuu´-ti-leit, *v*
mutilare

mutineer, miuu-ti-nir´, *n*
ammutinato *m*

mutinous, miuu´-ti-nos,
adj ammutinato

mutiny, miuu´-ti-ni, *n*
ammutinamento *m*

mutter, mŏt´-*a*, *v*
mormorare

mutton, mŏt´-*on*, *n*
montone *m*

mutual, miuu´-chiu-*al*, *adj*
mutuo

muzzle, mŏs´-l, *n*
museruola *f*; (snout)
muso *m*; (gun) bocca *f*

my, mai, *adj* mio, mia,
miei, mie

myrrh, m*e*r, *n* mirra *f*

myrtle, m*e*r´-tl, *n* mirto *m*

myself, mai-self´, *pron refl*
mi; (after prep) me

mysterious*, mis-tir´-ri-
os, *adj* misterioso

mystery, mis´-*te*-ri, *n*
mistero *m*

mystify, mis´-ti-fai, *v*
mistificare

myth, miZ, *n* mito *m*

mythology, miZ-ol´-*o*-chi,
n mitologia *f*

nag, nagh, *v* assillare; *n*
(horse) ronzino *m*

nail, neil, *n* chiodo *m*;
(human) unghia *f*; *v*
inchiodare

nailbrush, neil´-brŏsh, *n*
spazzolino per unghie *m*

nailfile, neil´-fail, *n*
limetta per unghie *f*

naive*, nai-iiv´, *adj*
ingenuo

naked, nei´-kid, *adj* nudo

name, neim, *n* nome *m*

nameless, neim´-lis, *adj*
senza nome; anonimo

namely, neim´-li, *adv* cioè

namesake, neim´-seik, *n*
omonimo *m*

nanny, nan´-i, *n*
bambinaia *f*

nap, nap, *n* sonnellino *m*;
(cloth) pelo *m*

nape, neip, *n* nuca *f*

napkin, nap´-kin, *n*
tovagliolo *m*

Naples, nei´-pls, *n*
Napoli *f*

nappy, nap´-i, *n*
pannolino *m*

narcissus, naar-sis´-*us*, *n*
narciso *m*

narcotic, naar-kot´-ik, *n*
narcotico *m*

narrate, na-eeit´, *v* narrare

narrative, na´-ra-tiv, *n*
narrazione *f*

narrow, na´-rou, *adj*
stretto

narrow-minded, na-rou-
main´-did, *adj* di idee
ristrette

narrowness, na´-rou-nis,
n strettezza *f*

nasal*, nei´-sal, *adj* nasale

nasturtium, nas-ter´-
sh*um*, *n* nasturzio *m*

nasty, naas´-ti, *adj* cattivo;
brutto

nation, nei´-shon, *n*
nazione *f*

national*, nash´-on-al, *adj*
nazionale

nationality, nash-on-al´-i-
ti, *n* nazionalità *f*

native, nei´-tiv, *n*
(country) natale;
indigeno *m*

natural*, nat´-iu-ral, *adj*
naturale

naturalization, nat-iu-ra-
lai-sei´-shon, *n*
naturalizzazione *f*

nature, nei´-cha, *n*
natura *f*

naughty, noo´-ti, *adj*
cattivo

nausea, noo´-si-a, *n*
nausea *f*

nauseous, noo´-si-os, *adj*
nauseabondo

nautical*, noo´-ti-kl, *adj*
nautico

naval, nei´-val, *adj* navale

naval officer, nei´-val of´-
is-a, *n* ufficiale di
marina *m*

navel, nei´-vel, *n*
ombelico *m*

navigate, nav´-i-gheit, *v*
navigare

navigation, nav-i-ghei´-
shon, *n* navigazione *f*

navigator, nav´-i-ghei-*ta*, n navigatore m

navvy, nav´-i, n manovale m

navy, nei´-vi, n marina f

navy blue, nei´-vi bluu, adj blu; n blu m

near, nir, adv vicino; prep vicino a; adj vicino, prossimo; v avvicinarsi

nearby, nir´-bai, adj & adv vicino

nearly, nir´-li, adv quasi

near-sighted, nir-sai´-tid, adj miope

neat*, niit, adj (tidy) ordinato; (spruce) accurato; (not diluted) liscio

necessarily, nes´-i-se-ri-li, adv necessariamente

necessary, nes´-i-se-ri, adj necessario

necessitate, ni-ses´-i-teit, v necessitare

necessity, ni-ses´-i-ti, n necessità f

neck, nek, n collo m

necklace, nek´-las, n collana f

need, niid, v aver bisogno di; n bisogno m

needle, nii´-dl, n ago m; (on record player) puntina f

needless*, niid´-lis, adj inutile

needy, nii´-di, adj bisognoso

negation, ni-ghei´-shon, n negazione f

negative, neg´-a-tiv, n negativa f; adj* negativo

neglect, nigh-lekt´, v trascurare

neglected, nigh-lek´-tid, adj trascurato

neglectful, nigh-lekt´-ful, adj negligente

negligence, negh´-lich-ens, n negligenza f

negligent, negh´-lich-ent, adj negligente

negotiate, ni-gou´-shi-eit, v negoziare, trattare

negotiation, ni-gou-shi-ei´-shon, n negoziato m, trattativa f

neigh, nei, v nitrire; n nitrito m

neighbour, nei´-ba, n vicino m

neighbourhood, nei´-be-hud, n vicinato m

neighbouring, nei´-be-ring, adj vicino

neighbourly, nei´-be-li, adj da buon vicino

neither, nai´-Da, adj & pron né l'uno né l'altro; adv né; nemmeno; – ... **nor,** né... né

neon, nii´-on, n neon m

nephew, ne´-iuu, n nipote (di zii) m

nerve, nerv, n nervo m;

(pluck) sangue freddo m; (cheek) faccia tosta f

nervous*, ner´-vos, adj nervoso; agitato; emozionato

nest, nest, n nido m; v nidificare

nestle, nes´-l, v accoccolarsi

net, net, n rete f; adj (weight etc.) netto

Netherlands, neD´-e-lands, npl Paesi Bassi mpl

nettle, net´-l, n ortica f

nettle rash, net´-l rash, n orticaria f

network, net´-uerk, n rete f

neurotic, niur-rot´-ik, adj nevrotico

neuter, niuu´-ta, adj gram neutro

neutral, niuut´-ral, adj neutrale; neutro

never, nev´-a, adv mai

nevertheless, nev-e-De-les´, adv ciononostante, tuttavia

new*, niuu, adj nuovo

newborn, niuu´-boorn, adj neonato

news, niuus, npl notizie fpl; (radio, TV) notiziario m

newsagent, niuus-ei´-chent, n giornalaio m

newspaper, niuus-pei´-pa,

n giornale *m*; quotidiano *m*

New Year, niuu iir, *n* anno nuovo *m*

New Year's Day, niuu´-iirs dei, *n* capodanno *m*

New Year's Eve, niuu´-iirs iiv, *n* la notte di San Silvestro *f*

New York, niu ioork, *n* New York *f*

New Zealand, niu sii´-land, *n* Nuova Zelanda *f*

next, nekst, *adj* vicino; seguente; prossimo; *adv* dopo, poi; **– to,** *prep* vicino a

nibble, nib´-l, *v* sgranocchiare; (rats) rosicchiare; (fish) abboccare

nice*, nais, *adj* gentile; bello; simpatico

nick, nik, *n* tacca *f*; **in the – of time,** appena in tempo

nickel, nik´-l, *n* nickel *m*

nickname, nik´-neim, *n* soprannome *m*

nicotine, ni´-ko-tiin, *n* nicotina *f*

niece, niis, *n* nipote (di zii) *f*

night, nait, *n* notte *f*

night-dress, nait´-dres, *n* camicia da notte *f*

nightfall, nait´-fool, *n* calar della notte *m*

nightingale, nait´-ing-gheil, *n* usignolo *m*

nightlife, nait´-laif, *n* vita notturna *f*

nightly, nait´-li, *adv* di notte; ogni notte

nightmare, nait´-mer, *n* incubo *m*

Nile, nail, *n* Nilo *m*

nimble, nim´-bl, *adj* agile

nine, nain, *adj* nove

nineteen, nain-tiin´, *adj* diciannove

nineteenth, nain-tiinZ´, *adj* diciannovesimo; (date) diciannove

ninetieth, nain´-ti-eZ, *adj* novantesimo

ninety, nain´-ti, *adj* novanta

ninth, nainZ, *adj* nono; (date) nove

nip, nip, *v* pizzicare; **– off,** staccare

nipple, nip´-l, *n* capezzolo *m*

nitrate, nait´-reit, *n* nitrato *m*

nitrogen, nait´-ro-chen, *n* azoto *m*

no, nou, *adv* no

nobility, no-bil´-i-ti, *n* nobiltà *f*

noble, nou´-bl, *adj* nobile

nobody, nou´-bod-i, *pron* nessuno

nod, nod, *v* far un cenno col capo; *n* cenno del

capo *m*

noise, nois, *n* rumore *m*

noiseless*, nois´-lis, *adj* silenzioso

noisily, noi´-si-li, *adv* rumorosamente

noisy, noi´-si, *adj* rumoroso

nomad, nou´-mad, *n* nomade *m/f*

nominal, nom´-i-nal, *adj* nominale

nominate, nom´-i-neit, *v* candidare; nominare

nomination, nom´-i-nei´-shon, *n* candidatura *f*; nomina *f*

nominee, nom-i-nii´, *n* candidato *m*; persona designata *f*

non-commissioned officer, non-ko-mish´-nd of´-is-a, *n* sottufficiale *m*

none, nŏn, *pron* nessuno

nonplussed, non-plŏst´, *adj* sconcertato

nonsense, non´-sens, *n* assurdità *f*

non-skid, non´-skid, *adj* antisdrucciolo

non-smoker, non-smouk´-a, *n* non fumatore *m*

non-stop, non´-stop, *adj* continuo; (train, flight) diretto

nook, nuk, *n* cantuccio *m*

noon, nuun, *n*

mezzogiorno *m*

no one, nou´-uŏn, *pron*
nessuno

noose, nuus, *n* nodo
scorsoio *m*

nor, noor, *conj* né

norm, noorm, *n* norma *f*

normal, noor´-mal, *adj*
normale

north, noorZ, *n* nord *m*,
settentrione *m*

North Sea, noorZ sii, *n*
Mare del Nord *m*

northerly, noor´-De-li, *adj*
del nord; verso nord

northern, noor´-Den, *adj*
settentrionale

Norway, noor´-uei, *n*
Norvegia *f*

Norwegian, noor-uii-
chan, *adj* norvegese

nose, nous, *n* naso *m*

nostril, nos´-tril, *n*
narice *f*

nosy, nou´-si, *adj* curioso

not, not, *adv* non

notable, nou´-ta-bl, *adj*
notevole

notary, nou´-ta-ri, *n*
notaio *m*

notch, noch, *v* intagliare;
n tacca *f*

note, nout, *v* notare; *n*
nota *f*; banconota *f*;
(letter) biglietto *m*

notebook, nout´-buk, *n*
bloc-notes *m*

notepaper, nout´-pei-pa, *n*

carta da lettere *f*

noted, nou´-tid, *adj*
famoso, celebre

noteworthy, nout´-uer-Di,
adj degno di nota

nothing, nŏ´-Zing, *adv*
niente ; **for –,** per
niente; invano

notice, nou´-tis, *v* notare;
accorgersi di; *n* avviso
m; attenzione *f*; (to quit)
preavviso *m*

noticeable, nou´-tis-*a*-bl,
adj percettibile;
notevole

notice board, nou´-tis
boorD, *n* bacheca *f*

notify, nou´-ti-fai, *v*
comunicare; avvisare

notion, nou´-shon, *n*
nozione *f*

notoriety, nou-to-rai´-i-ti,
n notorietà *f*

notorious*, no-toor´-ri-os,
adj famigerato

notwithstanding, not-
uiD-stan´-ding, *conj* &
prep malgrado

nought, noot, *n* zero *m*

noun, naun, *n* gram
sostantivo *m*

nourish, nŏ´-rish, *v* nutrire

nourishing, nŏ´-rish-ing,
adj nutritivo

nourishment, nŏ´-rish-
ment, *n* nutrimento *m*

novel, nov´-el, *n*
romanzo *m*

novelist, nov´-el-ist, *n*
romanziere *m*

novelty, nov´-el-ti, *n*
novità *f*

November, no-vem´-ba, *n*
novembre *m*

novice, nov´-is, *n* novizio
m, novizia *f*; (beginner)
principiante *m/f*

now, nau, *adv* ora, adesso;
– and then, di tanto in
tanto; **just –,** proprio ora

nowadays, nau´-a-deis,
adv oggigiorno, al giorno
d'oggi

nowhere, nou´-uer, *adv* in
nessun luogo

noxious, nok´-shos, *adj*
nocivo

nozzle, nos´-l, *n* (of hose)
bocchetta *f*

nuclear, niu´-klir, *adj*
nucleare; atomico

nucleus, niu´-kli-os, *n*
nucleo *m*

nude, niuud, *adj* nudo

nudge, nŏch, *v* toccare col
gomito; *n* gomitata *f*

nugget, nŏ´-ghit, *n* pepita *f*

nuisance, niuu´-sens, *n*
fastidio *m*; seccatura *f*

numb, nŏm, *adj*
intorpidito

number, nŏm´-ba, *v*
numerare; (count)
contare; *n* numero;
(figure) cifra *f*; (many)
gran quantità *f*

number plate, nŏm´-ba
pleit, numero di targa *m*

numberless, nŏm´-be-lis,
adj innumerevole

numbness, nŏm´-nis, *n*
intorpidimento *m*

numerous, niuu´-me-ros,
adj numeroso

nun, nŏn, *n* suora *f*,
monaca *f*

nuptial, nŏp´-shal, *adj*
nuziale

nurse, ners, *n* infermiera *f*;
(male) infermiere *m*; *v*
curare

nursery, ner´-se-ri, *n*
camera dei bambini *f*;
(plants) vivaio *m*

nursery rhyme, ner´-se-ri
raim, *n* filastrocca *f*

nursery school, ner´-se-ri
skuul, *n* scuola
materna *f*

nut, nŏt, *n* noce *f*; (hazel)
nocciola *f*; (peanut)
nocciolina *f*; *mech*
dado *m*

nut-cracker, nŏt´-krak-a,
n schiaccianoci *m*,

nutmeg, nŏt-megh, *n* noce
moscata *f*

nutrition, niu-trish´-on, *n*
nutrizione

nutritious, niu-trish´-os,
adj nutritivo; nutriente

nutshell, nŏt´-shel, *n*
guscio di noce *m*; **in a –,**
fig in breve

oak, ouk, n quercia f

oar, oor, n remo m

oarsman, oors´-man, n rematore m

oasis, ou-ei´-sis, n oasi f

oath, ouZ, n giuramento m; (curse) imprecazione f, bestemmia f; **take an –,** v prestare giuramento

oatmeal, out´-miil, n farina d'avena f

oats, outs, npl avena f

obdurate*, ob´-diu-rat, adj caparbio

obedience, o-bii´-di-ens, n ubbidienza f

obedient, o-bii´-di-ent, adj ubbidiente

obese, o-biis, adj obeso

obesity, o-bii´-si-ti, n obesità f

obey, o-bei´, v ubbidire

obituary, o-bit´-iu-a-ri, n necrologio m

object, ob-chekt´, v obiettare; (oppose) opporsi

object, ob´-chekt, n oggetto m; (aim) scopo m

objection, ob-chek´-shon, n obiezione f

objectionable, ob-chek´-shon-a-bl, adj riprovevole

objective, ob-chek´-tiv, n obiettivo m

obligation, ob-li-ghei´-shon, n obbligo m; impegno m

obligatory, ob-li´-ga-to-ri, adj obbligatorio

oblige, ob-laich´, v obbligare; (favour) fare una cortesia

obliging*, ob-laich´-ing, adj gentile; servizievole

obliterate, ob-lit´-e-reit, v cancellare

oblivion, ob-liv´-i-on, n oblio m

oblivious, ob-liv´-i-os, adj ignaro

oblong, ob´-long, adj oblungo; n rettangolo m

obnoxious, ob-nok´-shos, adj detestabile; ripugnante

obscene*, ob-siin´, adj osceno

obscure, ob-skiur´, adj* oscuro; v oscurare

observance, ob-ser´-vans, n osservanza f

observant, ob-ser´-vant, adj osservante

observation, ob-se-vei´-shon, n osservazione f

observatory, ob-ser´-va-to-ri, n osservatorio m

observe, ob-serv´, v osservare

obsess, ob-ses´, v ossessionare

obsession, ob-se´-shon, n ossessione f

obsolete, ob´-so-liit, adj obsoleto

obstacle, ob´-sti-kl, n ostacolo m

obstinacy, ob´-sti-na-si, n ostinazione f

obstinate*, ob´-sti-nat, *adj* ostinato

obstreperous*, ob-strep´-e-ros, *adj* turbolento

obstruct, ob-strŏkt´, *v* ostruire

obstruction, ob-strŏk´-shon, *n* ostruzione *f*; ostacolo *m*

obtain, ob-tein´, *v* ottenere

obtrude, ob-truud´, *v* imporsi

obtrusive*, ob-truu´-siv, *adj* importuno

obtuse*, ob-tiuus´, *adj* ottuso

obviate, ob´-vi-eit, *v* ovviare; evitare

obvious*, ob´-vi-os, *adj* ovvio, evidente

occasion, o-kei´-shon, *n* occasione *f*; (cause) motivo *m*

occasional*, o-kei´-shon-al, *adj* occasionale; sporadico

occult, o-kŏlt´, *adj* occulto

occupation, ok-iu-pei´-shon, *n* occupazione *f*; professione *f*, mestiere *m*

occupier, ok-iu-pai-a, *n* (tenant) inquilino *m*

occupy, ok-iu-pai, *v* occupare; occuparsi

occur, o-ker´, *v* (to the mind) venire in mente; (happen) accadere;

(opportunity) presentarsi

occurrence, o-kŏ´-rens, *n* evento *m*

ocean, ou´-shan, *n* oceano *m*

ochre, ou´-ka, *n* ocra *f*

o'clock, o-klok´, *adv* one —, l'una; six —, le sei

octagonal, ok-tagh´-on-al, *adj* ottagonale

octane, ok´-tein, *n* ottano *m*

octave, ok´-tiv, *n* ottava *f*

October, ok-tou´-ba, *n* ottobre *m*

octopus, ok´-to-pus, *n* polpo *m*; piovra *f*

oculist, ok´-iu-list, *n* oculista *m/f*

odd, od, *adj* (number) dispari; (single) spaiato; (strange) strano

oddly, od´-li, *adv* stranamente

odds, ods, *npl* probabilità *f*; – and ends, cianfrusaglie *fpl*

odour, ou´-da, *n* odore *m*

of, ov, *prep* di

off, of, *prep* da; *adv* lontano; via; spento; chiuso; – and on, di tanto in tanto

offal, of´-l, *n* frattaglie *fpl*

offence, o-fens´, *n* offesa *f*; reato *m*

offend, o-fend´, *v*

offendere

offensive, o-fen´-siv, *adj** offensivo; *n* mil offensiva *f*

offer, of´-a, *v* offrire; *n* offerta *f*

offering, of´-e-ring, *n* offerta *f*

office, of´-is, *n* ufficio *m*; carica *f*

office hours, of´-is au´-es, *n* orario d'ufficio *m*

officer, of´-is-a, *n* ufficiale *m*; agente *m*

official, o-fish´-l, *n* funzionario *m*; *adj* ufficiale

officious*, o-fish´-os, *adj* ufficioso

off-licence, of´-lai-sens, *n* negozio di vini e liquori *m*

off-peak, of´-piik, *adj* (rate) ridotto

off-side, of´-said, *adj* (sport) in fuorigioco

offspring, of´-spring, *n* figlio *m*, figlia *f*

often, of´-n *adv* spesso

ogle, ou´-gl, *v* adocchiare

oil, oil, *n* olio *m*; petrolio *m*; *v* oliare; lubrificare

oil-cloth, oil´-kloZ, *n* tela cerata *f*

ointment, oint´-ment, *n* unguento *m*

old, ould, *adj* vecchio; antico

old-fashioned, ould-fash´-ond, *adj* all'antica; fuori moda, antiquato

olive, ol´-iv, *n* oliva *f*

olive oil, ol´-iv oil, *n* olio d'oliva *m*

Olympic Games, o-lim´-pik gheims, *npl* Olimpiadi *fpl*

omelet, om´-lit, *n* frittata *f*

omen, ou´-men, *n* presagio *m*

ominous, om´-i-nos, *adj* infausto; di malaugurio

omission, o-mish´-on, *n* omissione *f*

omit, o-mit´, *v* omettere; tralasciare

omnipotent, om-nip´-o-tent, *adj* onnipotente

on, on, *prep* su, sopra; *adv* (upon) sopra; (onward) avanti; (date) il; – **foot,** a piedi

once, uŏns, *adv* una volta; (formerly) un tempo; **all at –,** improvvisamente; **at –,** subito; – **more,** ancora una volta

one, uŏn, *adj* uno; (sole) unico; *pron,* uno, una; (impersonal) si; **this –,** questo; **that –,** quello

oneself, uŏn-self´, *pron refl* si; sé, se stesso, se stessa

one-way, uŏn´-uei, *adj* (street) a senso unico; (ticket) di sola andata

ongoing, on´-gou-ing, *adj* in corso

onion, ŏn´-ion, *n* cipolla *f*

on-line, on´-lain, *adj* in linea

only, oun´-li, *adv* solamente; *adj* solo, unico

onslaught, on´-sloot, *n* attacco *m*

onto, on´-tu, *prep* su, sopra

onward, on´-uad, *adv* in avanti

onyx, on´-iks, *n* onice *f*

ooze, uus, *v* stillare; sprizzare; *n* melma *f*

opal, ou´-pal, *n* opale *m*

opaque, o-peik´, *adj* opaco

open, ou´-pen, *v* aprire; *adj** aperto

opener, oup´-na, *n* apriscatole *m*

opening, oup´-ning, *n* opportunità *f*; apertura *f*

opera, op´-e-ra, *n* opera *f*

opera glasses, op´-e-ra ghlaas´-is, *npl* binocolo da teatro *m*

opera house, op´-e-ra haus, *n* teatro dell' opera *m*

operate, op´-e-reit, *v* operare

operation, op-e-rei´-shon, *n* operazione *f*

operator, op´-e-rei-ta, *n* operatore *m*; centralinista *m/f*

opinion, o-pin´-ion, *n* opinione *f*

opium, ou´-pi-um, *n* oppio *m*

opossum, o-pos´-um, *n* opossum *m*

opponent, o-pou´-nent, *n* avversario *m*

opportune*, op´-o-tiuun, *adj* opportuno

opportunity, oo-o-tiuu´-ni-ti, *n* opportunità *f*

oppose, o-pous´, *v* opporre

opposite, op´-o-sit, *n* contrario *m*; *adv* dirimpetto; di fronte

opposition, op-o-si´-shon, *n* opposizione *f*

oppress, o-pres´, *v* opprimere

oppression, o-presh´-on, *n* oppressione *f*

oppressive*, o-pres´-iv, *adj* oppressivo; opprimente

optician, op-tish´-an, *n* ottico *m*

optimism, op´-ti-mism, *n* ottimismo *m*

optimist, op´-ti-mist, *n* ottimista *m/f*

optimistic, op-ti-mis´-tik, *adj* ottimistico

option, op´-shon, *n* scelta *f*; opzione *f*

optional*, op´-shon-al, *adj* facoltativo

opulent, op´-iu-lent, *adj* opulento

or, oor, *conj* o, oppure; **–
else,** altrimenti

oral*, oor´-ral, *adj* orale

orange, o´-rinch, *n*
arancia *f; adj* (colour)
arancione

orator, o´-ra-ta, *n*
oratore *m*

oratory, o´-ra-to-ri, *n*
(speaking) oratoria *f;*
(chapel) oratorio *m*

orbit, oor´-bit, *n* orbita *f*

orchard, oor´-chad, *n*
frutteto *m*

orchestra, oor´-kis-tra, *n*
orchestra *f*

orchid, oor´-kid, *n*
orchidea *f*

ordain, oor-dein´, *v*
decretare; (clergy)
ordinare

ordeal, oor´-diil, *n*
durissima prova *f*

order, oor´-da, *n* ordine *m;
v* ordinare

orderly, oor´-de-li, *adj*
ordinato, metodico; *n
mil* attendente *m*

ordinary, oor´-di-na-ri, *adj*
ordinario; comune

ore, oor, *n* minerale
grezzo *m*

organ, oor´-gan, *n* organo
m

organic, oor-gan´-ik *adj*
organico; (vegetables)
biologico

organisation, oor-gan-ai-

sei´-shon, *n*
organizzazione *f*

organize, oor´-gan-ais, *v*
organizzare

orgasm, oor´-gasm, *n*
orgasmo *m*

orgy, oor´-chi, *n* orgia *f*

orient, oor´-ri-ent, *n*
oriente *m*

oriental, oor-ri-en´-tal, *adj*
orientale

origin, o´-ri-chin, *n*
origine *f*

original, o-rich´-in-al, *adj*
originale

originate, o-rich´-in-eit, *v*
dare origine a; aver
origine da

ornament, oor´-na-ment,
n ornamento *m*

ornamental, oor-na-men´-
tal, *adj* ornamentale

orphan, oor´-fan, *n*
orfano *m*

orphanage, oor´-fan-ich, *n*
orfanotrofio *m*

orthodox, oor´-Zo-doks,
adj ortodosso

oscillate, os´-il-eit, *v*
oscillare

ostentatious*, os-tin-tei´-
shos, *adj* ostentato

ostrich, os´-trich, *n* struzzo
m

other, ŏD´-a, *adj* altro,
altra, altri, altre; **the –
one,** l'altro, l'altra

otherwise, ŏD´-e-uais, *adv*

altrimenti

otter, ot´-a, *n* lontra *f*

ought, oot, *v* dovere;
bisognare

ounce, auns, *n* oncia *f*
(28.35 g)

our, aur, *adj* nostro,
nostra, nostri, nostre

ours, aurs, *pron* il nostro,
la nostra, i nostri, le
nostre; **a friend of –,** un
nostro amico

ourselves, aur-selvs´, *pron
refl* ci; noi stessi

out, aut, *adv* fuori;
(extinguished) spento

outbid, aut-bid´, *v* fare
un'offerta maggiore

outbreak, aut´-breik, *n*
scoppio *m*; epidemia *f*

outburst, aut´-berst, *n*
scoppio *m*

outcry, aut´-krai, *n*
protesta *f*

outdo, aut-duu´, *v*
superare

outdoor, aut´-door, *adj*
all'aperto

outer, aut´-a, *adj* esterno

outfit, aut´-fit, *n*
completo *m*; tenuta *f*;
attrezzatura *f*

outgrow, aut-grou´, *v*
diventare troppo grande
per

outing, au´-ting, *n* gita *f*

outlast, aut-laast´, *v*
sopravvivere a

outlaw, aut´-loo, n
fuorilegge m/f; v bandire

outlet, aut´-lit, n sbocco
m; valvola di sfogo f;
comm punto vendita m

outline, aut´-lain, n
abbozzo m; contorno m;
profilo m; v descrivere a
grandi linee

outlive, aut-liv´, v
sopravvivere a

outlook, aut´-luk, n
prospettiva f; visione f;
vista f

outlying, aut-lai´-ing, adj
remoto

outnumber, aut-nŏm´-ba,
v superare
numericamente

out-patient, aut´-pei-
shent, n paziente
esterno m

outpost, aut´-poust, n
avamposto m

output, aut´-put, n
rendimento m;
produzione f

outrage, aut´-reich, n
oltraggio m; atrocità f

outrageous*, aut-rei´-
chŏs, adj scioccante;
stravagante

outright, aut-rait´, adv
completamente

outrun, aut-rŏn´, v
superare in velocità

outside, aut-said´, adv
(outdoors) fuori,

all'esterno; n esterno m;
adj esterno

outsize, aut´-sais, n taglia
forte f

outskirts, aut´-skerts, npl
periferia f

outstanding*, aut-stan´-
ding, adj eccellente;
saliente; (debts) non
pagato

outward, aut´-uad, adv
verso l'esterno; adj
esteriore

outwit, aut-uit´, v
mostrarsi più astuto di

oval, ou´-val, n ovale m;
adj ovale

oven, ŏv´-en, n forno m

over, ou´-va, prep su;
sopra; al di sopra di; di
là di; più di; adv al di
sopra; (finished) finito;
– **here,** qui; – **there,** là;
all –, (everywhere)
dappertutto

overalls, ou´-ve-rools, npl
tuta da lavoro f

overbearing, ou-ve-ber´-
ring, adj prepotente;
autoritario

overboard, ou´-ve-boord,
adv fuori bordo

overcast, ou´-ve-kaast, adj
coperto

overcharge, ou-ve-
chaarch´, v far pagare
troppo

overcoat, ou´-ve-kout, n

cappotto m

overcome, ou-ve-kŏm´, v
vincere; superare

overdo, ou-ve-duu´, v
strafare; esagerare;
(cooking) cuocere
troppo

overdraft, ou´-ve-draaft, n
scoperto di conto m

overdraw, ou-ve-droo´, v
avere uno scoperto di
conto

overdue, ou-ve-diuu´, adj
in ritardo; (debt)
scaduto

overflow, ou-ve-flou´, v
traboccare

overgrow, ou-ve-grou´, v
crescere troppo

overhang, ou-ve-hang´, v
sporgere

overhaul, ou-ve-hool´, v
rivedere; revisionare

overhead, ou-ve-hed´, adv
in alto

overhear, ou-ve-hir´, v
sentire per caso

overjoyed, ou-ve-choid´,
adj pazzo di gioia

overland, ou´-ve-land, adv
per via (di) terra

overlap, ou-ve-lap´, v
sovrapporsi

overload, ou-ve-loud´, v
sovraccaricare

overlook, ou-ve-luk´, v
(view) dare su; (miss)
trascurare; (pardon)

passare sopra a

overnight, ou-ve-nait´, *adv* (durante) la notte; (stay) di una notte; *fig* improvviso

overpower, ou-ve-pau´-a, *v* sopraffare

overrate, ou-ve-reit´, *v* sopravvalutare

overrule, ou-ve-ruul´, *v* (set aside) respingere

overrun, ou-ve-rŏn´, *v* protrarsi

overseas, ou-ve-siis´, *adv* all'estero

oversee, ou-ve-sii´, *v* sorvegliare

oversight, ou´-ve-sait, *n* svista *f*

oversleep, ou-ve-sliip´, *v* non svegliarsi in tempo

overstep, ou-ve-step´, *v* eccedere

overtake, ou-ve-teik´, *v* sorpassare

overthrow, ou-ve-Zrou´, *v* rovesciare

overtime, ou´-ve-taim, *n* (work) straordinario *m*

overturn, ou-ve-tern´, *v* rovesciare; rovesciarsi

overweight, ou-ve-ueit´, *adj* sovrappeso

overwhelm, ou-ve-uelm´, *v* sopraffare

overwork, ou-ve-uerk´, *v* lavorare troppo

owe, ou, *v* dovere

owing, ou´-ing, *adj* (money) dovuto; **– to,** *prep* a causa di

owl, aul, *n* gufo *m*

own, oun, *v* possedere; ammettere; *adj* proprio

owner, ou´-na, *n* proprietario *m*

ox, oks, *n* bue *m*

oxygen, ok´-si-chen *n* ossigeno *m*

oyster, ois´-ta, *n* ostrica *f*

ozone, ou´-soun, *n* ozono *m*

ozone-friendly, ou´-soun frend´-li, *adj* che rispetta l'ozono

ozone layer, ou´-soun lei´-a, *n* ozonosfera *f*

pace, peis, *v* camminare su e giù; *n* passo *m*; (speed) velocità *f*

pacific, pa-si´-fik, *adj* pacifico

pacify, pas´-i-fai, *v* placare

pack, pak, *v* imballare; fare i bagagli; *n* pacco *m*; (wolves) branco *m*; (cards) mazzo *m*

package, pa´-kich, *n* pacchetto *m*

package holiday, pa´-kich hol´-i-dei, *n* vacanza organizzata *f*

packed lunch, pakt lönch´, *n* pranzo al sacco *m*

packet, pak´-it, *n* pacchetto *m*

packing, pak´-ing, *n* imballaggio *m*

pact, pakt, *n* patto *m*

pad, pad, *v* imbottire; *n* imbottitura *f*; (ink) tampone *m*; (paper) bloc-notes *m*

padding, pad´-ing, *n* imbottitura *f*

paddle, pad´-l, *v* remare con la pagaia; (feet) sguazzare; *n* pagaia *f*

paddock, pad´-ok, *n* (meadow) pascolo *m*; (at races) recinto *m*

padlock, pad´-lok, *n* lucchetto *m*; *v* chiudere col lucchetto

paediatrician, pii-di-a-tri´-shan, *n* pediatra *m/f*

pagan, pei´-gan, *n* pagano *m*

page, peich, *n* pagina *f*

pageant, pach´-ent, *n* corteo *m*; parata *f*

pager, pei´-cha, *n* cercapersone *m*

pail, peil, *n* secchio *m*

pain, pein, *n* dolore *m*

painful*, pein´-ful, *adj* doloroso

painless, pein´-lis, *adj* indolore

paint, peint, *v* dipingere, verniciare; *n* pittura *f*, vernice *f*, colore *m*

painter, pein´-ta, *n* pittore *m*, pittrice *f*; imbianchino *m*

painting, pein´-ting, *n* pittura *f*; dipinto *m*, quadro *m*

pair, per, *n* paio *m*

palace, pal´-is, *n* palazzo *m*

palatable, pal´-i-ta-bl, *adj* gustoso

palate, pal´-it, *n* palato *m*

pale, peil, *adj* pallido; *v* impallidire

paleness, peil´-nis, *n* pallore *m*

palette, pal-et´, *n* tavolozza *f*

pallid, pal´-id, *adj* pallido

palm, paam, *n* palma *f*; palmo *m*

palpitation, pal-pi-tei´-shon, *n* palpitazione *f*

paltry, pool´-tri, *adj* meschino

pamper, pam´-pa, *v* coccolare, viziare

pamphlet, pam´-flit, n opuscolo m

pan, pan, n padella f; casseruola f

pancake, pan´-keik, n frittella f; crêpe f

pander, pan´-da, v assecondare

pane, pein, n vetro m; (large) vetrata f

panel, pan´-l, n pannello m; giuria f

pang, pang, n dolore m; (mental) angoscia f

panic, pan´-ik, n panico m

pansy, pan´-si, n viola del pensiero f

pant, pant, v ansimare

panther, pan´-Za, n pantera f

pantomime, pan´-to-maim, n pantomima f; (Xmas) spettacolo di Natale m

pantry, pan´-tri, n (food) dispensa f

pants, pants, npl mutande fpl

pap, pap, n pappa f

papal, pei´-pal, adj papale

paper, pei´-pa, n carta f; (newspaper) giornale m; v tappezzare

par, paar, n pari f; adj alla pari

parable, pa´-ra-bl, n parabola f

parachute, pa´-ra-shuut, n paracadute m

parade, pa-reid´, n sfilata f; parata f; (troops) rivista f

paradise, pa´-ra-dais, n paradiso m

paraffin, pa´-ra-fin, n paraffina f; cherosene m

parallel, pa´-ra-lel, adj parallelo

paralyse, pa´-ra-lais, v paralizzare

paralysis, pa-ral´-i-sis, n paralisi f

parapet, pa´-ra-pet, n parapetto m

parasite, pa´-ra-sait, n parassita m

parcel, paar´-sel, n pacco m

parched, paarcht, adj disseccato, riarso; (person) assetato

parchment, paarch´-ment, n pergamena f

pardon, paar´-dn, v perdonare; (grant) graziare; n perdono m; grazia f

parents, per´-rents, npl genitori mpl

Paris, pa´-ris, n Parigi f

parish, pa´-rish, n parrocchia f

park, paark, n parco m; v parcheggiare

parking, paar´-king, n parcheggio m; "no –", "sosta vietata"

parking ticket, paar´-king tik´-it, n multa per sosta vietata f

parliament, paar´-la-ment, n parlamento m

parlour, paar´-la, n salottino m

parrot, pa´-rot, n pappagallo m

parry, pa´-ri, v parare

parse, paars, v fare l'analisi grammaticale

parsimonious*, paar-si-mou´-ni-os, adj parsimonioso

parsley, paars´-li, n prezzemolo m

parsnip, paars´-nip, n pastinaca f

parson, paar´-son, n parroco m

parsonage, paar´-son-ich, n casa parrocchiale f

part, paart, v dividere, separare; n parte f

partake, paar-teik´, – in, v partecipare a; – of, prendere

partial, paar´-shal, adj parziale; – to, favorevole a

partiality, paar-shi-al´-i-ti, n parzialità f

participate, paar-tis´-i-peit, v partecipare

participle, paar´-ti-si-pl, n participio m

particle, paar´-ti-kl, *n*
particella *f*

particular*, pa-tik´-iu-la,
adj particolare;
(fastidious) esigente;
(exact) minuzioso

particulars, pa-tik´-iu-las,
npl particolari *mpl*,
dettagli *mpl*; (personal)
dati *mpl*

parting, paar´-ting, *n*
separazione *f*; (hair)
scriminatura *f*, riga *f*

partition, paar-tish´-on, *n*
divisione *f*

partly, paart´-li, *adv*
parzialmente, in parte

partner, paart´-na, *n*
(business) socio *m*;
(cards) compagno *m*;
(dance) cavaliere *m*,
dama *f*

partnership, paart´-ne-
ship, *n* associazione *f*;
società *f*

partridge, paar´-trich, *n*
pernice *f*

party, paar´-ti, *n* partito
m; festa *f*

pass, paas, *v* passare;
(examination) superare

passage, pas-ich, *n*
passaggio *m*; corridoio
m; (travel) traversata *f*

passbook, paas´-buk, *n*
libretto di risparmio *m*

passenger, pas´-in-cha, *n*
passeggero *m*

passer-by, pas-e-bai´, *n*,
passante *m/f*

passion, pash´-on, *n*
passione *f*

passionate*, pash´-on-at,
adj appassionato

Passover, paas´-ou-va, *n*
Pasqua ebraica *f*

passport, paas´-poort, *n*
passaporto *m*

past, paast, *n* passato *m*;
adj passato; *prep* oltre

paste, peist, *n* colla *f*;
impasto *m*; *v* incollare

pastel, past´-l, *n* pastello *m*

pastime, paas´-taim, *n*
passatempo *m*

pastor, paas´-ta, *n relig*
pastore *m*

pastries, peis´-tris, *npl*
pasticcini *mpl*

pastry, peis´-tri, *n* pasta *f*

pasture, paas´-cha, *n*
pascolo *m*

pat, pat, *v* battere
dolcemente; *n*
colpetto *m*

patch, pach, *n* pezza *f*,
toppa *f*; *v* rattoppare

patent, pei´-tent, *n*
brevetto *m*; *v* brevettare

patent leather, pei´-tent
leD´-a, *n* vernice *f*

paternal*, pa-ter´-nal, *adj*
paterno

path, paaZ, *n* sentiero *m*

pathetic, pa-Zet´-ik, *adj*
patetico

patience, pei´-shens, *n*
pazienza *f*

patient, pei´-shent, *adj*
paziente; *n* paziente *m/f*

patriot, pei´-tri-ot, *n*
patriota *m/f*

patriotic, pei-tri-ot´-ik, *adj*
patriottico

patrol, pa-troul´, *n*
pattuglia *f*; *v* pattugliare

patronize, pat´-ron-ais, *v*
trattare con
condiscendenza

pattern, pat´-en, *n* motivo
m, disegno *m*; modello
m, cartamodello *m*

paunch, poonch, *n*
pancia *f*

pauper, poo´-pa, *n*
indigente *m/f*

pause, poos, *n* pausa *f*; *v*
fare una pausa

pave, peiv, *v* lastricare

pavement, peiv´-ment, *n*
marciapiede *m*

pavilion, pa-vil´-ion, *n*
padiglione *m*

paw, poo, *n* zampa *f*

pawn, poon, *v* impegnare;
n pegno *m*; (chess)
pedina *f*

pawnbroker's, poon´-
brou-kes, *n* monte di
pietà *m*

pay, pei, *v* pagare

payable, pei´-a-bl, *adj*
pagabile

payment, pei´-ment, *n*

pagamento m

payphone, pei´-foun, n
telefono pubblico m

pea, pii, n pisello m

peace, piis, n pace f

peaceful*, piis´-ful, adj
pacifico

peach, piich, n pesca f

peacock, pii´-kok, n
pavone m

peak, piik, n picco m;
punta f; apice m

peak hours, piik´-au-es,
npl ore di punta fpl

peal, piil, n (bells)
scampanio m; (thunder)
rimbombo m; v suonare

peanut, pii´-nöt, n
arachide f, nocciolina
americana f

peanut butter, pii´-nöt
böt´-a, n burro
d'arachidi m

pear, per, n pera f; (tree)
pero m

pearl, perl, n perla f

peasant, pes´-ant, n
contadino m,
contadina f

peat, piit, n torba f

pebble, peb´-l, n
ciottolo m

peck, pek, v beccare; n
beccata f

peculiar*, pi-kiuu´-li-a,
adj bizzarro, strano

pecuniary, pi-kiuu´-ni-a-
ri, adj pecuniario

pedal, ped´-l, n pedale m;
v pedalare

pedantic, pi-dan´-tik, adj
pedante

pedestal, ped´-is-tl, n
piedistallo m

pedestrian, pi-des´-tri-an,
n pedone m

pedigree, ped´-i-grii, adj di
razza pura

pedlar, ped´-la, n
venditore ambulante m

peel, piil, n buccia f; v
sbucciare; spellare

peep, piip, v sbirciare; n
sbirciata f

peer, pir, n pari m

peerage, pir´-ich, n dignità
di pari f

peevish, pii´-vish, adj
scontroso

peg, pegh, n (tent)
picchetto m; (hats)
attaccapanni m;
(clothes) molletta f

pellet, pel´-it, n pallottola
f; (shot) pallino m

pelt, pelt, v colpire con; n
(fur) pelliccia f

pen, pen, n penna f;
(sheep) ovile m

penal, pii´-nal, adj penale

penalty, pen´-al-ti, n pena
f; ammenda f; (football)
rigore m

penance, pen´-ans, n
penitenza f

pence, pens, npl penny m

pencil, pen´-sil, n matita f

pendant, pen´-dant, n
pendente m

pending, pen´-ding, adj
pendente; prep durante

pendulum, pen´-diu-lum,
n pendolo m

penetrate, pen´-i-treit, v
penetrate

penfriend, pen´-frend, n
amico di penna m

penguin, peng´-guin, n
pinguino m

penicillin, pen-i-si´-lin, n
penicillina f

peninsula, pen-in´-siu-la,
n penisola f

penis, pii´-nis, n pene m

penitent, pen´-i-tent, adj
penitente

penknife, pen´-naif, n
temperino m

penniless, pen´-i-lis, adj
senza un soldo

penny, pen´-i, n penny m

pension, pen´-shon, n
pensione f

pensioner, pen´-shon-a, n
pensionato m,
pensionata f

pensive*, pen´-siv, adj
pensieroso

people, pii´-pl, n gente f;
persone fpl; popolo m

pepper, pep´-a, n pepe m

peppermint, pep´-e-mint,
n menta piperita f

per, per, prep per

perceive, pe-siiv´, v
percepire

per cent, pe-sent´, adv per
cento

percentage, pe-sen´-tich, n
percentuale f

perception, pe-sep´-shon,
n percezione f

perceptive, pe-sep´-tiv, adj
perspicace

perch, perch, n posatoio
m; (fish) pesce persico m

peremptory, pi-remp´-to-
ri, adj perentorio

perfect, per´-fikt, adj*
perfetto; v perfezionare

perfection, pe-fek´-shon, n
perfezione f

perfidious*, pe-fid´-i-os,
adj perfido

perfidy, per´-fi-di, n
perfidia f

perforate, per´-fo-reit, v
perforare

perform, pe-foorm´, v
eseguire; (fulfill)
compiere; (stage)
rappresentare

performance, pe-foorm´-
ans, n prestazioni
fpl; (stage)
rappresentazione f

perfume, per´-fiuum, n
profumo m; v profumare

perhaps, pe-haps´, adv
forse

peril, pe´-ril, n pericolo m

period, pir´-ri-od, n

periodo m; (woman)
mestruazioni fpl

periodical, pir-ri-od´-i-kl,
adj periodico; n
periodico m

periscope, pe´-ris-koup, n
periscopio m

perish, pe´-rish, v perire;
deteriorarsi

perishable, pe´-ri-sha-bl,
adj deperibile

perjury, per´-chu-ri, n
spergiuro m; falso
giuramento m

perm, perm, n
permanente f

permanent, per´-ma-nent,
adj permanente

permeate, per´-mi-eit, v
permeare

permission, pe-mish´-on,
n permesso m

permit, pe-mit´, v
permettere

permit, per´-mit, n
permesso m,
autorizzazione f

perpendicular, per-pen-
dik´-iu-la, adj
perpendicolare; n
perpendicolare f

perpetrate, per´-pi-treit, v
perpetrare

perpetual*, pe-pet´-iu-al,
adj perpetuo

perplex, pe-pleks´, v
lasciare perplesso

persecute, per´-si-kiuut, v

perseguitare

persecution, per-si-kiuu´-
shon, n persecuzione f

perseverance, per-si-vir´-
rens, n perseveranza f

persevere, per-si-vir´, v
perseverare

persist, pe-sist´, v
persistere

person, per´-son, n
persona f

personal, per´-son-al, adj
personale

personality, per-so-na´-li-
ti, n personalità f

personify, pe-so´-ni-fai, v
personificare

perspective, pe-spek´-tiv,
n prospettiva f

perspiration, per-spi-rei´-
shon, n traspirazione f

perspire, pe-spair´, v
traspirare

persuade, pe-sueid´, v
persuadere

persuasion, pe-suei´-shon,
n persuasione f

pert*, pert, adj
impertinente

pertain, pe-tein´, v
appartenere a;
riguardare

pertinent, per´-ti-nent, adj
pertinente

perturb, pe-terb´, v
turbare

perverse*, pe-vers´, adj
perverso

pervert, pe-vert´, v
pervertire; traviare

pessimism, pes´-i-mism, n
pessimismo m

pessimist, pes´-i-mist, n
pessimista m/f

pessimistic, pes-i-mis´-tik,
adj pessimistico

pest, pest, n peste f

pester, pes´-ta, v
tormentare, dare
fastidio a

pet, pet, v coccolare; n
(animal) animale
domestico m; (person)
favorito m

petal, pet´-l, n petalo m

petition, pi-tish´-on, n
petizione f

petrified, pet´-ri-faid, adj
terrorizzato

petrol, pet´-rol, n
benzina f

petroleum, pi-trou´-li-om,
n petrolio m

petroleum jelly, pi-trou´-
li-om chel´-i, n
vaselina f

petrol pump, pet´-rol
pŏmp, n distributore di
benzina m

petrol station, pet´-rol
stei´-shon, stazione di
servizio f

petticoat, pet´-i-kout, n
sottoveste f

petty, pet´-i, adj
insignificante; meschino

pew, piuu, n banco di
chiesa m

pewter, piu´-ta, n peltro m

phantom, fan´-tom, n
fantasma m

pharmacist, faar´-ma-sist,
n farmacista m/f

pharmacy, faar´-ma-si, n
farmacia f

phase, feis, n fase f

pheasant, fes´-ant, n
fagiano m

phenomenon, fi-nom´-i-
non, n fenomeno m

phial, fai´-al, n fiala f

philosopher, fi-los´-o-fa, n
filosofo m

phlegm, flem, n flemma m

phobia, fou´-bi-a, n fobia f

phone, foun, n telefono m;
v telefonare

phosphate, fos´-feit, n
fosfato m

phosphorus, fos´-fo-ros, n
fosforo m

photo, fou´-tou, n foto f

photocopy, fou-to-kop´-i,
n fotocopia f; v
fotocopiare

photograph, fou´-to-graaf,
n fotografia f

photographer, fo-togh´-ra-
fa, n fotografo m,
fotografa f

phrase, freis, n frase f

physical*, fis´-i-kl, adj
fisico

physician, fi-sish´-an, n

medico m

physics, fi´-siks, n fisica f

piano, pi-an´-ou, n
pianoforte m

pick, pik, n piccone m; v
scegliere; (gather)
cogliere; – up,
raccogliere; passare a
prendere; rimorchiare

pickle, pik´-l, v conservare
in aceto

pickles, pik´-ls, npl
sottaceti mpl

pickpocket, pik´-pok-it, n
borsaiolo m

picnic, pik´-nik, n
picnic m

picture, pik´-cha, n
quadro m; illustrazione f;
foto f

pie, pai, n pasticcio m;
torta f

piece, piis, n pezzo m

piecemeal, piis´-miil, adv
poco alla volta

pier, pir, n molo m

pierce, pirs, v forare; fig
penetrare

piercing, pir´-sing, adj
penetrante

piety, pai´-i-ti, n pietà f

pig, pigh, n maiale m

pigeon, pich´-in, n
piccione m

pigeonhole, pich´-in-houl,
n (division) casella f

pig-iron, pigh´-ai-on, n
ghisa f

pigsty, pigh´-stai, *n* porcile *m*

pike, paik, *n* (fish) luccio *m*

pilchard, pil´-chad, *n* sardina *f*

pile, pail, *n* (heap) pila *f*; mucchio *m*; *v* ammucchiare

piles, pails, *npl med* emorroidi *fpl*

pile-up, pail´-ŏp, *n* tamponamento a catena *m*

pilfer, pil´-fa, *v* rubacchiare

pilgrim, pil´-grim, *n* pellegrino *m*

pilgrimage, pil´-gri-mich, *n* pellegrinaggio *m*

pill, pil, *n* pillola *f*

pillage, pil´-ich, *n* saccheggio *m*

pillar, pil´-a, *n* pilastro *m*, colonna *f*

pillow, pil´-ou, *n* guanciale *m*

pillowcase, pil´-ou-keis, *n* federa *f*

pilot, pai´-lot, *n* pilota *m/f*; *v* pilotare

pimple, pim´-pl, *n* foruncolo *m*

pin, pin, *n* spillo *m*; *v* fissare con spilli

pinafore, pin´-a-foor, *n* grembiulino *m*

pincers, pin´-ses, *npl* pinze

fpl; tenaglie *fpl*

pinch, pinch, *n* pizzicotto *m*; *v* pizzicare; (shoes) far male

pine, pain, *n* pino *m*; – **for,** *v* languire

pineapple, pain´-ap-l, *n* ananas *m*

pink, pingk, *adj* rosa; *n* rosa *m*

pint, paint, *n* pinta *f* (= 0,57 l)

pioneer, pai-o-nir´, *n* pioniere *m*

pious*, pai´-us, *adj* pio

pip, pip, *n* seme *m*

pipe, paip, *n* tubo *m*; (tobacco) pipa *f*

pirate, pair´-rat, *n* pirata *m*; *v* riprodurre abusivamente

Pisces, pai´-siis, *n* Pesci *mpl*

pistol, pis´-tl, *n* pistola *f*

piston, pis´-ton, *n* pistone *m*

pit, pit, *n* fosso *m*; (theatre) platea *f*

pitch, pich, *n* (sport) campo *m*; (tar) pece *f*; *mus* tono *m*; *v* (throw) lanciare

pitcher, pich´-a, *n* brocca *f*

pitchfork, pich´-foork, *n* forcone *m*

pitfall, pit´-fool, *n* trabocchetto *m*

pith, piZ, *n* midollo *m*;

essenza *f*

pitiable, pit´-i-a-bl, *adj* pietoso

pitiful, pit´-i-ful, *adj* compassionevole

pitiless, pit´-i-lis, *adj* senza pietà

pity, pit´-i, *n* compassione *f*; **what a –!** che peccato!

pivot, piv´-ot, *n* perno *m*; *v* imperniare

placard, plak´-aard, *n* cartello *m*

placate, pla-keit´, *v* placare

place, pleis, *n* luogo *m*; posto *m*; *v* mettere

placid*, plas´-id, *adj* placido

plagiarism, plei´-chia-rism, *n* plagio *m*

plague, pleigh, *n* peste *f*; *v* tormentare

plaice, pleis, *n* sogliola *f*

plain, plein, *n* pianura *f*; *adj** (simple) semplice; (looks) ordinario; (clear) chiaro

plait, plat, *n* treccia *f*; *v* intrecciare

plan, plan, *n* piano *m*, progetto *m*; (draft) schema *m*; *v* progettare; organizzare

plane, plein, *v* piallare; *n* pialla *f*; (geom) piano *m*; (tree) platano *m*;

aereo m

planet, plan´-it, n
pianeta m

plank, plangk, n tavola f,
asse f

plant, plaant, v piantare; n
pianta f; impianto m;
stabilimento m

plantation, plaan-tei´-
shon, n piantagione f

plaster, plaas´-ta, v
ingessare; n gesso m;
(building) intonaco m

plastic, plas´-tik, adj di
plastica; n plastica f

plastic surgery, plas´-tik
ser´-che-ri, n chirurgia
plastica f

plate, pleit, v (metal)
placcare; n (food) piatto
m; targa f

platform, plat´-foorm, n
piattaforma f

platinum, plat´-i-num, n
platino m

play, plei, v giocare;
suonare; interpretare; n
gioco m;
rappresentazione f

player, plei-a, n giocatore
m, giocatrice f; musicista
m/f; attore m, attrice f

playful*, plei´-ful, adj
giocoso; scherzoso

playground, plei´-graund,
n (school) cortile per la
ricreazione m; (park)
campo giochi m

plea, plii, n appello m;
supplica f; pretesto m

plead, pliid, v supplicare;
law difendere

pleasant, ples´-ant, adj
gradevole, piacevole

please, pliis, interj per
favore; v piacere a

pleased, pliisd, adj
contento; soddisfatto

pleasing, pliis´-sing, adj
piacente; gradevole

pleasure, plesh´-a, n
piacere m

pledge, plech, n pegno m;
promessa f; v impegnare;
promettere

plenty, plen´-ti, n
abbondanza f; molto

pliable, plai´-a-bl, adj
malleabile

pliers, plai´-as, npl pinze
fpl

plight, plait, n situazione f

plimsolls, plim´-sols, npl
scarpe da tennis fpl

plod, plod, v (work)
sgobbare; – along,
camminare a fatica

plodder, plod´-a, n
sgobbone m

plot, plot, n complotto m;
(story) intreccio m;
(land) lotto m; v
complottare

plough, plau, v arare; n
aratro m

ploughman, plau´-man, n

aratore m

ploughman's lunch, plau´-
mans-lönch, n piatto a
base di formaggio, pane
e sottaceti

pluck, plök, v cogliere;
spennare; n fig fegato m

plug, plögh, v tappare;
infilare la spina di; n
tappo m; (electric)
spina f

plum, plöm, n prugna f;
susina f; (tree) susino m

plumage, pluu´-mich, n
piumaggio m

plumb, plöm, n piombo m

plumber, plöm´-a, n
idraulico m

plump, plömp, adj
grassoccio

plunder, plön´-da, n
saccheggio m; v
saccheggiare

plunderer, plön´-de-ra, n
saccheggiatore m

plunge, plönch, v tuffarsi;
immergere; n tuffo m

plural, pluur´-ral, n
plurale m

plus, plös, n più m; prep
più

plush, plösh, n felpa f

ply, plai, v (trade)
esercitare; n (wool)
capo m

plywood, plai´-uud, n
compensato m

pneumatic, niu-mat´-ik,

adj pneumatico

pneumonia, niu-mou´-ni-a, *n* polmonite *f*

poach, pooch, *v* cacciare di frodo; (cook) affogare

poacher, pooch´-a, *n* bracconiere *m*

P.O. box, pii-ou´-boks, *n* casella postale *f*

pocket, pok´-it, *v* intascare; *n* tasca *f*

pod, pod, *n* guscio *m*, baccello *m*

poem, pou´-im, *n* poesia *f*

poet, pou´-it, *n* poeta *m/f*

poetry, pou´-it-ri, *n* poesia *f*

point, point, *v* indicare; mostrare; (sharpen) appuntire; *n* (tip) punta *f*; (punctuation, position) punto *m*

pointer, poin´-ta, *n* indicatore *m*

pointless, point´-lis, *adj* inutile, vano

poise, pois, *n* portamento *m*

poison, poi´-son, *n* veleno *m*; *v* avvelenare

poisonous, poi´-son-os, *adj* velenoso

poke, pouk, *n* colpetto *m*; *v* dare colpetti; (fire) attizzare

poker, pou´-ka, *n* attizzatoio *m*; (cards) poker *m*

pole, poul, *n* palo *m*; (arctic) polo *m*

police, po-liis´, *n* polizia *f*

policeman, po-liis´-man, *n* poliziotto *m*

policewoman, po-liis´-uu-man, *n* donna poliziotto *f*

police station, po-liis´ stei´-shon, *n* centrale di polizia *f*

policy, pol´-i-si, *n* politica *f*, linea di condotta *f*; (insurance) polizza *f*

polish, pol´-ish, *v* lucidare; *n* lucido *m*

polite, po-lait´, *adj* educato, cortese

politeness, po-lait´-nis, *n* educazione *f*, cortesia *f*

political, po-lit´-i-kl, *adj* politico

politician, pol-i-tish´-an, *n* personaggio politico *m*

politics, pol´-i-tiks, *n* politica *f*

poll, poul, *n* votazione *f*; *v* votare

pollen, pol´-en, *n* polline *m*

pollute, po-luut´, *v* inquinare

pollution, po-luu´-shon, *n* inquinamento *m*

polyester, pol-i-es´-ta, *n* poliestere *m*

polystyrene, pol-i-stai´-riin, *n* polistirolo *m*

pomegranate, pom´-i-gra-nit, *n* melagrana *f*; (tree) melograno *m*

pomp, pomp, *n* pompa *f*, fasto *m*

pompous*, pom´-pos, *adj* pomposo

pond, pond, *n* laghetto *m*

ponder, pon´-da, *v* ponderare

ponderous*, pon´-de-ros, *adj* ponderoso, pesante

pontiff, pon´-tif, *n* pontefice *m*

pony, pou´-ni, *n* pony *m*

poodle, puu´-dl, *n* barboncino *m*

pool, puul, *n* (pond) stagno *m*; (puddle, blood) pozza *f*; (swimming) piscina *f*; *v* mettere insieme

poor, poor, *adj** povero; *n* povero *m*

pop, pop, *v* scoppiettare; *n* scoppiettio *m*; *mus* pop *m*

popcorn, pop´-koorn, *n* popcorn *m*

Pope, poup, *n* Papa *m*

poplar, pop´-la, *n* pioppo *m*

popper, pop´-a, *n* bottone automatico *m*

poppy, pop´-i, *n* papavero *m*

popular, pop´-iu-la, *adj* popolare

populate, pop´-iu-leit, *v*
popolare

population, pop-iu-lei´-shon, *n* popolazione *f*

populous, pop´-iu-los, *adj*
popoloso

porcelain, poor-si-lin, *n*
porcellana *f*

porch, poorch, *n*
portico *m*

porcupine, poor´-kiu-pain, *n* porcospino *m*

pore, poor, *n* poro *m*; –
over, *v* essere
immerso in

pork, poork, *n* carne di
maiale *f*

pornographic, poor-no-gra´-fik, pornografico

pornography, poor-no-gra-fi, *n* pornografia *f*

porous, poor´-ros, *adj*
poroso

porpoise, poor´-pos, *n*
focena *f*

porridge, po´-rich, *n*
porridge *m*, pappa
d'avena *f*

port, poort, *n* porto *m*;
naut babordo *m*

portable, poor´-ta-bl, *adj*
portatile

porter, poor´-ta, *n* (door)
portinaio *m*; (luggage)
portabagagli *m*,
facchino *m*

portfolio, poort-fou´-li-ou,
n cartella *f*; (ministerial)

portafoglio *m*

porthole, poort´-houl, *n*
oblò *m*

portion, poor´-shon, *n*
porzione *f*

portly, poort´-li, *adj*
(stout) corpulento

portrait, poort´-reit, *n*
ritratto *m*

portray, poor-trei´, *v*
ritrarre; (describe)
descrivere

Portugal, poor´-tiu-gal, *n*
Portogallo *m*

Portuguese, poor´-tiu-ghiis, *adj* portoghese

pose, pous, *n* posa *f*; *v*
posare; – **as,** farsi passare
per

position, po-sish´-on, *n*
posizione *f*

positive*, pos´-i-tiv, *adj*
positivo; (certain) certo

possess, po-ses´, *v*
possedere

possession, po-sesh´-on, *n*
possesso *m*

possessive, po-ses´-iv, *adj*
possessivo

possessor, po-ses´-a, *n*
possessore *m*

possibility, pos-i-bil´-i-ti,
n possibilità *f*

possible, pos´-i-bl, *adj*
possibile

possibly, pos´-i-bli, *adv*
forse

post, poust, *v* impostare; *n*

posta *f*; (wood, iron)
palo *m*; (job) posto *m*

postage, pous´-tich, *n*
affrancatura *f*

postal, pous´-tl, *adj* postale

postbox, poust´-boks, *n*
buca delle lettere *f*

postcard, poust´-kaard, *n*
cartolina *f*

postcode, poust´-koud, *n*
codice postale *m*

postdate, poust-deit´, *v*
postdatare

poster, pous´-ta, *n*
affisso *m*

posterior, pos-tir´-ri-a, *n*
didietro *m*; *adj*
posteriore

posterity, pos-te´-ri-ti, *n*
posterità *f*

postgraduate, poust-grad´-iu-*at*, *n* laureato che
segue un corso di
specializzazione

postman, poust´-man, *n*
postino *m*

postmark, poust´-maark, *n*
timbro postale *m*

postmortem, poust-moor´-tem, *n* autopsia *f*

post office, poust´-of-is, *n*
ufficio postale *m*

postpone, pous-poun´, *v*
posticipare, rinviare

postscript, poust´-skript, *n*
post scriptum *m*

posture, pos´-cha, *n*
postura *f*

pot, pot, n vaso m; pentola f; (tea) teiera f; (coffee) caffettiera f; v mettere in vaso

potato, po-tei´-tou, n patata f

potent, pou´-tent, adj potente

potion, pou´-shon, n pozione f

pottery, pot´-e-ri, n ceramica f

pouch, pauch, n borsa f; marsupio m

poulterer, poul´-te-ra, n pollivendolo m

poultice, poul´-tis, n impiastro m, cataplasma m

poultry, poul´-tri, n pollame m

pounce, pauns, v (on, upon) piombare addosso

pound, paund, n sterlina f; (weight) libbra f (= 453 g); v pestare, polverizzare

pour, poor, v versare; (rain) piovere a dirotto; – out, (serve) versare

pout, paut, v fare il broncio; n broncio m

poverty, pov´-e-ti, n povertà f

powder, pau´-da, v polverizzare; (face) incipriarsi; n polvere f; cipria f

power, pau´-a, n potere m; mech forza f, energia f

powerful*, pau´-e-ful, adj potente

powerless, pau´-e-lis, adj impotente

practicable, prak´-ti-ka-bl, adj attuabile

practical*, prak´-ti-kl, adj pratico

practice, prak´-tis, n pratica f; (custom) consuetudine f

practise, prak´-tis, v far pratica; (doctor) esercitare

practitioner, prak-tish´-on-a, n medico m

praise, preis, v lodare; n lode f

praiseworthy, preis´-uer-Di, adj lodevole

pram, pram, n carrozzina f

prance, praans, v impennarsi; fig pavoneggiarsi

prank, prangk, n burla f

prattle, prat´-l, v chiacchierare

prawn, proon, n gamberetto m

pray, prei, v pregare

prayer, prer, n preghiera f

preach, priich, v predicare

preacher, prii´-cha, n predicatore m

precarious*, pri-ker´-ri-os, adj precario

precaution, pri-koo´-shon, n precauzione f

precede, pri-siid´, v precedere

precedence, pres´-i-dens, n precedenza f

precedent, pres´-i-dent, n precedente m

precinct, prii´-singkt, n distretto m

precious*, presh´-os, adj prezioso

precipice, pres´-i-pis, n precipizio m

precipitate, pri-sip´-i-teit, v precipitare

precise*, pri-sais´, adj preciso

precision, pri-sish´-on, n precisione f

preclude, pri-kluud´, v escludere, precludere

precocious, pri-kou´-shos, adj precoce

predatory, pred´-a-to-ri, adj rapace

predecessor, prii-di-ses´-a, n predecessore m

predicament, pri-dik´-a-ment, n posizione difficile f

predicate, pred´-i-ket, n gram predicato m

predict, pri-dikt´, v predire

prediction, pri-dik´-shon, n predizione f

predominant, pri-dom´-inant, *adj* predominante

pre-eminent, prii-em´-i-nent, *adj* preminente

preface, pref´-is, *n* prefazione *f*

prefer, pri-fer´, *v* preferire

preferable, pref´-e-ra-bl, *adj* preferibile

preference, pref´-e-rens, *n* preferenza *f*

prefix, prii-fiks´, *n* prefisso *m*

pregnancy, pregh´-nan-si, *n* gravidanza *f*

pregnant, pregh´-nant, *adj* incinta

prejudice, prech´-u-dis, *v* pregiudicare; *n* pregiudizio *m*

prejudiced, prech´-u-dist, *adj* prevenuto

prejudicial*, prech-u-dish´-al, *adj* pregiudizievole

preliminary, pri-lim´-i-na-ri, *adj* preliminare; *n* preliminare *m*

prelude, pre´-liuud, *n* preludio *m*

premature*, prem´-a-tiur, *adj* prematuro

premeditate, pri-med´-i-teit, *v* premeditare

premier, prem´-i-a, *n* primo ministro *m*; *adj* principale

premises, prem´-i-sis, *npl* locali *mpl*

premium, prii´-mi-um, *n* premio *m*

preparation, prep-a-rei´-shon, *n* preparazione *f*

prepare, pri-per´, *v* preparare

prepay, prii-pei´, *v* pagare in anticipo

prepossessing, prii-po-ses´-ing, *adj* attraente

preposterous*, pri-pos´-te-ros, *adj* assurdo

prerogative, pri-rogh´-a-tiv, *n* prerogativa *f*

presage, pres´-ich, *n* presagio *m*

prescribe, pri-skraib´, *v* prescrivere

prescription, pri-skrip´-shon, *n* (medical) ricetta *f*

presence, pres´-ens, *n* presenza *f*

presence of mind, pres´-ens ov maind, *n* presenza di spirito *f*

present, pri-sent´, *v* presentare; (give) donare

present, pres´-ent, *n* dono *m*, regalo *m*; *adj* presente

presentation, pres-en-tei´-shon, *n* presentazione *f*

presenter, pre-sen´-ta, *n* presentatore *m*, presentatrice *f*

presentiment, pri-sen´-ti-ment, *n*

presentimento *m*

presently, pres´-ent-li, *adv* ora, subito

preservation, pres-e-vei´-shon, *n* conservazione *f*

preserve, pri-serv´, *v* proteggere; conservare

preserves, pri-servs´, *npl* conserve *fpl*

preside, pri-said´, *v* presiedere

president, pres´-i-dent, *n* presidente *m/f*

press, pres, *n mech* pressa *f*; (editorial) stampa *f*; *v* premere; (fruit) spremere

pressing, pres´-ing, *adj* urgente

pressure, presh´-a, *n* pressione *f*; *v* fare pressioni

presume, pri-siuum´, *v* presumere

presumption, pri-sŏmp´-shon, *n* presunzione *f*

pretence, pri-tens´, *n* pretesto *m*; pretesa *f*

pretend, pri-tend´, *v* fingere

pretentious*, pri-ten´-shos, *adj* pretenzioso

pretext, prii´-text, *n* pretesto *m*

pretty, pri´-ti, *adj* grazioso, carino

prevail, pri-veil´, *v* prevalere; (upon)

persuadere

prevalent, prev´-a-lent, *adj* prevalente

prevaricate, pri-va´-ri-keit, *v* tergiversare

prevent, pri-vent´, *v* prevenire; impedire

prevention, pri-ven´-shon, *n* prevenzione *f*

preventive*, pri-ven´-tiv, *adj* preventivo

preview, pri-viu, *n* anteprima *f*

previous, prii´-vi-os, *adj* anteriore, precedente

prevision, pri-vi´-shon, *n* previsione *f*

prey, prei, *n* preda *f*

price, prais, *n* prezzo *m*

priceless, prii´-lis, *adj* inestimabile

prick, prik, *n* puntura *f*; *v* pungere

prickle, prik´-l, *n* pizzicore *m*; (thorn) spina *f*

prickly, prik´-li, *adj* pungente; (thorny) spinoso

pride, praid, *n* orgoglio *m*; *v* (oneself) essere orgoglioso

priest, priist, *n* prete *m*

prig, prigh, *n* borioso *m*

prim, prim, *adj* per benino

primary, prai´-ma-ri, *adj* primario; (main) principale

primary school, prai´-ma-ri skuul, *n* scuola elementare *f*

prime, praim, *adj* (quality) migliore; *v* (prepare) preparare; **in the – of life,** *n* nel fiore degli anni

prime minister, praim min´-is-ta, *n* primo ministro *m*

primer, prai´-ma, *n* (paint) vernice base *f*

primitive, prim´-i-tiv, *adj* primitivo

primrose, prim´-rous, *n* primula *f*

prince, prins, *n* principe *m*

princely, prins´-li, *adj* principesco

princess, prin´-ses, *n* principessa *f*

principal, prin´-si-pl, *n* (school) preside *m/f*; *adj* principale

principle, prin´-si-pl, *n* principio *m*; **on –,** per principio

print, print, *n* stampa *f*; (photo) copia *f*; *v* stampare

printer, prin´-ta, *n* stampante *f*

printing, prin´-ting, *n* stampa *f*

prior, prai´-a, *adj* precedente

priority, prai-o´-ri-ti, *n* priorità *f*

prism, prism, *n* prisma *m*

prison, pris´-on, *n* prigione *f*, carcere *m*

prisoner, pris-o-na, *n* prigioniero *m*

privacy, pri´-va-si, *n* intimità *f*

private*, prai´-vit, *adj* privato; particolare

privation, prai-vei´-shon, *n* privazione *f*

privilege, pri´-vi-lich, *n* privilegio *m*; *v* privilegiare

privy, priv´-i, *adj* privato

Privy Council, pri´-vi kaun´-sil, *n* consiglio della Corona *m*

prize, prais, *n* premio *m*; *v* valutare

pro, prou, *prep* per, a favore di; **the –s and cons,** *n* i pro e i contro

probable, prob´-a-bl, *adj* probabile

probation, pro-bei´-shon, *n* libertà vigilata *f*; periodo di prova *m*

probe, proub, *v* sondare; *n* sonda *f*

problem, prob´-lem, *n* problema *m*

procedure, pro-sii´-cha, *n* procedimento *m*, procedura *f*

proceed, pro-siid´, *v* procedere

proceedings, pro-sii´-

dings, npl procedura f; provvedimenti mpl

proceeds, prou´-siids, npl ricavato m

process, prou´-ses, n processo m

procession, pro-sesh´-on, n processione f

proclaim, pro-kleim´, v proclamare

proclamation, prok-la-mei´-shon, n proclamazione f

procure, pro-kiur´, v procurare

prod, prod, n colpetto m; v dare un colpetto

prodigal*, prod´-i-gal, adj prodigo

prodigious*, pro-dich´-os, adj prodigioso

prodigy, prod´-ich-i, n prodigio m

produce, prod´-iuus, n prodotto agricolo m

produce, pro-diuus´, v produrre

producer, pro-diuu´-sa, n produttore m

product, pro´-dŏkt, n prodotto m

production, pro-dŏk´-shon, n produzione f

profane, pro-fein´, adj* profano; v profanare

profess, pro-fes´, v professare

profession, pro-fesh´-on, n professione f

professional, pro-fesh´-on-al, adj professionale

professor, pro-fes´-a, n docente m/f; professore m

proficiency, pro-fish´-en-si, n progresso m; capacità f

proficient, pro-fish´-ent, adj competente; provetto

profile, prou´-fail, n profilo m

profit, prof´-it, n profitto m, utile m; vantaggio m, beneficio m; v ricavare beneficio da

profitable, prof-it´-a-bl, adj redditizio; vantaggioso

profiteer, pro-fi-tir´, n speculatore m

profligate, pro´-fli-gat, adj dissoluto

profound*, pro-faund´, adj profondo

profuse*, pro-fius´, adj copioso

prognosticate, progh-nos´-ti-keit, v pronosticare

program, prou´-gram, n comp programma m; v programmare

programme, prou´-gram, n programma m

progress, prou´-gres, n

progresso m

progress, pro-gres´, v progredire; avanzare

prohibit, pro-hib´-it, v proibire

prohibition, prou-ib-ish´-on, n proibizione f

project, pro´-chekt, n progetto m

project, pro-chekt´, v progettare

projectile, pro-chek´-tail, n proiettile m

projection, pro-chek´-shon, n proiezione f

prologue, prou´-logh, n prologo m

prolong, pro-long´, v prolungare

promenade, prom-i-naad´, n passeggiata f; v passeggiare

prominent, prom´-i-nent, adj prominente; (person) in vista

promiscuous*, pro-mis´-kiu-os, adj promiscuo

promise, pro´-mis, n promessa f; v promettere

promissory note, prom´-is-o-ri nout, n pagherò m

promote, pro-mout´, v promuovere

promoter, pro-mou´-ta, n promotore m; promoter m

promotion, pro-mou´-shon, n promozione f

prompt, prompt, *adj**
pronto, immediato; *v*
(stage) suggerire;
(induce) spingere

prompter, promp´-ta, *n*
suggeritore *m*

prone, proun, *adj* a faccia
in giù, prono; propenso

prong, prong, *n* rebbio *m*,
dente *m*

pronoun, prou´-naun, *n*
pronome *m*

pronounce, pro-nauns´, *v*
pronunciare

pronunciation, pro-nŏn-
si-ei´-shon, *n*
pronuncia *f*

proof, pruuf, *n* prova *f*;
bozza *f*

prop, prop, *n* sostegno *m*,
puntello *m*; *v* sostenere,
puntellare

propagate, prop´-a-gheit, *v*
propagare

propel, pro-pel´, *v*
spingere

propeller, pro-pel´-a, *n*
elica *f*

proper*, prop´-a, *adj*
appropriato; corretto

property, prop´-e-ti, *n*
proprietà *f*

prophecy, prof´-i-si, *n*
profezia *f*

prophesy, prof´-i-sai, *v*
profetizzare

prophet, prof´-it, *n*
profeta *m*

propitious*, pro-pish´-os,
adj propizio

proportion, pro-poor´-
shon, *n* proporzione *f*

proposal, pro-pou´-sal, *n*
proposta *f*

propose, pro-pous´, *v*
proporre

proprietor, pro-prai´-e-ta,
n proprietario *m*

propriety, pro-prai´-e-ti, *n*
proprietà *f*

proscribe, pro-skraib´, *v*
proscrivere

prose, prous, *n* prosa *f*

prosecute, pros´-i-kiut, *v*
processare

prosecution, pros-i-kiu´-
shon, *n* processo *m*;
accusa *f*

prosecutor, pros´-i-kiu-ta,
n pubblico ministero *m*

prospect, pros´-pekt, *n*
prospettiva *f*

prospective, pros-pek´-tiv,
adj probabile

prospectus, pros-pek´-tus,
n prospetto *m*

prosper, pros´-pa, *v*
prosperare

prosperity, pros-pe´-ri-ti, *n*
prosperità *f*

prosperous*, pros´-pe-ros,
adj prospero, fiorente

prostitute, pros´-ti-tiut, *n*
prostituta *f*; *v* prostituire

prostrate, pros-treit´, *v*
(oneself) prostrarsi; *adj*

(sorrow) prostrato

prostration, pros-trei´-
shon, *n* prostrazione *f*

protagonist, pro-ta´-go-
nist, *n* protagonista *m/f*

protect, pro-tekt´, *v*
proteggere

protection, pro-tek´-shon,
n protezione *f*

protein, prou´-tiin, *n*
proteina *f*

protest, prou´-test, *n*
protesta *f*

protest, pro-test´, *v*
protestare

protract, pro-trakt´, *v*
protrarre

protrude, pro-truud´, *v*
protrudere

proud*, praud, *adj*
orgoglioso

provable, pruu´-va-bl, *adj*
provabile

prove, pruuv, *v* provare

proverb, prov´-erb, *n*
proverbio *m*

provide, pro-vaid´, *v*
fornire, provvedere

provided, pro-vai´-did,
conj a condizione che

providence, prov´-i-dens,
n provvidenza *f*

provident, prov´-i-dent,
adj previdente

province, prov´-ins, *n*
provincia *f*

provision, pro-vish´-on, *n*
provvista *f*; riserva *f*;

condizione f

provisional, pro-vish´-on-al, *adj* provvisorio

provisions, pro-vish´-ons, *npl* viveri *mpl*, provviste *fpl*

provocation, prov-*o*-kei´-shon, *n* provocazione f

provoke, pro-vouk´, *v* provocare

prow, prau, *n* prua f

prowess, prau´-is, *n* prodezza f

prowl, praul, *v* aggirarsi con fare sospetto

proximity, prok-sim´-i-ti, *n* prossimità f

proxy, prok´-si, *n* procura f; mandatario *m*; by –, per procura

prude, pruud, *n* puritano *n*

prudence, pruud´-dens, *n* prudenza f

prudent, pruu´-dent, *adj* prudente

prudish, pruu´-dish, *adj* puritano

prune, pruun, *n* prugna f; *v* potare

pry, prai, *v* ficcare il naso

psalm, saam, *n* salmo *m*

pseudonym, siuu´-do-nim, *n* pseudonimo *m*

psychiatric, sai-ki-at´-rik, *adj* psichiatrico

psychiatrist, sai-kai´-a-trist, *n* psichiatra *m/f*

psychoanalyst, sai-kou-an´-a-list, *n* psicanalista *m/f*

psychological, sai-ko-lo´-chi-kl, *adj* psicologico

psychology, sai-kol´-o-chi, *n* psicologia f

psychopath, sai´-ko-paZ, *n* psicopatico *m*

pub, pŏb, *n* pub *m*

public, pŏb´-lik, *adj** & *n* pubblico *m*

publican, pŏb´-li-kan, *n* gestore di un pub *m*

publication, pŏb-li-kei´-shon, *n* pubblicazione f

public house, pŏb´-lik haus, *n* pub *m*

publicity, pŏb-li´-si-ti, *n* pubblicità f

publish, pŏb´-lish, *v* pubblicare

publisher, pŏb´-li-sha, *n* editore *m*, casa editrice f

pucker, pŏk´-a, *v* corrugare; (fold) increspare

pudding, pud´-ing, *n* budino *m*; dessert *m*

puddle, pŏd´-l, *n* pozza f

puerile, piur-rail, *adj* puerile

puff, pŏf, *n* sbuffo *m*; *v* soffiare; (swell) gonfiarsi

puff pastry, pŏf peis´-tri, *n* pasta sfoglia f

puffy, pŏf´-i, *adj* gonfio

pull, pul, *n* tirata f,

strattone *m*; *v* tirare; – **down,** tirare giù; (demolish) abbattere; – **out,** estrarre, strappare; – **up,** issare

pulley, pul´-i, *n* puleggia f

pulp, pŏlp, *n* polpa f

pulpit, pul´-pit, *n* pulpito *m*

pulse, pŏls, *n* polso *m*

pulverize, pŏl´-ve-rais, *v* polverizzare

pumice stone, pŏm´-is stoun, *n* pietra pomice f

pump, pŏmp, *n* pompa f; *v* pompare

pun, pŏn, *n* gioco di parole *m*

punch, pŏnch, *v* dare un pugno; (pierce) punzonare; *n* pugno *m*; (tool) punzone *m*; (drink) ponce *m*

punctilious*, pŏngk-til´-i-os, *adj* scrupoloso

punctual, pŏngk´-tiu-al, *adj* puntuale

punctuate, pŏngk´-tiu-eit, *v* punteggiare

punctuation, pŏngk´-tiu-ei´-shon, *n* punteggiatura f

puncture, pŏngk´-cha, *n* (tyre) foratura f

pungency, pŏn´-chen-si, *n* asprezza f

pungent, pŏn´-chent, *adj* pungente

punish, pŏn´-ish, v punire

punishable, pŏn´-ish-a-bl, adj punibile

punishment, pŏn´-ish-ment, n punizione f; castigo m

punitive, piuu´-ni-tiv, adj punitivo

punt, pŏnt, v puntare

puny, piuu´-ni, adj gracile

pupil, piuu´-pil, n allievo m; (eye) pupilla f

puppet, pŏp´-it, n marionetta f, burattino m

puppy, pŏp´-i, n cucciolo m

purchase, per´-chis, n acquisto m; v acquistare

purchaser, per-chis´-a, n compratore m

pure*, piur, adj puro; (chaste) casto

purgative, per´-ga-tiv, n purgante m

purgatory, per´-ga-to-ri, n purgatorio m

purge, perch, v purgare

purify, piur´-ri-fai, v purificare

purity, piur´-ri-ti, n purità f

purloin, pe-loin´, v sottrarre

purple, per´-pl, adj viola; n viola m

purport, pe-poort´, v pretendere

purpose, per´-pos, n scopo m, intenzione f

purposely, per´-pos-li, adv di proposito

purr, per, v fare le fuse

purse, pers, n borsellino m

pursue, pe-siuu´, v inseguire; (aim) perseguire

pursuit, pe-siuut´, n inseguimento m; aspirazione f

purveyor, pe-vei´-a, n fornitore m

pus, pŏs, n pus m

push, push, v premere; spingere; n spinta f

pushchair, push´-cher, n passeggino m

pushing, push´-ing, adj intraprendente

pussy(-cat), pu´-si(-kat), n micio m

put, put, v mettere; (express) dire; – off, rimandare; – on, indossare

putrefy, piut´-ri-fai, v putrefare

putrid, piut´-rid, adj putrido

putty, pŏt´-i, n stucco m, mastice m

puzzle, pŏs´-l, v confondere; essere perplesso; n indovinello m

pyjamas, pi-chaa´-mas, npl pigiama m

pylon, pai´-lon, n pilone m

pyramid, pi´-ra-mid, n piramide f

Pyrenees, pi-re-niis, npl Pirenei mpl

python, pai´-Zon, n pitone m

quack, kuak, *n* ciarlatano *m*

quadruped, kuod´-ru-ped, *n* quadrupede *m*

quadruple, kuod´-ru-*pl*, *n* quadruplo *m*; *adj* quadruplo

quagmire, kuogh´-mair, *n* pantano *m*

quail, kueil, *n* quaglia *f*; *v* tremare di paura

quaint*, kueint, *adj* bizzarro

quaintness, kueint´-nis, *n* bizzarria *f*

quake, kueik, *v* tremare

quaker, kuei´-ka, *n* quacchero *m*

qualification, kuol-i-fi-kei´-shon, *n* qualifica *f*

qualified, kuol´-i-faid, *adj* qualificato; abilitato; diplomato

qualify, kuol´-i-fai, *v* qualificare

quality, kuol´-i-ti, *n* qualità *f*

quandary, kuon´-da-ri, *n* perplessità *f*

quantity, kuon´-ti-ti, *n* quantità *f*

quarantine, kuo´-ran-tiin, *n* quarantena *f*

quarrel, kuo´-rel, *n* litigio *m*; *v* litigare

quarrelsome, kuo´-rel-som, *adj* litigioso

quarry, kuo´-ti, *n* cava *f*

quarter, kuoor´-ta, *n* quarto *m*; (period) trimestre *m*

quarterly, kuoor´-te-li, *adj* trimestrale; *adv* trimestralmente

quartet, kuoor-tet´, *n* quartetto *m*

quartz, kuoorts, *n* quarzo *m*

quash, kuosh, *v* reprimere; (verdict) cassare, annullare

quaver, kuei´-va, *v* tremare; *n* (music) croma *f*

quay, kii, *n* molo *m*

queasy, kuii´-si, *adj* nauseato

queen, kuiin, *n* regina *f*

queer*, kuir, *adj* strano, bizzarro

quell, kuel, *v* reprimere

quench, kuench, *v* estinguere; (thirst) togliere

querulous*, kue´-riu-los, *adj* querulo

query, kuir´-ri, *n* interrogativo *m*; dubbio *m*; *v* mettere in dubbio

quest, kuest, *n* ricerca *f*

question, kues´-chon, *n* domanda *f*; questione *f*; *v* interrogare; (doubt) dubitare; – **mark**, *n* punto interrogativo *m*

questionable, kues´-chon-a-bl, *adj* discutibile

queue, kiu, *n* coda *f*; *v* fare la coda

quibble, kuib´-l, *v* cavillare; *n* cavillo *m*

quick, kuik, *adj** veloce, rapido; svelto; *interj* & *adv* presto

quicken, kuik´-en, *v* accelerare; affrettare

quickness, kuik´-nis, *n* rapidità *f*

quicksand, kuik´-sand, *n* sabbie mobili *fpl*

quicksilver, kuik´-sil-va, *n* mercurio *m*

quiet, kuai´-et, *adj** calmo; tranquillo; *n* quiete *f*

quill, kuil, *n* penna d'oca *f*

quilt, kuilt, *n* piumino *m*; trapunta *f*

quince, kuins, *n* mela cotogna *f*

quinine, kuin´-iin, *n* chinino *m*

quintet, kuin-tet´, *n* quintetto

quit, kuit, *v* lasciare; smettere

quite, kuait, *adv* completamente; piuttosto

quits, kuits, *adj* pari

quiver, kuiv´-a, *v* fremere

quiz, kuis, *n* quiz *m*

quorum, kuoor´-rum, *n* quorum *m*, numero legale *m*

quota, kuou´-ta, *n* quota *f*

quotation, kuou-tei´-shon, *n* citazione *f*; (price) preventivo *m*; (shares) quotazione *f*

quote, kuout, *v* citare; fare un preventivo; quotare

R

rabbi, rab´-ai, n rabbino m

rabbit, rab´-it, n
coniglio m

rabid*, rei´-bid, adj
rabbioso; fanatico

rabies, rei´-biis, n rabbia f

race, reis, v correre; n razza
f; (contest) gara f; (cars)
corsa f

racecourse, reis´-koors, n
ippodromo m

racehorse, reis´-hoors, n
cavallo da corsa m

racetrack, reis´-trak, n
pista f

racial, reish´-l, adj razziale

racism, rei´-sism, n
razzismo m

racist, rei´-sist, n razzista
m/f; adj razzista

rack, rak, n rastrelliera f;
(luggage) rete

portabagagli f; v (brain)
scervellarsi

racket, rak´-it, n
racchetta f

radiant, rei´-di-ant, adj
raggiante, radioso

radiate, rei´-di-eit, v
irradiare

radiation, rei-di-ei´-shon,
n radiazione f

radiator, rei´-di-ei-ta, n
radiatore m

radical, ra´-di-kl, adj
radicale

radio, rei´-di-ou, n radio f

radioactive, rei-di-ou-ak´-
tiv, adj radioattivo

radish, rad´-ish, n
rafano m

radium, rei´-di-um, n
radio m

radius, rei´-di-us, n

raggio m

raffle, raf´-l, n lotteria f; v
mettere in palio

raft, raaft, n zattera f

rafter, raaf´-ta, n
travicello m

rag, ragh, n cencio m

rage, reich, n rabbia f; v
infuriarsi

raid, reid, n incursione f;
(air) attacco m; (police)
irruzione della polizia f;
v fare incursione in

rail, reil, n rotaia f; (stairs)
ringhiera f

railway, reil´-uei, n
ferrovia f

rain, rein, v piovere; n
pioggia f

rainbow, rein´-bou, n
arcobaleno m

raincoat, rein´-kout, n
impermeabile m

rainy, rei´-ni, adj piovoso

raise, reis, v alzare;
sollevare; (increase)
aumentare; (cultivate)
coltivare; (breed)
allevare; (funds)
raccogliere

raisin, rei´-sin, n uva
passa f, zibibbo m

rake, reik, n rastrello m; v
rastrellare

rally, ral´-i, v riunire; n
riunione f; (car) rally m;
(tennis) scambio m

ram, ram, n montone m;

(battering) ariete *m*; *v* sfondare; speronare

ramble, ram´-bl, *v* gironzolare; (mind) divagare; *n* escursione *f*

rampant, ram´-pant, *adj* che dilaga

rampart, ram´-paart, *n* bastione *m*

rancid, ran´-sid, *adj* rancido

rancour, rang´-ka, *n* rancore *m*

random, ran´-dom, **at –**, *adv* a casaccio

range, reinch, *v* variare; *n* gamma *f*; portata *f*; (mountains) catena *f*

ranger, rein´-cha, *n* guardia forestale *f*

rank, rangk, *v* classificare; *adj* (taste, smell) rancido; *n* grado *m*; fila *f*; (taxi) posteggio *m*; **the – and file**, la base

ransack, ran´-sak, *v* saccheggiare

ransom, ran´-som, *n* riscatto *m*; *v* riscattare

rap, rap, *v* bussare; *n* colpo *m*; *mus* rap *m*

rapacious, ra-pei´-shos, *adj* rapace

rape, reip, *v* violentare; *n* violenza carnale *f*

rapid*, rap´-id, *adj* rapido

rapidity, ra-pid´-i-ti, *n* rapidità *f*

rapids, rap´-ids, *npl* rapide *fpl*

rapier, rei´-pi-a, *n* spadino *m*

rapture, rap´-cha, *n* estasi *f*

rare*, rer, *adj* raro; (air) rarefatto; (steak) al sangue

rarity, rer´-ri-ti, *n* rarità *f*

rascal, raas´-kl, *n* furfante *m*

rash, rash, *n* (skin) eruzione *f*; *adj** avventato

rasher, rash´-a, *n* fettina di pancetta *f*

rashness, rash´-nis, *n* avventatezza *f*

rasp, raasp, *n* raspa *f*; *v* raspare

raspberry, raas´-be-ri, *n* lampone *m*

rat, rat, *n* sorcio *m*, ratto *m*

rate, reit, *n* tasso *m*; (proportion) percentuale *f*; (price) tariffa *f*; (speed) velocità *f*; *v* valutare, stimare

rather, raa´-Da, *adv* piuttosto; (prefer) preferibilmente

ratify, ra´-ti-fai, *v* ratificare

ratio, rei´-shi-ou, *n* rapporto *m*; proporzione *f*

ration, rash´-on, *n* razione *f*; *v* razionare

rational, rash´-on-al, *adj* razionale

rattle, rat´-l, *v* strepitare; *n* (noise) strepito *m*; (toy) sonaglio *m*

rattlesnake, rat´-l-sneik, *n* serpente a sonagli *m*

ravage, rav´-ich, *v* devastare; *n* devastazione *f*

rave, reiv, *v* delirare; **– about**, *fig* andare in estasi per

raven, reiv´-n, *n* corvo *m*

ravenous, rav´-en-os, *adj* vorace

ravine, ra-viin´, *n* burrone *m*

raving, reiv´-ing, *adj* delirante

ravishing, rav´-ish-ing, *adj* incantevole

raw, roo, *adj* crudo; (rough) greggio; (wound) in carne viva

ray, rei, *n* raggio *m*

raze, reis, *v* radere; (trees) abbattere

razor, rei´-sa, *n* rasoio *m*

razor blade, rei´-sa bleid, *n* lametta da barba *f*

reach, riich, *v* arrivare a; raggiungere; estendersi; *n* portata *f*

react, rii-akt´, *v* reagire

reaction, rii-ak´-shon, *n*

reazione f

read, riid, v leggere

reader, rii´-da, n lettore m, lettrice f

readily, red´-i-li, adv prontamente; volentieri

reading, rii´-ding, n lettura f

ready, red´-i, adj pronto

real, riil, adj reale; (genuine) vero

realistic, rii-al-is´-tik, adj realistico

reality, rii-al´-i-ti, n realtà f

realize, rii´-al-ais, v rendersi conto di; (sell) realizzare

really, rii-al´-i, adv realmente

realm, relm, n regno m, reame m

ream, riim, n (paper) risma f

reap, riip, v mietere, raccogliere

rear, rir, v allevare; adj di dietro, posteriore; n didietro m

reason, rii´-son, v ragionare; n ragione f

reasonable, rii´-son-a-bl, adj ragionevole

reassure, rii-a-shoor´, v rassicurare

rebate, rii´-beit, n rimborso m

rebel, reb´-l, n ribelle m/f

rebel, ri-bel´, v ribellarsi

rebellion, ri-bel´-ion, n ribellione f

rebound, rii´-baund, n rimbalzo m

rebound, ri-baund´, v rimbalzare

rebuff, ri-böf´, v rifiutare; n rifiuto m

rebuke, ri-biuuk´, n rimprovero m; v rimproverare

recall, ri-kool´, v richiamare; (mind) rammentarsi

recapitulate, rii-ka-pit´-iu-leit, v ricapitolare

recede, ri-siid´, v ritirarsi

receipt, ri-siit´, n ricevuta f; (reception) ricevimento m

receive, ri-siiv´, v ricevere

receiver, ri-sii´-va, n ricevitore m; (bankruptcy) curatore fallimentare m; (stolen goods) ricettatore m

recent, rii´-sent, adj & adv recente

recently, rii´-sent-li, adv recentemente

receptacle, ri-sep´-ta-kl, n ricettacolo m

reception, ri-sep´-shon, n accoglienza f; ricevimento m; (hotel) reception f

receptionist, ri-sep´-shon-

ist, n receptionist m/f

recess, ri-ses´, n recesso m; parl vacanze fpl

recession, ri-se´-shon, n recessione f

recipe, res´-i-pi, n ricetta f

reciprocate, ri-sip´-ro-keit, v ricambiare

recital, ri-sai´-tl, n recital m

recite, ri-sait´, v recitare

reckless, rek´-lis, adj imprudente

reckon, rek´-n, v contare, calcolare; pensare

reclaim, ri-kleim´, v reclamare; (land) bonificare

recline, ri-klain´, v reclinare

recluse, ri-kluus´, n recluso m

recognition, rek-ogh-nish´-on, n riconoscimento m

recognize, rek´-ogh-nais, v riconoscere

recoil, ri-koil´, v rinculare; n rinculo m

recollect, rek-o-lekt´, v ricordarsi

recollection, rek-o-lek´-shon, n ricordo m

recommence, rii-ko-mens´, v ricominciare

recommend, rek-o-mend´, v raccomandare

recommendation, rek-o-

men-dei´-shon, n
raccomandazione f

recompense, rek´-om-
pens, v ricompensare; n
ricompensa f

reconcile, rek´-on-sail, v
riconciliare

reconsider, rii-kon-sid´-a,
v riconsiderare

record, ri-koord´, v
ricordare; registrare

record, rek´-oord, n record
m; disco m; pratica f;
archivio m

recoup, ri-kuup´, v rifarsi

recourse, ri-koors´, n
ricorso m

recover, ri-kŏv´-a, v
ricuperare; riprendersi

re-cover, rii-kŏv´-a, v
ricoprire

recovery, ri-kŏv´-e-ri, n
ricupero m; ripresa f

recreation, rek-ri-ei´-
shon, n ricreazione f

recreation ground, rek-ri-
ei´-shon graund, n
campo giochi m

recruit, ri-kruut´, n
recluta f; v reclutare

rectangular, rek-tang´-
ghiu-la, adj rettangolare

rectify, rek´-ti-fai, v
rettificare

rector, rek´-ta, n rettore
m; parroco m

rectory, rek´-to-ri, n casa
parrocchiale f

recuperate, ri-kuu´-pe-
reit, v ricuperare;
ristabilirsi

recur, ri-ker´, v ricorrere

red, red, adj rosso; n rosso
m

red-hot, red´-hot, adj
arroventato

reddish, red´-ish, adj
rossiccio

redeem, ri-diim´, v
riscattare, disimpegnare;
(soul) redimere

redemption, ri-demp´-
shon, n redenzione f

red-light district, red-lait´
dis´-trikt, n quartiere a
luci rosse m

redouble, rii-dŏb´-l, v
raddoppiare

redress, ri-dres´, n
riparazione f; v riparare

red tape, red teip´, n
burocrazia f

reduce, ri-diuus´, v ridurre

reduction, ri-dŏk´-shon, n
riduzione f

redundancy, ri-dŏn´-dan-
si, n licenziamento per
esubero m

redundant, ri-dŏn´-dant,
adj licenziato per
esubero

reed, riid, n canna f

reef, riif, n banco di
scogli m

reek, riik, v puzzare di

reel, riil, n rocchetto m;

(film) rullino m; v
(sway) barcollare

refer, ri-fer´, v riferirsi;
(apply) rivolgersi;
(consult) consultare

referee, ref-e-rii´, n arbitro
m

reference, ref´-e-rens, n
referenza f; with – to, in
riferimento a

referendum, re-fe-rend´-
um, n referendum m

refine, ri-fain´, v raffinare

refined*, ri-faind´, adj
raffinato

refinement, ri-fain´-ment,
n raffinatezza f

reflect, ri-flekt´, v
riflettere

reflection, ri-flek´-shon, n
riflessione f; riflesso m

reflector, ri-flek´-ta, n
riflettore m

reform, ri-foorm´, v
riformare; (moral)
correggere; n riforma f

refrain, ri-frein´, v
astenersi; n ritornello m

refresh, ri-fresh´, v
rinfrescare

refreshment, ri-fresh´-
ment, n rinfresco m

refrigerator, ri-frich´-e-
rei-ta, n frigorifero m

refuge, ref´-iuuch, n
(place) rifugio m

refugee, ref-iu-chii´, n
profugo m

refund, ri-fŏnd´, v
rimborsare

refusal, ri-fiuu´-sal, n
rifiuto m

refuse, ri-fiuus´, v
rifiutare

refuse, ref´-ius, n rifiuti
mpl

regain, rii-ghein´, v
riguadagnare

regal*, rii´-gal, adj regale

regard, ri-gaard´, v
riguardare; considerare;
n riguardo m; **kind –s,**
cordiali saluti mpl; **with
– to,** in relazione a

regardless, ri-gaard´-lis,
adv lo stesso; **– of** senza
tener conto di

regatta, ri-gat´-a, n
regata f

regenerate, ri-chen´-e-
reit, v rigenerare

regent, rii´-chent, n
reggente m

regiment, rech´-i-ment, n
reggimento m

region, rii´-chon, n
regione f

register, rech´-is-ta, n
registro m; v registrare

registrar, rech´-is-traar, n
ufficiale di stato civile m

registration, rech-is-trei´-
shon, n registrazione f

registry, rech´-is-tri, n
archivio m; segreteria f

regret, ri-gret´, v

rammaricarsi di; n
rammarico m

regrettable, ri-gret´-a-bl,
adj deplorevole

regular*, regh´-iu-la, adj
regolare

regulate, regh´-iu-leit, v
regolare

regulation, regh´-iu-lei´-
shon, n regolamento m

rehearsal, ri-her´-sal, n
(stage) prova f

rehearse, ri-hers´, v far le
prove

reign, rein, v regnare; n
regno m

reimburse, rii-im-bers´, v
rimborsare

rein, rein, n redine f

reindeer, rein´-dir, n
renna f

reinforce, rii-in-foors´, v
rinforzare

reinstate, rii-in-steit´, v
reintegrare

re-insure, re-in-shoor´, v
riassicurare

reject, ri-chekt´, v
respingere; rifiutare

rejoice, ri-chois´, v
rallegrarsi

rejoicing, ri-chois´-ing, n
festeggiamento m

rejuvenate, ri-chuu´-ven-
eit, v ringiovanire

relapse, ri-laps´, n ricaduta
f; v ricadere

relate, ri-leit´, v

raccontare

related, ri-lei´-tid, adj
parente; collegato

relation, ri-lei´-shon, n
(reference) rapporto m;
(kinship) parente m/f

relationship, ri-lei´-shon-
ship, n relazione f;
parentela f

relative, re´-la-tiv, n
parente m/f; adj relativo

relax, ri-laks´, v rilassare;
rilassarsi

relaxation, rii-lak-sei´-
shon, n relax m

relating, ri-lei´-ting, **– to,**
prep che riguarda

relay, rii´-lei, v
trasmettere; n (race)
corsa a staffetta f

release, ri-liis´, n rilascio
m; (film, record) uscita
f; v rilasciare

relent, ri-lent´, v cedere

relentless*, ri-lent´-lis, adj
implacabile

relevant, rel´-i-vant, adj
pertinente; relativo

reliable, ri-lai´-a-bl, adj
affidabile; attendibile

reliance, ri-lai´-ans, n
fiducia f

relic, rel´-ik, n reliquia f

relief, ri-liif´, n sollievo m;
(raised) rilievo m; mil
cambio m; (help)
soccorsi mpl

relieve, ri-liiv´, v

alleviare; soccorrere

religion, ri-lich´-on, n
religione f

religious*, ri-lich´-os, adj
religioso

relinquish, ri-ling´-kuish,
v rinunziare a

relish, rel´-ish, n gusto m;
v gustare

reluctance, ri-lŏk´-tans, n
riluttanza f

reluctant*, ri-lŏk´-tant,
adj riluttante

rely, ri-lai´, v contare su

remain, ri-mein´, v
rimanere

remand, ri-maand´, v law
rinviare a giudizio

remark, ri-maark´, v
osservare ; n
osservazione f

remarkable, ri-maark´-a-
bl, adj notevole

remedy, rem´-i-di, n
rimedio m; v rimediare

remember, ri-mem´-ba, v
ricordarsi

remembrance, ri-mem´-
brans, n ricordo m

remind, ri-maind´, v
ricordare

remit, ri-mit´, v rimettere

remnant, rem´-nant, n
avanzo m; scampolo m

remonstrate, re´-mon-
streit, v protestare

remorse, ri-moors´, n
rimorso m

remote*, ri-mout´, adj
remoto

removal, ri-muu´-val, n
trasloco m

remove, ri-muuv´, v
togliere, rimuovere

remunerate, ri-miuu´-ne-
reit, v rimunerare

remunerative, ri-miuu´-
ne-ra-tiv, adj
rimunerativo

render, ren´-da, v rendere

rendering, ren´-de-ring, n
interpretazione f

renegade, ren´-i-gheid, n
rinnegato m

renew, ri-niuu´, v
rinnovare

renewal, ri-niuu´-al, n
rinnovo m

renounce, ri-nauns´, v
rinunciare a

renovate, ren´-o-veit, v
rinnovare

renown, ri-naun´, n fama f

rent, rent, v affittare; n
affitto m

renunciation, ri-nŏn-si-
ei´-shon, n rinunzia f

reorganize, ri-oor´-gan-
ais, v riorganizzare

repair, ri-per´, n
riparazione f; v riparare

repartee, rep-aar-tii´, n
botta e risposta f

repeal, ri-piil´, v abrogare;
n abrogazione f

repeat, ri-piit´, v ripetere

repel, ri-pel´, v respingere

repellent, ri-pel´-ent, adj
ripugnante

repent, ri-pent´, v pentirsi

repetition, re-pi-tish´-on,
n ripetizione f

replace, ri-pleis´, v
sostituire; (put back)
rimettere a posto

replenish, ri-plen´-ish, v
riempire di nuovo;
reintegrare

reply, ri-plai´, n risposta f;
v rispondere

report, ri-poort´, v far
rapporto; n rapporto m,
resoconto m

reporter, ri-poor´-ta, n
reporter m/f, cronista
m/f

repose, ri-pous´, v
riposare; n riposo m

repository, ri-pos´-i-to-ri,
n deposito m

represent, rep-ri-sent´, v
rappresentare

representation, rep-ri-
sen-tei´-shon, n
rappresentazione f

representative, rep-ri-
sen´-ta-tiv, n
rappresentante m/f

repress, ri-pres´, v
reprimere

reprieve, ri-priiv´, n
commutazione f; v
commutare

reprimand, rep´-ri-maand,

n rimprovero *m*; *v*
rimproverare

reprint, rii´-print, *n*
ristampa *f*

reprint, ri-print´, *v*
ristampare

reprisal, ri-prai´-*s*al, *n*
rappresaglia *f*

reproach, ri-prouch´, *n*
rimprovero *m*; *v*
rimproverare

reproduce, rii-pro-diuus´,
v riprodurre

reproduction, rii-pro-
dŏk´-shon, *n*
riproduzione *f*

reproductive, rii-pro-
dŏk´-tiv, *adj* riproduttivo

reproof, ri-pruuf´, *n*
riprovazione *f*

reprove, ri-pruuv´, *v*
biasimare

reptile, rep´-tail, *n*
rettile *m*

republic, ri-pŏb´-lik, *n*
repubblica *f*

repudiate, ri-piuu´-di-eit,
v ripudiare

repugnant, ri-pŏgh´-nant,
adj ripugnante

repulse, ri-pŏls´, *v*
respingere

repulsive*, ri-pŏl´-siv, *adj*
ripulsivo

reputable, rep´-iu-*t*a-bl,
adj degno di fiducia

reputation, rep-iu-tei´-
pshon, *n* reputazione *f*

repute, ri-piuut´, *n*
reputazione *f*

request, ri-kuest´, *n*
richiesta *f*; *v* richiedere

require, ri-kuair´, *v* (need)
aver bisogno di;
(demand) richiedere

requirement, ri-kuair´-
ment, *n* esigenza *f*,
bisogno *m*; requisito *m*

requisite, rek´-ui-sit, *n*
requisito *m*; *adj* richiesto

rescue, res´-kiuu, *v*
soccorrere; *n* soccorso *m*

research, ri-serch´, *n*
ricerca *f*

resemble, ri-sem´-bl, *v*
rassomigliare a

resent, ri-sent´, *v* risentirsi
di

resentful*, ri-sent´-ful, *adj*
risentito; pieno di
risentimento

resentment, ri-sent´-
ment, *n* risentimento *m*

reservation, res-e-vei´-
shon, *n* prenotazione *f*

reserve, ri-serv´, *n* riserva
f; *v* riservare

reservoir, res´-e-vuaar, *n*
serbatoio *m*; bacino
idrico *m*

reside, ri-said´, *v* risiedere

residence, res´-i-dens, *n*
residenza *f*

resident, res´-i-dent, *adj*
residente; *n* residente
m/f

resign, ri-sain´, *v* dare le
dimissioni; (claim)
rinunciare a; – **oneself,**
rassegnarsi

resin, res´-in, *n* resina *f*

resist, ri-sist´, *v* resistere

resistance, ri-sis´-*t*ans, *n*
resistenza *f*

resolute*, res´-o-luut, *adj*
risoluto

resolution, res-o-luu´-
shon, *n* risoluzione *f*;
risolutezza *f*

resolve, ri-solv´, *v*
risolvere

resort, ri-soort´, *n* località
f; risorsa *f*; – **to,** *v*
ricorrere a

resound, ri-saund´, *v*
risuonare

resource, ri-soors´, *n*
risorsa *f*

resources, ri-soor´-sis, *npl*
mezzi *mpl*, risorse *fpl*

respect, ris-pekt´, *v*
rispettare; *n* rispetto *m*

respectability, ris-pek-*t*a-
bil´-i-ti, *n* rispettabilità *f*

respectable, ris-pek´-*t*a-bl,
adj rispettabile

respectful*, ris-pekt´-ful,
adj rispettoso

respite, res´-pait, *n* respiro
m, tregua *f*

respond, ris-pond´, *v*
rispondere

response, ris-pons´, *n*
risposta *f*

responsibility, ris-pon-si-bi´-li-ti, *n* responsabilità *f*

responsible, ris-pon´-si-bl, *adj* responsabile

rest, rest, *n* (repose) riposo *m*; (remainder) resto *m*; *v* (repose) riposarsi

restless*, rest´-lis, *adj* irrequieto

restaurant, res´-to-rant, *n* ristorante *m*

restore, ris-toor´, *v* (give back) restituire; (repair) restaurare

restrain, ris-trein´, *v* (to check) frenare

restraint, ris-treint´, *n* restrizione *f*; ritegno *m*

restrict, ris-trikt´, *v* restringere, limitare

restriction, ris-trik´-shon, *n* restrizione *f*

result, ri-sölt´, *n* risultato *m*; *v* risultare

resume, ri-siuum´, *v* riassumere

resumption, ri-sŏmp´-shon, *n* ripresa *f*

resurrection, res-e-rek´-shŏn, *n* resurrezione *f*

retail, ri-teil´, *v* vendere al minuto

retail, rii´-teil, *n* dettaglio *m*

retailer, rii´-tei-la, *n* dettagliante *m/f*

retain, ri-tein´, *v* ritenere

retaliate, ri-tal´-i-eit, *v* vendicarsi

retard, ri-taard´, *v* ritardare

reticent, ret´-i-sent, *adj* reticente

retinue, ret´-i-niuu, *n* seguito *m*

retire, ri-tair´, *v* ritirarsi; andare in pensione

retirement, ri-tair´-ment, *n* pensionamento *m*; pensione *f*

retort, ri-toort´, *n* rimbeccata *f*; *v* rimbeccare

retract, ri-trakt´, *v* ritrattare

retreat, ri-triit´, *v* ritirare; *n* ritirata *f*

retrieve, ri-triiv´, *v* ricuperare

return, ri-tern´, *v* ritornare; (give back) restituire; *n* ritorno *m*; restituzione *f*; (ticket) biglietto di andata e ritorno *m*

returns, ri-terns´, *npl* (turnover) guadagno *m*

reveal, ri-viil´, *v* rivelare

revel, rev´-el, *v* gozzovigliare

revenge, ri-vench´, *v* vendicarsi; *n* vendetta *f*

revenue, rev´-e-niuu, *n* reddito *m*; (state)

fisco *m*

reverse, ri-vers´, *v* fare marcia indietro; *n* (back) rovescio *m*; (car) retromarcia *f*; (contrary) contrario *m*

revert, ri-vert´, *v* ritornare

review, ri-viuu´, *v* (consider) esaminare; (edit) recensire; *n* recensione *f*; rivista *f*

revile, ri-vail´, *v* insultare

revise, ri-vais´, *v* rivedere; ripassare

revision, ri-vish´-on, *n* revisione *f*; ripasso *m*

revive, ri-vaiv´, *v* rianimare

revoke, ri-vouk´, *v* revocare

revolt, ri-voult´, *v* ribellarsi; *n* rivolta *f*

revolution, re-vo-luu´-shon, *n* rivoluzione *f*

revolve, ri-volv´, *v* girare

revolver, ri-vol´-va, *n* rivoltella *f*

revolving door, ri-vol´-ving door, *n* porta girevole *f*

reward, ri-uoord´, *v* ricompensare; *n* ricompensa *f*

rheumatism, ruu´-ma-tism, *n* reumatismo *m*

rhinoceros, rai-nos´-e-ros, *n* rinoceronte *m*

rhubarb, ruu´-baarb, *n*

rabarbaro *m*

rhyme, raim, *n* rima *f*; *v* rimare

rib, rib, *n* costola *f*

ribbon, rib´-on, *n* nastro *m*

rice, rais, *n* riso *m*

rich*, rich, *adj* ricco; (food) grasso

richness, rich´-nis, *n* ricchezza *f*

rickety, rik´-it-i, *adj* (shaky) vacillante

rid, rid, *v* sbarazzare; liberare; **get – of,** sbarazzarsi di

riddle, rid´-l, *n* (puzzle) enigma *m*; *v* (perforate) crivellare

ride, raid, *v* andare a cavallo; (cycle) andare in bicicletta; *n* cavalcata *f*; giro in bicicletta *m*

rider, rai´-da, *n* cavallerizzo *m*, amazzone *f*; ciclista *m/f*

ridge, rich, *n* (mountain) crinale *m*

ridicule, rid´-i-kiuul, *v* ridicolizzare

ridiculous*, ri-dik´-iu-los, *adj* ridicolo

rifle, raif´-l, *n* carabina *f*

rift, rift, *n* (crack) crepa *f*; *fig* spaccatura *f*

rig, righ, *n* piattaforma petrolifera *f*; *v* truccare

right, rait, *n* diritto *m*; (side) destra *f*; *adj*

diritto; giusto; destro; *adv* a destra; **all –,** benissimo; **on the –,** a destra

rigid*, rich´-id, *adj* rigido

rigorous*, ri´-go-ros, *adj* rigoroso

rigour, ri´-ga, *n* rigore *m*

rim, rim, *n* orlo *m*; (wheel) cerchio *m*

rind, raind, *n* (fruit) scorza *f*; (cheese) crosta *f*; (bacon etc.) cotenna *f*

ring, ring, *n* circolo *m*; (metal) anello *m*; (napkin) portatovagliolo *m*; (bell) squillo *m*; *v* suonare

ringleader, ring´-lii-da, *n* capobanda *m*

ring road, ring´ roud, *n* circonvallazione *f*

rinse, rins, *v* sciacquare

riot, rai´-ot, *n* tumulto *m*

rip, rip, *v* squarciare; (cloth) strappare

ripe, raip, *adj* maturo

ripen, raip´-n, *v* maturare

ripple, rip´-l, *n* increspatura *f*; (sound) mormorio *m*

rise, rais, *v* alzarsi; (prices) aumentare; (revolt) insorgere; *n* aumento *m*; salita *f*

risk, risk, *n* rischio *m*; *v* rischiare

rite, rait, *n* rito *m*

rival, rai´-val, *n* rivale *m/f*; (competitor) concorrente *m/f*

river, riv´-a, *n* fiume *m*

rivet, riv´-it, *n* (metal) ribattino *m*

road, roud, *n* strada *f*

road works, roud´-uerks, *npl* lavori stradali *mpl*

roam, roum, *v* vagabondare

roar, roor, *n* ruggito *m*; *v* ruggire

roast, roust, *n* arrosto *m*; *v* arrostire

rob, rob, *v* rubare

robbery, rob´-e-ri, *n* furto *m*

robe, roub, *n* veste *f*; (bath) accappatoio *m*; (lawyer's) toga *f*

robin, rob´-in, *n* pettirosso *m*

robot, rou´-bot, *n* robot *m*

robust*, ro-bŏst´, *adj* robusto

rock, rok, *n* scoglio *m*; roccia *f*; *mus* rock *m*; *v* dondolare; (cradle) cullare; (quake) far tremare

rocket, rok´-it, *n* razzo *m*; rucola *f*

rocking chair, rok-ing´-cher, *n* sedia a dondolo *f*

rocking horse, rok-ing´-hoors, *n* cavallo a dondolo *m*

rocky, rok´-i, *adj* roccioso; traballante

rod, rod, n canna f; bacchetta f

roe, rou, n (deer) capriolo m; (of fish) uova *fpl*

rogue, rough, n briccone m

roll, roul, n rullio m; (bread) panino m; *v* rullare; **– up,** arrotolare

roll call, roul´-kool, n appello m

roller, roul´-a, n rullo m; (hair) bigodino m

rollerskate, rou´-le-skeit, *v* pattinare

roller skates, rou´-le skeits, *npl* pattini a rotelle *mpl*

romance, ro-mans´, n storia d'amore f

romantic, ro-man´-tik, *adj* romantico

Rome, roum, n Roma f

romp, romp, *v* giocare chiassosamente

roof, ruuf, n tetto m; (mouth) palato m

rook, ruk, n cornacchia f

room, ruum, n stanza f, camera f; (space) spazio m

room service, ruum ser´-vis, n servizio in camera m

roomy, ruu´-mi, *adj* spazioso

roost, ruust, *v* appollaiarsi; n posatoio m

root, ruut, n radice f; *v* mettere radici

rope, roup, n corda f, fune f

rosary, rou´-sa-ri, n rosario m

rose, rous, n rosa f

rosemary, rous´-ma-ri, n rosmarino m

rosy, rou´-si, *adj* roseo

rot, rot, n marciume m; *v* imputridire

rotate, rou-teit´, *v* ruotare

rotten, rot´-n, *adj* putrido; marcio

rough*, röf, *adj* ruvido; (rude) rozzo; (sea) grosso; (bumpy) accidentato

round, raund, *adj* rotondo; *prep* intorno a; *v* arrotondare; n giro m; (boxing) round m

roundabout, raund´-a-baut, n rotatoria f

roundness, raund´-nis, n rotondità f

rouse, raus, *v* svegliare; (anger) suscitare

rout, raut, n disfatta f

route, ruut, n itinerario m; percorso m

routine, ru-tiin´, n routine f

row, rou, n fila f; *v* remare

row, rau, n lite f; *v* litigare

royal*, roi´-al, *adj* reale

royalty, roi´-al-ti, n famiglia reale f; (author's) diritti d'autore *mpl*

rub, röb, *v* fregare; **– off,** venir via; **– out,** cancellare

rubber, röb´-a, n gomma f

rubbish, röb´-ish, n rifiuti *mpl*; (trash) robaccia f

ruby, ruu´-bi, n rubino m

rucksack, rök´-sak, n zaino m

rudder, röd´-a, n timone m

ruddy, röd´-i, *adj* rosso

rude*, ruud, *adj* rozzo, cafone

rudiments, ruu´-di-ments, *npl* rudimenti *mpl*

ruffle, röf´-l, *v* arruffare

rug, rög, n coperta da viaggio f; tappeto m

rugby, rög´-bi, n rugby m

rugged*, rög´-id, *adj* scabro; frastagliato

ruin, ruu´-in, *v* rovinare; n rovina f

rule, ruul, *v* rigare; (govern) governare; n regola f

ruler, ruul´-a, n capo m; (drawing) riga f, righello m

rum, röm, n rum m

rumbling, röm´-bling, n

brontolio *m*; ronzio *m*

rummage, rŏm´-ich, *v*
frugare

rumour, ruu´-m*a*, *n* voce
f, pettegolezzo *m*

run, rŏn, *v* correre;
dirigere; gestire; *n* corsa
f; **– away,** *v* fuggire,
scappare

rupture, rŏp´-ch*a*, *n*
rottura *f*; *med* ernia *f*

rural*, rur´-ral, *adj* rurale

rush, rŏsh, *n* ressa *f*; fretta
f; *v* precipitarsi

Russia, rŏsh-*a*, *n* Russia *f*

Russian, rŏsh-*a*n, *adj*
russo

rust, rŏst, *n* ruggine *f*; *v*
arrugginire

rusty, rŏs´-ti, *adj*
arruginito

rustic, rŏs´-tik, *adj* rustico

rustle, rŏs´-l, *v* frusciare; *n*
fruscio *m*

rut, rŏt, *n* solco *m*

rye, rai, *n* segale *f*

sable, seib´-l, n (fur) zibellino m

sabre, sei´-ba, n sciabola f

sack, sak, n sacco m; v licenziare; mil saccheggiare

sacrament, sa´-kra-ment, n sacramento m

sacred*, seik´-rid, adj sacro

sacrifice, sak´-ri-fais, n sacrificio m; v sacrificare

sacrilege, sak´-ri-lich, n sacrilegio m

sad*, sad, adj triste

saddle, sad´-l, n sella f; v sellare

sadness, sad´-nis, tristezza f

safe, seif, adj* salvo; sicuro; n cassaforte f

safeguard, seif´-gaard, n

salvaguardia f

safety, seif´-ti, n salvezza f; sicurezza f

safety pin, seif´-ti pin, n spilla da balia f

sag, sagh, v afflosciarsi

sagacious*, sa-ghei´-shos, adj sagace

sage, seich, n saggio m; (herb) salvia f

Sagittarius, sach-i-ter´-ri-os, n Sagittario m

sail, seil, n vela f; v veleggiare; (leave) salpare

sailing, sei´-ling, n sport della vela m

sailor, sei´-la, n marinaio m

saint, seint, n santo m

sake, seik, n for ...'s –, per amore di...

salad, sal´-ad, n insalata f

salad dressing, sal´-ad dres´-ing, n condimento per insalata m

salary, sal´-a-ri, n stipendio m

sale, seil, n vendita f; (bargains) svendita f, saldi mpl; (auction) asta f

sales assistant, seils a-sis´-tant, n commesso m, commessa f

salesman, seils´-man, n venditore m

salient, sei´-li-ent, adj saliente

saliva, sa-lai´-va, n saliva f

sallow, sal´-ou, adj giallastro

salmon, sam´-on, n salmone m

saloon, sa-luun´, n salone m

salt, solt, n sale m; adj salato

salt cellar, solt sel´-a, n saliera f

salty, sol´-ti, adj salato

salute, sa-luut´, n mil saluto m; v salutare

salvage, sal´-vich, n salvataggio m; v ricuperare

salvation, sal-vei´-shon, n salvezza f

salver, sal´-va, n vassoio m

same, seim, the –, pron lo

stesso, la stessa, gli
stessi, le stesse; *adj*
stesso, medesimo

sample, saam´-*pl*, *v*
assaggiare; provare; *n*
campione *m*

sanctify, sangk´-ti-fai, *v*
santificare

sanction, sangk´-shon, *n*
sanzione *f*; *v* sanzionare

sanctity, sangk´-ti-ti, *n*
santità *f*

sanctuary, sangk´-tiu-ri, *n*
santuario *m*

sand, sand, *n* sabbia *f*

sandal, san´-dl, *n*
sandalo *m*

sandpaper, sand´-pei-pa, *n*
carta vetrata *f*

sandwich, sand´-uich, *n*
tramezzino *m*; panino
imbottito *m*

sandy, san´-di, *adj*
sabbioso

sane*, sein, *adj* sano

sanitary, san´-i-te-ri, *adj*
sanitario

sanitary towels, san´-i-te-
ri tau´-els, *npl* assorbenti
igienici *mpl*

sanity, san´-i-ti, *n* sanità *f*;
igiene *f*

sap, sap, *n* linfa *f*; *v* minare

sapphire, saf´-air, *n*
zaffiro *m*

sarcasm, saar´-kasm, *n*
sarcasmo *m*

sarcastic, saar-kas´-tik, *adj*

sarcastico

sardine, saar-diin´, *n*
sardina *f*

sash, sash, *n* corda *f*;
(belt) fascia *f*

satchel, sach´-l, *n* (school)
cartella *f*

satellite, sa´-ti-lait, *n*
satellite *m*

satellite dish, sa´-ti-lait
dish, *n* antenna
parabolica *f*

satiate, sei´-shi-eit, *v*
saziare

satin, sat´-in, *n* raso *m*; *adj*
di raso

satire, sat´-air, *n* satira *f*

satisfaction, sat-is-fak´-
shon, *n* soddisfazione *f*

satisfactory, sat-is-fak´-*to*-
ri, *adj* soddisfacente

satisfy, sat´-is-fai, *v*
soddisfare

saturate, sat´-iu-reit, *v*
saturare

Saturday, sat´-*e*-di, *n*
sabato *m*

sauce, soos, *n* salsa *f*

saucepan, soos´-pan, *n*
casseruola *f*

saucer, soo´-sa, *n*
piattino *m*

saunter, soon´-*ta*, *v*
girovagare

sausage, sos´-ich, *n*
salsiccia *f*

savage, sav´-ich, *n*
selvaggio *m*; *adj**

selvaggio

save, seiv, *v* salvare;
(economize)
risparmiare; (keep)
conservare

saving, sei´-ving, *n*
risparmio *m*

savings, sei´-vings, *npl*
risparmi *mpl*

savoury, sei´-ve-ri, *adj*
saporito; (not sweet)
salato

saw, soo, *n* sega *f*; *v* segare

say, sei, *v* dire

saying, sei´-ing, *n* detto *m*

scab, skab, *n* crumiro *m*;
crosta *f*

scaffold, skaf´-old, *n*
(execution) patibolo *m*

scaffolding, skaf´-ol-ding,
n impalcatura *f*

scald, skoold, *v* scottare

scale(s), skeil(s), *npl*
bilancia *f*; (fish) squama
f; (measure, music) scala
f; *v* scalare

scallop, skal´-op, *n* cappa
santa *f*

scalp, skalp, *n* cuoio
capelluto *m*

scamper, skam´-pa, *v*
filarsela

scan, skan, *v* scrutare;
leggere; *n* ecografia *f*

scandal, skan´-dl, *n*
scandalo *m*

scanty, skan´-ti, *adj* scarso;
succinto

scapegoat, skeip´-gout, n capro espiatorio m

scar, skaar, n cicatrice f; v lasciare delle cicatrici su; cicatrizzarsi

scarce, skers, adj scarso, raro

scarcely, skers´-li, adv raramente; appena

scarcity, sker´-si-ti, n scarsità f

scare, sker, v impaurire; – **away**, spaventare

scarecrow, sker´-krou, n spaventapasseri m

scarf, skaarf, n sciarpa f

scarlet, skaar´-let, adj scarlatto

scarlet fever, skaar´-let fii´-va, n scarlattina f

scathing, skei´-Ding, adj sferzante

scatter, skat´-a, v spargere

scene, siin, n scena f

scenery, sii´-ne-ri, n panorama f; (stage) scenario m

scent, sent, n profumo m; (trail) pista f; v profumare

sceptical*, skep´-ti-kl, adj scettico

sceptre, sep´-ta, n scettro m

schedule, shed´-iuul, n tabella di marcia f; lista f; v stabilire; **on** –, in orario

scheduled flight, shed´-iuuld flait, n volo di linea m

scheme, skiim, n piano m, progetto m; v progettare

scholar, skol´-a, n erudito m, studioso m

school, skuul, n scuola f

schoolmaster, skuul-maas´-ta, n maestro m; professore m

schoolmistress, skuul-mis´-tris, n maestra f; professoressa f

sciatica, sai-at´-ka, n sciatica f

science, sai´-ens, n scienza f

scientific, sai-en-tif´-ik, adj scientifico

scissors, sis´-os, npl forbici fpl

scoff, skof, v papparsi; – **at**, farsi beffe di

scold, skould, v sgridare; n sgridata f

scoop, skuup, n paletta f; – **out**, v scavare

scope, skoup, n campo d'azione m; (aim) scopo m

scorch, skoorch, v bruciacchiare

score, skoor, n punteggio m; mus colonna sonora f; v segnare; incidere

scorn, skoorn, n disprezzo m; v disprezzare

scornful*, skoorn´-ful, adj sdegnoso

Scorpio, skoor´-pi-ou, n Scorpione m

scorpion, skoor´-pi-on, n scorpione m

Scotland, skot´-land, n Scozia f

Scottish, skot´-ish, adj scozzese

scoundrel, skaun´-drel, n briccone m

scour, skaur, v fregare

scourge, skerch, n flagello m

scout, skaut, v esplorare; n esploratore m

scowl, skaul, v guardare torvo

scraggy, skragh´-i, adj scheletrico

scramble, skram´-bl, v (eggs) strapazzare; – **for**, azzuffarsi

scrap, skrap, n pezzo m; rottame m; v scartare

scrape, skreip, v raschiare

scratch, skrach, n graffio m; v graffiare; (rub itch) grattare; (glass) scalfire; – **out**, cancellare

scream, skriim, v gridare; n grido m

screen, skriin, v proteggere; n (cinema) schermo m; (room) paravento m

screw, skruu, n vite f; v

avvitare

screwdriver, skruu´-drai-va, n cacciavite m

scribble, skrib´-l, n scarabocchio m; v scribacchiare

scroll, skroul, n rotolo m

scrub, skrŏb, v fregare; n (bush) macchia f

scruple, skruu´-pl, n scrupolo m

scrupulous*, skruu´-piu-los, adj scrupoloso

scrutinize, skruu´-ti-nais, v scrutare

scuffle, skŏf´-l, n rissa f

sculptor, skŏlp´-ta, n scultore m

sculpture, skŏlp´-cha, n scultura f

scum, skŏm, n schiuma f; feccia f

scythe, saiD, n falce f

sea, sii, n mare m

seal, siil, n sigillo m; (animal) foca f; v sigillare

sealskin, siil´-skin, n pelle di foca f

seam, siim, n cucitura f; (mine) vena f, filone m

seaman, sii´-man, n marinaio m

sear, sir, v scottare; bruciare

search, serch, n ricerca f; perquisizione f; v cercare, frugare;

perquisire

searchlight, serch´-lait, n riflettore m

seasick, sii´-sik, adj che soffre il mal di mare

seaside, sii´-said, n spiaggia f

season, sii´-son, n stagione f; v (food) condire

seasoning, sii´-son-ing, n condimento m

season ticket, sii´-son tik´-it, n abbonamento m, tessera f

seaweed, sii´-uiid, n alga f

seat, siit, n sedile m; posto m; (trousers) fondo m; (politics) seggio m

seat belt, siit´-belt, n cintura di sicurezza f

secluded, si-kluu´-did, adj appartato

seclusion, si-kluu´-shon, n ritiro m

second, sek´-ond, n secondo m; adj secondo; (date) due; v (support) appoggiare

secondary, sek´-on-da-ri, adj secondario

secondary school, sek´-on-da-ri skuul, n scuola secondaria f

second-hand, sek´-ond hand, adj di seconda mano

secondly, sek´-ond-li, adv in secondo luogo

secrecy, sii´-kri-si, n segretezza f

secret, sii´-krit, adj* segreto; n segreto m

secretary, sek´-ri-ta-ri, n segretario m; segretaria f

secrete, si-kriit´, v (glands) secernere

secretion, si-krii´-shon, n secrezione f

sect, sekt, n setta f

section, sek´-shon, n sezione f

secure, si-kiur´, adj* sicuro; v assicurare

security, si-kiur´-ri-ti, n sicurezza f; garanzia f

sedative, sed´-a-tiv, n sedativo m

sedentary, sed´-en-tri, adj sedentario

sediment, sed´-i-ment, n sedimento m

seduce, si-diuus´, v sedurre

see, sii, v vedere; (visit) visitare; – **through,** (glass, a person etc.) vedere attraverso; – **to,** occuparsi di

seed, siid, n seme m

seek, siik, v cercare

seem, siim, v sembrare

seethe, siiD, v bollire; ribollire

seize, siis, v prendere; sequestrare

seizure, sii´-sha, n

attacco m

seldom, sel´-dom, *adv*
raramente

select, si-lekt´, *v* scegliere;
adj scelto

selection, si-lek´-shon, *n*
selezione *f*, scelta *f*

self-, self, *prefix* auto-

self-catering, self-kei´-te-
ring, *adj* in cui si
provvede da sé ai pasti

self-conscious, self-kon´-
shos, *adj* timido

selfish, sel´-fish, *adj*
egoista

selfishness, sel´-fish-nis, *n*
egoismo *m*

self-service, self-ser´-vis, *n*
self-service *m*

sell, sel, *v* vendere

semblance, sem´-blans, *n*
sembianza *f*

semi-, sem´-i, *prefix* semi-

semicircle, se´-mi-ser-kl, *n*
semicerchio *m*

semicolon, se-mi-kou´-
lon, *n* punto e virgola *m*

seminary, sem´-i-na-ri, *n*
seminario *m*

semolina, sem-o-lii´-na, *n*
semolino *m*

senate, sen´-it, *n* senato *m*

send, send, *v* mandare;
spedire; – **away,** mandar
via; – **back,** rinviare; –
for, *v* mandare a
chiamare; – **off,** spedire;
(footballer) espellere

sender, sen´-da, *n*
mittente *m/f*

senile, sii´-nail, *adj* senile

senior, sii´-ni-a, *adj*
maggiore, più anziano;
di grado superiore

seniority, sii-ni-o´-ri-ti, *n*
anzianità *f*; superiorità *f*

senior partner, sii´-ni-a
paart´-na, *n* socio più
anziano *m*

sensation, sen-sei´-shon, *n*
sensazione *f*

sense, sens, *n* senso *m*

senseless*, sens´-lis, *adj*
svenuto; insensato

sensible, sen´-si-bl, *adj*
sensato

sensitive, sen´-si-tiv, *adj*
sensibile

sensual*, sen´-siu-al, *adj*
sensuale

sentence, sen´-tens, *n*
frase *f*; *law* sentenza *f*

sentiment, sen´-ti-ment, *n*
sentimento *m*;
(conviction) opinione *f*

sentimental, sen-ti-men´-
tl, *adj* sentimentale

sentinel, sen´-ti-nal, *n*
sentinella *f*

sentry, sen´-tri, *n*
sentinella *f*

separate, sep´-a-reit, *v*
separare; separarsi

separate, sep´-a-rat, *adj**
separato

separation, sep-a-rei´-

shon, *n* separazione *f*

September, sep-tem´-ba, *n*
settembre *m*

septic, sep´-tik, *adj* settico;
infetto

sequel, sii´-kuel, *n*
risultato *m*; sequenza *f*;
seguito *m*

sequence, sii´-kuens, *n*
serie *f*; ordine *m*

serenade, se-ri-neid´, *n*
serenata *f*

serene*, si-riin´, *adj*
sereno

sergeant, saar´-chent, *n*
sergente *m*

serial, siir´-ri-al, *n* serial *m*

series, siir´-ris, *n* serie *f*

serious*, siir´-ri-os, *adj*
serio

sermon, ser´-mon, *n*
predica *f*

servant, ser´-vant,
n domestico *m*,
domestica *f*

serve, serv, *v* servire;
(prison sentence)
scontare

service, ser´-vis, *n*
servizio *m*

service charge, ser´-vis
chaarch, *n* servizio *m*

service station, ser´-vis
stei´-shon, *n* stazione di
servizio *f*

servile, ser´-vail, *adj*
servile

servitude, ser´-vi-tiuud, *n*

servitù f

session, sesh´-n, n
sessione f

set, set, v (trap) tendere;
(clock) regolare;
(example) dare; (task)
imporre; (solidify)
rapprendere; (jewels)
montare; (sun)
tramontare; n serie f;
(china etc.) servizio m;
(radio, TV) apparecchio
m; **– on fire,** dare fuoco
a; **– on music,** mettere
in musica

set menu, set men´-iu, n
menù fisso m, menù
turistico m

settee, set´-ii, n divano m

settle, set´-l, v (accounts)
regolare; (argument)
appianare; (domicile)
stabilirsi

settlement, set´-l-ment, n
(accounts) saldo m;
(argument) risoluzione f;
(agreement) accordo m

seven, sev´-en, adj sette

seventeen, sev-en-tiin´,
adj diciassette

seventeenth, sev-en-
tiinZ´, adj
diciassettesimo; (date)
diciassette

seventh, sev´-enZ, adj
settimo; (date) sette

seventieth, sev-en-ti-eZ,
adj settantesimo

seventy, sev´-en-ti, adj
settanta

sever, sev´-a, v recidere;
interrompere

several, sev´-e-ral, adj
diversi, alcuni

severe*, si-vir´, adj severo;
serio, grave

severity, si-ve´-ri-ti, n
severità f; gravità f

sew, sou, v cucire

sewage, siu´-ich, n acque
di scolo fpl

sewer, siu´-a, n fogna f

sewing, sou´-ing, n cucito
m

sewing machine, sou´-ing
ma-shiin´, n macchina
da cucire f

sex, seks, n sesso m

sexist, sek´-sist, adj sessista

sexual, sek´-siu-al, adj
sessuale

sexy, sek´-si, adj sexy

shabby, shab´-i, adj
malandato; trasandato

shade, sheid, n ombra f;
(colour) tinta f; (lamp)
paralume m; v
proteggere, riparare

shadow, shad´-ou, n
ombra f; v (follow)
pedinare

shady, shei´-di, adj
ombreggiato; fig losco

shaft, shaaft, n albero di
trasmissione m; (mine)
pozzo m

shaggy, shagh´-i, adj ispido

shake, sheik, v scuotere;
agitare; tremare; (hand)

shaky, shei´-ki, adj
malfermo; tremolante

shallow, shal´-ou, adj poco
profondo

sham, sham, n finta f; v
fingere

shame, sheim, n vergogna
f; v far vergognare

shameful*, sheim´-ful, adj
vergognoso

shameless*, sheim´-lis, adj
sfacciato

shampoo, sham-puu´, n
shampoo m

shamrock, sham´-rok, n
trifoglio m

shape, sheip, n forma f; v
formare

share, sher, v dividere;
condividere; n parte f;
(stock) azione f

shareholder, sher´-houl-
da, n azionista m/f

shark, shaark, n pescecane
m, squalo m

sharp*, shaarp, adj
affilato; acuto; pungente

sharpen, shaarp´-en, v
affilare; fare la punta a

sharpener, shaar´-pe-na, n
temperamatite m

shatter, shat´-a, v
mandare in frantumi;
distruggere

shave, sheiv, v radere;

radersi

shaving, shei´-ving, n
rasatura f

shaving brush, shei´-ving
brŏsh, n pennello da
barba m

shaving cream, shei´-ving
kriim, n crema da
barba f

shavings, shei´-vings, npl
trucioli mpl

shawl, shool, n scialle m

she, shii, pron lei, ella

sheaf, shiif, n (corn)
covone m; (papers)
fascio m

shear, shir, v tosare

shears, shirs, npl cesoie fpl

sheath, shiiZ, n guaina f

shed, shed, n capanno m;
v (tears, blood) versare;
(leaves, feathers)
perdere

sheen, shiin, n
lucentezza f

sheep, shiip, n pecora f

sheer, shiir, adj puro,
semplice; (steep)
verticale; (transparent)
velatissimo

sheet, shiit, n (bed)
lenzuolo m; (paper)
foglio m

shelf, shelf, n mensola f;
scaffale m

shell, shel, n conchiglia f;
(nut, egg) guscio m;
(artillery) granata f; v

sgusciare; bombardare

shellfish, shel´-fish, n
crostacei mpl

shelter, shel´-ta, n riparo
m; v ripararsi; proteggere

shepherd, shep´-ed, n
pastore m

sheriff, she´-rif, n
sceriffo m

sherry, she´-ri, n sherry m

shield, shiild, n scudo m; v
difendere

shift, shift, n (workers)
turno m; v spostare

shin, shin, n stinco m

shine, shain, v
risplendere; luccicare;
brillare; n splendore m

shingle, shing´-gl, n
(stones) ciottoli mpl

ship, ship, n nave f; v
spedire via mare

shipwreck, ship´-rek, n
naufragio m

shipyard, ship´-iaard, n
cantiere navale m

shire, shair, n contea f

shirk, sherk, v schivare

shirt, shert, n camicia f

shiver, shiv´-a, v tremare;
n brivido m

shoal, shoul, n (fish)
banco di pesci m

shock, shok, n scossa f;
(fright) shock m; v
scioccare

shock absorber, shok ab-
soor´-ba, n

ammortizzatore m

shocking*, shok´-ing, adj
scioccante

shoddy, shod´-i, adj
(goods) scadente

shoe, shuu, n scarpa f;
(horse) ferro di
cavallo m

shoot, shuut, v sparare;
(film) girare;
(grow) germinare;
n germoglio m

shooting, shuu´-ting, n
sparatoria f

shooting star, shuu´-ting
staar, n stella cadente f

shop, shop, n negozio m; v
fare acquisti; fare la
spesa

shop assistant, shop a-
sis´-tant, n commesso m,
commessa f

shopkeeper, shop-kii´-pa,
n negoziante m/f

shopping, shop´-ing, n
acquisti mpl; spesa f

shopping centre, shop´-
ing sen´-ta, n centro
commerciale m

shore, shoor, n spiaggia f;
(river, lake) riva f

short*, shoort, adj corto;
(small) basso

shortage, shoor´-tich, n
carenza f

short cut, shoort´-kŏt, n
scorciatoia f

shorten, shoort´-n, v

accorciare, ridurre

short-sighted, shoort-sai´-tid, *adj* miope

shot, shot, *n* sparo *m*; tiro *m*

shoulder, shoul´-da, *n* spalla *f*; *v fig* addossarsi

shoulder strap, shoul´-de-strap, *n* bretellina *f*

shout, shaut, *n* grido *m*; *v* gridare

shove, shŏv, *n* spinta *f*; urto *m*; *v* spingere

shovel, shŏv´-l, *n* pala *f*; *v* spalare

show, shou, *v* mostrare; *n* mostra *f*; (play) spettacolo *m*; (exhibition) esposizione *f*

shower, shau´-a, *n* doccia *f*; acquazzone *m*

showroom, shou´-ruum, salone d'esposizione *m*

showy, shou´-i, *adj* vistoso

shred, shred, *n* brandello *m*

shrewd*, shruud, *adj* astuto

shriek, shriik, *n* strillo *m*; *v* strillare

shrill, shril, *adj* squillante

shrimp, shrimp, *n* gamberetto *m*

shrine, shrain, *n* santuario *m*

shrink, shringk, *v* restringersi

shrivel, shriv´-l, **– up,** *v*

avvizzire

shroud, shraud, *n* sudario *m*

Shrove Tuesday, shrouv tiuus´-di, *n* martedì grasso *m*

shrub, shrŏb, *n* arbusto *m*

shrug, shrŏgh, *v* (shoulders) fare spallucce

shudder, shŏd´-a, *n* fremito *m*; *v* fremere

shuffle, shŏf´-l, *v* (cards) mescolare; strascicare i piedi

shun, shŏn, *v* evitare

shut, shŏt, *v* chiudere; **– up,** star zitto

shutter, shŏ´-ta, *n* imposta *f*; (camera) otturatore *m*

shuttle, shŏt´-l, *n* spola *f*, navetta *f*

shy*, shai, *adj* timido

shyness, shai´-nis, *n* timidezza *f*

sick, sik, *adj* malato; nauseato

sicken, sik´-n, *v* nauseare

sickle, sik´-l, *n* falcetto *m*

sickly, sik´-li, *adj* malaticcio

sickness, sik´-nis, *n* malattia *f*

side, said, *v* prendere le parti di; *n* lato *m*, parte *f*

side effect, said´-i-fekt, *n* effetto collaterale *m*

sideways, said´-ueis, *adv*

di fianco, di lato

siege, siich, *n* assedio *m*

sieve, siv, *n* setaccio *m*; *v* setacciare

sift, sift, *v* setacciare

sigh, sai, *n* sospiro *m*; *v* sospirare

sight, sait, *v* avvistare; *n* (eye) vista *f*; (spectacle) spettacolo *m*; (gun) mira *f*; **by –,** di vista

sights, saits, *npl* luoghi di maggiore interesse *mpl*

sign, sain, *n* segno *m*; (board) insegna *f*; *v* firmare

signal, sigh´-nal, *n* segnale *m*; *v* segnalare

signature, sigh´-na-cha, *n* firma *f*

significant*, sigh-nif´-i-kant, *adj* significativo

signify, sigh´-ni-fai, *v* significare

silence, sai´-lens, *n* silenzio *m*; *interj* silenzio!; *v* imporre il silenzio

silencer, sai´-len-sa, *n* silenziatore *m*

silent*, sai´-lent, *adj* silenzioso

silk, silk, *n* seta *f*

sill, sil, *n* davanzale *m*

silly, sil´-i, *adj* sciocco

silver, sil´-va, *n* argento *m*; *adj* d'argento

similar*, sim´-i-la, *adj*

simile

similarity, sim-i-la´-ri-ti, *n* somiglianza *f*

simmer, sim´-a, *v* cuocere a fuoco lento

simple, sim´-pl, *adj* semplice

simplicity, sim-plis´-i-ti, *n* semplicità *f*

simplify, sim´-pli-fai, *v* semplificare

simultaneous*, sim-ul-tei´-ni-os, *adj* simultaneo

sin, sin, *n* peccato *m*; *v* peccare

since, sins, *prep* da; *adv* da allora; *conj* poiché

sincere*, sin-sir´, *adj* sincero

sinew, sin´-iuu, *n* tendine *m*

sing, sing, *v* cantare

singe, sinch, *v* bruciacchiare

singer, sing´-a, *n* cantante *m/f*

single, sing´-gl, *adj* solo; (unmarried) single; *n* (ticket) biglietto d'andata *m*

single room, sing´-gl ruum, *n* camera singola *f*

singly, sing´-ghli, *adv* separatamente

singular, sing´-ghiu-la, *adj** singolare; *n* singolare *m*

sinister, sin´-is-ta, *adj*

sinistro

sink, singk, *v* affondare; *n* (kitchen) lavello *m*

sinner, sin´-a, *n* peccatore *m*

sip, sip, *n* sorso *m*; *v* sorseggiare

siphon, sai´-fon, *n* sifone *m*

siren, sair´-ren, *n* sirena *f*

sirloin, ser´-loin, *n* controfiletto *m*

sister, sis´-ta, *n* sorella *f*

sister-in-law, sis´-te-rin-loo, *n* cognata *f*

sit, sit, *v* sedere; – **down,** sedersi

sitting room, sit´-ing ruum, *n* salotto *m*

site, sait, *n* località *f*; sito *m*; (building) cantiere *m*

situated, sit´-iu-ei-tid, *adj* situato

situation, sit-iu-ei´-shon, *n* situazione *f*

six, siks, *adj* sei

sixteen, siks-tiin´, *adj* sedici

sixteenth, siks-tiinZ´, *adj* sedicesimo; (date) sedici

sixth, siksZ, *adj* sesto; (date) sei

sixtieth, siks´-ti-eZ, *adj* sessantesimo

sixty, siks´-ti, *adj* sessanta

size, sais, *n* dimensioni *fpl*; (clothes) misura *f*, taglia *f*; (shoes) numero *m*; *v*

incollare

skate, skeit, *v* pattinare; *n* pattino *m*; (fish) razza *f*

skateboard, skeit´-boord, *n* skateboard *m*

skater, skei´-ta, *n* pattinatore *m*

skating, skei´-ting, *n* pattinaggio *m*

skating rink, skei´-ting rink, *n* pista di pattinaggio *f*

skein, skein, *n* matassa *f*

skeleton, skel´-i-ton, *n* scheletro *m*

sketch, skech, *n* schizzo *m*; abbozzo *m*; *v* fare uno schizzo

skewer, skiuu´-a, *n* spiedo *m*

ski, skii, *n* sci *m*; *v* sciare

skid, skid, *v* slittare; *n* slittamento *m*

skiing, skii´-ing, *n* (activity) sci *m*

skilful*, skil´-ful, *adj* abile

skill, skil, *n* abilità *f*

skim, skim, *v* scremare

skin, skin, *n* pelle *f*; (peel) buccia *f*; *v* spellare; (peel) sbucciare

skip, skip, *v* saltare; (omit) sorvolare

skipper, skip´-a, *n* capitano *m*

skirmish, sker´-mish, *n* scaramuccia *f*

skirt, skert, *n* gonna *f*

skittle, skit´-l, n birillo m

skull, sköl, n cranio m; (skeleton) teschio m

skunk, sköngk, n puzzola f

sky, skai, n cielo m

skyscraper, skai´-skrei-pa, n grattacielo m

slab, slab, n lastra f

slack, slak, adj (loose) allentato; (business) fiacco

slacken, slak´-n, v allentare; (pace) rallentare

slam, slam, v sbattere

slander, slaan´-da, n diffamazione f

slang, slang, n gergo m

slant, slaant, n pendenza f; fig angolazione f; v inclinare

slanting, slaan´-ting, adj obliquo; inclinato

slap, slap, n manata f, pacca f; schiaffo m; v dare una manata a; schiaffeggiare

slash, slash, v sfregiare; tagliare

slate, sleit, n ardesia f; tegola f; lavagnetta f

slaughter, sloo´-ta, n macello m; v macellare

slave, sleiv, n schiavo m; v lavorare come uno schiavo

slavery, slei´-ve-ri, n schiavitù f

slay, slei, v trucidare

sledge, slech, n (vehicle) slitta f

sledgehammer, slech-ham´-a, n mazza ferrata f

sleek*, sliik, adj liscio; (manners) mellifluo

sleep, sliip, n sonno m; v dormire

sleeper, sliip´-a, n vagone letto m

sleeping bag, sliip´-ing bagh, n sacco a pelo m

sleepless, sliip´-lis, adj insonne

sleeplessness, sliip´-lis-nis, n insonnia f

sleepwalker, sliip´-uoo-ka, n sonnambulo m

sleepy, slii´-pi, adj assonnato

sleet, sliit, n nevischio m

sleeve, sliiv, n manica f

sleigh, slei, n slitta f

sleight, slait, – of hand, n gioco di prestigio m

slender, slen´-da, adj snello, sottile

slice, slais, n fetta f; v affettare

slide, slaid, v scivolare; n scivolo m; diapositiva f; vetrino m

slight*, slait, adj leggero; insignificante

slim, slim, adj snello, magro; v dimagrire

slime, slaim, n melma f

slimy, slai´-mi, adj melmoso; fig viscido

sling, sling, n fionda f; med fascia al collo f; v (throw) scagliare

slip, slip, v scivolare

slipper, slip´-a, n pantofola f

slippery, slip´-e-ri, adj sdrucciolevole

slip road, slip´ roud, n rampa di accesso f

slit, slit, n fessura f; v tagliare

slope, sloup, n china f; v essere in pendio

slot, slot, n fessura f

slouch, slauch, v camminare pesantemente

slovenly, slöv´-en-li, adj trasandato

slow*, slou, adj lento; be –, v (watch) ritardare

slug, slögh, n lumaca f

sluggish*, slö´-ghish, adj lento

sluice, sluus, n chiusa f

slum, slöm, n tugurio m

slumber, slöm´-ba, n sonno m

slump, slömp, n caduta f

slur, sler, v biascicare

slush, slösh, n fanghiglia f

slut, slöt, n sgualdrina f

sly*, slai, adj sornione, scaltro

smack, smak, n schiaffo m;

v dare scapaccioni a

small, smool, *adj* piccolo

smart, smaart, *adj**
elegante; intelligente,
sveglio; *v* (pain) far
male

smash, smash, *n* scontro
m; *comm* successo *m*; *v*
frantumare

smattering, smat´-e-ring, *n*
conoscenza superficiale *f*

smear, smir, *v* imbrattare;
n imbrattatura *f*; *med*
striscio *m*

smell, smel, *n* odore *m*; *v*
odorare

smelly, smel´-i, *adj*
puzzolente

smile, smail, *n* sorriso *m*; *v*
sorridere

smog, smogh, *n* smog *m*

smoke, smouk, *n* fumo *m*;
v fumare

smokeless, smouk´-lis, *adj*
senza fumo

smoker, smouk´-a, *n*
fumatore *m*

smoky, smouk´-i, *adj*
fumoso

smooth, smuuD, *adj**
liscio; *v* lisciare

smother, smŏD´-a, *v*
soffocare

smoulder, smoul´-da, *v*
covare sotto la cenere

smudge, smŏch, *n*
sbavatura *f*; *v* sporcare

smug, smŏgh, *adj*

soddisfatto, compiaciuto

smuggle, smŏgh´-l, *v*
contrabbandare

smuggler, smŏgh´-la, *n*
contrabbandiere *m*

snack, snak, *n* spuntino *m*

snail, sneil, *n* lumaca *f*

snake, sneik, *n* serpente *m*

snap, snap, *n* (noise)
schiocco *m*; (catch)
fermaglio *m*; *v* (break)
spezzarsi; (fingers)
schioccare; – **at,** cercar
di mordere

snapshot, snap´-shot, *n*
istantanea *f*

snare, sner, *n* trappola *f*; *v*
intrappolare

snarl, snaarl, *v* ringhiare

snatch, snach, – **at,** *v*
cercare di afferrare; –
from, strappare da

sneak, sniik, – **away,** *v*
andarsene alla
chetichella

sneer, snir, *n* ghigno *m*; *v*
sogghignare

sneeze, sniis, *n* starnuto
m; *v* starnutire

sniff, snif, *v* annusare

snip, snip, – **off,** *v*
ritagliare

snipe, snaip, *n* beccaccino
m

sniper, snaip´-a, *n* tiratore
scelto *m*

snob, snob, *n* snob *m/f*

snobbish, snob´-ish,

adj snob

snore, snoor, *v* russare

snort, snoort, *n* sbuffata *f*;
v sbuffare

snout, snaut, *n* muso *m*;
(pig) grugno *m*

snow, snou, *n* neve *f*; *v*
nevicare

snowflake, snou´-fleik, *n*
fiocco di neve *m*

snowstorm, snou´-stoorm,
n tempesta di neve *f*

snub, snŏb, *n* affronto *m*;
v snobbare

snub-nosed, snŏb´-nousd,
adj dal naso a patata

snug, snŏgh, *adj* comodo

so, sou, *adv* così; *conj* così
da

soak, souk, *v* inzuppare

soap, soup, *n* sapone *m*

soar, soor, *v* elevarsi

sob, sob, *n* singhiozzo *m*; *v*
singhiozzare

sober*, sou´-ba, *adj* sobrio

soccer, so´-ka, *n* calcio *m*

sociable, sou´-sha-bl, *adj*
socievole

social, sou´-shal, *adj*
sociale

social worker, sou´-shal
uer´-ka, *n* assistente
sociale *m/f*

socialism, sou´-shal-ism, *n*
socialismo *m*

socialist, sou´-shal-ist, *adj*
socialista; *n* socialista
m/f

society, so-sai´-i-ti, *n*
società *f*

sock, sok, *n* calzino *m*

socket, sok´-it, *n* incavo
m; (eyes) orbita *f*;
(electricity) presa di
corrente *f*

sod, sod, *n* zolla erbosa *f*

soda, sou´-da, *n* soda *f*

soft*, soft, *adj* molle

soft drink, soft dringk, *n*
bibita analcolica *f*

soften, sof´-en, *v*
ammorbidire; attenuare

softness, soft´-nis, *n*
mollezza *f*

software, soft´-uer, *n*
software *m*

soil, soil, *n* suolo *m*; *v*
imbrattare

solace, sol´-is, *n*
consolazione *f*

solder, soul´-da, *n*
saldatura *f*; *v* saldare

soldier, soul´-cha, *n*
soldato *m*

sole, soul, *v* risuolare; *n*
(shoe) suola *f*; (foot)
pianta del piede *f*; (fish)
sogliola *f*; *adj* solo, unico

solemn*, sol´-em, *adj*
solenne

solicit, so-lis´-it, *v*
sollecitare; adescare

solicitor, so-lis´-i-ta, *n*
avvocato *m*; notaio *m*

solicitude, so-lis´-i-tiuud,
n sollecitudine *f*

solid*, sol´-id, *adj* solido

solidify, so-lid´-i-fai, *v*
solidificare

solitary, sol´-i-ta-ri, *adj*
solitario

solitude, sol´-i-tiuud, *n*
solitudine *f*

soluble, sol´-iu-bl, *adj*
solubile

solution, so-luu´-shon, *n*
soluzione *f*

solve, solv, *v* risolvere

solvency, sol´-ven-si, *n*
solvibilità *f*

solvent, sol´-vent, *adj*
solvibile; (chemistry)
solvente

sombre, som-ba, *adj* cupo;
triste

some, sŏm, *adj* del, dello,
della, delle, degli;
qualche; *pron* alcuni,
alcune; un po'

somebody, sŏm´-bod-i,
pron qualcuno

somehow, sŏm´-hau, *adv*
in un modo o nell'altro;
per qualche motivo

someone, sŏm´-uŏn, *pron*
qualcuno

something, sŏm´-Zing,
pron qualcosa

sometimes, sŏm´-taim,
adv un giorno; uno di
questi giorni

sometime, sŏm´-taims,
adv qualche volta

somewhat, sŏm´-uot, *adv*

piuttosto, alquanto

somewhere, sŏm´-uer, *adv*
da qualche parte

somersault, sŏm´-e-solt, *n*
capriola *f*

somnambulist, som-nam´-
biu-list, *n* sonnambulo
m

son, sŏn, *n* figlio *m*

song, song, *n* canzone *f*

son-in-law, sŏn-in-loo, *n*
genero *m*

soon, suun, *adv* presto; **as
– as,** non appena

soot, sut, *n* fuliggine *f*

soothe, suuD, *v* calmare

sorcerer, soor´-se-ra, *n*
stregone *m*

sorcery, soor´-se-ri, *n*
stregoneria *f*

sordid*, soor´-did, *adj*
sordido

sore, soor, *n* piaga *f*; *adj*
che fa male

sorrow, so´-rou, *n*
dolore *m*

sorrowful*, so´-rou-ful,
adj addolorato

sorry, so´-ri, *adj* spiacente;
addolorato; **I am –,** mi
dispiace; **–!** scusi!

sort, soort, *n* specie *f*,
genere *m*; *v* ordinare;
smistare

soul, soul, *n* anima *f*

sound, saund, *n* rumore *m*;
suono *m*; *v* suonare; *adj**
(healthy) sano; (safe)

solido; (thorough)
giudizioso

soundproof, saund´-pruuf,
adj insonorizzato

soup, suup, *n* minestra *f*;
zuppa *f*

sour*, sau-a, *adj* agro,
acido, aspro

source, soors, *n* sorgente *f*

south, sauZ, *n* sud *m*,
meridione *m*

southerly, sŏD´-e-li, *adj*
del sud; verso sud

southern, sŏD´-en, *adj*
meridionale

souvenir, su´-ven-iir, *n*
ricordo *m*

sow, sou, *v* seminare

sow, sau, *n* scrofa *f*

soya, soi´-a, *n* soia *f*

space, speis, *n* spazio *m*;
(time) intervallo *m*

spacious*, spei´-shos, *adj*
spazioso

spade, speid, *n* vanga *f*

Spain, spein, *n* Spagna *f*

span, span, *n* palmo *m*; *fig*
durata *f*; *v* attraversare

spangle, spang´-gl, *n*
lustrino *m v* costellare

spaniel, span´-iel, *n*
spaniel *m*

Spanish, span´-ish, *adj*
spagnolo; *n* (language)
spagnolo *m*

spanner, span´-a, *n* chiave
inglese *f*

spar, spaar, *v* (boxing)

allenarsi

spare, sper, *v* (life)
risparmiare; (afford)
dare; (part with) fare a
meno di; *adj* di riserva;
in più; *n* pezzo di
ricambio *m*

sparing*, sper´-ring, *adj*
(thrifty) economo

spark, spaark, *n* scintilla *f*;
v scintillare

spark plug, spaark´ plŏgh,
n candela *f*

sparkle, spaark´-l, *v*
scintillare; (wine)
spumare

sparkling, spaark´-ling, *adj*
scintillante; frizzante

sparrow, spa´-rou, *n*
passero *m*

spasm, spasm, *n*
spasimo *m*

spasmodic, spas-mo´-dik,
adj spasmodico;
intermittente

spatter, spat´-a, *v* schizzare

spawn, spoon, *n* (fish,
frog) uova *fpl*; *v* deporre
le uova

speak, spiik, *v* parlare

speaker, spii´-ka, *n*
oratore *m*

spear, spir, *n* lancia *f*

special*, spesh´-al, *adj*
speciale

speciality, spe-shi-al´-i-ti,
n specialità *f*

species, spii´-shis, *n*

specie *f*

specific, spi-si´-fik, *adj*
specifico

specification, spes-i-fi-
kei´-shon, *n*
specificazione *f*

specify, spes´-i-fai, *v*
specificare

specimen, spes´-i-min, *n*
esemplare *m*

speck, spek, *n* macchia *f*,
punto *m*

spectacle, spek´-ta-kl, *n*
spettacolo *m*

spectacles, spek´-ta-kls,
npl occhiali *mpl*

spectator, spek-tei´-ta, *n*
spettatore *m*

spectre, spek´-ta, *n*
spettro *m*

speculate, spek´-iu-leit, *v*
speculare

speech, spiich, *n* parola *f*;
(discourse) discorso *m*

speechless, spiich´-lis, *adj*
senza parole;
ammutolito

speed, spiid, *n* velocità *f*; *v*
andare a velocità
eccessiva

speed limit, spiid lim´-it, *n*
limite di velocità *m*

speedy, spii´-di, *adj*
pronto; celere

spell, spel, *v* compitare; *n*
(charm) incantesimo *m*;
(time) periodo *m*

spend, spend, *v* spendere

sphere, sfir, n sfera f

spice, spais, n spezia f; v condire con spezie

spicy, spai´-si, adj piccante

spider, spai´-da, n ragno m

spike, spaik, n spunzone m

spill, spil, v spandere

spin, spin, v far girare

spinach, spin´-ich, n spinaci mpl

spinal, spain´-l, adj dorsale

spindle, spin´-dl, n fuso m

spine, spain, n spina f

spinster, spin´-sta, n zitella f

spiral, spair´-ral, n spirale f; adj spirale

spire, spair, n guglia f

spirit, spi´-rit, n spirito m; (alcohol) alcol m; (vitality) energia f; (drinks) alcolici mpl

spiritual, spi´-rit-iu-al, adj spirituale

spit, spit, v sputare; n sputo m; (roasting) spiedo m

spite, spait, n dispetto m; v causare dispetto; **in – of,** conj nonostante

spiteful*, spait´-ful, adj dispettoso

spittle, spit´-l, n sputo m

splash, splash, n spruzzo m; v spruzzare

splendid*, splen´-did, adj splendido

splendour, splen´-da, n splendore m

splint, splint, n (surgical) stecca f

splinter, splin´-ta, n scheggia f; v scheggiarsi

split, split, n scissione f; spaccatura f; v spaccarsi; dividere

spoil, spoil, v guastare; (child) viziare

spoils, spoils, npl bottino m

spoke, spouk, n raggio m

spokesman, spouks´-man, n portavoce m

spokeswoman, spouks´-uu-man, n portavoce f

sponge, spŏnch, n spugna f

sponsor, spon´-sa, n sponsor m; v sponsorizzare

spontaneous*, spon-tei´-ni-os, adj spontaneo

spool, spuul, n rocchetto m

spoon, spuun, n cucchiaio m

spoonful, spuun´-ful, n cucchiaiata f

sport, spoort, n sport m

sporty, spoor´-ti, adj sportivo

spot, spot, n punto m; (dirt) macchia f; (pimple) foruncolo m; (place) luogo m; v chiazzare

spot check, spot chek´, n controllo casuale m

spotless*, spot´-lis, adj immacolato

spotted, spot´-id, adj maculato; a puntini

spout, spaut, n (gutter) grondaia f; (pot or jug) becco m; v zampillare

sprain, sprein, n distorsione f; v storcere

sprawl, sprool, v stravaccarsi; (town, plant) crescere in modo disordinato

spray, sprei, v spruzzare; n spruzzo m

spread, spred, v estendersi; (butter etc.) spalmare; (news) diffondere

sprig, sprigh, n ramoscello m

sprightly, sprait´-li, adj arzillo

spring, spring, n primavera f; (leap) salto m; (water) sorgente f; (metal) molla f; v saltare

springy, spring´-i, adj elastico

sprinkle, spring´-kl, v spruzzare; spargere

sprout, spraut, n germoglio m; cavolino di Bruxelles m; v germogliare

spur, sper, n sperone m; incentivo m; v spronare

spurious*, spiur´-ri-os, *adj*
falso

spurn, spern, *v* disprezzare

spy, spai, *n* spia *f*; *v* spiare

squabble, skuob´-l, *n* lite *f*;
v litigare

squad, skuod, *n* squadra *f*

squalid*, skuol´-id, *adj*
squallido

squall, skuool, *n* raffica *f*;
burrasca *f*

squalor, skuol´-a, *n*
squallore *m*

squander, skuon´-da, *v*
dissipare

square, skuer, *adj**
quadrato; *n* quadrato *m*;
piazza *f*

squash, skuosh, *v*
schiacciare; *n* squash *m*;
(drink) spremuta *f*

squat, skuot, *adj* (figure)
tozzo; *n* casa occupata *f*;
v occupare
abusivamente;
accovacciarsi

squeak, skuiik, *v* squittire

squeeze, skuiis, *n* stretta *f*;
v spremere; stringere

squid, skuid, *n* calamaro *m*

squint, skuint, *n* strabismo
m; *v* strabuzzare gli occhi

squirrel, skui´-rel, *n*
scoiattolo *m*

squirt, skuert, *v* schizzare

stab, stab, *n* pugnalata *f*; *v*
pugnalare

stability, sta-bil´-i-ti, *n*

stabilità *f*

stable, steib´-l, *n* scuderia
f; *adj* stabile

stack, stak, *n* catasta *f*,
mucchio *m*; (chimney)
ciminiera *f*; *v*
ammucchiare

stadium, stei´-di-um, *n*
stadio *m*

staff, staaf, *n* personale *m*

stag, stagh, *n* cervo *m*

stage, steich, *n* (theatre)
scena *f*, palcoscenico *m*;
(step) fase *f*; *v* mettere
in scena

stagger, stagh´-a, *v*
vacillare; (astonish)
sbalordire

stagnate, stagh-neit´, *v*
stagnare

stag party, stagh´-paar-ti,
n festa di addio al
celibato *f*

staid*, steid, *adj* posato,
serio

stain, stein, *v* tingere;
(soil) macchiare; *n*
macchia *f*

stainless, stein´-lis, *adj*
(metal) inossidabile

stair, ster, *n* gradino *m*,
scalino *m*

staircase, ster´-keis, *n*
scala *f*

stairs, sters, *npl* scale *fpl*

stake, steik, *n* paletto *m*; *v*
scommettere

stale, steil, *adj* (bread)

stantio; (beer) svaporato

stalk, stook, *n* gambo *m*; *v*
seguire

stall, stool, *n* bancarella *f*;
(theatre) platea *f*; *v*
(car) spegnersi

stalwart, stool´-uat, *adj*
fedele

stamina, stam´-i-na, *n*
resistenza *f*

stammer, stam´-a, *v*
balbettare; *n* balbuzie *f*

stamp, stamp, *n* (postage)
francobollo *m*; (rubber
etc.) timbro *m*; *v*
(letters) affrancare;
(imprint) timbrare;
(foot) pestare i piedi

stampede, stam-piid´, *n*
fuga precipitosa *f*

stand, stand, *n* posizione *f*;
tribuna *f*; (taxi)
posteggio *m*;
(exhibition) stand *m*; *v*
stare; stare in piedi;
(endure) sopportare;
– by, rimanere vicino;
sostenere; **– up,** alzarsi
in piedi

standard, stan-dad, *n*
modello *m*, standard *m*;
adj normale; (weights
etc.) tipo

standing, stan´-ding, *adj* in
piedi; fisso; *n* posizione *f*

standing room, stan´-ding
ruum, *n* posto in piedi *m*

standstill, stand´-stil, *n*

punto morto *m*

staple, steip´-l, *adj*
principale; *n* punto
metallico *m*

stapler, steip´-la, *n*
cucitrice *f*

star, staar, *n* stella *f*

starch, staarch, *n* amido
m; *v* inamidare

stare, ster, *n* sguardo fisso
m; *v* guardare fisso

starling, staar´-ling, *n*
storno *m*

starry, staar´-ri, *adj*
stellato

start, staart, *n* inizio *m*;
(departure) partenza *f*; *v*
iniziare, cominciare;
mech mettere in moto;
(depart) partire

startle, staart´-l, *v*
trasalire; far trasalire

starvation, staar-vei´-
shon, *n* inedia *f*; fame *f*

starve, staarv, *v* morire
d'inedia; morire di fame

state, steit, *v* dichiarare; *n*
stato *m*; (condition)
condizione *f*

stately, steit´-li, *adj*
maestoso

statement, steit´-ment, *n*
dichiarazione *f*; (bank)
estratto conto *m*

statesman, steits´-man, *n*
statista *m*

station, stei´-shon, *n*
(railway) stazione *f*;

(police, fire) caserma *f*;
v disporre

stationary, stei´-shon-a-ri,
adj fermo

stationer's, stei´-shon-es,
n cartoleria *f*

stationery, stei´-shon-e-ri,
n articoli di cancelleria
mpl

statistics, sta-tis´-tiks, *n*
statistica *f*

statue, stat´-iuu, *n* statua *f*

statute, stat´-iut, *n* statuto
m

staunch, stoonch, *adj*
fedele

stave, steiv, *v* – **in,**
sfondare; – **off,** evitare

stay, stei, *n* soggiorno *m*; *v*
(remain) rimanere

steadfast, sted´-faast, *adj*
saldo, fermo

steady, sted´-i, *adj* serio;
costante; stabile; solido

steak, steik, *n* bistecca *f*

steal, stiil, *v* rubare

stealth, stelZ, *n* **by –,**
furtivamente

steam, stiim, *n* vapore *m*;
v cuocere al vapore

steamy, stii´-mi, *adj*
appannato; pieno di
vapore

steel, stiil, *n* acciaio *m*

steep, stiip, *adj* erto; *v*
(soak) inzuppare

steeple, stiip´-l, *n*
campanile *m*

steer, stir, *v* guidare

steering wheel, stir´-ring
uil, *n* volante *m*

stem, stem, *n* stelo *m*;
(fruit) picciolo *m*; –
from, derivare da

stench, stench, *n* tanfo *m*

step, step, *n* passo *m*;
(stair) gradino *m*; *v* fare
un passo

stepbrother, step´-brŏ-Da,
n fratellastro *m*

stepfather, step´-faa-Da, *n*
patrigno *m*

stepladder, step´-lad-a, *n*
scala a libretto *f*

stepmother, step´-mŏ-Da,
n matrigna *f*

stepsister, step´-sis-ta, *n*
sorellastra *f*

stereo, ste´-ri-ou, *adj*
stereo; *n* stereo *m*

sterile, ste´-rail, *adj* sterile

sterilize, ste´-ri-lais, *v*
sterilizzare

sterling, ster´-ling, *adj*
puro; *n* sterlina *f*

stern*, stern, *adj* austero

stew, stiuu, *n* stufato *m*; *v*
cuocere in umido

steward, stiuu´-ed, *n*
steward *m*, assistente di
volo *m*

stewardess, stiuu-ed-es´, *n*
hostess *f*, assistente di
volo *f*

stick, stik, *n* bacchetta *f*;
(walking etc.) bastone

m; *v* attaccare; incollare

sticky, stik´-i, *adj*
appiccicoso

stiff, stif, *adj* duro; rigido

stiffen, stif´-n, *v* irrigidire

stifle, staif´-l, *v* soffocare

stigmatize, stigh´-ma-**tais**,
v stigmatizzare

still, stil, *adj* quieto;
calmo; *adv* ancora;
tuttavia

still life, stil laif´, *n* natura
morta *f*

stimulate, stim´-iu-leit, *v*
stimolare

sting, sting, *v* pungere; *n*
puntura *f*; pungiglione *m*

stingy, stin´-chi, *adj*
spilorcio

stink, stingk, *v* puzzare; *n*
puzzo *m*

stint, stint, *v* lesinare

stipulate, stip´-iu-leit, *v*
stipulare

stipulation, stip-iu-lei´-
shon, *n* stipulazione *f*

stir, ster, *v* mescolare; (to
move) commuovere

stirrup, sti´-rop, *n* staffa *f*

stitch, stich, *v* cucire; *n*
punto *m*; (knitting)
maglia *f*; (pain) fitta *f*

stock, stok, *n* (store) stock
m; (broth) brodo *m*;
(live) bestiame *m*; *v*
(keep) avere in
magazzino

stockbroker, stok´-brou-

ka, *n* agente di borsa *m/f*

stock cube, stok´-kiuub, *n*
dado per brodo *m*

stock exchange, stok iks-
cheinch, *n* borsa valori *f*

stocking, stok´-ing, *n*
calza *f*

stock market, stok
maar´-kit, *n* mercato
azionario *m*

stocktaking, stok´-tei-
king, *n* inventario *m*

stocks, stoks, *npl* valori di
borsa *mpl*

stoke, stouk, *v* attizzare

stolid, stol´-id, *adj*
flemmatico

stomach, stôm´-ak, *n*
stomaco *m*

stone, stoun, *n* pietra *f*;
(pebble) ciottolo *m*; (of
fruit) nocciolo *m*; *v*
lapidare; (fruit)
snocciolare

stool, stuul, *n* sgabello *m*

stoop, stuup, *v* abbassarsi

stop, stop, *n* fermata *f*;
(punctuation) punto *m*;
v fermare; (payment)
sospendere; (cease)
interrompere; – **up,**
otturare

stopper, stop´-a, *n*
tappo *m*

storage, stoor´-rich, *n*
magazzinaggio *m*

store, stoor, *v*
immagazzinare; *n* (shop)

magazzino *m*

stork, stoork, *n* cicogna *f*

storm, stoorm, *n*
temporale *m*; *v* prendere
d'assalto

stormy, stoor´-mi, *adj*
tempestoso

story, stoor´-ri, *n* racconto
m; storia *f*

storybook, stoor´-ri-buk,
n libro di racconti *m*

stout*, staut, *adj*
corpulento; *n* birra
scura *f*

stove, stouv, *n* stufa *f*;
(range) fornello *m*

stow, stou, *v* stivare

stowaway, stou´-a-uei,
n passeggero
clandestino *m*

straggle, stragh´-l, *v* (lag)
rimanere indietro

straight, streit, *adj* diritto;
onesto; *adv* diritto

straighten, streit´-n, *v*
raddrizzare

straightforward, streit-
foor´-uad, *adj* semplice;
onesto

strain, strein, *n* (effort)
sforzo *m*; (tendon)
strappo *m*; *v* sforzarsi;
(tendon) strappare;
(liquid) filtrare

strainer, strein´-a, *n*
colino *m*

straits, streits, *npl*
(channel) stretto *m*

strand, strand, *n* filo *m*;
(hair) ciocca *f*

stranded, stran´-did, *adj*
bloccato

strange*, streinch, *adj*
strano

stranger, strein´-cha, *n*
sconosciuto *m*;
estraneo *m*

strangle, strang´-gl, *v*
strangolare

strap, strap, *n* cinghia *f*;
bretellina *f*

straw, stroo, *n* paglia *f*

strawberry, stroo´-be-ri, *n*
fragola *f*

stray, strei, *adj* randagio; *v*
smarrirsi

streak, striik, *n* striscia *f*

streaky, strii´-ki, *adj*
striato

stream, striim, *n*
corrente *f*

street, striit, *n* via *f*

strength, strengZ, *n* forza *f*

strengthen, streng´-Zen, *v*
rinforzare

strenuous*, stren´-iu-os,
adj energico

stress, stres, *n* accento *m*;
pressione *f*; stress *m*; *v*
accentare; sottolineare

stretch, strech, *n* distesa *f*;
v tendere; estendersi;
stiracchiarsi

stretcher, strech´-a, *n*
barella *f*

strewn, struun, *adj* –

with, cosparso di

strict*, strikt, *adj* severo;
stretto

stride, straid, *n* passo
lungo *m*; *v* camminare a
passi lunghi

strife, straif, *n* disputa *f*

strike, straik, *n* sciopero
m; *v* (work) scioperare;
(hit) colpire; (match)
accendere; **– out,**
(delete) depennare

striker, straik´-a, *n*
scioperante *m/f*

string, string, *n* spago *m*;
(violin) corda *f*

stringency, strin´-chen-si,
n rigore *m*

strip, strip, *n* striscia *f*;
(comic) fumetto *m*; *v*
spogliarsi

stripe, straip, *n* striscia *f*

strive, straiv, *v* sforzarsi,
lottare

stroke, strouk, *n* (blow)
colpo *m*; *med* attacco *m*;
(pen) tratto *m*; (piston)
corsa *f*

stroll, stroul, *n* giro *m*; *v*
far un giro

strong*, strong, *adj* forte;
(firm) solido

structure, strŏk´-cha, *n*
struttura *f*

struggle, strŏgh´-l, *n* lotta
f; *v* lottare

strut, strŏt, *v*
pavoneggiarsi

stubborn*, stŏb´-en, *adj*
testardo

stud, stŏd, *n* (nail)
borchia *f*; (shoes)
tacchetto *m*; (horse)
stallone *m*

student, stiuu´-dent, *n*
studente *m*, studentessa
f

studio, stiuu´-di-ou, *n*
studio *m*

studio flat, stiuu´-di-ou
flat, *n* monolocale *m*

studious*, stiuu´-di-os, *adj*
studioso

study, stŏd´-i, *n* studio *m*;
v studiare

stuff, stŏf, *v* (pad)
imbottire; (preserve)
impagliare; (cookery)
farcire; (gorge)
rimpinzarsi; *n* roba *f*

stuffing, stŏf´-ing, *n*
imbottitura *f*; (cookery)
ripieno *m*

stuffy, stŏf´-i, *adj* mal
ventilato

stumble, stŏm´-bl, *v*
inciampare

stump, stŏmp, *n* (limb)
moncone *m*; (tree etc.)
ceppo *m*; (cigar etc.)
mozzicone *m*

stun, stŏn, *v* stordire

stunning, stŏn´-ing, *adj*
fantastico

stunted, stŏn´-tid, *adj*
(growth) stentato

stupefy, stiuu´-pi-fai, *v* stordire

stupendous*, stiu-pen´-dos, *adj* stupendo

stupid*, stiu´-pid, *adj* stupido

stupidity, stiu-pi´-di-ti, *n* stupidaggine *f*

stupor, stiu´-pa, *n* torpore *m*

sturdy, ster´-di, *adj* vigoroso; robusto

sturgeon, ster´-chon, *n* storione *m*

stutter, stŏt´-a, *v* balbettare; *n* balbuzie *f*

sty, stai, *n* (eye) orzaiolo *m*

style, stail, *n* stile *m*; classe *f*

stylish, stai´-lish, *adj* elegante, distinto

subdue, sub-diuu´, *v* soggiogare

subdued, sub-diuud´, *adj* sommesso

subject, sub-chekt´, *v* assoggettare

subject, sŏb´-chikt, *n* soggetto *m*; (a national) cittadino *m*; – to, *adj* soggetto a

subjunctive, sub-chŏngk´-tiv, *n* congiuntivo *m*

sublime, sub-laim´, *adj* sublime

submarine, sŏb-ma-riin´, *n* sottomarino *m*

submerge, sub-merch´, *v* sommergere

submission, sub-mish´-on, *n* sottomissione *f*

submit, sub-mit´, *v* sottomettere

subordinate, sub-oor´-di-nat, *adj* subordinato

subpoena, sub-pii´-na, *n* mandato di comparizione *m*

subscribe, sub-skraib´, *v* abbonarsi; – to, condividere

subscriber, sub-skraib´-a, *n* abbonato *m*

subscription, sub-skrip´-shon, *n* sottoscrizione *f*; abbonamento *m*

subsequent*, sŏb´-si-kuent, *adj* seguente

subside, sub-said´, *v* cedere; (abate) calmarsi

subsidiary, sub-sid´-i-a-ri, *adj* accessorio

subsidize, sŏb´-si-dais, *v* sovvenzionare

subsidy, sŏb´-si-di, *n* sussidio *m*

subsistance, sub-sis´-tans, *n* sussitenza *f*

substance, sŏb´-stans, *n* sostanza *f*

substantial, sub-stan´-shal, *adj* sostanzioso; notevole

substantiate, sub-stan´-shi-eit, *v* provare

substitute, sŏb-sti-tiut, *n* (person) sostituto *m*; (thing) surrogato *m*; *v* sostituire

subterranean, sub-te-rei´-ni-an, *adj* sotterraneo

subtitles, sŏb-tai´-tls, *npl* sottotitoli *mpl*

subtle, sŏt´-l, *adj* fino; sottile

subtract, sub-trakt´, *v* sottrarre

suburb, sŏb´-erb, *n* sobborgo *m*

subway, sŏb´-uei, *n* sottopassaggio *m*

succeed, suk-siid´, *v* succedere a; riuscire

success, suk-ses´, *n* successo *m*

successful*, suk-ses´-ful, *adj* riuscito

succession, suk-sesh´-on, *n* successione *f*

successive, suk-ses´-siv, *adj* successivo

succumb, su-kŏm´, *v* soccombere

such, sŏch, *adj* tale; *adv* talmente; – a, un tale

suck, sŏk, *v* succhiare

suction, sŏk´-shon, *n* aspirazione *f*

sudden*, sŏd´-n, *adj* improvviso

sue, siuu, *v* citare in giudizio

suet, suu´-it, *n* grasso di

rognone m

suffer, sŏf´-a, v soffrire

suffering, sŏf´-e-ring, n
sofferenza f

suffice, su-fais´, v bastare

sufficient*, su-fish´-ent,
adj sufficiente

suffocate, sŏf´-o-keit, v
soffocare

suffrage, sŏf´-rich, n
suffragio m

sugar, shu´-ga, n zucchero
m; v zuccherare

suggest, su-chest´, v
suggerire, proporre

suggestion, su-ches´-chon,
n suggerimento m,
proposta f

suicide, suu´-i-said, n
suicidio m

suit, suut, v convenire;
(dress etc.) star bene; n
abito completo m; law
causa f

suitable, suut´-a-bl, adj
adatto; conveniente

suitcase, suut´-keis, n
valigia f

suite, suiit, n (rooms)
appartamento m;
(furniture) mobilia f

sulk, sŏlk, v fare il broncio

sulky, sŏlk´-i, adj
imbronciato

sullen*, sŏl´-n, adj cupo

sulphur, sŏl´-fa, n zolfo m

sultry, sŏl´-tri, adj
soffocante, afoso

sum, sŏm, n somma f; –
up, v ricapitolare

summary, sŏm´-a-ri, n
sommario m; adj
sommario

summer, sŏm´-a, n estate f

summit, sŏm´-it, n
sommità f, cima f;
(politics) vertice m

summon, sŏm´-on, v
citare; (call) convocare

summons, sŏm´-ons, n
(legal) citazione f

sumptuous*, sŏmp´-tiu-
os, adj sontuoso

sun, sŏn, n sole m

sunbathe, sŏn´-beiD, v
prendere il sole

sunburn, sŏn´-bern, n
scottatura f

sun cream, sŏn´ criim, n
crema solare f

Sunday, sŏn´-di, n
domenica f

sundries, sŏn´-dris, npl,
diversi mpl

sundry, sŏn´-dri, adj vario

sunflower, sŏn-flau´-a, n
girasole m

sunglasses, sŏn-ghlaas´-is,
npl occhiali da sole

sunken, sŏng´-ken, adj
(features) incavato

sunny, sŏn´-i, adj assolato;
soleggiato; (day) di sole

sunrise, sŏn´-rais, n alba f

sunscreen, sŏn´-scriin,
n lozione solare

protettiva f

sunset, sŏn´-set, n
tramonto m

sunshine, sŏn´-shain, n
sole m

sunstroke, sŏn´-strouk, n
colpo di sole m,
insolazione f

suntan, sŏn´-tan, n
abbronzatura f

super, suu´-pa, adj
splendido

superb*, su-perb´, adj
superbo

superficial*, suu-pe-fi´-
shal, adj superficiale

superfluous*, su-per´-flu-
os, adj superfluo

superior, su-pir´-ri-a, adj
superiore; n superiore m

superlative, su-per´-la-tiv,
n superlativo m

supermarket, suu-pe-
maar´-kit, n
supermercato m

supernatural, suu-pe-
nat´-chu-ral, adj
soprannaturale; n
soprannaturale m

superstition, suu-pe-
stish´-on, n superstizione
f

superstitious*, suu-pe-
stish´-os, adj
superstizioso

supervise, suu´-pe-vais, v
soprintendere;
sorvegliare

supervision, suu-pe-vish´-on, n supervisione f; sorveglianza f

supervisor, suu-pe-vais´-a, n soprintendente m/f; sorvegliante m/f

supper, sŏp´-a, n cena f

supple, sŏp´-l, adj flessibile

supplement, sŏp´-li-ment, n supplemento m

supplier, sup-lai´-a, n fornitore m

supply, sup-lai´, v (with) fornire; n fornitura f

support, su-poort´, n sostegno m; v sostenere

suppose, su-pous´, v supporre

supposition, sŏp-o-sish´-on, n supposizione f

suppress, su-pres´, v sopprimere; (conceal) nascondere

supremacy, su-prem´-a-si, n supremazia f

supreme*, su-priim´, adj supremo

surcharge, ser´-chaarch, n sovrapprezzo m

sure*, shoor, adj sicuro, certo

surety, shoor´-ri-ti, n cauzione f; (person) garante m

surf, serf, n spuma del mare f

surface, ser´-fis, n superficie f; v venire in superficie

surfboard, serf´-boord, n tavola da surf f

surfing, serf´-ing, n surf m

surge, serch, v sollevarsi; n ondata f

surgeon, ser´-chon, n chirurgo m

surgery, ser´-che-ri, n chirurgia f; ambulatorio m

surgical, ser´-chik-l, adj chirurgico

surly, ser´-li, adj burbero; irascibile

surmise, su-mais´, n supposizione f; v supporre

surmount, su-maunt´, v sormontare

surname, ser´-neim, n cognome m

surpass, su-paas´, v superare

surplus, ser´-plus, n eccedenza f

surprise, su-prais´, n sorpresa f; v sorprendere

surrender, su-ren´-da, n resa f, capitolazione f; v capitolare; arrendersi

surround, su-raund´, v circondare

surroundings, su-raun-dings, npl dintorni mpl

survey, ser´-vei, n perizia f; rilevamento m; fare una perizia; (to glance) ispezionare

surveyor, su-vei´-a, n geometra m; perito m

survival, su-vai´-val, n sopravvivenza f

survive, su-vaiv´, v sopravvivere

survivor, su-vai´-va, n superstite m/f

susceptible, su-sep´-ti-bl, adj suscettibile

suspect, sus-pekt´, v sospettare

suspect, sŏs´-pekt, n sospetto m

suspend, sus-pend´, v sospendere

suspenders, sus-pen´-des, npl giarrettiere fpl

suspense, sus-pens´, n suspense f

suspension, sus-pen´-shon, n sospensione f

suspicion, sus-pish´-on, n sospetto m

suspicious*, sus-pish´-os, adj sospettoso

sustain, sus-tein´, v sostenere; mantenere; (loss) subire

sustenance, sŏs´-ti-nans, n mantenimento m

swagger, suagh´-a, n spavalderia f; v fare lo spavaldo

swallow, suol´-ou, v inghiottire; n rondine f

swamp, suomp, n palude f;

v sommergere

swan, suon, *v* cigno *m*

swap, suop, *v* fare uno scambio

swarm, suoorm, *n* sciame *m*; *v* sciamare

sway, suei, *n* (influence) influenza *f*; *v* influenzare; (to rock) oscillare; (to reel) vacillare

swear, suer, *v* giurare; (curse) bestemmiare

sweat, suet, *n* sudore *m*; *v* sudare

sweater, suet´-a, *n* maglione *m*

sweatshirt, suet´-shert, *n* felpa *f*

Sweden, suiid´-n, *n* Svezia *f*

Swedish, suiid´-ish, *adj* svedese; *n* (language) svedese

sweep, suiip, *v* spazzare

sweet, suiit, *n* dolce *m*; *adj** dolce

sweeten, suiit´-n, *v* zuccherare; *fig* addolcire

sweetheart, suiit´-haart, *n* innamorato *m*, innamorata *f*; tesoro *m*

sweetness, suiit´-nis, *n* dolcezza *f*

sweet pea, suiit pii´, *n* pisello odoroso *m*

swell, suel, *v* gonfiarsi; *n* (sea) mare lungo *m*

swelling, suel´-ing, *n* gonfiore *m*

swerve, suerv, *v* deviare; sterzare; (skid) slittare

swift*, suift, *adj* veloce, rapido

swim, suim, *n* nuotata *f*; *v* nuotare

swimming, suim´-ing, *n* nuoto *m*

swimming costume, suim´-ing kos´-tiuum, *n* costume da bagno *m*

swimming pool, suim´-ing puul, *n* piscina *f*

swimming trunks, suim´-ing trŏngks, *npl* calzoncini da bagno *mpl*

swindle, suin´-dl, *n* truffa *f*; truffare

swindler, suin´-dla, *n* imbroglione *m*

swine, suain, *n* porco *m*

swing, suing, *n* oscillazione *f*; (child's) altalena *f*; *v* dondolare, oscillare

Swiss, suis, *adj* svizzero

switch, suich, *n* interruttore *m*; *v* scambiare; – **off**, spegnere; – **on**, accendere

switchboard, suich´-boord, *n* centralino *m*

Switzerland, suit´-se-land, *n* Svizzera *f*

swivel, sui´-vel, *n* perno *m*

swoon, suun, *v* svenire

swoop, suup, – **down,** *v* piombare dall'alto

sword, soord, *n* spada *f*

sworn, suoorn, *adj* giurato

syllable, sil´-a-bl, *n* sillaba *f*

syllabus, sil´-a-bus, *n* (school) programma *m*

symbol, sim´-bol, *n* simbolo *m*

symmetry, sim´-it-ri, *n* simmetria *f*

sympathetic, sim-pa-Zet´-ik, *adj* comprensivo, compassionevole

sympathize, sim-pa-Zais´, *v* compatire

sympathy, sim´-pa-Zi, *n* compassione *f*

symptom, simp´-tom, *n* sintomo *m*

synchronize, sing´-kro-nais, *v* sincronizzare

syndicate, sin´-di-kat, *n* consorzio *m*

synonymous*, si-non´-i-mos, *adj* sinonimo

synthetic, sin-Zet´-ik, *adj* sintetico

syphilis, sif´-il-is, *n* sifilide *f*

syringe, si-rinch´, *n* siringa *f*; *v* siringare

syrup, si´-rop, *n* sciroppo *m*

system, sis´-tem, *n* sistema *m*

tabernacle, tab´-e-nak-l, n
tabernacolo m

table, teib´-l, n tavolo m,
tavola f; (list) tabella f

tablecloth, teib´-l-kloZ, n
tovaglia f

tablespoon, teib´-l-spuun,
n cucchiaio da tavola m

tablet, tab´-lit, n tavoletta
f; pastiglia f

table tennis, teib´-l ten´-
is, n ping pong m

tack, tak, n (nail) bulletta
f; v imbullettare

tackle, tak´-l, n (fishing)
arnesi da pesca mpl; v
affrontare

tact, takt, n tatto m

tactful*, takt´-ful, adj
pieno di tatto, discreto

tactics, tak-tiks, n tattica f

tactless, takt´-lis, adj senza

tatto, indelicato

tadpole, tad´-poul, n
girino m

tag, tagh, n cartellino m;
– **along**, v seguire

tail, teil, n coda f

tailor, tei´-la, n sarto m

taint, teint, v infangare

take, teik, v prendere;
accompagnare; portare;
– **away**, portar via; – **off**,
togliere; decollare

takings, tei´-kings, npl
incasso m

talcum powder, tal´-kum
pau´-da, n talco m

tale, teil, n racconto m;
(fairy) favola f

talent, tal´-ent, n
talento m

talk, took, v parlare; n
conversazione f;

chiacchiere fpl;
(politics) colloquio

talkative, took´-a-tiv, adj
loquace

tall, tool, adj alto; grande

tallow, tal´-ou, n sego m

tally, tal´-i, v (agree)
corrispondere

talon, tal´-on, n artiglio m

tame, teim, adj mansueto;
v domare

tamper, tam´-pa, v – **with**,
manomettere

tampon, tam´-pon, n
assorbente interno m

tan, tan, n abbronzatura f;
v abbronzarsi

tangerine, tan´-che-riin, n
mandarino m

tangible, tan´-chib-l, adj
tangibile

tangle, tang´-gl, n
groviglio m; v
ingarbugliare

tank, tangk, n cisterna f;
(fish) acquario m

tankard, tang´-kad, n
boccale m

tantalize, tan´-ta-lais, v
tormentare

tantamount, tan´-ta-
maunt, adj equivalente

tap, tap, v bussare; (barrel)
spillare; n rubinetto m

tape, teip, n nastro m

tape measure, teip mesh´-
a, n metro a nastro m

taper, tei´-pa, v terminare

a punta

tape recorder, teip ri-koor´-da, n registratore a cassetta m

tapestry, tap´-is-tri, n arazzo m

tapeworm, teip´-uerm, n tenia f

tar, taar, n catrame m; v incatramare

tardy, taar´-di, adj (slow) lento

target, taar´-ghit, n bersaglio m; obiettivo m

tariff, ta´-rif, n tariffa f

tarnish, taar´-nish, v ossidarsi

tarpaulin, taar-poo´-lin, n telone incerato m

tarragon, ta´-ra-gon, n dragoncello m

tart, taart, n crostata f; adj* agro

tartar sauce, taar´-ta soos, n salsa tartara f

task, taask, n compito m

tassel, tas´-l, n nappina f

taste, teist, n gusto m; v gustare

tasteful*, teist´-ful, adj di gusto

tasteless, teist´-lis, adj insipido; di cattivo gusto

tasty, teis´-ti, adj saporito

tatters, tat´-es, npl brandelli mpl

tattoo, ta-tuu´, n tatuaggio m; v tatuare

taunt, toont, n scherno m; v schernire

Taurus, toor´-ros, m Toro m

tawdry, too´-dri, adj pacchiano

tax, taks, n tassa f; v tassare

taxi, tak´-si, n taxi m

taxi driver, tak´-si drai´-va, n tassista m/f

taxpayer, taks´-pei-a, n contribuente m/f

tax return, taks ri-tern´, n dichiarazione dei redditi f

tea, tii, n tè m; merenda f; cena f

tea bag, tii´-bagh, n bustina di tè f

teach, tiich, v insegnare

teacher, tiich´-a, n insegnante m/f; maestro m, maestra f

teaching, tiich´-ing, n insegnamento m

team, tiim, n squadra f, équipe f

teamwork, tiim´-uerk, n lavoro d'équipe m

teapot, tii´-pot, n teiera f

tear, ter, n strappo m; v lacerare

tear, tir, n lacrima f

tearoom, tii´-ruum, n sala da tè f

tease, tiis, v stuzzicare

teaspoon, tii´-spuun, n

cucchiaino m

teat, tiit, n tettarella f

tea towel, tii tau´-el, n telo da cucina m

technical*, tek´-nik-l, adj tecnico

technician, tek-ni´-shan, n tecnico m

technology, tek-no´-lo-chi, n tecnologia f

teddy bear, te´-di-ber, n orsacchiotto m

tedious*, tii´-di-os, adj tedioso

teem, tiim, v formicolare

teenager, tiin-eich´-a, n adolescente m/f

teething, tii´-Ding, n dentizione f

teetotaller, tii´-tou-ta-la, n astemio m

telegram, tel´-i-gram, n telegramma m

telegraph, tel´-i-graaf, v telegrafare

telephone, tel´-i-foun, n telefono m; v telefonare

telephone box, tel´-i-foun boks, n cabina telefonica f

telephone call, tel´-i-foun kool, n telefonata f

telephone number, tel´-i-foun nŏm´-ba, n numero di telefono m

telescope, tel´-i-skoup, n telescopio m

television, tel´-i-vish-on,

n televisione f

television set, tel´-i-vish-on set, n televisore m

tell, tel, v dire; (relate) raccontare

temper, tem´-pa, n umore m; collera f

temperament, tem´-pe-ra-ment, n temperamento m

temperance, tem´-pe-rans, n temperanza f

temperate, tem´-pe-ret, adj (moderate) moderato, (habits) sobrio

temperature, tem´-pe-ra-cha, n temperatura f

tempest, tem´-pist, n tempesta f

temple, tem´-pl, n tempio m; (head) tempia f

temporary, tem´-po-ra-ri, adj temporaneo

tempt, tempt, v tentare

temptation, temp-tei´-shon, n tentazione f

ten, ten, adj dieci

tenable, ten´-a-bl, adj sostenibile

tenacious*, ti-nei´-shos, adj tenace

tenacity, ti-nas´-i-ti, n tenacia f

tenancy, ten´-an-si, n locazione f

tenant, ten´-ant, n locatario m, inquilino m

tend, tend, v aver

tendenza; badare a

tendency, tend´-en-si, n tendenza f

tender, ten´-da, v fare un'offerta; n offerta d'appalto f; adj* tenero

tenderness, ten´-de-nis, n tenerezza

tenement, ten´-i-ment, n casamento m

tennis, ten´-is, n tennis m

tennis court, ten´-is koort, n campo da tennis m

tennis racket, ten´-is rak´-it, n racchetta da tennis f

tenor, ten´-a, n tenore m

tense, tens, adj* teso; gram tempo m

tension, ten´-shon, n tensione f

tent, tent, n tenda f

tentative, ten´-ta-tiv, adj esitante

tenth, tenZ, adj decimo; (date) dieci

tenure, ten´-ia, n (job) incarico m

tepid, tep´-id, adj tiepido

term, term, n espressione f; (quarter) trimestre m

terminal, ter´-mi-nal, adj* terminale; n comp terminale m; (airport) terminal m

terminate, ter´-mi-neit, v terminare

terminus, ter´-mi-nus, n capolinea m

terms, terms, npl condizioni fpl

terrace, te´-ris, n terrazza f

terraces, te´-ris-is, npl gradinate fpl

terrible, te-ri-bl, adj terribile

terrific, te-rif´-ik, adj fantastico

terrify, te´-ri-fai, v terrorizzare

territory, te´-ri-to-ri, n territorio m

terror, te´-ra, n terrore m

terrorism, te´-ro-rism, n terrorismo m

terrorist, te´-ro-rist, n terrorista m/f

terrorize, te´-ro-rais, v terrorizzare

terse*, ters, adj terso

test, test, n prova f; esame m; analisi f; compito in classe m; v provare; esaminare

Testament, tes´-ta-ment, n Testamento m

testicle, tes´-tik-l, n testicolo m

testify, tes´-ti-fai, v testimoniare

testimony, tes´-ti-mo-ni, f testimonianza f

text, tekst, n testo m

textbook, tekst´-buk, n libro di testo m

textile, teks´-tail, *adj*
tessile

texture, teks´-cha, *n*
consistenza *f*

Thames, tems, Tamigi *m*

than, Dan, *conj* che; (with
numerals, pronouns
etc.) di

thank, Zangk, *v*
ringraziare; – **you!** *interj*
grazie!

thankful*, Zangk´-ful, *adj*
grato, riconoscente

thanks, Zangks, *npl* grazie
fpl; – **to,** *prep* grazie a

Thanksgiving, Zangk´-ful,
n giorno del
ringraziamento *m*

that, Dat, *adj* quello,
quella; *pron* quello,
quella; ciò; che; cui; *conj*
che; *adv* così

thatched, Zacht, *adj* (roof)
di paglia; (cottage) col
tetto di paglia

thaw, Zoo, *n* disgelo *m; v*
scongelare

the, Di, *art* il, lo, la, i, gli,
le; – **more… – more…,**
più… più…; – **sooner –
better,** prima è, meglio è

theatre, Zi-*a*-ta, *n* teatro
m; med sala operatoria *f*

theft, Zeft, *n* furto *m*

their, Der, *adj* loro

theirs, Ders, *pron* il loro,
la loro, i loro, le loro; **a
friend of –,** un loro

amico

them, Dem, *pron* li, le,
loro, essi, esse

theme, Ziim, *n* tema *m*

themselves, Dem-selvs´,
pron refl si; loro stessi,
loro stesse

then, Den, *adv* allora; poi;
conj dunque, quindi

theology, Zi-ol´-*o*-chi, *n*
teologia *f*

theoretical,* Zi-o-ret´-i-
kl, *adj* teorico

theory, Zi´-*o*-ri, *n* teoria *f*

therapy, Ze´-*ra*-pi, *n*
terapia *f*

there, Der, *adv* li, là; – **is,**
c'è; – **are,** ci sono

thereafter, Der-aaf´-*ta*,
adv da allora in poi

thereby, Der-bai´, *adv* con
ciò

therefore, Der´-foor, *adv*
perciò

thermal, Zer´-mal, *adj*
termale

thermometer, Ze-mom´-*i*-
ta, *n* termometro *m*

these, Diis, *pron & adj*
questi, queste

thesis, Zi´-sis, *n* tesi *f*

they, Dei, *pron* essi, esse,
loro

thick*, Zik, *adj* spesso,
denso; (big) grosso

thicken, Zik´-n, *v*
condensarsi; addensare

thicket, Zik´-it, *n*

boscaglia *f*

thickness, Zik´-nis, *n*
spessore *m*

thief, Ziif, *n* ladro *m*

thigh, Zai, *n* coscia *f*

thimble, Zim´-bl, *n*
ditale *m*

thin, Zin, *adj** sottile;
(lean) magro; *v*
assottigliare

thing, Zing, *n* cosa *f*

think, Zingk, *v* pensare;
(believe) credere; –
over, riflettere su

third, Zerd, *adj* terzo;
(date) tre

thirdly, Zerd´-li, *adv* in
terzo luogo

thirst, Zerst, *n* sete *f*

thirsty, Zers´-ti, *adj*
assetato

thirteen, Zer-tiin´, *adj*
tredici

thirteenth, Zer-tiinZ´, *adj*
tredicesimo; (date)
tredici

thirtieth, Zer´-ti-eZ, *adj*
trentesimo; (date)
trenta

thirty, Zer´-ti, *adj* trenta

this, Dis, *pron & adj*
questo, questa; *adv* così

thistle, Zis´-l, *n* cardo *m*

thong, Zong, *n* cinghia *f*

thorn, Zoorn, *n* spina *m*

thorny, Zoorn´-i, *adj*
spinoso

thorough*, Zð´-ra, *adj*

minuzioso; profondo

thoroughbred, Zŏ'-robred, adj purosangue

thoroughfare, Zŏ'-rofer, n strada transitabile f; **no –**, divieto di transito m

those, Dous, pron quelli, quelle; adj quei, quegli, quelle

though, Dou, conj benché; adv comunque

thought, Zoot, n pensiero m

thoughtful*, Zoot'-ful, adj pensieroso; premuroso

thoughtless*, Zoot'-lis, adj sconsiderato

thousand, Zau'-sand, adj mille; mila

thousandth, Zau'-sandZ, adj millesimo

thrash, Zrash, v battere

thrashing, Zrash'-ing, n percosse fpl, botte fpl

thread, Zred, n filo m; v infilare

threadbare, Zred'-ber, adj logoro

threat, Zret, n minaccia f

threaten, Zret'-n, v minacciare

threatening*, Zret'-n-ing, adj minaccioso

three, Zrii, adj tre

thresh, Zresh, v battere

threshold, Zresh'-hould, n soglia f

thrift, Zrift, n parsimonia f

thrifty, Zrift'-ti, adj parsimonioso

thrill, Zril, n fremito m; v entusiasmare

thrilling, Zril'-ing, adj entusiasmante; ricco di suspense

thrive, Zraiv, v prosperare

throat, Zrout, n gola f

throb, Zrob, v pulsare; (heart) palpitare

throne, Zroun, n trono m

throng, Zrong, n calca f; v accalcarsi

throttle, Zrot'-l, v (kill) strangolare; n mech valvola a farfalla f

through, Zruu, prep attraverso; per

throughout, Zru-aut', prep in tutto; per tutto; adv dappertutto

throw, Zrou, v gettare; n lancio m, tiro m

thrush, Zrŏsh, n tordo m

thrust, Zrŏst, n colpo m; v dare una puntata

thud, Zŏd, n tonfo m

thumb, Zŏm, n pollice m

thump, Zŏmp, n (blow) colpo m; v dar un colpo

thunder, Zŏn'-da, n tuono m; v tuonare

thunderbolt, Zŏn'-deboult, n fulmine m

thunderstorm, Zŏn'-destoorm, n temporale m

thundery, Zŏn'-de-ri, adj temporalesco

Thursday, Zers'-di, n giovedì m

thus, Dŏs, adv così

thwart, Zuoort, v contrastare

thyme, taim, n timo m

Tiber, tai'-ba, Tevere m

tick, tik, n zecca f; segno m; v (clock) fare tic tac; (check) spuntare

ticket, tik'-it, n biglietto m; (parking) multa f

ticket office, tik'-it of'-is, n biglietteria f

tickle, tik'-l, v solleticare

ticklish, tik'-lish, adj che soffre il solletico

tidal, taid'-l, adj di marea

tide, taid, n (high) alta marea f; (low) bassa marea f

tidy, tai'-di, adj in ordine, ordinato; v mettere in ordine, riordinare

tie, tai, n cravatta f; v legare; (bow etc.) annodare; (sport) pareggiare

tier, tir, n piano m

tiff, tif, n battibecco m

tiger, tai'-ga, n tigre f

tight*, tait, adj stretto; teso

tighten, tait'-n, v stringere; tendere

tights, taits, npl

collant *mpl*

tile, tail, *n* (roof) tegola *f;* (floor and wall) piastrella *f; v* rivestire di tegole; piastrellare

till, til, *n* registratore di cassa *m*

till, til, *conj & prep* = **until**

tilt, tilt, *v* inclinare, pendere

timber, tim´-ba, *n* legname da costruzione *m*

time, taim, *v* cronometrare; *n* tempo *m;* (hour) ora *f;* (occasion) volta *f*

time bomb, taim´-bom, *n* bomba a orologeria *f*

timeless, taim´-lis, *adj* eterno; senza tempo

timely, taim´-li, *adj* opportuno; tempestivo

time off, taim-´of, *n* tempo libero *m*

timetable, taim´-tei-bl, *n* orario *m*

timid*, tim´-id, *adj* timido

tin, tin, *n* stagno *m;* latta *f;* lattina *f,* scatoletta *f*

tin foil, tin foil´, *n* carta stagnola *f*

tinge, tinch, *n* sfumatura *f*

tingle, ting´-gl, *v* formicolare; *n* formicolio *m*

tinkle, ting´-kl, *v* tintinnare; *n*

tintinnio *m*

tinned, tind, *adj* in scatola

tin-opener, tin´-oup-na, *n* apriscatole *m*

tinsel, tin´-sel, *n* fili argentati *mpl*

tint, tint, *n* tinta *f*

tiny, tai´-ni, *adj* minuscolo

tip, tip, *n* punta *f;* (hint) suggerimento *m;* (gratuity) mancia *f; v* capovolgere; (waiters etc.) dare la mancia

tiptoe, tip´-tou, *n* on –, in punta di piedi

tire, tair, *v* stancare; – of, stancarsi di

tired, taird, *adj* stanco

tireless*, tair´-lis, *adj* instancabile

tissue, tish´-uu, *n* tessuto *m;* fazzolettino di carta *m*

tissue paper, tish´-uu pei´-pa, *n* carta velina *f*

title, tai´-tl, *n* titolo *m*

titter, tit´-a, *v* ridacchiare

to, tu, *prep* (direction) a; in; (to a place or person) da; (until) fino; (intention) per; (time) ten – seven, le sette meno dieci

toad, toud, *n* rospo *m*

toast, toust, *n* (bread) pane tostato *m;* (health) brindisi *m; v* (bread) tostare; (health)

brindare

tobacco, to-bak´-ou, *n* tabacco *m*

tobacconist, to-bak´-o-nist, *n* tabaccaio *m*

toboggan, to-bogh´-an, *n* toboga *m*

today, tu-dei´, *adv* oggi

toddler, tod´-la, *n* bambino che muove i primi passi *m*

toe, tou, *n* dito del piede *m*

toffee, tof´-i, *n* caramella mou *f*

together, to-gheD´-a, *adv* insieme

toil, toil, *n* fatica *f; v* affaticarsi

toilet, toi´-lit, *n* gabinetto *m*

toilet paper, toi´-lit pei´-pa, *n* carta igienica *f*

toiletries, toi´-lit-ris, *npl* articoli da toaletta *mpl*

token, tou´-ken, *n* segno *m;* buono *m*

tolerable, tol´-e-ra-bl, *adj* tollerabile

tolerance, tol´-e-rans, *n* tolleranza *f*

tolerant, tol´-e-rant, *adj* tollerante

tolerate, tol´-e-reit, *v* tollerare

toll, toul, *n* (tax) pedaggio *m; v* (bell) suonare

tomato, to-maa´-tou, *n*

pomodoro *m*

tomb, tuum, *n* tomba *f*

tombstone, tuum´-stoun, *n* pietra tombale *f*

tomboy, tom´-boi, *n* maschiaccio *m*

tomcat, tom´-kat, *n* gatto maschio *m*

tomfoolery, tom-fuul´-e-ri, *n* sciocchezze *fpl*

tomorrow, tu-mo´-rou, *adv* domani

ton, tŏn, *n* tonnellata *f*

tone, toun, *n* tono *m*

tongs, tongs, *npl* molle *fpl*

tongue, tŏng, *n* lingua *f*

tonic, ton´-ik, *n* tonico *m*

tonight, tu-nait´, *adv* stanotte

tonsil, ton´-sil, *n* tonsilla *f*

too, tuu, *adv* troppo; (also) anche; **– much,** troppo; **– many,** troppi, troppe

tool, tuul, *n* arnese *m*

tooth, tuuZ, *n* dente *m*

toothache, tuuZ´-eik, *n* mal di denti *m*

toothbrush, tuuZ´-brŏsh, *n* spazzolino da denti *m*

toothpaste, tuuZ´-peist, *n* dentifricio *m*

toothpick, tuuZ´-pik, *n* stuzzicadenti *m*

top, top, *n* cima *f*; parte superiore *f*; coperchio *m*; *adj* primo; migliore; **on –,** in cima, sopra

topic, top´-ik, *n* argomento *m*

topical, top´-ik-l, *adj* di attualità

topless, top´-lis, *adj* in topless

topple, top´-l, *v* (headlong fall) capitombolare; (car etc.) rovesciarsi

topsy-turvy, top´-si-ter´-vi, *adv* sottosopra

torch, toorch, *n* torcia *f*

torment, toor´-ment, *n* tormento *m*; *v* tormentare

tornado, toor-nei´-dou, *n* tornado *m*

torpedo, toor-pii´-dou, *n* siluro *m*

torpid*, toor´-pid, *adj* intorpidito

torpor, toor´-pa, *n* torpore *m*

torrent, to´-rent, *n* torrente *m*

torrid, to´-rid, *adj* torrido

tortoise, toor´-tos, *n* tartaruga *f*

tortoiseshell, toor´-tos-shel, *adj* di tartaruga

torture, toor´-cha, *n* tortura *f*; *v* torturare

toss, tos, *v* gettare in aria; (coin) fare a testa o croce; **to – and turn,** agitarsi nel sonno

total, tout´-l, *n* totale *m*; *v* sommare; *adj** totale

totter, tot´-a, *v* barcollare

touch, tŏch, *v* toccare; *n* (contact) tocco *m*; (feeling) tatto *m*

touching*, tŏch´-ing, *adj* commovente

touchy, tŏch´-i, *adj* suscettibile

tough*, tŏf, *adj* duro

tour, tur, *n* viaggio *m*; visita *f*; tournée *f*; *v* visitare

tourist, tur´-rist, *n* turista *m/f*

tourist office, tur´-rist of´-is, *n* ufficio d'informazione turistica *m*

tournament, toor´-na-ment, *n* torneo *m*

tout, taut, *v n* bagarino *m*

tow, tou, *v* rimorchiare

towards, to´-uoords, *prep* verso

towel, tau´-el, *n* asciugamano *m*; (kitchen) strofinaccio *m*

tower, tau´-a, *n* torre *f*

tower block, tau´-a blok, *n* palazzone *m*

town, taun, *n* città *f*

town centre, taun-sen´-ta, *n* centro *m*

town hall, taun hool, *n* municipio *m*

toy, toi, *n* giocattolo *m*

trace, treis, *n* traccia *f*; *v* tracciare; (track)

rintracciare; (copy) ricalcare

tracing, trei´-sing, n ricalco m

tracing paper, trei´-sing pei´-pa, n carta da ricalco f

track, trak, n traccia f; pista f; v seguire le tracce

tract, trakt, n tratto m

traction, trak´-shon, n trazione f

tractor, trak´-ta, n trattore m

trade, treid, v commerciare; n commercio m; (craft) mestiere m

trademark, treid´-maark, n marchio registrato m

trade union, treid iuu´-ni-on, n sindacato m

tradition, tra-dish´-on, n tradizione f

traditional*, tra-dish´-on-al, adj tradizionale

traffic, traf´-ik, n traffico m

traffic jam, traf´-ik cham, n ingorgo m

traffic lights, traf´-ik laits, npl semaforo m

tragedy, trach´-i-di, n tragedia f

tragic, trach´-ik, adj tragico

trail, treil, n pista f; scia f;

v strascicare

trailer, trei´-la, n (van) rimorchio m

train, trein, v addestrare; allenare; (educate) formare; n (railway) treno m; (dress) strascico m

trainer, trei´-na, n allenatore m; addestratore m

trainers, trei´-nes, npl scarpe da ginnastica fpl

training, trei´-ning, n addestramento m; allenamento m; formazione f

traitor, trei´-ta, n traditore m

tram, tram, n tram m

tramp, tramp, n vagabondo m

trample, tram´-pl, v calpestare

trance, traans, n trance f

tranquil*, trang´-kuil, adj tranquillo

tranquilizer, trang´-kuil-ai-sa, n tranquillante m

transaction, tran-sak´-shon, n transazione f

transcribe, tran-skraib´, v trascrivere

transfer, trans-fer´, v trasferire; n trasferimento m; autoadesivo m

transform, trans-foorm´, v

trasformare

transit, tran´-sit, n transito m

translate, trans-leit´, v tradurre

translation, trans-lei´-shon, n traduzione f

translator, trans-lei´-ta, n traduttore m, traduttrice f

transmit, trans-mit´, v trasmettere

transparent, trans-pa´-rent, adj trasparente

transplant, trans´-plaant, v trapiantare; n trapianto m

transport, tran´-spoort, n trasporto m

transport, tran-spoort´, v trasportare

transpose, trans-pous´, v trasporre

transverse, trans-vers´, adj trasversale

trap, trap, n trappola f; v intrappolare

trapdoor, trap´-door, n trabocchetto m

trappings, trap´-ings, npl ornamenti mpl

trash, trash, n robaccia f; (nonsense) sciocchezze fpl

trashy, trash´-i, adj scadente

trauma, troom´-a, n trauma m

travel, trav´-el, v viaggiare

travel agency, trav´-el ei´-chen-si, n agenzia di viaggi f

traveller, trav´-e-la, v viaggiatore m

traveller's cheque, trav´-el-es chek, n traveller's cheque m

travel sickness, trav´-el sik´-nis, n mal d'auto m

travesty, trav´-is-ti, n parodia f

trawler, trool´-a, n peschereccio m

tray, trei, n vassoio m

treacherous*, trech´-e-ros, adj infido

treachery, trech´-e-ri, n tradimento m

treacle, triik´-l, n melassa f

tread, tred, n (tyre) battistrada m; v camminare; – **upon,** calpestare

treason, trii´-son, n tradimento m

treasure, tresh´-a, n tesoro m; v valutare

treasurer, tresh´-u-ra, n tesoriere m

treasury, tresh´-u-ri, n tesoreria f

treat, triit, n (enjoyment) piacere m; v trattare; fig offrire

treatment, triit´-ment, n trattamento m

treaty, trii´-ti, n trattato m

treble, treb´-l, adj triplice; v triplicare

tree, trii, n albero m

trellis, trel´-is, n graticcio m

tremble, trem´-bl, v tremare

tremendous*, tri-men´-dos, adj fantastico

tremulous*, trem´-iu-los, adj tremulo

trench, trench, n trincea f

trend, trend, n tendenza f

trespass, tres´-pas, v violare

trespasser, tres´-pas-a, n trasgressore m

trestle, tres´-l, n cavalletto m

trial, trai´-al, n law processo m; (test) collaudo m; (hardship) tribolazioni fpl

triangle, trai´-ang´-gl, n triangolo m

triangular, trai-ang´-ghiu-la, adj triangolare

tribe, traib, n tribù f

tribunal, trai-biuu´-nal, n tribunale m

tributary, trib´-iu-ta-ri, n (stream) affluente m

tribute, trib´-iuut, n tributo m

trick, trik, n (fraud) trucco m; (joke) burla f; (dexterity) gioco m; v

ingannare

trickle, trik´-l, n rivolo m; gocciolare

trifle, traif´-l, n bagatella f

trifling, traif´-ling, adj insignificante

trigger, trigh´-a, n (gun) grilletto m

trill, tril, n trillo m

trim, trim, v (dress) guarnire; (hair) spuntare; adj curato; snello; (hair) spuntatina f

trimming, trim´-ing, n guarnizione f

trinket, tring´-kit, n ciondolo m; ninnolo m

trio, trii´-ou, n trio m

trip, trip, n (journey) gita f; v (stumble) inciampare

tripe, traip, n trippa f

triple, trip´-l, adj triplo

triplets, trip´-lits, npl tre gemelli mpl

tripod, trai´-pod, n treppiede m

triumph, trai´-omf, n trionfo m

trivial*, triv´-i-al, adj triviale

trolley, trol´-i, n carrello m

trombone, trom´-boun, n trombone m

troop, truup, n truppa f

trophy, trou´-fi, n trofeo m

tropical, trop´-ik-l, *adj*
tropicale

tropics, trop´-iks, *npl*
tropici *mpl*

trot, trot, *v* trottare; *n*
trotto *m*

trotter, trot´-a, *n*
trottatore *m*; (pig)
zampone *m*

trouble, trŏb´-l, *n* noia *f*,
guaio *m*; disturbo *m*; *v*
darsi la pena; disturbare

troublesome, trŏb´-l-som,
adj seccante

trough, trof, *n*
abbeveratoio *m*;
trogolo *m*

trousers, trau´-ses, *npl*
pantaloni *mpl*

trout, trout, *n* trota *f*

trowel, trau´-el, *n*
cazzuola *f*

truant, truu´-ant, **play –,**
v marinare la scuola

truce, truus, *n* tregua *f*

truck, trŏk, *n* carro merci
m; autocarro *m*

truck driver, trŏk drai´-
va, *n* camionista *m/f*

truculent*, trŏk´-iu-lent,
adj truculento

trudge, trŏch, *v* marciare
penosamente

true, truu, *adj* vero;
(faithful) leale

truffle, trŏf´-l, *n* tartufo *m*

truism, truu´-ism, *n* verità
lapalissiana *f*

trumpet, trŏm´-pit, *n*
tromba *f*

truncheon, trŏn´-shon, *n*
manganello *m*

trunk, trŏngk, *n* (tree,
body) tronco *m*;
(elephant) proboscide *f*;
(travelling) baule *m*

truss, trŏs, *n* cinto
erniario *m*; *v* (poultry)
legare

trust, trŏst, *n* fiducia *f*; *v*
fidarsi

trustee, trŏs-tii´, *n*
amministratore
fiduciario *m*

trustworthy, trŏst´-uer-Di,
adj fidato

truth, truuZ, *n* verità *f*

truthful*, truuZ´-ful, *adj*
veritiero

try, trai, *v* provare; (taste)
assaggiare; *law*
processare

trying, trai´-ing, *adj*
penoso

T-shirt, tii´-shert, *n*
maglietta *f*

tub, tŏb, *n* tinozza *f*;
(bath) vasca da bagno *f*

tube, tiuub, *n* tubo *m*;
(London Underground)
metropolitana *f*

tuck, tŏk, *n* piega *f*; *v*
ripiegare; **– in,**
rimboccare; **– up,**
rimboccare le coperte

Tuesday, tiuus´-di, *n*

martedì *m*

tuft, tŏft, *n* ciuffo *m*

tug, tŏgh, *n* strattone *m*; *v*
tirare; (tow) rimorchiare

tugboat, tŏgh´-bout, *n*
rimorchiatore *m*

tug-of-war, tŏgh´-ov-uoor,
n tiro alla fune *m*

tuition, tiu-ish´-on, *n*
lezioni *fpl*

tulip, tiuu´-lip, *n*
tulipano *m*

tumble, tŏm´-bl, *n*
capitombolo *m*; *v*
(person) inciampare;
(things) cadere

tumble dryer, tŏm´-bl
drai´-a, *n*
asciugabiancheria *f*

tumbler, tŏm´-bla, *n*
bicchiere da whisky *m*

tumour, tiuu´-ma, *n*
tumore *m*

tumult, tiuu´-mŏlt, *n*
tumulto *m*

tuna, tiuu´-na, *n* tonno *m*

tune, tiuun, *n* melodia *f*; *v*
accordare

tuneful, tiuun´-ful, *adj*
melodioso

tunic, tiuu´-nik, *n mil*
giubba *f*

tuning fork, tiuu´-ning
foork, *n* diapason *m*

tunnel, tŏn´-l, *n* galleria *f*,
tunnel *m*; *v* traforare

turbine, ter´-bain, *n*
turbina *f*

turbot, ter´-bot, n (fish)
rombo m

turbulent*, ter´-biu-lent,
adj turbolento

tureen, tu-riin´, n
zuppiera f

turf, terf, n tappeto
erboso m

turkey, ter´-ki, n
tacchino m

Turkey, ter´-ki, n
Turchia f

Turkish, ter´-kish, adj
turco

turmoil, ter´-moil, n
tumulto m

turn, tern, v girare;
(become) diventare; n
(order of succession)
turno m; – **about**, v fare
dietrofront; – **back**,
tornare indietro; – **into**,
v trasformarsi in; – **off**,
chiudere; – **on**, aprire; –
out, rivelarsi;
(extinguish) spegnere; –
over, voltare; voltarsi; –
to, ricorrere a

turning, ter´-ning, n
svolta f

turning point, ter´-ning
point, n fig svolta
decisiva f

turnip, ter´-nip, n rapa f

turnover, ter´-nou-va, n
volume d'affari m

turnstile, tern´-stail, n
cancelletto girevole m

turpentine, ter´-pen-tain,
n trementina f

turret, tŏ´-rit, n torretta f

turtle, ter´-tl, n testuggine
f, tartaruga marina f

turtledove, ter´-tl-dŏv, n
tortora f

turtleneck, ter´-tl-nek,
n maglione col collo
alto m

tusk, tŏsk, n zanna f

tussle, tŏs´-l, n baruffa f; v
far baruffa

tutor, tiuu´-ta, n
insegnante m/f;
precettore m

TV, tii vii, n TV f, tivù f

twang, tuang, n accento
nasale m

tweezers, tuii´-ses, npl
pinzette fpl

twelfth, tuelfZ, adj
dodicesimo; (date)
dodici

twelve, tuelv, adj dodici

twentieth, tuen´-ti-eZ, adj
ventesimo; (date) venti

twenty, tuen´-ti, adj venti

twice, tuais, adv due volte

twig, tuigh, n
ramoscello m

twilight, tuai´-lait, n
crepuscolo m

twill, tuil, n (fabric)
spigato m

twin, tuin, n gemello m;
adj gemello

twine, tuain, n spago m; v

intrecciare

twinge, tuinch, n fitta f; v
tormentare

twinkle, tuing´-kl, v
sfavillare

twirl, tuerl, v volteggiare;
(twist) torcere

twist, tuist, v torcere

twit, tuit, n fam cretino m

twitch, tuich, n tic m; v
contrarsi

twitter, tuit´-a, v
cinguettare; n
cinguettio m

two, tuu, adj due

tycoon, tai-kuun´, n
magnate m

type, taip, n tipo m;
(printing) carattere m; v
scrivere a macchina

typewriter, taip´-rai-ta, n
macchina da scrivere f

typhoid, tai´-foid, n febbre
tifoidea f

typical*, tip´-i-kl, adj
tipico

typist, tai´-pist, n
dattilografo m,
dattilografa f

tyrannical*, ti-ran´-i-kl,
adj tirannico

tyrannize, ti´-ra-nais, v
tiranneggiare

tyrant, tai´-rant, n
tiranno m

tyre, tair, n pneumatico m

ubiquitous, iu-bik´-ui-tos, *adj* onnipresente

udder, ŏd´-a, *n* mammella *f*

ugly, ŏgh´-li, *adj* brutto

ulcer, ŏl´-sa, *n* ulcera *f*; (mouth) afta *f*

ulterior, ŏl-tir´-ri-a, *adj* ulteriore

ultimate*, ŏl´-ti-mat, *adj* ultimo; supremo

ultimatum, ŏl-ti-mei´-tum, *n* ultimatum *m*

ultra, ŏl´-tra, *adj* ultra

umbrella, ŏm-brel´-a, *n* ombrello *m*

umpire, ŏm´-pair, *n* arbitro *m*

unable, ŏn-eib´-l, *adj* **be-to,** non potere; essere incapace di

unacceptable, ŏn-ak-sep´-ta-bl, *adj* inaccettabile

unaccountable, ŏn-a-kaun´-ta-bl, *adj* inesplicabile

unacquainted, ŏn-a-kuein´-tid, *adj* **be-with,** non conoscere

unaffected, ŏn-a-fek´-tid, *adj* naturale; impassibile

unaided, ŏn-ei´-did, *adj* da solo

unaltered, ŏn-ool´-ted, *adj* inalterato

unanimity, iu-nan-i´-mi-ti, *n* unanimità *f*

unanimous*, iu-nan´-i-mos, *adj* unanime

unapproachable, ŏn-a-prouch´-a-bl, *adj* inaccessibile

unarmed, ŏn-aarmd´, *adj* inerme

unattended, ŏn-a-ten´-did, *adj* incustodito; solo

unavoidable, ŏn-a-voi-da-bl, *adj* inevitabile

unaware, ŏn-a-uer´, *adj* ignaro

unawares, ŏn-a-uers´, *adv* alla sprovvista

unbearable, ŏn-ber´-ra-bl, *adj* insopportabile

unbelievable, ŏn-bi-lii´-va-bl, *adj* incredibile

unbiased, ŏn-bai´-ast, *adj* imparziale

unblemished, ŏn-blem´-isht, *adj* senza macchia

unbounded, ŏn-baun´-did, *adj* illimitato

unbreakable, ŏn-breik´-a-bl, *adj* infrangibile

unburden, ŏn-berd´-n, *v* sfogarsi

unbutton, ŏn-bŏt´-n, *v* sbottonare

uncalled-for, ŏn-koold´-foor, *adj* fuori luogo

uncanny, ŏn-kan´-i, *adj* strano

uncared-for, ŏn-kerd´-foor, *adj* trascurato

unceasing*, ŏn-sii´-sing, *adj* incessante

uncertain*, ŏn-ser´-tan, *adj* incerto

unchanged, ŏn-cheinchd´, *adj* immutato

uncivil, ŏn-siv´-il, *adj* scortese

unclaimed, ŏn-kleimd´, *adj* non reclamato

uncle, ong´-kl, *n* zio *m*

unclean*, ŏn-kliin´, *adj* sporco; *fig* immondo

uncomfortable, ŏn-kŏm´-fo-ta-bl, *adj* scomodo; a disagio

uncommon*, ŏn-kom´-on, *adj* non comune

unconcerned, ŏn-kon-sernd´, *adj* indifferente

unconditional*, ŏn-kon-dish´-on-al, *adj* incondizionato

unconscious*, ŏn-kon´-shos, *adj* incoscio; inconsapevole; svenuto

uncontrollable, ŏn-kon-trou´-la-bl, *adj* irrefrenabile

unconventional, ŏn-kon-ven´-shon-al, *adj* privo di convenzioni

uncork, ŏn-koork´, *v* stappare

uncover, ŏn-kŏv´-a, *v* scoprire

uncultivated, ŏn-kŏl´-ti-vei-tid, *adj* incolto

undaunted*, ŏn-doon´-tid, *adj* non intimidito

undecided, ŏn-di-sai´-did, *adj* indeciso

undelivered, ŏn-di-liv´-ed, *adj* non recapitato

undeniable, ŏn-di-nai´-a-bl, *adj* innegabile

under, ŏn´-da, *adv* & *prep* sotto; al di sotto di

under-age, ŏn´-de-reich, *adj* minorenne

underdone, ŏn´-de-dŏn, *adj* poco cotto

underestimate, ŏn´-de-res´-ti-meit, *v* sottovalutare

undergo, ŏn-de-gou´, *v* sottoporsi a; subire

undergraduate, ŏn´-de-grad´-iu-at, *n* studente universitario *m*

underground, ŏn´-de-graund, *adj* sotterraneo; *n* metropolitana *f*

underline, ŏn-de-lain´, *v* sottolineare

undermine, ŏn-de-main´, *v* minare

underneath, ŏn-de-niiZ´, *prep* sotto, al di sotto di

underrate, ŏn-de-reit´, *v* sottovalutare

understand, ŏn-de-stand´, *v* capire, comprendere

understanding, ŏn-de-stan´-ding, *adj* comprensivo; *n* intesa *f*; **on the –,** *conj* a condizione che

understate, ŏn-de-steit´, *v* minimizzare; sminuire

undertake, ŏn´-de-teik´, *v* intraprendere

undertaker, ŏn´-de-teik-a, *n* impresario di pompe funebri *m*

undertaking, ŏn´-de-teik-ing, *n* impresa *f*

underwear, ŏn´-de-uer, *n* biancheria intima *f*

underworld, ŏn´-de-uerld, *n* malavita *f*

undeserved*, ŏn-di-servd´, *adj* immeritato

undesirable, ŏn-di-sair´-ra-bl, *adj* sgradito

undignified, ŏn-digh´-ni-faid, *adj* poco dignitoso

undisturbed, ŏn-dis-terbd´, *adj* tranquillo

undo, ŏn-duu´, *v* disfare; slacciare

undoubted*, ŏn-dau´-tid, *adj* indubbio

undress, ŏn-dres´, *v* svestirsi

undue, ŏn-diuu´, *adj* eccessivo

undulating, ŏn´-diu-lei-ting, *adj* ondeggiante; ondulato

unduly, ŏn-diuu´-li, *adv* eccessivamente

unearth, ŏn-erZ´, *v* dissotterrare; *fig* scoprire

unearthly, ŏn-erZ´-li, *adj* soprannaturale

uneasy, ŏn-ii´-si, *adj* inquieto; a disagio

uneducated, ŏn-ed´-iu-kei-tid, *adj* senza istruzione

unemployed, ŏn-imploíd´, adj disoccupato

unemployment, ŏn-im-ploí´-ment, n disoccupazione f

unequal, ŏn-íi´-kual, adj disuguale

unerring*, ŏn-er´-ring, adj infallibile

uneven, ŏn-íi´-ven, adj ineguale; irregolare

unexpected*, ŏn-iks-pek´-tid, adj inatteso; imprevisto

unfailing*, ŏn-fei´-ling, adj inesauribile; infallibile

unfair*, ŏn-fer´, adj ingiusto

unfaithful*, ŏn-feiZ´-ful, adj infedele

unfashionable, ŏn-fash´-on-a-bl, adj fuori moda

unfasten, ŏn-faas´-n, v slacciare; sciogliere

unfathomable, ŏn-faD´-om-a-bl, adj imperscrutabile

unfavourable, ŏn-fei´-vo-ra-bl, adj sfavorevole

unfit, ŏn-fit´, adj inadatto; fuori forma

unflagging, ŏn-fla´-ghing, adj instancabile

unflinching*, ŏn-flin´-ching, adj risoluto

unfold, ŏn-fould´, v spiegare; (reveal) svelare

unforeseen, ŏn-fo-siin´, adj imprevisto

unfortunate*, ŏn-foor´-tiu-nat, adj sfortunato

unfounded, ŏn-faun´-did, adj infondato

unfriendly, ŏn-frend´-li, adj poco amichevole; ostile

unfulfilled, ŏn-ful-fild´, adj non realizzato

unfurl, ŏn-ferl´, v spiegare

unfurnished, ŏn-fer´-nisht, adj non ammobiliato

ungainly, ŏn-ghein´-li, adj sgraziato, goffo

ungrateful*, ŏn-greit´-ful, adj ingrato

unguarded, ŏn-gaar´-did, adj indifeso; fig imprudente

unhappy, ŏn-hap´-i, adj infelice; scontento

unharmed, ŏn-haarmd´, adj illeso, incolume

unhealthy, ŏn-hel´-Zi, adj malsano; (person) malaticcio

unheard-of, ŏn-herd´-ov, adj inaudito

unheeded, ŏn-hii´-did, adj ignorato

unhinged, ŏn-hinchd´, adj (mind) sconvolto

unhurt, ŏn-hert´, adj sano e salvo

uniform, iuu´-ni-foorm, n uniforme f; divisa f; adj

uniforme

unimaginable, ŏn-i-mach´-in-a-bl, adj inconcepibile

unimpaired, ŏn-im-perd´, adj intatto

unimpeachable, ŏn-im-piiich´-a-bl, adj irreprensibile

unimportant, ŏn-im-poor´-tant, adj insignificante

uninhabitable, ŏn-in-hab´-i-ta-bl, adj inabitabile

unintelligible, ŏn-in-tel´-ich-i-bl, adj incomprensibile

unintentional*, ŏn-in-ten´-shon-al, adj involontario

uninviting, ŏn-in-vai´-ting, adj poco attraente; poco invitante

union, iuu´-ni-on, n unione f; sindacato m

unique, iu-niik´, adj unico

unit, iuu´-nit, n unità f

unite, iu-nait´, v unire

unity, iuu´-ni-ti, n unità f

universal*, iuu-ni-ver´-sl, adj universale

universe, iuu´-ni-vers, n universo m

university, iuu-ni-ver´-si-ti, n università f

unjust*, ŏn-chŏst´, adj ingiusto

unkind*, ŏn-kaind´, *adj* poco gentile

unknown, ŏn-noun´, *adj* sconosciuto

unlawful*, ŏn-loo´-ful, *adj* illegale; illecito

unleaded, ŏn-led´-id, *adj* senza piombo

unless, un-les´, *conj* a meno che

unlike, ŏn-laik´, *adj* poco somigliante; *prep* a differenza di

unlikely, ŏn-laik´-li, *adj* improbabile

unlimited, ŏn-lim´-i-tid, *adj* illimitato

unload, ŏn-loud´, *v* scaricare

unlock, ŏn-lok´, *v* aprire

unlooked-for, ŏn-lukt´ foor, *adj* inatteso

unlucky, ŏn-lŏk´-i, *adj* sfortunato

unmarried, ŏn-ma´-rid, *adj* (man) celibe; (woman) nubile

unmerciful*, ŏn-mer´-si-ful, *adj* spietato

unmistakable, ŏn-mis-tei´-ka-bl, *adj* inconfondibile; indubbio

unmoved, ŏn-muuvd´, *adj* indifferente

unnatural, ŏn-nat´-chu-ral, *adj* innaturale; anormale

unnecessary, ŏn-nes´-is-a-ri, *adj* non necessario

unnerving, ŏn-ner´-ving, *adj* inquietante

unnoticed, ŏn-nou´-tist, *adj* inosservato

unobtainable, ŏn-ob-tei´-na-bl, *adj* introvabile

unoccupied, ŏn-ok´-iu-paid, *adj* non occupato, libero; vuoto

unopposed, ŏn-o-pousd´, *adj* senza opposizione

unpack, ŏn-pak´, *v* disfare; disfare i bagagli

unpleasant*, ŏn-ples´-ant, *adj* spiacevole; sgradevole; antipatico

unpopular, ŏn-pop´-iu-la, *adj* impopolare

unprecedented, ŏn-pres´-i-den-tid, *adj* senza precedenti

unpredictable, ŏn-pri-dik-ta-bl, *adj* imprevedibile

unprepared, ŏn-pri-perd´, *adj* impreparato

unproductive, ŏn-pro-dŏk´-tiv, *adj* improduttivo

unprofitable, ŏn-prof´-i-ta-bl, *adj* non redditizio

unpromising, ŏn-prom´-is-ing, *adj* non promettente

unprotected, ŏn-pro-tek´-tid, *adj* non protetto

unqualified, ŏn-kuol´-i-faid, *adj* non qualificato

unquestionable, ŏn-kues´-chon-a-bl, *adj* incontestabile

unravel, ŏn-rav´-el, *v* sbrogliare

unread, ŏn-red´, *adj* non letto

unreadable, ŏn-rii´-da-bl, *adj* illeggibile

unreasonable, ŏn-rii´-son-a-bl, *adj* irragionevole

unrelated, ŏn-ri-lei´-tid, *adj* senza nesso; non imparentato

unrelenting, ŏn-ri-len´-ting, *adj* implacabile

unreliable, ŏn-ri-lai´-a-bl, *adj* inaffidabile

unremitting, ŏn-ri-mit´-ing, *adj* incessante

unreserved, ŏn-ri-servd´, *adj* non riservato; senza riserve

unrest, ŏn-rest´, *n* agitazioni *fpl*

unrestrained, ŏn-ri-streind´, *adj* sfrenato

unrestricted, ŏn-ri-strik´-tid, *adj* illimitato

unripe, ŏn-raip´, *adj* acerbo; non maturo

unroll, ŏn-roul´, *v* srotolare

unruly, ŏn-ruu´-li, *adj* turbolento; (hair) ribelle

unsafe, ŏn-seif´, *adj* poco sicuro

unsaleable, ŏn-seil´-a-bl, adj invendibile

unsatisfactory, ŏn-sat-is-fak´-to-ri, adj poco soddisfacente

unscrew, ŏn-skruu´, v svitare

unscrupulous, ŏn-skruu´-piu-los, adj senza scrupoli

unseasonable, ŏn-sii´-son-a-bl, adj fuori stagione

unseemly, ŏn-siim´-li, adj indecoroso

unseen, ŏn-siin´, adj inosservato

unselfish, ŏn-sel´-fish, adj altruista

unsettled, ŏn-set´-ld, adj instabile

unshaken, ŏn-sheik´-n, adj risoluto

unshaven, ŏn-shei´-ven, adj non rasato

unshrinkable, ŏn-shring´-ka-bl, adj irrestringibile

unsightly, ŏn-sait´-li, adj sgradevole

unskilled, ŏn-skild´, adj non specializzato

unsociable, ŏn-sou´-sha-bl, adj poco socievole

unsold, ŏn-sould´, adj invenduto

unsolicited, ŏn-so-lis´-i-tid, adj non richiesto

unsolved, ŏn-solvd´, adj insoluto, non risolto

unsteady, ŏn-sted´-i, adj instabile; tremante

unsuccessful*, ŏn-suk-ses´-ful, adj senza successo; vano

unsuitable, ŏn-suu´-ta-bl, adj inadatto

unsurpassed, ŏn-su-paast´, adj insuperato

unsympathetic, ŏn-sim-pa-Zet´-ik, adj poco comprensivo

untangle, ŏn-tang´-gl, v sbrogliare

untarnished, ŏn-taar´-nisht, adj senza macchia

untenable, ŏn-ten´-a-bl, adj insostenibile

untested, ŏn-tes´-tid, adj non collaudato

unthinkable, ŏn-Zing´-ka-bl, adj impensabile

unthinking, ŏn-Zing´-king, adj sconsiderato

untidy, ŏn-tai´-di, adj disordinato

untie, ŏn-tai´, v slegare; slacciare

until, un-til´, prep fino a; conj finché non; – now, finora

untimely, ŏn-taim´-li, adj prematuro; fuori luogo

untiring, ŏn-tair´-ring, adj instancabile

untold, ŏn-tould´, adj incalcolabile; indicibile

untouched, ŏn-tŏcht´, adj intatto

untranslatable, ŏn-trans-lei´-ta-bl, adj intraducibile

untried, ŏn-traid´, adj intentato; non processato

untrue, ŏn-truu´, adj falso

untrustworthy, ŏn-trŏst´-uer-Di, adj non degno di fiducia; inattendibile

untruth, ŏn-truuZ´, n falsità f

unusual*, ŏn-iuu´-shu-al, adj insolito

unvaried, ŏn-ver´-rid, adj invariato

unvarying, ŏn-ver´-ri-ing, adj invariabile

unveil, ŏn-veil´, v svelare; scoprire

unwarranted, ŏn-uo´-ran-tid, adj ingiustificato

unwavering, ŏn-uei´-ve-ring, adj incrollabile

unwelcome, ŏn-uel´-kom, adj non gradito; sgradito

unwell, ŏn-uel´, adj indisposto

unwholesome, ŏn-houl´-som, adj malsano; cattivo

unwieldy, ŏn-uiil´-di, adj poco maneggevole

unwilling, ŏn-uil´-ing, adj riluttante

unwind, ŏn-uaind´, v srotolare; rilassarsi

unwise*, ŏn-uais´, *adj* imprudente

unwittingly, ŏn-uit´-ing-li, *adj* senza volerlo

unworthy, ŏn-uer´-Di, *adj* indegno

unwrap, ŏn-rap´, *v* disfare; scartare

unwritten, ŏn-rit´-n, *adj* non scritto

unyielding, ŏn-iiil´-ding, *adj* inflessibile

up, ŏp, *adv* & *prep* su; – **and down**, su e giù; – **here**, quassù; – **there**, lassù; – **to**, fino a

upbraid, ŏp-breid´, *v* rimproverare

upbringing, ŏp´-bring-ing, *n* educazione *f*

upheaval, ŏp-hii´-val, *n* sconvolgimento *m*

uphill, ŏp-hil´, *adj* in salita

uphold, ŏp-hould´, *v* difendere; confermare

upholster, ŏp-houl´-sta, *v* tappezzare

upkeep, ŏp´-kiip, *n* manutenzione *f*

uplift, ŏp-lift´, *v* elevare; sollevare

upon, *u*p-on´, *prep* sopra

upper, ŏp´-a, *adj* superiore

uppermost, ŏp´-e-moust, *adj* più alto

upright, ŏp´-rait, *adj* dritto; (honest) onesto

uprising, ŏp´-rai-sing, *n* insurrezione *f*

uproar, ŏp´-roor, *n* clamore *m*

uproot, ŏp-ruut´, *v* sradicare

upset, ŏp-set´, *v* capovolgere; (plans) scombussolare; (feelings) sconvolgere

upside down, ŏp´-said daun, *adj* & *adv* sottosopra

upstairs, ŏp´-sters, *adv* di sopra

upstart, ŏp´-staart, *n* parvenu *m*

upwards, ŏp´-uads, *adv* in su, verso l'alto

urban, er´-ban, *adj* urbano

urchin, er´-chin, *n* monello *m*

urge, erch, *v* esortare

urgency, er´-chen-si, *n* urgenza *f*

urgent*, er´-chent, *adj* urgente

urinate, iur´-ri-neit, *v* orinare

urine, iur´-rin, *n* orina *f*

urn, ern, *n* urna *f*

us, ŏs, *pron* ci, ce, noi

use, iuus, *v* usare; servirsi di; – **up**, consumare

use, iuus, *n* uso *m*; utilità *f*

used to, iuust tu, *adj* abituato a

useful*, iuus´-ful, *adj* utile

useless*, iuus´-lis, *adj* inutile; inefficace

usher, ŏsh´-a, *n* usciere *m*; – **in**, *v* introdurre

usherette, ŏsh-e-ret´, *n* (cinema) mascherina *f*

usual*, iuu´-shu-al, *adj* solito

utensil, iu-ten´-sil, *n* utensile *m*

utility, iu-til´-i-ti, *n* utilità *f*

utilize, iuu´-til-ais, *v* utilizzare

utmost, ŏt´-moust, *adj* estremo; **do one's –**, *n* fare tutto il possibile

utter, ŏt´-a, *v* (word) pronunciare; (sound) emettere; *adj** totale

vacancy, vei´-kan-si, n
posto vacante m;
(emptiness) vuoto m

vacant, vei´-kant, adj
(empty) vuoto; (free)
libero; (mind) distratto

vacate, va-keit´, v lasciare
libero; sgombrare;
lasciare

vacation, va-kei-shon, n
vacanza f; ferie fpl

vaccinate, vak´-si-neit, v
vaccinare

vacillate, vas´-i-leit, v
vacillare

vacuum, vak´-iu-um, n
vuoto m

vacuum cleaner, vak´-iu-
um klii´-na, n
aspirapolvere m

vagabond, vagh´-a-bond,
n vagabondo m

vagary, vei´-gha-ri, n
capriccio m

vagina, va-chai´-na, n
vagina f

vagrancy, vei´-gran-si, n
vagabondaggio m

vague*, veigh, adj vago

vain*, vein, adj vanitoso;
in –, invano

valet, val´-ei, n valletto m

valiant*, val´-iant, adj
valoroso

valid*, val´-id, adj valido

valley, val´-i, n valle f

valour, val´-a, n valore m

valuable, val´-iu-a-bl, adj
di valore; prezioso

valuables, val´-iu-a-bls,
npl oggetti di valore mpl

valuation, val-iu-ei´-shon,
n valutazione f

value, val´-iu, n valore m;

v valutare

valuer, val´-iu-a, n
stimatore m

valve, valv, n valvola f

vampire, vam´-pair, n
vampiro m

van, van, n furgone m;
(train) vagone m

vandal, van´-dl, n vandalo
m

vane, vein, n banderuola f;
(windmill) pla f

vanilla, va-nil´-a, n
vaniglia f

vanish, van´-ish, v svanire

vanity, van´-i-ti, n vanità f

vanquish, vang´-kuish, v
vincere

vaporize, vei´-po-rais, v
vaporizzare

vapour, vei´-pa, n
vapore m

variable, ver´-ri-a-bl, adj
variabile

variation, ver-ri-ei´-shon,
n variazione f

varicose vein, va´-ri-kos
vein, n varice f, vena
varicosa f

varied, ver´-rid, adj vario,
diverso

variegated, ver´-ri-i-ghei-
tid, adj variegato

variety, va-rai´-i-ti, n
varietà f; (show) varietà
m

various*, ver´-ri-os, adj
vario; diverso

varnish, vaar´-nish, n vernice f; v verniciare

vary, ver´-ri, v variare

vase, vaas, n vaso m

vaseline, vas´-e-liin, n vaselina f

vast*, vaast, adj vasto

vat, vat, n tino m

vault, voolt, n volta f; (church) cripta f; (burial) tomba f; v saltare

veal, viil, n vitello m

veer, vir, v girare; naut virare

vegetables, vech´-i-tab-ls, npl verdure fpl

vegetarian, vech-i-ter´-ri-an, n vegetariano m, vegetariana f

vegetation, vech-i-tei´-shon, n vegetazione f

vehement*, vii´-i-ment, adj veemente

vehicle, vii´-i-kl, n veicolo m

veil, veil, n velo m; v velare

vein, vein, n vena f; (geological) filone m

vellum, vel´-um, n pergamena f

velocity, vi-los´-i-ti, n velocità f

velvet, vel´-vit, n velluto m

velveteen, vel-vi-tiin´, n vellutino m

vending machine, ven´-ding ma-shiin´, n distributore automatico m

vendor, ven´-da, n venditore m

veneer, vi-nir´, n impiallacciatura f; v impiallacciare

venerable, ven´-e-ra-bl, adj venerabile

veneration, ven-e-rei´-shon, n venerazione f

venereal, vi-nir´-ri-al, adj venereo

vengeance, ven´-chans, n vendetta f; **with a –,** furiosamente

venial, vii´-ni-al, adj veniale

Venice, ven´-is, n Venezia f

venison, ven´-i-son, n carne di cervo f

venom, ven´-om, n veleno m

venomous, ven´-o-mos, adj velenoso

vent, vent, n presa d'aria f; **give – to,** v sfogare

ventilate, ven´-ti-leit, v ventilare

ventilator, ven´-ti-lei-ta, n ventilatore m

ventriloquist, ven-tril´-o-kuist, n ventriloquo m

venture, ven´-cha, n impresa f; v rischiare

veranda, vi-ran´-da, n veranda f

verb, verb, n verbo m

verbal*, ver´-bal, adj verbale

verbatim, ve-bei´-tim, adv letteralmente

verbose, ve-bous´, adj verboso

verdict, ver´-dikt, n verdetto m

verge, verch, v rasentare; n orlo m

verger, ver´-cha, n sagrestano m

verify, ve´-ri-fai, v verificare

vermilion, ve-mil´-ion, n vermiglio m

vermin, ver´-min, n insetti e animali nocivi mpl

vernacular, ve-nak´-iu-la, n vernacolo m; adj vernacolare

versatile, ver´-sa-tail, adj versatile

verse, vers, n verso m; (Bible) versetto m

versed, verst, adj versato

version, ver´-shon, n versione f

versus, ver´-sus, prep contro

vertical*, ver´-tik-l, adj verticale

vertigo, ver´-ti-gou, n vertigine f

very, ve´-ri, adv molto;

tanto; proprio

vessel, ves´-l, *n* recipiente *m; naut* nave *f*

vest, vest, *n* canottiera *f*; maglia intima *f*

vested, ves´-tid, *adj* (interest, rights) acquisito

vestige, ves´-tich, *n* vestigio *m*

vestment, vest´-ment, *n* paramento liturgico *m*

vestry, vest´-ri, *n* sagrestia *f*

vet, vet, *n* veterinario *m*

veteran, vet´-e-ran, *n* veterano *m*

veterinary, vet´-ri-na-ri, *adj* veterinario

veto, vii´-tou, *n* veto *m; v* porre il veto

vex, veks, *v* contrariare

vexation, vek-sei´-shon, *n* contrarietà *f*

via, vai´-a, *prep* via; per mezzo di

viaduct, vai´-a-dŏkt, *n* viadotto *m*

vibrate, vai´-breit, *v* vibrare

vibration, vai-brei´-shon, *n* vibrazione *f*

vicar, vik´-a, *n* pastore anglicano *m*

vicarage, vik´-e-rich, *n* canonica anglicana *f*

vice, vais, *n* vizio *m; mech* morsa *f*

vice-, vais, *prefix* vice-

vice-president, vais-pres´-i-dent, *n* vicepresidente *m/f*

viceroy, vais´-roi, *n* viceré *m*

vice versa, vai´-si ver´-sa, *adv* viceversa

vicinity, vi-sin´-i-ti, *n* vicinanze *fpl*

vicious*, vish´-os, *adj* brutale; (animal) feroce; vizioso

viciousness, vish´-os-nis, *n* ferocia *f*; cattiveria *f*

victim, vik´-tim, *n* vittima *f*

victimize, vik´-tim-ais, *v* perseguitare

victor, vik´-ta, *n* vincitore *m*

victorious*, vik-toor´-ri-os, *adj* vittorioso

victory, vik´-to-ri, *n* vittoria *f*

video, vi´-di-ou, *n* video *m*; (tape) videocassetta *f*; (recorder) videoregistratore *m*

vie, vai, *v* gareggiare

view, viuu, *n* vista *f*; opinione *f; v* visitare

vigil, vich´-il, *n* veglia *f*

vigilance, vich´-il-ans, *n* vigilanza *f*

vigilant, vich´-il-ant, *adj* vigile

vigorous*, vi´-go-ros, *adj* vigoroso

vigour, vi´-ga, *n* vigore *m*

vile, vail, *adj* abbietto; pessimo

vilify, vil´-i-fai, *v* diffamare

villa, vil´-a, *n* villa *f*

village, vil´-ich, *n* paese *m*; villaggio *m*

villager, vil´-ich-a, *n* paesano *m*, paesana *f*

villain, vil´-an, *n* mascalzone *m*; (in play, film) cattivo *m*

villainous, vil´-a-nos, *adj* infame

villainy, vil´-a-ni, *n* infamia *f*

vindicate, vin´-di-keit, *v* confermare

vindication, vin-di-kei´-shon, *n* conferma *f*

vindictive*, vin-dik´-tiv, *adj* vendicativo

vindictiveness, vin-dik´-tiv-nis, *n* spirito vendicativo *m*

vine, vain, *n* vite *f*

vinegar, vin´-i-ga, *n* aceto *m*

vineyard, vin´-iaard, *n* vigna *f*, vigneto *m*

vintage, vin´-tich, *n* vendemmia *f*; (year) annata *f*

vinyl, vai´-nil, *n* vinile *m*

viola, vi-ou´-la, *n* viola *f*

violate, vai´-o-leit, *v*

violare

violence, vai´-o-lens, n
violenza f

violent*, vai´-o-lent, adj
violento

violet, vai´-o-let, n
violetta f; adj violetto; n
violetto m

violin, vai-o-lin´, n
violino m

violinist, vai-o-lin´-ist, n
violinista m/f

viper, vai´-pa, n vipera f

virgin, ver´-chin, adj
vergine; n vergine f

Virgo, ver´-gou, n
Vergine f

virile, vi´-rail, adj virile

virtual*, ver´-tiu-al, adj
virtuale

virtue, ver´-tiuu, n virtù f

virtuous*, ver´-tiu-os, adj
virtuoso

virulent*, vi´-riu-lent, adj
virulento

virus, vai´-ros, n virus m

visa, vii´-sa, n visto m

viscount, vai´-kaunt, n
visconte m

viscountess, vai´-kaun-
tes, n viscontessa f

visibility, vis-i-bil´-i-ti, n
visibilità f

visible, vis-i-bl, adj
visibile

vision, vish´-on, n
visione f

visit, vis´-it, n visita f; v

visitare; (person) andare
a trovare; **–ing-card,** n
biglietto da visita m

visitor, vis´-i-ta, n
visitatore m

visual, vis´-iu-al, adj
visivo

vital*, vait´-l, adj vitale

vitality, vai-tal´-i-ti, n
vitalità f

vitamin, vi´-ta-min, n
vitamina f

vitriol, vit´-ri-ol, n
vetriolo m

vivacious*, vi-vei´-shos,
adj vivace

vivid*, viv´-id, adj vivido

vixen, vik´-sen, n volpe
femmina f; fig megera f

viz (= namely), neim´-li,
adv cioè

vocabulary, vo-kab´-iu-la-
ri, n vocabolario m

vocal, vou´-kl, adj vocale

vocal cords, vou´-kl
koords, npl corde
vocali fpl

vocation, vo-kei´-shon,
n vocazione f;
professione f

vociferous*, vo-sif´-e-ros,
adj rumoroso

vogue, voug, n moda f;
voga f

voice, vois, n voce f

void, void, adj vuoto;
nullo; n vuoto m

volatile, vol´-a-tail, adj

volatile

volcano, vol-kei´-nou, n
vulcano m

volley, vol´-i, n volée f; mil
scarica f, salva f

volt, voult, n volt m

volume, vol´-iuum, n
volume m

voluminous, vo-luu´-mi-
nos, adj voluminoso

voluntary, vol´-on-ta-ri,
adj volontario

volunteer, vol-on-tir´,
n volontario m,
volontaria f

voluptuous*, vo-lŏp´-tiu-
os, adj voluttuoso

vomit, vom´-it, v vomitare

voracious*, vo-rei´-shos,
adj vorace

vortex, voor´-teks, n
vortice m

vote, vout, n voto m; v
votare

voter, vou´-ta, n votante
m/f

vouch, vauch, v attestare;
– for, garantire per

voucher, vauch´-a, n
buono m, coupon m

vow, vau, n voto m; v fare
voto; giurare

vowel, vau´-el, n vocale f

voyage, voi´-ich, n
viaggio m

vulgar, vŏl´-ga, adj volgare

vulnerable, vŏl´-ne-ra-bl,
adj vulnerabile

wad, uod, *n* fascio *m*; batuffolo *m*; tampone *m*

wadding, uod´-ing, *n* imbottitura *f*

waddle, uod´-l, *v* camminare come una papera

wade, ueid, *v* guadare; sguazzare

wafer, uei´-fa, *n* cialda *f*; *relig* ostia *f*

wag, uagh, *v* scodinzolare; *n* burlone *m*

wage, ueich, *v* – war on, dichiarare guerra a

wager, uei´-cha, *n* scommessa *f*; *v* scommettere

wages, uei´-chis, *npl* salario *m*, stipendio *m*, paga *f*

waggle, uagh´-l, *v* scodinzolare, dimenare

waggon, uagh´-n *n* carro *m*; (railway) vagone *m*

waif, ueif, *n* (child) fanciullo abbandonato *m*

wail, ueil, *n* gemito *m*; *v* gemere

waist, ueist, *n* vita *f*

waistcoat, ueist´-kout, *n* panciotto *m*; gilè *f*

wait, ueit, *v* aspettare; (at table) servire; **– for,** aspettare

waiter, uei´-ta, *n* cameriere *m*

waiting, uei´-ting, *n* attesa *f*

waiting room, ueit´-ing ruum, sala d'attesa *f*

waitress, ueit´-ris, *n* cameriera *f*

waive, ueiv *v* rinunciare a

wake, ueik, *v* (to awake) svegliarsi; (to call *or* be called) svegliare; *n* (ship's) scia *f*

Wales, ueils, *n* Galles *m*

walk, uook, *v* camminare; passeggiare; *n* camminata *f*; passeggiata *f*

wall, uool, *n* muro *m*; parete *f*

wallet, uol´-it, *n* portafoglio *m*

wallflower, uool´-flau-a, *n* violaciocca *f*

wallow, uol´-ou, *v* rotolarsi in; crogiolarsi in

wallpaper, uool-pei´-pa, *n* carta da parati *f*

walnut, uool´-nŏt, *n* noce *f*

walrus, uool´-ros, *n* tricheco *m*

waltz, uolts, *n* valzer *m*; *v* ballare il valzer

wander, uon´-da, *v* gironzolare senza meta; (mind) vagare

wane, uein, *v* calare

want, uont, *n* (lack) mancanza *f*; (distress) bisogno *m*; *v* volere; aver bisogno di

wanton, uon´-ton, *adj* gratuito, ingiustificato

war, uoor, *n* guerra *f*;

lotta f

warble, uoor´-bl, v
gorgheggiare

warbler, uoor´-bla, n
uccello canoro m

ward, uoord, n (hospital)
corsia f, sala f; (minor)
minore sotto tutela m/f;
– off, v respingere

warden, uoord-n, n
custode m/f; direttore m,
direttrice f

warder, uoor´-da,
secondino m

wardrobe, uoord´-roub, n
guardaroba m

warehouse, uer´-haus, n
magazzino m

wares, uers, npl merci fpl

warily, uer´-ri-li, adv
cautamente

warlike, uoor´-laik, adj
bellicoso

warm, uoorm, adj* caldo;
v riscaldare

warmth, uoormZ, n
calore m

warn, uoorn, v avvertire

warning, uoor´-ning, n
avvertimento m;
ammonimento m;
preavviso m

warp, uoorp, v (wood)
deformarsi; (mind)
corrompere

warrant, uo´-rant, n (for
arrest) mandato di
cattura m; (voucher)

mandato m

warranty, uo´-ran-ti, n
garanzia f

warrior, uo´-ri-a, n
guerriero m

Warsaw, uoor´-soo, n
Varsavia f

warship, uoor´-ship, n
nave da guerra f

wart, uoort, n porro m,
verruca f

wary, uer´-ri, adj cauto

wash, uosh, n lavata f; v
lavare; lavarsi; **– up**,
lavare i piatti

washbasin, uosh´-bei´-sin,
n lavabo m, lavandino m

washer, uosh´-a, n mech
rondella f

washing, uosh´-ing, n
(laundry) biancheria f,
bucato m

washing machine, uosh´-
ing ma-shiin, n
lavatrice f

washing powder, uosh´-
ing pau´-da, n detersivo
in polvere per bucato m

washing up, uosh´-ing ŏp,
do the –, lavare i piatti

washing-up liquid, uosh-
ing-ŏp´ lik´-uid, n
detersivo liquido per i
piatti m

wasp, uosp, n vespa f

waste, ueist, n spreco m;
(refuse) rifiuti mpl;
(land) distesa desolata f;

v sprecare; **– away**,
deperire

wasteful, ueist´-ful, adj
sprecone

waste paper, ueist pei´-pa,
n cartaccia f

wastepaper basket, ueist´-
pei-pa baas´-kit, n
cestino della cartaccia m

watch, uoch, n orologio
m; (look-out) guardia f;
v guardare; sorvegliare; **–
over**, v (guard) vegliare
su

watch-dog, uoch´-dogh, n
cane da guardia m

watchful, uoch´-ful, adj
vigile

watchmaker, uoch´-mei-
ka, n orologiaio m

watchman, uoch´-man, n
guardia notturna f

water, uoo´-ta, v
annaffiare; (cattle etc.)
abbeverare; n acqua f

water bottle, uoo´-ta bot´-
l, n borraccia f

water closet, uoo´-ta
klos´-it, n (W.C.)
gabinetto m

watercolour, uoo´-te-kŏl-
a, n acquerello m

watercress, uoo´-te-kres, n
crescione m

waterfall, uoo´-te-fool, n
cascata f

water lily, uoo´-te lil-i, n
ninfea f

waterlogged, uoo´-te-logd, *adj* impregnato d'acqua

watermark, uoo´-te-maark, *n* (paper) filigrana *f*

watermelon, uoo´-te-mel-on, *n* anguria *f*, cocomero *m*

waterproof, uoo´-te-pruuf, *adj* impermeabile

watering can, uoo´-te-ring kan, *n* annaffiatoio *m*

water-skiing, uoo´-te-skii-ing, *n* sci nautico *m*

watertight, uoo´-te-tait, *adj* a tenuta stagna

watery, uoo´-te-ri, *adj* acquoso; annacquato

wave, ueiv, *n* onda *f*; *v* agitare; (hand) salutare con la mano; (hair) ondulare

waver, uei´-va, *v* vacillare

wavering, uei´-ve-ring, *adj* vacillante

wavy, uei´-vi, *adj* ondulato

wax, uaks, *n* cera *f*; *v* incerare; (moon) crescere

waxworks, uaks´-uerks, *npl* museo delle cere *m*

way, uei, *n* via *f*; strada *f*; (manner) modo *m*; – **in,** entrata *f*; – **out,** uscita *f*; – **through,** passaggio *m*

wayward, uei´-uad, *adj* capriccioso

we, uii, *pron* noi

weak*, uiik, *adj* debole; leggero

weaken, uiik´-n, *v* indebolire

weakening, uiik´-ning, *n* indebolimento *m*

weakness, uiik´-nis, *n* debolezza *f*

wealth, uelZ, *n* ricchezza *f*

wealthy, uel´-Zi, *adj* ricco

wean, uiin, *v* svezzare

weapon, uep´-n, *n* arma *f*

wear, uer, *n* (wear and tear) logorio *m*; (clothes) uso *m*; *v* portare; (last) durare; – **out,** consumare; (fatigue) stancare

weariness, uir´-ri-nis, *n* stanchezza *f*

weary, uir´-ri, *adj* stanco; *v* stancare

weasel, ui´-sel, *n* donnola *f*

weather, ueD´-a, *n* tempo *m*

weather forecast, ueD-e-foor´-kaast, *n* previsioni del tempo *fpl*

weathervane, ueD´-e-vein, *n* banderuola *f*

weave, uiiv, *v* tessere

weaver, uii´-va, *n* tessitore *m*

web, ueb, *n* ragnatela *f*

web-footed, ueb-fut´-id, *adj* palmipede

wed, ued, *v* sposare,

sposarsi

wedding, ued´-ing, *n* matrimonio *m*; nozze *fpl*

wedding ring, ued´-ing ring, *n* fede *f*

wedge, uech, *n* cuneo *m*

wedlock, ued´-lok, *n* matrimonio *m*

Wednesday, uel´-ens-di, *n* mercoledì *m*

weed, uiid, *n* erbaccia *f*; *v* strappare le erbacce

week, uiik, *n* settimana *f*

weekday, uiik´-dei, *n* giorno feriale *m*; giornata lavorativa *f*

weekend, uiik-end´, *n* fine settimana *m*

weekly, uiik´-li, *adj* settimanale

weep, uiip, *v* piangere

weigh, uei, *v* pesare; considerare

weight, ueit, *n* peso *m*

weighty, uei´-ti, *adj* (serious) grave

weir, uir, *n* sbarramento *m*

weird, uird, *adj* strano; bizzarro

welcome, uel´-kom, *v* accogliere; dare il benvenuto; *adj* benvenuto; *n* benvenuto *m*

weld, ueld, *v* saldare

welfare, uel´-fer, *n* benessere *m*; assistenza sociale *f*

well, uel, n pozzo m; adv bene

well-being, uel-bii´-ing, n benessere m

well-bred, uel-bred´, adj ben educato

well-done, uel-dŏn´, adj ben cotto

well-known, uel-noun, adj famoso

Welsh, welsh, adj gallese; n (language) gallese

west, uest, n ovest m, occidente m

westerly, uest´-e-li, adj dell'ovest, verso ovest

western, uest´-en, adj occidentale

wet, uet, n bagnato; umido; (weather) piovoso; (paint) fresco; v bagnare; inumidire

wet nurse, uet' ners, n balia f

wetsuit, uet´-suut, n muta subacquea f

whack, uak, n ceffone m; v dare un ceffone a

whale, ueil, n balena f

whale-bone, ueil´-boun, n stecca di balena f

whaler, uei´-la, n (ship) baleniera f

wharf, uoorf, n molo m

what, uot, adj che; pron che (cosa), ciò, ciò che, quello che

whatever, uot-ev´-a, pron & adj qualunque; tutto quello che

wheat, uiit, n frumento m

wheel, uiil, n ruota f

wheelbarrow, uiil´-ba-rou, n carriola f

wheelchair, uiil´-cher, n sedia a rotelle f

wheel clamp, uiil' klamp, n ceppo bloccaruote m

wheezy, uii´-si, adj col respiro affannoso

whelk, uelk, n buccino m

when, uen, adv quando

whenever, uen-ev´-a, conj quando; ogni volta che

where, uer, adv & conj dove

whereas, uer´-ras, conj mentre

wherever, uer-ev´-a, adv & conj ovunque

whet, uet, v (appetite) stuzzicare

whether, ueD´-a, conj se

which, uich, adj quale; pron quale; che; il quale, la quale, cui

whichever, uich-ev´-a, adj & pron qualunque; quello che

while, uail, n un po' (di tempo) m; conj mentre; v passare; **be worth –,** valer la pena

whim, uim, n capriccio m

whimper, uim´-pa, v gemere; n gemito m

whine, uain v guaire; n guaito m

whip, uip, n frusta f; v frustare; (cream) montare

whirl, uerl, n turbine m

whirlpool, uerl´-puul, n vortice m

whirlwind, uerl´-uind, n mulinello m

whisk, uisk, n frullino m; v frullare

whiskers, uis´-kes, npl baffi mpl

whisky, uis´-ki, n whisky m

whisper, uis´-pa, v sussurrare; n sussurro m

whistle, uis´-l, n fischietto m; (sound) fischio m; v fischiare

white, uait, adj bianco; n bianco m

whiteness, uait´-nis, n biancore m

whitewash, uait´-uosh, n calce f; v imbiancare

Whitsun, uit´-sun, n Pentecoste f

whiz, uis, v sibilare

who, huu, pron chi, che

whoever, hu-ev´-a, pron chiunque

whole, houl, n intero m; tutto m; adj tutto; intero

wholemeal, houl´-miil, adj integrale

wholesale, houl´-seil, adj

all'ingrosso

wholesome, houl´-som, *adj* sano; salubre

wholly, hou´-li, *adv* interamente

whom, huum, *pron* chi, che, cui

whoop, huup, n urlo m; v urlare

whooping-cough, huu´-ping-kof, n pertosse f, tosse asinina f

whore, hoor, n puttana f

whose, huus, *pron* di cui; di chi

why, uai, *adv* perché

wick, uik, n stoppino m

wicked*, uik´-id, *adj* malvagio

wickedness, uik´-id-nis, n malvagità f

wicker, uik´-a, n vimini m

wicket, uik´-it, n (cricket) porta f

wide*, uaid, *adj* largo; ampio; – **awake,** completamente sveglio

widespread, uaid´-spred, *adj* diffuso

widen, uaid´-n, v allargare

widow, uid´-ou, n vedova f

widower, uid´-ou-a, n vedovo m

width, uidZ, n larghezza f; ampiezza f

wield, uiild, v maneggiare

wife, uaif, n moglie f

wig, uigh, n parrucca f

wild*, uaild, *adj* selvaggio; selvatico; *fig* folle

wilderness, uil´-de-nis, n deserto m

wildlife, uaild´-laif, n natura f

wilful*, uil´-ful, *adj* intenzionale; premeditato

will, uil, n volontà f; testamento m; v volere

willing*, uil´-ing, *adj* volonteroso; disponibile

willingness, uil´-ing-nis, n buona volontà f

will-o´-the-wisp, uil-o-De-uisp´, n fuoco fatuo m

willow, uil´-ou, n salice m; **weeping –,** salice piangente m

wily, uai´-li, *adj* astuto

win, uin, v vincere

wince, uins, v trasalire

winch, uinch, n argano m

wind, uaind, v serpeggiare; snodarsi ; – **up,** v caricare; (business) liquidare

wind, uind, n vento m; flatulenza f

windfall, uind´-fool, fortuna insperata f

winding, uain´-ding, *adj* serpeggiante; tortuoso; (stairs) a chiocciola

windmill, uind´-mil, n mulino a vento m

window, uin´-dou, n finestra f; finestrino m; vetrina f

windpipe, uind´-paip, n trachea f

windscreen, uind´-skriin, n parabrezza m

windscreen wiper, uind´-skriin uai´-pa, n tergicristalli m

windsurfer, uind´-ser-fa, n windsurf m

windy, uin´-di, *adj* ventoso

wine, uain, n vino m

wineglass, uain´-ghlaas, n bicchiere da vino m

wing, uing, n ala f

wink, uingk, v fare l'occhiolino; n occhiolino m

winner, uin´-a, n vincitore m, vincitrice f

winning, uin´-ing, *adj* vincente; affascinante

winning post, uin´-ing poust, n traguardo m

winnings, uin´-ings, npl vincita f

winter, uin´-ta, n inverno m

winter sports, uin´-ta spoorts, npl sport invernali mpl

wipe, uaip, n pulita f; v pulire; – **off,** cancellare

wire, uair, n fil di ferro m; filo elettrico m

wisdom, uis´-dom, n

saggezza f

wisdom tooth, uis´-dom tuuZ, n dente del giudizio m

wise*, uais, adj saggio

wish, uish, n desiderio m; v desiderare

wishful, uish´-ful, adj desideroso

wisp, uisp, n ciuffo m

wistaria, uis-ter´-ri-a, n glicine m

wistful*, uist´-ful, adj pensoso

wit, uit, n spirito m

witch, uich, n strega f

witchcraft, uich´-kraaft, n stregoneria f

with, uiD, prep con

withdraw, uiD´-droo, v ritirare

wither, uiD´-a, v appassire

withering, uiD´-e-ring, adj (look) fulminante

withhold, uiD-hould´, v trattenere

within, uiD-in´, prep dentro

without, uiD-aut´, prep senza

withstand, uiD-stand´, v resistere

witness, uit´-nis, n testimone m/f; v testimoniare

wits, uits, npl sensi mpl

witticism, ui´-ti-sism, n arguzia f

witty, uit´-i, adj spiritoso

wizard, uis´-ad, n stregone m, mago m

wobble, uob´-l, v traballare

wolf, uulf, n lupo m

woman, uu´-man, n donna f

womb, uuum, n utero m; fig grembo m

wonder, uŏn´-da, n meraviglia f; v meravigliarsi; (ask oneself) domandarsi

wonderful*, uŏn´-de-ful, adj meraviglioso

woo, uuu, v corteggiare

wood, uud, n legno m; (forest) bosco m

wooden, uud-n, adj di legno

woodpecker, uud´-pek-a, n picchio m

wool, uul, n lana f

woollen, uul´-en, adj di lana

word, uerd, n parola f

wording, uer´-ding, n formulazione f

word processor, uerd prou´-ses-a, n word processor m

work, uerk, v lavorare; funzionare; n lavoro m

worker, uer´-ka, n lavoratore m, lavoratrice f

workman, uerk´-man, n

operaio m

workmanship, uerk´-man-ship, n abilità professionale f

works, uerks, npl fabbrica f; mech meccanismo m

workshop, uerk´-shop, n officina f

world, uerld, n mondo m

worldly, uerld´-li, adj mondano

worm, uerm, n verme m

worm-eaten, uerm´-iit-n, adj bacato; tarlato

worry, uŏ´-ri, n preoccupazione; v preoccupare, preoccuparsi

worse, uers, adj peggiore; adv peggio

worship, uer´-ship, n adorazione f; v adorare

worst, uerst, adj & n il peggiore m, la peggiore f; adv il peggio; **get the – of it,** aver la peggio

worth, uerZ, n valore m; adj be –, valere

worthless, uerZ´-lis, adj senza valore; (person) indegno

worthwhile, uerZ´-uail, adj che vale la pena

worthy, uer´-Di, adj degno

would, uud, v he – do, lui farebbe; **he – have done,** lui avrebbe fatto; **– you like some tea?** gradisce del tè?

would-be, uud´-bii, *adj* aspirante

wound, uuund, *n* ferita *f*; *v* ferire

wrangle, rang´-gl, *v* litigare; *n* litigio *m*

wrap, rap, *n* scialle *m*; – up, *v* avvolgere; (oneself) imbacuccarsi

wrapping paper, rap´-ing pei´-pa, *n* carta da regalo *f*; carta da pacchi *f*

wreath, riiZ, *n* corona *f*

wreck, rek, *n* naufragio *m*; *v* far naufragare; (destroy) distruggere; *fig* rovinare

wreckage, rek´-ich, *n* relitto *m*; rottami *mpl*

wren, ren, *n* scricciolo *m*

wrench, rench, *n* strattone *m*; (tool) chiave inglese *f*; *v* torcere; strappare

wrestle, res´-l, *v* lottare

wrestler, res´-la, *n* lottatore *m*

wretch, rech, *n* disgraziato *m*

wretched, rech´-id, *adj* disgraziato

wriggle, righ´-l, *v* contorcersi; (eels etc.) guizzare

wring, ring, *v* (clothes) strizzare; (hands, neck) torcere

wrinkle, ring´-kl, *n* ruga *f*; grinza *f*; *v* raggrinzirsi

wrist, rist, *n* polso *m*

writ, rit, *n* mandato *m*

write, rait, *v* scrivere

writer, rai´-ta, *n* scrittore *m*, scrittrice *f*

writhe, raiD, *v* contorcersi

writing, rai´-ting, *n* scrittura *f*; in –, *adv* per iscritto

writing-paper, rai´-ting pei´-pa, *n* carta da lettere *f*

written rit´-n *adj* scritto

wrong, rong, *n* torto *m*; *v* far torto a; *adj** sbagliato; cattivo; ingiusto

wrought iron, root ai´-on, *n* ferro battuto *m*

wry, rai, *adj* beffardo

Xmas (= Christmas),
kris´-mas, n Natale m

Xmas eve, kris´-mas iiv, n
vigilia di Natale f

X-ray, eks´-rei, n raggio X
m; (X-ray photography)
radiografia f; v
radiografare

xylophone, sai´-lo-foun, n
xilofono m

yacht, iŏt, *n* yacht *m*

yachting, iŏt´-ing, *n* yachting *m*

yard, iaard, *n* cortile *m*; (measure) iarda *f*

yarn, iaarn, *n* filato *m*; (tale) storia *f*, racconto *m*

yawn, ioon, *v* sbadigliare; *n* sbadiglio *m*

year, iir, *n* anno *m*

yearly, iir´-li, a, annuo, annuale; *adv* annualmente

yearn, iern, *v* bramare

yearning, ier´-ning, *n* brama *f*

yearningly, ier´-ning-li, *adv* bramosamente

yeast, iiist, *n* lievito *m*

yell, iel, *v* strillare; *n* strillo *m*, urlo *m*

yellow, iel´-ou, *adj* giallo; *n* giallo *m*

yelp, ielp, *v* guaire; *n* guaito *m*

yes, ies, *adv* sì

yesterday, ies´-te-di, *adv* ieri

yet, iet, *adv* ancora; già; *conj* eppure

yew, iuu, *n* (tree) tasso *m*

yield, iiild, *n* rendita *f*; ricavo *m*; *v* fruttare; produrre; (give way) cedere

yoga, iou´-ga, *n* yoga *m*

yog(h)urt, io´-gut, *n* yogurt *m*

yoke, iouk, *n* giogo *m*; *v* aggiogare

yokel, iouk´-l, *n* zotico *m*

yolk, iouk, *n* tuorlo *m*

you, iuu, *pron* tu; voi; lei; loro

young, iŏng, *adj* giovane; **the –,** *npl* (of animals) i piccoli *mpl*

youngster, iŏng´-sta, *n* giovane *m/f*

your, ioor, *adj* tuo, tua, tuoi, tue; suo, sua, suoi, sue; vostro, vostra, vostri, vostre

yours, ioors, *pron* il tuo, la tua, i tuoi, le tue; il suo, la sua, i suoi, le sue; il vostro, la vostra, i vostri, le vostre; **a friend of –,** un tuo amico; un suo amico; un vostro amico

yourself, ioor-self´, *pron refl* ti; si; te; sé

yourselves, ioor-selvs´, *pron* (refl) vi; si; voi; loro

youth, iuZ, *n* gioventù *f*; (lad) giovane *m*

youthful, iuZ´-ful, *adj* giovanile

youthfulness, iuZ´-ful-nis, *n* giovinezza *f*

youth hostel, iuZ-hos´-tel, *n* ostello della gioventù *m*

zeal, siil, *n* zelo *m*

zealous*, sel´-os, *adj* zelante

zebra, sii´-bra, *n* zebra *f*

zenith, sen´-iZ, *n* zenit *m*

zero, sir´-rou, *n* zero *m*

zest, sest, *n* gusto *m*; (of orange, lemon) scorza *f*

zigzag, sigh´-sagh, *adj* a zigzag; *v* zigzagare

zinc, singk, *n* zinco *m*

zip (fastener), sip (faas´-en-a), *n* cerniera lampo *f*

zone, soun, *n* zona *f*

zoo, suu, *n* zoo *m*

zoological, suu-o-loch´-i-kl, *adj* zoologico

zoology, suu-ol´-o-chi, *n* zoologia *f*

zoom, suum, *v* sfrecciare

zoom lens, suum-lens´, *n* zoom *m*